DATE DUE

AG, 1 2 10			

DEMCO 38-296

HANDBOOK OF AMERICAN POPULAR CULTURE

HANDBOOK OF AMERICAN POPULAR CULTURE

Second Edition, Revised and Enlarged

Advertising–Graffiti

Edited by M. THOMAS INGE

Greenwood Press
NEW YORK
WESTPORT, CONNECTICUT
LONDON

Library of Congress Cataloging-in-Publication Data

Handbook of American popular culture / edited by M. Thomas Inge.—
2nd ed., rev. and enlarged.
    p. cm.
  Includes index.
  ISBN 0–313–25406–0 (lib. bdg. : alk. paper)
  1. United States—Popular culture. 2. United States—Popular
culture—History—Sources. 3. United States—Popular culture—
Bibliography. I. Inge, M. Thomas.
E169.1.H2643 1989
306'.4'0973—dc19   88–39092

British Library Cataloguing in Publication Data is available.

Library of Congress Catalog Card Number: 88–39092
ISBN: 0–313–25406–0
ISBN: 0–313–27241–7 (v. 1)
ISBN: 0–313–27242–5 (v. 2)
ISBN: 0–313–27243–3 (v. 3)

First published in 1989

Greenwood Press, Inc.
88 Post Road West, Westport, Connecticut 06881

Printed in the United States of America

The paper used in this book complies with the
Permanent Paper Standard issued by the National
Information Standards Organization (Z39.48–1984).

10 9 8 7 6 5 4 3 2 1

Copyright Acknowledgment

The editor and publisher gratefully acknowledge permission to reprint material from the
following copyrighted source.

William Howland Kenney. "Jazz: A Bibliographical Essay" (*American Studies International*,
25, April 1987, Vol. XXV, No. 1).

For Tonette

*Mistress of herself
though china fall.*

Contents

About the Contributors   xi

Introduction   xxi

Advertising   1
Donald A. McQuade and Elizabeth Williamson

Almanacs   41
Robert K. Dodge

Animation   59
Thomas W. Hoffer

Architecture   79
Richard Guy Wilson

The Automobile   107
Michael L. Berger and Maurice Duke

Business   133
Richard F. Welch

Catalogs   157
Evelyn Beck

Circus and Outdoor Entertainment   173
  Don B. Wilmeth

Comic Strips   205
  M. Thomas Inge

Computers   229
  Michael G. Wessells

Dance   259
  Loretta Carrillo

Death   279
  Robert A. Armour and J. Carol Williams

Debate and Public Address   307
  Robert H. Janke

Editorial Cartoons   367
  Nancy Pogel and Paul Somers, Jr.

Fashion   417
  Vicki L. Berger

Film   445
  Robert A. Armour

Foodways   475
  Charles Camp

Games and Toys   497
  Bernard Mergen

Gardening   525
  Patsy G. Hammontree

Graffiti   549
  Lisa N. Howorth

Illustration   567
  James J. Best

Jazz   591
  William Howland Kenney III and Bill Bennett

Leisure Vehicles, Pleasure Boats, and Aircraft   615
  Bernard Mergen

Magazines   641
  Dorothy S. Schmidt

Magic and Magicians   671
  Steven S. Tigner

Medicine and the Physician   721
  Anne Hudson Jones

Minorities   745
  Faye Nell Vowell

Music   771
  Mark W. Booth

Musical Theater and the Revue   791
  Don B. Wilmeth

Newspapers   817
  Richard A. Schwarzlose

The Occult   851
  Robert Galbreath

Photography   887
  Richard N. Masteller

Physical Fitness   925
  Marilyn J. Gibbs and Claudius W. Griffin

Pornography   957
  Joseph W. Slade

Propaganda   1011
  Richard Alan Nelson

Radio   1127
  Thomas A. Greenfield and Nicholas A. Sharp

Records and the Recording Industry   1155
  James Von Schilling

Regionalism   1185
  Anne E. Rowe

Science   1203
  Elizabeth Barnaby Keeney

Self-Help Tradition and Popular Religion   1229
  Roy M. Anker

Sports   1277
  Robert J. Higgs

Stage Entertainment   1297
  Don B. Wilmeth

Stamp and Coin Collecting   1329
  John Bryant

Television   1367
  Robert S. Alley

Trains and Railroading   1405
  Arthur H. Miller, Jr.

Women   1425
  Jeanie K. Forte and Katherine Fishburn

Appendix: The Study of Popular Culture   1459
  Michael J. Bell

Name Index   1485

Subject Index   1571

About the Contributors

ROBERT S. ALLEY is Professor of Humanities and Chair of Area Studies at the University of Richmond. His publications include *The Producer's Medium,* written with Horace Newcomb, and *Television: Ethics for Hire?* In 1977 he produced and wrote the PBS film, *Television: For Better or Worse.* He has co-directed several symposia dealing with television and its portrayal of women. He is currently working on two books with his colleague, Irby Brown, one dealing with the role of women on television, the other on "The Mary Tyler Moore Show."

ROY M. ANKER is Professor of English at Calvin College in Grand Rapids, Michigan, where he teaches courses in literature, film, and popular religion. He is currently completing a book surveying the role of the self-help tradition in American popular religion and culture.

ROBERT A. ARMOUR is Professor of English at Virginia Commonwealth University, a fellow at VCU's Center for Educational Development and Faculty Resources, and co-director of the Central Virginia Faculty Consortium. He has published widely on literature, film, and popular culture. His most recent book is *The Gods and Myths of Ancient Egypt.*

EVELYN BECK is a staff writer for the Anderson *Independent-Mail,* a daily South Carolina newspaper. She has taught English at Florida State University, Clemson University, and Tri-County Technical College. She has published fiction and is a freelance writer for a number of regional and national publications.

MICHAEL J. BELL is Associate Professor of American Studies and Anthropology and the Chairman of the American Studies Department at Grinnell College, Grinnell, Iowa. He is the author of *The World from Brown's Lounge: An Ethnography of Black Middle Class Play* as well as numerous articles on Afro-American performance styles, workers' culture, and the history of critical theory.

BILL BENNETT, jazz critic and former production coordinator for the Smithsonian Collection of Recordings, is now employed in the Technical Systems Sector of Hewlett Packard in California.

MICHAEL L. BERGER is Professor in the Division of Human Development at St. Mary's College of Maryland. His research interests center on the impact of technology on society and human behavior, especially as it relates to automotive history. He is the author of *The Devil Wagon in God's Country: The Automobile and Social Change in Rural America, 1893–1929* and is currently completing *The Automobile: A Reference Guide* for Greenwood Press.

VICKI L. BERGER is Head of the Collections Branch and Curator of Textiles at the North Carolina Museum of History in Raleigh. Her professional service includes active membership in the Costume Society of America, Popular Culture Association, and the North Carolina Museums Council. Before Joining the Museum of History, Dr. Berger taught clothing and textiles at East Carolina University where she was the recipient of the ECU Alumni Association's Award for Teaching Excellence.

JAMES J. BEST is Associate Professor of Political Science at Kent State University, where he also teaches a course on the history of American illustration for the American Studies Program. He is the author of *American Popular Illustration* and is currently completing a book dealing with the social, economic, and cultural context of the Golden Age of American illustration.

MARK W. BOOTH is Professor and Chairman of the English Department at the University of Wyoming. He has written *The Experience of Songs,* a study of the nature and uses of folk, popular, and literary song verse, and *American Popular Music: A Reference Guide.* He has also written about and teaches courses in eighteenth-century English literature.

JOHN BRYANT is Associate Professor of English at Hofstra University. His articles on Melville have appeared in *American Literature, Nineteenth-*

Century Fiction, Philological Quarterly, and *Melville Society Extracts.* Editor and contributor to *The Companion to Melville Studies* (1986), he is also at work on *American Repose,* a book-length study of Melville's comic sensibility. His work on television sitcoms has appeared in *Journal of Popular Culture* and *Studies in American Humor.* Of an evening, he will fiddle with a stamp collection that he has maintained since the age of ten.

CHARLES CAMP has served as Maryland State Folklorist at the Maryland State Arts Council since 1976. He served as Executive Secretary/Treasurer of the American Folklore Society from 1980 through 1985 and has published more than forty articles on traditional music, crafts, architecture, and cookery in various scholarly journals. Among his activities at the Arts Council have been the production of three documentary films, four exhibitions on regional folk artists, and eight festivals. He has taught courses on food and culture in American life at the University of Maryland and Indiana University.

LORETTA CARRILLO is Lecturer in the Romance Studies Department at Cornell University. She has published articles on dance, fashion, and U. S. Hispanic popular culture.

ROBERT K. DODGE is Professor of English at the University of Nevada, Las Vegas, where he teaches American literature. He is co-editor of *Voices from Wah Kon-tah,* and of *New and Old Voices of Wah Kon-tah,* anthologies of poetry by contemporary native Americans. He is editor of *Early American Almanac Humor* and is currently working on two indexes of almanacs of the early American republic to be published by Greenwood Press.

MAURICE DUKE is Professor of English at Virginia Commonwealth University in Richmond and the author and editor of books and articles on American literature. He was for twelve years the Book Page editor and a weekly book columnist for the Richmond Times-Dispatch. Professing a lifelong interest in automobiles—he thinks he has owned about fifty—Duke was for five years a licensed amateur race car driver, competing often on tracks from Charlotte Motor Speedway to Pocono. In addition, he worked briefly as a volunteer pit crew member for a professional team for several Daytona International Speedway races. Duke is currently at work on a historical anthology of the Chesapeake Bay, on which he regularly sails.

KATHERINE FISHBURN is Professor of English at Michigan State University, where she teaches courses in women's literature, feminist critical theory, modern American fiction, and contemporary literature. She is author of *Richard Wright's Hero, Women in Popular Culture, The Unexpected Universe of Doris Lessing,* and *Doris Lessing: Life, Work and Criticism.* Recent essays of hers have appeared in *Science-Fiction Studies, Studies in the Novel, Regionalism and the Female Imagination,* and *Doris Lessing: The Alchemy of Survival.* She is currently at work on a full-length study of Buchi Emecheta's fiction, and she serves as the managing editor of the *Doris Lessing Newsletter.*

JEANIE K. FORTE is Assistant Professor of English at the University of Tennessee, Knoxville. Her research interests include women's performance art, women in film, feminist theory, and modern drama. Her publications include articles in *Theatre Journal, Theater, High Performance,* and *Women and Performance;* her book, *Women in Performance Art: Feminism and Postmodernism,* is forthcoming from Indiana University Press.

ROBERT GALBREATH is Assistant University Librarian for Collection Management at Loyola University of Chicago. An intellectual historian by training, his research interests focus on modern occultism, gnosticism, and visionary and apocalyptic literature. He edited *The Occult: Studies and Evaluations,* contributed chapters to such books as *The Occult in America* and *The End of the World,* and has published articles and essays in the *Journal of Religion, Political Theory, Science-Fiction Studies,* and elsewhere.

MARILYN J. GIBBS is Assistant Professor of Health and Sport Science at the University of Richmond, where she teaches professional preparation courses for the undergraduate program and sport sociology for the sport management graduate program. Her research interests are in pedagogy, sport administration, as well as sport and the arts. She has published material on the concepts of teaching sport and sport poetry.

THOMAS A. GREENFIELD is Dean of Arts and Sciences and Professor of English at Bellarmine College. He is the author of *Radio: A Reference Guide* (Greenwood Press), the editor of *Scholar and Educator,* and a regular reviewer for *Comparative Drama.* In 1983 his book, *Work and the Work Ethic in American Drama, 1920–1970,* was nominated for the Freedley Award for the outstanding book in Theater Arts.

CLAUDIUS W. GRIFFIN is Professor of English at Virginia Commonwealth University. He has published essays on teaching composition, edited a collection of essays on writing across the curriculum, and written a textbook on business writing. He is currently working on a book about teaching Shakespeare through film and performance.

PATSY G. HAMMONTREE is Assistant Professor of English at the University of Tennessee, Knoxville. She is the author of *Elvis Presley* (Greenwood Press), and her publications have appeared in the *Southern Quarterly,* the *Country Music Journal,* and the *Association for Communication Administration Bulletin.* She is working on a bio-bibliography about Shirley Temple Black for Greenwood Press and a drama anthology for Harcourt Brace Jovanovich.

ROBERT J. HIGGS is Professor of English at East Tennessee State University, where he teaches courses in Appalachian and Southern literature and the literature of sports. He is the author of *Laurel and Thorn: The Athlete in American Literature* (1981) and *Sports: A Reference Guide* (1982) and co-editor with Neil D. Isaacs of *The Sporting Spirit: Athletes in Literature and Life* (1977). He is presently at work on a book on sports and religion entitled *God in the Stadium, Muscle in the Church.*

THOMAS W. HOFFER is Professor of Communication and a filmmaker at the College of Communication, Florida State University, Tallahassee. His film, video, and print publications include studies in American television docudrama, broadcasting, Vietnam and Southeast Asia, Florida regional folklore, music and medical technology, Florida and American film history, aging, and national defense. He is author of *Animation: A Reference Guide* (Greenwood Press, 1981), an encyclopedic organization of the literature in cel, stop-action, drawing-on-film, and computer technologies, and is completing a book-length treatment of docudrama in American television for Greenwood Press. He is President of a videocassette production and packaging company, Dunecrest Video Corporation, Eastpoint, Florida.

LISA N. HOWORTH is Instructor in Art History at the University of Mississippi and a research bibliographer at the Center for the Study of Southern Culture. With the Center and the United States Information Agency, she has written and produced a series of slide and videotape programs on American art, and she is co-editor of a forthcoming bibliographic guide to the blues. She has contributed articles on popular culture and architecture to the *Encyclopedia of Southern Culture.*

M. THOMAS INGE is Robert Emory Blackwell Professor of Humanities at Randolph-Macon College in Ashland, Virginia. He has edited many reference guides in popular culture for Greenwood Press, including the *Handbook of American Popular Literature.* In addition to his research on the history, development, and appreciation of comic strips and comic books, he is general editor of the "Studies in Popular Culture" series for the University Press of Mississippi.

ROBERT H. JANKE is Associate Professor in the School of the Arts, Virginia Commonwealth University, where he teaches and serves as director of the school's program in speech communication. He is a past president of the Virginia Speech Communication Association, and his work includes articles published in *The Speech Communication Teacher, Perceptual and Motor Skills,* and *The Ideabook: For Teaching the Basic Speech Communication Course.*

ANNE HUDSON JONES is Associate Professor of Literature and Medicine at the Institute for the Medical Humanities of the University of Texas Medical Branch at Galveston. She is the editor of *Literature and Medicine: Images of Healers* (1983) and *Images of Nurses: Perspectives from History, Art, and Literature* (1988), and the author of numerous articles on various aspects of literature and medicine. Since 1985 she has been editor of the annual journal *Literature and Medicine,* published by Johns Hopkins University Press.

ELIZABETH BARNABY KEENEY is Lecturer on the History of Science and Allston Burr Senior Tutor at Harvard University. Her teaching and research interests focus on popular science and medicine in nineteenth-century America. She is currently working on a history of botany as popular culture in America.

WILLIAM HOWLAND KENNEY III is Associate Professor of History and Coordinator of the American Studies Program at Kent State University. His scholarly articles have appeared in *American Studies, American Music, American Studies International,* and the *Black Perspective in Music.* He is General Editor of the monographic series "Jazz: History, Culture & Criticism" at Wayne State University Press and is presently at work on a cultural history of jazz in Chicago, 1906–1930.

RICHARD N. MASTELLER is Associate Professor of English at Whitman College, where he teaches American literature and participates in an interdisciplinary General Studies program. Trained in American Studies, he has published in *The New England Quarterly* (with Jean Carwile Masteller), *Prospects: An Annual of American Cultural Studies,* and *Smithsonian Studies in American Art.* He organized the photographic exhibition, "Auto as Icon," for the International Museum of Photography at George Eastman House and recently completed the exhibition and catalogue, *"We, the People?" Satiric Prints of the 1930s,* with support from the Washington Commission for the Humanities and the Swann Foundation. His teaching and research interests include the 1930s, the 1960s, photographic history, and twentieth-century American literature.

DONALD A. McQUADE is Professor of English at the University of California, Berkeley. He has written extensively on American literature and culture. His publications on advertising include *Popular Writing in America*

(1973, 1988) and *Edsels, Luckies, and Frigidaires: Advertising the American Way* (1979). In 1985–86 he served as the guest curator of an exhibition on advertising and American social history at the Smithsonian Institution's Cooper-Hewitt Museum in New York. Most recently, he has contributed to the *Columbia Literary History of the United States* and served as both general and contributing editor to *The Harper American Literature,* a two-volume comprehensive regathering and reassessment of the American literary canon. He is currently at work on *The Culture of Efficiency,* a study of the impact of Frederick Taylor's principles of scientific management on twentieth-century American culture.

BERNARD MERGEN is Professor of American Civilization at George Washington University and associate editor of the *American Quarterly.* His research interests include the history of children's play, material culture, and environmental history. He is the author of *Play and Playthings: A Reference Guide* and *Recreational Vehicles and Travel: A Resource Guide.* Currently he is working on a cultural and technological history of snow in America.

ARTHUR H. MILLER, JR., is College Librarian at Lake Forest College. He supervises the Elliott Donnelley Railroad Collection in the college's Donnelley Library and is a member of the American Studies Program committee. He has taught in the American Studies Program and has published articles on library topics.

RICHARD ALAN NELSON Is Professor and Public Relations Sequence Head in the A. Q. Miller School of Journalism and Mass Communications at Kansas State University, following a long academic association with the University of Houston. Accredited by the Public Relations Society of America, he regularly serves as a consultant to business and government. Nelson is on the editorial board of *American journalism* and authored numerous refereed articles. In addition, Nelson is the author of *Florida and the American Motion Picture Industry, 1898–1980* and co-author of *Issues Management: Corporate Public Policymaking in an Information Society,* and is completing *Propaganda: A Reference Guide* for Greenwood Press.

NANCY POGEL is Professor of American Thought and Language at Michigan State University. Her articles and reviews on American humor, film comedy, and women in popular culture appear in *Literature/Film Quarterly, MidAmerica, American Literature, The Dictionary of Literary Biography,* and *American Women by Women.* She is the author of *Woody Allen* (Twayne, 1987). With Paul P. Somers, Jr., she has written a chapter on "Literary Humor" in *Humor in America* (Greenwood Press, 1988). She is currently working on a book about women in film comedy. She has been named an American Council on Education Fellow for 1988–89.

ANNE E. ROWE is Professor of English at Florida State University, Tallahassee. Her research interests are in Southern literature. She is the author of *The Enchanted Country: Northern Writers in the South, 1865–1910,* and *The*

Idea of Florida in the American Literary Imagination. She is presently at work on a book on the Southern domestic novel.

DOROTHY S. SCHMIDT is Associate Professor of English at Pan American University. Founder of Pan American University Press as well as the small presses riverSedge and Double SS Press, she is also an advisor for the prize-winning student literary magazine, *Gallery.*

RICHARD A. SCHWARZLOSE is Professor in the Medill School of Journalism, Northwestern University, where he teaches media history, law and ethics, and press-government relations. His articles on these subjects have appeared in several academic and trade publications. His *Newspapers: A Reference Guide* was published in 1987 by Greenwood Press, and a two-volume history of the American wire services is scheduled for publication. He spent seven years as a reporter and telegraph editor in daily newspaper journalism.

NICHOLAS A. SHARP is Director of Nontraditional Studies at Virginia Commonwealth University. Primarily interested in the relationships of language, literature, and values, he has published articles and essays on Shakespeare, Renaissance literature, popular culture, and adult education.

JOSEPH W. SLADE is Director of the Communications Center and Chairman of the Department of Media Arts at Long Island University, Brooklyn Campus. He is editor of *The Markham Review,* an interdisciplinary journal of American culture, and co-editor of the forthcoming *Essays on Science, Technology, and Literature.* Author of *Thomas Pynchon* (1974) and some sixty articles on communications, film, television, American literature, technology, and other subjects, he is currently working on two books, the first a study of the Maxim family of inventors and the second a history of the clandestine cinema.

PAUL SOMERS, JR., is Professor of American Thought and Language at Michigan State University and Contributing Editor to *National Lampoon.* He has published short stories and numerous articles on American literature and humor. He is the author of *Johnson J. Hooper* (1984).

STEVEN S. TIGNER is Professor of Philosophy at the University of Toledo. His non-magical research interests and publications lie mainly in ancient Greek philosophy and philology and in moral education. He was founding editor of the *Journal of Magic History* and has lectured widely on magic and fraud in human culture as well as on numerous other topics in the liberal arts.

JAMES VON SCHILLING is Assistant Professor in the Humanities Division of Northampton Community College in Bethlehem, Pennsylvania, where he teaches writing and journalism. A semiprofessional musician on weekends, he has written on contemporary music for the *Popular Culture Reader, Creem,* and other publications, and has taught popular music at Bowling Green State University.

FAYE NELL VOWELL is Associate Vice President for Academic Affairs at Emporia State University. She compiled the section on black Americans for *A Comprehensive Bibliography for the Study of American Minorities,* edited by Wayne C. Miller. Her current research interests are the Chicano novel and minorities on the Great Plains. As part of a National Endowment for the Humanities grant, she has written and directed a number of educational television programs about minorities on the Great Plains.

RICHARD F. WELCH is Associate Professor of Communication at Kennesaw State College, Georgia, where he teaches journalism and public address. He is the Chair of the Mass Communication and Public Relations Division of the Popular Culture Association and is presently working on a book about Hollywood's vision of the Vietnam War. He has worked as a reporter, advertising copywriter and photographer, and corporate advertising supervisor and was co-owner of a communication research firm.

MICHAEL G. WESSELLS is Associate Professor of psychology and Assistant Dean of Academic Planning at Randolph-Macon College. He studied computers and culture on a Kellogg Fellowship from 1983–1986 and has taught numerous courses for faculty and students on social and ethical issues in the use of computers. He is the author of *Computer, Self and Society,* published by Prentice-Hall.

J. CAROL WILLIAMS was formerly Assistant Professor of Philosophy and Religious Studies at Virginia Commonwealth University. Her philosophical articles on perception and semantics have appeared in the *Southern Journal of Philosophy* and *Man and World.* She has also written several essays on aspects of death ranging from images of death in popular music to the rhetoric of the funeral industry. She is now an attorney practicing in Washington, D.C.

ELIZABETH WILLIAMSON is a freelance writer and an adjunct Instructor of English at Camden County Community College in Blackwood, New Jersey. She is married to an ad man and has two small sons who want to write jingles when they grow up.

DON B. WILMETH, Professor of Theatre and English at Brown University, administered the Program and then the Department of Theatre, Speech and Dance there for thirteen years until 1987. The author, editor, or co-editor of nine books,including the award-winning *George Frederick Cooke* (1980), his most recent projects have included co-editing *The Cambridge Guide to World Theatre* (1988), writing the text for *Mud Show: American Tent Circus Life* (1988), and compiling and editing documents for the period 1865–1915 for Cambridge University Press's series on theatre documents. He is advisory editor for four journals, was book review editor for *Theatre Journal,* and theater editor/columnist for the magazine *Usa Today.* In 1982 he was selected as a Guggenheim Fellow.

RICHARD GUY WILSON is Professor of Architectural History at the University of Virginia. His specialty is American and European architecture of the nineteenth and twentieth centuries. He has been the curator of a number of museum exhibitions and author of books and articles, among them *The American Renaissance, 1876–1917* (1979), *McKim, Mead and White Architects* (1983), *The AIA Gold Medal* (1984), *The Machine Age in America* (1986), as well as a contributor to *"The Art That Is Life" : The Arts and Crafts Movement in America* (1987).

Introduction

The development of the field of popular culture as a legitimate subject of critical scrutiny and scholarly investigation in America began with the declaration of Gilbert Seldes in his audacious and ground-breaking book published in 1924, *The 7 Lively Arts,* where he asserted that

> entertainment of a high order existed in places not usually associated with Art, that the place where an object was to be seen or heard had no bearing on its merits, . . . and that a comic strip printed on newspulp which would tear and rumple in a day might be as worthy of a second look as a considerable number of canvasses at most of our museums.[1]

While the guardians of high culture and the New York critics looked on in disbelief, Seldes issued a series of propositions which threatened the foundations of the intellectual establishment. Among them were the following:

> That there is no opposition between the great and the lively [i.e., popular] arts.
> That except in a period when the major arts flourish with exceptional vigour, the lively arts are likely to be the most intelligent phenomenon of their day.
> That the lively arts as they exist in America today are entertaining, interesting, and important.
> That with a few exceptions these same arts are more interesting to the adult cultivated intelligence than most of the things which pass for art in cultured society.[2]

While outrage met his propositions, Seldes established the point of view that twentieth-century America had an artistic tradition of its own different from but no less respectable than the European, and most of the work done in the study of popular culture since is but an extrapolation of ideas expressed in his book. It was not until the 1950s, however, that serious discussion began, with such critics as Henry Nash Smith, who looked to the popular literature of the dime novel as a way of understanding American culture in *Virgin Land* (1950), and Dwight MacDonald's several essays, later collected in *Against the American Grain* (1962), in which he expressed alarm over what he saw as the trivialization of American culture through the mass media. Critics of the 1960s—Leo Lowenthal, Marshall McLuhan, Benjamin DeMott, Susan Sontag, Leslie Fiedler, and Tom Wolfe among them— approached popular culture in a variety of ways, distinctive but nearly always for reasons that had little to do with a proper appreciation for the subject. Then in the 1970s criticism of the popular arts matured with such standard works as Russel B. Nye's comprehensive history *The Unembarrassed Muse* (1970) and John Cawelti's definitive study of formula in Western fiction and film, *The Six-Gun Mystique* (1971).

Academic study of popular culture began with early investigations within the established disciplines, such as sociologists who examined the mass media for what they revealed about social attitudes and mores, and English teachers who turned to film when they discovered that some of the same critical tools applied to literature could also be used in an appreciation of the motion picture. Likewise, those engaged in research in folklore, history, mass communications, and anthropology often found it profitable to include popular culture in their purview.

The development of popular culture as a separate field began with the establishment of the *Journal of Popular Culture* in the summer of 1967 and the founding of the Popular Culture Association in 1969, both through the leadership of Ray B. Browne and the support of such scholars as Russel B. Nye, John Cawelti, Carl Bode, and Marshall Fishwick. Also in 1969 Ray B. Browne established the Center for the Study of Popular Culture at Bowling Green State University in Ohio, which coordinates archival and research activities and the publication of books and several journals and supports degree-granting programs in the Department of Popular Culture. The Popular Culture Association, as an affiliate organization, supports scholarly sessions at the national and regional meetings of the Modern Language Association and the American Historical Association, as well as other professional societies, and has held its own national convention on a regular basis since 1971. There are also eleven regional and state associations which meet regularly, and there is a Canadian Popular Culture Association and a Japanese Popular Culture Association, which were developed with the assistance of the American association.

All of this scholarly study has had its impact on curriculum. In a survey published in 1980, *Currents of Warm Life: Popular Culture in Higher Education,* Mark Gordon and Jack Nachbar reported that almost 2,000 courses in popular culture were then being offered in the United States among 260 four-year colleges and universities surveyed, and on the basis of the data gathered, they projected the actual existence of nearly 20,000 courses throughout the nation. The seven most frequently offered subjects were popular literature (especially detective and science fiction), film, mass media, ethnic studies, television and radio, history and popular culture, and popular music. These courses were most commonly offered by departments of English, Speech/ Communications, Sociology, History, Journalism, American Studies, Ethnic Studies, and Art (in descending order of frequency). While the growth and expansion of courses has been remarkable, only one other school besides Bowling Green State University has developed a degree program in popular culture—Morgan State University in Baltimore—but then all humanities and liberal arts programs have experienced little growth under the economic conditions of the last few decades in higher education.

The serious and systematic study of popular culture may be the most significant and potentially useful of the trends in academic research and teaching in the last half of this century in the United States. Scholarly study in this area will help modern society understand itself better and provide new avenues and methods of bringing to bear on contemporary problems the principles and traditions of humanism. It is no longer necessary to justify the study of popular culture by an alliance with some other social or cultural purpose. We have come to recognize that each form or medium of expression has its own aesthetic principles, techniques, and ways of conveying ideas. Each has been subject to misuse and ineptitude, but each has witnessed levels of artistic accomplishment remarkable by any measure, although finally each must be evaluated within and by its own self-generated set of standards and objectives. This last may be the most immediate task ahead for those who wish to fulfill the vision and propositions of Gilbert Seldes offered over sixty years ago.

WHY STUDY POPULAR CULTURE?

Why is it important that we study popular culture? Because there is no more revealing index to the total character and nature of a society than an examination of its popular arts and the way it spends its leisure time. Norman F. Cantor and Michael S. Werthman have put it most aptly:

Play is not frivolous; it is a serious matter centering on how men treat one another, a reflection of man's needs, aspirations, and nature. The rules which regulate the games people play differ from those prescribed for most human activities inasmuch as a man may choose to play or be a spectator or absent himself altogether. These choices are not open in the larger, more public game of life that depends on political and economic compulsion. The quality of volition therefore informs the whole history of popular culture. In that history is described what men have done and are doing with their capabilities, and further, it measures human potentiality not by showing what man can be forced to do, but by demonstrating what he can do when left to his own devices, free to follow the inclinations of his mind and spirit.[3]

In other words, popular culture shows man at his best, at his most capable and creative, and in his most liberated state. Thus the health of a society is directly reflected in the liveliness and quality of its entertainment.

Popular culture is also the place to look for the emerging art forms of the future. Drama and poetry have been with us since classical times and earlier, while the novel in the West developed in the eighteenth century and came to flower in the nineteenth and twentieth centuries. Painting and sculpture have lengthy pedigrees in Western civilization, while the print and the graphic arts came into being with the invention of printing. In this century, however, a great variety of new forms have come into being for creative expression. At least one of them, film, has in a very short time matured and become in the eyes of many a fine art, as has photography. Jazz has been acclaimed as well, as a distinctive form of American art. Other examples of new art forms developed within the last hundred years include radio drama, television drama, comic strips and comic books, animated films, docudramas, and many varieties of popular music. None of these has quite achieved the maturity found in film, but each has the potential of becoming the focus for creative energy and striking accomplishment. Some of these will drop from view, undoubtedly, but others may not fully blossom until the twenty-first century. In any case, there are a large number of cultural possibilities available to the artist, more than ever before in the known history of civilization.

Finally, Americans in particular should study their popular arts the better to understand themselves. The media inform their environment, make suggestions about ways to view themselves, provide role models from infancy through old age, give information and news as it happens, provide education, influence their opinions, and open up opportunities for creative expression. Culture emanates from society, voices its hopes and aspirations, quells its fears and insecurities, and draws on the mythic consciousness of an entire civilization or race. It is an integral part of life and a permanent record of what we believe and are. While future historians will find the accumulated popular culture invaluable, the mirror is there for us to look into immediately. America's popular culture is known throughout the world and serves as a silent ambassador. We should know what it says about us.

THE DEFINITION OF POPULAR CULTURE

What exactly is popular culture? So varied are its forms and so diverse its implications that most definitions are either too narrow or too inclusive. Ray B. Browne's definition may be both the briefest and the broadest: "all the experiences in life shared by people in common, generally though not necessarily disseminated by the mass media"[4] While the qualifying phrase helps, the term "experience" seems much too general and the meaning of "people in common" too vague. (How many people must share the experience before it becomes common enough to be popular?).

The British critic C.W.E. Bigsby in his effort probes at the ambiguities inherent in the two words, the adjective "popular" and the noun "culture":

Part of the difficulty over the meaning of the term 'popular culture' arises from the differing meanings attributable to the word 'popular' itself, for as the OED makes evident it can mean both 'intended for and suited to ordinary people,' or 'prevalent or current among, or accepted by, the people generally.' The latter includes everyone; the former excludes all but the 'ordinary.' Hence popular culture is sometimes presented as that which appeals only to the community ('mass culture') or to the average ('middlebrow'), thus confirming the social fragmentation of society, and sometimes as a phenomenon cutting across class lines. For some, therefore, it is a simple opiate, for others a subversive and liberating force, linking those of differing social and educational background.

There is further difficulty still in that the word 'culture' is susceptible both of a general and a specialized meaning. In the former sense it implies the attitudes and values of a society as expressed through the symbolic form of language, myths, rituals, life-styles, establishments (political, religious, educational); in the latter it is closer to the meaning implied by Matthew Arnold and defined by the OED as 'the training, development, and refinement of mind, taste, manners: the condition of being thus trained and refined, the intellectual side of civilization.' . . . Thus, by analogy, popular culture is sometimes defined as the attitudes and values of those excluded from the intellectual elite and expressed through myths, rituals and life-styles specific to this excluded group, and sometimes as the popular, as opposed to the intellectual arts.[5]

What is useful here is the identification of culture as "language, myths, rituals, life-styles, establishments," all symbolic forms for the expression of the attitudes and values of society. But this seems to suggest that culture is somehow automatic, unconscious, and not a willful expression of man's creative urges, as it has been in the post-industrial society.

Michael J. Bell has suggested a useful definition which pays attention simultaneously to purpose, form, and function:

At its simplest popular culture is the culture of mass appeal. A creation is popular when it is created to respond to the experiences and values of the majority, when it is produced in such a way that the majority have easy access to it, and when it can be understood and interpreted by that majority without the aid of special knowledge or experience.[6]

This may be the most serviceable of the definitions reviewed so far, except for the repetition of the problematic word—"majority." Are we speaking of the majority of the people on the face of the earth, in one nation, among one ethnic group, within one economic class, or what? And what constitutes a majority?

Perhaps the most useful definition has been offered by the historians Norman F. Cantor and Michael S. Werthman:

Man's culture is the complex of all he knows, all he possesses, and all he does. His laws and religious beliefs, his art and morals, his customs and ideas are the content of his culture.... And cutting across cultural and subcultural boundaries is the fundamental distinction between work and play: between what is done of necessity and what is done by choice.

George Santayana, writing about the distinctions between work and play, indicated the importance of the things men do when they are not engaged in the fight for survival or the avoidance of pain. He said:

We may measure the degree of happiness and civilization which any race has attained by the proportion of its energy which is devoted to free and generous pursuits, to the adornment of life and the culture of the imagination. For it is in the spontaneous play of his faculties that man finds himself and his happiness. Slavery is the most degrading condition of which he is capable, and he is as often a slave to the niggardliness of the earth and the inclemency of heaven, as to a master or an institution. He is a slave when all his energy is spent on avoiding suffering and death, when all his action is imposed from without, and no breath or strength is left him for free enjoyment. . . . Work and play here take on a different meaning and become equivalent to servitude and freedom. . . . We no longer mean by work all that is done usefully, but only what is done unwillingly and by the spur of necessity. By play, we are designating, no longer what is done fruitlessly, but whatever is done spontaneously and for its own sake, whether it have or not an ulterior utility.

Popular culture may be seen as all those things man does and all those artifacts he creates for their own sake, all that diverts his mind and body from the sad business of life. Popular culture is really what people do when they are not working; it is man in pursuit of pleasure, excitement, beauty, and fulfillment.[7]

I would refine this definition for my purposes one step further: popular culture is what we do by choice to engage our minds and our bodies when we are not working or sleeping. This can be active—playing baseball, driving an automobile, dancing—or passive—watching television, sunbathing, or reading a book. It can be creative—painting a portrait, writing a poem, cooking a meal—or simply responsive—playing a game, watching a circus, or listening to music. While highly inclusive, and perhaps imprecise, such a definition allows for the great diversity of form and the wide degree of latitude for engagement of mind and body necessary for any discussion of popular culture in the twentieth century.

HIGH CULTURE AND POPULAR CULTURE

In the effort to define popular culture, nearly all commentators have assumed that there are clear distinctions to be made between high or elite culture and popular or mass culture. For those trained in the traditional methods of cultural analysis, it is easy to draw up a list of seemingly opposite distinctions in form, function, and methods of evaluation. I will mention here only the most obvious.

Form

High culture is generally thought to be fairly exclusive in its style and content, the individual and subjective expression of an artist who aims to be different and daring in his approach, with the intention of stretching the boundaries and limitations of the form of art practiced. A premium is placed on originality and novelty; the work is often complex and intricate in its structure, the end result often being mystification and a recognition of the refusal of existence to answer to man's rational categories. Form, then, is but an extension of a philosophical attitude that recognizes mutability, temporality, and free will as influential factors in the scheme of things and the universe.

Popular culture, however, is thought to be comprehensive or relevant to a large part of the population in its style and content. It is often an anonymous or seemingly objective product of a team or an individual creative technician who follows traditional or tried-and-true approaches to the material. The patterns tend to be highly formulaic, occasionally with a different twist for surprise effect but nothing radical to disturb expectations. Situations and moral dilemmas are often oversimplified so that no mistake can be made about right and wrong, and complex questions are made easy by clarifying them in terms of standard theological categories. Mystery and the irrational have little place here since everything can ultimately be explained or has a rational basis. Form, then, reflects an attitude that embraces stability, security, and even determinism as essential factors in human existence.

Function

The function of high culture is to validate the experience of the individual. Creation is a purely aesthetic act in pursuit of truth and beauty, and, that being so, therefore self-justifying. "Art for art's sake" is a phrase generally applied to allow for creations that are non-representational and totally without use or even meaning. Whether or not the object answers our efforts to understand it, it is assumed that enlightenment is the artist's purpose, that we are better educated for having been exposed to the artist's vision, no matter how solitary or absurd. The art piece is designed aggressively to confront us, to challenge our assumptions and beliefs about art and life, and to identify the unanswered questions about existence. Rather than provide answers, it poses the questions and posits irresolvable conflicts and dilemmas.

Popular culture, on the other hand, validates the common experience of the larger part of the population. The creative act is a social act with clear economic or political consequences. It is "art for society's sake," with explicit functions to fulfill in addressing a social problem, supporting a political attitude, or selling a product which answers a psychological need, such as supporting our self-confidence. While a kind of subtle instruction is going on, or subliminal suggestion, the primary purpose is to entertain us, to cause us to relax and escape the pressures of our jobs, our problems, and our personal relationships. We want to laugh and forget, not be reminded of the tragedies and injustices of the world. We also seek in popular culture to have our attitudes and biases confirmed, to know that there are others just like us with the same thoughts, and be encouraged to believe that everything will come out right in the end. By providing a vicarious outlet for our emotional tendencies and a safety valve for our aggressions, the cultural act has a therapeutic effect and makes us feel better physically and psychologically. The answers to questions are given, and every situation has a happy ending.

Evaluation

In our efforts to appreciate and evaluate high culture, we have developed a carefully formulated, if not entirely agreed–upon, set of critical standards designed as measures against which each piece of art of its kind can be compared and found worthy or lacking. In many forms, and certainly this seems true of literature, the standards derive from the classical principles set down by the Greek critics and thinkers, and a special premium is placed on the longevity of an idea or technique, as if age is a sign of validity. Some would argue, in fact, that only with the passage of time can a piece of art be properly evaluated as it gains in reputation among the cultural arbiters of an age. Its final value, then, derives from the respect it garners among critics, the body of commentary and appreciative criticism that gathers around it. Since high culture appeals to the intellect and the noble aspirations of people, it is to be cherished and protected against the ravages of time and the whims of changing social and political systems.

Popular culture, designed to appeal to the common man and the largest part of the population, is to be evaluated only by the personal taste of the individual consumer. Its success and reputation are based on how widely distributed it is or how many people it reaches. Sales charts and the money earned by the creators are the only methods of determining its value. Because it appeals to our emotions and panders to our needs, it satisfies the baser side or non–intellectual part of human nature. Ultimately, therefore, it may be debasing, corrupting, and potentially evil, even though it never challenges the mores or principles of the larger society. Perhaps there is some of the Puritanic in this attitude—if it's fun, it must be sinful.

While such an elaborate listing of comparative features between high and popular culture would seem reflective of a substantial body of empirical data and scientifically verifiable theory, the fact of the matter is that the whole thing is an elaborate fiction, an intellectual concoction generated by the American academy and critical establishment (with the help of the British). So effectively have these arguments and points of cultural theology been preached by the critical priesthood of scholars and teachers that we are inclined to agree with them without reservation. Yes, we agree, there is a vast difference between Shakespeare and Neil Simon, forgetting in the face of cultural authority that both directed their plays to the widest possible audiences, that both addressed the basic human problems of their societies, and that both are enormously popular on the commercial stage with or without the approval of the priesthood. Shakespeare has not survived because of the enormous body of criticism generated by scholars of his work (enough to fill entire buildings) but because of the actability, durability, and continuing appeal of his plays to people of all nations and cultures.

In his influential sociological study *Popular Culture and High Culture,* Herbert J. Gans accepts the two as given separate phenomena but goes on to argue in behalf of cultural pluralism:

I believe both to be cultures and my analysis . . . rests on two value judgments: (1) that popular culture reflects and expresses the aesthetic and other wants of people (thus making it culture and not just commercial menace); and (2) that all people have a right to the culture they prefer, regardless of whether it is high or popular.[8]

Ray B. Browne has suggested that perhaps the best metaphorical figure to describe all art and culture is that of a flattened ellipse or lens:

In the center, largest in bulk and easiest seen through is Popular Culture, which includes Mass Culture. On either end of the lens are High and Folk Cultures, both looking fundamentally alike in many aspects and both having a great deal in common, for both have keen direct vision and extensive peripheral insight and acumen. All four derive in many ways and to many degrees from one another, and the lines of demarcation between any two are indistinct and fluid.[9]

I wish to go one step further than both Gans and Browne. What I wish to argue is that there are *no* distinctions between what we call high culture and popular culture, at least not in this century in the United States, which has witnessed the deep social changes wrought by industrialism, technology, and democracy. What we have is simply American culture. In the mass society in which we have lived, the older cultural distinctions make no sense, and we must seek new ways to understand the forms, functions, and ways of evaluating our arts and creative achievements. Then Americans might stop apologizing for the fact that our only indigenous art forms have been jazz and the comics, and that primarily in film have we had an international cultural impact. In fact, we might then begin to take pride in those particular accomplishments.

Where would Americans go if they wished to participate in highbrow culture? To the art gallery, the museum, the opera, the symphony concert, or the ballet? If they attended any of these in Washington, D.C., for example, at the Kennedy Center say, would they find themselves rubbing shoulders with the cultural elite? A few scholars might be present from one of the local universities, a few wealthy patrons of the arts, an ambassador or two, some political figures, and the critic from the *Washington Post,* but the vast majority of those attending are government white-collar workers, young executives and lawyers, American and foreign students, tourists, and other middle-class people—well educated perhaps, even some Ph.D.s among them, but by and large a typical cross-section of the American populace of all ages, classes, and ethnic groups. Such cultural events are open to and attended by all Americans, who by no stretch of the imagination could be called cultural elites. They may discuss the performance or exhibition, sometimes knowledgeably and sometimes on the basis of individual taste, but they do not constitute any sort of select society. In the United States, wealth has never gone hand in hand with sophistication or education, so except for a handful of philanthropists, we have had few patrons of the arts in the original sense. The patrons are the thousands of ordinary people who pay the price of admission or the taxes to subsidize the museum or program.

The extent to which high and popular culture merge in America is illustrated by a magazine called *Connoisseur.* According to a promotional flyer sent to thousands of homes in the United States, *Connoisseur* is a "clear and comprehensive guide for people 'in the know' about enduring values of art and beauty." The audience is identified in this way: "If you are classic and aristocratic in your tastes, but democratic and modern in their application [never mind the inherent contradictions here], you are the best of the breed— a contemporary connoisseur." The magazine promises to introduce the reader to the finest hotels and restaurants in the world, the loveliest precious stones, secrets of successful bidding at art auctions, how to select an architect or a decorator, or how to find a trustworthy art dealer to assess the value of his or her collection of paintings. Advertisements in selected issues promote Ming dynasty ceramics, rare works of art, antiques, horses, and exclusive hotels.

While much of this is merely Madison Avenue rhetoric and advertising hype, are we to assume that the readers of this magazine are the highbrows who support high culture? Are they a small and select group of the tasteful and wealthy? According to the statement of ownership and circulation required by the U.S. Post Office to be published in all magazines once a year to maintain fourth-class mailing privileges, on October 1, 1987, over 374,600 copies of *Connoisseur* were printed, sold, and distributed that month. According to the Internal Revenue Service tax returns, in the latest year for which the information is available, there are only about 17,266 people in the United States who annually earn a million dollars or more. So, who are all the current and potential readers? They are the middle-class people who use *Connoisseur* magazine as a wish book or enjoy the status of having a copy on display on the coffee table. The audience of connoisseurs, which a recent subscription campaign seeks to expand, is a fantasy, a non-existent group. For only $9.99 a year, the reader can be included among "those who are confident that they know the best and are proud of it." The inexpensive price of the magazine and the mass mailing of subscription appeals are indicators of its actual market—the aspiring American middle class, not the actual connoisseurs, who would hardly need a magazine to tutor them in taste.

There are simply too many examples of high and popular art which cross the boundaries to argue with any conviction that a firm line of demarcation exists. Such pieces of popular art as the film *Citizen Kane,* the comic strips *Krazy Kat* and *Little Nemo in Slumberland,* or the comedy of Charlie Chaplin have come to be recognized as classics in their own right, and each has inspired large quantities of critical commentary. On the other hand, such examples of high art as Shakespeare's *Hamlet,* Picasso's *Guernica,* or da Vinci's *Mona Lisa* have entered the popular consciousness and would be promptly recognized, and to a large extent even understood, by just about everyone. Valid aesthetic distinctions may be made between Tolstoy's *War and Peace* and Margaret Mitchell's *Gone with the Wind,* yet both have been profoundly influential in shaping the attitudes of Americans toward the events they portray and the meaning of history. Which of the two has been read by more people? Mitchell's extremely popular novel, of course, not to mention the countless millions who have seen the motion picture version, which has never ceased to be shown in some part of the world since it was first released fifty years ago.

It would seem to make better sense to describe all of this we have been discussing—high culture, low culture, mass media, popular culture, or whatever—as simply culture. Culture is a creative response to our environment, an effort to make sense out of disorder, a desire to discover beauty and meaning in the ugliness and absurdity of our world. Whether it be simple or complex, elite or democratic, individually crafted or mass produced, we should drop the adjectives "high" and "popular" and address ourselves to the total culture of twentieth-century American society without maintaining false distinctions that have no reality in the modern world. Until that time comes, however, it will continue to be necessary to use the term "popular culture" as I have in the title of this reference work in the traditional sense.

Basically, this work is a revision of the *Handbook of American Popular Culture,* which was published in three sequential volumes between 1978 and 1981. Here the volumes are published at once as a set, and there have been many modifications. New subjects have been added, including chapters on business, catalogs, computers, dance, fashion, gardening, graffiti, musical theater, and the study of popular culture. Some articles have been completely recast; some are contributed by different authors. All others have been extensively revised and updated, with special attention given to recent bibliography.

The essays on aspects of popular literature originally included in the three-volume handbook (1978–81) have been revised, expanded, and published as a separate volume, the *Handbook of American Popular Literature* (1988), as popular literature seems to have become a discrete and well-defined area of study unto itself. In any case, the *Handbook of American Popular Literature* should be considered a companion to the present set of volumes. There the reader will find essays on best sellers, Big Little Books, children's literature, comic books, detective and mystery novels, fantasy, gothic novels, historical fiction, popular history and biography, pulps and dime novels, romantic fiction, science fiction, verse and popular poetry, Westerns, and young adult fiction.

The intent of the *Handbook of American Popular Culture,* both the first and present editions, is to assemble in one place the basic bibliographical data needed to begin the study of most of the major areas of popular culture. Each chapter, prepared by an authority on the subject, provides a brief chronological survey of the development of the medium or topic; a critical guide in essay form to the standard or most useful reference works, bibliographies, histories, critical studies, and journals; a description of existing research centers and collections of primary and secondary materials; and a bibliography of works cited in the text. With this handbook, the student, scholar, librarian, or general reader can easily locate the kind of information needed to complete a research paper or project, answer a question, build a basic library, or read about a topic or personality as a matter of interest.

Just as this revised edition of the *Handbook* was going to press, an invaluable reference work appeared which, had it been available, would have been mentioned in every chapter in these volumes. The *Directory of Popular Culture Collections* by Christopher D. Geist, Ray B. Browne, Michael T. Marsden, and Carole Palmer (Phoenix, Arizona: Oryx Press, 1989) is an indexed survey of the collections of 667 libraries and institutions holding significant materials available to students and scholars in the field. As the first effort of its kind, it is necessarily incomplete, but the authors are already soliciting information for a future revision. In the meantime, the work fills a gap in a substantial and authoritative way.

I wish to express my appreciation to all the contributors to this and the first edition of the *Handbook*. Without them, of course, it would not have been possible. Also, I wish to thank James Sabin and Marilyn Brownstein at Greenwood Press, who insisted that it could become a reality. Finally, thanks must go to John Baldwin and Michael G. Bond for many a helping hand cheerfully rendered.

M. Thomas Inge
Randolph-Macon College
Ashland, Virginia 23005

NOTES

1. Gilbert Seldes, *The Seven Lively Arts,* rev. ed. (New York: Harper and Brothers, 1957), p. 3.

2. Ibid., pp. 294–95.

3. Norman F. Cantor and Michael S. Werthman, *The History of Popular Culture to 1815* (New York: Macmillan, 1968), pp. xxiii–xxiv.

4. Ray B. Browne, *Popular Culture and the Expanding Consciousness* (New York: Wiley, 1973), p. 6.

5. C. W. E. Bigsby, *Approaches to Popular Culture* (London: Edward Arnold, 1976), pp. 17–18.

6. Micheal J. Bell, "The Study of Popular Culture," in *Concise Histories of American Popular Culture,* ed. M. Thomas Inge (Westport, Conn.: Greenwood Press, 1982), p. 443. This essay has been revised and appears in this edition of the *Handbook of American Popular Culture.*

7. Cantor and Werthman, pp. xxi–xxii.

8. Herbert J. Gans, *Popular Culture and High Culture* (New York: Basic Books, 1974), p. vii.

9. Ray B. Browne, *Popular Culture and Curricula* (Bowling Green, Ohio: Bowling Green University Popular Press, 1972), p. 10.

Advertising

DONALD A. McQUADE
and ELIZABETH WILLIAMSON

Advertising remains an inescapable fact of everyday life in contemporary America. According to recent estimates, most Americans see or hear nearly two thousand advertisements a day. The promises and pleas of Madison Avenue compete for our attention no matter where we are or what we are doing—whether at work or at play, on the road or in what advertisers call "the privacy of your own home." Advertising beckons us even when we try to imagine ourselves going off to a remote, tranquil location seemingly free from commercial appeals. No place, no object, no person, no activity, no life style, and no way of thinking or talking can be completely exempt from advertising. Ours is a commercial world.

The advertising industry has changed remarkably in the past one hundred years—from the simplicity of brokering space in newspapers to the complexity of integrating the informational necessities and nuances of effective copywriting with the alluring qualities of elegantly purposeful graphics into promotional "campaigns" with demonstrably successful results. In 1880, American business spent approximately $175 million on advertising. By the turn of the century, that figure had grown to $300 million. In 1987, American corporations spent nearly $100 billion advertising their goods and services. With each new fiscal year, advertising, through its own ever-increasing personnel and expenditures, more and more vigorously underwrites the very acts of consumption it promotes.

The look and sound of advertisements have undergone similar dramatic transformations. From their origins as individual efforts to sell items by circulating unvarnished news about their availability, advertisements have developed in the twentieth century into corporate efforts to invent memorable relationships between people and products. Along the way, advertisers have helped change irrevocably the American public's relation to products. We were once a nation in which people searched for products in order to survive; we are now a nation in which products relentlessly search for people in order to survive.

In the public eye, advertising has generally been perceived as a world populated by more than its fair share of creative geniuses, eccentric egos, reprobates, and scoundrels, as well as bright and energetic professionals—an almost insistently ephemeral industry with little patience for success and no tolerance of failure, and a craft distinguished by its verbal cleverness, graphic inventiveness, and a great deal of memorable, zany talk ("When you got it, flaunt it!"). But the world of Madison Avenue and the effects of its work on the attitudes, behavior, and economy of Main Street are far more complex—and significant—than the limitations of that popular image allow.

Behind advertising's enormous outlay of intelligence and imagination lies at least one truth that both the practitioners and the critics of advertising agree on: advertising is an aggressive, creative force that helps stimulate the public's desire for particular goods and services as well as reflecting—and affecting—virtually every dimension of the American public's daily life. Yet fascinated, if not preoccupied, with discovering—and purchasing—better ways to live, few Americans pause to consider how advertising influences—and mirrors—our changing individual hopes and fears, our shifting collective expectations and anxieties.

Advertisements capitalize on the real and idealized textures of everyday experience—its frustrations and satisfactions, its ambiguities and its rewards. As such, advertisements constitute one of the most valuable cultural artifacts available to those interested in tracing the changes and continuities in American popular culture. This chapter offers multiple perspectives and approaches to the graphic record of this nation's peoples, products, and pastimes.

Advertising has been described as an institution, a business, an industry, a discipline, a profession, a science, an art, and a talent. It has been defined as news, salesmanship in print, and mass communication. Some of the best minds in, outside, and on the fringes of the business have attempted to define and deal with this elusive and controversial subject. Scholars—as well as prominent figures in the industry itself—have examined the political, economic, social, ethical, historical, and religious aspects of advertising. Each of these researchers and commentators has told us what advertising is, how it works, how it should work, and why it does not work; each has told us that advertising either informs, deceives, pleases, or frightens the American public.

Advertising has been attacked and defended by almost every segment of society. When advantageous, some will admit to having been influenced by or even drawn to advertisements. When it is not, the vindictiveness against advertising pours forth, even from public relations, marketing, and retailing specialists. An increasing number of studies of American popular culture discuss advertising but more often than not emphasize advertising's deleterious effects on this nation's life and culture. Standard American history books contain few, if any, references to advertising, although recent studies of American social history have begun to attend more rigorously to the scholarly import of advertising. Yet, to examine the advertisements of a nation is essentially to view most aspects of its existence. Advertising is the story of a nation's people. And, although advertising certainly did not originate in America, this country has probably done more than any other to foster advertising's growth and development. It has been said that some foreign politicians have studied American advertisements as a gauge for measuring and understanding America's tastes and values. Advertising is probably the most pervasive form of popular culture but, surprisingly, has rarely been examined from this perspective.

Dealing with the fullness of that perspective is an enormous challenge, but one that is limited by the scope of this chapter. By providing a history of advertising and a survey of the most important books on the subject, this chapter might well convince readers of the pervasiveness of advertising in American life and culture as well as stimulate further research and investigation of advertising as a form of popular culture.

HISTORIC OUTLINE

Although the origins of advertising have been traced back to several extremely early sources, no one is exactly sure when the trade began. Anthropologists, however, have discovered evidence of several written advertisements and offered them as the first recorded efforts in selling. The ones most often noted are a Babylonian clay tablet announcing the services of an ointment dealer, scribe, and shoemaker, as well as a piece of papyrus from the ruins of Thebes offering a reward for the return of runaway slaves. The early history of advertising, replete with its accounts of Grecian town criers and Roman shop signs, is a fascinating one, and readers are encouraged to consult the definitive histories listed elsewhere in this chapter for thorough treatments of the subject.

The earliest publications about the New World suggest that America itself was presented to the European imagination in advertising terms. The publication of the first book about America written in English, Thomas Hariot's *A Brief and True Report of the New Found Land of Virginia* (1588), may well be regarded as an advertising brochure. Sir Walter Raleigh had chosen Hariot, a well-known Oxford mathematician, to serve in the official capacity of natural scientist and surveyor on the second expedition Raleigh sponsored to explore and colonize Virginia, the huge tract of land Queen Elizabeth had given him in 1584. Accompanying Hariot was John White, a London artist commissioned to supply drawings that would document Hariot's notes and observations. The tumultuous events in Europe in 1588 prevented the Hariot/White collaboration from being published in its original form. Growing fears and preparations for war with Spain diverted potential support from the additional expeditions to the New World Raleigh had planned, as did the reports of hardships encountered in the earlier voyages to the Virginia colony. At Raleigh's urging, Hariot set aside his "scholarly" account of the Virginia expedition and prepared a brief promotional pamphlet that both "advertised" the advantages of settling the Virginia colony and rebuked what Hariot labelled "the slanderous and shameful reports" of his fellow voyagers.

Yet the Hariot/White collaboration would not have had much influence beyond courtly circles had it not been for the ambition of Theodore DeBry, a Flemish engraver and bibliophile, who set out to publish a collection of writing about the European expeditions to the New World. DeBry learned of Hariot and White's work, published it in a volume entitled *America I,* and recast White's starkly simple watercolors as elaborate engravings depicting the New World as a cornucopia inhabited by natives in classic poses and garb. DeBry's rendition became the standard, "advertised" image of the New World that defined the expectations of immigrants lured to America for the next three centuries.

Advertising *in* America, which developed in conjunction with the expanding colonial economy, began with its first product, tobacco. But as the colonies grew, advertising found its greatest impetus in shop signs and posted notices as well as in newspapers, once the press had won its right to exist. In 1690, Benjamin Harris, the celebrated colonial printer of *The New England Primer* and *A Brief and True Narrative of Some Remarkable Passages Relating to Sundry Persons Afflicted by Witchcraft at Salem Village,* secured a license to open a coffee house in Boston, where he sold the first advertised patent medicine in America and the first brand name:

That Excellent Antidote against all manner of Gripings, called Aqua anti Torminalis, which if timely taken, it not only cures the Griping of the Guts, and the Wind Cholic; but preventeth that awful Distemper of the Dry Belly Ach; With Printed Directions for the use of it. Sold by Benjamin Harris, at the London Coffee-House in Boston. Price Three Shillings the half pint Bottle.

In 1704, the *Boston Newsletter* carried advertisements for the return of some men's clothing and for the reward and capture of a thief. By the time of the Revolution, there were some thirty newspapers in America, each carrying a substantial number of advertisements, mostly classified and local.

Although American advertising had reached an appreciable level of sophistication and circulation, it was Benjamin Franklin who did much to spur the growth of advertising in America. As a printer and a newspaperman, Franklin made important improvements in advertising methods; he also made major changes in the style and format of American advertisements. Most newspaper advertisements, which consisted of three- and four-line notices, were printed in various and uneven typefaces and were difficult to read. Franklin cleaned up the ads by separating individual notices with white spaces and then by adding bolder headings, thereby making one ad distinct from the next. To emphasize the differences in the advertisements, Franklin began using illustrations representative of the individual advertiser. He experimented with such different symbols as ships, tools, horses, and books, which indicated the general contents of the advertisements. These symbols ranged in size from one and one-quarter inches to half and full columns; they also served as either borders or major graphics for the advertisements.

In addition to showing graphic expertise, Franklin also demonstrated his mastery of early American advertising copy. His knowledge of effective, persuasive copy is obvious in the notice he wrote advertising his famous Franklin stove. He stressed not only the functional features of his invention but also the pleasures and comforts it would bring to women. In effect, he promoted a very early version of Thomas Edison's proposition that the woman of the future would be a "domestic engineer." But Franklin wrote much more copy than the ad for his stove. Advertising his brother's super fine crown soap, he created such persuasive copy as: "It cleanses fine Linens, Muslins, Laces, Chinces, Cambricks, etc. with Ease and Expedition, which often suffer more from the long and hard rubbing of the Washer, through the ill qualities of the soap than the wearing."

Despite Franklin's improvements, the general state of advertising in colonial America remained relatively inauspicious. Most ads amounted to little more than simple notices for goods, services, land out west, slaves, or lost items. Merchants also used advertisements to attack competitors and to announce the newest wonder drugs. Fraudulent medical hucksters and their patent medicines, largely responsible for advertising's early disreputable public image, would continue to haunt the advertising industry well into the twentieth century.

Late eighteenth-century shopkeepers directed most of their advertisements toward the upper classes. Long notices informed the wealthy readers of the latest imported goods from England, Holland, and the Far East. Quality fabrics like chintzes and taffetas, and fragrant balms, spices, and perfumes had become signs of wealth and prestige in the New World. The words "imported" and "just arrived" in an advertisement spoke well of colonial America's taste and of the advertiser's audience, both of which changed after the revolutionary war. After the long struggle with England for independence, America experienced drastic economic and social changes, and the advertisements of the early nationalistic period reflected those changes. Whereas it had once been fashionable to own goods "just imported," it soon became as prestigious and more feasible to purchase "American-made" products, a tag that began to appear regularly in advertisements.

Newspaper growth matched the increasing American population and income, and by 1820 some 500 newspapers served more than nine million Americans. Although newspaper advertisements remained of uneven quality, they were almost certain to be read since they, along with legal notices, occupied the majority of newspaper space. Newspapers prided themselves on the number, not the quality, of the ads that appeared in their pages. And the American reading public had little difficulty distinguishing between the ever-present advertisements and the highly partisan editorials of the new nation's leading newspapers.

Technological advances in the early 1800s created—and accelerated—frequent changes in newspaper format and production, especially in price reduction. The most prominent of the so-called Penny Press newspapers, the *New York Sun,* was a 9 × 12 tabloid that rapidly reached a circulation of 20,000. Benjamin Day, its founder, soon met competition from James Gordon Bennett, a very shrewd editor, reporter, and founder of the *New York Herald.* Bennett charged two pennies for his paper, and soon its circulation doubled that of the *Sun.* Gradually, the lurid details and miraculous cures of the patent medicine ads that crowded these and most other newspapers began to compete with these newspapers' increasingly sensational crime reporting. Both men continually experimented with a wide range of advertisements. Day created a section called "Wants" and charged advertisers fifty cents per ad per day. Bennett immediately created the "Personals" column, whose contents read much like those of today.

Bennett saw the power and profit in advertising and soon added restrictions to advertisers in his newspapers. At first he limited the time that a single advertisement could run to two weeks, but he later changed the limitation to one day. He also banned the use of illustrations. His idea was to give all advertisements equal importance and impact. Advertisers protested, but the *Herald's* circulation and the need for and effectiveness of advertising forced the advertisers to submit to Bennett's strictures.

Bennett successfully implemented his restrictions for a brief time—until Robert Bonner of the *New York Ledger* matched wits with Bennett and won. Bonner, whose pulp magazine itself accepted no advertisements, did advertise for his magazine elsewhere. Deciding to break Bennett's boycott, Bonner bought whole pages in the *Herald* and simply repeated the announcement for his magazine in bold type over and over again. Sometimes he repeated a complete advertisement as many as ninety-three times in a single issue of the *Herald.*

Such chaotic competition demanded some sort of order, which soon arose in the form of a new commercial service, the advertising agent. Someone had to inform advertisers about the various newspapers, rates, and promotional options available to them, and someone had to help newspaper editors fill their pages with advertisements. The first advertising agent, Volney B. Palmer, began as a newspaper advertising solicitor, then decided to go "independent"; he established several offices selling space for a few newspapers and charged 25 percent commission for each advertisement. His first competitor was his own protégé, S. M. Pettingill, whom Palmer tried to run out of business by waging a slanderous war against him. Palmer's efforts failed, however; he eventually lost his fortune as well as his sanity. During the same period, Pettingill prospered; he became one of the industry's earliest—and most successful—advertising agents and copywriters.

The success of the advertising agent soon created its own competition and new challenges. In the early years following the Civil War, some twenty agents operated in ten cities. Although they claimed to follow the advertising rates established by the newspapers, they often dickered to the point of cutting the editors' rates a healthy percentage, thereby increasing their own commissions. The shrewd advertising agent often easily—and quickly—became a wealthy entrepreneur.

Despite the intense competitive pressures of the marketplace, the advertising agent added stability and respectability to a still floundering, but nonetheless promising industry. George P. Rowell bought mass space in one hundred papers across the country and contracted it to advertisers. Rowell also guaranteed payment to the newspapers for any ads for which he received a commission. He believed in truth in advertising and solemnly declared that "honesty is by all odds the very strongest point which can be crowded in an ad." In addition to his devotion to honesty, Rowell is best known as the founder of *Printer's Ink* and as the publisher of the first American directory that gave estimates of the nation's newspaper rates and circulations. Although Rowell stressed the need for integrity in advertising, he and many other agents made fortunes during—and after—the Civil War by advertising patent medicines. Even religious publications—the predecessors of magazines and the most influential medium in post-Civil War America—contained inordinate amounts of patent medicine advertisements. In fact, patent medicine advertising comprised 75 percent of all advertising in religious publications. Many temperance papers, for example, carried advertisements for medicines later found to contain eighty-proof alcohol. Apparently, the success of most patent medicines depended on what William James would later call "the will to believe."

Once the secret formulas of patent medicine began to be exposed (only the names, rather than the ingredients, of the patent medicines were registered with the U.S. Patent Office), the public responded by showing disapproval of both the products and the advertising agencies that promoted them. As consumer behavior gradually changed, several advertising agents also tried to clean up their increasingly unsavory reputation. F. Wayland Ayer, founder of N. W. Ayer and Son, became personally interested in the reputation of advertising after an associate made disparaging remarks about the nature of Ayer's business. Ayer responded by trying further to stabilize Rowell's efforts to establish rates between and among advertiser, publisher, and client. Ayer initiated the open contract, which stipulated not only the exact amount of money that would be spent on advertising but also included the agent's 15 percent commission, which soon became the standard for the industry. The greatest impact of Ayer's system was felt in new corporate alliances and interests: it was now clear that the agent represented the advertiser, not the newspaper. Ayer is also credited with first studying the needs and wants of the public and for having produced the first marketing survey.

Most efforts to establish a greater rapport between agents and clients focused on newspaper activity since the few magazines that were successful in the mid-century steadfastly resisted carrying advertisements. J. Walter Thompson was the first advertising agent to convince magazine publishers to accept advertisements. His success, as well as several events in the last three decades of the nineteenth century, made magazines and magazine advertising the new American corporate craze. Technological advances such as the Hoe high-speed rotary press and the halftone method of reproducing photographs, in addition to a reduction in second-class postal rates and a 50 percent increase in the literacy rate, all contributed to the mass circulation of magazines. Popular magazines introduced Americans to the nationwide sale of products, brand names, and to national advertising. *Harper's*, which initially shunned advertisements, carried 135 pages of ads and 163 pages of editorial content by 1899. J. Walter Thompson, who continued to control much of the advertising in existing magazines—principally women's—was not the only person to recognize the profit in this area. Cyrus Curtis, magazine magnate, created magazines expressly for the purpose of advertising. Among his creations were *Ladies' Home Journal, Cosmopolitan,* and *McClure's.*

The twentieth century heralded a new—and far more momentous—era in American advertising history. Industry leaders quickly converted outdoor advertising, the oldest form of the craft, into the latest rage when the first electric sign was erected in New York in 1891. Retailers actively engaged in—and depended on—advertising to boost sales. Copywriter Claude Hopkins gave Americans a breakfast product "shot from guns" as well as conferring a new status on the importance of copywriting in developing a successful advertising campaign. By the 1920s, American public—and private—consciousness was saturated with advertising. Newspapers, magazines, transit ads, billboards, posters, and window displays proclaimed America's commercial and social progress. The age of mass production, mass selling, and mass advertising had arrived. And most Americans appeared to thrive on it. Broadway, "The Great White Way," attracted thousands of tourists, as did Hudson River steamboat excursions to Albany, during which passengers gazed at lighted billboards lining the riverbanks.

At the same time, many Americans began to worry about the moral, psychological, and physical effects that such mass production and mass selling would have on American life and culture. On the one hand, outsiders (and insiders, too) wrote exposés attacking the new American way advocated in advertising as well as denouncing the fraudulent claims of irresponsible hucksters. On the other hand, advertisers themselves grouped together to create organizations and associations to regulate their own business. Vigilance committees and campaigns to promote truth in advertising sprang up overnight. Federal and local agencies such as the Federal Trade Commission, the Better Business Bureau, the Association of National Advertising Managers, and the American Association of Advertising Agencies developed policies to improve the effectiveness of advertising and to protect the consumer from fraudulent claims. *Printer's Ink,* the leading advertising trade paper, created a model statute for regulating advertising; it vowed to "punish untrue, deceptive, or misleading advertising." In 1916, advertising gained some crucial respectability when President Woodrow Wilson addressed the Associated Advertising Clubs of the World in Philadelphia.

The struggle between advertising groups and consumer groups escalated, as did American prosperity, through the 1920s. Advertising benefited greatly from the booming economy and published self-congratulatory messages proclaiming its contributions to America's financial growth and its sociocultural development. This booster spirit is amply evident in the December 7, 1929 issue of the *Saturday Evening Post,* which carried 154 pages of advertising in a 268-page publication that sold for five cents. Another new medium of the 1920s, the radio, brought advertising billings to $3.5 billion by the end of the decade.

Despite the stock market crash of 1929 and the ensuing economic upheavals, advertisers continued to prosper. Advertising revenue increased steadily during the Great Depression as Americans imagined attractive, corporate-designed alternatives to the daily financial traumas they faced. Yet advertisers had to struggle against other factors throughout the 1930s. Muckrakers launched new attacks; the Robinson-Patman Act of 1936 protected the little merchant from unfair competition by big business; the Wheeler-Lea Act of 1938 gave the Federal Trade Commission more power over advertising; and the Federal Food, Drug, and Cosmetic Act of 1938 gave the federal government authority over packaging and labeling.

In spite of controls and criticism, advertising continued to prosper. Radio remained the major advertising medium until the emergence of television, which soon became advertising's major new source of expression, new opportunities, new challenges, and new problems. American advertising undoubtedly will continue to flourish in the electronic age, despite the problems of shortages and an uncertain American economic future.

REFERENCE WORKS

Although a massive amount of material has been written about advertising, very little has been done to organize this available body of material to make it more readily accessible and useful to researchers. Some standard reference works do exist, but most are directed to the advertising industry and serve as basic trade information sources. John M. Richard's *A Guide to Advertising Information Sources* is a fifty-nine-page pamphlet annotating 277 sources, mostly yearbooks, directories, and standard rate and data information. The material is divided into seventeen categories with such diverse and confusing titles as art, bibliographies, fairs and shows, legal, and general works. The *Guide,* compiled mostly for professionals, has a somewhat limited use as a general source book; it is also marred by typographical errors. Eleanor Blum's *Basic Books in the Mass Media* contains a chapter entitled "Advertising and Public Relations" with over sixty items annotated in alphabetical order. Yet, much like Richard's *Guide,* Blum's checklist contains some highly specialized and widely diverse sources. While neither of these books contains material dated after 1971, together they provide an adequate resource for the standard advertising directories, handbooks, histories, and bibliographies. Both are indexed by subject, author, and title, and Blum's book contains a popular culture index.

A more practical basic bibliography for the uninitiated, but somewhat dated and generally difficult to locate, is *One Hundred Books on Advertising,* compiled by Richard W. Haverfield. *Advertising: An Annotated Bibliography,* compiled by the J. Walter Thompson Company with an introduction by J. Treasure, is an equally hard to find publication but with a British slant. The Thompson checklist, however, is fairly recent and, although slight, contains a solid list of references useful to British and American readers. Treasure's introduction is lively, his organization of the checklist practical, and his annotations informative. Of course, many books on advertising contain bibliographies of varying quality, but a particularly helpful one can be found at the end of Roy Nelson's *The Design of Advertising.* Although Nelson's checklist is not annotated, it is thorough and divided into handy categories that mirror the book's organization. In addition, Nelson's bibliography provides a solid overview of advertising's many dimensions; each section of the checklist also contains a list of related specialized periodicals.

The most recent—and comprehensive—bibliographical source on advertising for scholars is Richard Pollay's *Information Sources in Advertising History.* Pollay has dedicated himself to the proposition that advertising will be "a central focus in the history of the 20th century." The book opens with Pollay's plea to counter the advertising industry's almost insistently ephemeral self-image by urging historians to address advertising's importance in American business and culture as well as urging industry leaders to establish corporate archives and to encourage scholarly access to these materials. Extensive bibliographical essays follow—Julian Simon on economic data on advertising, Margaret A. Miller on professional data, Quentin J. Schultze on trade periodicals, and Pollay on types of literature available to historians. The remaining sections, gathered under such subject headings as histories, psychology, sociology, textbooks, and vocational guides, include brief but incisive bibliographical annotations and are completed by as detailed a listing as is available of advertising archives and special collections. A thorough index and a reliable system of cross-referencing make Pollay's *Information Sources in Advertising History* an easy-to-use and indispensable reference tool.

Several marketing and public relations bibliographies are useful sources for locating materials on advertising. Scott Cutlip's *A Public Relations Bibliography* contains a section on advertising. Under the heading "Mass Media," Cutlip cites ninety-three items, principally articles, which treat advertising as a public relations tool. Robert Bishop's *Public Relations: A Comprehensive Bibliography* extends Cutlip's work and provides a more thorough treatment of advertising, annotating some 160 items in a special section devoted to advertising. Bishop arranges the items, both books and articles, in alphabetical order by author, and although he makes no attempt to categorize items within the section, he does provide an index and cross-references. Several bibliographies on marketing also treat advertising in considerable detail. Among the most reliable are *A Basic Bibliography on Marketing Research* by Robert Ferber et al., Nevin W. Raber and Richard Coachys's *Marketing: A Select List of Current Titles,* and David A. Revzan's *A Comprehensive Classified Marketing Bibliography.* Two specialized checklists covering articles on advertising are *Copy Testing: An Annotated Bibliography, 1960–1972* and *Continuity in Advertising: A Selected Abstract Bibliography.*

No single index to advertising exists. After consulting the bibliographies listed above for articles on advertising, researchers might well want to consult the *Readers' Guide to Periodical Literature* and then, given a particular subject, examine any of the following—or kindred—indexes: *Accountants' Index; Applied Science and Technology Index; Art Index; Biological and Agricultural Index; Business Periodicals Index; Education Index; Index to Legal Periodicals; Public Affairs Information Index; Sociological Abstracts; Psychological Abstracts;* and *Women's Studies Abstracts,* to cite the indexes of but a few of the relevant academic disciplines.

Numerous encyclopedias, handbooks, texts, and how-to books on advertising exist, and, given the scholarly focus of this chapter, it would be unnecessary and inadvisable to list them all in these pages. The ones cited here either are representative of the kinds of books available or are considered particularly useful as primary and secondary sources. One of the earliest encyclopedias of advertising was published in 1897. *Fowler's Publicity* is a 1,000-page compendium of early advertising information and trivia. Although difficult to locate and of questionable practical use to contemporary researchers, Nathaniel Fowler's encyclopedia remains an important historical source and an unfailingly odd work to consult.

The Encyclopedia of Advertising by Irvin Graham is a classic reference manual that lists over 1,000 terms related to advertising and its many branches. Divided into three sections, this encyclopedia consists principally of alphabetically arranged and highly detailed definitions of advertising terms in the first section; the second section groups terms according to subject matter; and the third section prints a directory of advertising associations, with addresses and statements of aim. Yet this volume contains far more than a directory of advertising resources; it remains an excellent working manual meant to provide clear and instant access to the vocabulary of advertising. Another massive work with a similar format is S. Watson Dunn's *International Handbook of Advertising.*

Four reliable dictionaries in which to locate advertising terms are *Media/ Scope's Dictionary of Terms;* the *Ayer Glossary of Advertising and Related Terms;* Laurence Urdang's *Dictionary of Advertising Terms;* and, most recently, the *Macmillan Dictionary of Marketing and Advertising,* edited by Michael John Baker. Valerie Noble's *The Effective Echo: A Dictionary of Advertising Slogans* provides an excellent history of the advertising slogan and also presents a thorough discussion of the features of an effective slogan as well as a chronology of slogan lists published in *Printer's Ink.* In more recent years, David P. Cleary has studied the formulas for success of the most famous names in *Great American Brand Names,* and Paul Duncan has analyzed the ingredients of one of twentieth-century America's most popular advertising strategies in *Testimonial Advertising.*

Several handbooks on various aspects of advertising exist, and, although directed to the business community, they can serve as solid, basic reference works for researchers as well. Roger Barton's *Handbook of Advertising Management* contains thirty-two essays in nine parts that attempt to examine the principles, rather than the details, of advertising. In the preface, Barton explains to advertisers that they cannot disregard the effects of their profession on the tastes and social mores of their audiences. Barton's handbook contains a glossary of terms and is indexed. *The Dartnell Advertising Manager's Handbook* by Richard H. Stansfield and *The Dartnell Direct Mail and Mail Order Handbook* by Richard S. Hodgson cannot be overlooked, if only because of their sheer size. Those interested in understanding the interrelations of public relations and advertising should consult Howard Stephenson's *Handbook of Public Relations: The Standard Guide to Public Affairs and Communications.*

Printing and Promotion Handbook: How to Plan, Produce, and Use Printing, Advertising, and Direct Mail, by Daniel Melcher and Nancy Larrick, remains an important work that covers many facets of advertising and production. Other handbooks that deal with the production aspects of advertising include Irving Settel and Norman Glenn's *Television Advertising and Production Handbook* and Martin Padley's *A Handbook to Television Advertising*. Settel and Glenn's *Handbook* is somewhat dated, while Padley's more recent publication defines terms and discusses issues in the television industry. Jack Sissors and Jim Surmonek's *Advertising Media Planning* is one of the most recent—and instructional—titles in an expanding list on this subject. Among the many books directed to the advertising artist, the following three are fairly representative sources of information: John Snyder's *Commercial Artist's Handbook;* John Quick's *Artists' and Illustrators' Encyclopedia;* and Johnny A. Gazurian's *The Advertising and Graphic Arts Glossary*. For handbooks on copywriting, see *Advertising Writing* by W. Keith Hafer and Gordon E. White as well as *The Compleat Copywriter: A Comprehensive Guide to All Phases of Advertising Communication* by Hanley Norins. Roy S. Durstine's *Making Advertisements and Making Them Pay,* first published in 1920, remains a classic—and still useful—primer for copywriters.

In a field such as advertising, textbooks often serve as good reference guides and handbooks. A few of the major texts are *Advertising Theory and Practice* by Charles H. Sandage and Vernon Fryburger, *Advertising Procedure* by Otto Kleppner, *Advertising* by John S. Wright and Willis Winter, *Advertising:Its Role in Modern Marketing* by S. Watson Dunn and Arnold M. Barban, and *Advertising in America: An Introduction to Persuasive Communication* by Stanley M. Ulanoff. *The Commercial Connection,* edited by John W. Wright, contains one of the most expansive recent collections of essays on the role of advertising in contemporary American mass media. Wright's collection can be supplemented by the latest edition of *American Mass Media: Industries and Issues,* edited by Robert Atwan, Barry Orton, and William Vesterman, a volume with a first-rate section on advertising.

A useful directory of advertising is the *Madison Avenue Handbook,* which includes a guide to the city and an outdated listing of addresses and telephone numbers of advertising agencies, along with a still useful basic guide to sources for media, talent, photography, illustration, television, film, and copy. *The Creative Black Book,* another directory of major services, includes indexing by regional subdivisions. However, the definitive advertising directories remain the *Standard Directory of Advertising Agencies* and the *Standard Directory of Advertisers.* Commonly called "The Red Books," these two directories contain the most updated lists of agencies and advertisers available: the *Standard Directory of Advertisers* lists some 17,000 companies and issues an annual geographical index; the *Standard Directory of Advertising Agencies,* published three times a year, lists some 4,000 United States and 400 foreign agencies. *Marketing Strategies of America's 125 Largest Advertisers,* published by the weekly trade journal *Advertising Age,* gives detailed accounts of the sales, expenses, and earnings of America's largest corporations. This reference work also contains a complete list of marketing, advertising, and sales personnel, along with the names of the advertising agencies that handle the accounts.

RESEARCH COLLECTIONS

Collections of advertisements are widely scattered among trade associations, advertising agencies, university libraries, public libraries, and historical societies. If one is interested in collections of advertisements of a particular product—for example, pharmaceuticals—one should consult the *Subject Directory of Special Libraries and Information Centers* by Margaret Labash Young et al. to locate pharmaceutical companies that maintain collections of their products' advertisements. Although many companies preserve collections of their advertisements, these materials generally are not available for public inspection. However, the Advertising Research Foundation and the Association of National Advertisers are two advertising associations that maintain readily accessible research collections, consisting mostly of print advertisements, vertical clipping files, and copies of speeches.

The J. Walter Thompson Company's Information Center in New York has established the most comprehensive corporate archive on advertising, and such agencies as N. W. Ayer, Doyle Dane Bernbach, and Ogilvy and Mather have undertaken similar curatorial programs in recent years. The J. Walter Thompson collection of print advertisements, clippings, news reports, studies, and press releases now numbers nearly 200,000 items. The University of Wisconsin houses the Frank Thayer Collection on the Law of Mass Communications, and the University of Illinois Communication Library's collection focuses on communication theory and its effects. Political advertisements and posters are the emphasis of the collection at the University of Michigan Library. Yale University maintains a strong graphic arts collection, with special emphasis on eighteenth and nineteenth-century trade cards. The Friendship Library at Fairleigh Dickinson University serves as the official depository for the outdoor advertising industry, and included among its 2,500 items are fifteen original billboards. Other notable university libraries with special collections of advertising are the Bancroft Library at the University of California, Berkeley, which has extensive holdings on advertising in the American West, as well as the Baker Library in the Graduate School of Business Administration at Harvard University.

The Prints and Photographs Division of the Library of Congress contains extensive holdings on advertising. The Ayer Collection of Business Americana at the Smithsonian Institution includes at least 400,000 advertisements from the *Saturday Evening Post*. The Smithsonian also serves as the repository of the Warshow Collection of Business Americana, an extraordinary compilation of the eclectic collecting tastes of its founder. The Cooper-Hewitt Museum in New York, the graphic arts and design wing of the Smithsonian

Institution, maintains extensive holdings on American advertising, as was amply evident in its 1985–86 exhibition entitled "Advertising America," for which Donald McQuade served as guest curator.

Some years ago, the New York Public Library established the history of advertising and advertising periodicals as two of its corporate research interests, and the Cincinnati Art Museum Library enjoys a deserved national reputation for its collection of prints and engravings in advertising and the graphic arts. The Bella C. Landauer collections at the New-York Historical Society and at New York's Metropolitan Museum are remarkable both for the nature and the extent of the advertising material gathered in each, especially eighteenth-, nineteenth-, and early twentieth-century American print advertisements and trade cards. The New-York Historical Society, the Massachusetts Historical Society, and the Chicago Historical Society are but the most prominent local institutions that maintain large collections of pre-twentieth-century American print advertisements and advertising trade cards, along with city directories replete with elegant ads as well as industry and corporate catalogs. A remarkably good collection of American advertising cards can also be found at the American Antiquarian Society.

HISTORY AND CRITICISM

The first detailed history of advertising appeared in 1874, but *A History of Advertising from the Earliest Times* by Henry Sampson is slanted toward British advertising and is not especially useful as a source for American advertising. In fact, chapter 19 attacks colonial American advertisements on the grounds of naïveté, immorality, flippancy, and greed. From its first publication in 1929, Frank Presbrey's *The History and Development of Advertising* has remained the definitive history of advertising. Presbrey's text surveys British and American advertising and remains the soundest and most unbiased early history of the profession. Yet, in light of the book's date of publication as well as the remarkable developments in advertising over the past sixty years, Presbrey's history must be supplemented by more recent work.

A sound, thorough, and complete history of American advertising has yet to be published. Thirty years after Presbrey's history, James Playsted Wood's *The Story of Advertising* appeared; it treats advertising as "a story of people" and as the primary expression of democracy. The most recent history of American advertising, Stephen Fox's *The Mirror Makers,* is also the most engaging and reliable survey of advertising since 1958, when Wood's text was published. Fox creates a gracefully written narrative history of advertising's development, and especially of the very different selling strategies of the industry's leading figures. Fox's study focuses on the people who have created twentieth century American advertising, and how their work reflects the quirks and personalities of the producers. Fox carried into the project the impression that advertising has the independent power to create and shape mass tastes and behavior, but he eventually concluded that advertising serves merely as a mirror that reflects society. Fox begins his history of American advertising in the late nineteenth century, chronicles the importance of such early agency founders as J. Walter Thompson and Albert Lasker, and then studies the most prominent figures on Madison Avenue today, including David Ogilvy, Shirley Polykoff, and Jerry Della Femina. The controlling idea of his study is that "advertising gathered power early in this century, reached a peak of influence in the 1920s, and since then—despite consistent gains in volume and omnipresence—has steadily lost influence over American life."

Three recent—and more focused—studies, when combined with Stephen Fox's general overview, provide readers with a clear, engaging, detailed, and reliable chronology of the development of modern American advertising. *The Making of Modern Advertising* by Daniel Pope traces the economic circumstances in the period between the Civil War and 1920 that led to the formation of advertising agencies, the articulation of ethical standards, and the emergence of distinctive advertising styles and persuasive strategies. In this respect, Pope's work draws on two earlier studies, Ralph M. Hower's *The History of an Advertising Agency* and George P. Rowell's *Forty Years an Advertising Agent: 1865–1905*. In the final chapter Pope takes a longer view when he compares and contrasts these early developments to the current state of advertising. He examines, for example, the impact on advertising of such factors as technological advances, new theoretical work in the social sciences, and recent shifts in ethical and social standards. Pope's thoroughly researched and highly readable study makes a substantial contribution to advancing our knowledge of both American advertising's most formative years and its most formidable institutions and leaders.

Published two years later, after *The Making of Modern Advertising,* Roland Marchand's *Advertising the American Dream: Making Way for Modernity, 1920–1940* extends and enriches Pope's work by examining the social context of American advertising during the 1920s and 1930s. Marchand's study is the most comprehensive and lucid account we have of the specific ways in which the advertising profession complicated the American public's adjustment to the psychological and social intricacies of modern life by introducing new products and assisting corporations to respond more profitably to changing consumer needs, wants, and whims. Challenging the notion that advertising is a reliable and simple mirror of social behavior, Marchand argues that advertising drew much of its influence by borrowing freely from the other forms of popular culture that also gained prominence during this same period—principally radio, and especially soap operas, as well as photography, cartoons, and the tabloid press. Marchand's exemplary work is supported by a thorough bibliographical essay detailing important sources of information about the role of advertising in early twentieth-century American business and culture. *Advertising the American Dream* establishes a scholarly standard for the work needed on other areas and periods in advertising history.

A less scholarly analysis of "the golden age of American advertising" can be found in *When Advertising Tried Harder: the Sixties.* . . . Adapting the title from the famous Avis campaign of that period, Larry Dobrow, a former advertising executive, pays tribute to the agencies and the people—Mary Wells, Jack Tinker, George Lois, Jerry Della Femina, and especially David Ogilvy and William Bernbach—who led the "revolution" in advertising creativity during the 1960s. Replete with excellent—and memorable—illustrations, Dobrow's oversize volume may itself serve as a visually attractive alternative to many of today's less-than-appealing advertisements.

More specialized "histories" of advertising have appeared with greater frequency. James Harvey Young, for example, documents the fascinating rise and fall of patent medicines and their advertising in his excellent study *Toadstool Millionaires: A Social History of Patent Medicines.* The advertisements Young prints can be supplemented by two generous collections of patent medicine advertisements: Gerald Carson's fairly whimsical *One for a Man, Two for a Horse* as well as Grace Hechtlinger's *The Great Patent Medicine Era.* A far less appreciative assessment of advertising's history in this country can be found in E.S. Turner's historical exposé, *The Shocking History of Advertising!* In the preface, Turner admits to a pessimistic view of humankind; individuals are, he observes, without grace, and advertisers, unless they affirm their commitment to an unequivocal code of ethics, will continue to contribute to American society's downfall. Frank Rowsome adopts a far less moralistic tone in *They Laughed When I Sat Down: An Informal History of Advertising in Words and Pictures,* which provides a lighthearted history of magazine advertising between the Civil War and World War II. Rowsome, who titled his history after John Caples's famous advertisement, looks at the entertaining aspects of advertising as well as the informative and personal memoirs of prominent early advertising agents. Clarence P. Hornung and Fridolf Johnson's *200 Years of American Graphic Art* traces the history of American printing from 1639, when the first printing press in the American colonies cranked out broadsides and Bibles in Cambridge, Massachusetts. This fast-paced, breezy survey of the role of graphic art in American newspapers, magazines, almanacs, trade cards, posters, print advertisements, and sundry forms of advertising ephemera includes a great deal of attention to advertising and its importance in the development of commercial art.

Most critical books on advertising are either exposés or defenses of the profession. However, there are a few which, for various reasons, have become important books in the study of advertising. One such study, Otis Pease's *The Responsibilities of American Advertising,* helped set a direction—and a moral tone—for subsequent discussions of advertising. Neil H. Borden's *The Economic Effects of Advertising* is a landmark study of the effects of advertising within a capitalistic society. In his 1954 study, *People of Plenty,* David Potter analyzes the role that advertising has played in America's history of economic abundance. Julian Simon's *Issues in the Economics of Advertising* is another standard reference for this aspect of advertising. More recently, Mark Albion and Paul W. Farris have published a valuable assessment of advertising's impact on the American economy, *The Advertising Controversy: Evidence on the Economic Effects of Advertising.*

In *Motivation in Advertising,* Pierre Martineau suggest that advertising's primary function is to help people express their convictions and not to manipulate consumers. In *Reality in Advertising,* advertising executive Rosser Reeves formulates such influential theories about advertising as a product's "U.S.P.—Unique Selling Proposition"—and argues that advertising agents must begin to look objectively at their craft. Leo Bogart's *Strategy in Advertising* deals with the generic characteristics of mass communications, focusing on media strategy. Bogart, in directing his media plans, suggests that advertising remains the most visible aspect of modern society's values. Walter Taplin, in *Advertising: A New Approach,* attempts to overcome some of the negative judgments of advertising by looking at such issues as human wants and the role of information in persuasion tactics. Raymond A. Bauer and Stephen A. Greyser study consumer judgment of advertising in *Advertising in America: The Consumer View.* In addition to providing a historical review of consumer attitudes toward advertising, Bauer and Greyser supply data analyzing Americans' reactions to advertisements as well as criticizing advertising in America. Eugene Linden's *Affluence and Discontent: The Anatomy of Consumer Societies* provides a provocative and informative assessment of advertising's impact on consumer behavior. More recently, Daniel Horowitz in *The Morality of Spending* examines the ways in which Americans have characteristically greeted a rising standard of living with a mixture of pleasure and disquiet. Focusing on the years from 1875 to 1940, Horowitz analyzes American attitudes toward patterns of consumption and studies the striking similarities in the ways such social theorists as Alexis de Tocqueville, Thorstein Veblen, Robert and Helen Lynd, and Daniel Bell have viewed the effects of consumption on American life and culture.

A countless number of books attack advertising and propose consumer rights policies. Interestingly enough, many of these books are written by former advertising agents. A 1934 exposé by James Rorty, *Our Master's Voice: Advertising,* vilifies advertising agents as dull and hopeless demons and sadists. The book also includes an attack on Bruce Barton's contention in his best seller, *The Man Nobody Knows,* that Jesus was the first ad man. Another early twentieth-century best seller is Frederick Wakeman's *The Hucksters.* In *The Clowns of Commerce,* insider Walter Goodman explains that the extreme defensiveness of advertising agents arises out of their own inner turmoils. The most widely circulated—and popular—analyses of advertising, however, remain those of Marshall McLuhan and Vance Packard. Among his many books, McLuhan's *The Mechanical Bride: Folklore of Industrial Man* and *Understanding Media: The Extensions of Man* deal most directly with advertising. In *Understanding Media,* McLuhan argues that advertising is the most faithful reflection of human activities but that in its attempt to achieve universal programmed harmony, advertising will also create its own demise. Vance Packard's *The Hidden Persuaders* unpacks the premise that advertisers manipulate the American public through psychological and social-scientific techniques.

Joseph J. Seldin's *The Golden Fleece* describes the postwar upheaval of American society and traces advertising's exploitation of the new middle class in their search for "the good life." Another book that traces the roots of American industrialism and the relationship between capitalism and advertising is Stuart Ewen's highly regarded *Captains of Consciousness: Advertising and the Social Roots of the Consumer Culture,* a study that is extended in his *Channels of Desire: Mass Images and the Shaping of American Consciousness,* coauthored with Elizabeth Ewen. The past three decades have witnessed an increasing number of Marxist critiques of advertising, led most notably by such prominent European theorists as Raymond Williams and Henri Lefebvre. In this country, such efforts are ably represented by Stuart Ewen's work as well as by such volumes as *Monopoly Capital* by Paul Baran and Paul Sweezy.

Recent commentators have also devoted a great deal of time and intelligence to studying the ideological dimensions of advertising, and with intriguing results. *Rhetoric and Ideology in Advertising* by Gunnar Andren et al. offers some alarming answers to the two questions its authors pose:" 1) What methods are used by advertising to get the readers to accept a message? 2) What kind of ideological content—if any—is found in advertising in the USA?" Gillian Dyer's *Advertising as Communication* provides a similarly transatlantic view of advertising and offers a critical perspective on the linkages between and among semiotics, language, rhetoric, and the "birth" of an advertisement. Additional incisive (and transatlantic) views of this subject include those of Judith Williamson in *Decoding Advertisements: Ideology and Meaning in Advertising* and, more recently, those of John Sinclair in *Images Incorporated: Advertising as Industry and Ideology.* Yet, the most consistently incisive assessments of the semiotic elements of advertising and their ideological significance can be found in the essays of Roland Barthes.

The exploitation of the consumer in this country has been documented in *The Permissible Lie: The Inside Truth About Advertising.* Author Samm Sinclair Baker admits that in 1933 he decided to make his fortune in advertising and then later to expose its evils. Baker's book, first published in 1968, is an attempt to eliminate the evils of advertising and to enlarge its benefits for the entire nation. In 1972, Robin Wight argued that there exists an unseen but powerful consumer revolution against advertising and marketing. *The Day the Pigs Refused to Be Driven to Market* admits that the revolution has no marches, no manifestos, no leaders, and few formal followers, but that the movement is powerful. Three years later Jeffrey Schrank's *Deception Detection: An Educator's Guide to the Art of Insight* appeared, which reads as though it were the manifesto to the movement described by Wight. Schrank's book presents a collection of ideas that could be part of a consumer education course or a shopper's survival kit. In a similar vein, Ivan L. Preston's *The Great American Blow-Up: Puffery in Advertising and Selling* argues that the consumer movement should stop nothing short of complete elimination of false, deceptive advertising.

Advertising has taken advantage of some particular American weaknesses, according to several commentators. Wilson Bryan Key's two books of the 1970s examine advertising's seductive techniques. *Subliminal Seduction* and *Media Sexploitation* conclude that through visual, auditory, and olfactory techniques the media program Americans into using cigarettes and alcohol and trade on our sexual insecurity and obsessions. The health industry promoted by advertising is attacked in Ralph Lee Smith's *The Health Hucksters* and in Arthur Kallet and F. J. Schlink's *100 Million Guinea Pigs*. Thomas Whiteside exposes the tobacco industry and pleads for strong federal regulation of cigarette advertising in his 1971 book *Selling Death: Cigarette Advertising and Public Health*.

The susceptibility of Americans to seductive political advertising has been amply documented in the years following the publication in 1969 of Joe McGinniss's *The Selling of the President 1968*. In *Politics and Public Service* (1977), David L. Paletz provides a primer not only on "the process by which the [television] spots are produced" but also on the messages they communicate to the American public. Robert Spero's *The Duping of the American Voter: Dishonesty and Deception in Presidential Television Advertising* (1980) challenges the principle that political advertising is "protected speech" under the First Amendment and therefore "required to meet no broadcast standards of behavior and ethics." Spero suggests implementing a series of twelve possible remedies, including requiring candidates to appear in each of their ads and creating a political advertising code. Kathleen Jamieson's impressive study *Packaging the Presidency* (1984) presents a history of campaign advertising—from the pre-television era of handbills, whistle-stop rallies, and newsreels to the broadcast messages of campaigns from 1952 through 1980. *The Spot: The Rise of Political Advertising on Television* (1984) by Edwin Diamond and Stephen Bates offers a history of the political commercial (the "polispot") and recounts the effects of televised "polispots" on presidential elections by analyzing more than 650 political commercials in the archives of the New Study Group at MIT, which Diamond heads. The most recent treatments of this subject are *New Perspectives on Political Advertising* (1986), edited by Lynda Lee Kaid et al., and Philip Gold's *Advertising, Politics, and American Culture* (1987), in which Gold offers an expansive view of advertising: as full of contradictions and paradoxes.

Commentators on advertising have addressed not only its effects on politics but also its impact on individual, group, and racial and ethnic identity. And controversy has continually swirled around the images of children, minorities, and women in advertising. As early as 1938, an advertising-sponsored study of children and advertising appeared. E. Evalyn Grumbino's *Reaching Juvenile Markets: How to Advertise, Sell, and Merchandise Through Boys and Girls* attempted to study the changing interests of children and thereby to "create better appeals to the juvenile market and so eliminate much of the exploitation of boys and girls, which is resented by all interested in the welfare of children." But the welfare of children has not been considered, argues Ron Goulart in *The Assault on Childhood*. Goulart exposes many of the commercial assaults on children, including comics, the media, and advertising. Bruce Brown catalogues—and analyzes—the changing images of family life in American magazine advertising between 1920 and 1978, and D. Parke Gibson reports on how advertisers reach black consumers in *The $30 Billion Negro*. More recently, an informative exhibition on the changing image of blacks and other minorities in advertising, entitled "Ethnic Images in Advertising" and under the direction of curator Gail F. Stern, has traveled the nation under the sponsorship of the Smithsonian Institution's Traveling Exhibition Series before returning to its permanent display at the the Balch Institute for Ethnic Studies in Philadelphia. *Edsels, Luckies, and Frigidaires: Advertising the American Way*, by Robert Atwan, Donald McQuade, and John W. Wright, contains the most thorough documentation of the changing images of blacks, women, and men in American advertising. For a contrasting assessment of advertising's impact on American culture, see Ronald Berman's *Advertising and Social Change*.

The changing image of women in advertising has been the focus of increasing attention. In *Ladies of the Avenue*, Patricia E. Tierney bitterly discusses the sexism and prejudice within the advertising business world. A 1975 publication, *Advertising and Women*, sponsored by a consultative panel of the National Advertising Review Board, examines the portrayal of women in advertising. The panel readily documented the unfavorable image of women in commercials. Gillian Dyer extended that work in a 1987 publication, *Boxed In: Women and Television*. Carl Naether published *Advertising to Women* in 1926, the first detailed inquiry into the specific strategies advertisers use to establish memorable relationships between women and the products agencies are hired to promote. Although originally published in England, *Images of Women: Advertising in Women's Magazines* by Trevor Millum and *Advertising in Women's Magazines, 1956–1974* by Janice Winship have much to offer on the study of that subject. Kathryn Weibel devotes a chapter to women and magazine advertising in *Mirror Mirror: Images of Women Reflected in Popular Culture*. Joseph Dispenza's 1975 study *Advertising the American Woman* cataloged advertising images that highlight the extent to which Americans have been conditioned to limit their view of the roles of women in our society. In *Gender Advertisements*, the social anthropologist Erving Goffman analyses selected print advertisements and photographs to illustrate how Americans "display" themselves. Goffman argues that advertising both shapes and reflects what have been for generations such socially acceptable curiosities of human behavior as the long-standing depiction of men instructing women (but rarely vice versa) and the traditional childlike poses of women. The most recent—and incisive—studies of the images of women in advertising include John S. Straiton's 1984 publication *Of Women and Advertising*; Joseph Hansen and Evelyn Reed's *Cosmetics, Fashions, and the Exploitation of Women*, published in 1986; and Gillian Dyer's 1987 study, *Boxed In: Women and Television*. Despite the more favorable recent portrayals of women in advertising initiated by public utilities and other public service companies, advertisers remain reluctant to permit women to abandon their principal identity as the purchasers of most day-to-day goods and services.

Numerous studies of the cultural consequences of advertising have appeared in recent years. Denys Thompson's *Voice of Civilisation: An Enquiry into Advertising* did much to set the direction and tone of later efforts. Most distinguished among these are Merle Curti's remarkably incisive essay "The Changing Concept of 'Human Nature' in the Literature of American Advertising," Jackson Lears's *No Place of Grace,* a brilliant critique of modernism and the transformation of American culture from 1880 to 1920, as well as such first-rate studies as James Sloan Allen's *The Romance of Commerce and Culture,* Adrian Forty's *Objects of Desire,* and, most recently, Jennifer Wicke's *Advertising Fictions: Literature, Advertisement, and Social Reading. The Culture of Consumption,* edited by Richard Wightman Fox and Jackson Lears, presents a series of six finely wrought and learned essays on the effects of our consumer society on American journalism, literature, politics, science, and advertising. The first two essays focus on advertising and mass-market magazines in the late nineteenth century. Jackson Lears illustrates the ways in which advertising helped shape a consumer culture by promoting the therapeutic value of self-fulfillment and self-gratification. In a related essay, Christopher Wilson demonstrates the connections between the mass-market magazine, which served as a forum for advertisements, and the subsequent development of consumer culture. An "insider's" view of the political, sociological, psychological, and moral aims, responsibilities, and consequences of advertising can be found in *Advertising: Its Cultural and Political Effects* by Giancarlo Buzzi, a former advertising executive.

Michael Schudson provides the most balanced and exhaustive view of advertising's effects on both consumer behavior and, more broadly, on American culture. His study of the impact of advertising on American society, entitled *Advertising, the Uneasy Persuasion,* rejects both the inflated claims of practitioners and the exaggerated fears of critics. Schudson finds advertising as a business to be not nearly as important, influential, or scientifically grounded as either its advocates or its critics proclaim. Schudson also convincingly demonstrates how businesses hedge the bets they place on the powers of advertising. He notes, for example, that in most cases advertisers target their pitches toward heavy users, rather than infrequent or new users of products. Advertisers correctly assume, Schudson asserts, that most consumers do not pay much attention to most ads most of the time. To understand better advertising's effects on our growing "materialism," Schudson traces the nineteenth-century roots of America's consumer culture and offers a fascinating case study of advertising's role in introducing women to the cigarette market. Schudson concludes that advertising mainly reinforces, not creates, consumer preferences already deeply ingrained by traditional purchase patterns, population growth, rises and falls in real income, and other demographic and cultural forces.

Advertising executives take special pleasure and pride in writing about themselves and each other, and there is no paucity of biographies and autobiographies of these most prominent men and women in the field. A sampling of the most interesting and informative life stories follows. Chalmers Lowell Pancoast's *Trail Blazers of Advertising* is a thoroughly engaging collection of personal anecdotes and stories about advertising when it was a "game and an adventure," not a "science or profession." Pancoast writes in what is at once a lively, dramatic, and nostalgic style. Claude C. Hopkins, one of the giants of early advertising, wrote two important books, *Scientific Advertising* and *My Life in Advertising*. Estelle Hamburger's *It's a Woman's Business* is one of the first memoirs of advertising written by a woman. It should be read in conjunction with Jane Maas's *Adventures of an Advertising Woman,* the most recently published memoir of a female advertising executive. Earnest Elmo Calkins, author of several books on advertising, published the story of his many years as an ad man in *"And Hearing Not—."* John Gunther chronicles the life and times of perhaps the most influential early twentieth-century advertising agent in *Taken at the Flood: The Story of Albert D. Lasker.* James Webb Young's book *How to Become an Advertising Man* grew out of his lectures delivered at the University of Chicago to the trainees of the J. Walter Thompson Company. David G. Lyon's *Off Madison Avenue* and Jim Ellis's *Billboards to Buicks* offer not only autobiographical insights into the advertising world but also suggestions on how to start an advertising agency. In *My First Sixty-five Years in Advertising,* Maxwell Sackheim tells about his life in direct mail and offers hints about this lucrative aspect of advertising. *The Blue Streak: Some Observations Mostly About Advertising* contains a chronology of the personal memoirs of Fairfax M. Cone; Cone's own autobiography is *With All Its Faults: A Candid Account of Forty Years in Advertising.* Perhaps the most well known—and celebrated—public representative of the contemporary advertising industry is David Ogilvy, who captures the spirit and substance of his years in the business in *Confessions of an Advertising Man; Blood, Brains*

& *Beer,* and, most recently, in *Ogilvy on Advertising.* Other prominent contemporary autobiographies are: Jerry Della Femina's *From Those Wonderful Folks Who Gave You Pearl Harbor,* George Lois's *George, Be Careful,* Charlie Brower's *Me and Other Advertising Geniuses,* Shirley Polykoff's *Does She or Doesn't She? And How She Did It,* and John O'Toole's *The Trouble with Advertising,* each of which attests to the variety of backgrounds, personalities, experiences, opinions, and philosophies that exists in the world of advertising, as does Bart Cummings's recently published series of interviews, entitled *The Benevolent Dictators,* with the current leaders of the advertising industry.

Since advertising pervades virtually every area of mass communications, it is possible here to discuss only the most basic books relating advertising to a particular branch of communications. Readers are therefore advised to consult other chapters in this handbook if they are interested in the role of advertising within a particular area of the mass media. (See, for example, the chapter on television for material on advertising's relation to that medium.) *Outdoor Advertising: History and Regulation,* edited by John W. Houck, contains nine essays dealing with the oldest form of advertising. Although most of the essays deal with regulatory and aesthetic goals, one essay by Philip Tucker, former president of the Outdoor Advertising Association of America, provides a solid survey of the history of outdoor advertising in America. Frank Luther Mott's *American Journalism* traces the historical development of newspapers in the United States, while *National Advertising in Newspapers* by Neil H. Borden et al., although published in 1946, offers some sound and still applicable newspaper advertising principles.

Histories of American magazines that also discuss advertising are Frank Mott's *History of American Magazines,* James Playsted Wood's *Magazines in the United States,* Theodore Peterson's *Magazines in the Twentieth Century,* and James L. C. Ford's *Magazines for Millions: The Story of Specialized Publications.* Wood's history addresses the state of both early and mid-twentieth-century magazine advertisements, while Ford's study describes some of the serialized publications in the advertising profession.

In *A Decade of Radio Advertising,* Herman Hettinger gives a general survey of broadcast advertising and attempts to define and evaluate its basic structure and its economic and social roles. *Television and Radio* by Giraud Chester et al. and *Advertising in the Broadcast Media* by Elizabeth J. Heighton and Don R. Cunningham are two reliable basic texts that provide broad overviews of the finer details about the workings of the business. These volumes should be supplemented by Erik Barnouw's more recent study, *The Sponsor.* Although they are essentially how-to books, *Anatomy of Local Radio-TV Copy* by William A. Peck and *The Power Technique of Radio-TV Copywriting* by Neil Terrell contain some suggestions on the structure of commercials. The standard history of television remains Erik Barnouw's *Tube of Plenty.* Readers might also want to consult Martin Mayer's *About Television.* Lincoln Diamant's *Television's Classic Commercials: The Golden Years 1948–1958* provides a historical background for television commercials and also reprints sixty-nine television commercial classics. In *The Sponsored Film,* Walter J. Klein deals with the public relations and commercial aspects of the sponsored film industry. A pictorial history of motion picture, newspaper, and magazine advertising through the 1940s can be found in Russell C. Sweeney's *Coming Next Week: A Pictorial History of Film Advertising.*

Few critical studies of advertising copy and design exist. Manuel Rosenberg's *The Art of Advertising* is a 1930 version of a book of basic design for the advertising artist. Roy Paul Nelson's *The Design of Advertising,* first published in 1967, appeared in its fifth edition in 1985. Nelson's text contains an excellent bibliography in addition to being a solid sourcebook on typography and design. An overview of American advertising art is presented in a bicentennial edition, *200 Years of American Graphic Art: A Retrospective Survey of the Printing Arts and Advertising Since the Colonial Period* by Clarence Hornung and Fridolf Johnson, who admit that it would take years and ten volumes to do justice to such a topic. Hornung and Johnson's scope is broad and sketchy, whereas Theodore Menten's range is far more focused in *Advertising Art in the Art Deco Style,* a volume containing some 300 art deco ads and posters from nine countries originally produced between 1924 and 1940. Menten argues that advertising art really came into its own as never before in history during the art deco period. Stephen Baker, in *Visual Persuasion: The Effect of Pictures on the Subconscious,* contends that Americans have always demanded realism in their art and that advertising artists have yet to understand fully the effects of pictures on the subconscious. *Making Ads Pay* by John Caples, author of the famous ad, "They Laughed When I Sat Down," is a study of creativity and effective copywriting. Although it is a British publication, Geoffrey N. Leech's *English in Advertising: A Linguistic Study of Advertising in Great Britain* suggests the possibility of a similar study of American advertising and signals an ever-increasing interest in the language of advertising, as is now evident most notably in such studies as *The Language of Television Advertising* by Michael L. Geis and in *The Language of Advertising* by Torbin Vestergaard and Kim Schroder.

Virtually nothing has been done to study speciality advertising, with the noteworthy exception of the work of George L. Herpel and Richard A. Collins in *Speciality Advertising in Marketing.* In addition to merchandising techniques, Herpel and Collins discuss the role, concept, and history of speciality advertising. Relatively little has also been done with classified ads. A 1975 study, *Help Wanted: Case Studies of Classified Ads* by John Walsh, Miriam Johnson, and Marged Sugarman, tests the accuracy and effectiveness of classified ads listed in San Francisco and Salt Lake City newspapers. The findings show that in spite of the popularity of classified ads, they are often inadequate, unscrupulous, and generally ineffective.

Robert Glatzer studies the twenty most successful advertising campaigns

in his book *The New Advertising: The Great Campaigns from Avis to Volkswagen,* while Frank Rowsome, Jr., retells the stories of two highly successful
campaigns in *The Verse by the Side of the Road: The Story of the Burma-Shave
Signs and Jingles* and *Think Small: The Story of Those Volkswagen Ads.* Michael
Arlen's best-selling *Thirty Seconds* recounts the making of AT & T's highly
successful "Reach Out and Touch Someone" campaign and provides valuable insights into an industry which routinely seeks to create an advertised
reality that is often "more real than real." A compendium of ideas, along
with reprints, commentaries, and anecdotes, can be found in *Humor in
Advertising . . . And How to Make It Pay* by Don Herold.

There is a wealth of material available to readers interested in collections
of short, critical pieces about advertising. Books of advertising-related readings are widely used and are dependable resources for general information
about virtually any aspect of modern advertising. A sampling of these
university course readers includes *The Role of Advertising: A Book of Readings,*
edited by Charles H. Sandage and Vernon Fryburger; *Advertising in America,*
edited by Poyntz Tyler; *Speaking of Advertising,* edited by John S. Wright
and Daniel S. Warner; *Exploring Advertising,* edited by Otto Kleppner and
Irving Settel; *Advertising and Society,* edited by Yale Brozen; and *Advertising
and the Public Interest,* edited by Salvatore F. Divita. Historian Daniel Boorstin provides another, and more culturally intricate, reading of advertising's
role in American popular culture in his excellent essay "Advertising and
American Civilization," published in his collection *Democracy and Its Discontents.* Three special editions compiled by *Advertising Age* also serve as
useful general readers: *The New World of Advertising* reprints articles from
Advertising Age; How It Was in Advertising, a bicentennial edition, is an
informative and entertaining selection of readings with a historical slant;
and *Twentieth Century Advertising and the Economy of Abundance* reviews fifty
years of American advertising, its economics and social importance, and its
contribution to the American standard of living. Two anthologies on popular culture co-edited by Bernard Rosenberg and David Manning White,
Mass Culture: The Popular Arts in America and *Mass Culture Revisited,* contain
several essays on advertising, all of which are disparaging. Donald McQuade
and Robert Atwan present a more balanced view of advertising in the
opening section of *Popular Writing in America,* in which they reprint seventy-
five print advertisements as well as several essays on the cultural importance
of advertising.

The advertising industry supports an extraordinary number of advertising
and related periodicals. In scope and importance, *Advertising Age,* a weekly
publication that includes news about all trade-related industries, dominates
the others but faces increasingly stiff competition from *Ad Week,* a younger
and more aggressive trade journal. In addition to news items, *Advertising
Age* and *Ad Week* often include critical articles and print special issues as
well as producing useful bibliographies. In 1967, *Marketing/Communications*

superseded *Printer's Ink,* the oldest advertising journal in America, and remained an important publication until 1972, when it ceased publication. Special serialized publications abound for media, marketing, broadcasting, print, illustration, photography, graphics, and design. A brief list of these advertising periodicals appears at the end of this chapter, and readers are also encouraged to check section nine of Eleanor Blum's *Basic Books in the Mass Media* for annotations of other serialized publications.

ANTHOLOGIES AND REPRINTS

Reprint collections run the gamut from the whimsical to the professional and the scholarly. Julian Lewis Watkins's *The 100 Greatest Advertisements: Who Wrote Them and What They Did* includes a reproduction of each selected great advertisement along with extensive textual commentary by the author. Watkins's book, which first appeared in 1949, was followed in 1959 by a second edition with an additional thirteen advertisements. Edgar R. Jones takes a random look at some turn-of-the-century magazine advertisements in *Those Were the Good Old Days: A Happy Look at American Advertising, 1880–1930.* The book is a nostalgic collection, and Jones admits to no sound rationale for including particular ads; he intentionally refrains from editorial comments. Another reprint of early American advertisements is *Floyd Clymer's Scrapbook: Early Advertising Art,* an anthology that also contains Clymer's personal musings about advertising. *The Wonderful World of American Advertisements, 1865–1900* by Leonard DeVries and Ilonka Van Amstel reprints many of the most popular advertisements of the post-Civil War era and documents America's seemingly limitless interest in the curious and exotic.

While these books represent the whimsical, nostalgic approach to the reprinting of advertisements, two more serious attempts to reprint collections are Bella Landauer's *Early American Trade Cards* and Mary Black's *American Advertising Posters of the Nineteenth Century.* Both of these books, which reflect efforts to organize the massive collections of New York socialite Bella C. Landauer, contain useful annotations, critical notes, and indexes. *Early American Trade Cards* gives the definition and history of printed trade cards, while Mary Black, in her edition of posters from the Landauer collection, adds valuable notes and separate indexes of artists, engravers, and advertisers. In a similarly serious vein, readers might also want to examine Brian Holme's generously and handsomely illustrated *Advertising: Reflections of a Century,* which at once documents the changing styles in advertising illustration, surveys the progress of graphic design, and provides a kaleidoscopic view of what American life has looked like for the past century. In *The Promise and the Product,* Victor Margolin, Ira Brichta, and Vivian Brichta use numerous illustrations to support their claim that the art of the poster has been the art of the people and has reflected the ever-changing life styles and aspirations of "average" Americans as well as documenting time-altered attitudes towards its citizens, especially women and blacks.

Collecting and reprinting advertisements devoted to one subject seems to be a favorite avocation of many people. Just a few examples of such books are Arnold Fochs's *The Very Idea: A Collection of Retail Advertising Ideas,* containing what he considers the most effective local retail advertisements; Robert Karolevitz's *Old Time Agriculture in the Ads: Being a Compendium of Magazine and Newspaper Sales Literature Reminiscent of the Days When Farming Was the Way of Life and Horsepower Came in Horses!,* whose title reveals the nature of the book; and Lawrence Dietz's *Soda Pop: The History, Advertising Art, and Memorabilia of Soft Drinks in America,* a textual and pictorial survey of the soda pop industry, with emphasis on Coke and its advertisements. Auto buffs seem to be particularly interested in examining advertisements as inducements to the consumer to participate in an already uniquely American cultural phenomenon—the automobile. Howard Garrett's *The Poster Book of Antique Auto Ads, 1898–1920,* Michael Frostick's *Advertising and the Motor-Car,* and Q. David Bowers's *Early American Car Advertisements* reprint automobile ads more for their "artsy" and "quaint" qualities; Jane and Michael Stern and Peter Roberts go beyond merely reproducing advertisements in *Auto Ads* and *Any Color So Long as It's Black: The First Fifty Years of Automobile Advertising.* These authors attempt to relate advertisements to consumer preferences and needs as well as to what is perhaps America's quintessential cultural product.

Many professional groups and organizations publish annuals that contain the advertisements considered the best of that year. *Art Directors Annual, Communication Arts Annual, Graphics Annual, Illustrators, Modern Publicity, The Penrose Annual,* and *The Print Casebooks* are but a few of the professional reprints produced yearly. Finally, advertising men themselves are beginning to reprint their individual work. George Lois's *The Art of Advertising* is a collection of his major ads and reflects not only the accomplishments of his corporate efforts but also the tastes and culture of the American consumer. More books of this sort are beginning to appear and offer a legitimate cataloging of American popular culture.

BIBLIOGRAPHY

Books and Articles

Advertising Age, ed. *How It Was in Advertising: 1776–1976.* Chicago: Crain Books, 1976.
————. *Marketing Strategies of America's 125 Largest Advertisers.* Chicago: Crain Communications, 1970.

————. *Twentieth Century Advertising and the Economy of Abundance*. Chicago: Crain Communications, 1980.

Advertising and Women: A Report on Advertising Portraying or Directed to Women. New York: National Advertising Review Board, March 1975.

Albion, Mark S., and Paul W. Farris. *The Advertising Controversy: Evidence on the Economic Effects of Advertising*. Boston: Auburn House, 1981.

Allen, James Sloan. *The Romance of Commerce and Culture: Capitalism, Modernism, and the Chicago-Aspen Crusade for Cultural Reform*. Chicago: University of Chicago Press, 1983.

Andren, Gunnar, et al. *Rhetoric and Ideology in Advertising*. Stockholm: Liber Forlag, 1978.

Arlen, Michael. *Thirty Seconds*. New York: Farrar, Straus and Giroux, 1980.

Ash, Lee, ed. *Subject Collections: A Guide to Special Book Collections and Subject Emphases as Reported by University, College, Public, and Special Libraries and Museums in the United States and Canada*. 6th ed. New York: R. R. Bowker, 1985.

Atwan, Robert, Donald McQuade, and John W. Wright. *Edsels, Luckies, and Frigidaires: Advertising the American Way*. New York: Dell, 1979.

Atwan, Robert, Barry Orton, and William Vesterman. *American Mass Media: Industries and Issues*. 3rd ed. New York: Random House, 1986.

Ayer Glossary of Advertising and Related Terms. 2nd ed. Philadelphia: Ayer Press, 1977.

Baker, Michael John, ed. *Macmillan Dictionary of Marketing and Advertising*. New York: Nichols, 1984.

Baker, Samm Sinclair. *The Permissible Lie: The Inside Truth About Advertising*. Cleveland: World, 1968.

Baker, Stephen. *Visual Persuasion: The Effect of Pictures on the Subconscious*. New York: McGraw-Hill, 1961.

Baran, Paul, and Paul Sweezy. *Monopoly Capital: An Essay on the American Economic and Social Order*. New York: Monthly Review Press, 1966.

Barnouw, Erik. *The Sponsor: Notes on a Modern Potentate*. New York: Oxford University Press, 1978.

————. *Tube of Plenty: The Evolution of American Television*. Rev. ed. New York: Oxford University Press, 1982.

Barthes, Roland. *Mythologies*. New York: Hill and Wang, 1972.

Barton, Bruce. *The Book Nobody Knows*. Indianapolis: Bobbs-Merrill, 1926.

————. *The Man Nobody Knows: A Discovery of Jesus*. Indianapolis: Bobbs-Merrill, 1925.

Barton, Roger, ed. *Handbook of Advertising Management*. New York: McGraw-Hill, 1970.

Bauer, Raymond A., and Stephen A. Greyser. *Advertising in America: The Consumer View*. Boston: Graduate School of Business Administration, Harvard University, 1968.

Berman, Ronald. *Advertising and Social Change*. Beverly Hills: Sage, 1981.

Bishop, Robert L., comp. *Public Relations: A Comprehensive Bibliography*. Ann Arbor, Mich.: A. G. Leigh-James, 1974.

Black, Mary. *American Advertising Posters of the Nineteenth Century*. New York: Dover, 1976.

Blum, Eleanor. *Basic Books in the Mass Media*. 2nd ed. Urbana: University of Illinois Press, 1980.

Bogart, Leo. *Strategy in Advertising: Matching Media and Messages to Markets and Motivation*. New York: Harcourt, Brace and World, 1967; 2nd ed. Chicago: Crain Books, 1984.

Boorstin, Daniel J. *Democracy and Its Discontents: Reflections on Everyday America*. New York: Random House, 1971.

Borden, Neil H. *The Economic Effects of Advertising*. Chicago: R. D. Irwin, 1942. Reprint. New York: Arno Press, 1976.

Borden, Neil H., Malcolm D. Taylor, and Howard T. Hovde. *National Advertising in Newspapers*. Cambridge, Mass.: Harvard University Press, 1946.

Bowers, Q. David. *Early American Car Advertisements*. New York: Bonanza Books, 1966.

Brower, Charlie. *Me and Other Advertising Geniuses*. Garden City, N.Y.: Doubleday, 1974.

Brown, Bruce. *Images of Family Life in Magazine Advertising: 1920–1978*. New York: Praeger, 1981.

Brozen, Yale, ed. *Advertising and Society*. New York: New York University Press, 1974.

Buzzi, Giancarlo. *Advertising: Its Cultural and Political Effects*. Minneapolis: University of Minnesota Press, 1968.

Calkins, Earnest Elmo. *"And Hearing Not—." Annals of an Adman*. New York: Scribner's, 1946.

Caples, John. *Making Ads Pay*. New York: Harper and Row, 1957.

Carson, Gerald. *One for a Man, Two for a Horse: A Pictorial History, Grave and Comic, of Patent Medicines*. New York: Bramhall House, 1961.

Chester, Giraud, Garnet R. Garrison, and Edgar E. Willis. *Television and Radio*. 5th ed. New York: Appleton-Century-Crofts Educational Division, 1978.

Cleary, David P. *Great American Brands: The Success Formulas that Made Them Famous*. New York: Fairchild Publications, 1981.

Clymer, Floyd. *Floyd Clymer's Scrapbook: Early Advertising Art*. New York: Bonanza Books, 1955.

Cone, Fairfax M. *The Blue Streak: Some Observations Mostly About Advertising*. Chicago: Crain Communications, 1973.

———. *With All Its Faults: A Candid Account of Forty Years in Advertising*. Boston: Little, Brown, 1969.

Continuity in Advertising: A Selected Abstract Bibliography. New York: McGraw-Hill, 1966.

Copy Testing: An Annotated Bibliography, 1960–1972. New York: Advertising Research Foundation, 1972.

The Creative Black Book. New York: Friendly Publications, 1970.

Cummings, Bart. *The Benevolent Dictators: Interviews with Advertising Greats*. Chicago: Crain Books, 1984.

Curti, Merle. "The Changing Concept of 'Human Nature' in the Literature of American Advertising." *Business History Review*, 61 (Winter 1967), 335–57.

Cutlip, Scott M., comp. *A Public Relations Bibliography*. 2nd ed. Madison: University of Wisconsin Press, 1965.

DeBry, Theodore. *America, I*. Frankfurt: I. Wechel, 1590.

Della Femina, Jerry. *From Those Wonderful Folks Who Gave You Pearl Harbor.* Edited by Charles Sopkin. New York: Simon and Schuster, 1970.

DeVries, Leonard, and Ilonka Van Amstel. *The Wonderful World of American Advertisements, 1865–1900.* Chicago: Follett, 1972.

Diamant, Lincoln. *Television's Classic Commercials: The Golden Years 1948–1958.* Communication Art Books. New York: Hastings House, 1971.

Diamond, Edwin, and Stephen Bates. *The Spot: The Rise of Political Advertising on Television.* Cambridge, Mass.: MIT Press, 1984.

Dietz, Lawrence. *Soda Pop: The History, Advertising Art, and Memorabilia of Soft Drinks in America.* New York: Simon and Schuster, 1973.

Dispenza, Joseph E. *Advertising the American Woman.* Dayton, Ohio: Pflaum Publishing, 1975.

Divita, Salvatore F., ed. *Advertising and the Public Interest.* Chicago: American Marketing Association, 1974.

Dobrow, Larry. *When Advertising Tried Harder: The Sixties, the Golden Age of American Advertising.* New York: Friendly Press, 1984.

Duncan, Paul. *Testimonial Advertising: An Empirical Perspective.* Berkeley: University of California Press, 1982.

Dunn, S. Watson, ed. *International Handbook of Advertising.* New York: McGraw-Hill, 1964.

Dunn, S. Watson, and Arnold M. Barban. *Advertising: Its Role in Modern Marketing.* 4th ed. Hinsdale, Ill.: Dryden Press, 1978.

Durstine, Roy S. *Making Advertisements and Making Them Pay.* New York: Scribner's, 1920.

Dyer, Gillian. *Advertising as Communication.* New York: Methuen, 1982.

———. *Boxed In: Women and Television.* New York: Pandora Press, 1987.

Ellis, Jim. *Billboards to Buicks: Advertising as I Lived It.* New York: Abelard-Schuman, 1968.

Ewen, Stuart. *Captains of Consciousness: Advertising and the Social Roots of the Consumer Culture.* New York: McGraw-Hill, 1976.

Ewen, Stuart, and Elizabeth Ewen. *Channels of Desire: Mass Images and the Shaping of American Consciousness.* New York: McGraw-Hill, 1982.

Ferber, Robert, Alain Cousineau, Millard Crask, and Hugh G. Wales, comps. *A Basic Bibliography on Marketing Research.* 3rd ed. New York: American Marketing Association, 1974.

Fochs, Arnold, comp. and ed. *The Very Idea: A Collection of Retail Advertising Ideas.* Duluth, Minn.: A. J. Publishing, 1971.

Ford, James L. C. *Magazines for Millions: The Story of Specialized Publications.* Carbondale: Southern Illinois University Press, 1969.

Forty, Adrian. *Objects of Desire: Design and Society from Wedgewood to IBM.* New York: Pantheon Books, 1986.

Fowler, Jib. *Mass Advertising as Social Forecast: A Method for Futures Research.* Westport, Conn.: Greenwood Press, 1976.

Fowler, Nathaniel Clark. *Fowler's Publicity: An Encyclopedia of Advertising and Printing, and All that Pertains to the Public-Seeking Side of Business.* New York: Publicity Publishing, 1897.

Fox, Richard Wightman, and T. J. Jackson Lears, eds. *The Culture of Consumption:*

Critical Essays in American History, 1880–1980. New York: Pantheon Books, 1983.

Fox, Stephen. *The Mirror Makers: A History of American Advertising and Its Creators.* New York: William Morrow, 1984.

Frostick, Michael. *Advertising and the Motor-Car.* London: Lund Humphries, 1970.

Garrett, Howard, comp. *The Poster Book of Antique Auto Ads, 1898–1920.* Secaucus, N.J.: Citadel Press, 1974.

Gazurian, Johnny A. *The Advertising and Graphic Arts Glossary.* Los Angeles: Los Angeles Trade-Technical College, 1966.

Geis, Michael L. *The Language of Television Advertising.* New York: Academic Press, 1982.

Gibson, D. Parke. *The $30 Billion Negro.* New York: Macmillan, 1969.

Glatzer, Robert. *The New Advertising: The Great Campaigns from Avis to Volkswagen.* New York: Citadel Press, 1970.

Goffman, Erving. *Gender Advertisements.* Cambridge, Mass.: Harvard University Press, 1979.

Gold, Philip. *Advertising, Politics, and American Culture: From Salesmanship to Therapy.* New York: Paragon House, 1987.

Goodman, Walter. *The Clowns of Commerce.* New York: Sagamore Press, 1954.

Gossage, Howard Luck, et al., eds. *Is There Any Hope for Advertising?* Urbana: University of Illinois Press, 1986.

Goulart, Ron. *The Assault on Childhood.* Los Angeles: Sherbourne Press, 1969.

Graham, Irvin. *The Encyclopedia of Advertising.* 2nd ed. New York: Fairchild Publications, 1969.

Grumbino, E. Evelyn. *Reaching Juvenile Markets: How to Advertise, Sell, and Merchandise Through Boys and Girls.* New York; McGraw-Hill, 1938.

Gunther, John. *Taken at the Flood: The Story of Albert D. Lasker.* New York; Harper and Row, 1960.

Hafer, W. Keith, and Gordon E. White. *Advertising Writing.* St Paul: West Publishing, 1977.

Hamburger, Estelle. *It's a Woman's Business.* New York: Vanguard Press, 1939.

Hansen, Joseph, and Evelyn Reed. *Cosmetics, Fashions, and the Exploitation of Women.* New York: Pathfinder Press, 1986.

Hariot, Thomas. *A Brief and True Report of the New Found Land of Virginia.* London, 1588. Reprint. New York: Dover, 1972.

Haverfield, Richard W., comp. *One Hundred Books on Advertising.* Bul. Vol. 66, No. 3, Journalism Series No. 162, University of Missouri, 1965.

Hechtlinger, Grace. *The Great Patent Medicine Era.* New York: Galahad Books, 1970.

Heckor, Sidney, and Daniel V. Stewart, eds. *Nonverbal Communication in Advertising.* Lexington, Mass.: Lexington Books, 1988.

Heighton, Elizabeth J., and Don R. Cunningham. *Advertising in the Broadcast Media.* Belmont, Calif.: Wadsworth, 1976.

Herold, Don. *Humor in Advertising . . . And How to Make It Pay.* New York: McGraw-Hill, 1963.

Herpel, George L., and Richard A. Collins. *Speciality Advertising in Marketing.* Homewood, Ill.: Dow-Jones-Irwin, 1972.

Hettinger, Herman S. *A Decade of Radio Advertising*. Chicago: University of Chicago Press, 1933. Reprint. New York: Arno Press, 1971.

Hodgson, Richard S. *The Dartnell Direct Mail and Mail Order Handbook*. 3rd ed. Chicago: Dartnell Press, 1980.

Holme, Brian. *Advertising: Reflections of a Century*. New York: Viking Press, 1982.

Hopkins, Claude C. *My Life in Advertising*. New York: Harper and Brothers, 1927. Reprint. Chicago: Advertising Publications, 1966.

————. *Scientific Advertising*. New York: Harper and Brothers, 1923. Reprint. Chicago: Advertising Publications, 1966.

Hornung, Clarence P. *Handbook of Early Advertising Art*. 3rd ed. New York: Dover, 1956.

Hornung, Clarence P., and Fridolf Johnson. *200 Years of American Graphic Art: A Retrospective Survey of the Printing Arts and Advertising Since the Colonial Period*. New York: George Braziller, 1976.

Horowitz, Daniel. *The Morality of Spending: Attitudes Toward the Consumer Society in America, 1875–1940*. Baltimore: Johns Hopkins University Press, 1985.

Houck, John W., ed. *Outdoor Advertising: History and Regulation*. Notre Dame, Ind.: University of Notre Dame Press, 1969.

Hower, Ralph M. *The History of an Advertising Agency*. Cambridge, Mass.: Harvard University Press, 1939.

Jamieson, Kathleen Hall. *Packaging the Presidency: A History and Criticism of Presidential Campaign Advertising*. New York: Oxford University Press, 1984.

Jones, Edgar R. *Those Were the Good Old Days: A Happy Look at American Advertising, 1880–1930*. Rev. ed. New York: Simon and Schuster, 1979.

Jones, John Philip. *What's in a Name? Advertising and the Concept of Brands*. Lexington, Mass.: Lexington Books, 1986.

Kaid, Lynda Lee., et al., eds. *New Perspectives on Political Advertising*. Carbondale: Southern Illinois University Press, 1986.

Kallet, Arthur, and F. J. Schlink. *100 Million Guinea Pigs: Dangers in Everyday Foods, Drugs, and Cosmetics*. New York: Vanguard Press, 1933. Reprint. New York: Arno Press, 1976.

Karolevitz, Robert F. *Old Time Agriculture in the Ads: Being a Compendium of Magazine and Newspaper Sales Literature Reminiscent of the Days When Farming Was the Way of Life and Horsepower Came in Horses!* Aberdeen, S.D.: North Plains Press, 1970.

Key, Wilson Bryan. *Media Sexploitation*. Englewood Cliffs, N.J.: Prentice-Hall, 1976.

————. *Subliminal Seduction: Ad Media's Manipulation of a Not So Innocent America*. New York: New American Library, 1973.

Klein, Walter J. *The Sponsored Film*. New York: Hastings House, 1976.

Kleppner, Otto. *Advertising Procedure*. 7th ed. Englewood Cliffs, N.J.: Prentice-Hall, 1979.

Kleppner, Otto, and Irving Settel, eds. *Exploring Advertising*. Englewood Cliffs, N.J.: Prentice-Hall, 1970.

Landauer, Bella C. *Early American Trade Cards*. New York: William Edwin Rudge, 1927.

Lasker, Albert. *The Lasker Story*. Chicago: Advertising Publications, 1953.

Lears, T. J. Jackson. *No Place of Grace: Antimodernism and the Transformation of American Culture, 1880–1920.* New York: Pantheon Books, 1982.

Leech, Geoffrey N. *English Advertising: A Linguistic Study of Advertising in Great Britain.* London: Longmans, Green, 1966.

Lefebvre, Henri. *Everyday Life in the Modern World.* Translated by Sacha Rabinovitch. New York: Harper and Row, 1972. Originally published in Paris: Editions Gallimard, 1968.

Leiss, William, Stephen Kline, and Sut Jhally. *Social Communication in Advertising: Persons, Products, and Images of Well-Being.* New York: Methuen, 1986.

Levenson, Bob. *Bill Bernbach's Book: A History of the Advertising that Changed the History of Advertising.* New York: Villard Books, 1987.

Leymore, Varda Langholz. *Hidden Myth: Structure and Symbolism in Advertising.* New York: Basic Books, 1975.

Library of Congress, Division of Bibliography. "Advertising, with Special Reference to Its Social and Economic Effects; a List of Recent Writings." Washington, D.C.: Government Documents, 1930.

Linden, Eugene. *Affluence and Discontent: The Anatomy of Consumer Societies.* New York: Viking Press, 1979.

Lipstein, Benjamin. *Evaluating Advertising: A Bibliography of the Communications Process.* New York: Advertising Research Foundation, 1978.

Lodisle, Leonard M. *The Advertising and Promotion Challenge: Vaguely Right or Precisely Wrong?* New York: Oxford University Press, 1986.

Lois, George. *The Art of Advertising: George Lois on Mass Communication.* New York: Harry N. Abrams, 1977.

Lois, George, with Bill Pitts. *George, Be Careful.* New York: Saturday Review Press, 1972.

Lyon, David G. *Off Madison Avenue.* New York: Putnam's, 1966.

Maas, Jane. *Adventures of an Advertising Woman.* New York: St. Martin's Press, 1986.

McAuliffe, Robert E. *Advertising, Competition, and Public Policy: Theories and New Evidence.* Lexington, Mass.: Lexington Books, 1987.

McGinniss, Joe. *The Selling of the President 1968.* New York: Trident Press, 1969.

McLuhan, Marshall. *The Mechanical Bride: Folklore of Industrial Man.* New York: Vanguard Press, 1951.

———. *Understanding Media: The Extensions of Man.* New York: McGraw-Hill, 1964.

McQuade, Donald, and Robert Atwan. *Popular Writing in America: The Interactions of Style and Audience.* 4th ed. New York: Oxford University Press, 1988.

Madison Avenue Handbook. New York: Peter Glenn Publications, 1958-.

Marchand, Roland. *Advertising the American Dream: Making Way for Modernity, 1920–40.* Berkeley: University of California Press, 1985.

Margolin, Victor, Ira Brichta, and Vivian Brichta. *The Promise and the Product: 200 Years of American Advertising Posters.* New York: Macmillan, 1979.

Marin, Allan, comp. *50 Years of Advertising as Seen Through the Eyes of Advertising Age.* Chicago: Crain Communications, 1980.

Martineau, Pierre. *Motivation in Advertising: Motives that Make People Buy.* New York: McGraw-Hill, 1957.

Mayer, Martin. *About Television.* New York: Harper and Row, 1972.

———. *Madison Avenue, U.S.A.* New York: Harper and Row, 1958.

Media/Scope. Dictionary of Terms Useful to Buyers of Advertising. Skokie, Ill.: Standard Rate and Data Service, 1966.

Melcher, Daniel, and Nancy Larrick. *Printing and Promotion Handbook: How to Plan, Produce, and Use Printing, Advertising, and Direct Mail.* 3rd ed. New York: McGraw-Hill, 1966.

Menten, Theodore, comp. *Advertising Art in the Art Deco Style.* New York: Dover, 1975.

Meyers, William. *The Image Makers: Power and Persuasion on Madison Avenue.* New York: Times Books, 1984.

Millum, Trevor. *Images of Women: Advertising in Women's Magazines.* Totowa, N.J.: Rowman and Littlefield, 1975.

Mott, Frank Luther. *American Journalism: A History of Newspaper in the United States Through 260 Years: 1690 to 1950.* 3rd ed. New York: Macmillan, 1962.

———. *A History of American Magazines.* 5 vols. Cambridge, Mass.: Harvard University Press, 1957.

Naether, Carl. *Advertising to Women.* New York: Prentice-Hall, 1926.

Nelson, Roy Paul. *The Design of Advertising.* 5th ed. Dubuque, Iowa: William C. Brown, 1985.

The New World of Advertising. Chicago: Crain Books, 1975.

Noble, Valerie. *The Effective Echo: A Dictionary of Advertising Slogans.* New York: Special Libraries Association, 1970.

Norins, Hanley. *The Compleat Copywriter: A Comprehensive Guide to All Phases of Advertising Communication.* New York: McGraw-Hill, 1966.

Ogilvy, David. *Blood, Brains & Beer: The Autobiography of David Ogilvy.* New York: Atheneum, 1978.

———. *Confessions of an Advertising Man.* New York: Atheneum, 1971.

———. *Ogilvy on Advertising.* New York: Crown, 1983.

Olins, Wally. *The Corporate Personality: An Inquiry into the Nature of Corporate Identity.* New York: Mayflower Books, 1979.

Olsen, Jerry, and Keith Sentis, eds. *Advertising and Consumer Psychology.* New York: Praeger, 1986.

O'Toole, John. *The Trouble with Advertising.* New York: Chelsea House, 1981.

Packard, Vance. *The Hidden Persuaders.* New York: David McKay, 1957.

———. *The Status Seekers.* New York: David McKay, 1959.

———. *The Waste Makers.* New York: David McKay, 1960.

Padley, Martin, ed. *A Handbook to Television Advertising.* New York: National Retail Merchants Association, 1969.

Paletz, David L. *Politics in Public Service: Advertising on Television.* New York: Praeger, 1977.

Pancoast, Chalmers Lowell. *Trail Blazers of Advertising.* New York: Grafton Press, 1926. Reprint. New York: Arno Press, 1976.

Pease, Otis. *The Responsibilities of American Advertising: Private Control and Public Influence, 1920–1940.* New Haven: Yale University Press, 1958.

Peck, William A. *Anatomy of Local Radio-TV Copy.* 4th ed. Blue Ridge Summit, Pa.: TAB Books, 1976.

Peterson, Theodore. *Magazines in the Twentieth Century.* Urbana: University of Illinois Press, 1964.

Pollay, Richard W., comp. *Information Sources in Advertising History*. Westport, Conn.: Greenwood Press, 1979.

Polykoff, Shirley. *Does She or Doesn't She? And How She Did It*. Garden City, N.Y.: Doubleday, 1975.

Pope, Daniel. *The Making of Modern Advertising*. New York: Basic Books, 1983.

Potter, David Morris. *People of Plenty: Economic Abundance and the American Character*. Chicago: University of Chicago Press, 1954.

Presbrey, Frank. *The History and Development of Advertising*. Garden City, N.Y.: Doubleday, Doran, 1929. Reprint. Westport, Conn.: Greenwood Press, 1968.

Preston, Ivan L. *The Great American Blow-Up: Puffery in Advertising and Selling*. Madison: University of Wisconsin Press, 1975.

Quick, John. *Artists' and Illustrators' Encyclopedia*. 2nd ed. New York: McGraw-Hill, 1977.

Raber, Nevin W., and Richard Coachys, comps. *Marketing: A Select List of Current Titles*. Bloomington: Indiana University, Division of Research, Graduate School of Business, n.d.

Reeves, Rosser. *Reality in Advertising*. New York: Alfred A. Knopf, 1960.

Revzan, David A. *A Comprehensive Classified Marketing Bibliography*. Berkeley: University of California Press, 1951, with supplements, 1963.

Richard, John M. *A Guide to Advertising Information Sources*. Scottsdale Ariz.: MacDougal, 1969.

Robbins, Celia Dame, ed. *Slogans*. Detroit: Gale Research, 1984.

Roberts, Peter. *Any Color So Long as It's Black: The First Fifty Years of Automobile Advertising*. New York: William Morrow, 1976.

Rorty, James. *Our Master's Voice: Advertising*. New York: John Day, 1934. Reprint. New York: Arno Press, 1976.

Rosenberg, Bernard, and David Manning White, eds. *Mass Culture Revisited*. New York: Van Nostrand Reinhold, 1971.

———. *Mass Culture: The Popular Arts in America*. London: Free Press, 1957.

Rosenberg, Manuel. *The Art of Advertising*. New York: Harper and Brothers, 1930.

Rowell, George P. *Forty Years an Advertising Agent: 1865–1905*. New York: Printer's Ink, 1906.

Rowsome, Frank, Jr. *They Laughed When I Sat Down: An Informal History of Advertising in Words and Pictures*. New York: McGraw-Hill, 1959.

———. *Think Small: The Story of Those Volkswagen Ads*. Brattleboro, Vt.: Stephen Greene Press, 1970.

———. *The Verse by the Side of the Road: The Story of the Burma-Shave Signs and Jingles*. Brattleboro, Vt.: Stephen Greene Press, 1965.

Sackheim, Maxwell. *My First 65 Years in Advertising*. Blue Ridge Summit, Pa.: TAB Books, 1975.

Sampson, Henry. *A History of Advertising from the Earliest Times*. London: Chatto and Windus, 1874. Reprint. Detroit: Gale Research, 1974.

Sandage, Charles H., and Vernon Fryburger. *Advertising Theory and Practice*. 11th ed. Homewood, Ill.: Richard D. Irwin, 1983.

———. eds. *The Role of Advertising: A Book of Readings*. Homewood, Ill.: Richard D. Irwin, 1960.

Schrank, Jeffrey. *Deception Detection: An Educator's Guide to the Art of Insight.* Boston: Beacon Press, 1975.

Schudson, Michael. *Advertising, the Uneasy Persuasion: Its Dubious Impact on American Society.* New York: Basic Books, 1984.

Seldin, Joseph J. *The Golden Fleece.* New York: Macmillan, 1963.

Settel, Irving, and Norman Glenn. *Television Advertising and Production Handbook.* New York: Crowell, 1953.

Sharp, Harold. *Advertising Slogans of America.* Metuchen, N.J.: Scarecrow Press, 1984.

Simon, Julian. *Issues in the Economics of Advertising.* Urbana: University of Illinois Press, 1970.

Sinclair, John. *Images Incorporated: Advertising as Industry and Ideology.* New York: Croom Helm, in association with Methuen, 1987.

Sissors, Jack Z., and Jim Surmonek. *Advertising Media Planning.* Chicago: Crain Books, 1982.

Smith, Ralph Lee. *The Health Hucksters.* New York: Crowell, 1960.

Snyder, John. *Commercial Artist's Handbook.* New York: Watson-Guptill, 1973.

Spero, Robert. *The Duping of the American Voter: Dishonesty and Deception in Presidential Television Advertising.* Philadelphia: Lippincott and Crowell, 1980.

Standard Directory of Advertisers: The Agency Red Book. New York: National Register Publication Co., 1964.

Standard Directory of Advertising Agencies. New York: National Register Publication Co., 1964.

Stansfield, Richard H. *The Dartnell Advertising Manager's Handbook.* 3rd ed. Chicago: Dartnell, 1982.

Stein, Gail F. *Exhibition Catalogue, Ethnic Images in Advertising.* Philadelphia: Balch Institute for Ethnic Studies and Anti-Defamation League of B'nai B'rith, 1984.

Stephenson, Howard, ed. *Handbook of Public Relations: The Standard Guide to Public Affairs and Communications.* 2nd ed. New York: McGraw-Hill, 1971.

Stern, Jane, and Michael Stern. *Auto Ads.* New York: David Obst Books, 1978.

Straiton, John S. *Of Women and Advertising.* Toronto: McClelland and Stewart, 1984.

Sweeney, Russell C. *Coming Next Week: A Pictorial History of Film Advertising.* Cranbury, N.J.: A. S. Barnes, 1973.

Taplin, Walter. *Advertising: A New Approach.* Boston: Little, Brown, 1960.

Terrell, Neil. *The Power Technique of Radio-TV Copywriting.* Blue Ridge Summit, Pa.: TAB Books, 1971.

Thompson, Denys. *Voice of Civilisation: An Enquiry into Advertising.* London: F. Muller, 1947.

Thompson, J. Walter Company. *Advertising: An Annotated Bibliography.* New York: National Book League, 1972.

Tierney, Patricia E. *Ladies of the Avenue.* London: Bartholomew House, 1971.

Turner, E. S. *The Shocking History of Advertising!* New York: E. P. Dutton, 1953.

Tyler, Poyntz, ed. *Advertising in America.* The Reference Shelf. Vol. 31, No. 5. New York: H. W. Wilson, 1959.

Ulanoff, Stanley M. *Advertising in America: An Introduction to Persuasive Communication.* New York: Hastings House, 1977.

Urdang, Laurence, ed. *Dictionary of Advertising Terms*. Chicago: Tatham, Laird and Kudner, 1977.

Vestergaard, Torbin, and Kim Schroder. *The Language of Advertising*. New York: Basil Blackwell, 1985.

Wakeman, Frederick. *The Hucksters*. New York: Rinehart, 1946.

Walsh, John, Miriam Johnson, and Marged Sugarman. *Help Wanted: Case Studies of Classified Ads*. Salt Lake City, Utah: Olympus Publishing, 1975.

Warner, Kenneth E. *Selling Smoke: Cigarette Advertising and Public Health*. Washington, D.C.: American Public Health Association, 1986.

Watkins, Julian Lewis. *The 100 Greatest Advertisements: Who Wrote Them and What They Did*. New York: Dover, 1949.

Weibel, Kathryn. *Mirror Mirror: Images of Women Reflected in Popular Culture*. Garden City, N.Y.: Anchor Books, Doubleday, 1977.

White, John. *America, 1585: The Complete Drawings of John White*. Edited by Paul Hulton. Chapel Hill: University of North Carolina Press, 1984.

Whiteside, Thomas. *Selling Death: Cigarette Advertising and Public Health*. New York: Liveright, 1971.

Wicke, Jennifer. *Advertising Fictions: Literature, Advertisement, and Social Reading*. New York: Columbia University Press, 1988.

Wight, Robin. *The Day the Pigs Refused to Be Driven to Market: Advertising and the Consumer Revolution*. New York: Random House, 1972.

Williams, Raymond. *The Long Revolution*. New York: Columbia University Press, 1961. Reprint. Westport, Conn.: Greenwood Press, 1975.

————. "The Magic System." *New Left Review* (July–August 1960), 27–32.

Williamson, Judith. *Decoding Advertisements: Ideology and Meaning in Advertising*. London: Calder and Boyars, 1978.

Winship, Janice. *Advertising in Women's Magazines, 1956–1974*. Birmingham, Eng.: Centre for Contemporary Cultural Studies, University of Birmingham, 1980.

Wood, James Playsted. *Magazines in the United States*. 3rd ed. New York: Ronald Press, 1971.

————. *The Story of Advertising*. New York: Ronald Press, 1958.

Wright, John S., and Daniel S. Warner. *Speaking of Advertising*. New York: McGraw-Hill, 1963.

Wright, John S., and Willis Winter. *Advertising*. 5th ed. New York: McGraw-Hill, 1982.

Wright, John W., ed. *The Commercial Connection: Advertising and the American Mass Media*. New York: Dell, 1979.

Young, James Harvey. *Toadstool Millionaires: A Social History of Patent Medicines in America Before Federal Regulation*. Princeton, N.J.: Princeton University Press, 1961.

Young, James Webb. *How to Become an Advertising Man*. Chicago: Advertising Publications, 1963.

Young, Margaret Labash, Brigette T. Darnay, et al. *Subject Directory of Special Libraries and Information Centers*. 8th ed. Detroit: Gale Research, 1983.

Annuals

Advertising Age Yearbook. Chicago: Advertising Age.

Art Directors Annual. (Also called *The Annual of Advertising Editorial and Television Art and Design*.) New York: Watson-Guptill.

The Best in Advertising. New York: R. C. Publications, 1975, 1977–81.
Communication Arts Annual. Palo Alto, Calif.: Coyne and Blanchard.
Current Issues and Research in Advertising. Graduate School of Business Administration, University of Michigan, 1977- .
Graphics Annual. New York: Hastings House.
Illustrators. New York: Hastings House.
Modern Publicity. New York: Viking Press.
The Penrose Annual. New York: Hastings House.
The Print Casebooks. New York: Watson-Guptill.

Periodicals

Accountants' Index. New York, 1920-.
Advertising Age. Chicago, 1930-.
Advertising World. New York, 1985-.
Ad Week. New York, Los Angeles, 1980-.
Applied Science and Technology Index. New York, 1958- .
Art Direction. New York, 1949-.
Art Index. New York, 1929-.
Biological and Agricultural Index (formerly *Agricultural Index*). New York, 1964-.
Broadcasting. Washington, D.C., 1931-.
Business History Review. Cambridge, Mass., 1926.
Business Marketing. Chicago, 1983-.
Business Periodicals Index. New York, 1958-.
Communication Arts. Palo Alto, Calif., 1959-.
Education Index. New York, 1929-.
Gallagher Report. New York, 1951-.
Graphics: USA. New York, 1964-.
Illustrator. Minneapolis, 1916-.
Index to Legal Periodicals. Buffalo, N.Y., 1926-.
Journal of Advertising. Provo, Utah, 1972-.
Madison Avenue. New York, 1958-.
Marketing and Media Decisions. New York, 1984-.
Marketing/Communications (formerly *Printer's Ink*). New York, 1967–72.
Print. New York, 1939-.
Printer's Ink. New York, 1888–1967. See also *Marketing/Communications.*
Psychological Abstracts. Washington, D.C., 1927-.
Public Affairs Information Index. New York, 1915-.
Quarterly Report: Advertising Research Foundation. New York, 1983-.
Readers' Guide to Periodical Literature. New York, 1900-.
Sociological Abstracts. New York, 1953-.
Television/Radio Age. New York, 1953-.
Women's Studies Abstracts. Rush, N.Y., 1972-.

Almanacs

ROBERT K. DODGE

Americans today are only vaguely aware of the importance of almanacs during the first 250 years of American history. Most of us can quote a few of Poor Richard's sayings and associate them with an almanac; most of us probably remember the story of Abraham Lincoln and his use of an almanac to prove the innocence of a client; and many of us may remember reading in our history books that a Bible and an almanac constituted the only reading matter for most of our pioneers.

Anything else we remember about early American almanacs is probably associated with a sense of the quaint, of people who spelled with a final "k" and who attempted to predict the weather a year in advance.

Almanacs were much more than quaint. They were the forerunners of modern magazines and city directories. They served as calendars and road maps. They helped to publicize the U.S. Constitution. They served as vehicles for advertising and for politics and religion, and they spread humor throughout the country. They provide us an important source of information about American life and attitudes in the seventeenth, eighteenth, and nineteenth centuries.

HISTORIC OUTLINE

In 1639 Stephen Daye printed America's first almanac in Cambridge, Massachusetts. For the next two and a half centuries and longer, almanacs constituted an important part of American life.

Most seventeenth-century almanacs appear quite modest. Almost all of them are sixteen-page pamphlets. A few extended to twenty-four or even thirty-two pages, beginning the gradual but steady tendency of American almanacs to lengthen. The sixteen-page almanacs devoted a separate page to each month. (Some of today's "factual" almanacs of a thousand or more pages devote fewer pages to the calendar.) Another page was often used to introduce the calendar and to give information concerning the dates of eclipses. Two of the three additional pages consisted of the front and back covers. The remaining page, usually the inside of the back cover, was sometimes used for advertisements, sometimes to provide information on events of the coming year, and sometimes to present an essay on the science of astronomy.

The calendar, considered the heart of the almanac, contained such information as the time of sunrise and sunset, the beginning date of each season (under the old-style calendar more variable than today), the phases of the moon, and usually some astrological information as well. If the intended readership included commercial fishermen or shippers, the calendar would include information on tides. The longer almanacs often allotted two pages to each month, although at least one twenty-four-page almanac included a nine-page explanation of its twelve-page calendar.

In the eighteenth century the almanac industry became more competitive. After all, the printing of an almanac had become a very profitable sideline for many American printers. They had a guaranteed market among farmers, commercial fishermen, and sailors. Naturally each almanac maker wanted to capture as large a share of the market as possible. It was perhaps competition more than any other influence that led to the changes in the eighteenth-century almanac, changes that make them more interesting to the student of American popular culture than are the majority of the almanacs from the seventeenth century.

Early competition concentrated on the accuracy of the calendar. Almanac makers extolled the virtues of their own calendars and often pointed out real or imagined inaccuracies in their competitors'. Sometimes a free errata sheet for the calendar of a major competitor was offered with the purchase of an almanac.

Another form of competition involved piracy. One of the reasons that bibliographies list so many editions of such popular titles as Thomas Greenleaf's and Abraham Weatherwise's almanacs appears to be that some of the editions were piracies. In at least one case the piracy had more involved motives, at least if Nathaniel Ames, publisher of one of America's first best-selling almanacs, was correct in his assessment of the competition. Ames complained that his competitors had banded together to produce a fraudulent and inaccurate almanac under his name in order to discredit him and his calendars.[1]

Ames and James Franklin can be credited with beginning to change the rules of almanac competition. They realized that the accuracy of a calendar as a sales inducement could be pushed only to a certain point, and they began the process of including other material to sell their almanacs. Ames often included short paragraphs on current events and on morality in general. James Franklin invented the character of Poor Robin, who gave his readers the sayings of Poor Robin.

While Ames and James Franklin began the process of changing the rules of competition, it was Benjamin Franklin who carried the process to its completion. Benjamin Franklin's first almanac burst upon the Philadelphia scene with the creation of Poor Richard and the prediction of the death of Titan Leeds, at the time the most popular almanac maker in the city.

Both the sayings of Poor Richard and the prediction, to which Leeds foolishly responded, helped Franklin's almanac to capture the attention of Philadelphia, and as Franklin saw the popularity of Poor Richard's sayings grow, he increased their number. The idea for the prediction, like the idea for the sayings, was borrowed: the prediction from Jonathan Swift, a well-known British almanac maker who later developed a reputation for satire; the sayings from his brother. But, while Franklin treated the prediction almost exactly as Swift had, he developed the sayings far beyond what his brother had done.

Other almanac makers soon accepted the idea that material other than the calendar could make their almanacs sell. In the decades following the introduction of Poor Richard, almanacs grew longer and longer as publishers competed to include more and more material that the public would buy. It is such material that makes eighteenth-and nineteenth-century almanacs so interesting to the student of American popular culture.

For example, historians of farming in early America will find hundreds of "valuable receipts" for improving soil, increasing crop yields, and curing diseases in livestock. Many of the receipts appear to be based on superstition, and a few appear to be based on even less than that, but many more seem to represent a real interest in the establishment of an empirical science of farming. Two of the better suggestions include the use of lime as a fertilizer (useful only when the soil is acidic) and the addition of green organic material to the soil.

Other receipts offered cures for various human ailments. The gout, bloody flux, toothache, and nosebleed are provided with "sure and certain" cures. The science of medicine appears even less advanced than that of agriculture, but a trial-and-error methodology was beginning here as well.

Some almanacs included recipes for the preparation and preservation of food. Such recipes impress the modern reader with their emphasis on preservation and with the large quantities they were intended to serve. Measurements tended to be imprecise.

Many of the almanacs contained descriptions of American customs. One almanac printed an essay in favor of the New England custom of bundling.

According to the essay, bundlers were almost always pure, and that new fangled innovation, the sofa, was far more dangerous to a woman's chastity. A long poem against bundling appeared in one of the Andrew Beers almanacs for 1793. Unlike the essay, the moralistic poem includes much detail about what its author thought took place in the bundling bed. One quatrain describes a man and a woman who had bundled together, each wearing a full set of clothing and wrapped in a separate sheet. The man, however, caught the itch from the woman, and she caught a bastard from him.[2]

Other described customs included bees and peddling. A few publishers, most notably Robert Thomas of *The (Old) Farmer's Almanack,* opposed the custom of social gatherings known as bees as wasteful of time and property. Thomas believed that a family had plenty of time during the long winter to husk its corn as it became necessary without the expense of entertaining all of the neighbors. Most almanac makers, however, considered bees of all kinds to be either harmless entertainment or positive ways for neighbors to help each other.

Peddlers constituted an important method of distribution for the almanac industry. Other media might criticize the peddler and, perhaps, deservedly so, but, as many of today's newspapers romanticize the newsboy, so did almanacs tend to romanticize the peddler.

Judging from what was printed in almanacs, early Americans must have liked to read about the exotic and the horrible. Indian captivity narratives and other stories of Indian cruelty abound, as do stories of Indian stoicism. Stories of cannibalism in America and Africa are common. Some almanacs described exotic animals, such as the giraffe and the elephant. The myth of the elephant's memory was demonstrated. Sentimental stories were popular as well. Some of the sentimental stories appear grotesque, at best, to the modern reader, but they do represent one form of popular story for the time.

By the last half of the eighteenth century, many of the almanacs had begun to provide pure information in the style of the present *World Almanac and Book of Facts* or the other large present-day almanacs familiar to most of us. The information was usually local, but a selection of almanacs would provide such information for most of the United States. What clubs existed in a particular city? What were the roads and their condition? Who were the political officers? What were the churches and who were the clergymen? Most localities had one or more almanacs that attempted to answer such questions. A few even attempted to name every family in the locality.

Other kinds of information dealt with current events, including politics. The first balloon ascension was noted in many almanacs and even inspired the publication of the *Balloon Almanac.* The settlement of the frontier was a popular topic, as was the American Revolution and later the adoption of the Constitution. Laws and tariffs were reprinted. George Washington's

"Farewell Address" was widely reprinted, as were many of the writings of Benjamin Franklin.

Another topic that must interest the student of popular culture is humor. Comic almanacs flourished in the nineteenth century. The David Crockett almanacs are probably the best known, but Josh Billings (Henry Wheeler Shaw), Commodore Rollingpin (John Henton Carter), and others produced comic almanacs. *All-My-Nack, Allminax,* and *Allmaniac* were among the comic misspellings. In addition, many of the serious almanacs contained comic material, much as *Reader's Digest* and other magazines do today. Such comic material constitutes one of the few sources of early popular humor still available to us. Between 1776 and 1800, for example, more than 1,500 comic items were published in serious American almanacs. Certainly much of the comedy was literary rather than popular, and much of it was not even very comic. In some cases the comic items seem to have been copied directly from British sources. Nevertheless, this body of humor is worthy of study simply because it does constitute almost the only source of written popular humor before the *Spirit of the Times* and its competing journals, and the almanac remained an important source even after that.

The nineteenth century saw the development of advertising almanacs, especially those advertising patent medicines. Milton Drake says that about fifty patent medicine almanacs were published in the century, many of them in continuous publication for several years.[3] Many other groups used almanacs for advertising in the nineteenth century. Drake lists religious groups, uplift groups, political groups, labor and professional groups, fraternal groups, and pressure groups, as well as straightforward sales-related advertisers such as those printing and distributing almanacs in this century. The *Christian Almanac,* one of the religious almanacs, grew to have a circulation of 300,000 in 1850.[4]

The twentieth century has brought about additional changes in U.S. almanacs. The almanac of pure information has certainly become the dominant form. For some publishers, the word *almanac* has come to mean any yearly compilation of information and statistics, whether in a particular field (for example, the *Nurse's Almanac* and the *Standard Educational Almanac)* or more general (the *World Almanac and Book of Facts).* The calendar, if it exists at all, has been relegated to a very minor role. In the case of a few publications, such as *The People's Almanac* by David Wallechinsky and Irving Wallace, even the characteristic of yearly publication has been dropped. A few old-time or family almanacs are still published. Most prominent among them is the *Old Farmer's Almanac,* a direct descendant of Robert B. Thomas's *Farmer's Almanac.* Its appeal to a sense of nostalgia and quaintness had gained it a circulation of two million in 1970.

Scholars interested in American ethnic groups will find that U.S. almanacs have been published in at least twenty languages including twelve European languages and six American Indian languages.

REFERENCE WORKS

Two bibliographies are essential to the study of American almanacs. The first, *American Bibliography* by Charles Evans, is a fourteen-volume work which claims to be a dictionary of all "books, pamphlets and periodical publications" printed in America before 1821. Before his death, however, Evans had carried the bibliography only through part of 1799. The American Antiquarian Society (AAS) finished 1799, 1800, and the index, which has a separate heading for almanacs. The Evans-American Antiquarian Society publication lists more than 5,000 almanacs as having been printed in America before the end of 1800. It is somewhat confusing that these listings include almanacs published *for* 1801. With few exceptions almanacs were published in the fall or winter of the year preceding the year of their calendar.

Evans's entries, some of which were taken from advertisements and other sources, contain some ghosts. In at least one case an almanac appears to be listed under two different titles. Nevertheless, Evans's bibliography is important for at least two reasons. Evans and the American Antiquarian Society were among the first to consider the almanacs an important scholarly resource. Besides, this bibliography and its supplement provides access to *Early American Imprints,* a Readex Microprint Edition edited by Clifford K. Shipton and published by the American Antiquarian Society.

Any library with a set of these microcards and the later supplement, also edited by Shipton, holds a representative collection of seventeenth- and eighteenth-century American almanacs. It may appear that the collection is biased toward almanacs published in the Northeast, but it must be remembered that by far the majority of almanac publishers, especially in these two centuries, were located in the Northeast.

Access to the supplement to *Early American Imprints* is provided by the two-volume *Supplement to Charles Evans' American Bibliography* by Roger P. Bristol, which has a separate heading for almanacs in the index. The index lists nearly a thousand almanacs not included in *American Bibliography*.

From 1958 to 1966, Ralph Shaw and Richard Shoemaker published twenty-two additional volumes of *American Bibliography* on a less comprehensive plan than that of Evans. Their work is subtitled A *Preliminary Checklist for 1801–1819,* and they call it "a preliminary step in filling the gap in American bibliography."[5] Like the Evans-AAS volumes, the Shaw-Shoemaker volumes locate entries whose locations are known, but, because there is no separate listing for almanacs in the index, it is necessary to search each volume in order to find all of the almanacs.

In 1967, Richard Shoemaker again began expanding *American Bibliography* by publishing A *Checklist of American Imprints*. Beginning with 1820, that series now extends through 1833. In addition to Shoemaker, Gayle and M. Frances Cooper and Scott and Carol Bruntjen have worked as compilers. There are comprehensive title and author indexes for 1820 to 1829, but, as with the Shaw-Shoemaker volumes of *American Bibliography,* the student of almanacs must search each volume or read through the entire title index. These volumes provide locations. Most useful for the almanac researcher, then, are the Evans-AAS volumes and the supplement, which have a more usable index and provide access to the AAS microcard collection.

The second indispensable bibliography is Milton Drake's two-volume *Almanacs of the United States,* which attempts to list and locate all American almanacs published before 1850. In addition, for some states, notably those in the Confederacy and some of the western states, Drake carries the list into the 1870s. Drake's work contains 14,385 entries and locates nearly 75,000 copies. Drake canvassed 558 libraries and read about "four hundred bibliographical works in search of defunct issues."[6] Drake believes that he has, in fact, listed 85 percent or more of the almanacs published before 1850. As a bibliography of almanacs, Drake obviously supersedes Evans. Evans, however, is still essential to most almanac researchers for the access it gives to the AAS microcard collection.

In addition to his list, Drake provides an interesting and informative introduction. We learn, for example, that the old story of Lincoln saving a client with an almanac is supported by Illinois court records of an account of a British lawyer who had earlier used a fraudulent almanac to save his client in the same way. Drake also includes a list of American towns and cities where almanacs were published and the date of the earliest listed almanac for each town. He lists about 350 such cities and towns. Finally, Drake includes a bibliography of secondary source material, most of which his work has superseded.

To seek out almanacs published after 1850 is much more difficult because there is no specialized almanac bibliography such as Drake's, and many of the compilers of general bibliographies did not consider almanacs worthy of inclusion. Those general bibliographies that do include almanacs often seem to include too few. The *American Catalogue* is one of only a few general bibliographies that list almanacs. For the period from 1895 to 1900 it lists only forty almanacs and forty-seven calendars and yearbooks. *The American Catalogue,* founded by F. Leypoldt and continued by Lynds E. Jones and R. R. Bowker, lists books in print from 1876 to 1910. Its subject index has a heading for almanacs and another for calendars and yearbooks. *The Catalogue of Public Documents* put out by the Superintendent of Documents lists calendars and nautical almanacs published by agencies of the U.S. government.

RESEARCH COLLECTIONS

The first library to collect almanacs aggressively was that of the American Antiquarian Society under the direction of Clarence Brigham. Consequently, the AAS has perhaps the largest collection of early American almanacs of any library. It is this collection that formed the basis for the almanac representation in their microcard edition of *Early American Imprints*.

The holdings of the AAS are so great that when Milton Drake began work on his *Almanacs of the United States* he believed that a canvass of the AAS holdings together with those of the Library of Congress, the New York Public Library, Rutgers University, the New York Historical Society, "and a scattering of others" would serve to find "everything that matters."[7] That search did net Drake 10,000 entries and located 20,000 copies, but his expansion of the search to more than 500 libraries netted an additional 4,000 entries and 55,000 located copies.

Most of the almanacs of early America were produced for a specific locality. It may be expected that state and local libraries will provide good sources for almanacs originally published within the locality or state that they serve and that they will, perhaps, hold copies not found in such giant collections as the AAS and the Library of Congress.

It is no surprise, then, that researchers interested in almanacs published in early Virginia will find copies, often unique, in the College of William and Mary, the Colonial Williamsburg Library, and the Virginia Historical Society Library, as well as in the Library of Congress. It is somewhat surprising that for very early Virginia almanacs the Huntington Library in San Marino, California, is an important source, as is the Washington State Historical Library and the William L. Clements Library in Ann Arbor, Michigan. The Huntington Library has collected many of the earliest almanacs from several of the states that have a colonial history. It owns the only extant copy of *An Almanack* for 1646, published in Cambridge, Massachusetts, by Stephen Daye. According to Drake, it is the earliest almanac still extant.

For almanacs published in Alabama, the important local libraries include the University of Alabama and the Alabama Department of Archives and History in Montgomery; for those published in California, the important local libraries are the Bancroft Library and the University of California Library in Berkeley, the California State Library in Sacramento, the California Historical Society in San Francisco, and, somewhat less important, the University of California at Los Angeles.

For Connecticut, the following local libraries have important holdings: the Connecticut Historical Society and the Connecticut State Library in Hartford, Yale University in New Haven, and local historical societies in New Haven, Litchfield, and New London. The Western Reserve Historical Society in Cleveland, Ohio, also has several Connecticut almanacs.

For Delaware, the Henry Francis DuPont Winterthur Museum in Winterthur has an important collection of early almanacs. The University of Delaware in Newark has a collection of nineteenth-century almanacs. The Pennsylvania Historical Society Library in Philadelphia appears to have a larger collection than either of the in-state libraries.

For the District of Columbia, the best local resources are, of course, the Library of Congress and the Public Library of the District of Columbia.

The De Renne Georgia Library in Athens is the best in-state source for almanacs published in Georgia. Emory University in Atlanta and the Georgia Historical Society in Savannah as well as the Atlanta Public Library have some holdings.

For Illinois, the Newberry Library and the Chicago Historical Society in Chicago and the Illinois Historical Library in Springfield provide the best local sources for almanac research.

For Indiana, consult the Indiana Historical Society and the Indiana State Library in Indianapolis, as well as Earlham College in Richmond and Indiana University in Bloomington. The Ohio State Historical Society in Columbus, Ohio, also has several Indiana almanacs.

The Kentucky Historical Society in Frankfort, the Louisville Free Public Library, the Lexington Public Library, and the University of Kentucky Library in Lexington have holdings of almanacs published in Kentucky, as do the Indiana Historical Society and the Washington State Historical Society.

Of the almanacs published in Louisiana, only a few are listed by Drake as being held in Louisiana libraries. The Howard-Tilton Memorial Library at Tulane University in New Orleans has all of them.

For Maine, the important in-state sources include the Maine Historical Society and Longfellow House in Portland as well as the Bowdoin College Library in Brunswick and the Bangor Public Library.

For Maryland there are two important local libraries: the Enoch Pratt Library and the Maryland Historical Society, both in Baltimore.

Massachusetts, along with Pennsylvania and New York, was one of the top three almanac-producing states. There are many libraries with important holdings of almanacs published in Massachusetts. Probably the most important in-state library for Massachusetts is the American Antiquarian Society Library in Worcester, but the Massachusetts Historical Society and the Boston Public Library in Boston and Harvard University in Cambridge rival it as far as in-state almanacs are concerned. In addition, both the New York and Pennsylvania historical societies have significant holdings of Massachusetts almanacs, and many libraries throughout the state have some almanacs. The (Old) Farmer's Almanack was originally published in Massachusetts and appears to be the most widely collected of all American almanacs. Drake lists eighty libraries in twenty-four states holding copies of the 1850 edition of this Boston almanac.

Few almanacs were published in Michigan. Consult the Burton Historical Collection and the Detroit Public Library in Detroit as well as the Michigan State Library in Lansing. Even fewer were published in Minnesota, and there are no significant in-state holdings of Minnesota almanacs. The only significant in-state holdings of Mississippi almanacs are at the State Department of Archives and History in Jackson. For Missouri, the most significant holdings are at the Missouri Historical Society in St. Louis, but the Missouri State Historical Society in Columbia and the Mercantile Library Association in St. Louis are worth consulting.

For New Hampshire, whose presses produced about 500 almanacs, the most important in-state library is that of the New Hampshire Historical Society in Concord. The State Library in Concord and the Dartmouth College Library are also important.

New Jersey has two important libraries of almanac holdings: Rutgers University in New Brunswick and the New Jersey Historical Society in Newark.

New York produced far more almanacs than any other state. Several libraries hold significant numbers of New York almanacs, including the New York Public Library, the New York Historical Society, the Long Island Historical Society, and the Pierpont Morgan Library, all of New York City, and the New York State Library in Buffalo. In addition to the national collections, such out-of-state libraries as the John Carter Brown Library in Providence, Rhode Island, the Pennsylvania Historical Society, the American Philosophical Society, and the Rosenbach Foundation of Philadelphia, and the Huntington Library have collections that are significant.

In North Carolina, the University of North Carolina at Chapel Hill and Duke University at Durham have the two largest collections. The North Carolina Historical Commission and the State Library in Raleigh have smaller collections.

Several Ohio libraries have significant holdings of Ohio almanacs. They are: the Ohio State Library in Columbus, the Public Library of Cincinnati and Hamilton County, the Historical and Philosophical Society of Ohio, which is also in Cincinnati, the Western Reserve Historical Society in Cleveland, the Dayton Public Library, and Marietta College.

Few almanacs were published in Oregon. The Oregon Historical Society in Portland has most of them. The Library Association of Portland and the University of Oregon in Eugene also have holdings.

Pennsylvania is the third largest almanac-producing state. The Historical Society of Pennsylvania and the American Philosophical Society, both in Philadelphia, have large holdings of Pennsylvania almanacs. Each has some unique copies, as does the Library Company of Philadelphia. The Rosenbach Foundation of Philadelphia has several almanacs, at least one of which is unique, as do the New York Historical Society and the John Carter Brown Library.

The Rhode Island Historical Society has large holdings of Rhode Island almanacs as does the John Carter Brown Library. Both are in Providence. For South Carolina, the most significant in-state holdings are in the Charleston Library and the South Carolina Historical Society. Both are located in

Charleston. The South Carolina State Library in Columbia also has some almanacs.

The Tennessee State Library in Nashville has succeeded in collecting most of the almanacs published in that state. All but one of the few almanacs published in Utah are held by the Library of the Church of Jesus Christ of Latter Day Saints in Salt Lake City. In-state libraries that have collected Vermont almanacs include the Vermont State Library and the Vermont Historical Society in Montpelier and the University of Vermont in Burlington.

Apart from the five national collections already listed and the in-state collections, some libraries have significant national or regional holdings, although they are not comparable to those of the AAS or the Library of Congress. Such historical societies as the Western Reserve, the Washington State, the Massachusetts, and the Pennsylvania have collected actively both inside and outside their states. The Harvard, Yale, Indiana, Brown, and Texas university libraries have also accumulated large holdings of out-of-state almanacs, as have the American Philosophical Society and the Huntington Library.

Any scholar interested in examining American almanacs should realize how very spread out they are. To be sure, they are concentrated in the Northeast, from Washington, D.C., to Boston, but many unique copies can be found in California and throughout the state libraries. A scholar should probably begin by consulting a copy of Drake's bibliography, from which much of the above information has been taken, deciding which almanacs he or she needs to examine and planning a reasonable travel schedule. He or she should also bear in mind that many U.S. libraries have several thousand copies of almanacs published before 1801 available on microcard.

HISTORY AND CRITICISM

Like many other articles of popular culture, almanacs have too often been considered beneath the efforts of scholarship. Aside from biographers of Franklin, few scholars gave much attention to American almanacs until George Lyman Kittredge wrote *The Old Farmer and His Almanack* and Clarence Brigham began his efforts to build up the AAS collection of almanacs.

The Old Farmer and His Almanack deals with the almanacs of Robert B. Thomas. Kittredge brilliantly discusses the divisions of Thomas's almanac, including The Farmer's Calendar, the letters to the editor, the sayings, and the anecdotes. Kittredge's best chapters deal with Thomas's folk wisdom, the characters he created for The Farmer's Calendar, and the letters. Perhaps the most significant aspect of Kittredge's book, however, was that it gave a certain respectability to the study of almanacs. If the great scholar of Shakespeare and early British literature considered almanacs important enough to devote an entire book to one almanac, then perhaps other almanacs deserved a closer look.

Samuel Briggs's *The Essays, Humor and Poems of Nathaniel Ames, Father and Son, of Dedham, Massachusetts from Their Almanacks, 1726–1775* reprinted much of the Ames almanacs, omitting the calendars. It also contains several essays by Briggs: "Almanacks," "The Rise of the Almanack in America," "The Ames Family, and the Town of Dedham," "The Old Tavern," "Notes on Each Almanack." Of the essays "The Rise of the Almanack in America" is one of the most interesting.

Richard M. Dorson edited *Davy Crockett: American Comic Legend,* which contains material on the Crockett almanacs. Joseph Leach's *The Typical Texan: Biography of an American Myth* is important as a scholarly book on a subject other than almanacs that uses almanacs as an important source of material.

Milton Drake's *Almanacs of the United States* has already been fully discussed under the Reference Works section. It is an essential book for anyone who wants to study American almanacs.

Robb Sagendorph's *America and Her Almanacs: Wit, Wisdom and Weather* is less a scholarly book than an exercise in nostalgia. At the time he wrote *America and Her Almanacs,* Sagendorph had been editor of the *Old Farmer's Almanac* for thirty-one years. He claims, with some accuracy, that "reading the early almanacs is the only way to see into the heart of Colonial America." It may not be the only way, but it is an excellent way, and Sagendorph's book provides a great deal of almanac material to read and more than 200 woodcuts reproduced from the almanacs. One chapter is devoted to *Poor Richard.*

In 1970 Henry Wheeler Shaw's *Josh Billings' Farmers' Allminax* was reprinted in a volume called *Old Probability: Perhaps Rain—Perhaps Not. Old Probability* is nothing more than a reprint of the Josh Billings's almanacs.

Marion Barber Stowell's *Early American Almanacs: The Colonial Weekday Bible* may be the most important almanac book since Drake's bibliography. *Early American Almanacs* is one of only a few books that attempts to deal with the entire spectrum of American almanacs for a specific period. Stowell studied some 450 almanacs of the seventeenth and eighteenth century. She described many of the almanac makers and provided many examples from the almanacs. It is possible that she could have been more successful in her immense task if there had been a larger body of competent scholarship preceding her. She does succeed in showing the importance of almanacs to early America and in creating the first systematic, broadly based study of early American almanacs that is not primarily bibliographical.

Clarence Brigham wrote two articles for the *Proceedings of the American Antiquarian Society,* "An Account of American Almanacs and Their Value for Historical Study" and "Report of the Librarian," which contains a summary of the AAS collection of American almanacs. Both articles helped encourage the use of almanacs as documentary sources. The AAS had already begun using its *Proceedings* to encourage almanac study. As early as 1907 Victor Hugo Paltsits had published "The Almanacs of Roger Sherman, 1750–1761," and in 1914 George Emery Littlefield published "Notes on the Calendar and the Almanac" in the *Proceedings*.

Bernard S. Capp's *English Almanacs, 1500–1800: Astrology and the Popular Press* deals entirely with almanacs published in Britain. It serves, however, to provide a general view of the background out of which American almanacs grew.

Robert K. Dodge's *Early American Almanac Humor* is a selection of humorous items drawn from the almanacs of the early American republic (1776–1800). Dodge claims to have found early examples of Yankee trickster stories, of American tall tales, and of other stories that entered the mainstream of American humor. Dodge is also working on two forthcoming books about almanacs to be published by Greenwood Press.

Both Tanis Thorne and Robert Dodge have published articles making the case for the study of almanacs. Thorne's "The Almanacs of the San Francisco Bay Region, 1850–1861: A Neglected Historical Source" appeared in 1978. Dodge's "Access to Popular Culture: Early American Almanacs" was published in 1979.

A number of articles have dealt with the almanacs of one publisher or of one author. Alfred B. Page covered the almanacs of John Tulley from 1687 to 1702, and Frank H. Severance published "The Story of Phinney's Western Almanack, with Notes on Other Calendars and Weather Forecasters of Buffalo." Jasper Marsh wrote "Amos Pope and His Almanacs," and Arthur D. Graeff published a series of articles in volumes 5 and 6 (1938 and 1939) of the *American-German Review*. The articles, seldom more than two pages long, are entitled "Pennsylvania German Almanacs." F. G. Woodward published "An Early Tennessee Almanac and Its Maker: Hill's Almanac 1825–1862," and Robert T. Sidwell wrote "An Odd Fish: Samuel Keimer and a Footnote to American Educational History." Keimer was a publisher of an almanac in Philadelphia, but Sidwell deals with him primarily as an educator.

In 1968 two articles were published dealing with John Henton Carter, the author of *Commodore Rollingpin's Almanac*. John T. Flanagan's "John Henton Carter, Alias 'Commodore Rollingpin' " and James T. Swift's "From Pantry to Pen: The Saga of Commodore Rollingpin" both concentrate on the man as well as his work.

Another article that deals with comic almanacs is David Kesterson's "Josh Billings 'Defolks' Rural America," in which Kesterson compares Billings's parody with the farmer's almanac tradition that inspired it. Nancy Merrill's "Henry Ranlet: Exeter Printer" deals with an important almanac maker and printer of the early republic.

Also of interest are articles that use almanacs as source material. Chester

E. Eisinger's "The Farmer in the Eighteenth Century Almanac" uses almanacs to determine the strength of the agrarian view of life in eighteenth-century America. Elsie H. and Curtis Booker's "Patent Medicines Before the Wiley Act of 1906" uses almanac advertising as a source. Robert Dodge's "Didactic Humor in the Almanacs of Early America," "The Irish Comic Stereotype in the Almanacs of the Early Republic," and his two notes and short article on Americanisms in *American Speech* also use almanacs as sources. Giles E. Gobetz's "Slovenian Ethnic Studies" and Jon Stanley Wenrick's "Indians in Almanacs, 1783–1815" find almanacs to be sources for ethnic studies.

Marion Barber Stowell's excellent work "The Influence of Nathaniel Ames on the Literary Taste of His Time" serves as a model of the kind of article for which almanacs can serve as sources. Three other important works include Maxine Moore's *That Lonely Game: Melville, Mardi, and the Almanac,* Allan R. Raymond's "To Reach Men's Minds: Almanacs and the American Revolution, 1760–1777," and Rose Lockwood's "The Scientific Revolution in Seventeenth-Century New-England," which sees the almanacs as one of the battlegrounds between the Puritans' belief in a finite and largely Ptolemaic universe and the astronomers' scientific belief in an infinite Copernican universe. Dick Goddard's "Six Inches of Partly Cloudy" focuses on methods of predicting the weather before the development of meteorology.

NOTES

1. Samuel Briggs, *The Essays, Humor and Poems of Nathaniel Ames, Father and Son, of Dedham, Massachusetts from Their Almanacks, 1726–1775* (Detroit: Singing Tree Press, 1969), p. 372.

2. "A Song Upon Bundling," *Beers's Almanac for 1793* (Hartford, Conn.: Hudson and Goodwin, 1792), pp. 26–27.

3. Milton Drake, *Almanacs of the United States* (New York: Scarecrow Press, 1962) 1; xiii.

4. Drake, p.x.

5. Ralph R. Shaw and Richard H. Shoemaker, *American Bibliography: A Preliminary Checklist for 1801* (New York: Scarecrow Press, 1958), p. iii.

6. Drake, 1; xv.

7. Drake, 1; xv.

BIBLIOGRAPHY

Booker, Elsie H., and Curtis Booker, "Patent Medicines Before the Wiley Act of 1906,"*North Carolina Folklore,* 18 (November 1970), 130–42.

Briggs, Samuel. *The Essays, Humor and Poems of Nathaniel Ames, Father and Son, of Dedham, Massachusetts from Their Almanacks, 1726–1775.* Cleveland: Western Reserve Press, 1891. Reprint. Detroit: Singing Tree Press, 1969.

Brigham, Clarence. "An Account of American Almanacs and Their Value for Historical Study."*Proceedings of the American Antiquarian Society*, n.s. 34 (October 1925), 3–28.

———. "Report of the Librarian."*Proceedings of the American Antiquarian Society*, n.s. 35 (October 1926), 190–218.

Bristol, Roger P. *Supplement to Charles Evans' American Bibliography*. Charlottesville: University Press of Virginia, 1970.

Capp, Bernard S. *English Almanacs, 1500–1800: Astrology and the Popular Press*. Ithaca, N.Y.: Cornell University Press, 1979.

Danforth, Samuel. *An Almanack for the Year of Our Lord 1646*. . . . Cambridge, Mass.: Printed by Stephen Daye, 1646.

Dodge, Robert. "Access to Popular Culture: Early American Almanacs."*Kentucky Folklore Record*, 25 (January-June 1979), 11–15.

———. "Damn Yankee."*American Speech*, 57 (Fall 1982), 240.

———. "Didactic Humor in the Almanacs of Early America." *Journal of Popular Culture*, 5 (Winter 1971), 592–605.

———. *Early American Almanac Humor*. Bowling Green, Ohio: Bowling Green University Popular Press, 1987.

———. "Four Americanisms Found in Early Almanacs." *American Speech*, 60 (Fall 1985), 270–71.

———. "The Irish Comic Stereotype in the Almanacs of the Early Republic."*Eire-Ireland*, 19 (Fall 1984), 111–20.

———. "Twistical."*American Speech*, 56 (Fall 1981), 218.

Dorson, Richard M. *Davy Crockett: American Comic Legend*. New York: Spiral Editions, 1939.

Drake, Milton. *Almanacs of the United States*. 2 vols. New York: Scarecrow Press, 1962.

Eisinger, Chester E. "The Farmer in the Eighteenth Century Almanac."*Agricultural History*, 28 (July 1954), 107–12.

Evans, Charles. *American Bibliography*. 14 vols. Worcester, Mass.: American Antiquarian Society, 1903–55. Reprint. New York: Peter Smith, 1941–67.

Flanagan, John T. "John Henton Carter, Alias 'Commodore Rollingpin.' " *Missouri Historical Review*, 63 (October 1968), 38–64.

Gobetz, Giles E. "Slovenian Ethnic Studies."*Journal of Ethnic Studies*, 2 (Winter 1975), 99–103.

Goddard, Dick. "Six Inches of Partly Cloudy."*Inland Seas*, 41 (Winter 1985), 244–54.

Graeff, Arthur D. "Pennsylvania German Almanacs." *American-German Review*, 5 (April-May 1939), 4–7, 36; 5 (June-July 1939), 30–33, 37–38; 5 (August-September 1939), 24–29; 6 (October-November 1939), 10–12, 40; 6 (December 1939-January 1940), 12–19; 6 (April-May 1940), 10–13, 37; 6 (June-July 1940), 9–12; 6 (August-September 1940), 10–14.

Kesterson, David. "Josh Billings 'Defolks' Rural America." *Tennessee Folklore Society Bulletin*, 41 (1975), 57–64.

Kittredge, George Lyman. *The Old Farmer and His Almanack*. Cambridge, Mass.: Harvard University Press, 1920. Reprint. New York: Benjamin Blom, 1967.

Leach, Joseph. *The Typical Texan: Biography of an American Myth*. Dallas: Southern Methodist University Press, 1952.

Leypoldt, F., Lynds E. Jones, and R. R. Bowker. *The American Catalogue.* New York: Bowker, 1880–1911. Reprint. New York: Peter Smith, 1941.

Littlefield, George Emery. "Notes on the Calendar and the Almanac."*Proceedings of the American Antiquarian Society,* n.s. 24 (October 1914), 11–64.

Lockwood, Rose. "The Scientific Revolution in Seventeenth-Century New-England."*New England Quarterly,* 53 (Spring 1980), 76–95.

McDowell, Marion Barber (now Marion Barber Stowell). "Early American Almanacs: The History of a Neglected Literary Genre." Ph.D. dissertation, Florida State University, 1974.

Marsh, Jasper. "Amos Pope and His Almanacs."*Danvers Historical Society, Historical Collections,* 10 (1922), 93–114.

Merrill, Nancy. "Henry Ranlet: Exeter Printer, 1762–1807." *History of New Hampshire,* 37 (Winter 1982), 250–82.

Moore, Maxine. *That Lonely Game: Melville, Mardi, and the Almanac.* Columbia: University of Missouri Press, 1975.

Page, Alfred B. "The Almanacs of John Tulley: 1687–1702." *Publications of the Colonial Society of Massachusetts,* 13 (July 1912), 207–23.

Paltsits, Victor Hugo. "The Almanacs of Roger Sherman, 1750–1761."*Proceedings of the American Antiquarian Society,* n.s. 18 (April 1907), 213–58.

Raymond, Allan R. "To Reach Men's Minds: Almanacs and the American Revolution, 1760–1777."*New England Quarterly,* 51 (Fall 1978), 370–95.

Rowland, Howard S., and Beatrice Rowland. *The Nurses' Almanac.* Germantown, Md.: Aspen Systems, 1978.

Sagendorph, Robb. *America and Her Almanacs: Wit, Wisdom and Weather.* Boston: Yankee-Little, Brown, 1970.

Severance, Frank H. "The Story of Phinney's Western Almanack, with Notes on Other Calendars and Weather Forecasters of Buffalo."*Buffalo Historical Society Publications,* 24 (December 1920), 343–58.

Shaw, Henry Wheeler. *Old Probability: Perhaps Rain—Perhaps Not.* New York: G. W. Carleton, 1876. Reprint. Upper Saddle River, N.J.: Literature House/ Gregg Press, 1970.

Shaw, Ralph R., and Richard H. Shoemaker. *American Bibliography: A Preliminary Checklist for 1801–1819.* 20 vols. New York: Scarecrow Press, 1958–64.

Shipton, Clifford K. *Early American Imprints, 1639–1800.* Worcester, Mass.: American Antiquarian Society, 1956–64.

———. *Early American Imprints, 1639–1800. Supplement.* Worcester, Mass.: American Antiquarian Society, 1966–68.

Shoemaker, Richard, et al. *A Checklist of American Imprints, 1820–1833,*yearly. Metuchen, N. J.: Scarecrow Press, 1964–.

Sidwell, Robert T. "An Odd Fish: Samuel Keimer and a Footnote to American Educational History."*History of Education Quarterly,* 6 (Spring 1966), 16–30.

The Standard Education Almanac. Los Angeles: Academic Media, 1968–.

Stowell, Marion Barber. *Early American Almanacs: The Colonial Weekday Bible.* New York: Burt Franklin, 1977.

———. "The Influence of Nathaniel Ames on the Literary Taste of His Time."*Early American Literature,* 18 (Summer 1983), 127–45.

Superintendent of Documents. *The Catalogue of Public Documents.* Washington,

D.C.: Government Printing Office, 1896–1941. Reprint. New York: Johnson Reprint/Kraus Reprint, 1963.

Swift, James T. "From Pantry to Pen: The Saga of Commodore Rolling-pin."*Missouri Historical Bulletin,* 24 (January 1968), 113–21.

Throne, Tanis. "The Almanacs of the San Francisco Bay Region, 1850–1861: A Neglected Historical Source."*Journal of the West,* 17 (Summer 1978), 36–45.

Wallechinsky, David, and Irving Wallace. *The People's Almanac.* Garden City, N.Y.: Doubleday, 1975.

Wenrick, Jon Stanley. "For Education and Entertainment—Almanacs in the Early American Republic, 1783–1815." Ph.D. dissertation, Claremont Graduate School, 1974.

———. "Indians in Almanacs, 1783–1815."*Indian Historian,* 8 (Winter 1977), 36–42.

Woodward, F. G. "An Early Tennessee Almanac and Its Maker: Hill's Almanac 1825–1862."*Tennessee Folklore Society Bulletin,* 18 (March 1952), 9–14.

The World Almanac and Book of Facts. New York: Press Publishing (1868–1923), New York World (1924–31), New York World-Telegram (1932–66), and Newspaper Enterprise Association (1967–).

Animation

THOMAS W. HOFFER

Animated motion pictures of the kind known to mass audiences in the United States from the early 1920s to the 1950s were literally created and photographed frame by frame. Of course, all moving pictures are photographed in this way, usually twenty-four frames taken in one second, processed and projected on a screen at the same rate, and fused into the appearance of motion by our mind's eye in which the vision of a previous frame persists for a split second until the next frame is put in place on the screen. All of this happens so rapidly that we pay little heed to the technology involved or the psychology and physiology of our own mechanisms.

There are five capabilities in the film or television technologies which allow a filmmaker to express any idea with some telling impact or recognition. Animators and live-action filmmakers can manipulate image sizes such as closeups, medium views, or long shots, all defined in the context of the first shot used in a given sequence. A second element involves changing the angle that the camera has to the subject-action, whether it be straight-away to the action, low, high, moving into or away from the action, or moving at some angle to the subject-action, as in a tracking shot. A third categorical element involves the composition of mass, line, tone (lighting), and color; all those manipulatable items we would commonly assign to the realm of the animator. For the live-action filmmaker, the single shot is the basic unit of film structure. The single shot, of course, has dozens of compositional elements that work to convey meaning to an audience. But animation's range of manipulation extends far beyond the single shot. In each category, up to now, we can find numerous counterparts to film in other art forms: sculpture, still photographs, painting, theater, for example. Only the fourth expressive element, editing, will separate film and television tape from those other art forms and help us understand the film process and the basis for animation. The complex process of editing makes possible the manipulation of space (the single shot, for example) and time.

In live-action cinematography, the intervals between shots are timed fairly precisely, about twenty-four exposures every second. There is a stability in the twenty-four-frame-per-second shot that matches the reality of the sound we hear, recorded in synchronism with that shot. In editing, we can interrupt this first sound shot by inserting a picture and sound of something else, or overlap the sound from the first shot with a new piece of material, to create the impression that the second shot was photographed (and is occurring) at the same time as the first. Let us say, for example, that we interrupt the shot of a speaker with a view of someone sleeping. With this juxtaposition, we have altered the spatial arrangements of speaker and sleeper to create the impression that both are in the same room, yet they were photographed some distance apart. If we were to continue intercutting the sleeping listener with the speaker, we would as editors begin to alter time, at least as it is perceived in this sequence. The time alteration occurs on two levels: reel time and real time. Real time is altered because two shots at twenty-four frames per second must flow in front of our eyes, taking at least twice as long to view as one shot of similar length. But we alter the length of the cutaway shot of the sleeping listener, thereby directly affecting the length of the shot as originally photographed. The intercutting back and forth may help, with other factors, to build up to some high point in the relationship between our speaker and the sleeping listener, altering the timing of each action.

Something else is at work here that provides a new perspective arising from the two shots, however. The first view of the speaker contains a literal or physical meaning, as does the second shot of the sleeper. When the two are intercut, the second view (sleeper) takes on a compound, secondary meaning as a result of this shot being seen after the view of the speaker. For example, we can now conclude that there is some kind of relationship between the speaker and the sleeper which we would not be able to determine without the edited second shot. We may continue to examine this newly discovered related action of the sleeper only to learn that he is completely oblivious to the speaker and what he is saying. Or, if the sleeper and speaker are animated in their own actions, intercutting the two views may produce some funny or startling results which were not expressed in either shot when originally photographed. This combination of shots in editing is what adds the new and secondary meanings, which tend to compound themselves as the sequence is unreeled. Indeed, the timing (a duration of a screen action) is now the product of the juxtaposition of the edited shots, not a fragment of real time. The edited film, in reel time, is what pulls us out of our reality and into the cinema. This is what distinguishes film and television tape from all other art forms, such as sculpture, still photographs, painting, or theater.

We are conditioned through previous films and television programs to see and learn what is evolving in the sequence of the two shots, speaker and sleeper. The manipulator or filmmaker is now conditioning our perception of these events, not in the real time of their occurrence, but in the timings and resulting rhythm (buildup of tension in a sequence) associated with careful selection of screen actions in the sequence. Thus, the heart of the expressive process in film or television tape is editing. Of course, the other categorical elements contribute to expression, as indicated above. Changing image sizes of the sleeper and speaker could potentially heighten the buildup of tension, as could alternating camera angles.

Finally, sound recording, subjected to editing and dozens of other manipulations, is a fifth expressive element in this process. The traditional types of sound are dialogue, sound effects, and music, but numerous variations are possible, edited in consonance or contradiction to the images. The animator, as well as the viewer in search of greater appreciation or understanding of the animated film, draws upon these five categorial elements of expression, as does the live-action filmmaker.

John Halas, in his *Masters of Animation,* reminds us that film technology and the medium's capacity to express ideas are closely interrelated and interdependent.

Unlike live-action film, however, animation has the greater flexibility of using motion creatively. That is to say, it can exaggerate physical possibilities by slowing movement down, speeding it up and using it comically or expressively. Herein lies the starting point of the art of animation.[1]

The professional animator has mastered the five categorical expressive elements because he or she must manifest timings and rhythm over a series of drawings built into shots; these shots are then built into sequences. But, unlike the live-action filmmaker, the animator also works at a microlevel, within the individual shot or series of drawings making up the shot, beginning with his drawing. In Norman McLaren's definition of animation, we see an approach that embraces all forms of animation, from cel through computer generated images:

Animation is not the art of drawings that move, but the art of movements that are drawn. What happens between each frame is more important than what exists on each frame. Animation is therefore the art of manipulating the invisible interstices that lie between frames. The interstices are the bones, flesh and blood of the movies, what is on each frame, merely the clothing.[2]

Various kinds of animated drawings or objects have evolved in film since the turn of the century. These include the stop-action tricks of Emil Cohl, silhouette cutouts of Lotte Reiniger, puppet films of George Pal, animated photographs by Bob Godfrey, and drawings of images and sound tracks on film by Norman McLaren. Our subject here is another type of animated material that reached mass audiences as the moving picture evolved in the United States and became a distinct product of our popular culture. These were the animated cartoons of Walt Disney, Max and Dave Fleischer, Ub Iwerks, Tex Avery, Bob Clampett, Chuck Jones, Art Babbit, Shamus Culhane, and hundreds of others who created their films frame by frame by drawing them individually for the camera through the use of celluloid overlays. The works of those hundreds of artists resulted in more than movement of simple objects; they created characters, told stories, used and exploited stereotypes, and caricatured life and personalities.

HISTORIC OUTLINE

The following few highlights in the evolution of the animated film in the United States after 1900 are certainly no substitute for a definitive history. Indeed, the field is in need of more histories that attempt some assessment of the art form in the context of American film and the broader social, economic, and political environments.

Depending upon whether you define animation as movement or photography, our story could start with successive drawings of animals on cave walls originating thousands of years ago or with early attempts around 1900 to fuse the moving picture camera and single drawings to create the illusion of movement. One likely contender for the first animated cartoon made in the United States was a project of the Edison Company entitled *The Enchanted Drawing,* registered for copyright on November 16, 1900. Running a bit over one minute at today's projection speeds, the story line consisted of a cartoonist interacting with a one-line caricature of a man drawn on a nearby easel. The cartoonist was J. Stuart Blackton, an employee of Edison, who would later become very prominent in the American silent film.

Space does not permit tracing the evolution of film cartoons through a series of characters, studios, principal directors, animators, or new techniques and technologies. One major characteristic of the period from 1900 to 1928 was the gradually diminishing role of the sole animator as author as complex organizations, using divided labor to conceive, draw, photograph, and manufacture animated cartoons, formed.

A number of important animators influenced the early medium with their individual styles, techniques, and inventions; they include Winsor McCay, John Bray, Earl Hurd, Raoul Barre, Max Fleischer, Paul Terry, Sidney Smith, Henry Mayer, and Emil Cohl. McCay, using rice paper cels, had produced an animated film for Vitagraph release in 1911, followed by "Gertie the Dinosaur," a vaudeville act using film, copyrighted in 1914. That same year, John Bray and Earl Hurd were using nitrate acetate cels with separately drawn backgrounds. Barre was instrumental in developing a technique for redrawing only the successive cels for those portions of a character that moved, using the same cel for the stationary portions of the character. Shamus Culhane places the beginning of the theatrical cartoon at about 1916.

Soon, symbiosis set in; animated cartoons drew their content, characters, and form from the comic strips. Animators also copied each other as well as the characters created by such actors as Charlie Chaplin.

All the commercial animators were cartoonists who had worked on strips or comic magazines. Raoul Barre and Charlie Bowers produced *Mutt and Jeff,* and Hearst's International Studio flooded the market with animated cartoon versions of *Happy Hooligan,* the *Katzenjammer Kids, Krazy Kat* and the like.[3]

Instead of using movement to show emotions, a number of devices from the comic strips were copied in the films. For example, a drawing of a light bulb suddenly appearing over the head of an animated character would symbolize an idea. Dialogue was contained in balloons floating at the top of the frame, connected to a character. Some borrowed from D. W. Griffith and exploited an iris in the frame.

Many cartoon characters were wooden and conveyed little personality through the silent medium. Others were strings of visual gags, trite story lines, and chases. By the mid–1920s, the animated cartoon was relegated to minor status on most playbills, sometimes used as a chaser at the end of a program and the start of another. Distributors and exhibitors placed little value on them, and in some instances with justification. One exception was a character animated by Otto Messmer for Pat Sullivan: Felix the Cat.

The period from 1928 to about 1950 has been characterized as the "golden age" of film animation partly because it began with the exploitation of sound and, by 1932, color. Indeed, the real growth of the mass audience for theatrical cartoons began with the innovation of sound, marked by Walt Disney's *Steamboat Willie.* The genius of Disney flowered during this time, first with his exploitation of the new sound medium, followed with the application of Technicolor, and, by the late 1930s, the release of *Snow White.* Both Disney and Max Fleischer innovated the use of the storyboard in their organizations, allowing their animators to plan entire films more efficiently, but the Disney organization placed greater emphasis on education and training. Disney insisted on the best-quality work; he maximized every opportunity to strengthen the creative process of production yet maintained control over the final result. Following the success of *Flowers and Trees* (1932), the first three-strip Technicolor cartoon, and the popular *Three Little Pigs* (1933), which was promoted in other media with the hit tune "Who's

Afraid of the Big Bad Wolf" (itself an appeal against the Depression), Disney resisted the general industry practice of following a winner with a duplicate offering. This practice, epitomized in the trade motto "Nothing succeeds like success," is still followed in today's phonograph, radio, television, and film industries. His shrewd deal with Technicolor, insuring exclusive use of the new process for two years, undoubtedly nourished new exhibitor and distributor interest in the animated film and seemed to be quite consistent with the high ideals of competitive bidding in the marketplace. Of course, his competitors did not think so.

The Disney organization also exploited their own characters through merchandising contracts, later emulated by Walter Lantz and the Fleischers. Such symbiotic activity was critically important in keeping Disney credit active for more investment, particularly for feature-length production in the form of *Snow White and the Seven Dwarfs* (1937). While it was not the first animated feature, *Snow White* was the most economically and artistically successful for many years. In that picture and an earlier short subject, Disney innovated the multiplane techniques that provided a greater sense of depth.

There is abundant evidence that the major achievement of the 1930s, beyond the innovation of sound and color, was the Disney organizational configuration, which made possible successful feature film, and new artistic heights of character animation. Checkpoints in the animation process were implemented to maintain quality. These included the conference technique, key drawings, pencil tests, and stereophonic sound. In the early 1940s, *Fantasia* did badly at the box office but since has won success, demonstrating that many of Disney's products now achieve new leases on life with new generations, enhanced by a weekly television program plugging Disney theme parks and upcoming animated and live-action theatrical features. Few could lay claim to such longevity, but the secret is not attributed exclusively to art in animation.

World War II eclipsed theatrical animation to some degree and brought forward more applications in education and training, particularly in the films commissioned by the U.S. military. Animated theatrical films were released from other studios as well, including Warner Brothers, Metro-Goldwyn-Mayer, 20th Century Fox, Paramount, Universal, and Columbia. The Fleischer studio animated *Betty Boop* (1930), *Popeye* (1933), and *Superman* (1941), but in 1942 the Fleischer unit was dissolved by Paramount. Under their new banner, Famous Studios, the *Superman* theatricals continued, followed by *Casper, the Friendly Ghost* (1946), *Herman and Katnip* (1948), and *Little Audrey* (1949). Paul Terry's studio, releasing through 20th Century Fox, animated *Gandy Goose* (1938), *Dinky Duck* (1939), *Mighty Mouse* (1943), and *Heckle and Jeckle* (1946). Walter Lantz released his theatrical cartoons through Universal beginning with *Andy Panda* (1939) and *Woody Woodpecker* (1940). Columbia's animation unit manufactured *Krazy Kat* (1930), *Scrappy* (1931), *Barney Google* (mid–1930s), and *The Fox and the Crow* (1941).

Following some labor troubles in the Disney organization in 1941, a number of animators established United Productions of America (UPA), with a cartoon style in considerable contrast to Disney's character animation. In the UPA cartoons, there was more abstraction, as in the character and backgrounds of *Mr. Magoo* (1949) and *Gerald McBoing Boing* (1951), who spoke in sound effects. The two-dimensionality of the UPA style did not bode well for their attempts in feature production. As more animators attempted to tackle feature production, a new word came into the vocabulary: "Disneyfication," which included the exploitation of strong story, personality coupled with character animation, and a fantasy form based on realism to some degree and cultivated through constant training of animators and numerous checkpoints. Metro-Goldwyn-Mayer characters came later than those of other studios, probably the most well known being *Tom and Jerry* (1939). Warner Brothers began with *Bosko* (1930) and *Porky Pig* (1935) and later introduced *Bugs Bunny and Elmer Fudd* (1940), *Tweetie Pie* (1944), *Sylvester* (1945), and the clever *Roadrunner and the Coyote* (1948).

With such a stable of characters and personalities competing for audiences, it was indeed a golden era for animation, probably not to be repeated again in the American marketplace.

The Disney characters were fewer in number compared to most studios but included *Mickey Mouse* (1928), *Goofy* (1932), *Pluto* (1930), *Donald Duck* (1934), and *Chip and Dale* (1943). Major efforts turned toward feature production, although the studio always had short subject cartoons in production until 1955. *Snow White* (1937) was an immediate box office success. Others followed, including *Pinocchio* (1940), *Fantasia* (1940), *The Reluctant Dragon* (1941), *Dumbo* (1941), and *Bambi* (1942), some live-action, combinations of live-action and animation, or all animation pictures. In contrast to the Disney artistic and box office successes, the Fleischer organization, as the only credible competitor to Disney, did not fare nearly as well. There were many differences between the two organizations and their products. From an artistic standpoint, Shamus Culhane concluded:

Fleischerites always defended their work by stoutly maintaining that if they had more time the quality of their work would rival, or be better than, Disney's. They never could accept the fact that time wasn't the factor; it was education. Disney's artists and writers were working with principles of their craft which had been arrived at by intensive study. Fleischer people were operating from instinct and a scornful rejection of the idea that principles of writing and animation even existed.[4]

From a business standpoint, the Fleischers did not own their commercially successful characters, a lesson learned early by Walt Disney when he lost Oswald the Rabbit. Max Fleischer spurned the pencil tests as a device to check and improve animation in a system of divided labor. In a letter quoted at length by Culhane, Max Fleischer asserted that the film animation industry must pull "away from the tendencies toward realism. . . . The cartoon must be a portrayal of the expression of the true cartoonist, in simple, unhampered cartoon style."[5] Disney's success, on the other hand, was based on the study of realism and movement, as these revealed emotional qualities which could be exploited in characters and strong story lines.

After 1950 the American film industry was undergoing a restructuring in which the studios were divesting themselves of their theaters and abandoning certain practices, such as block booking, considered unlawful and in restraint of competition. The vertically integrated film business involved the studios distributing their own films to major exhibitors they controlled or owned. Block booking, for example, required that an exhibitor take all of a given studio's output, including the budget films and short subjects, if it wanted the Class A pictures, which would reap higher gains. Such a guaranteed channel from studio to local theater for all kinds of films at least brought films to potential audiences in an efficient manner and minimized the usual risks of not finding enough screens to exhibit them for paying audiences. This system undoubtedly contributed to the continued existence of the expensive animation units at the major studios in the 1940s.

But there were other reasons for the demise of the theatrical cartoon as the guaranteed screens disappeared. The cost of manufacturing theatrical cartoons increased enormously, from $8,000 to $25,000 or more for a split reel (less than seven minutes). Television's capturing of the nighttime radio and film audience was an important reason for the decline of film audiences. At the same time, television began to provide new opportunities for animation in terms of advertising and children's programming. Network television in the 1950s was growing, opening new opportunities for films of all types, and by 1960 the electronic medium had devoured both the mundane and the classic animated short films formerly seen only in theaters. With the adoption of limited cel techniques, and later stop-action animation, coupled with computer-assisted technologies, animated programming increased sharply. Other forms of stop-action, object, or dimensional animation found new outlets in television. For example, NBC-TV's *Project Twenty* documentary series used stills-in-motion techniques.

Scientists at Bell Laboratories made the first computer-animated films in 1963. Others developed and exploited theory, hardware, and software to evolve computer graphics, first used in auto and aircraft industries as an aid in design. Experimentalists such as Stan Vanderbeek and John Whitney connected with programmers and the new technology. In the late 1960s, Scanimate, Animac, Caesar, Video Cel, and Antics offered computer graphics for television production. With the invention of computer-assisted animation, or motion control, it was possible to incorporate streaks and slit-scan techniques such as those used in the titles for *Superman: The Movie* (1983) or the stargate sequence in *2001: A Space Odyssey* (1968).

By the mid–1980s, computer image-making came from three methods:

motion control, analogue systems, and digital systems. Motion control involved the use of a computer to control the operation of an animation stand for special effects such as streaking. Analogue systems manipulate artwork on videotape by stretching, flipping, distorting, and colorizing the material. Digital systems, however, generate their own images and animate them, using either vector or raster graphics. The chief difference from the analogue system is that the digital image is based on mathematically derived information, while the analogue image is based on a televised image. Landmark films incorporating the digital technologies include *Tron* (1982) and *The Last Starfighter* (1984), where the computer-generated images simulated reality.

According to John Halas, the prolific animator and writer, the opportunity for a new "golden age" is even riper. The television commercial has provided the window for the exploitation of new ideas and technologies. Joined by a much larger flow of international contributors and nourished by television exposure, the future of film animation continues to remain bright.

REFERENCE WORKS

Readers interested in animation will discover that a number of useful references have been devised in the last fifteen years to make library research much easier. There is one aid devoted to the major classes of animation, Thomas W. Hoffer's *Animation: A Reference Guide* (1981), published by Greenwood Press. This is an encyclopedic survey and guide to the animation literature in cel, stop-action, drawing-on-film, experimental, and computer graphic modes and begins with an extensive historical overview. Citing the trustworthy and important reference aids, together with production literature in conventional animated forms and computerized devices, the book concludes with seven appendixes about major research centers, a chronology, sources for collectors, and annotated listings from the trade press. This is a critical guide to the published literature in animation, not a dictionary of animators, technologies, or films.

Two indexes are critically important to the scholar in animation desiring to keep up with new periodical materials published in the trades, critical magazines, and the popular press. Surveying the international setting is the *International Index to Film Periodicals* (an annual since 1972, compiled by the Federation Internationale des Archives du Film [FIAF]), which includes eighty of the most important film serials. *The Film Literature Index*, edited by Fred Silva and others, issued quarterly and in an annual supplement, encompasses over 300 film periodicals. With over 1,000 subject headings, the alphabetical subject-author index is among the most comprehensive finding aids for contemporary data. This index is far superior to the FIAF index because the *Film Literature Index* derives topic headings from the literature itself instead of using a prescribed protocol, which inevitably creates more classification problems as the literature evolves. For example, when one decides on a specific list of categories into which all sorts of materials are to be classified, there is little room for growth, either in the natural divisions of topics, or the addition of topics. On the other hand, if one constructs a category list from the normal and dynamic growth of film literature, as it occurs naturally, those categories are easily inserted into a flexible protocol, ever-changing as the film literature itself changes. In short, the *Film Literature Index* is not saddled with revising a protocol as the literature changes, and the topical index can take the form of very discrete categories and more generalized topics in the same index.

Additional indexes, facilitating historical work, include *The New Film Index* by Richard Dyer MacCann and Edward S. Perry; *Retrospective Index to Film Periodicals (1930–71)* by Linda Batty; *The Critical Index (1946–73),* edited by John C. Gerlach and Linda Gerlach; and *The Film Index: A Bibliography. Volume 1: The Film as Art,* edited by Harold Leonard. In 1987, Kraus International Publications announced the availability of volumes 2 and 3 of *The Film Index: A Bibliography,* bringing to the researcher over 20,000 annotated citations. Volume 2 (*The Film as Industry*) embraces advertising and publicity, associations, distribution, exhibition, finance, history, jurisprudence, labor relations, and production topics. Volume 3 (*The Film in Society*) contains the topics of censorship, culture, education, Hollywood, moral and religious aspects, social and political aspects, and special applications. All of the preceding titles, except for the older *Film Index: A Bibliography,* are compared by journal coverage, time coverage, and other aspects in an article by Abigail Nelson, "Guide to Indexes of Periodical Literature on Film."

Except for titles included in *Business Periodicals Index, Music Index,* and *Film Literature Index,* none of the motion picture trade journals is currently indexed systematically, and certainly not back to their various years of inception. *Variety* is selectively indexed in those mentioned above but with different criteria for selection of material. In the reference guide to the animation literature by Hoffer, cited above, Appendix 6 contains 409 annotated citations from the trade and popular press on animation subjects, extracted from a larger indexing project of *Variety, Moving Picture World,* and *Billboard* begun at Florida State University, College of Communication, in 1974. The appendix contains an index to the annotations.

Additional indexes of the general film literature that include works on animation are George Rehrauer's *Cinema Booklist* (with supplement), Frank Manchel's *Film Study: A Resource Guide,* Peter J. Bukalski's *Film Research: A Critical Bibliography with Annotations and Essay,* and Marietta Chicorel's *Chicorel Index to Film Literature.*

RESEARCH COLLECTIONS

Compared to general film collections, the number of archives containing even a fraction of animation material is very small. Some libraries and museums across the United States do contain animated films, and a smaller number collect and have available papers, memorabilia, and ephemera on this subject.

William C. Young's *American Theatrical Arts: Guide to Manuscripts and Special Collections in the United States and Canada* is a useful but slightly dated list of theater and film collections organized by name and subject. One does need to read carefully when utilizing this directory and perhaps follow up hunches with a letter. For example, the references to the State Historical Society of Wisconsin Mass Communication History Center do not note animation subjects, but the center does indeed have a collection of several hundred animated films open to scholars. These are found under the Warner Brothers and United Artists collections. The Brigitte T. Darnay et al. *Subject Directory of Special Libraries and Information Centers* is a multivolume collection of special libraries. Audiovisual and art and theater collections can be located in this set. Olga S. Weber's *North American Film and Video Directory* is a more comprehensive locator of film collections. Nineteen animation collections are separately listed in the index, and more can be located with a careful reading of descriptors. *Subject Collections* by Lee Ash has numerous leads to film collections, some of which contain materials on animation. Listings are more detailed than in the Weber work.

The Library of Congress, National Archives, and the American Film Institute collections certainly constitute the largest film resources in the United States at the same location, Washington, D.C. Library of Congress holdings include the paper print collection of early United States and some foreign films (1894–1912) and over 60,000 titles systematically gathered since 1942. In the Motion Picture Section of the Prints and Photographs Division, projection facilities are available to individual scholars upon appointment. Reading room facilities containing extensive files on directors, production companies, yearbooks, press books, and other reference aids are also open to serious researchers.

The American Film Institute deposits its holdings in the Library of Congress. At the institute's West Coast Center for Advanced Studies, the Charles K. Feldman Library archives contain some animation materials.

The National Archives hold United States government films in a collection exceeding forty million feet of film. Photographic and paper holdings are organized under more than 400 Record Groups representing several hundred past and present United States government agencies. Interested parties should write to the General Services Administration, National Archives and Records Service, Washington, D.C. 20408, for a list of Record Groups, in addition to raising specific research questions.

Outside of the District of Columbia, other major archives are located in New York City, including the Film Department of the Museum of Modern Art and Anthology Film Archives. Appendix 2 in Hoffer's *Animation: A Reference Guide* contains detailed information about these archives and other research centers.

HISTORY AND CRITICISM

The literature about animation has been growing since the first edition of this Handbook was published. John Canemaker's *Winsor McCay: His Life and Art,* the only biography of one of America's most influential animators and cartoon artists, is the book most appropriate to head the list of animation historical studies. Using individual rice paper cels, McCay fully animated a cartoon as early as 1911, in a Vitagraph project, "Little Nemo." Although McCay did not fully exploit the commercial potential between his commercially successful comic strip *Little Nemo* and the film medium, his film animations became a model for the fully animated film in later years. Indeed, McCay's process of animation included a form of "inbetweening," as it was later called, dubbed the "McCay Split System." Even in his first animated film, there is clear evidence that McCay drew movements of his characters, as in the example of a rotating character in the Nemo film, with lines of the figure overlapping to enhance the illusion of the character's rotation on screen. While this illusion appears as a rotation when projected, only a close, frame-by-frame inspection will reveal McCay's genius in overlapping the figure's lines in several frames, and at the same time seeming to foretell Norman McLaren's definition by some sixty-odd years! By 1913, McCay began a new animation to be called *Gertie the Dinosaur,* which incorporated the split system as well as a method of recycling the same action. These and other innovations were painstakingly researched by Canemaker, providing a full perspective of McCay's life and his work in art and the animated film. The handsome book contains a detailed text, notes, bibliography, supporting art examples, frame enlargements, and photographs obtained from McCay's surviving family and other sources. *The Sinking of the Lusitania,* released in July 1918, is McCay's animated reenactment of the 1915 calamity which helped precipitate American entry into the European war. Canemaker wrote:

The dark somber mood, the superb realistic draftsmanship, the timing of the actions, the excellent dramatic choices of "camera" angles and editing—all these qualities would reappear only with Disney's mature work in certain sequences of his feature-length cartoons and some of his World War II propaganda cartoon shorts.[6]

Thus, through such examples, has the case been made that Winsor McCay was the forerunner in American film animation.

Before Mickey: The Animated Film 1896–1928 by Donald Crafton is based on his doctoral dissertation at Yale University, "Emile Cohl and the Origins of the Animated Film." Both works are undoubtedly important scholarly landmarks in research on the silent animated film. The studies devote some attention to Emile Cohl, a French caricaturist who after 1908 established himself as a pioneer in film animation. Crafton based his study on the artist's surviving papers, Gaumont records, and European film archives.

Not surprisingly, Walt Disney is the subject of several books on animation. One of the earliest to attempt a serious review of his art and organization was Robert D. Feild's *The Art of Walt Disney*. However, two works, taken together, provide a much fuller, more detailed perspective. *Walt Disney: An American Original* by Bob Thomas provides an important historical review. Thomas based his biography on interviews with Disney and others, interoffice memoranda, verbatim minutes of studio meetings, and Disney correspondence. The second work, by Frank Thomas and Ollie Johnston, addressed a sizable task in *Disney Animation: The Illusion of Life*. Their original intention was simply to write a book on how to animate, but the volume flowered into a definitive record on how Disney character animation evolved. This primer is not designed to teach animation per se, but the reader can decidedly gain a strong understanding of the process Disney's personnel exploited in reaching the high standards embraced in character animation. Authors Thomas and Johnston point out that Disney did not build an organization in terms of command and control; rather, he stimulated a unified "group of talented people with particular abilities who could work together in continually changing patterns."[7] Perhaps this was his greatest contribution to the development of character animation: the creation of an organizational structure with the required divisions of labor, yet flexible at every stage, from beginning concept through production design, story, character development, and the complex animation production process, while evolving high standards of quality. Shamus Culhane expressed these Disney ideals this way:

I think of Walt Disney as the ideal philosopher-capitalist, a towering figure in this shoddy machine age. At a time when cars by the thousands have to be sent back to the factories because of faulty work; when companies knowingly endanger lives by concealing dangerous faults in airplane design . . . when planned obsolescence is a way of life, Disney's vision of excellence, demanding that his workers do their best possible work at all times, shines out like a beacon through this murk.[8]

Culhane found that this division of labor, and eventually the move toward quality, began when Disney appointed Burt Gillett and Wildred Jackson as full-time directors in 1929. They were released from the usual tasks performed by directors in other studios, such as writing stories, drawing layouts, designing characters, or animating key scenes.

Like the conductor of an orchestra, the director could now supervise writers, character designers, layout men, animators, and background painters, seeing to it that each member of the team was following a definite plan.[9]

Culhane has pointed out that Disney refined the entire structure of work allocation, establishing teams consisting of an animator, an assistant, an inbetweener, all working in the same room so that the animator could supervise the others.[10]

Disney made other changes in the "traditional" cel animation process. Animators at Disney now drew only rough drawings, leaving the details for the assistant and the inbetweener. Pencil tests, or films made of those rough drawings, were made and screened to check the animation before inking and painting. At the beginning of each project, the writers would meet with the entire animation department, and anyone could contribute to the discussion. Disney paid many $25 or more for each gag submitted. When the films were completed, a screening was held and questionnaires were distributed, asking for evaluations in order to encourage frank criticism. Disney made the rounds to each office during the day and, if confronted with a problem, he would participate in the solution, on the spot. For most, the site visit of the boss in every phase of a project might be enough incentive, but Disney also provided additional rewards for good work. A bonus system was started in which artists were paid a bonus on a sliding scale for the best animation, up to $12 a foot. This was the "Disney version," which has never been fully revealed or understood, especially by those who have never photographed or edited films.[11]

Bridging animation's history from Disney to other studios and media, Shamus Culhane has written a personal, incisive narrative of his experiences with the organizations and personalities of Max Fleischer, Ub Iwerks, Walt Disney, and Walter Lantz, taking the reader through his transition to Paramount's Famous Studio, the Culhane Studio, and television. Here is the view of an insider stripped of all the ambiguities found in polite language. Culhane provides a candid, sometimes abrasive, but honest assessment of studio organizations, styles, major personalities in animation, businessmen, and union leadership. In his book, *Talking Animals and Other People,* we learn the basic differences between the Disney operation and style and their competition in the 1930s and 1940s. Moreover, the differences between the silent era and the sound film, through the teaching of Don Graham at Disney, and Disney's move into character animation are starkly drawn. Consequently, the book is a strong complement to Thomas and Johnston's *Disney Animation: The Illusion of Life.* The Culhane work is also unique because his story and informed opinions are conditioned by successes and failures cut from the cloth of sixty years of the animation history he lived. When the subject of animation unions is undertaken, Culhane's commentary is about as subtle as a cleaver thrown on a butcher's block. There are plenty of laughs too, and some carefully articulated and constructive recommendations about the problems of animation in today's business environment.

Among the technique books, Susan Rubin's *Animation: The Art and the Industry* is a volume on technique in the business context written by a working specialist. While the work covers methods, techniques, and the industry, the reader will discover a fascinating section comprised of edited interviews with professionals discussing their experiences in making animated films, from producers through every important stage in animation including directors, illustrators, in-betweeners, inkers and checkers, cameramen, editors, and computer graphics personnel. The volume concludes with a glossary. An alternate selection would be John Halas and Roger Manvell's *The Technique of Film Animation*.

Leonard Maltin's *Of Mice and Magic: A History of American Animated Cartoons* remains the only history of American theatrical animation from the silent period up through the 1960s. He has organized the book by studio or producer organization, such as Disney, Fleischer, United Productions of America, and Warner Brothers, and gives a detailed account of personalities, procedures, and products of the minor studios, such as Paul Terry, A. J. Van Beuren, MGM, Famous Studios, and Columbia Screen Gems. The most disappointing aspect of Maltin's work is the lack of documentation except for casual and incomplete references to names of other interviewers or to published and unpublished data. There is no bibliography in the 1980 version. As history, Maltin does fill in the presumably factual story, but none of the chapters attempts to bring the producer organizations into any other context or assessment. The concluding chapter, "The Rest of the Story," does little to draw the entire work together for some assessment, interpretation, or concluding set of arguments. While some changes are identified in the conclusion, other factors contributing to high costs of production and competition for audiences are omitted, although these matters directly influenced the demise of the theatrical cartoon in the United States. The early 1970s is a good place to conclude the history, but not without some assessment of American animation and a fuller picture of the American animated film in related contexts, such as the film industry. Maltin is given to oversimplification or exaggeration in spots. From his description of Charles Mintz (p. 206), who "stole Disney's staff and starring character," one gets an incomplete and inaccurate picture. His statement that *Gertie the Dinosaur,* animated by Winsor McCay, launched an entire industry is an exaggeration that potentially misleads the reader. And whether sound sent "shock waves" through the film industry depends upon the point of view at the time. Leonard Maltin also compiled an exhaustive survey, *The Disney Films,* which includes credit lists and synopses of this major studio through the 1960s. The encyclopedic scope of the work enhances its value as a reference tool.

Leslie Cabarga's *The Fleischer Story* attempts to fill the void concerning

Dave and Max Fleischer, animators of Betty Boop and Popeye. While his scrapbook approach is appealing to the eye, with hundreds of model drawings, cartoons, magazine reprints, and film frames, the book lacks documentation and attribution to the large number of animators and studio personnel interviewed. Fortunately, the recent work by Shamus Culhane goes far to fill in the perspective for the Fleischer operation.

Tex Avery: King of Cartoons by Joe Adamson covers the life and work of the late animator responsible for some of the funniest and wildest Warner Brothers cartoons. Adamson brings a refreshing sense of accuracy to his work, coupled with views on the state of animation research and writing, including his favored fault in animation writing, the "sociological sidestep." He takes several authors to task, such as Lewis Jacobs, Richard Schickel, Ralph Stephenson, and Roger Manvell. The book concludes with a long interview with Avery and his longtime associate, Heck Allen. Another major work by Adamson is *The Walter Lantz Story, with Woody Woodpecker and Friends,* a chatty and fond reminiscence from the early days up through the exploitation of the woodpecker character on television. In 1972, Walter Lantz closed his studio for the last time, indicating that it did not stop producing cartoons because their popularity waned but because "we could not afford to make them."

Doing Their Bit: Wartime American Animated Short Films, 1939–1945 by Michael S. Shull and David E. Wilt is a systematic content analysis of war-related cartoons released by the major American studios, providing some insight into popular culture and the "establishment" handling of war themes. For example, the animated output of Warner Brothers in 1943 contained more blatantly racist references to the Japanese that of the other studios. MGM cartoons contained far fewer references to war-related topics compared to all other studios. Slightly less than one-half (46 percent) of commercial animated shorts released in the United States from 1939 to 1945 contained war-related themes, and this finding by the authors closely parallels the number of war-related live-action features. The authors screened most of the films and supplemented their information from copyright records and other published sources. The practice of "rotating credits" at some studios has complicated the problem of accurately determining roles in these historic remnants. Some studios would only identify one or two animators even though a given cartoon might have been the work product of several persons. Also, many animators used nicknames or other variants over the years, resulting in many inconsistencies in credits, but Shull and Wilt have provided a list of variant names to help solve that problem. Another work, *The Warner Brothers Cartoons* by Will Friedwald and Jerry Beck, consisting of extensive filmography of Warner Brothers cartoons from its beginnings to closure, complements the Shull and Wilt work. On a broader level, Jeff Lenburg's *The Encyclopedia of Animated Cartoon Series: 1909–1979* lists pertinent data of theatrical and television animated films released as part of a series, most typically under the banner of a character.

On the international front, a panorama of world animation, including a historical sketch, is the thrust of John Halas's recent book, patterned after the BBC-TV series of the same title, *Masters of Animation*. The book is divided into three major areas: the animation medium, international aspects (focusing on twelve national cinemas), and a brief review of the computer in the modern animation age. Halas concludes his overview with the generalization that the biggest transition in animation has been the innovation of machine-generated images, largely conditioned by television, at least in America, and shaped further by the demands for programs and advertising. Biographical sketches on dozens of world animators elevate the work into an important reference as well.

Animation history has been given short shrift in most film histories. Even a casual perusal of the animation literature reveals a distinct lack of historical study, although the current publication emphasis on individual studios, animators, and case studies of films is a valuable historical contribution. A great deal of this literature is bound to the aesthetic appreciation of the film or artist, for understandable reasons. There ought to be a little room for "romancing" the subject matter and perhaps some adulation of personalities, but the historical aspects of much of this literature are still anchored to the need to identify and validate facts and assertions. Memoranda are often discarded, office records and rosters are destroyed, personnel move on— typical problems when the historian attempts to reconstruct an event for whatever purpose. The American film industry has already earned a reputation for discarding everything not directly contributing to the return of investment on the original negatives, or box office. The story is not any different in the animation phase of filmmaking, except that the documentation trail is becoming more decentralized and the technology more complex. Complicating matters has been the demise in recent years of two publications, *Funnyworld* and *Animania,* which served to catalyze dormant interest in animation. These publications began as newsletters circulated to small numbers of highly motivated fans and later evolved into regular publications with editorial staffs and informed columnists. While some "fanzine" characteristics persisted, these journals brought forward new authors and, above all, new information and leads to new sources. They also served new agendas along with their detailed attention to history. There are still important assessments to be made about many phases of the animation media, many beyond the "golden age." The artistic factors are important. The economic and organizational conditions within which that art is produced need to be understood, as do the political, social, and psychological conditions as perceived by mass or specialized audiences.

NOTES

1. John Halas, *Masters of Animation* (Topsfield, Mass.: Salem House, 1987), p. 9.
2. Quoted in John Halas, ed., *Computer Animation* (New York: Hastings House, 1974), p. 97.

3. Shamus Culhane, *Talking Animals and Other People* (New York: St. Martin's Press, 1986), p. 2.

4. Ibid., pp. 226–27.

5. Ibid., p. 62.

6. John Canemaker, *Winsor McCay: His Life and Art* (New York: Abbeville Press, 1987), p. 156.

7. Frank Thomas and Ollie Johnston, *Disney Animation: The Illusion of Life* (New York: Abbeville Press, 1984), p. 45.

8. Culhane, p. 184.

9. Ibid., pp. 95–96.

10. Ibid., p. 96.

11. *The Disney Version* by Richard Schickel attempts to cut through the so-called Disney myths and present an objective overview of cartoon content and organization in American culture. Schickel surveyed much of the enormous periodical material on the Disney organization, and numerous references are included in the concluding bibliography.

BIBLIOGRAPHY

Books and Articles

Adamson, Joe. *Tex Avery: King of Cartoons*. New York: Popular Library, 1975.
———. *The Walter Lantz Story, with Woody Woodpecker and Friends*. New York: Putnam's, 1985.
Ash, Lee. *Subject Collections: A Guide to Special Book Collections and Subject Emphases as Reported by University, College, Public, and Special Libraries and Museums in the United States and Canada*. 6th ed. New York: R. R. Bowker, 1985.
Batty, Linda. *Retrospective Index to Film Periodicals (1930–71)*. New York: R. R. Bowker, 1975.
Beaver, Frank E. *Dictionary of Film Terms*. New York: McGraw-Hill, 1983.
Bukalski, Peter J. *Film Research: A Critical Bibliography with Annotations and Essay*. Boston: G. K. Hall, 1972.
Business Periodicals Index. New York: Wilson, 1958.
Cabarga, Leslie. *The Fleischer Story*. Franklin Square, N.Y.: Nostalgia Press, 1976.
Canemaker, John. *Winsor McCay: His Life and Art*. New York: Abbeville Press, 1987.
Chicorel, Marietta. *Chicorel Index to Film Literature*. New York: Chicorel Library Publishing Corp., 1975.
Crafton, Donald. *Before Mickey: The Animated Film 1896–1928*. Cambridge, Mass.: MIT Press, 1982.
———. *Emile Cohl and the Origins of the Animated Film*. Ph.D. dissertation, Yale University, 1977.
Culhane, Shamus. *Talking Animals and Other People*. New York: St. Martin's Press, 1986.
Darnay, Brigitte T., et al., eds. *Subject Directory of Special Libraries and Information Centers*. 11th ed. Detroit: Gale Research, 1988.

Federation Internationale des Archives du Film. *International Index to Film Periodicals.* New York: R. R. Bowker, 1972-.

Feild, Robert D. *The Art of Walt Disney.* New York: Macmillan, 1944.

Friedwald, Will, and Jerry Beck. *The Warner Brothers Cartoons.* Metuchen, N.J.: Scarecrow Press, 1981.

Gerlach, John C., and Linda Gerlach. *The Critical Index (1946–73).* New York: Teachers College Press, 1974.

Halas, John. *Masters of Animation.* Topsfield, Mass.: Salem House, 1987.

————., ed. *Computer Animation.* New York: Hastings House, 1974.

————, and Roger Manvell. *The Technique of Film Animation.* London: Focal Press, 1968.

Hoffer, Thomas W. *Animation: A Reference Guide.* Westport, Conn.: Greenwood Press, 1981.

Lenburg, Jeff. *The Encyclopedia of Animated Cartoon Series: 1909–1979.* New York: Arlington House, 1981.

Leonard, Harold, ed. *The Film Index: A Bibliography.* 3 vols. New York: Kraus, 1987.

MacCann, Richard Dyer, and Edward S. Perry. *The New Film Index.* New York: E. P. Dutton, 1975.

Maltin, Leonard. *The Disney Films.* New York: Harry N. Abrams, 1973.

————. *Of Mice and Magic: A History of American Animated Cartoons.* New York: McGraw-Hill, 1980.

Manchel, Frank. *Film Study: A Resource Guide.* Rutherford, N.J.: Fairleigh Dickinson University Press, 1973.

Mehr, Linda Harris. *Motion Pictures, Television and Radio: A Union Catalogue of Manuscript and Special Collections in the Western United States.* Boston: G. K. Hall, 1977.

————. *Music Index.* Detroit: Information Service, 1949-.

Nelson, Abigail. "Guide to Indexes of Periodical Literature on Film." *University Film Study Newsletter,* 6 (October 1975), 3.

Rehrauer, George. *Cinema Booklist.* Metuchen, N.J.: Scarecrow Press, 1972. (With supplement, 1974.)

Rubin, Susan. *Animation: The Art and the Industry.* Englewood Cliffs, N.J.: Prentice-Hall, 1984.

Sadoul, Georges. *Dictionary of Filmmakers.* Translated by Peter Morris. Berkeley: University of California Press, 1972.

————. *Dictionary of Films.* Translated by Peter Morris. Berkeley: University of California Press, 1972.

Schickel, Richard. *The Disney Version.* New York: Simon and Schuster, 1968.

Shull, Michael, and David E. Wilt. *Doing Their Bit: Wartime American Animated Short Films, 1939–1945.* Jefferson, N.C.: McFarland and Co., 1987.

Silva, Fred, et al. *Film Literature Index.* Albany, N.Y.: Filmdex, 1974.

Theater Arts Library, University of California (Los Angeles). *Motion Pictures: A Catalogue of Books, Periodicals, Screenplays and Production Stills.* Boston: G. K. Hall, 1976.

Thomas, Bob. *The Art of Animation.* New York: Simon and Schuster, 1958.

————. *Walt Disney: An American Original.* New York: Simon and Schuster, 1976.

Thomas, Frank, and Ollie Johnston. *Disney Animation: The Illusion of Life*. New York: Abbeville Press, 1984.
Weber, Olga S. *North American Film and Video Directory*. New York: R. R. Bowker, 1975.
Wheaton, Christopher D., and Richard B. Jewell. *Primary Cinema Resources: An Index to Screenplays, Interviews and Special Collections at the University of Southern California*. Boston: G. K. Hall, 1975.
Young, William C. *American Theatrical Arts: Guide to Manuscripts and Special Collections in the United States and Canada*. Chicago: American Library Association, 1971.

Periodicals

American Cinematographer. Los Angeles, 1919–.
American Film: Journal of the Film and Television Arts. Washington, D.C., 1975–.
Billboard. Cincinnati, 1894–.
Cartoonist Profiles. Fairfield, Conn., 1969–.
Cinefantastique. Oak Park, Ill., 1970–.
Film Comment. New York, 1962–.
Filmmakers' Newsletter. New York, 1967–.
Films and Filming. London, 1954–.
Films in Review. New York, 1950–.
Journal of Popular Film. Bowling Green, Ohio, 1972–.
Journal of the University Film and Video Association. Philadelphia, 1949–.
Millimeter. New York, 1973–.
Moving Picture World. New York, 1907–1927.
Photon. Brooklyn, N.Y., 1963–.
Print. Aspley Guise, Eng., 1964–.
University Film Study Newsletter. Cambridge, Mass. 1972–.
Variety. New York, 1905–.

Architecture

RICHARD GUY WILSON

Architecture is the most conspicuous "art" that makes up our world. You can turn off Madonna, refuse to watch *Dallas,* ignore the *60 Minute Wonder Diet,* be revolted by Big Macs, and reject the message of Mr. Clean, and yet unless you become a hermit and retire to the mythical cave, the manmade environment intrudes. Buildings, whether they serve work, play, or sleep, reveal personal and cultural values; they are records, and, properly understood, they are our permanent diaries. William Morris, the English designer, poet, and revolutionary, observed in 1881: "Architecture embraces the consideration of the whole external surroundings of the life of man; we cannot escape from it if we would so long as we are part of civilization, for it means a moulding and altering to human needs of the very face of the earth itself, except in the outermost desert."[1] Morris saw architecture as virtually everything, not simply the top 5 percent of high design. Today that includes both the homes of the wealthy and ranch houses, courthouses and fast-food outlets, sculpture in public places and the real sculpture of our world, plastic flamingos in the front yard and superhighway interchanges, and designer furniture to Ethan Allen "Olde Colonial."

In recent years—since the mid–1970s—architecture has risen considerably in popularity. As an academic "growth industry" it has reached the status of "edutainment," or a field in which avocational interest is merged with scholarly vocation. There have been on public television two programs devoted to American architecture, and we are promised more. Architectural "superstars" such as Philip Johnson, Robert Stern, and I. M. Pei grace the covers of magazines, and a sure sign of approval can be found in the countless articles that have appeared in airliner magazines. Museums have discovered architecture, and while collecting entire buildings is generally hard—Old Sturbridge Village or the Ford Greenfield Village are the examples—a museum or gallery can show architectural drawings, photographs, fragments of buildings, and furniture. Tours are popular, from a day with the garden club to a coach tour of the remains of old U.S.1. Where twenty-five years ago only one newspaper, the great, venerable *New York Times,* had a critic of architecture, now there are many. And architectural book publishing has flourished; books of all types, from studies of fast-food architecture to the most recondite subjects, have appeared. Ten years ago this chapter had little to report on; since then a number of books have appeared, and articles on diners, drive-in theaters, and roadside stands appear with frequency in places as diverse as the *Smithsonian* and the local op-ed page.

Popular architecture (or, alternatively, modern vernacular) constitutes at least 95 percent of our built surroundings. There is a need to understand this environment in all its aspects, not simply the current "in" subjects of fast-food palaces and the strip, but also urban sprawl, shopping centers, ranch-style homes, and the symbolic meanings people ascribe to or invest in their construction. Since the late eighteenth century and the development of a modern consciousness, most historians have felt that buildings are concrete expressions of a culture and world view. While this is perhaps more easily acceptable in terms of such public or semi-public monuments as the East Wing of the National Gallery of Art in Washington, D.C., or St. Peter's Cathedral, to take two extremes, there recently have been other views. Richard Oliver and Nancy Ferguson, in writing about fast-food restaurants, diners, gas stations, and historical villages, claim that "by their very familiarity, they can and do act as mirrors of our culture."[2] The profound shifts created by the industrial revolution have affected the built environment in many ways, most of which have been ignored. A radical discrepancy exists between the tastes, needs, and preferences of professionals—historians, critics, architects, urban designers, and planners, and the decision makers whose policies they inform—and the people whose lives they influence.

Popular architecture, as does all architecture, generally fulfills two functions: first, it allows some type of activity, and second, it communicates. The methods of communication through different signs and symbol systems are at the core of the study of popular architecture. The physical elements of coach lanterns and shutters on a house, the twisting nudes in front of Caesar's Palace in Las Vegas, and the blinking "Over a Billion Sold" convey messages of social status, association with the past, and information. To understand popular architecture it must be looked at as not simply an art of building, but as a tangible expression of a way of life.

HISTORIC OUTLINE

In the West before the late eighteenth century nearly all architecture was of two basic types: either folk (or vernacular or traditional) or academic high art. By folk architecture is meant buildings of a preindustrial society, whether houses, shops, or barns that are based on one or a very few types that admit only a few individual variations. In the vernacular traditions, the specialized architect or a designer did not exist; the building type was carried in the collective consciousness of the culture. Construction took place either by the final consumer or by a tradesman not far removed from the consumer, and the materials used were local. Academic high art architecture refers to specialized buildings, each one an original or unique creation (self-consciously in a "style"); the designer is a professional or an amateur who specializes in or has aspirations to the creation of significant monuments.

Popular architecture emerged with the industrial revolution. With popular architecture production is changed; building materials and even entire buildings are produced on a mass scale by a team or teams of specialists who are generally far removed from the ultimate consumer. Instead of one prevailing building type, there are many, with innumerable variations within each. The forms, plans, and images of the building are products of fashion and are acquired through popular magazines, trade journals, books, governmental agencies, travel, and the media. The images refer to history, high art, technology, status, patriotism, and individual fantasies. Semiotically, popular architecture is fashion- or style-consciousness, and the symbols are generally chosen for their immediate impact.

Who designs popular architecture? The answer is many people. Buildings by academically trained architects are not necessarily examples of high art, and in fact architects have been responsible for the mass-produced Mobil service station, ranch-style houses, and Miami Beach hotels. There is hardly a building activity of the modern age that architects have not participated in; they serve on the design staffs of Holiday Inns, Disney World, the Rouse Corporation, and Winnebago. But there are others, such as industrial designers, who have also designed mass-produced commercial buildings. The profession of the industrial designer did not emerge until the 1930s, but he quickly became the hero of the new technological mass production age. Walter Dorwin Teague, one of the first, designed the enamel-paneled, machine-like Texaco service station, reproduced in over 20,000 units. Another source for the designs of popular architecture is the builder or contractor. The increasingly technological nature of building precludes much design by actual workers, an old and honored tradition; today instead buildings are increasingly prefabricated or come from kits. Finally, the consumer, who decides to add a clip-on mansard to his storefront, or put a French Provincial door on her ranch house and a plastic deer in the front yard, is also a designer.

Between popular architecture and high art architecture the relationship has never been stable, and in spite of the elitist "trickle-down" theory that high art always informs low art, or that popular architecture "rips off" high art architecture, the reverse is often true. Taste that used to be a sign of class and wealth is no longer an operable guide. Who or what actually informs the taste and the processes by which it trickles down, or up, or sideways must always be considered in any study of popular architecture. But it is evident that plans, forms, and images constantly shift from one level to another. Recently there has been a great spurt of interest by academic high art architects in the archetypal image of the 1930s and 1940s, the sleek, shiny, streamlined diner. Now, as they are passing out of existence to be replaced by colonial and Mediterranean style diners, they are discovered and appropriated. A number of "postmodern" architects have actually designed "new diners." Or one can look at materials such as shingles which have moved over the years from a vernacular exterior covering into the range of high art, back into the hands of the builder and Levittown, and once again back to becoming a chic material.

The emergence of postmodernism since the mid–1970s (though its roots can be traced back to the mid–1960s; see R. G. Wilson, "Abstraction Versus Figuration") has blurred some of the distinctions between high art architecture and popular architecture. With the advent of architectural modernism in the 1920s many architects consciously eschewed historical images and embraced abstract art as a source. Such abstract modernism was never the exclusive property of high art architecture; indeed, many contemporary strip and shopping malls owe a great deal to this source. Within high art architecture a shift began in the 1960s when the pop art movement of Andy Warhol, Roy Lichtenstein, and others, along with Susan Sontag's concept of "camp," was picked up by Charles Moore and Robert Venturi. Architecturally, this meant an interest in, and an appropriation of, the imagery and symbolism of popular architecture for the purposes of high art. Consequently, much of the current interest in popular architecture is seen through a postmodernist sensibility of irony, wit, and condescension. This has been coupled with a nostalgia craze for the most arcane bits of the popular past, i.e., Big Little Books, diner food, and 1950s tail fins. Yet, as at least one critic (Tom Wolfe in *From Bauhaus to Our House*) has claimed, the postmodernist architectural sensibility retains an elitist code accessible only to the initiated.

The styles and motifs of popular architecture are communicated by one of two methods: experimentally through observation and travel, or secondhand through books, magazines, and trade journals. The first, of course, is nebulous and depends on study of specific individuals; the second has left a more tangible record.

Media influence can be followed by looking briefly at the development of the American house. The ideal of the single family house available to all classes of citizens is one of the unique aspects of American architecture. During the nineteenth century in the United States books began to appear intended for mass circulation that spread knowledge of stylistic details. The earliest were builder's guides such as Asher Benjamin's *The American Builder's Companion* and Minard Lafever's *The Modern Builder's Guide*. The contents were plates illustrating details of ornament and construction, with possibly a few elevations and plans of complete buildings. They helped spread the fashion for first Federal, then Greek Revival, and finally Gothic Revival styles to builders, carpenters, and, of course, consumers. Their continuation in print, in some cases nearly thirty years after first publication, accounts for the *retardare* appearance of some buildings in more provincial areas. About mid-century a new type of publication appears, the house pattern book, which is filled with plans and designs of complete buildings. The most popular of these were Andrew Jackson Downing's *Cottage Residences* and *The Architecture of Country Houses*. In these books, along with large, pretentious homes, there were "Working Men's Cottages," "Laborer's Cottages," and small houses, along with details that would allow anybody with either skills or some funds to update their homes. This type of publication continued throughout the nineteenth century in a virtual flood of titles and editions, such as George Woodward's *Woodward's National Architect,* E. C. Gardner's *Homes and How to Make Them,* and the Palliser Company's *New Cottage Homes and Details.* These books served as dream manuals for the masses. House details could be adapted from them by a local builder or architect, and in many cases complete sets of plans could be purchased at a nominal cost, such as those of the Palliser Company. The men responsible for these books were a varied lot; a few had some architectural background, but many were simply glorified carpenters who adopted aspects of high art styles for mass consumption.

Another method of communication was through magazines. *Godey's Lady's Book* published, between 1846 and 1892, 450 house designs. In the 1860s several magazines such as the *American Builder* and the *Architectural Review and American Builder's Journal* came into being that were directed specifically at the builder and carpenter. The first professional architectural magazine in the United States, the *American Architect and Building News,* was not founded until 1876. While magazines for professional architects always carry house designs, far more important were periodicals such as Gustav Stickley's *Craftsman* (1901–16) and Henry L. Wilson's *Bungalow Magazine* (1909–18), which actively promoted the low-slung middle-class house. Both Stickley and Wilson collected their designs in book format.

With small modifications these same media patterns have persisted into the 1970s. Certainly one of the greatest influences on home design has been the mass circulation homemaker magazine. A study of these magazines, which advocate different approaches to architectural style, interior furnishings, and gardens, is essential to any understanding of the popular culture of the home. Some at times advocated strong points of view. *The House Beautiful* in its early years supported the Art and Crafts movement and bungalow design. More famous was the *Ladies Home Journal*, which at the turn of the century sponsored home design by architects such as Frank Lloyd Wright. It is through Wright's designs in the *Journal* that many builders and home owners learned to imitate his work. Other *Journal* architects were more conservative and advocated styles ranging from colonial to Mediterranean. Other magazines such as *American Home* have been almost single-minded in their sponsoring of "Early American" as the fit style for Americans. Today two strong directions can be seen in homemaker magazines such as *Better Homes and Gardens:* the first is a natural trend, the second a rich eclecticism.

Tangential to the homemaker magazines are how-to-do-it magazines such as *Early American Life*, which is filled with nostalgia for the good old days. The advertisement states: "Your Dream Home—there's at least one house in every issue of *Early American Life*, complete with floor plans." These can be in any number of styles, but most frequently in the Stockcode and Cape Cod. *Popular Mechanics*, the best known of the how-to-do-it magazines, has always exercised a strong influence on taste in home and furniture design.

Specialized trade journals are probably the major new contribution of the twentieth century. Professional architectural magazines such as *Progressive Architecture* and *Architectural Record* have minimally affected popular taste, but they are important for tracing ideas. Far more important are magazines such as *House and Home: The Magazine of Housing, Qualified Remodeler,* and *Professional Builder and Apartment Business,* which are directed at the construction industry. They deal with such topics as "Bathroom Design: The Opulent Look" and "How to Facelift Old Buildings Without Losing Their Charm."

Books or specialized issues of magazines devoted to home design have had a long history in the twentieth century. Most have been on the order of the house pattern books and present images and ideas that can be adapted or copied at will. Collections of designs by architects such as *The Architectural Record's Book of Vacation Houses* or *A Treasury of Contemporary Houses* are important since a vast range of styles, from radical to conservative, is shown. *The Building Guide* of *House and Garden* magazine for 1963–64 offered forty houses and plans ranging from the "contemporary" to the "traditional" and included designs such as "A Combination of Ranch and Colonial" and "The Plantation House in Miniature." Some, such as *The Book of Houses* by John F. Dean and Simon Breines, convey conventional wisdom, advising under a chapter entitled "What Price Style?" that "style, of course, is a subjective factor and if a family is emotionally drawn toward a 'Cape Cod' or a 'Georgian,' serious consideration should be given to a home of that type."

Also a creature of the media were the catalogues issued by house manufacturers. These catalogues paraded a variety of house sizes and styles in varying price ranges that the public could purchase in the form of kits. Perhaps the most important were published by companies such as the Aladdin Concrete Home Company of Bay City, Michigan, and Sears, Roebuck and Company of Chicago. The Sears designs accounted for nearly 100,000 homes in the years 1908–40. Their designs have been collected in K. C. Stevenson and H. W. Jande, *Houses by Mail: A Guide to Houses from Sears, Roebuck and Company.*

Images of other building types are communicated in much the same manner. There are specialized trade journals of industries such as service stations and restaurants. The impact of fast food can be felt in many magazines such as *Restaurant Business* and *Nation's Restaurant News.* Many feature articles on designs and images of the fast-food industry. Books on office design and shopping centers abound, though they are, of course, directed at the professional in the field rather than at the public. But books such as *Architectural Record's Motels. Hotels and Restaurants* have influenced buildings around the world.

While popular architecture began to emerge in the eighteenth century with the industrial revolution, it and the associated components in the manmade environment have not been the subject of serious study until very recently. Among architects and historians the reasons are fairly obvious: popular architecture was not serious and lacked the imprint of *Kultur.* The study of architecture, whether historical or contemporary, has usually been confined to monuments: churches, temples, memorials, theaters, forums, palaces, homes of the elite, and buildings designed by architects that aspire to greatness. As a result of Germanic pedantic scholarship and English dilettantism, architecture is usually studied chronologically and concentration is on a critical and evaluative analysis of the styles, forms, plans, ornament, and details. While sometimes the culture and the purpose of a building are noted, in general the building is seen as existing independently in space and time. The preoccupation from the 1930s onward in both the United States and Europe with "modern architecture" led to a further separation from the field of popular architecture. Concerned with totally abstract designing in modern materials and techniques, and completely removed from the area of historical recall, nostalgia, or recognizable motifs, modern architecture developed its own language. While the historians of modern architecture have paid some attention to issues of prefabrication and industrial warehouses and factories, still it has been largely a history of designs by major architects. In these studies, as in the more traditional historical studies, the appearance of a Howard Johnson's, a Cozy Cape Cod Cottage from Mount Vernon Estates, or an entryway to Forest Lawn Cemetery in Southern California would be only in the most negative of terms.

Variations from the study of certifiable monuments can be seen in the interest in early American and vernacular architecture. Early American architecture is basically pre-industrial vernacular, and the study of both this and nineteenth-century vernacular has grown spectacularly in recent years. The Vernacular Forum, an association of scholars, publishes an annual, *Perspectives in Vernacular Architecture,* edited by Camile Wells. An introductory book is Dell Upton, editor, *America's Architectural Roots: Ethnic Groups that Built America,* which is a sort of style manual for vernacular buildings. The most provocative author in the area of vernacular architecture, Henry Glassie, has come from a folklore background; his major works are *Pattern in the Material Folk Culture of the Eastern United States* and *Folk Housing in Middle Virginia.* In the latter book Glassie applies the structuralism of Claude Lévi-Strauss and Noam Chomsky to vernacular houses, and while the results are dense and open to question, he offers some suggestions for the study of popular architecture.

Along with the other revolutions of the 1960s, a sense of crisis in the architectural and design world led in the 1970s and 1980s to a greater recognition of popular architecture and the necessity of understanding the entire man-made environment. One significant change was the sense of failure of modern architecture; the brave new world envisioned in the 1930s, where "Total Design" could improve man's life, was a hoax. Most consumers disliked, if not downright hated, modern buildings, not only for their sterile quality and uncomfortable feeling, but also because they simply did not work well. Urban renewal, a product of modern architectural city planning, proved to be worse than the illness it was supposed to correct. Jane Jacobs's book, *The Death and Life of Great American Cities,* was viewed as heretical for her celebration of the messy vitality of the street when published in 1961. Today it is the received orthodoxy. While there are still many architects and critics who profess an admiration for modern architecture, the continuous bombardment of questions and alarming failures has opened the doors for some recognition of popular architecture.

The Museum of Modern Art in New York, the citadel of avant-garde modern chic, provided several new directions in the mid–1960s. In 1964 the exhibit "Architecture Without Architects" by Bernard Rudofsky (and book of same name) presented the thesis that centuries-old buildings executed by common men without the aid of designers could present eternal themes of architecture. Shown were not only homes and temples of primitive peoples but also granaries and fertilizer bins. Rudofsky has gone on to exploit this unself-conscious theme in *The Prodigous Builders.* In 1966 the Museum of Modern Art published Robert Venturi's *Complexity and Contradiction in Architecture,* the first openly critical look at the theories of modern architecture.

The leaders of postmodernism, Venturi and Moore, have helped to spur the study of popular architecture. Venturi's *Complexity and Contradiction* was concerned more with a rather obtuse design philosophy, and except for the notorious phrase, "Main Street is almost alright," was not really concerned with popular architecture. The book Venturi produced with Denise Scott Brown and Steven Izenour, *Learning from Las Vegas,* was concerned with popular architecture and argued that architects should look at the strip, for in spirit if not style it approached the grandeur of the Roman Forum, or "Las Vegas is to the strip what Rome is to the piazza." Charles Moore's writings have been felicitous, with significant comments on suburban and motel culture. Another harbinger of the change has been the example of Peter Blake. In 1964 he published *God's Own Junkyard,* a great diatribe against popular architecture. But within ten years he was writing admiring articles on the virtues of Disney World and the strip. *Progressive Architecture* magazine, the high priest of modern architecture, devoted its June 1978 issue to "Taste in America"; it contained articles on McDonald's design evolution and suburbia.

The other critical shift that began in the 1960s and still continues is the burgeoning historic preservation movement. Historic preservation as a movement can be traced back to the mid-nineteenth century in the United States and abroad. Up until the 1960s it was generally viewed as elitist and concerned with historic houses and recreations of olden time in Williamsburg and other museum villages. But in the 1960s historic preservation became more populist in outlook, less concerned with the individual high art buildings and more with entire neighborhoods. Nods of approval have been given to lesser classes of structures; service stations, billboards, and diners now appear on the National Register of Historic Places. The Rhode Island Historical Preservation Commission has registered seventeen Quonset huts located at the U.S. Navy air station at Quonset, Rhode Island. The championing by preservationists of the large hillside sign for Hollywood and a current battle to resurrect a giant Coca-Cola neon sign in Boston are indications of a changing climate toward popular architecture. Preservation studies have been carried out on working-class neighborhoods such as the Old West Side in Ann Arbor, Michigan, a blue-collar German enclave.

Others in the last few years, such as architectural and art historians, sociologists, planners, and anthropologists, have produced a variety of papers, articles, and books that have contributed to knowledge in the area. However, while some research is under way on such diverse topics as gas stations, fast-food restaurants, and amusement parks, the field is still virtually wide open. Basic research needs to be done in every area, and methodological approaches need to be discussed. Societies dealing with different aspects of popular architecture have been founded, including the Society for Commercial Archaeology and the Society for Industrial Archaeology.

REFERENCE WORKS

There are no major reference works devoted specifically to popular architecture, and here, as elsewhere, one has to make piecemeal use of other sources. Among dictionaries, the *Dictionary of Architecture and Construction,* edited by Cyril M. Harris, it is undoubtedly the best and most complete. Well illustrated with abundant references, it is directed at the professional.

To be able to understand properly the allusions and references popular architecture makes, identification of the style or styles of a building has a place. For the United States two books are available, Marcus Whiffen's *American Architecture Since 1780,* and *What Style Is It?* by John Poppeliers et al. While recognition of a building's style is important, the problem with both of these books is the implication that style and how accurately a building falls within stylistic perimeters are the important questions. Obviously buildings have other elements.

Biographical information on American architects can be found in Withey's *Biographical Dictionary of American Architects (Deceased).* All levels of architects are included, but it is by no means complete. Also of use is Columbia University's *Avery Obituary Index of Architects and Artists,* which includes even more obscure figures. Finally there is the *Macmillan Encyclopedia of Architects,* edited by Adolf Plazeck; however, it is exclusively concerned with high art architects.

For access to periodicals the major work is the *Avery Index to Architectural Periodicals,* produced by the staff at the Avery Architectural Library at Columbia University. This is a retrospective index of most English-language architectural periodicals and selected foreign and other periodicals. It is updated with supplements every few years and is now available on computer. While primarily concerned with architectural periodicals, the *Avery Index* contains a vast gold mine of information that is conveniently indexed not only under authors, architects, and locations, but also under subject headings such as "moving picture theaters" and "restaurants." Unfortunately, there is no heading for "diners" or "fast food."

There is no comprehensive bibliography of American architectural books. Though limited in scope, Henry-Russell Hitchcock's *American Architectural Books: A List of Books, Portfolios, and Pamphlets on Architecture and Related Subjects Published in America Before 1895* is the best for the period. It does contain a comprehensive listing of builder's guides and pattern books, which are a major source for studying the dissemination of popular architectural idioms. Keith Morgan and Richard Cheek are preparing an update to extend that work to 1940.

RESEARCH COLLECTIONS

Architecture by its very nature is generally a static entity, and while one can point to mobile homes and the ephemeral creations of the strip, most architecture is hardly collectable. Most research on architecture can be divided into two aspects: actual field work and collection of data, and library or archival work where drawings, plans, photographs, magazines, and books devoted to buildings as well as materials devoted to their creators can be pursued. While the collecting of architectural records and drawings (both presentation and working drawings) has grown in recent years, there is no collection specifically devoted to popular architecture. Many university libraries are avidly pursuing collections for their local area, but storage and study space for the bulky materials is always a problem. The Committee for the Preservation of Architectural Records, located at the Prints and Photographs Division, Library of Congress, Washington, D.C. 20540, acts as a clearinghouse for information and publishes a free newsletter that contains information and research queries. A new form of research guide containing lists of local depositories has been produced by committees in Philadelphia, New York, Chicago, and other cities.

Most collections of architectural records tend to emphasize the unique architect, and the depositing of materials relating to popular creations is not common. The major collections are in the Avery Architectural Library at Columbia, the Smithsonian Institution's Museum of History and Technology in Washington, the Cooper-Hewitt Museum in New York, the Library of Environmental Design at the University of California, Berkeley, the Architectural Drawings Collection at the University of California, Santa Barbara, the Kahn Archives at the University of Pennsylvania, and the Northwest Architectural Archive at the University of Minneapolis. These collections may have materials that are related to popular architecture. Guides exist for some collections.

Much documentation on popular architecture remains in the hands of the original owners or patrons. Large corporations such as Mobil Oil, Sunoco, Austin, McDonald's, and White Tower have opened their files to qualified researches. No published work has been done on popular housing, but the Levit Corporation, Jim Walter Corporation, and local builders should be contacted.

For extensive collections of books and periodicals that relate to popular architecture, the Avery Architectural Library at Columbia is easily the best in the United States, if not the world. Other extensive collections are the architectural or design libraries at the University of California, Berkeley, the University of Michigan, and the University of Virginia.

Photographs are, of course, one of the primary records of architecture and the sometimes transient creations of popular architecture. Local collections in libraries, newspapers, and museums should always be consulted. Undoubtedly the major national collection is at the Library of Congress, Prints and Photographs Division. Photographs of all types, from amateur to professional, including the Farm Security Administration's records of the 1930s, are deposited there. A wealth of material on the popular landscape waits to be used.

Also housed in the photographic division at the Library of Congress are the deposited records of the Historic American Buildings Survey (HABS).

A division of the National Park Service, HABS was founded during the Depression as an attempt to record through field research, photographs, and scale drawings many of the fast-disappearing creations of the built environment. After a period of hiatus HABS was refounded in 1957 and continues today to send field teams throughout the United States and territories to record architecture. While much of the focus of HABS has been on high art architecture, attention in recent years has been paid to movie theaters, service stations, and middle-class housing. As projects are completed, the records, along with drawings, photographs, and negatives, are deposited in the Library of Congress. Unfortunately, no complete index exists to HABS; the first catalogue published in 1941, is long out of date. In recent years catalogs for individual states, cities, and special subjects, such as Robert Vogel's compilation, *The New England Textile Mill Survey,* have been issued. In 1969 the Historic American Engineering Record (HAER) was established; it performs essentially the same function as HABS but is more concerned with bridges, locks, railroad stations, piers, and factories. HAER also publishes catalogues.

Finally, one might note the National Register of Historic Places, also in the National Park Service, and the various state preservation agencies that, while not officially research collections, frequently contain significant amounts of information and materials on both common and extravagant structures. The 1966 Historic Preservation Act mandated that every state have a historic preservation office and the methods of accomplishing a statewide survey of notable structures.

HISTORY AND CRITICISM

Because so little research has been done on popular architecture, there are no books devoted specifically to the topic as a whole. To gain a perspective on popular architecture one has to refer to a wide range of books and articles.

Writings on the theory and methodology of the study of popular architecture are few and far between. Smatterings of ideas can be found in essays by J. Meredith Neil, Marshall Fishwick, and Dennis Alan Mann, and one can turn back to the standards on popular culture such as works by Herbert J. Gans. Probably, though, the most important search for a methodology has been done by Alan Gowans, first in his *The Unchanging Arts,* which, while devoted largely to the other arts, does have some comments on architecture, and then in his rather ponderously titled *On Parallels in Universal History Discoverable in Arts and Artifacts.* This last, subtitled "An Outline Statement," is a theory that what is art has changed over time, that the arts must be interpreted in their historic terms, and that "taste is determined by ideology." The implications for popular architecture are manifest, and while much needs to be fleshed out, it is an important beginning. George

Kubler's *The Shape of Time* has a somewhat different emphasis and argues that all man-made things can be viewed as art existing in a linked succession. As indicated above, the works by Henry Glassie offer several possibilities, and one should also look at Amos Rapoport's *House: Form and Culture,* which, while devoted to the building of primitive peoples, offers many suggestions.

Theoretical fads such as structuralism or semiotics come and go in architecture. Ten years ago semiotics, or the application of linguistic theory of signs, developed by Ferdinand de Saussure and C. S. Pierre, was the hot topic. Most of the writing was jargon-ridden and obscure, but it demonstrated that all buildings and their furnishings carry meanings, intended or not. The most understandable introduction is Geoffrey Broadbent's article, "A Plain Man's Guide to the Theory of Signs in Architecture." One should also look at Charles Jencks and George Baird's collection of essays, *Meaning in Architecture,* and a three-part essay by Jencks in *Architecture and Urbanism.* Structuralism has found surprisingly few adherents. Glassie's book on Virginia houses cited earlier is perhaps the most important example. The field of deconstructionism and hermeneutics has its current advocates; however, no attention has been focused on popular architecture.

Another area for the student to be aware of is the actual impact of the intangibles of space and form on humans. This is also is an undeveloped field, surprisingly little research having been done on perception and cultural usages of space. Beginnings have been made by anthropologists such as Edward T. Hall in *The Hidden Dimension* and by psychologists such as Robert Sommer in *Personal Space* and *Design Awareness.* Kent Bloomer and Charles Moore's *Body, Memory and Architecture,* which is written from an architect's point of view, while slim, offers some important insights. There are numerous other technical articles and research reports the student can pursue if needed.

The book that comes the closest to a general history of American architecture and pays some attention to popular culture is Alan Gowans's *Images of American Living: Four Centuries of Architecture and Furniture as Cultural Expression.* While Gowans's concentration is on high art architecture, he does attempt to note some of the popular permeations. Published in 1964, the book needs to be updated. James Marston Fitch's *American Building: The Historical Forces that Shaped It,* while a general history, focuses more on physical and technological factors. He is very good for the period prior to the twentieth century. Again the focus is almost completely on high art. John Kouwenhoven's *The Arts in Modern American Civilization,* while published in 1948, is the only book that has seriously attempted to take a fresh look at American artifacts and study their uniqueness as typically American. His comments on the vernacular tradition are still worth reading.

Technological or construction history is a separate category from architecture due to its specialized nature. The best overall study of the American contribution is Carl Condit's two-volume work, *American Building Art,* which has been condensed and revised into one volume, *American Building: Materials and Techniques.* A virtue of these pioneer attempts is that Condit understands technical language but can write literate English. James Marston Fitch has made a contribution here with his second study, *American Building: The Environmental Forces that Shaped It.* A physiological study of the different sensory elements that make buildings, it is an important work. The title of Siegfried Giedion's *Mechanization Takes Command: A Contribution to Anonymous History* is self-explanatory; it is the first serious attempt to trace many contributions to modern life such as bathtubs, kitchen ranges, and heating. Reyner Banham's *The Architecture of the Well-Tempered Environment* is more narrowly focused and deals with the period from the late nineteenth century to the 1960s and with the uses high art architects have made of air conditioning, dropped ceilings, fluorescent lighting, and forced-air heating. Critical and prescriptive in nature, Banham's hero, if he has one, is Willis Carrier. However, Banham's perceptions are astute and his thinking, as always, is original. The book is a must.

Books on furniture, interiors, and the decorative arts proliferate and encompass everything from how to collect Victorian to serious studies of specific furniture types. All are of some value, but for the student looking for a broad overview, there is little. Russell Lynes's *The Tastemakers,* published in 1954, is dated, but it is a popular history of American interior design that pays considerable attention to mass taste. The term "interior design" indicates status, while the terms "interior decoration" and "decorator" are generally avoided by high art architects and decorators. As the title of C. Ray Smith's *Interior Design in Twentieth Century America: A History* indicates, the concern is exclusively with name designers and high-style furniture makers; the popular styles—French Provincial, Early American— receive little coverage. Far too rare are studies that attempt to interpret individual tastes in interior decoration. M H. Harmon's *Psycho-Decorating: What Homes Reveal About People,* is based on interviews with one hundred middle-income women who have decorated their own homes. Extremely limited and filled with unsupportable interpretative generalizations, still it indicates a direction that should be investigated. See also *Dining in America,* edited by Kathryn Grover. Not strictly concerned with decorative arts, and far more inclusive, and yet a book that must be mentioned, is *I'll Buy That! Fifty Small Wonders and Big Deals that Revolutionized the Lives of Consumers,* by the editors of *Consumer Reports.* While the fifty wonders deal with everything from "the pill" to automobiles to Levittown, the major portion of the book is devoted to appliances and home goods. This is a book that no student of popular culture can afford to be without.

The recent revival of interest in art deco or moderne of the 1920s and 1930s has resulted in several books that deal with the decorative arts from a popular point of view. Bevis Hillier's *Art Deco* and his essay in the Minneapolis Institute of Art's *The World of Art Deco* introduced a broad range of objects. The best coverage of the decorative arts, including mass-produced objects, is in Dianne Pilgrim's essay in Wilson, Pilgrim, and Tashjian, *The Machine Age in America, 1918–1941*. A collection of thirties and forties decorative trivia can be found in Lester Glassner and Brownie Harris, *Dime-Store Days*.

Hillier's later book, *The Decorative Arts of the Forties and Fifties: Austerity/Binge,* is mainly devoted to England, but the parallels with the United States are close enough for it to be of value. This is an attempt to deal with what is jokingly known in the trade as "Art Yucko." Filled with illustrations is *Fifties Style: Then and Now* by Richard Horn.

The role of the industrial designer has been assessed in books such as Donald Bush, *The Streamlined Decade,* Jeffrey L. Meikle, *Twentieth Century Limited: Industrial Design in America, 1925–1939,* Arthur Pulos, *American Design Ethic: A History of Industrial Design,* and Wilson, Pilgrim, and Tashjian, *The Machine Age in America, 1918–1941*. Contemporary accounts by the designers themselves include Raymond Loewy's *Industrial Design,* Walter Dorwin Teague's *Design This Day,* and Harold Van Doren's *Industrial Design*.

The history of the American landscape, urban, suburban, and rural, and how to analyze it has a significant number of books of some importance. John Reps's *The Making of Urban America: A History of City Planning in the United States,* while focusing on the more formal or designed creations, includes everything from garden cities to railroad speculator towns. It is very good and has plenty of illustrations. For a wider view of the landscape in all its guises, John Brinckerhoff Jackson is clearly superior. His magnum opus on the history of the American landscape is not completed, and we have to be content with collections of his essays, *Landscapes,* his one book, *American Space: The Centennial Years, 1865–1876,* and old copies of *Landscape* magazine, which he used to edit. A good history which reflects Jackson's wide perspective is John R. Stilgoe's *Common Landscape of America, 1580 to 1845*. Another volume covering the later period is under way. In this regard see Stilgoe's more specialized work, *Metropolitan Corridor*. An incomparable source for the historical study of the landscape is the WPA Guide Series to the different states, which is slowly being reissued. Another class of books is the critical-analytical studies that generally contain some history along with a methodology of how to look at the landscape. Most of them prejudicially call the popular environment "goop" and "crap" and contain prescriptive remedies; however, used with care, they are important. Examples are Kevin Lynch, *The Image of the City,* Donald Appleyard, Kevin Lynch, and John R. Meyer, *The View from the Road,* Ian Nairn, *The American Landscape: A Critical View,* Richard Saul Wurman, *Making the City Observable,* and Grady Clay, *Close-up: How to Read the American City*. Clay's book contains an extensive analysis of the strip.

There are many books on American cities, but the best one from a visual point of view is Harold M. Mayer and Richard C. Wade's *Chicago: Growth of a Metropolis*. Attention is paid to the everyday realities of common building. The WPA Guide Series devoted several books to cities which should be looked at. Quite clearly the entry point for the study of popular architecture in a city should be Tom Wolfe's seminal essay on the "Versailles" of Las Vegas. Following this there is the previously mentioned work by Venturi, Brown, and Izenour, *Learning from Las Vegas*. This is written from an architect's and urban planner's point of view and provides an insightful look at all the elements of the American strip, gas stations, signs, parking lots, and "ugly and ordinary architecture." The actual history is slim, but the interpretation is challenging.

If Las Vegas is the Versailles of popular architecture, then Los Angeles is the Holy City. Reyner Banham's *Los Angeles: The Architecture of Four Ecologies* is every bit as important as *Learning from Las Vegas* and probably offers a more profound interpretation. Banham's book is a mix between high art and popular architecture, and he identifies as the four ecologies the ocean front, the foothills, the Plains of Id, and the freeway world or autotopia. An Englishman, he appreciates the American scene as only an outsider can. Also to be looked at concerning Los Angeles is David Gebhard and Harriette Von Brenton's *L.A. in the 30s*. While containing many examples of high art architecture, it also looks at the early drive-ins, freeways, and movie lots.

Several exhibits have led to some rather ephemeral documents on popular architecture. *Signs of Life: Symbols in the American City* is a slim catalog of an important exhibit organized by Venturi and Brown and others at the Renwick Gallery of the Smithsonian Institution in 1976. The exhibit documented popular taste in the American home, strip, and street. An earlier catalog for the Institute of Contemporary Art in Philadelphia, *The Highway*, contains essays by Venturi and Brown. In 1978 the Cooper-Hewitt branch of the Smithsonian held an exhibit on architectural packaging and looked at four popular American building types; fast-food restaurants, diners, gasoline stations, and museum-village restorations. An article by Richard Oliver and Nancy Ferguson, the curators of the exhibit, appeared in *Architectural Record* for February 1978 and also as a reprint catalog. Finally, a planned exhibit on Catskill resort hotels has resulted in an article in *Progressive Architecture* by John Margolies and Elizabeth Cromly.

One area of popular architecture studies that has received a great deal of attention has been the American penchant for movement and travel, and specifically the highway. Of course, Americans moved by other means before the automobile—and indeed they would continue to in the twentieth-century—but in general canals and railroads have been overlooked. The vast area of railroad buffdom includes thousands of books on virtually every aspect of trains, but these are generally very specialized. The best book that transcends the rail fan's narrow focus is Stilgoe's *Metropolitan Corridor: Rail-*

roads and the American Scene, mentioned above. Stilgoe treats the period 1880–1930 and deals with the railroad as a cultural phenomenon. Attention is paid to the structures that used to border the right-of-way and the industrial scene.

However, it is the twentieth-century American highway that has inspired most of the studies of popular architecture. The model study is Thomas J. Schlereth's *US 40: A Roadscape of the American Experience,* which covers only the state of Indiana. He pays attention to the pre-twentieth-century road and covers paving and grading changes extensively as well as service stations, diners, and roadside structures. A far less scholarly and more openly nostalgic book is Phil Patton's *Open Road: A Celebration of the American Highway.* Older, and written from the point of view of a professional landscape architect (and indeed an award-winning designer), is Lawrence Halprin's *Freeways.* He deals with the aesthetics of freeway design and its many images. David Brodsly's *L.A. Freeway: An Appreciative Essay* expands upon some of the observations of Reyner Banham noted above and gives a history of the Mecca of freeways. The odd and frequently overscaled sculptures one finds alongside the road have been analyzed—not very perceptively—by Karal Ann Marling in *The Colossus of Roads: Myth and Symbol Along the American Highway.* The book is devoted to Minnesota and has a lot of footnotes and poor illustrations, but it is an opening gambit in a neglected area. Billboards are architecture and also art, but they have received scant attention from historians. *Billboard Art* by Sally Henderson and Robert Landau provides some history, though the concentration is on the recent past (i.e., post–1960) and California. One of the great designers of billboards, Otis Shepard, is barely known today; the only treatment of him is in Steve Strauss, *Moving Images.* The world of tourist attractions, from giant rattlesnakes to twine balls, is humorously told in Jack Barth, Doug Kirby, Ken Smith, and Milk Wilkins's *Roadside America.* Chester Liebs's *Main Street to Miracle Mile: American Roadside Architecture* is an ambitious attempt to deal with several types of structures. Unfortunately, the book becomes something of a catalog. Certainly the most entertaining is John Baeder's *Gas, Food and Lodging,* which is something of a personal memoir. Baeder is a contemporary painter infatuated with the relics of the road as well as postcards. The book is an interesting attempt to "do" history from postcards and succeeds very well.

Highway or roadside architecture has been the great growth area of popular architecture studies in recent years. Liebs's book, *Main Street,* is the starting point with his chapters on drive-in theaters, motels, gas stations, and other kinds of architecture. *California Crazy: Roadside Vernacular Architecture* by Jim Heimann and Rip Georges is primarily photographs of oversized flower pots and pigs acting as buildings. It does have an introduction by architectural historian David Gebhard that contains valuable information on designs found in the U.S. Patent Office. Daniel I. Veyra's

"Fill'er Up" : *An Architectural History of America's Gas Stations* is primarily pictures, though it does have an important listing of source materials. However, the book's text hardly does justice to the subject. Master's theses from the many graduate programs in architectural history and historic preservation undoubtedly provide information in many of these areas; one example is Gary Wolf's on the Sunoco station. John Margolies is a noted photographer who has concentrated in the area; a collection of his photographs with minimal text is *The End of the Road: Vanishing Highway Architecture in America*.

A very good book on the early history of roadside accommodations is Warren James Belasco's *Americans on the Road: From Autocamp to Motel, 1910–1945*. The book is carefully researched and documented, and the conclusions are sound.

Surprisingly, the auto-directed shopping mall or shopping center has received little academic study. The only book—other than professional architects' how-to manuals—is British, though it looks at American developments; see Barry Maitland, *Shopping Malls*. Richard Longstreth, an American architectural historian, is writing a history of the Southern California shopping center. Longstreth has also published as an article a history of the Country Club Plaza in Kansas City, an important source for American shopping center design. Also to be looked at is Meredith L. Clausen, "Northgate Regional Shopping Center—Paradigm from the Provinces."

The subspecialty of roadside food buildings has attracted a lot of interest. Many of the above-mentioned books by Margolies, Liebs, Schlereth, and others deal with the subject. Richard Gutman has been the historian of the diner, first with an article, and then with a book, *American Diner,* co-authored by Elliott Kaufman. John Baeder, a popular contemporary painter, has collected his paintings of them in a book, *Diner*. Alan Hess has written *Googie: Fifties Coffee Shop Architecture,* which is an interesting story of a California specialty that went nationwide. Actually, the original name of the restaurant was Googie's; it was designed by a high art architect named John Lautner, a follower of Frank Lloyd Wright. The exuberant image of Googie's caught on and led to a nationwide architectural phenomenon. Two employes of Robert Venturi, Paul Hirshorn and Steven Izenour, have written *White Towers,* which chronicles with excellent photographs the chain that began in the 1920s. Warren Belasco has written an article on the Howard Johnson's chain. There has also been a nostalgic interest in the food of the roadside, as exemplified by Tabori Stewart's *Roadside Food*. The best book overall on the subject of roadside food architecture is Philip Langdon's *Orange Roofs, Golden Arches,* which, as the title indicates, covers the subject in an engaging manner, with plenty of illustrations.

There is a sub-subspecialty in this area, and that is—as might be expected—McDonald's. Langdon is good on it; in addition there are histories and cultural considerations of the company, such as John F. Love's *Mc-*

Donald's: Behind the Arches; Marshal Fishwick, ed., "The World of Ronald McDonald,"*Journal of American Culture;* and, of course, *Grinding It Out,* the memoirs of Ray Kroc, who founded the company—or perhaps more accurately, who made it into a national institution. In 1984 the American press was consumed by reports that the original McDonald's was closing. At the time this was reported as a stand in Des Plaines, Illinois, constructed in 1955. Alan Hess has put the story right; the first McDonald's was in San Bernardino, California, while the first of the eye-catching stands was designed by Stanley Meston and erected in Phoenix in 1953. That one has been demolished, but the second McDonald's is in near-mint condition in Downey, California. See Hess's article in the *Journal of the Society of Architectural Historians.* Finally, one should look at the thesis by Abbott and Grosvenor on McDonald's.

Movie theaters have received some attention. There is a Theater Historical Society—headquartered in Notre Dame, Indiana—which publishes a newsletter titled *Marquee* and holds conventions. Simon Tidworth's *Theatres: An Architectural and Cultural History,* and Dennis Sharp's *The Picture Palace* offer an English picture of the history of movie palaces. From the American point of view there are two books, both conspicuously illustrated and popularly written: Ben Hall, *The Best Remaining Seats,* and David Naylor, *American Picture Palaces.*

The house as popular architecture really has not received serious study. The extensive background of original sources one might use for such a history has been outlined earlier in this chapter. The best book from an American point of view is Clifford Clark's *The American Family Home, 1800–1960;* it is comprehensive in that all types of houses, from architect-designed to pattern book and Levittown, are included. Clark attempts to see the family house as a social institution and also as architecture. Gwendolyn Wright's *Building the Dream: A Social History of Housing in America* is also important, but marred by an excessive zeal to prove that the single-family middle-class house is wrong and that everybody should live in apartments. The history of the type of housing popular at the turn of the century is surveyed in Robert Winter, *The California Bungalow.* Alan Gowans in *The Comfortable House: North American Suburban Architecture 1890–1930* has some important information, though he tries to prove that all modern houses are bad and has a tendency to catalog. Some preliminary information on trailers and the mobile home industry can be found in Carlton M. Edwards, *Homes for Travel and Living.* Along this line, Robert Landau and James Phillippi's *Airstream* is unacademic but entertaining. Unfortunately, the history of the modern ranchburger, or the Cape Cod, still remains to be written.

There are numerous books on foreign housing; among them, Maurice W. Barley, *The House and Home,* covers 900 years of England, while Martin Pawley, *Architecture Versus Housing,* treats the large housing block and is polemical in outlook. Also, Robin Boyd's *Australia's Home* should be looked at.

Some other areas suggestive of future examination are indicated by Alan Crawford and Robert Thorne's pamphlet, *Birmingham Pubs, 1890–1939*. The architecture of amusement parks and recreation has similarly received little attention in the United States. Critical articles abound on Disneyland/World and others; they can be located through the periodical indexes. There is one picture book: Gary Kyriazi's *The Great American Amusement Park*.

The study of popular architecture still is in its infancy. Many of the above noted books suffer from a lack of perspective and sound scholarship with regard to notes, research, and methodology, and too frequently disintegrate into a nostalgic cry for the past. Others are excessively polemical or simply picture books. There is room for plenty of work!

ANTHOLOGIES AND REPRINTS

There has been little anthologization of literature on popular architecture. About the only anthologies have been those issued from the Popular Culture Press at Bowling Green University. *Popular Architecture,* edited by Marshall Fishwick and J. Meredith Neil, collects articles dealing with a variety of subjects, some appropriate, such as those by Neil, Brown, Attoe and Latus, Gowans, and others, but some far afield from the subject. Other essays on popular architecture subjects have appeared in *The Arts in a Democratic Society,* edited by Dennis Alan Mann, and *Icons of America,* edited by Ray B. Browne and Marshall Fishwick.

Reprints have proven to be the major source of builder's guides and house pattern books. The major publishers in this line have been Dover Publications, Da Capo Press, and the American Life Foundation and Study Institute. The list would be very long if the hundred or so reprinted were noted. Instead, reprinted works that have been referred to earlier are so noted in the bibliography at the end of this chapter.

NOTES

1. William Morris, "The Prospects of Architecture in Civilization," in *The Collected Works of William Morris,* ed. May Morris (London: Longmans, Green, 1910–15), vol. 22, p. 120.
2. Richard Oliver and Nancy Ferguson, "Place, Product, Packaging," *Architectural Record,* 163 (February 1978), 116.

BIBLIOGRAPHY

Books and Articles

Abbott, James G., and John R. Grosvenor. "Corporate Architecture and Design Theory: A Case Study of McDonald's." Master's thesis, Miami University, 1976.

Appleyard, Donald, Kevin Lynch, and John R. Meyer. *The View from the Road.* Cambridge, Mass.: MIT Press, 1964.

Architectural Record. *The Architectural Record Book of Vacation Houses.* New York: McGraw-Hill, 1977.

———. *Motels, Hotels and Restaurants.* 2nd ed. New York: F. W. Dodge, 1960.

———. *A Treasury of Contemporary Houses.* New York: F. W. Dodge, 1954.

Baeder, John. *Diners.* New York: Harry N. Abrams, 1978.

———. *Gas, Food and Lodging.* New York: Abbeville Press, 1982.

Banham, Reyner. *The Architecture of the Well-Tempered Environment.* Chicago: University of Chicago Press, 1969.

———. *Los Angeles: The Architecture of Four Ecologies.* New York: Harper and Row, 1971.

Barley, Maurice W. *The House and Home: A Review of 900 Years of House Planning and Furnishing in Britain.* Greenwich, Conn.: New York Graphic Society, 1971.

Barth, Jack, et al. *Roadside America.* New York: Simon and Schuster, 1986.

Belasco, Warren J. *Americans on the Road: From Autocamp to Motel, 1910–1945.* Cambridge, Mass.: MIT Press, 1979.

———. "Towards a Culinary Denominator: The Rise of Howard Johnson's, 1925–1940." *Journal of American Culture,* 2 (Fall 1979), 508–12.

Benjamin, Asher. *The American Builder's Companion.* 1827. 6th ed. New York: Dover, 1969.

Blake, Peter. *God's Own Junkyard: The Planned Deterioration of America's Landscape.* New York: Holt, Rinehart and Winston, 1964.

Bloomer, Kent C., and Charles W. Moore. *Body, Memory and Architecture.* New Haven: Yale University Press, 1977.

Boyd, Robin. *Australia's Home: Its Origins, Builders and Occupiers.* Ringwood, Victoria: Penguin Books, 1968.

Broadbent, Geoffrey. "A Plain Man's Guide to the Theory of Signs in Architecture." *Architectural Design,* 47 (July–August 1977), 474–82.

Brodsly, David. *L.A. Freeway: An Appreciative Essay.* Berkeley: University of California Press, 1981.

Browne, Ray B., and Marshall Fishwick, eds. *Icons of America.* Bowling Green, Ohio: Bowling Green University Popular Press, 1978.

Bush, Donald J. *The Streamlined Decade.* New York: George Braziller, 1975.

Clark, Clifford Edward, Jr. *The American Family Home, 1800–1960.* Chapel Hill: University of North Carolina Press, 1986.

Clausen, Meredith L. "Northgate Regional Shopping Center—Paradigm from the Provinces." *Journal of the Society of Architectural Historians,* 43 (May 1984), 144–61.

Clay, Grady. *Close-up: How to Read the American City.* New York: Praeger, 1973.

Columbia University. *Avery Index to Architectural Periodicals.* 2nd ed. 15 vols. plus supplements. Boston: G. K. Hall, 1973.

———. *Avery Obituary Index of Architects and Artists.* Boston: G. K. Hall, 1963.

Committee for the Preservation of Architectural Records. *Architectural Research Materials in New York City: A Guide to Resources in All Five Boroughs.* 2 vols. New York: Committee for the Preservation of Architectural Records, 1977.

Condit, Carl W. *American Building Art*. 2 vols. New York: Oxford University Press, 1960, 1961.

———. *American Building: Materials and Techniques*. Chicago: University of Chicago Press, 1968.

Crawford, Alan, and Robert Thorne. *Birmingham Pubs, 1890–1930*. Birmingham, England: Center for Urban and Regional Studies, University of Birmingham and the Victorian Society, Birmingham Group, 1975.

Dean, John F., and Simon Breines. *The Book of Houses*. New York: Crown, 1946.

Downing, Andrew Jackson. *The Architecture of Country Houses*. 1850. Reprint. New York: Dover, 1969.

———. *Cottage Residences*. 1842. Reprint. Watkins Glen, N.Y.: Library of Victorian Culture, 1967.

Editors of Consumer Reports. *I'll Buy That!: Fifty Small Wonders and Big Deals that Revolutionized the Lives of Consumers*. Mount Vernon, N.Y.: Consumers Union, 1986.

Edwards, Carlton M. *Homes for Travel and Living: The History and Development of the Recreational Vehicle and Mobile Home Industry*. Lansing: Carl Edwards and Assoc., 1977.

Fishwick, Marshall, ed. "The World of Ronald McDonald." *Journal of American Culture*, 1 (Summer 1978), 336–471.

Fishwick, Marshall, and J. Meredith Neil, eds. *Popular Architecture*. Bowling Green, Ohio: Bowling Green University Popular Press, [1975].

Fitch, James M. *American Building: The Environmental Forces that Shaped It*. Boston: Houghton Mifflin, 1972.

———. *American Building: The Historical Forces that Shaped It*. Boston: Houghton Mifflin, 1966.

Gans, Herbert J. *Popular Culture and High Culture*. New York: Basic Books, 1975.

Gardner, Eugene C. *Houses and How to Make Them*. Boston: J. B. Osgood. 1885.

Gebhard, David, and Harriette Von Brenton. *L.A. in the 30s*. Santa Barbara: Peregrine Smith, 1975.

Giedion, Siegfried. *Mechanization Takes Command: A Contribution to Anonymous History*. New York: Oxford University Press, 1948.

Glassie, Henry. *Folk Housing in Middle Virginia: A Structural Analysis of Historic Artifacts*. Knoxville: University of Tennessee Press, 1975.

———. *Pattern in the Material Folk Culture of the Eastern United States*. Philadelphia: University of Philadelphia Press, 1968.

Glassner, Lester, and Brownie Harris. *Dime Store Days*. New York: Viking Press, 1980.

Gowans, Alan. *The Comfortable House: North American Suburban Architecture, 1890–1930*. Cambridge, Mass.: MIT Press, 1986.

———. *Images of American Living: Four Centuries of Architecture and Furniture as Cultural Expression*. New York: J. B. Lippincott, 1964.

———. *On Parallels in Universal History Discoverable in Arts and Artifacts: An Outline Statement*. Watkins Glen, N.Y.: Institute for the Study of Universal History, 1974.

———. *The Unchanging Arts: New Forms for the Traditional Functions of Art in Society*. New York: J. B. Lippincott, 1971.

Grief, Martin. *Depression Modern: The Thirties Style in America*. New York: Universe Books, 1975.

Grover, Kathryn, ed. *Dining in America, 1850–1900*. Amherst: University of Massachusetts Press, 1987.

Gutman, Richard J. S., and Elliott Kaufman. *American Diner*. New York: Harper and Row, 1979.

Hall, Ben M. *The Best Remaining Seats*. New York: Clarkson N. Potter, 1961.

Hall, Edward T. *The Hidden Dimension*. New York: Doubleday, 1966.

Halprin, Lawrence, *Freeways*. New York: Reinhold, 1966.

Harmon, M. H. *Psycho-Decorating: What Homes Reveal About People*. New York: Wyden Books, 1977.

Harris, Cyril M., ed. *Dictionary of Architecture and Construction*. New York: McGraw-Hill, 1975.

Heimann, Jim, and Rip Georges. *California Crazy: Roadside Vernacular Architecture*. San Francisco: Chronicle Books, 1980.

Henderson, Sally, and Robert Landau. *Billboard Art*. San Francisco: Chronicle Books, 1980.

Hess, Alan. *Googie: Fifties Coffee Shop Architecture*. San Francisco: Chronicle Books, 1985.

———. "The Origins of McDonald's Golden Arches." *Journal of the Society of Architectural Historians*, 45 (March 1986), 60–67.

Hillier, Bevis. *Art Deco*. London: Studio Vista, 1965.

———. *The Decorative Arts of the Forties and Fifties: Austerity/Binge*. New York: Clarkson N. Potter, 1975.

Hirshorn, Paul, and Steven Izenour. "Learning from Hamburgers." *Architecture Plus*, 1 (June 1973), 46–55.

Historic American Building Survey. National Park Service. *Historic American Building Survey*. Washington, D.C.: Department of the Interior, 1941.

Hitchock, Henry-Russell. *American Architectural Books: A List of Books, Portfolios, and Pamphlets on Architecture and Related Subjects Published in America Before 1895*. New York: Da Capo Press, 1975.

Horn, Richard. *Fifties Style: Then and Now*. New York: Beech Tree Books, 1975.

House and Garden. *Building Guide, Fall-Winter, 1963–64*. New York: Conde Nast, 1963.

Institute for Contemporary Art. *The Highway*. Philadelphia: Institute for Contemporary Art, 1970.

Jackson, John Brinckerhoff. *American Space: The Centennial Years, 1865–1876*. New York: W. W. Norton, 1972.

———. *Landscapes: Selected Essays*. Edited by Irvin H. Zobe. Amherst: University of Massachusetts Press, 1970.

Jacobs, Jane. *The Death and Life of Great American Cities*. New York: Random House, 1961.

Jencks, Charles. "The Architectural Sign." *Architecture and Urbanism*, 78 (April, May, June 1978), 3–10, 70–78, 128.

Jencks, Charles, and George Baird, eds. *Meaning in Architecture*. New York: George Braziller, 1970.

Kouwenhoven, John. *The Arts in Modern American Civilization*. New York: W. W. Norton, 1948.

Kroc, Ray. *Grinding It Out*. Chicago: Henry Regnery, 1977.

Kubler, George. *The Shape of Time*. New Haven: Yale University Press, 1962.

Kyriazi, Gary. *The Great American Amusement Park*. Secaucus: Citadel Press, 1976.

Lafever, Minard. *The Modern Builder's Guide*. New York: Sleight, 1833.

Landau, Robert, and James Phillippi. *Airstream*. Salt Lake City: Peregrine Smith, 1984.

Langdon, Philip. *Orange Roofs, Golden Arches: The Architecture of American Chain Restaurants*. New York: Alfred A. Knopf, 1986.

Liebs, Chester. *Main Street to Miracle Mile: American Roadside Architecture*. Boston: New York Graphic Society, 1985.

Loewy, Raymond. *Industrial Design*. Woodstock, N.Y.: Overlook Press, 1979.

Longstreth, Richard. "J. C. Nichols, the Country Club Plaza, and Notions of Modernity." *Harvard Architecture Review* (1986), 121–35.

Love, John F. *McDonald's: Behind the Golden Arches*. New York: Bantam Books, 1986.

Lynch, Kevin. *The Image of the City*. Cambridge, Mass: Technology Press and Harvard University Press, 1960.

Lynes, Russell. *The Tastemakers*. New York: Harper, 1954.

Maitland, Barry. *Shopping Malls*. London: Construction Press, 1985.

Mann, Dennis Alan, ed. *The Arts in a Democratic Society*. Bowling Green, Ohio: Bowling Green University Popular Press, 1977.

Margolies, John. *The End of the Road: Vanishing Highway Architecture in America*. New York: Penguin Books, 1981.

Margolies, John, and Elizabeth Cromly. "Upward and Inward with Time." *Progressive Architecture*, 59 (February 1978), 46–51.

Marling, Karal Ann. *The Colossus of Roads: Myth and Symbol Along the American Highway*. Minneapolis: University of Minnesota Press, 1984.

Mayer, Harold M., and Richard C. Wade. *Chicago: Growth of a Metropolis*. Chicago: University of Chicago Press, 1969.

Meikle, Jeffrey L. *Twentieth Century Limited: Industrial Design in America, 1925–1939*. Philadelphia: Temple University Press, 1979.

Minneapolis Institute of Art. *The World of Art Deco*. New York: E. P. Dutton, 1971.

Moore, Charles, Gerald Allen, and Donlyn Lyndon. *The Place of Houses*. New York: Holt, Rinehart and Winston, 1974.

Nairn, Ian. *The American Landscape: A Critical View*. New York: Random House, 1965.

National Trust for Historic Preservation, Tony P. Wren, and Elizabeth D. Mulloy. *America's Forgotten Architecture*. New York: Pantheon, 1976.

Naylor, David. *American Picture Palaces: The Architecture of Fantasy*. New York: Van Nostrand Reinhold, 1981.

Neil, J. Meredith. "What About Architecture?" *Journal of Popular Culture*, 5 (1971), 280–88.

Oliver, Richard, and Nancy Ferguson. "Place, Product, Packaging." *Architectural Record*, 163 (February 1978), 116–20.

Palliser, Palliser and Co. *New Cottage Homes and Details*. 1887. Reprint. New York: Da Capo Press, 1975.

Palmes, J. C. *Sir Banister Fletcher's A History of Architecture*. London: University of London, Athlone Press, 1975.

Patton, Phil. *Open Road: A Celebration of the American Highway*. New York: Simon and Schuster, 1986.

Pawley, Martin. *Architecture Versus Housing*. New York: Praeger, 1971.

Plazeck, Adolf. *Macmillan Encyclopedia of Architects*. New York: Macmillan, 1982.

Poppeliers, John, et al. *What Style Is It? Guide to American Architectural Styles*. Washington, D.C.: National Trust for Historic Preservation, 1982.

Pulos, Arthur J. *American Design Ethic: A History of Industrial Design*. Cambridge, Mass.: MIT Press, 1983.

Rapoport, Amos. *House: Form and Culture*. Englewood Cliffs, N.J.: Prentice-Hall, 1969.

Renwick Gallery, National Collection of Fine Arts, Smithsonian Institution. *Signs of Life: Symbols in the American City*. New York: Aperture, 1976.

Reps, John W. *The Making of Urban America: A History of City Planning in the United States*. Princeton, N.J.: Princeton University Press, 1965.

Rudofsky, Bernard. *Architecture Without Architects*. Garden City, N.Y.: Doubleday, 1964.

―――. *The Prodigious Builders*. New York: Harcourt, Brace Jovanovich, 1977.

Schlereth, Thomas J. *US 40: A Roadscape of the American Experience*. Indianapolis: Indiana Historical Society, 1985.

Sharp, Dennis. *The Picture Palace*. New York: Praeger, 1969.

Sloan, Samuel. *The Model Architect*. Philadelphia: E. S. Jones, 1852.

Smith, C. Ray. *Interior Design in Twentieth Century America: A History*. New York: Harper and Row, 1987.

Sommer, Robert. *Design Awareness*. San Francisco: Rinehart, 1972.

―――. *Personal Space*. Englewood Cliffs, N.J.: Prentice-Hall, 1969.

Stevenson, Katherine Cole, and H. Ward Jande. *Houses by Mail: A Guide to Houses from Sears, Roebuck and Company*. Washington, D.C.: Preservation Press, 1986.

Stewart, Tabori, and Chang Stewart. *Roadside Food*. New York: Workman, 1986.

Stilgoe, John R. *Common Landscape of America, 1580 to 1845*. New Haven: Yale University Press, 1981.

―――. *Metropolitan Corridor: Railroads and the American Scene*. New Haven: Yale University Press, 1983.

Strauss, Steve. *Moving Images: The Transportation Poster in America*. New York: Fullcourt Press, 1984.

Teague, Walter Dorwin. *Design This Day*. New York: Harcourt, Brace, 1940.

Tidworth, Simon. *Theatres: An Architectural and Cultural History*. New York: Praeger, 1975.

Upton, Del, ed. *America's Architectural Roots: Ethnic Groups that Built America*. Washington, D.C.: Preservation Press, 1986.

Van Doren, Harold. *Industrial Design: A Practical Guide*. New York: McGraw-Hill, 1940.

Venturi, Robert. *Complexity and Contradiction in Architecture*. New York: Museum of Modern Art, 1966.

Venturi, Robert, Denise Scott Brown, and Steven Izenour. *Learning from Las Vegas*. 1972. Rev. ed. Cambridge, Mass.: MIT, 1977.

Veyra, Daniel I. *"Fill'er Up": An Architectural History of America's Gas Stations*. New York: Collier, 1979.

Vogel, Robert. *The New England Textile Mill Survey*. Washington, D.C.: Historic American Building Survey, National Park Service, 1971.

Wells, Camile, ed. *Perspectives in Vernacular Architecture*. Annapolis: Vernacular Architecture Forum, 1982–. Annual.

Wheeler, Gervase. *Rural Homes, or Sketches of Houses Suited to American Country Life, with Original Plans, Designs, etc.* New York: C. Scribner, 1851.

Whiffen, Marcus. *American Architecture Since 1780*. Cambridge, Mass.: MIT Press, 1969.

White, Charles F. *The Bungalow Book*. New York: Macmillan, 1923.

Wilson, Richard Guy. "Abstraction Versus Figuration, Utopia Versus Context: The Place of Postmodernism in the Visual Arts." In *Critique of Modernity*. Edited by R. Langbaum. Charlottesville: Center for Advanced Studies, University of Virginia, 1986, pp. 87–95.

Wilson, Richard Guy, Dianne H. Pilgrim, and Dickran Tashjian. *The Machine Age in America, 1918–1941*. New York: Harry N. Abrams, 1986.

Wilson, Richard Guy, and Jeff Vaughn. *The Old West Side*. Ann Arbor: Old West Side Association, 1971.

Winter, Robert. *The California Bungalow*. Los Angeles: Hennessey and Ingalls, 1980.

Withey, Henry F., and Elsie R. Withey. *Biographical Dictionary of American Architects (Deceased)*. Los Angeles: New Age, 1956.

Wolf, Gary Herbert. "The Gas Station: The Evolution of a Building Type as Illustrated Through a History of the Sun Oil Company Gasoline Station." Master's thesis, University of Virginia, 1974.

Wolfe, Tom. *From Bauhaus to Our House*. New York: Farrar, Straus and Giroux, 1981.

Woodward, George. *Woodward's National Architect*. 1868. Reprint. Watkins Glen, N.Y.: American Life Foundation and Study Institute, 1977.

Wright, Gwendolyn. *Building the Dream: A Social History of Housing in America*. New York: Pantheon, 1981.

Wurman, Richard Saul. *Making the City Observable*. Minneapolis: Walker Art Center, and Cambridge, Mass.: MIT Press, 1971.

Periodicals

American Architect and Building News. Boston and New York, 1876–1938.
American Builder. Chicago and New York, 1865–1895.
The American Home. New York, 1928–.
The Architectural Record. New York, 1891–.
Architectural Review and American Builder's Journal. Philadelphia, 1868–70.
Better Homes and Gardens. Des Moines, 1922–.
Bungalow Magazine. Los Angeles, 1909–18.
The Craftsman Magazine. New York, 1901–16.
Early American Life. Harrisburg, Pennsylvania, 1970–.
Godey's Lady's Book and Lady's Magazine. Philadelphia, 1830–98.
Historic Preservation. Washington, D.C., 1949–.

House and Garden. New York, 1901–.

House and Home: The Magazine of Housing. New York, 1952–.

The House Beautiful. Chicago and New York, 1896–.

Ladies Home Journal. New York, 1883–.

Landscape. Santa Fe, N.M., and Berkeley, Calif., 1851–.

Nation's Restaurant News. New York, 1967–.

Popular Mechanics. New York, 1902–.

Professional Builder and Apartment Business. Chicago, 1936–.

Progressive Architecture. Stamford, Conn., 1926–.

Qualified Remodeler. Chicago, 1975–.

Restaurant Business. New York, 1902–   .

The Automobile

MICHAEL L. BERGER
and MAURICE DUKE

HISTORIC OUTLINE

Although man had dreamt of a self-propelled vehicle for centuries, it was not until the end of the nineteenth century that a practical road machine capable of sustained distances emerged for general use. Historians disagree on the actual inventor of the first American automobile. However, credit is usually given to Charles E. and J. Frank Duryea for the successful development (1893) and marketing of the gasoline motorcar that most resembles the one in use today. The Duryeas' success was abetted by their victory in the first American automobile race, held in 1895. This event was sponsored by the Chicago *Times-Herald,* and thus resulted in considerable publicity for the new means of transportation in general and the Duryea car in particular.

When the automobile first appeared, it was treated as an object of curiosity, a plaything for the rich and a tinkering project for inventors or the hapless blacksmith who might be called upon to aid a motorist who by some mechanical malfunction had suddenly become a pedestrian. The automobile quickly took hold, however, capturing people's minds as well as their pocketbooks. Races, such as the Vanderbilt Cup road races of 1904–16; reliability runs, like the Glidden Tours held between 1905 and 1913; and successful cross-country automobile trips, beginning in 1903 with that of Dr. H. Nelson Jackson, all helped establish the automobile as a viable means of transportation and a formidable challenger to the horse.

Although there was some early resistance to the motorcar, especially in rural areas, once its economic and social usefulness had been demonstrated this hostility disappeared. "For the first time in world history," historian George E. Mowry has written, "mass man became the master of a complicated piece of power machinery by which he could annihilate distance."[1] Born into an America that had virtually no paved road system, the auto soon began to shrink the size of the continent of whose vastness and inexhaustibility St. Jean deCrevecoeur had boasted just over a century before. Although still not completely trustworthy from a mechanical standpoint, automobiles became popular for cross-country expeditions—giving rise, incidentally, to a number of early automobile travel narratives and novels— and for exploring places that mere decades before were out of range of the traveller or adventurer who had to rely on the horse, the ship, and/or the train.

When the automobile emerged from its novelty stage, its influence on American life became markedly greater. The mass production of cars like Henry Ford's Model T, which began in the first decade of the twentieth century, ushered in a new era of attitudes and convictions about the auto. Ford showed that a mechanically efficient motorcar could be produced, sold at a moderate price, and still be the source of significant profits for the manufacturer. Both the joys and woes of owning a self-propelled vehicle were now within the means of the average American.

Although sudden death might lurk around the next curve, and the neighborhood horses might be terrified, not to mention the emerging noise and pollution problems, there was a new sense of freedom across the land. Urban dwellers could escape to the country for a day; isolated rural residents could visit each other and the nearby towns and cities more easily; and businessmen could move more quickly in their daily routines. As several automotive historians have noted, there was a good match between the nature of motor travel and the American character. The individualism and personal mobility Americans always had valued had found a new means of expression, and a new "escape valve" had been found for the stresses of modern society.

As the automobile became a way of life in America, so American life had to adjust to accommodate it. While the motorcar was shrinking the size of the continent, it was altering both its physical and social landscape as well. Service stations, garages, and parts warehouses popped up around the country at the same time that legislators and judges were pondering complex problems about how the use of the automobile should be governed. Also, culturally and socially, other changes were taking place. Clothing styles were altered to protect the motorist from the elements as he or she drove along in the open cars of the period. Hotels began giving way to auto camps, tourist cabins, and, eventually, the modern motel. The introduction of that word into our vocabulary showed that not even the language would remain unaffected by the cultural revolution brought forth by the automobile. City dwellers in increasing numbers found that they could live outside urban areas and motor to work, thus helping to create America's vast and sprawling suburbs.

Although the depression that began in 1929 brought the period of unbridled expansion to a close, the car remained an important part of life during the thirties. For the rich, a new era of American luxury cars was introduced with the appearance of the Cord, Duesenberg, and sixteen-cylinder Cadillacs. At the other end of the economic spectrum, the car was often the last refuge against the elements for the poor, the possession that was never sold, best exemplified by the Joad family's behavior in John Steinbeck's 1939 novel *The Grapes of Wrath*. The vast middle class of motorized Americans continued to set new records for motorized travel, though not new car purchases, even in these hard times.

The coming of World War II brought production of new cars to a standstill, as auto manufacturers re-tooled to produce the machinery of armed combat. Entering their first period of gasoline shortages, Americans now had to queue up to receive rationing stickers. "Is this trip necessary?" became the question of radio newscasters and politicians alike. The wheels of the country began to turn more slowly, but the speed was destined to be regained and even vastly accelerated in the next decade.

Emerging victorious from World War II, the American, as Lewis Mumford has written in *The Highway and the City*, "sacrificed his life as a whole to the motorcar."[2] The pent-up demand for cars, combined with postwar prosperity, led to record sales in the late forties and fifties. During the latter decade, often termed the "golden age" of the American automobile, cars became longer, more powerful, and more numerous, with two-car families no longer viewed as unusual. Design became more outlandish; witness the tailfin craze. Freeways and interstates took the place of the prewar highways, which now became relegated to secondary road status. And suburbs began the growth that was to allow them to surpass the cities in 1970 as the most populous residential areas.

More important from the sociocultural perspective, this decade saw the full flowering of outdoor drive-in movie theaters, dubbed "passion pits" by their critics; drive-in restaurants, where car-bound customers were often served by waitresses on roller skates; drive-in churches; and even drive-in funeral parlors. The popularity of automobile racing as a spectator sport grew enormously; new forms emerged, and greater commercialization occurred as it became a multimillion-dollar entertainment industry. The cars of yesteryear began reappearing on the nation's roads after having been reworked in various "customized" ways, "souped" up, and/or transformed into "hot rods," with their youthful creators maintaining that the cars reflected their innermost personalities.

Although there was some disenchantment with the automobile in the mid and late sixties, caused largely by questions of environmental pollution and safety, America's so-called love affair with the car continued relatively unabated in that decade, and a few new developments were added. Seemingly forever seeking vehicular freedom, many Americans yearned to leave the restricted confines of the highway for "off-road" adventures. Jeeps enjoyed a renaissance, specially produced recreational vehicles (RVs) made their appearance and were commercially successful, and motorized camping gained in popularity to the extent that national and state parks were no longer able to handle the demand effectively. The purchase and/or restoration of old cars gained in popularity as a hobby, with devotees apparently oblivious to the costs of a "pure" restoration. Finally, aspects of motoring that had long been considered exclusively European in nature, most notably sports cars and grand prix motor racing, began to achieve a level of acceptance that would make them important elements of the American automobile culture in the years to come.

By the early 1970s, cars were owned by 83 percent of American families, manufacturers could not keep up with demand, and the central place of the automobile in American life seemed assured for the foreseeable future. However, before the end of the decade, Americans were seriously questioning for the first time the role of the automobile (and its industry) in their lives and their dependency on it. The oil embargo of 1973 forced them to face the prospect that fossilized fuels might be depleted in the near future and the reality of gasoline prices that doubled before they levelled off. Americans witnessed the cost of new cars increasing two and sometimes threefold, and buyers experienced what was dubbed "sticker shock." Moreover, the motorcar, long suspected as a serious atmospheric pollutant, came under the study of scientists who proved such to be the case. Suddenly, the automobile and the industry that produced it became major problems for many Americans, and people began seriously to discuss controlling the sale and use of the automobile, and even its total prohibition.

However, such stringent regulation never occurred. Oil "shortages" eased, and gasoline prices actually went down. Inflation moderated, and the price of new cars stabilized. Federal and state emission control laws forced car manufacturers to produce less-polluting vehicles. But most important of all, for better or worse, the American public made it very clear that it wanted to keep the private automobile and the life-style it had helped create, irrespective of the social, economic, and political costs involved.

REFERENCE WORKS

There are many excellent one- or two-volume reference works that offer descriptions, technical data, and short summaries of the significance of the literally thousands of makes of cars that have been produced or planned since the 1890s. Unfortunately, they contain little or no information on the social or cultural significance of the vehicles.

The best available material for cultural historians is contained in three bibliographic reference volumes, from which one can cull automotive items of special interest. The broadest of these, *Technology and Values in American Civilization: A Guide to Information Sources* by Stephen H. Cutcliffe et al., is highly recommended. Composed of citations followed by brief annotations, this volume contains references to most of the significant books and articles up to 1980, all of which can be accessed through one of three indexes (author, title, or subject). A similar volume, *Motorsports: A Guide to Information Sources* by Susan Ebershoff-Coles and Charla Ann Leibenguth, ought to prove valuable to researchers in that area, although the items tend to be less scholarly (possibly by virtue of the subject) than the Cutcliffe volume. In addition, there is Bernard Mergen's *Recreational Vehicles and Travel: A Resource Guide,* which provides bibliographic essays on various aspects of the impact of RVs on American society. Finally, researchers interested in auto touring, or simply early motoring, should find Carey S. Bliss's *Autos Across America: A Bibliography of Transcontinental Automobile Travel, 1903–1940* to be particularly useful with its listing of personal accounts.

In preparation is Michael L. Berger's *The Automobile: A Reference Guide,* which will consist of a series of topical essays describing the contents and merits of some 3,000 scholarly books, articles, and dissertations that explore the impact of the car on American history and culture. Its publication will mark the first time a major bibliographic work has attempted to cover all aspects of the automobile's influence on American life.

While space considerations limit the citations in this chapter to books and doctoral dissertations, there is a wealth of scholarly material available in periodicals as well. An excellent reference source in this regard is *America: History and Life,* which is now available on-line for computer searches as well as in hard copy. The great advantage of this particular reference tool is that each bibliographic citation is followed by a full-paragraph description of its contents. Similar information for doctoral dissertations can be found in *Dissertation Abstracts.* In addition, *Writings on American History* and *Recently Published Articles,* both publications of the American Historical Association, can be useful sources of periodical citations. Furthermore, two scholarly journals, *Technology and Culture* and *Isis* (from the History of Science Society) publish yearly indexes of recently published books and articles, sometimes with brief annotations.

Finally, some mention should be made of the material that has been published in "auto buff" publications, those magazines and journals aimed at collectors and afficionados. Probably preeminent in this regard is *Automobile Quarterly,* a lavishly produced, beautifully illustrated hardbound quarterly. Although the articles usually lack citations, and the space devoted to the photographs often exceeds that for the text, the narrative is clearly research-based and can be of assistance to researchers interested in the impact of a particular person, vehicle, motor race, etc. *Automobile Quarterly* is indexed, and 1985 saw the publication of a cumulative index covering the first twenty volumes (1962–82). Also in this genre is the bimonthly publication of the Antique Automobile Club of America, *Antique Automobile,* and the quarterly magazine of the Veteran Motor Car Club of America, *Bulb Horn,* both of which are also indexed.

Access to these publications, and mass-circulation auto monthlies like *Road and Track* and *Car and Driver,* both of which regularly carry articles of popular cultural significance, can also be secured by using two privately printed periodical guides: *Automotive Literature Index,* compiled by A. Wallace, three volumes (1947–76, 1977–81, and 1982–86) of which have appeared; and *Auto Index,* which has been published every other month since 1973 and in yearly compilations by volume. Care should be taken in using these indexes, since the placement of specific articles under the topical headings is sometimes questionable.

RESEARCH COLLECTIONS

By far the best collection of materials available for the study of the automobile in America is housed in the National Automotive History Collection of the Detroit Public Library. Its holdings number approximately one million items, including over 17,000 books, 8,000 bound periodicals, 300,000 photographs, and hundreds of thousands of one-of-a-kind pieces of ephemera. Fortunately for researchers, these holdings have been cataloged, and a description, by subject and author, of their contents is readily available in a two-volume work entitled *The Automotive History Collection of the Detroit Public Library: A Simplified Guide to Its Holdings.*

Another major collection is housed in the Free Library of Philadelphia. Although there is no published guide to its holdings, this collection contains a total of some 13,000 volumes and is concerned with all aspects of the automotive industry and its history. Of particular importance to social historians are the 17,000 photographs of automobiles, ranging from the late nineteenth century to the present.

The Science and Technology Research Center of the New York Public Library also has extensive holdings on the automobile, as do the Cleveland, San Diego, and Flint (Michigan) public libraries.

Several major research universities also have amassed considerable collections. The DeGolyer Foundation Library of Southern Methodist University in Dallas holds over 90,000 volumes concerning the automobile, along with first editions by prominent authors, as well as manuscripts, photographs, and maps. At the Stuart A. Work Collection on automobile history at the University of California at Los Angeles, one can locate materials not only historical in nature, but also centering on racing, automobile shows, and promotional events concerning the automobile. Not surprisingly, the University of Michigan is another good source of information, especially its Highway Safety Research Institute Library, which houses some 26,000 items centering on the automobile.

Finally, each of the Big Three automobile companies has libraries and archives that concern its own history and that of the industry in general. Such facilities are usually open to scholars upon application. The best of the three is the Archives and Research Library of the Henry Ford Museum and Greenfield Village in Dearborn, Michigan, which has over 20,000 volumes and extensive collections of periodicals, trade catalogs, photographs, and newspaper clippings.

HISTORY AND CRITICISM

Histories of the automobile began appearing as early as 1917 and continue down to the present. Listed alphabetically below are some of the earlier ones that contain significant amounts of sociocultural information: Rudolph E. Anderson's *The Story of the American Automobile: Highlights and Sidelights;* Reginald M. Cleveland and S. T. Williamson's *The Road Is Yours: The Story of the Automobile and the Men Behind It;* David L. Cohn's *Combustion on Wheels: An Informal History of the Automobile Age;* Frank Donovan's *Wheels for a Nation;* C. B. Glasscock's *The Gasoline Age: The Story of the Men Who Made It;* Frank E. Hill's *The Automobile: How It Came, Grew, and Has Changed Our Lives;* Hiram P. Maxim's *Horseless Carriage Days;* and M. M. Musselman's *Get a Horse!: The Story of the Automobile in America.* Of these books, the Cohn and Donovan volumes will probably prove most valuable to the social or cultural historian.

Despite the good intentions of these works, they might best be classified as "popular histories," aimed at a general audience and comparatively weak in analysis. Pioneering scholarly works of a sociological nature during this period are best exemplified by John Mueller's 1928 dissertation entitled "The Automobile: A Sociological Study"; and by Robert S. Lynd and Helen M. Lynd's *Middletown: A Study in Contemporary American Culture* (1929) and *Middletown in Transition: A Study in Cultural Conflicts* (1937), both of which analyze the automobile's impact on the community of Muncie, Indiana.

It was not until 1965, with the publication of John B. Rae's *The American Automobile: A Brief History* that one got the first book-length, scholarly treatment of this subject. Rae's work opened up the field to serious study, and the next fifteen years saw the publication of several important works of interest to the social historian, beginning with James J. Flink's *America Adopts the Automobile, 1895–1910,* which explores the sociocultural milieu within which the automobile came of age. Flink's book was followed by Rae's *The Road and the Car in American Life,* Wik's *Henry Ford and Grassroots America,* Belasco's *Americans on the Road,* Berger's *The Devil Wagon in*

God's Country, and Preston's *Automobile Age Atlanta,* all of which are described below.

The scholarly movement that Rae set in motion in 1965 with his "brief history" reached a type of fruition with the publication of James Flink's *The Automobile Age* in 1988. Hailed by reviewers as a definitive treatment of the subject, Professor Flink's book is a comprehensive history that masterfully combines analysis of both industrial developments and societal impacts. While Flink's emphasis is on the American experience, he does a fine job of placing that experience in worldwide perspective. *The Automobile Age* should be the starting point for most serious students of the subject.

Two collections of essays have helped identify potentially rich areas for future sociocultural research. These volumes are *The Automobile in American Life,* edited by Charles L. Sanford, and *The Automobile and American Culture,* edited by David L. Lewis and Laurence Goldstein. Both are wide-ranging books, with selections concerning a number of social issues ignored, or casually treated, by most popular histories. Of the two, Sanford's is the more traditional, with the primary emphasis on the human dimensions of economic issues. Nonetheless, most of the readings wrestle with the question of social costs and benefits, for topics as diverse as the assembly line, automotive design, and possible replacements for the car.

The more recent Lewis and Goldstein volume is a pioneering one in that it is the first to bring together scholarly research exploring the car's influence on the cultural mainstream. Thus, essays are included that analyze that influence on art, music, film, literature, and poetry. In addition, such social concerns as sex, the status of women and teenagers, and the symbolic dimensions of the automobile are treated. It is also one of the first collections to include fictional treatments of the motor car as well.

Popular histories continued to be published in the seventies and eighties, benefiting from the concurrent scholarly research, and evidencing much more concern with sociocultural questions than their predecessors. Among the more notable works have been Raymond Flower and Michael W. Jones's *100 Years on the Road: A Social History of the Car,* which delivers what it promises, although with a heavily European focus; Leon Mandel's *Driven: The American Four-Wheeled Love Affair,* in which the author applies his version of social psychology to analyze what he sees as the multivariate impact of the car; Julian Pettifer and Nigel Turner's *Automania: Man and the Motor Car,* which provides an international overview of the auto's influence on several areas usually ignored in such volumes, e.g., courtship, art, music, movies, death, and Third World nations; and Stephen W. Sears's *The American Heritage History of the Automobile in America.* The most recent contribution to this area is the work of two British psychologists, Peter Marsh and Peter Collett. Entitled *Driving Passion: The Psychology of the Car,* it is one of the first book-length works to concentrate on the psychological satisfactions associated with car ownership and driving.

Although Americans have not always acknowledged it, the social impact of the automobile as a vehicle is inseparable from the roads it traverses. The first scholarly road conference held after World War II recognized this fact, as can be seen throughout its published proceedings, *Highways in Our National Life: A Symposium,* edited by Jean Labatut and Wheaton, J. Lane. Lewis Mumford in the *The Highway and the City* and John B. Rae in *The Road and the Car in American Life* start from the same premise but reach very different conclusions regarding the benefits/drawbacks of that pairing.

More recently, there has been renewed interest in this topic. Phil Patton's *Open Road: A Celebration of the American Highway* is a historical overview of the entire subject, with considerable attention to how the American lifestyle was changed by the growth of the interstate system. In a more popular vein, but useful nonetheless, is *Automerica: A Trip down U.S. Highways from World War II to the Future,* by the Ant Farm design group.

The evolution of the roadside area adjacent to one major highway is portrayed and analyzed by George R. Stewart in *U.S. 40: Cross Section of the United States of America,* Thomas R. Vale and Geraldine R. Vale in *U.S. 40 Today: Thirty Years of Landscape Change in America,* and Thomas J. Schlereth's *U.S. 40: A Roadscape of the American Experience.* All three books treat the historic National Road (now U.S. 40) and its adjacent landscape and buildings as an "outdoor museum" whose study provides information regarding the changing nature of American society.

Two more special accounts offer further insight into the culture of the road. *Blue Highways: A Journey into America,* by William L. H. Moon, offers vignettes of people who live and/or work along the two-lane-or-less "minor" highways that are usually portrayed in blue on road maps. In *L.A. Freeway: An Appreciative Essay,* David Brodsly explores the very nature of the freeway system and, as the *Los Angeles Times* notes, sees it "as the source of feelings, experiences and unique life patterns for the urban driver."[3]

Literary and Artistic Expression

The increased scholarly interest in the automobile has led to a number of books that treat specific cultural topics within the broader context of the car's impact on American life. One of these topics is the interaction between the car and literary and artistic expression. Preeminent in regard to the former is Cynthia Golomb Dettelbach's *In the Driver's Seat: The Automobile in American Literature and Popular Culture,* which analyzes the literary use to which many authors have put automobiles, especially in terms of formulating the American Dream. Another good analytical work, somewhat broader in focus, is Priscilla Lee Denby's doctoral dissertation, "The Self Discovered: The Car in American Folklore and Literature."

In *Man and Motor: The Twentieth Century Love Affair,* editor Derek Jewell collects and reprints myriad writings about the automobile from authors as distant in time as Rudyard Kipling and as contemporary as Henry Miller. In the same vein, but more restrictive in terms of the mode of expression, is *American Classic: Car Poems for Collectors,* edited by Mary Swope and Walter H. Kerr, which includes pieces by such well-known writers as e.e. cummings, Joyce Carol Oates, and Carl Sandburg. Finally, Henry Ford and the cars he made were so important that they evoked short stories and essays by literary figures of the day. One interesting collection, entitled *The Best of Ford,* compiled and edited by Mary Moline, includes pieces by such authors as John Dos Passos, Walter Lippmann, H. L. Mencken, and Will Rogers.

Finally, mention should be made of some highly praised novels that include motoring motifs. They include William Faulkner's *The Reivers,* F. Scott Fitzgerald's *The Great Gatsby,* Kenneth Grahame's *The Wind in the Willows,* Jack Kerouac's *On the Road,* Sinclair Lewis's *Babbit* and *Main Street,* Robert M. Pirsig's *Zen and the Art of Motorcycle Maintenance,* and John Steinbeck's *The Grapes of Wrath,* among others.

Although their designation as literature is questionable, advertisements do form a part of, and are influenced by, our culture, frequently telling us as much about the motoring public of yesteryear as the cars themselves. In this regard, *Auto Ads,* by Jane and Michael Stern, is clearly the best work. One hundred significant ads, spanning the history of the automobile, are reproduced and analyzed. Also good, but with a decidedly European emphasis, is Peter Roberts's *Any Colour So Long as It's Black: The First Fifty Years of Automobile Advertising.* Less satisfying from a scholarly perspective, but more extensive from the standpoint of reproducing specific American ads, are Q. David Bowers's *Early American Car Advertisements* and the more recent *The American Automobile: Advertising from the Antique and Classic Eras,* by Yasutoshi Ikuta. Finally, for a delightful look at a unique aspect of American advertising culture, see Frank J. Rowsome, Jr.'s *The Verse by the Side of the Road: The Story of the Burma-Shave Signs,* those innovative roadside serial placards.

Mark Williams's *Road Movies: The Complete Guide to Cinema on Wheels* deals with the use to which automobiles have been put in popular films, as does Raymond Lee's *Fit for the Chase: Cars and the Movies.* The former contains an interesting introductory essay and good descriptions of films from the past four decades. The latter collates a large number of movie stills that contain automobiles in them, but offers little discussion of the car's function in the scene in which it is pictured. Don Graham's *Cowboys and Cadillacs: How Hollywood Looks at Texas* is an interesting account of the relationship between two cultural icons that have very much affected American society. George Barris, in *Cars of the Stars,* provides captioned photographs of the specialized vehicles that have been built for particular Hollywood celebrities, as does Floyd Clymer in the earlier *Cars of the Stars and Movie Memories.* Similarly, John A. Conde's *Cars with Personalities* provides photographs and captions of 573 celebrities with their cars, from 1896 to 1982.

The Automobile and American Culture, edited by David L. Lewis and Laurence Goldstein, contains two essays pertinent to this discussion. In "A Runaway Match: The Automobile and Film, 1900–1920," Julian Smith links the development of these two inventions, claiming a symbiotic relationship for the period under study. "Cars and Films in American Culture, 1929–1959," by Kenneth Hey, carries the story forward for another generation. Both essays begin to define and answer the scholarly questions which are essentially missing from the previously mentioned books.

The automobile also has influenced the fine and applied arts. In regard to the former, the best work is *Automobile and Culture,* by Gerald Silk et al., an oversized book which combines fine color and black-and-white illustrations with a superior text. The latter provides a historical survey of the image of the car in art from Leonardo da Vinci to the present, and the factors that combine to influence automotive design. An earlier, less ambitious attempt at somewhat the same task was D. B. Tubbs's *Art and the Automobile,* which examines posters, paintings, sculpture, mascots, and car styling in general.

In a more popular vein, Sally Henderson and Robert Landau, in *Billboard Art,* do a good job of presenting and analyzing the history of outdoor advertising art and the societal values it represents. Warren H. Anderson's *Vanishing Roadside America* also concentrates on outdoor advertising, using fine color drawings by the author, rather than photographs, for illustrations to evoke nostalgia for the roadside of the 1930s and 1940s.

Architecture is well treated in a scholarly manner by Chester H. Liebs in *Main Street to Miracle Mile: American Roadside Architecture,* Karal Ann Marling in *The Colossus of Roads: Myth and Symbol Along the American Highway,* and in a more specific way in *"Fill'er Up": An Architectural History of America's Gas Stations* by Daniel I. Vieyra. More in the nature of photographic essays exploring commercial archeology are *The Well-Built Elephant and Other Roadside Attractions: A Tribute to American Eccentricity* by J. J. C. Andrews; *Souvenirs from the Roadside West* by Richard Ansaldi; *Highway as Habitat* by Ulrich Keller, with its emphasis on the road culture in the forties and fifties; *The End of the Road: Vanishing Highway Architecture in America* by John Margolies, which concentrates on motels, gas stations, and "enchanted villages"; and Samuel R. Ogden's *America the Vanishing: Road Life and the Price of Progress.*

Clearly related to artistic expression is the design and styling of automobiles themselves. A good survey of this topic through the mid-seventies is Paul C. Wilson's *Chrome Dreams: Automobile Styling Since 1893,* which includes sections regarding the influence of popular tastes on automotive design. A brief, popular overview of the same subject is available in *Fifty Years of American Automotive Design, 1930–1980,* by Dick Nesbitt, which attempts to explain the societal influences that inspired these changes. A more specialized work, *Fins and Chrome* by E. John DeWaard, focuses on American automobiles of the fifties. What distinguishes this picture book from others is the attention the author pays to the interaction between vehicular design and human personality traits, particularly in terms of customizing.

The individualized "hot rod" or "custom car" that reached its apogee in the fifties has never completely disappeared. One of the earliest books on this phenomenon is Eugene Jaderquist and Griffith Borgeson's *Best Hot Rods*. Done in the early 1950s, it is useful today because it gives reference data about the beginning of hot-rodding. Such practices are entertainingly described in Tom Wolfe's *The Kandy-Kolored Tangerine-Flake Streamline Baby*, which scrutinizes the fad of automobile customizing and hot-rod building on the West Coast. A more traditional approach to the subject is *Showtime: The Story of the International Championship Auto Shows and the Hot Rod/Custom Car World: A Twenty-Year History*, by Michael Sheridan and Sam Bushala, which provides both a factual catalog and an appreciation of these one-of-a-kind cars.

The Family and the Community

Of all the cultural dimensions of American life that the motorcar has influenced, one of the more neglected has been the study of its effects on family life and the community. It is from such case studies that we might learn how the motorcar has influenced schooling and other educational services, religious life, health care, and law and order. There are a few pioneering books in this regard, such as Reynold M. Wik's *Henry Ford and Grass-roots America*, a study of the rural response to Ford's life and work. Similar in subject to the Wik volume is Michael L. Berger's *The Devil Wagon in God's Country: The Automobile and Social Change in Rural America, 1893–1929*, which is one of the few purely social histories of the automobile, with chapters on the farm family, the rural community, leisure, religion, education, and health and the environment. The impact of the car on small-town life is analyzed by Norman T. Moline in *Mobility and the Small Town, 1900–1930*, a study of Oregon, Illinois. A somewhat different perspective is provided by John A. Jakle in *The American Small Town: Twentieth-Century Place Images*, which attempts to show how the transition from dependency on rail to motor transportation changed the stereotypic view of the small town as a place type.

Unfortunately, similar specialized studies for suburban America have yet to be written, a particularly ironic situation given the debt that such localities owe to the automobile for their existence. One possible explanation for this state of affairs is that the development of suburbia, particularly in the years following World War II, and that of the car are inseparably intertwined.

Thus, it could be argued that a separate book on the topic is probably unnecessary, since every study of suburbia must include a discussion of the automobile as one of the central themes. Two recent books do this in a prominent way. Kenneth T. Jackson's *Crabgrass Frontier: The Suburbanization of the United States,* easily the best study to date, does an excellent job of analyzing how the car, and other means of transportation, have influenced the development of residential areas. In *Contemporary Suburban America,* Peter O. Muller analyzes the socioeconomic functioning of such areas, and concludes that the auto-centered suburb is unlikely to change in the foreseeable future. Finally, with its regional focus, Ashleigh E. Brilliant's doctoral dissertation, "Social Effects of the Automobile in Southern California During the Twenties," offers valuable insights into how the car changed family life and community institutions in both suburbia and Los Angeles.

Urban America has been somewhat better served, in that we have some studies that exclusively devote themselves to the multiple influences of the car. From a historical vantage point there are Howard L. Preston's *Automobile Age Atlanta: The Making of a Southern Metropolis, 1900–1935* and Joel A. Tarr's lengthy essay *Transportation Innovation and Changing Spatial Patterns in Pittsburgh, 1850–1934.* Additional investigations of this type are needed, especially since national studies tend to blur distinctions among geographic regions, socioeconomic classes, ethnic and religious groups, etc. A more general treatment of the car's early influence on urban development is "American Cities and the Coming of the Automobile, 1870–1910," a doctoral dissertation by Clay McShane.

While most of the books mentioned in the previous three paragraphs pay some attention to the automobile's impact on family life, there has been surprisingly little scholarly analysis of how the car has specifically influenced the lives of women. Typical of what was available until recently were chapters like "Milady at the Wheel," in M. M. Musselman's 1950 popular history, *Get a Horse!: The Story of the Automobile in America;* essays such as Charles L. Sanford's " 'Woman's Place' in American Car Culture," which is reprinted in the Lewis and Goldstein collection cited earlier; and personal accounts of feminine motor exploits, e.g., Alice Huyler Ramsey's *Veil, Duster, and Tire Iron.* (In 1909, Ms. Ramsey became the first woman successfully to complete a transcontinental motor trip.)

Fortunately, 1987 saw the completion of two doctoral dissertations in this area: Beth Kraig's "Woman at the Wheel: A History of Women and the Automobile in America," and Virginia J. Scharff's "Reinventing the Wheel: American Women and the Automobile, 1910–1930." It is hoped that these works will soon emerge in book form and spark further scholarly interest in a neglected aspect of automotive history.

There are a number of scholarly studies that attempt to assess the influence of the automobile on the nature and availability of urban transportation, and the impact of that, in turn, on human behavior. Some of the earliest work in this regard was done by Lewis Mumford, one of America's most respected urban historians. Two of his books, *The City in History: Its Origins, Its Transformations, and Its Prospects* and *The Highway and the City*, judge the automobile to be a devastatingly negative force on America's cities. More recently, K. H. Schaeffer and Elliott Sclar, in *Access for All: Transportation and Urban Growth*, have maintained that the quality of human life depends on the amount of access we have to one another, and that the automobile has reached its limits in terms of enhancing such access.

The problem of balancing the advantages and disadvantages of the private automobile vis-à-vis the various forms of mass transit is an ongoing one. Its origins lie in governmental policies and regulations promulgated in the first third of this century, and this public policy issue has been the basis of several important works: Paul Barrett's *The Automobile and Urban Transit: The Formation of Public Policy in Chicago, 1900–1930*; Scott L. Bottles's *Los Angeles and the Automobile: The Making of the Modern City*; Mark S. Foster's *From Streetcar to Superhighway: American City Planners and Urban Transportation, 1900–1940*; David J. St. Clair's *The Motorization of American Cities*; Ronald A. Buel's *Dead End: The Automobile in Mass Transportation*; and John R. Meyer and Jose A. Gomez-Ibanez's *Autos, Transit, and Cities*, a comprehensive Twentieth Century Fund Report that explores the interaction between transportation and the quality of urban life. Finally, Helen Leavitt's *Superhighway—Superhoax*, a polemical attack on the motivations and actions of highway supporters, still makes interesting reading nearly two decades after its publication.

Recreation and Leisure

Almost from the beginning, Americans recognized the enormous potential of the car as a vehicle for recreational purposes. Easily the best introduction to this topic is *Americans on the Road: From Autocamp to Motel, 1910–1945* by Warren J. Belasco. The author does an excellent job of linking the emergence of the motel business with such social issues as class conflict, the growth of the consumer ethic, and the weakening of family ties. A broader perspective is offered by John A. Jakle in his *The Tourist: Travel in Twentieth-Century North America*, which contains four chapters devoted exclusively to the automobile. Also useful in this regard is John Baeder's *Gas, Food, and Lodging*, which uses postcards as illustrations to portray the changing face of roadside culture (including both people and places) that travelers encountered between 1918 and 1939. In a humorous vein, Jack Barth et al. have written *Roadside America*, which describes some of the more bizarre tourist attractions that have appeared alongside our nation's highways. (See the chapter on architecture above for additional references in this regard.)

Americans interested in motorized travel soon realized the advantages that might accrue from being able to bring something akin to their house along with them. Such thinking led to the commercial development of the car trailer, the mobile home, and the van. Two good introductions to the multiple aspects of this phenomenon are provided by Margaret J. Drury's *Mobile Homes: The Unrecognized Revolution in American Housing* and Michael A. Rockland's *Homes on Wheels. Airstream,* by Robert Landau and James Phillippi, is an uncritical description of the history and way of life associated with one of the most famous of these vehicles.

The car culture also has spawned a host of leisure-time hobbies that require little or no travel for participation. While probably the best known one is the restoration of antique cars, there are others such as the collection of automotive toys, mascots, ornaments, license plates, and even automotive art. A fine overview of the field can be found in *Automobile Quarterly's Complete Handbook of Automobile Hobbies,* edited by Beverly Rae Kimes. Also good are Jack Martells's *Antique Automobile Collectibles* and, with a more international flavor, Michael Worthington-Williams's *Automobilia: A Guided Tour for Collectors.*

In regard to automotive toys, the most recent, and probably definitive, work is Lillian Gottschalk's *American Toy Cars and Trucks, 1894–1942.* In addition to physically describing 475 different items—almost all American-made, Gottschalk does an excellent job of linking their histories to those of the real cars they represent. The text also is accompanied by superior photographic work. Another good work, covering a later period in which Japanese and German toy makers excelled to an extent unequalled since, is Dale Kelley's *Collecting the Tin Toy Car, 1950–1970.* Also worth examining is *The World of Model Cars,* edited by Vic Smeed, which discusses not only collecting and building such vehicles, but also the racing of radio-controlled models. The latter is covered in more detail in Robert Schleicher's *Model Car Racing.*

Not everyone into collecting model cars purchases the work of others. There is another group of hobbyists who enjoy making their own. Some insight into this form of leisure can be gained by perusing *The Complete Book of Model Car Building* by Dennis Doty, *Scratchbuilding Model Cars* by Saul Santos, and *The Complete Car Modeller* by Gerald A. Wingrove.

In addition to full-size and model cars, many Americans have chosen to collect ornamental parts of automobiles. Representative of the literature in this regard are William C. Williams's *Motoring Mascots of the World,* a study of hood ornaments; Keith Marvin's *License Plates of the World*; Scott Anderson's *Check the Oil: Gas Station Collectibles with Prices*; and Jim Evans's *Collectors Guide to Automotive Literature,* the latter defined as sales brochures, stock certificates, and other ephemera.

Racing

So much has been written on motor racing, some of it excellent and unfortunately some of it of dubious quality, that it is difficult to know where to begin research on the topic. The intent of this section is to send those interested to the books that will yield the most information on motor racing as a sport, as opposed to the drivers or their machines.

A comprehensive survey of the American scene, from its beginning in 1895 to 1973, can be found in Albert R. Bochroch's *American Automobile Racing*. For more in-depth examinations of two particular types of racing, see Lyle K. Engel's *Road Racing in America* and his *Stock Car Racing U.S.A.* The broader world of the latter is portrayed in *Grand National Stock Car Racing: The Other Side of the Fence* by W. Michael Lovern and Bob Jones, Jr., and *Fast as White Lightning: The Story of Stock Car Racing* by Kim Chapin, both of which attempt to capture the emotions of those involved in such racing, including drivers, mechanics, owners, sponsors, families, and fans.

The flavor of contemporary racing on dirt tracks is presented in John Sawyer's *The Dusty Heroes*. *Grand Prix: The Cars, the Drivers, the Circuits* by David Hodges et al. provides a contemporary history of this type of racing and American participation in it.

There are a number of books which focus on memorable automobile races. Many of the latter have had significant impact on American sports culture. *Great Auto Races,* a handsome volume written and lavishly illustrated by Peter Helck, centers on the early years of competition. Broader in coverage are *Great Moments in Speed* by Ross Olney, *The Shell Book of Epic Motor Races* by Peter Roberts, and *Great Moments in Auto Racing* by Irwin Stambler.

In a more specifically historical vein, there is Albert Bochroch's *Americans at LeMans: An Illustrated History of the Twenty-four Hour Race from 1923 to 1975,* and the same author's *Trans-Am Racing, 1966–1985: Detroit's Battle for Pony Car Supremacy*; Peter Helck's *The Checkered Flag,* which reviews early racing up to 1916; Fred J. Wagner's *The Saga of the Roaring Road: A Story of Early Auto Racing in America; Dirt Tracks to Glory: The Early Days of Stock Car Racing as Told by the Participants* by Sylvia Wilkinson; and *The Illustrated History of Sprint Car Racing, 1896–1942* and *The Mighty Midgets,* which traces developments in that area from 1933 to 1976, both by Jack C. Fox.

The annual Indianapolis 500, often dubbed the greatest spectacle in racing, has been the subject of uncounted articles as well as hundreds of books. In the latter category, among the more useful are *500 Miles to Go: The Story of the Indianapolis Speedway* by Al Bloemker; *Indy 500: More than a Race* by Tom Carnegie, which vividly describes the month-long preparations for the race and offers behind-the-scenes vignettes; *The Indianapolis 500: A Complete Pictorial History* by John and Barbara Devaney, a remarkably complete and well-illustrated study; and Brock W. Yates's *The Indianapolis 500: The Story of the Motor Speedway*. Finally, *The Indy 500: An American Institution Under Fire,* by Ron Dorson, describes the ill-fated 1973 race and its aftermath.

Four accounts of contemporary American racing by "outsiders" are worth the attention of those interested in an in-depth look at the sport. They are *Fast Lane Summer: North American Road Racing,* by Leon Mandel; *Fast Guys, Rich Guys and Idiots: A Racing Odyssey on the Border of Obsession,* by Sam Moses; *The Stainless Steel Carrot,* by Sylvia Wilkinson; and *Sunday Driver,* by Brock Yates. The Mandel volume offers some fine glimpses of what day-to-day life is like for those involved in road racing. Moses, the motorsports writer for *Sports Illustrated,* finds himself caught up, both physically and emotionally, in the world of professional motor racing as a result of a "typical" assignment and attempts to explain why. Wilkinson's book follows the ups and downs of a professional driver during an entire season. Automotive journalist Yates decided that in order to write well about racing he needed the actual experience on the track, and *Sunday Driver* chronicles his year of racing in the Trans Am series. Observations similar to those found in these books, but from a very different perspective, are provided in *Race Drivers' Wives: Twenty-four Women Talk About Their Lives,* by Jean and John Berry.

The types of motor racing mentioned above are spectator sports, run on tracks or marked road courses. However, one type of competition began on the streets, still remains there to some extent, and is largely participatory in nature—drag racing. A fair overview of this subject is provided in *Petersen's History of Drag Racing* by Dave Wallace, which chronicles the development of this sport over thirty years. *Street Was Fun in '51,* by Albert Drake, helps explain the factors that converged at that historical period to make drag racing so popular. These two works and others provide a non-scholarly background for the enthusiast. We still lack a serious sociological study of the phenomenon of drag racing.

Finally, some mention should be made of the spectacular increase in the use of off-road vehicles, the so-called RVs, for recreational purposes. They have evolved from the surplus World War II jeep to become a major class of vehicles unto themselves, with models sold by all the major car manufacturers. Researchers interested in this topic should begin by consulting Mergen's *Recreational Vehicles and Travel: A Resource Guide.*

Socioeconomic Problems

Despite the generally positive attitude shown by Americans toward the automobile, both the number and variety of critical appraisals have been increasing in recent years. One of the first books to view motorcars as less than desirable was John Keats's 1958 *The Insolent Chariots.* Aimed at a general audience, Keats's book provides a stinging indictment of the cars and management of the Detroit automotive industry. He also discusses that industry's failure to hear and heed the voice of the public in terms of production and safety. In a more recent and scholarly work, *The Car Culture,* James J. Flink turns away from his previously positive view of the automobile to attack the nature of the car industry and what it has done to American society and values. Although Flink's perspective is, by his own admission, a partisan one, this still is an important work of social history from one of our premier automotive historians.

Most criticism, however, has been of a more specific kind. One of the most controversial books in this regard was written by consumer advocate Ralph Nader in 1965. *Unsafe at Any Speed: The Designed-In Dangers of the American Automobile* accused General Motors of callous negligence in the design and manufacture of the rear-engine Corvair automobile, and eventually led to GM's abandonment of that model.

Actually, the question of safety in the car and on the road has been an ongoing one since the early days of motoring, in both mechanical and human terms. One of the pioneering scholarly works in this regard was *Passenger Car Design and Highway Safety,* the proceedings of a 1961 conference on research. Similar in concept to Nader's book and appearing the same year was *Safety Last: An Indictment of the Automobile Industry,* by Jeffrey O'Connell and Arthur Myers. For a more historical view, see Joel W. Eastman's *Styling vs. Safety: The American Automobile Industry and the Development of Automotive Safety, 1900–1966.* Finally, insight into what highway carnage meant in one era of American history is provided in Anedith J. B. Nash's doctoral dissertation entitled "Death on the Highway: The Automobile Wreck in American Culture, 1920–1940."

Another major socioeconomic problem associated with the automobile is that of pollution, with its air, solid waste, and visual dimensions. In the early and mid-seventies, there appeared a number of excellent, broadly based studies on this topic, including John Robinson's *Highways and Our Environment;* Frank P. Grad et al., *The Automobile and the Regulation of Its Impact on the Environment;* and, for a worldwide view, *The Automobile and the Environment: An International Perspective,* prepared by the Organisation for Economic Co-operation and Development and edited by Ralph Gakenheimer. More specifically, in *Yellowstone: A Wilderness Besieged,* Richard A. Bartlett assigns to the automobile a fair share of the blame for the ecological problems in what is probably our best-known national park.

These socioeconomic problems, in concert with threats to our gasoline supply, spiraling car prices, and increased sales of Japanese automobiles in the United States, led to a series of books in the 1970s challenging the place of the automobile in American society. For instance, Kenneth R. Schneider, in *Autokind vs. Mankind: An Analysis of Tyranny, a Proposal for Rebellion, a Plan for Reconstruction,* boldly asserts his thesis, which "challenges the automobile for what it does to life in the cities and the stranglehold it has on society," and concludes that the automobile must be removed from society. Automobile journalist John Jerome reaches the same conclusion in *The Death of the Automobile: The Fatal Effect of the Golden Era, 1955–1970.* Emma Rothschild attacks the corporate influence on consumers and auto workers in a collection of essays entitled *Paradise Lost: The Decline of the Auto-Industrial Age,* which also foresees the time when the automobile will be gone, replaced by a number of viable alternatives. Finally, in *Beyond the Automobile: Reshaping the Transportation Environment,* Tabor R. Stone offers a plan for a transportation system that would obviate the need for most motorcars.

During this period, the two positive voices were John B. Rae and B. Bruce-Biggs. Rae continued to defend both the automotive industry and the car's influence on American society in all his writing, but most notably in *The Road and the Car in American Life.* Bruce-Biggs's *The War Against the Automobile* is a direct counterattack against the anti-automobile forces, even including Ralph Nader.

NOTES

1. George E. Mowry, *The Urban Nation, 1920–1960,* vol. 6 of *The Making of America,* ed. David Donald, 6 vols. (New York: Hill and Wang, 1965–68), p. 17.

2. Lewis Mumford, *The Highway and the City* (New York: Harcourt, Brace and World, 1963), p. 235.

3. Edgardo Contini, "Passionate Ode to the Freeway," review of *L.A. Freeway: An Appreciative Essay* by David Brodsly, *Los Angeles Times,* January 14, 1982, p. 14.

BIBLIOGRAPHY

Books and Articles

Anderson, Rudolph E. *The Story of the American Automobile: Highlights and Sidelights.* Washington, D.C.: Public Affairs Press, 1950.

Anderson, Scott. *Check the Oil: Gas Station Collectibles with Prices.* Lombard, Ill.: Wallace-Homestead, 1987.

Anderson, Warren H. *Vanishing Roadside America.* Tucson: University of Arizona Press, 1981.

Andrews, J. J. C. *The Well-Built Elephant and Other Roadside Attractions: A Tribute to American Eccentricity.* New York: Congdon and Weed, 1984.

Ansaldi, Richard. *Souvenirs from the Roadside West.* New York: Harmony Books, 1978.

Ant Farm [Lord, Chip]. *Automerica: A Trip down U.S. Highways from World War II to the Future.* New York: E. P. Dutton, 1976.

The Automotive History Collection of the Detroit Public Library: A Simplified Guide to Its Holdings. 2 vols. Boston: G. K. Hall, 1966.

Baeder, John. *Gas, Food, and Lodging.* New York: Abbeville Press, 1982.

Barrett, Paul. *The Automobile and Urban Transit: The Formation of Public Policy in Chicago, 1900–1930.* Philadelphia: Temple University Press, 1983.

Barris, George. *Cars of the Stars.* Middle Village, N.Y.: Jonathan David, 1974.

Barth, Jack, et al. *Roadside America.* New York: Simon and Schuster, 1986.

Bartlett, Richard A. *Yellowstone: A Wilderness Besieged.* Tucson: University of Arizona Press, 1985.

Belasco, Warren J. *Americans on the Road: From Autocamp to Motel, 1910–1945*. Cambridge, Mass.: MIT Press, 1979.

Berger, Michael L. *The Automobile: A Reference Guide*. Westport, Conn.: Greenwood Press, forthcoming.

———. *The Devil Wagon in God's Country: The Automobile and Social Change in Rural America, 1893–1929*. Hamden, Conn.: Archon Books, 1979.

Berry, Jean, and John Berry. *Race Drivers' Wives: Twenty-four Women Talk About Their Lives*. Hazel Crest, Ill.: Berry Publishing, 1982.

Bliss, Carey S. *Autos Across America: A Biography of Transcontinental Automobile Travel, 1903–1940*. Los Angeles: Dawson's Book Shop, 1972.

Bloemker, Al. *500 Miles to Go: The Story of the Indianapolis Speedway*. New York: Coward-McCann, 1961.

Bochroch, Albert R. *American Automobile Racing*. New York: Viking, 1974.

———. *Americans at LeMans: An Illustrated History of the Twenty-four Hour Race from 1923 to 1975*. Tucson: Aztex, 1976.

———. *Trans-Am Racing, 1966–1985: Detroit's Battle for Pony Car Supremacy*. Osceola, Wis.: Motorbooks International, 1986.

Bottles, Scott L. *Los Angeles and the Automobile: The Making of the Modern City*. Berkeley: University of California Press, 1987.

Bowers, Q. David, ed. *Early American Car Advertisements*. New York: Crown, 1966.

Brilliant, Ashleigh E. "Social Effects of the Automobile in Southern California During the Twenties." Ph.D. dissertation, University of California, Berkeley, 1964.

Brodsly, David. *L.A. Freeway: An Appreciative Essay*. Berkeley: University of California Press, 1981.

Bruce-Biggs, B. *The War Against the Automobile*. New York: E. P. Dutton, 1977.

Buel, Ronald A. *Dead End: The Automobile in Mass Transportation*. Englewood Cliffs, N.J.: Prentice-Hall, 1972.

Carnegie, Tom. *Indy 500: More than a Race*. New York: McGraw-Hill, 1986.

Chapin, Kim. *Fast as White Lightning: The Story of Stock Car Racing*. New York: Dial Press, 1981.

Cleveland, Reginald M., and S. T. Williamson. *The Road Is Yours: The Story of the Automobile and the Men Behind It*. New York: Greystone Press, 1951.

Clymer, Floyd. *Cars of the Stars and Movie Memories*. Los Angeles: Floyd Clymer, 1954.

Cohn, David L. *Combustion on Wheels: An Informal History of the Automobile Age*. Boston: Houghton Mifflin, 1944.

Conde, John. *Cars with Personalities*. Keego Harbor, Mich.: Arnold Porter, 1982.

Cutcliffe, Stephen H., et al. *Technology and Values in American Civilization: A Guide to Information Sources*. Detroit: Gale Research, 1980.

Denby, Priscilla Lee. "The Self Discovered: The Car in American Folklore and Literature." Ph.D. dissertation, Indiana University, 1981.

Dettelbach, Cynthia Golomb. *In the Driver's Seat: The Automobile in American Literature and Popular Culture*. Westport, Conn.: Greenwood Press, 1976.

Devaney, John, and Barbara Devaney. *The Indianapolis 500: A Complete Pictorial History*. Chicago: Rand McNally, 1976.

DeWaard, E. John. *Fins and Chrome*. Greenwich, Conn.: Crescent Books, 1982.

Donovan, Frank. *Wheels for a Nation*. New York: Crowell, 1965.

Dorson, Ron. *The Indy 500: An American Institution Under Fire*. Newport Beach, Calif.: Bond/Parkhurst Books, 1974.

Doty, Dennis. *The Complete Book of Model Car Building*. Blue Ridge Summit, Pa.: TAB Books, 1981.

Drake, Albert. *Street Was Fun in '51*. Okemos, Mich.: Flat Out Press, 1982.

Drury, Margaret J. *Mobile Homes: The Unrecognized Revolution in American Housing*. New York: Praeger, 1972.

Eastman, Joel W. *Styling vs. Safety: The American Automobile Industry and the Development of Automotive Safety, 1900–1966*. Lanham, Md.: University Press of America, 1984.

Ebershoff-Coles, Susan, and Charla A. Leibenguth. *Motorsports: A Guide to Information Sources*. Detroit: Gale Research, 1979.

Engel, Lyle K. *Road Racing in America*. New York: Dodd, Mead, 1971.

———. *Stock Car Racing U.S.A.* New York: Dodd, Mead, 1973.

Evans, Jimmie R.H. *Collectors Guide to Automotive Literature*. Sioux City, Iowa: Larsen's Printing, n.d.

Faulkner, William. *The Reivers*. New York: Random House, 1962.

Fitzgerald, F. Scott. *The Great Gatsby*. New York: Scribner's, 1925.

Flink, James J. *America Adopts the Automobile, 1895–1910*. Cambridge, Mass.: MIT Press, 1970.

———. *The Automobile Age*. Cambridge, Mass.: MIT Press, 1988.

———. *The Car Culture*. Cambridge, Mass.: MIT Press, 1975.

Flower, Raymond, and Michael W. Jones. *100 Years on the Road: A Social History of the Car*. New York: McGraw-Hill, 1981.

Foster, Mark S. *From Streetcar to Superhighway: American City Planners and Urban Transportation, 1900–1940*. Philadelphia: Temple University Press, 1981.

Fox, Jack C. *The Illustrated History of Sprint Car Racing, 1896–1942*. Speedway, Ind.: Carl Hungness, 1985.

———. *The Mighty Midgets: The Illustrated History of Midget Auto Racing*. Speedway, Ind.: Carl Hungness, 1985.

Gakenheimer, Ralph, ed. *The Automobile and the Environment: An International Perspective*. Cambridge, Mass.: MIT Press, 1978.

Glasscock, C. B. *The Gasoline Age: The Story of the Men Who Made It*. Indianapolis: Bobbs-Merrill, 1937.

Gottschalk, Lillian. *American Toy Cars and Trucks, 1894–1942*. New York: Abbeville Press, 1986.

Grad, Frank P., et al. *The Automobile and the Regulation of Its Impact on the Environment*. Norman: University of Oklahoma Press, 1975.

Graham, Don. *Cowboys and Cadillacs: How Hollywood Looks at Texas*. Austin: Texas Monthly Press, 1984.

Grahame, Kenneth. *The Wind in the Willows*. New York: Scribner's, 1933.

Helck, Peter. *The Checkered Flag*. New York: Scribner's, 1967.

———. *The Great Auto Races*. New York: Harry N. Abrams, 1975.

Henderson, Sally, and Robert Landau. *Billboard Art*. San Francisco: Chronicle Books, 1980.

Hill, Frank E. *The Automobile: How It Came, Grew, and Has Changed Our Lives*. New York: Dodd, Mead, 1967.

Hodges, David, et al. *Grand Prix: The Cars, the Drivers, the Circuits.* New York: St. Martin's Press, 1981.

Ikuta, Yasutoshi. *The American Automobile: Advertising from the Antique and Classic Eras.* San Francisco: Chronicle Books, 1988.

Jackson, Kenneth T. *Crabgrass Frontier: The Suburbanization of the United States.* New York: Oxford University Press, 1985.

Jaderquist, Eugene, and Griffith Borgeson. *Best Hot Rods.* New York: Arco, 1953.

Jakle, John A. *The American Small Town: Twentieth-Century Place Images.* Hamden, Conn.: Archon Books, 1982.

————. *The Tourist: Travel in Twentieth-Century North America.* Lincoln: University of Nebraska Press, 1985.

Jerome, John. *The Death of the Automobile: The Fatal Effect of the Golden Era, 1955– 1970.* New York: W. W. Norton, 1972.

Jewell, Derek, ed. *Man and Motor: The Twentieth Century Love Affair.* New York: Walker, 1967.

Keats, John. *The Insolent Chariots.* Philadelphia: J. B. Lippincott, 1958.

Keller, Ulrich. *Highway as Habitat: A Roy Stryker Documentation, 1943–1955.* Santa Barbara: University Art Museum, University of California, Santa Barbara, 1985.

Kelley, Dale. *Collecting the Tin Toy Car, 1950–1970.* West Chester, Pa.: Schiffer Publishing, 1984.

Kerouac, Jack. *On the Road.* New York: Viking Press, 1958.

Kimes, Beverly Rae, ed. *Automobile Quarterly's Complete Handbook of Automobile Hobbies.* Princeton, N.J.: Princeton Publishing, 1981.

Kraig, Beth. "Woman at the Wheel: A History of Women and the Automobile in America." Ph.D. dissertation, University of Washington, 1987.

Labatut, Jean, and Wheaton J. Lane, eds. *Highways in Our National Life: A Symposium.* Princeton, N.J.: Princeton University Press, 1950.

Landau, Robert J., and James M. Phillippi. *Airstream.* Salt Lake City: Gibbs M. Smith, 1984.

Leavitt, Helen. *Superhighway—Superhoax.* New York: Doubleday, 1970.

Lee, Raymond. *Fit for the Chase: Cars and the Movies.* Cranbury, N.J.: A. S. Barnes, 1969.

Lewis, David L., and Laurence Goldstein, eds. *The Automobile and American Culture.* Ann Arbor: University of Michigan Press, 1983.

Lewis, Sinclair. *Babbitt.* New York: Harcourt, Brace, 1922.

————. *Main Street.* New York: Harcourt, Brace, 1920.

Liebs, Chester H. *Main Street to Miracle Mile: American Roadside Architecture.* Boston: New York Graphic Society/Little, Brown, 1985.

Lovern, W. Michael, and Bob Jones, Jr. *Grand National Stock Car Racing: The Other Side of the Fence.* Richmond, Va.: Fast Co. Ltd. of Virginia, 1982.

Lynd, Robert S., and Helen M. Lynd. *Middletown: A Study in Contemporary American Culture.* New York: Harcourt, Brace, 1929.

————. *Middletown in Transition: A Study in Cultural Conflicts.* New York: Harcourt, Brace, 1937.

McShane, Clay. "American Cities and the Coming of the Automobile, 1870–1910." Ph.D. dissertation, University of Wisconsin, Madison, 1975.

Mandel, Leon. *Driven: The American Four-Wheeled Love Affair*. New York: Stein and Day, 1977.

——. *Fast Lane Summer: North American Road Racing*. Mill Valley, Calif.: Squarebooks, 1981.

Margolies, John. *The End of the Road: Vanishing Highway Architecture in America*. New York: Viking Press, 1981.

Marling, Karal Ann. *The Colossus of Roads: Myth and Symbol Along the American Highway*. Minneapolis: University of Minnesota Press, 1984.

Marsh, Peter, and Peter Collett. *Driving Passion: The Psychology of the Car*. Boston: Faber and Faber, 1987.

Martells, Jack. *Antique Automobile Collectibles*. Chicago: Contemporary Books, 1980.

Marvin, Keith. *License Plates of the World*. Troy, N.Y.: Privately printed, 1963.

Maxim, Hiram P. *Horseless Carriage Days*. New York: Harper and Brothers, 1937.

Mergen, Bernard. *Recreational Vehicles and Travel: A Resource Guide*. Westport, Conn.: Greenwood Press, 1985.

Meyer, John R., and Jose A. Gomez-Ibanez. *Autos, Transit, and Cities*. Cambridge, Mass.: Harvard University Press, 1981.

Moline, Mary, ed. *The Best of Ford*. Van Nuys, Calif.: Rumbleseat Press, 1973.

Moline, Norman T. *Mobility and the Small Town, 1900–1930: Transportation Change in Oregon, Illinois*. Research Paper No. 132. Chicago: Department of Geography, University of Chicago, 1971.

Moon, William L. H. *Blue Highways: A Journey into America*. Boston: Atlantic-Little, Brown, 1983.

Moses, Sam. *Fast Guys, Rich Guys and Idiots: A Racing Odyssey on the Border of Obsession*. Jamestown, R.I.: September Press, 1986.

Mueller, John H. "The Automobile: A Sociological Study." Ph.D. dissertation, University of Chicago, 1928.

Muller, Peter O. *Contemporary Suburban America*. Englewood Cliffs, N.J.: Prentice-Hall, 1981.

Mumford, Lewis. *The City in History: Its Origins, Its Transformations, and Its Prospects*. New York: Harcourt, Brace and World, 1961.

——. *The Highway and the City*. New York: Harcourt, Brace and World, 1963.

Musselman, M. M. *Get a Horse!: The Story of the Automobile in America*. Philadelphia: J. B. Lippincott, 1950.

Nader, Ralph. *Unsafe at Any Speed: The Designed-In Dangers of the American Automobile*. New York: Grossman, 1965.

Nash, Anedith J. B. "The Automobile Wreck in American Culture, 1920–1940." Ph.D. dissertation, University of Minnesota, 1983.

Nesbitt, Dick. *Fifty Years of American Automobile Design, 1930–1980*. New York: Beekman House, 1985.

O'Connell, Jeffrey, and Arthur Myers. *Safety Last: An Indictment of the Automobile Industry*. New York: Random House, 1965.

Ogden, Samuel R. *America the Vanishing: Road Life and the Price of Progress*. Brattleboro, Vt.: Stephen Greene Press, 1969.

Olney, Ross. *Great Moments in Speed*. Englewood Cliffs, N.J.: Prentice-Hall, 1970.

Passenger Car Design and Highway Safety: Proceedings of a Conference on Research. New York: Association for the Aid of Crippled Children and Consumers Union of U.S., 1962.

Patton, Phil. *Open Road: A Celebration of the American Highway*. New York: Simon and Schuster, 1986.

Pettifer, Julian, and Nigel Turner. *Automania: Man and the Motor Car*. Boston: Little, Brown, 1984.

Pirsig, Robert M. *Zen and the Art of Motorcycle Maintenance*. New York: William Morrow, 1974.

Preston, Howard L. *Automobile Age Atlanta: The Making of a Southern Metropolis, 1900–1935*. Athens: University of Georgia Press, 1979.

Rae, John B. *The American Automobile: A Brief History*. Chicago: University of Chicago Press, 1965.

———. *The Road and the Car in American Life*. Cambridge, Mass.: MIT Press, 1971.

Ramsey, Alice Huyler. *Veil, Duster, and Tire Iron*. Covina, Calif.: Castle Press, 1961.

Roberts, Peter. *Any Colour So Long as It's Black: The First Fifty Years of Automobile Advertising*. Devon, England: David and Charles, 1976.

———. *The Shell Book of Epic Motor Races*. New York: Arco, 1965.

Robinson, John. *Highways and Our Environment*. New York: McGraw-Hill, 1971.

Rockland, Michael A. *Homes on Wheels*. New Brunswick, N.J.: Rutgers University Press, 1980.

Rothschild, Emma. *Paradise Lost: The Decline of the Auto-Industrial Age*. New York: Random House, 1973.

Rowsome, Frank J., Jr. *The Verse by the Side of the Road: The Story of the Burma-Shave Signs*. Brattleboro, Vt.: Stephen Greene Press, 1965.

St. Clair, David J. *The Motorization of American Cities*. New York: Praeger, 1986.

Sanford, Charles L., ed. *The Automobile in American Life*. Troy, N.Y.: Center for the Study of Human Dimensions of Science and Technology, Rensselaer Polytechnic Institute, 1977.

Santos, Saul. *Scratchbuilding Model Cars*. Blue Ridge Summit, Pa.: TAB Books, 1982.

Sawyer, John. *The Dusty Heroes*. Speedway, Ind.: Carl Hungness, 1978.

Schaeffer, K. H., and Elliott Sclar. *Access for All: Transportation and Urban Growth*. New York: Columbia University Press, 1980.

Scharff, Virginia J. "Reinventing the Wheel: American Women and the Automobile, 1910–1930." Ph.D. dissertation, University of Arizona, 1987.

Schleicher, Robert H. *Model Car Racing* Radnor, Pa.: Chilton Book, 1979.

Schlereth, Thomas J. *U.S. 40: A Roadscape of the American Experience*. Indianapolis: Indiana Historical Society, 1985.

Schneider, Kenneth R. *Autokind vs. Mankind: An Analysis of Tyranny, a Proposal for Rebellion, a Plan for Reconstruction*. New York: W. W. Norton, 1971.

Sears, Stephen W. *The American Heritage History of the Automobile in America*. New York: American Heritage, 1977.

Sheridan, Michael, and Sam Bushala. *Showtime: The Story of the International Championship Auto Shows and the Hot Rod/Custom Car World: A Twenty-Year History*. Pontiac, Mich.: Promotional Displays, 1980.

Silk, Gerald, et al. *Automobile and Culture*. New York: Harry N. Abrams, 1984.

Smeed, Vic, ed. *The World of Model Cars*. Secaucus, N.J.: Chartwell Books, 1980.

Stambler, Irwin. *Great Moments in Auto Racing*. New York: Scholastic Book Services, 1968.

Steinbeck, John. *The Grapes of Wrath*. New York: Viking Press, 1939.

Stern, Jane, and Michael Stern. *Auto Ads*. New York: Random House, 1979.

Stewart, George R. *U.S. 40: Cross Section of the United States of America*. Boston: Houghton Mifflin, 1953.

Stone, Tabor R. *Beyond the Automobile: Reshaping the Transportation Environment*. Englewood Cliffs, N.J.: Prentice-Hall, 1971.

Swope, Mary, and Walter H. Kerr, eds. *American Classic: Car Poems for Collectors*. College Park, Md.: SCOP Publications, 1985.

Tarr, Joel A. *Transportation Innovation and Changing Spatial Patterns in Pittsburgh, 1850–1934*. Chicago: Public Works Historical Society, 1978.

Tubbs, D. B. *Art and the Automobile*. London: Lutterworth Press, 1978.

Vale, Thomas R., and Geraldine R. Vale. *U.S. 40 Today: Thirty Years of Landscape Change in America*. Madison: University of Wisconsin Press, 1983.

Vieyra, Daniel I. *"Fill'er Up": An Architectural History of America's Gas Stations*. New York: Collier Books, 1979.

Wagner, Fred J. *The Saga of the Roaring Road: A Story of Early Auto Racing in America*. Los Angeles: Floyd Clymer, 1949.

Wallace, A. *Automotive Literature Index, 1947–1976*. Toledo: Privately printed, 1981.

———. *Automotive Literature Index, 1977–1981*. Toledo: Privately printed, 1983.

———. *Automotive Literature Index, 1982–1986*. Toledo: Privately printed, 1988.

Wallace, Dave. *Petersen's History of Drag Racing*. Los Angeles: Petersen Publishing, 1981.

Wik, Reynold M. *Henry Ford and Grass-roots America*. Ann Arbor: University of Michigan Press, 1972.

Wilkinson, Sylvia. *Dirt Tracks to Glory: The Early Days of Stock Car Racing as Told by the Participants*. Chapel Hill, N.C.: Algonquin Books, 1983.

———. *The Stainless Steel Carrot: An Auto Racing Odyssey*. Boston: Houghton Mifflin, 1973.

Williams, Mark. *Road Movies: The Complete Guide to Cinema on Wheels*. New York: Proteus, 1982.

Williams, William C. *Motoring Mascots of the World*. Osceola, Wis.: Motorbooks International, 1979.

Wilson, Paul C. *Chrome Dreams: Automobile Styling Since 1893*. Radnor, Pa.: Chilton Book, 1976.

Wingrove, Gerald A. *The Complete Car Modeller*. New York: Crown, 1978.

Wolfe, Tom. *The Kandy-Kolored Tangerine-Flake Streamline Baby*. New York: Farrar, Straus and Giroux, 1965.

Worthington-Williams, Michael. *Automobilia: A Guided Tour for Collectors*. New York: Hastings House, 1979.

Yates, Brock W. *The Indianapolis 500: The Story of the Motor Speedway*. Rev. ed. New York: Harper and Row, 1961.

———. *Sunday Driver*. New York: Farrar, Straus and Giroux, 1972.

Periodicals

America: History and Life. Santa Barbara, Calif., 1964–

Antique Automobile. Hershey, Pa., 1935–.

Auto Index. Suffern, N.Y., 1973–.

Automobile Quarterly. Newport Beach, Calif., 1962-.
Bulb Horn. Brookline, Mass., 1939-.
Car and Driver. Ann Arbor, Mich., 1955-.
Dissertation Abstracts. Ann Arbor, Mich., 1938-.
Isis. Philadelphia, 1912-.
Recently Published Articles. Washington, D.C., 1976-.
Road and Track. Newport Beach, Calif., 1947-.
Technology and Culture. Chicago, 1959-.
Writings on American History. Washington, D.C., 1918-.

Business

RICHARD F. WELCH

When you awoke this morning, you probably stumbled from bed, showered, rummaged through your closet looking for adequate clothes, wandered into the kitchen, and, glancing at the clock, decided if time allowed for a hearty breakfast or just a cup of coffee.

All these activities, and almost every other activity in our society, is influenced by—and in many cases dictated by—business. What we do first in the morning, what we wear, what we listen to and/or read, even what we plan to eat for lunch is controlled in large part by the business at which we labor. Of all the cultural institutions that affect our lives, none seems to be as all-pervasive, as all-encompassing, as business.

Among its numerous accomplishments, business has established and controls our monetary system—our money is based on the needs of business to monitor the flow of goods. It has created our national obsession with time—our idea of "weekend" would not exist without the workweek; and our news organizations set their schedules to accommodate business's time clocks. Business dictates who is a productive member of society and who is not, and sets the standards for what the culture expects of a "productive" life-style. Business influences fashion, mass media, food consumption, science, and even religion.

Business has provided popular artists with fodder for a variety of artifacts—literature like Sinclair Lewis's Zenith Trilogy, plays like *How to Succeed in Business Without Really Trying* and *Stop the World, I Want to Get Off,* films like *Citizen Kane* and *Baby Boom,* songs like "Allentown" and "Sixteen

Tons," and even sports teams like the Pittsburgh Steelers and the Green Bay Packers.

Nowhere has the influence of business been as pronounced as on our political and governmental institutions. One only needs to examine the federal executive branch to see the influence of business. We have a Secretary of Labor, a Secretary of Transportation, a Securities and Exchange Commission, a Federal Communication Commission, a Federal Trade Commission, an Internal Revenue Service, and countless other agencies—all directed at monitoring and controlling business.

In politics, we have reached an age when political divisions are influenced less by social, religious, or regional differences than by the type of work one does. Obviously, this political concept is not new. What is new is that the class structure created by business is not defined by economics but by life-style. This has reached its fulfillment in the young, upwardly mobile individuals who have flourished in the high-pressure worlds of finance, marketing, and hi-tech industry. These Yuppies are not "capitalists" in a traditional Marxian sense of the word. Where traditional capitalists designed transgenerational empires, the new capitalists create businesses that are nothing more than commodities to be sold as soon as the price is right. This "get rich now" atmosphere prevalent in the business world has carried over into "Yuppie" politics. This life-style revolution has created a politically conservative, but dishearteningly disinterested, pool of future business leaders who look to political leaders equally attuned to the here-and-now.

Trying to focus on the concept "business" clearly and concisely has been an endeavor that has taxed many historians for many centuries. Samuel Johnson's 1755 *A Dictionary of the English Language,* for instance, gives nine definitions for business—from "employment; multiplicity of affairs" to "to do one's business. To kill, destroy or ruin him." By the time we arrive at the modern *Oxford English Dictionary,* we find several pages devoted to "business."

There are four ways the popular culture researcher can view business—as a standardizing mechanism for society, as a formal context for personal interaction, as a cultural institution, and as a ritual. These last two have gained prominence in the last four decades, when "doing business" has come to mean more than to buy and sell commodities; now it stands for a pattern of living and a cultural institution. Each view has its own lexicon and direction. There is, fortunately, a wealth of documentation that offers access to the field in general no matter which view the researcher might care to address.

HISTORIC OUTLINE

History suggests that America was founded not on religious, cultural, militaristic, or geocentric grounds, but on the basic drive for unimpeded free enterprise. No one can deny the influence of business on the Puritan settlers, whose blend of Christianity and business ethic set a standard that continues in full force today.

Some of the earliest historical documents tell of business transactions—agrarian barter; stone, iron, and bronze manufacture; money lending; and the buying and selling of the necessities and amenities of life. Our modern American business institution, however, is rooted most directly in the aggressive entrepreneurial fervor of seventeenth-century Europe and the industrial revolution of eighteenth-century England.

From the time of Columbus, those who braved the dangers of crossing the Atlantic in wooden ships had, somewhere in their motivation, the desire to make their fortune in the New World. Even the Puritans, escaping the religious persecution of seventeenth-century England, had pragmatism intermingled with their religious fervor. The Robert Keayne case of 1639 clearly demonstrated that Puritanism had as much stock in assuring that business progressed smoothly as it did in enforcing a stringent adherence to the Bible. Keayne was censured by the civil authorities in Boston for inappropriate pricing practices. But his case also prompted John Cotton, a Puritan clergyman, to lay down rules of good business practice from the pulpit. These rules included not selling above current market price and not overcharging to compensate for losses incurred in the course of business. Cotton also proposed that the good Christian kept the faith if he worked at some acceptable livelihood—a philosophy that has evolved over the last three centuries into our Protestant work ethic. This concept surfaced again in 1657 in England through the writing of Richard Baxter, a Puritan preacher, who noted that the good Christian would attend to his or her business responsibilities diligently when not in the service of God.

America, with its natural resources and open spaces, was ripe for business. As early as 1660, English visitors to Boston were amazed by the wealth of the local merchants. And by 1700, the eastern seaboard was dotted with trading centers from Charleston in the south to Boston in the north. Entrepreneurs from England, Scotland, France, and Holland flocked to the New World to extract the limitless bounty that favored the land. They were especially pleased to be out from under the close scrutiny of their respective governments, although colonial regulations still thwarted unbridled trade in the New World. Some small manufacturing shops sprang up in New England to produce commodities, particularly iron kitchenware, that were too costly to import from England. The colonists, however, focused the full force of their business acumen on agriculture and trade, relying on Europe to provide the bulk of finished products.

In England, meanwhile, prosperity was being fueled by extended British trade, a rapidly growing population, bumper crops, and an endless source of raw materials from the British Empire. This situation fostered a burgeoning middle class willing to take over the mundane task of managing all this wealth—a task the landed gentry was unwilling and unable to assume. Among this new middle class was a group of dissenters, mostly Quakers, whose initiative eventually disrupted British life and helped set the colonists off on their Grand Adventure. One of these dissenters, James Watt, fired the first salvo of the industrial revolution when he adapted an obscure discovery of a Glasgow University professor to the need for cheap and efficient power. His invention, the steam engine, cut manufacturing loose from water power. It also allowed manufacturers to leave their mountainous isolation in the English highlands and build factories in the coal-rich midlands. Mills began producing an incredible array of goods at speeds unheard of twenty years earlier. Farm labor became factory labor—with steady wages, regulated hours, and a replaceability that made workers a very expendable commodity. As factory workers as young as eight slaved over machines eighteen hours a day, the factory owners grew wealthy and powerful.

The English north became more aggressive in its production and in its search for new consumers. And as England's home markets became saturated, these manufacturers turned their attention to America. Through political manipulation, the manufacturers forced the Crown to legislate controls that inhibited American business development. They wanted the colonies to remain primarily agrarian, and they used all the power at their disposal to guarantee that America remained an exclusively British market.

At first, the mercantile colonists conceded to England. Factories were closed and strict laws governing exports and imports imposed. Soon, however, business-minded colonists realized that such an arrangement greatly inhibited any growth. Businessmen up and down the eastern coast were fomenting dissent, calling for the removal of the restrictive laws that stymied trade. Unfortunately for England, these colonists propagandized their fellow colonists too well, and what started out as a conflict of business grew into a conflict of state—and eventually revolution.

Even as America suffered through its birth pains, commerce continued unabated. The colonists were now free, and the vast agricultural properties of the South, and the mills of the North that processed southern cotton, turned many of the former rebels into a moneyed upper class. The new Americans, however, did not take advantage of the unlimited resources, wide-open market, and growing work force to create an indigenous industrial base. The flow of goods from England and Europe satisfied most of the needs of the Americans, and local manufacturing was left to produce only those household items too marginal in profit to be imported.

As war loomed in Europe at the end of the eighteenth century, and the flow of imported goods began to dwindle, Americans sought alternatives to importation. In 1790, Samuel Slater, an English apprentice, defied strict laws against the export of English technology and arrived in America with the plans for steam-driven cloth machinery in his head. He put his knowledge to work in the northern mills and revolutionized cloth production. At the same time, Eli Whitney, whose cotton gin was facilitating higher yields from southern plantations, was setting up a mass-production plant in 1798 for the manufacture of muskets eventually used to arm the American army in 1812. His innovative production techniques—making interchangeable parts en masse—was adapted to numerous other products and sparked American business's interest in greater manufacturing self-sufficiency.

In 1825, English inventors put Watt's steam engine on wheels, and the industrial revolution became mobilized. Railroads arrived in America just as the heavily populated eastern seaboard was struggling to support its masses. With the newfound mobility, businesses could expand as far as tracks could be laid. The federal government, which at this point had little to offer the state-dominated society, took the lead in the expansionist drive to open the West. It undertook the development of major transportation systems, interconnecting roads, canals, and rail lines that not only afforded access to the West but generated the need for a new form of management once the systems fell into private hands—one that could deal with a more technologically intensive industry spread over great distances.

Matching the physical expansion of American business, equally radical changes were taking place in the way business was being conducted. William Mitchell wrote the first American text on accounting in 1796, revolutionizing the system that had been mired in ponderous English business practices. A trade boom between 1790 and 1808 caused by wars in Europe moved American merchants to the forefront of world trade, greatly expanding American shipping fleets and the attendant ship-building industries. With the infusion of working capital generated by this new trade, a sophisticated banking system quickly evolved that helped to pass this cash flow on to other sectors of the economy.

As industry and trade blossomed—and the western expansion opened new sources of raw materials and new population centers—the country became factionalized along lines of business specialization. The South, founded on its agricultural might, continued to develop its agrarian control; the North pushed ahead with its industrial specialization; and the West looked to mining and oil. The rapid expansion and overextension of the early 1800s, as well as the creation of large, diversified corporations consuming enormous amounts of capital, led to depressed markets and a stock market crash in 1857. This was just one of a series of financial crises that rocked the country from 1830 through the end of the century, causing bank closures and stock runs, and leading to the passage of protectionist laws in many states, laws that worked to isolate the South and led to rebellion.

Just as the Civil War caused a major shift in the social structure of the country, it sparked increased industrialization and capitalization in the North. And the fortunes made during the war were put to use extending the American frontier to California. By 1890 two-thirds of the American population lived outside the northeastern corridor and was growing at a rate twice as rapidly as Europe.

Although America was experiencing a population boom, there was still plenty of work and land that beckoned the impoverished peoples in Ireland, Italy, and eastern Europe who flocked to the "promised land." Although their lot in America may have been better than the lives many had left, the "promise" of America was not exactly as promised. As Thomas Griffin notes in his *Waist-High Culture:*

[In contrast to] Emma Lazarus' moving welcome inscribed on the Statue of Liberty . . . [America] did not want Europe's aged and sick; it wanted Europe's strong and willing arms. Come and pitch in—the work won't be pleasant at first because ditches must be dug, railroad tracks laid, coal mined and steel molded; the hours will be long and the cities congested. You may know nothing better than this all your lives, because you started late and your tongue is incomprehensible and you stink of garlic, but everything will be open to your children.[1]

With the influx of European labor on the East Coast and Chinese labor on the West Coast, industry prospered, absorbing the New Americans as rapidly as they disembarked. Many of these new workers had been witness to the infant labor movements rocking Europe, and they soon began to stir up unrest over the deplorable conditions in which they were forced to work. As the country moved into the twentieth century, the federal government, which had remained silent during business's expansionist period, was forced to confront the social misdeeds being committed in the name of free enterprise. Not only did the government attempt to better the lot of the working class through a range of legislation from child labor laws to wage controls, it took steps to insure that the growing corporate institution did not develop into an oligarchy. In a major reversal of policy, the federal government passed the Sherman Anti-trust Act in 1890, which limited the untethered growth of big business by outlawing price and market fixing. And in 1914, the Federal Trade Commission was created to give greater regulatory powers to the central government.

World War I not only gave American business a much needed economic boost, but demonstrated the power that could be unleashed by industry in a war effort. The war also generated greater concern for the needs of the individual, and by 1924, more than 1.5 million workers were represented by company-sanctioned worker organizations inside companies, although unions as such were still having difficulty making inroads because of strong industry resistance.

Although the future looked rosy for American business after World War I, there were storm clouds on the horizon. The single most devastating blow to American business was the Great Depression in the 1930s. Fomented by overextended banks, runaway speculation, and a tax structure that encouraged savings and discouraged investment, the Depression demonstrated how fragile an economic structure had been created by a business institution left relatively unimpeded by government.

After that fateful day in October 1929 when the stock market collapsed—with the resultant crumbling market and industrial systems—the federal government finally finished the job begun in 1890. It took control of the economy and established a structure that would prevent such catastrophes in the future through a series of legislative moves that put a halt to untethered business. There was the Securities and Exchange Act of 1934, which severely restricted the methods by which stock was traded and required businesses selling stock to publish annual financial statements for public scrutiny. The Banking Act of 1935 gave greater powers to the Federal Reserve Board in monitoring the national cash flow, including control over interest rates. The Social Security Act of 1935 set up a national system for unemployment insurance. The Wagner Act of 1935 established the National Labor Relations Board and opened industry to unimpeded unionization.

When the country entered World War II, the economy was well on its way to full recovery. Business and government had established a not-always-comfortable partnership in running the country's business. War once more showed how American industry could rise to the occasion as the nation's industrial might mobilized to meet the challenge of global warfare. During the war, technologies flourished, as did innovative manufacturing systems. When the war ended, America was well prepared to turn these new skills to peacetime production.

From World War II to the present, American business has once more become the nation's dominant institution. The relationship between business and government continues to be adversarial on a number of battlefields, but the regulators seem less strident and businesses more sophisticated in managing their relationship. Four major themes now dominate business—social consciousness, information orientation, merger motivation, and internationalism.

Companies today have come to realize that it is not enough to market a product; they must be good neighbors, caring as much about the environment, the growth of the nation, and the safety of their customers as they do about sales, quotas, and territories.

America has passed through the industrial age into the information age, with factories fully automated and all but the simplest jobs requiring some involvement with the computer. In the next twenty years, half of all jobs in America will involve communication in some form as the need to control and disseminate information becomes a major function of business.

As the cost of doing business rises, many corporations have turned to the merger as a means of spreading the risks. At first, merger-mania was confined to a few specialized industries such as steel and oil, usually involving major competitors buying out smaller companies. In today's world of mergers, however, there is greater emphasis on diversification—spreading the financial risks over a number of product lines to avoid a downturn in one market that could sink a specialized corporation.

Merger-mania has helped develop the final trend of modern business— that of creating corporations that extend beyond the borders of their home country. The differences in international wage structures, particularly in the Third World, have made cheap labor readily available to foreign companies. This, in turn, has lowered the cost of goods to a point where these same Third World countries have become viable markets for American goods. To accommodate this ever-expanding consumer world, corporations have extended themselves around the globe. And these corporations are quickly, but quietly, disrupting the age-old image of "nation." To whom does an American working for a Japanese construction company under the direction of a Swiss architect in the Egyptian desert owe his or her allegiance?

There is no denying that American business will lead the world into the future. But our business institution will not be the same as that envisioned by the Puritans in seventeenth-century New England, the colonial traders of the eighteenth century, the railroad barons of the nineteenth century, or the pre-Depression financial tycoons. The future business institution in America will envelop many nations and many people doing many different things for many different purposes.

REFERENCE WORKS

With a topic as broad as business, identifying the pertinent reference sources can be problematic. However, there are certain key documents that can give researchers entry points into the institutional structure of business. The obvious starting point is the dictionaries that provide us with the lingua franca of business. For a precise guide to "businessese," Jerry Rosenberg's *Dictionary of Business and Management* offers short, concise definitions for more than 8,000 business terms. A more esoteric (and historic) view of business terms can be found in the 1804 edition of *A Commercial Dictionary: Containing the Present State of Mercantile Law, Practice and Custom,* compiled by Joshua Montefiore. This book gives a fascinating insight into the business environment of the eighteenth century, including business geography. Other business dictionaries of note are Albert Giordano's *Concise Dictionary of Business Terminology,* J. Harold Janis's *Modern Business Language and Usage in Dictionary Form,* and Michael Rice's *Prentice-Hall Dictionary of Business, Finance and Law.* For more in-depth discussions of specific business terms, the three-volume *Encyclopedia of American Economic History: Studies of the Principal Movements and Ideas,* edited by Glenn Porter, offers detailed entries.

Although not exclusively American, another important primer for the business researcher is *The World of Business* by Edward C. Bursk and others from the Harvard Business School. It has synthesized the literature of business from Hammurabi to the twentieth century. Its introduction also provides an excellent overview of business in its broadest applications. Also of note is Michael Lavin's *Business Information: How to Find It, How to Use It*. Not only does it provide sources for information about individual companies, statistical data, and special topics, but it explains how to read these sources and how to set up searches for specific information. A good companion work is *Business and Economics Books 1876–1983*, which indexes more than 143,000 titles by subject, author, and title.

For earlier works on business and economics, *The Economic History of the United States Prior to 1860*, edited by Thomas Orsagh, and *Guide to Business History* by Henrietta Larson contain bibliographic data back to the 1600s. Both are divided by specific economic topics.

When seeking information concerning specific U.S. companies, the best sources are *Standard and Poor's Register of Corporations, Directors and Executives* and Dun and Bradstreet's *Million Dollar Directory*. Standard and Poor's, in three volumes, lists 45,000 corporations; each entry includes top management, gross revenue figures, number of employees, and a brief description of the company's business. The listing also notes if the company is a subsidiary and its board of directors if publicly held. Volume 2 focuses on individual businesspeople, noting their corporate positions and any directorships they might hold.

The *Million Dollar Directory* catalogs 160,000 businesses with net worth over $500,000. The alphabetic listings include sales and number of employees, S.I.C. codes, and top managers. A supplementary directory lists the "Top 50,000 Companies" whose net worth averages $1.8 million. Also included are cross-reference sections by geography and industrial classification.

Standard and Poor's also publishes its *Industry Surveys*, which provide statistical and marketing information for specific industries. The basic analysis sections are supplemented during the year with current analyses that provide more timely reports on activities within that industry. Any particular analysis begins with a narrative of activities for the past year that covers marketing, regulatory, and economic factors that have had impact on the industry. Each section has numerous graphs and charts drawn from government and private sources.

There are innumerable reference books that focus on specific aspects of the business institution. Two that are particularly interesting are Gary M. Fink's *Labor Unions* and *Professional Dissent: An Annotated Bibliography and Resource Guide* by James S. Bowman and others. *Labor Unions* contains sketches of more than 200 unions, including where and when they were founded as well as significant events in their development. *Professional Dissent*, although not exclusively focused on business, cites articles and books drawn from what the authors call the Age of the Whistle-Blower. Citations include works about dissent in business, government, science, and the professions, as well as citations on laws and court cases concerning internal dissent.

For information concerning individuals in business, one of the most complete sources is Marquis's *Who's Who in Finance and Industry*. It contains comprehensive biographical data on approximately 18,000 business executives. These leaders have been chosen more for their influence on the business community than exclusively because of income or position. The biographies include work resumé, family, club membership, and political affiliation.

Other reference works of note are *Business Periodicals Index, Predicast F&S Index, Where to Find Business Information: A Worldwide Guide for Everyone Who Needs the Answers to Business Questions* by David M. Brownstone and Gordon Carruth, *Business Information Sources* by Lorna M. Daniells, *The Encyclopedia of Business Information Sources, Ward's Directory of 51,000 Largest U.S. Corporations,* and *Who Owns Whom.*

Along with reference books, business is well represented in nationally accessible data banks. Information on these data bases is available through *ACBAS* from SLIGOS, which is an on-line directory of more than 1,000 data bases on business. Also of interest is *Area Business Databank* (from Information Access Company), which compiles citations from eighty regional, state, and local business publications; *BIS Informat Newsfile* (through Mead Data Central), which summarizes more than 300,000 stories from 500 international publications since 1983; and *BIZDATE,* from the SOURCE, which is actually the compilation of nine files ranging from THE BOARD ROOM, with reports on business from the American Enterprise Institute and the Business Roundtable, to FINANCIAL HEADLINES, with selected stories from UPI Business Wire.

RESEARCH COLLECTIONS

There are public, collegiate, and private business libraries around the country that offer extensive collections of works exclusively on business. Stanford University's Graduate School of Business houses more than 316,000 volumes, 300,000 corporate reports, and 2,344 periodical subscriptions. Columbia University's Thomas J. Watson Library of Business and Economics houses 340,000 volumes with business documents and materials dating from 1821. Cleveland Public Library's Business, Economics and Labor Department houses 116,000 volumes with extensive information concerning Cleveland-area businesses. The University of Pennsylvania's Lippincott Library of the Wharton School houses 118,000 volumes.

Pertinent business collections on microfilm (all from UMI Research Collections) include *American Association for Labor Legislation, 1905–1943,* which has collected the correspondence, organizational papers, and research materials of the AALL. *American Labor Unions: Constitutions and Proceedings*

1836–1982 contains the constitutions, reports, and debates of 250 active and inactive U.S. labor unions; a companion collection is *American Labor Union: Officer Reports*. Also available are the collected correspondence and writings of Eugene V. Debs, labor activist and leader of the Socialist Party in America. At the opposite end of the spectrum are the collected papers of Collis P. Huntington (1856–1901), the founder of the Central Pacific Railroad Company, the Southern Pacific Railroad Company, and the California Republican party. The writings of John Mitchell, the force behind the United Mine Workers Union, have been collected and include correspondence, union minutes, and eighty-three photographs of Mitchell and the union.

HISTORY AND CRITICISM

American business, as has been pointed out, started slowly. And those interested in writing about the theories underlying economics in the seventeenth and eighteenth centuries were in Britain. Because of this, there are few truly American sources of business writing prior to 1750. America had formulated its economic structure on the works of John Mill and Adam Smith, and Smith's *Wealth of Nations* was, during our early history, the primary guide for our economic development.

Some early works that bear mention, however, include two pamphlets, written in 1767 and 1786, that address the state of America's economy. The first, *The Commercial Conduct of the Province of New York Considered and the True Interest of That Colony Attempted to Be Shewn,* was twenty pages long and lamented the poor economic conditions found in New York despite what appeared to be thriving trade. It was authored by an individual identified only as "A Linen Draper" and was circulated among the members of the Society of Arts, Agriculture and Economy.

The second pamphlet, *The Commercial Conduct of the United States of America Considered,* follows the same theme as the earlier piece; the author is "A Citizen." It was written for public consumption but aimed explicitly at legislators. It begins, "The profession of a merchant is trade; they consult their own interest; but it is the Legislature only which can check and prohibit an intemperate, inpolitic, and luxurious commerce." The piece goes on to suggest that state government needed to take greater control of commerce to put a stop to ruthless business people.

One of the first works to examine American commerce closely actually was written by a Frenchman, Jacques Pierre Brissot de Warville, in 1795. The work, *The Commerce of America with Europe,* attempts to examine in some detail the exact commercial relationship established between the infant United States and its European trading partners. In his preface, Brissot de Warville reprints Lord Sheffield's comment that "England would always be the storehouse of the United States."

In 1806, Samuel Blodget compiled *Economica: A Statistical Manual for the*

United States of America, which summarized trade and commerce activity in the country. He produced a similar manual in 1810.

From a historical standpoint, little was done by American economic scholars before 1860. This may have been a result of the nation's dependence on foreign trade as well as a need to establish a business institution before writing about it. Ezra Seaman's *Essays on the Progress of Nations, in Productive Industry, Civilization, Population, and Wealth,* published in 1846, was one of the first retrospective looks at our economic development.

Around the turn of the century, there is a proliferation of works that attempt to review the short history of American business. William Babcock Weeden's *Economic and Social History of New England, 1620–1789* concentrates primarily on the agrarian nature of commerce. A. M. Simons's *Class Struggle in America* (1906) is unique for its application of Marxian theory to American business. Guy Stevens Callender's *Selections from the Economic History of the United States, 1765–1860* (1909) excerpts letters and pamphlets that deal with early American business. More comprehensive reviews of business history were Harold Underwood Faulkner's *American Economic History* (1924) and Clive Day's *History of the Commerce of the United States* (1925).

Two more recent works that present a definitive business history are *200 Years of American Business* and *The Evolution of the American Economy.* In *200 Years,* Thomas C. Cochran condenses the diverse development of the American business community into a descriptive narrative of the four major areas in business development—The Business Revolution, 1776–1840; A National Market, 1840–90; Adjusting to Bigness, 1890–1930; The Age of Demand, 1930–Present. In each era, he describes the technological advances that fomented expanding industry as well as the economic, political, and social trends in the nation that changed how business is conducted. *The Evolution of the American Economy* by Sidney Ratner, James Soltow, and Richard Sylla takes a more analytical view of American business, focusing on trends and statistical evidence to support the changes our economy has experienced. Although not a history of business, another important work is W. Jett Lauck's *Political and Industrial Democracy,* which traces the employer-worker relationship from 1776 to 1926. Its major thesis is that the spirit of cooperation created by World War I led to the democratization of business, specifically in the development of workers' councils that, by 1926, represented more than 1.5 million workers nationwide.

For an in-depth historical view of the individual in business, Miriam Beard has compiled a two-volume work, *A History of Business,* that analyzes the people who control business and how those people have changed in style and motivation. Volume 2 starts with the eighteenth century and covers both American and international business. Courtney Robert Hall, in his *History of American Industrial Science,* does a similar analysis for the development of technologies that fostered our present industrial complex.

Along with a general overview of industry, Hall includes detailed accounts of particular industries, from mining and rubber to paper and electronics.

Several authors have compiled historical anthologies that trace the development of American economic theory through the writings of America's premier economists. Henry William Spiegel's *The Rise of American Economic Thought* brings together the theories most influential in the early formation of the American system of business, including those of Benjamin Franklin, Mathew Carey, Thomas Cooper, and Simon Newcomb. Robert Heilbroner's *The Worldly Philosophers* also reviews the economic philosophies of European and American theorists and applies their thinking to modern American business. In a more pragmatic vein, John Brooks has compiled first-person accounts of the evolution of corporate America in *The Autobiography of American Business*. Among the accounts are those of Andrew Carnegie, Henry Ford, Helena Rubenstein, and Bernard Baruch.

Although innumerable histories of business exist, there is an equally large body of non-historical works that deal with business that could be of interest to researchers. These can be divided into two categories: theory and practice. The former works tend to explore the impact of capitalism on our society and the impact of society on capitalism. One of our most prolific writers in this area is John Kenneth Galbraith, who has produced, among other works, *American Capitalism* (1952, 1956), *The Affluent Society* (1958), and *The New Industrial State* (1967). In *American Capitalism,* he attempts to explain how a system that seems in total violation of sound economic practice has managed to succeed. He also confronts the ambiguities created by our rogue economy and the insecurities generated by those ambiguities. As he explains in his opening chapter, "Man cannot live without an economic theology—without some rationalization of the abstract and seemingly inchoate arrangements which provide him with his livelihood."

In *The Affluent Society,* he takes a critical view of the American passion for the acquisition of wealth and the apparent apathy toward advancing American economic thought caused by this passion. And in *The New Industrial State,* which Galbraith saw as a continuation of his earlier work, he postulates that the forces inducing human behavior are directed more by the market than by the individual. A counterpoint to this Galbraithian theory is that proposed by George Lodge in *The New American Ideology,* which suggests that, through our industrialization, we have passed beyond John Locke's sense of individualism into an ideology of communitarianism. This ideology exhibits itself in greater involvement of workers in management and in a shift in focus by corporations from consumers to community.

A writer as prolific as Galbraith is Milton Friedman, who has taken a long look at the tempestuous relationship between business and government and has concluded that much of what is wrong in business today is a result of an over-watchful federal government. In *Capitalism and Freedom,* written with his wife Rose, Friedman takes exception to the admonition offered by

John Kennedy in his inaugural—"Ask not what your country can do for you, but what you can do for your country." Friedman sees this as establishing an imbalance between the governed and the government. He suggests that what Kennedy should have said was, "What can the country offer me in my quest to accomplish my personal goals?" The body of the work attempts to outline how competitive capitalism can only work in a free enterprise system. In *Free to Choose: A Personal Statement,* written eighteen years after *Capitalism,* Milton and Rose Friedman continue to expand on Adam Smith's basic premise of economics—that successful enterprise is based on voluntary cooperation. They see this premise violated by the federal government's restrictive involvement in American business practices. In addition to these works, Friedman also has written *The Great Contraction 1929–1933* (with Anna J. Schwartz), *Essays in Positive Economics,* and *An Economist's Protest: Columns in Political Economy.*

A work that appeared soon after the publication of *American Capitalism,* which takes up the theme of economic change, is Adolf Berle's *The Twentieth Century Capitalist Revolution.* His primary thesis is that institutionalized American industry is at a crossroads, one path leading toward the assumption of a guiding role in our society, the other to destruction. He sees American business particularized in the modern corporation and suggests that dramatic changes in corporate life are needed to insure that industry makes the right choice. An equally dire harbinger of dramatic business change is Robert L. Heilbroner's *Business Civilization in Decline,* published in 1976. Despite its negative title, the work explicates how business in America will have to undergo both a structural and philosophic evolution to keep pace with societal and governmental shifts.

Another aspect of business that has received considerable attention is the concept of work. A seminal work in this area is Studs Terkel's *Working.* This is a collection of personal accounts of day-to-day life in the work setting told through the experiences of a diverse assemblage of workers— from miners to models, telephone operators to executives. Terkel points out in his introduction that "this book, being about work, is, by its very nature, about violence—to the spirit as well as the body." At the other end of the spectrum is Bernard Lefkowitz's *Breaktime,* which collects the impressions of people who have dropped out, and what the payoff is for not working.

A more theoretical approach to working is offered by Gale Miller in *It's a Living: Working in Modern Society,* which posits a typology ranging from peasant work through industrial, professional, and countercultural work. Miller discusses the applicable historical precedents that have influenced work as well as the social reality attendant on the type of work one does. An equally detailed examination of work is presented in Carl Kaufmann's *Man Incorporate: The Individual and His Work in an Organized Society.* The author focuses on how work has restructured our view of ourselves and our place in society from a historical perspective.

An area of particular interest in the modern business setting is the impact of corporate climate on the institution. Terrence Deal and Allan Kennedy investigate this aspect of business in *Corporate Cultures: The Rites and Rituals of Corporate Life.* Through case studies—Tandem Corporation, Procter and Gamble, etc.—the authors explore how culture, defined as an overriding value system, is fostered and maintained through corporate rituals.

Business writers also are fascinated with predicting the future. One of the most notable of these works is John Naisbitt's *Megatrends,* which isolates ten trends that portend radical changes in American society. Among these are the shift from an industrial to an information-based society, greater emphasis on innovation and self-reliance, the migration of workers from the North, and the obsolescence of representative democracy. A more specialized view of these changes is Max Ways's *The Future of Business: Global Issues in the Eighties and Nineties.*

As with any institution as volatile and ever-changing as business, there is a plethora of how-to books that attempt to arm the prospective business person with the knowledge, skills, and defenses needed to survive. Some take a lighter tone in discussing the subject, such as the "Peter" trilogy by Laurence J. Peter. Starting with *The Peter Principle,* written with Raymond Hull in 1969, the authors set forth his philosophy that business tends to promote individuals to the highest level of their incompetency. Within his less-than-serious message is the recommendation—to both employers and individuals—that people should avoid the ever-upward drive endemic to business. In *The Peter Prescription* (1972), he offers specific remedies to the "Peter Principle." And in *The Peter Pyramid,* published in 1986, he applies his theory on a larger scale to government, businesses, and institutions. Along the same line, Robert Townsend attempts to show "how to stop the Corporation from stifling people and strangling profits" in *Up the Organization.*

A more earnest approach to self-help is offered by *In Search of Excellence* by Thomas Peters and Robert Waterman, which explains those elements of modern business practice that guarantee success. Other works offering a more pragmatic approach to self-help include *How to Do Business and Succeed in It* by A. W. Astor, *Always Live Better than Your Clients* by Isadore Barmash, *The Corporate Prince: Machiavelli Reviewed for Today* by Richard D. Funk, *Business Wargames* by G. James Barrie, *Funny Business: A Senile Executive's Guide to Power and Success* by E. Alfred Osborne, *Game Plans: Sports Strategies for Business* by Robert Keidel, and *The Invisible War: Pursuing Self-Interest at Work* by Samuel A. Culbert and John J. McDonough.

On the darker side of business, a number of authors have dealt with the crimes, legal and ethical, committed in the name of higher profits. Addressing the ills of the corporate world has long been of interest to authors. Perhaps the earliest such antagonists were the "muckrakers" of the turn of the century. Named by Teddy Roosevelt for the character in *Pilgrim's Progress* who could not see the beauty of the world around him because he was too busy raking through the muck below his feet, the modern American muckraker relished exposing the foibles and follies of business and government. John Harrison and Harry Stein have collected a series of articles that explore the goals and motivations of these pioneers in *Muckraking: Past, Present and Future*. A new gang of muckrakers has taken the corporate world to task for its excesses in recent years. Vance Packard has carried the muckrakers' banner into the second half of the twentieth century. Among his numerous scathing exposés is *The Pyramid Climbers*, which strips away the veil of mystery surrounding the modern corporate executive to expose hustlers, trained, packaged, and programmed to succeed at any cost.

In *Up Against the Corporate Wall*, Prakash Sethi reviews a number of infamous business cases that, he suggests, have altered our view of corporate ethics. Included among these are Dow Chemical's reaction to nationwide protests over its production of napalm, the 1969 California farm workers' strike and subsequent grape boycott, and the battle between President Kennedy (and later President Johnson) and the American steel giants over price controls. Robert L. Heilbroner's *In the Name of Profit* puts the men running the super corporations under the microscope to explore their values and why they act the way they do. In the same vein, Roger D'Aprix notes, in the introduction to *In Search of a Corporate Soul*, "A truism about American society in the final third of a century is that almost every speck of it has been assigned to one organization or another." His book, following this premise, asks if the modern corporation has acted as a responsible steward for what the society has placed in its hands. In *The Gamesman*, Michael Maccoby creates a typology of the modern business manager, whom he sees as the beneficiary of the modern corporate system. Through an analysis of detailed interviews with 250 top executives, Maccoby identifies four basic managerial types: the craftsman, who enjoys the process of making something; the jungle fighter, whose motivation is the acquisition and defense of power; the company man, whose interest is maintaining organizational integrity; and the gamesman, who is a team player, but out to win for his employer and himself. Similarly, *The Naked Manager* by Robert Heller deals with the games managers play and how these games have led to mismanagement.

Besides the numerous books available on business, one source of interest to the researcher is the range of business magazines in circulation. America's desire to keep abreast of the happenings in business has a long history. Business magazines have been a part of our corporate world since the turn of the century. One magazine that stands out among the earliest business magazines is *Forbes*, founded in 1917, which continues today as our most prestigious business magazine. Created by Bertie Forbes, a Scot who had cut his journalistic teeth at the *New York Journal of Commerce* and the *Commercial and Financial Chronicle, Forbes* created a family publishing dynasty that still holds the reins of the magazine today. Although focused primarily on economic activity within the business community, *Forbes* also offers a forum for commentary, personality profiles, and life-style articles.

Forbes dominated the business community for eleven years before two serious contenders appeared. Both arrived on the eve of the Great Depression but survived the ensuing panic to take their place beside *Forbes* as the leaders in the business magazine field. *Business Week* hit the streets in 1929 with a no-nonsense approach to business that gave it a "workhorse" image in contrast to *Forbes's* executive style. *Fortune,* published by Time, Inc., came out in 1930 and challenged *Forbes* in style and content; it differentiated itself from its competition by instituting the single-company profile, later adopted by its two major competitors. Today, the three magazines vary little in content, although *Forbes* and *Fortune* still maintain the slick style they established at their inception.

Among the more recent entries into the general business magazine field are *Nation's Business* (1912), the house organ of the U.S. Chamber of Commerce; *Money* (1972) which, true to its name, focuses on the control and use of money by companies and corporate executives; *Inc.* (1979), written in a high-gloss style for the entrepreneur or middle manager with sights set on the executive boardroom; and *Venture* (1979), an all-out entrepreneurial guide for success. These general business magazines are joined by more than 10,000 other general and specialized magazines for every aspect of business. These are both horizontal (dealing with a particular business function, such as accounting, across industries) and vertical (dealing with a particular industry, such as advertising or steel production).

The academic community has been equally prolific in creating journals that monitor the activities of business. Perhaps the most famous of these is *Harvard Business Review,* which began publication in 1922. Although structured, as are most academic journals, with contributing scholars, it has avoided limiting readership only to academia. Other academic journals of note are *American Economic Review,* from the American Economic Association; *Business History Review,* from the Harvard Business School; *Journal of Business,* from the University of Chicago; *Journal of Economics and Business,* from Temple University; *Journal of Education for Business,* from the Helen Dwight Reid Educational Foundation; and *Quarterly Journal of Economics,* from Harvard University. Of equal importance for the popular culture researcher are the numerous state-based business reviews, usually published by state universities. Some of these, like *Indiana Business Review, Arkansas Business and Economic Review, Georgia Business and Economic Conditions,* and *Oklahoma Business Bulletin,* began before 1933.

NOTE

1. Thomas Griffith, *The Waist-High Culture* (New York: Grosset and Dunlap, 1959), p. 1.

BIBLIOGRAPHY

Astor, A. W. *How to Do Business and Succeed in It.* New York: Street and Smith, 1890.

Barmash, Isadore. *Always Live Better than Your Clients.* New York: Dodd, Mead, 1983.

Barrie, G. James. *Business Wargames.* New York: Penguin Books, 1986.

Beard, Miriam. *A History of Business.* 2 vols. Ann Arbor: University of Michigan Press, 1938.

Berle, Adolf A., Jr. *The Twentieth Century Capitalist Revolution.* New York: Harcourt, Brace, 1954.

Best, Fred, comp. *The Future of Work.* Englewood Cliffs, N.J.: Prentice-Hall, 1973.

Bining, Arthur. *The Rise of American Economic Life.* New York: Scribner's, 1943.

Blodget, Samuel. *Economica: A Statistical Manual for the United States of America.* 1806. Reprint. New York: A. M. Kelly, 1964.

Bowden, Witt. *The Industrial History of the United States.* New York: Adelphi, 1930.

Bowman, James S., Frederick A. Elliston, and Paula Lockhart. *Professional Dissent: An Annotated Bibliography and Resource Guide.* New York: Garland, 1984.

Brissot de Warville, Jacques Pierre. *The Commerce of America with Europe, Particularly with France and Great Britain.* 1795.

Brooks, John. *The Autobiography of American Business.* Garden City, N.Y.: Doubleday, 1974.

Brown, Richard D., and George J. Petrello. *Introduction to Business.* New York: Macmillan, 1979.

Brownstone, David M., and Gordon Carruth. *Where to Find Business Information: A Worldwide Guide for Everyone Who Needs Answers to Business Questions.* New York: Wiley, 1982.

Bryant, Keith L., Jr., and Henry C. Dethloff. *A History of American Business.* Englewood Cliffs, N.J.: Prentice-Hall, 1983.

Bursk, Edward, Donald T. Clark, and Ralph W. Hidy. *The World of Business.* New York: Simon and Schuster, 1962.

Business and Economics Books 1876–1983. 4 Vols, New York: R. R. Bowker, 1983.

Business, Economics Books and Serials in Print. New York: R. R. Bowker, 1973-. Annual.

Business Periodicals Index. New York: H. W. Wilson, 1958-.

Callender, Guy Stevens. *Selections from the Economic History of the United States, 1765–1860.* Boston: Ginn, 1909.

Caves, Richard. *American Industry: Structure, Conduct, Performance.* Englewood Cliffs, N.J.: Prentice-Hall, 1964.

Clapp, Jane. *Professional Ethics and Insignia.* Metuchen, N.J.: Scarecrow Press, 1974.

Cochran, Thomas C. *200 Years of American Business.* New York: Basic Books, 1977.

Corey, Lewis. *The Decline of American Capitalism.* New York: Covici Friede, 1934.

Costello, Patricia. *Stories from American Business*. Englewood Cliffs, N.J.: Prentice-Hall, 1987.

Culbert, Samuel A., and John J. McDonough. *The Invisible War: Pursuing Self-Interest at Work*. New York: Wiley, 1980.

Cunningham, William H. *Introduction to Business*. Cincinnati: SW Publishing, 1984.

Daniells, Lorna M. *Business Information Sources*. Berkeley: University of California Press, 1985.

D'Aprix, Roger M. *In Search of a Corporate Soul*. New York: AMACOM, 1976.

Day, Clive. *History of the Commerce of the United States*. New York: Longmans, 1925.

Deal, Terrence E., and Allan A. Kennedy. *Corporate Cultures: The Rites and Rituals of Corporate Life*. Reading, Mass.: Addison-Wesley, 1982.

Encyclopedia of Business Information Sources. Detroit: Gale Research, 1983.

Faulkner, Harold Underwood. *American Economic History*. 1924. New York: Harper and Row, 1976.

Fink, Gary M. *Labor Unions*. Westport, Conn.: Greenwood Press, 1977.

Fletcher, Gordon A. *The Keynesian Revolution and Its Critics*. New York: St. Martin's Press, 1987.

Frederick, John H. *The Development of American Commerce*. New York: Appleton, 1932.

Friedman, Milton. *An Economist's Protest: Columns in Political Economy*. Glen Ridge, N.J.: Thomas Horton, 1972.

———. *Essays in Positive Economics*. Chicago: University of Chicago Press, 1953.

Friedman, Milton, and Rose Friedman. *Capitalism and Freedom*. Chicago: University of Chicago Press, 1962.

———, and Rose Friedman. *Free to Choose: A Personal Statement*. New York: Harcourt Brace Jovanovich, 1980.

Friedman, Milton, and Anna Jacobson Schwartz. *The Great Contraction 1929–1933*. Princeton, N.J.: Princeton University Press, 1965.

Funk, Richard D. *The Corporate Prince: Machiavelli Reviewed for Today*. New York: Vantage Press, 1986.

Galbraith, John K. *The Affluent Society*. Boston: Houghton Mifflin, 1958.

———. *American Capitalism: The Concept of Countervailing Power*. Boston: Houghton Mifflin, 1956.

———. *Economic Development*. Cambridge, Mass.: Harvard University Press, 1964.

———. *The New Industrial State*. Boston: Houghton Mifflin, 1967.

Gilliland, Charles E., Jr., ed. *Readings in Business Responsibility*. Braintree, Mass.: D. H. Mark Publishing, 1969.

Giordano, Albert G. *Concise Dictionary of Business Terminology*. Englewood Cliffs, N.J.: Prentice-Hall, 1981.

Goodall, Francis. *Bibliography of Business History*. Brookfield, Vt.: Gower Publishing, 1987.

Gras, Norman S. *Business and Capitalism: An Introduction to Business History*. New York: A. M. Kelly, 1939.

Hall, Courtney Robert. *History of American Industrial Science*. New York: Library Publishers, 1954.

Harrison, John M., and Harry Stein. *Muckraking: Past, Present and Future*. University Park: Pennsylvania State University Press, 1973.

Hay, Robert D., and Edmund R. Gray. *Business and Society: Cases and Text*. Cincinnati: South-Western Publishing, 1981.

Hayek, F. A., ed. *Capitalism and the Historians*. Chicago: University of Chicago Press, 1954.

Heilbroner, Robert L. *Business Civilization in Decline*. New York: W. W. Norton, 1976.

———. *The Wordly Philosophers*. New York: Simon and Schuster, 1980.

———, ed. *In the Name of Profit*. Garden City, N.Y.: Doubleday, 1972.

Heller, Robert. *The Naked Manager: Games Executives Play*. New York: E. P. Dutton, 1985.

Hickman, Craig R., and Michael Silva. *Creating Excellence*. New York: NAL Books, 1984.

Howey, Richard S. *A Bibliography of General Histories of Economics 1692–1975*. Lawrence: Regents Press of Kansas, 1982.

Humphrey, Edward. *An Economic History of the United States*. New York: Century Historical Series, 1931.

Janis, J. Harold. *Modern Business Language and Usage in Dictionary Form*. Garden City, N.Y.: Doubleday, 1984.

Johnson, Harold L. *Business in Contemporary Society: Framework and Issues*. Belmont, Calif.: Wadsworth, 1971.

Jones, Donald G. *Business Ethics Bibliography, 1971–1975*. Charlottesville: University Press of Virginia, 1977.

Kaufmann, Carl. *Man Incorporate: The Individual and His Work in an Organized Society*. Garden City, N.Y.: Doubleday, 1967.

Keidel, Robert. *Game Plans: Sports Strategies for Business*. New York: E. P. Dutton, 1985.

Kirkland, Edward C. *A History of American Economic Life*. New York: Crofts, 1932.

Larson, Henrietta M. *Guide to Business History*. Cambridge, Mass.: Harvard University Press, 1948.

Lauck, W. Jett. *Political and Industrial Democracy 1776–1926*. New York: Funk and Wagnalls, 1926.

Lavin, Michael R. *Business Information: How to Find It, How to Use It*. Phoenix: Oryx Press, 1987.

Lefkowitz, Bernard. *Breaktime*. New York: Hawthorn Books, 1979.

Lodge, George C. *The New American Ideology*. New York: Alfred A. Knopf, 1976.

Lovett, Robert W. *American Economic and Business History: A Guide to Information Sources*. Detroit: Gale Research, 1971.

Maccoby, Michael J. *The Gamesman*. New York: Simon and Schuster, 1976.

Mayros, Van. *Business Information: Applications and Sources*. Radnor, Pa.: Chilton Publishing, 1983.

Miller, Gale. *It's a Living: Work in Modern Society*. New York: St. Martin's Press, 1981.

Million Dollar Directory. Parsippany, N.J.: Dun and Bradstreet, 1979-. Annual.

Montefiore, Joshua. *A Commercial Dictionary Containing the Present State of Mercantile Law, Practice and Custom*. Philadelphia: James Humphreys, 1804.

Moskowitz, Milton, Michael Katz, and Robert Levering. *Everybody's Business: An Almanac*. San Francisco: Harper and Row, 1980.

MOW International Research Team. *The Meaning of Work*. London: Harcourt Brace Jovanovich, 1987.

Naisbitt, John. *Megatrends*. New York: Warner Books, 1982.

Osborne, E. Alfred. *Funny Business: A Senile Executive's Guide to Power and Success*. New York: AMACOM, 1979.

Orsagh, Thomas, ed. *The Economic History of the United States Prior to 1860*. Santa Barbara, Calif.: ABC-CLIO, 1975.

Packard, Vance. *The Pyramid Climbers*. New York: McGraw-Hill, 1962.

Parkinson, C. Northcote. *Big Business*. Boston: Little, Brown, 1974.

Pascarella, Perry. *The New Achievers*. New York: Free Press, 1984.

Peter, Laurence J. and Raymond Hull. *The Peter Prescription*. New York: William Morrow, 1972.

———. *The Peter Principle*. New York: William Morrow, 1969.

———. *The Peter Pyramid or Will We Ever Get the Point?* New York: William Morrow, 1986.

Peters, Thomas J., and Nancy Austin. *A Passion for Excellence: The Leadership Difference*. New York: Random House, 1985.

———, and Robert H. Waterman, Jr. *In Search of Excellence*. New York: Harper and Row, 1982.

Porter, Glenn, ed. *Encyclopedia of American Economic History: Studies of the Principal Movements and Ideas*. 3 vols. New York: Scribner's, 1980.

Predicast F&S Index. Cleveland: Predicast, 1968-. Published monthly with quarterly and annual cumulations.

Pusateri, C. Joseph. *A History of American Business*. Arlington Heights, Ill.: Harlan Davidson, 1984.

Ratner, Sidney, James H. Soltow, and Richard Sylla. *The Evolution of the American Economy*. New York: Basic Books, 1979.

Rice, Michael Downey. *Prentice-Hall Dictionary of Business, Finance and Law*. Englewood Cliffs, N.J.: Prentice-Hall, 1983.

Rosenberg, Jerry M. *Dictionary of Business and Management*. New York: Wiley, 1978.

Saunders, Alta. *The Literature of Business: Contemporary*. Westport, Conn.: Greenwood Press, 1946.

Schlessinger, Bernard. *The Basic Business Library: Core Resources*. Phoenix: Oryx Press, 1983.

Seaman, Ezra C. *Essays on the Progress of Nations, in Productive Industry, Civilization, Population, and Wealth*. 1846.

Sethi, S. Prakash. *Up Against the Corporate Wall*. Englewood Cliffs, N.J.: Prentice-Hall, 1972.

Simons, A. M. *Class Struggle in America*. Chicago: Kerr, 1906.

Singewald, Frank D. *To Succeed in Business, Get There, Honestly if You Can, but Get There*. Pompano Beach, Fla.: Exposition Press, 1982.

Smith, Adam. *The Wealth of Nations*. Edited by Edwin Cannan. Chicago: University of Chicago Press, 1976.

Spiegel, Henry William. *The Rise of American Economic Thought*. Philadelphia: Chilton, 1960.

Standard and Poor's Industry Surveys. New York: Standard and Poor's, 1973-. Annual.

Standard and Poor's Register of Corporations, Directors and Executives. New York: Standard and Poor's, 1928-. Annual.

Sturdivant, Frederick D. *Business and Society: A Managerial Approach.* Homewood, Ill.: Richard D. Irwin, 1977.

Terkel, Studs. *Working.* New York: Random House, 1974.

Townsend, Robert. *Up the Organization.* New York: Alfred A. Knopf, 1970.

Tucker, Kenneth A., ed. *Business History: Selected Readings.* Totowa, N.J.: Biblio Distribution Center, 1977.

U.S. Department of Commerce Library Catalog. List of publications from the U.S. Government Printing Office from 1790 through 1950.

Vlahos, Olivia. *Doing Business: The Anthropology of Striving, Thriving, and Beating Out the Competition.* New York: Franklin Watts, 1985.

Voos, Henry. *Organizational Communication: A Bibliography.* Rutgers, N.J.: Rutgers University Press, 1967.

Ward's Directory of 51,000 Largest U.S. Corporations. Petaluma, Calif.: B. H. Ward Publishing, 1980-. Annual.

Ways, Max, ed. *The Future of Business: Global Issues in the Eighties and Nineties.* New York: Pergamon Press, 1978.

Weeden, William Babcock. *Economic and Social History of New England, 1620–1789.* 2 vols. Boston: Houghton Mifflin, 1890.

Who Owns Whom. London: Roskill, 1973-. (North American edition published annually.)

Who's Who in Finance and Industry. Chicago: Marquis Who's Who, 1936-. Annual.

Williamson, Harold, ed. *The Growth of the American Economy: An Introduction to the Economic History of the United States.* New York: Prentice-Hall, 1944.

Winch, Donald. *James Mill: Selected Economic Writings.* Chicago: University of Chicago Press, 1966.

Wright, Chester W. *Economic History of the United States.* New York: McGraw-Hill, 1941.

Periodicals

American Economic Review. Nashville, 1911-.

Arkansas Business and Economic Review. Fayetteville, Ark., 1933-.

Business History Review. Boston, 1926.-

Business Week. New York, 1929.-

Du Pont Magazine. Wilmington, Del., 1913-.

Forbes. New York, 1917-.

Fortune. New York, 1929-.

Georgia Business and Economic Conditions. Athens, Ga., 1929-.

Harvard Business Review. Boston, 1922-.

Inc. Magazine. Boston, 1979-.

Indiana Business Review. Bloomington, 1926-.

Journal of Business. Chicago, 1928-.

Journal of Economics and Business. Philadelphia, 1949-.

Journal of Education for Business. Washington D.C., 1928-.

Mississippi Business Review. Mississippi State, 1939-.

Money. New York, 1972-.

Nation's Business. Washington, D.C., 1911-.

Oklahoma Business Bulletin. Norman, Okla., 1928.-
Pennsylvania Business Survey. University Park, Pa., 1938.-
Quarterly Journal of Economics. New York, 1886-.
Venture, the Magazine for Entrepreneurs. New York, 1979-.

Catalogs

EVELYN BECK

As Kurt Vonnegut envisions the end of the world in his novel *Cat's Cradle,* it is made more bearable for the survivors by a bomb shelter equipped with all of life's necessities—a chemical toilet, a short-wave radio, twin beds, and a Sears, Roebuck catalog.

Catalogs—those elaborate advertising books—have inspired a peculiar kind of worship in the past century. In 1972, on the centennial of the Montgomery Ward catalog, Richard Nixon called catalogs "an American tradition."[1] And they are important, especially as an anthropological tool in discovering the desires of middle-class Americans. By showing us what men and women of the past century have wanted, needed, and done without to purchase, the catalog gives us an intimate, extraordinarily detailed glimpse into the American home.

There has not, however, been much scholarly writing on catalogs. The main attention has been business-oriented, with many articles appearing on the growing number and variety of catalogs, and nostalgic, with a flurry of reprints of old Sears catalogs. The publication of one reprint was initiated by an American history teacher who wanted to include an 1890s catalog in his college course in order to give his students an accurate sense of the period.

Most of the useful analysis of catalogs is, appropriately, historical, but very little has appeared in the past decade. A number of books were published in the 1940s, when Sears, Roebuck and Co. was the number one retail business in America. Since then, much of what has been written about catalogs is brief and scattered through a variety of news, business, and advertising magazines.

HISTORIC OUTLINE

The history of the catalog is actually a history of mail order, for the catalog served as the primary tool by which ambitious businessmen changed the buying habits of Americans. Because colonial America was not an industrial nation, merchandise ordered through the mail came from abroad. George Washington and Thomas Jefferson were among those who purchased goods from England before the American Revolution; after 1776, most mail order items came from France. The first native American mail order business began around 1830 on a very small scale in New England. Credit for the earliest known effort to sell exclusively by mail on a major scale goes to E. C. Allen of Augusta, Maine, who offered such merchandise as recipes for washing powder beginning in 1870. But it was not until 1872, when Montgomery Ward rented a small shipping room and distributed one-page price lists to farmers in a cooperative organization called the National Grange of the Patrons of Husbandry, that American mail order really got under way.

For years, farmers had bought all they required from the general store, which had become, even more than a source of goods, a local gathering place where people could catch up on the local gossip and engage in informal political debates. Perhaps more important, it was run by a townsman— often a leading citizen—who understood the insecurities of farm life and who thus extended annual credit to all. But farmers were growing increasingly dissatisfied with the abuses of middlemen, who raised the prices on merchandise as much as 100 percent, and with the limited selection from which to buy. Also a concern for busy farmers was having to travel to the general store, often many miles away, whenever they needed something. Tired of the lack of alternatives, farmers banded together in what became known as "The Grange" to eliminate the middleman and exercise more control over how and where they spent their money.

Montgomery Ward, a shrewd businessman, made himself their man and even labeled his mail order operation "The Original Grange Supply House." Because he worked out of Chicago, with its easy access to manufacturers and wholesalers, he boasted a large inventory and a much greater selection than the general store, and because the farmers bought in large quantities, Ward could offer them lower prices. But, most important, Ward offered his merchandise by mail. As farmers prospered, they had more money but less time to spend making their own clothes and tools. And as farming became more mechanized, the need for machinery increased. From the one-page price list grew "The Farmer's Bible," a mail order catalog designed to meet these needs.

Ward's success in the new mail order field soon led to competition. Richard Sears, also operating out of Chicago, began selling watches by mail in 1886, and then went into business with A. C. Roebuck, offering an increasingly varied catalog of merchandise that eventually established him as the mail order giant. In 1882, the Spiegel, May, Stern Company had begun offering goods by mail, followed by the Larkin Company in 1885 and the National Cloak and Suit Company in 1888. Montgomery Ward and Sears, the biggest firms, became fierce competitors, but the main threat to their enterprises came from outside their organizations.

Small-town merchants felt threatened by the mail order companies, whose lower prices were draining away their customers. Even more humiliating, the general-store owner was also the town postmaster, and he found himself delivering catalogs and sending off orders and then distributing the merchandise as it arrived. The tensions erupted into open warfare. Local merchants enlisted the country press, lecturers on the Chautauqua and Lyceum circuits, preachers, public officials, and banks to voice their opposition. Customers were denounced for "sending money off to the Chicago millionaires,"[2] and Sears and Montgomery Ward resorted to sending catalogs and goods in unmarked packages to protect their customers from harassment. Country merchants organized Saturday evening bonfires in the public square, offering prizes to those who brought the most catalogs to burn, and even giving a free moving picture ticket to every child who contributed a catalog to the blaze. Contests encouraged the writing of poetry denouncing mail order houses, and into the vocabulary came such euphemisms as "Monkey Ward," "Shears and Rawbuck," and "Rears and Soreback." In perhaps a greater, if less original, insult, catalog houses were also tagged "cat houses" in contempt.

Attempts to discredit the men behind the mail order houses flourished, too. Rumors that Richard Sears was a Negro were so widespread that the company published a photograph of a very white-faced Sears in several catalogs to end the gossip. Sears's merchandise, too, was smeared. The most popular story insisted that a sewing machine offered by the catalog actually turned out to be a needle and thread. Of course, some of the bad publicity was justified; none of the companies was above deceitful advertising to increase profits. Sears once sold miniature furniture in an ad that seemed to imply that it was lifesize, and as late as 1937, Spiegel introduced a line of clothing called "the famous Saindon Models," never mentioning that Saindon was not a famous designer but simply the company secretary.

People who bought from Sears and Montgomery Ward also had to be careful, as they were the object of many desperate threats. In one case, a man running for mayor of Warsaw, Iowa, threatened to fire any city employee caught buying through mail order. However, these attacks did little to discourage doing business with catalogs, and in fact served as free advertising, for the critics of mail order were often more hurt by public opinion than were the targets of their criticism.

Furthermore, mail order merchants won the biggest battle. Rural free delivery, which brought mail to the farms, and which had been strongly opposed by local store owners, was approved in 1893 and begun in 1896, making it easier for farmers to shop by mail and even less likely that they would shop in town. The adoption of parcel post in 1913 was an added bonus; postal rates fell, and packages, which previously could not exceed four pounds, now could weigh as much as eleven pounds, eliminating such practices as shipping an eight-pound overcoat in halves, in separate parcels, along with a needle and thread for assembly. The greatest advantage of local stores ceased to exist when mail order companies began to offer their customers credit.

As the mail order companies grew, so did their catalogs. An early price list from Montgomery Ward listed 163 items, most of them for one dollar, including hoop skirts, paper collars, and a backgammon set. Soon the catalogs were issued biannually and, except for a few financially difficult years, included progressively more pages. By 1874, Ward's catalog had 32 pages; by 1899, it numbered 1,036 pages. Today, these catalogs are several thousand pages thick. And except for a few unsuccessful years when Sears and Ward charged customers for the catalogs, they have been offered free or, more recently, for a fee that is refunded with the first purchase.

The design of the catalogs has also undergone tremendous change. Originally, detailed drawings and written descriptions along with editorial comments and customer testimonials crammed each page, leaving very little white space; eventually merchandise was more liberally spaced throughout. The artwork progressed from illustrations (which often used the heads of celebrities, such as Theodore Roosevelt) to halftones to black and white and then to the predominant use of color photographs using live models. Early catalogs did not include an index, since the merchants expected customers to read their tomes carefully from cover to cover.

Also interesting is the overall conservatism of the catalogs. Ward and Sears emphasized good taste, respectability, and wholesomeness. Sears's taboos have included "too full" brassieres, "sexy" legs in stocking ads, and illustrations of women (and later men) smoking or drinking. But times change, and by 1972, a Ward's cover featuring a young woman wearing only a bikini drew many complaints but also a noticeable increase in orders placed.

Both the design and the merchandise offered in the catalogs in many ways reflect American popular culture. One writer calls them "an invaluable record of American life . . . a diary of the times created by the people."[3] Through the additions and omissions, one can see many changes in American life. Liquor, for example, appeared in the 1874 Ward's catalog, but disappeared the following year after Prohibitionists objected. The obstacles faced by the struggling suffrage movement are suggested in the 1905 Sears catalog by a "(Bathing) Suit Worn by Man Who Opposed Votes for Women." Three decades later, however, women have evidently made strides, for birth control devices such as contraceptive jellies and vaginal sprays appear, though they are listed covertly as "feminine hygiene needs." As for blacks in the early twentieth century, we can sense their tenuous position by their labelling as "coons" and "darkies" in a 1905 catalog offering a group of records called "Negro Shouts," a chorus of "happy" blacks singing about their freedom.

The presence of American soldiers in two world wars becomes clear in the Sears catalogs published from the beginning of one conflict to the end of another. In 1918, "Dresses for Mourning and General War" are one sign of the U.S. entry into World War I. The higher prices in the 1920 catalog reflect the rapid inflation that followed American military involvement, and the crash of commodity prices caused by the depression of 1920–21 rendered 1920 catalogs useless. Indicative of the prosperity preceding World War II is a particularly sentimental page of the 1937 catalog headed "America looks forward," featuring a young man and woman holding hands as they prepare to venture down a road, presumably life's path.

But the newest war soon invades the pages, and the toy section of the 1941 catalog features an unusually large number of tanks, machine guns, and dive bombers. By 1942, the catalog reflects wartime shortages, as it has 196 fewer pages and 103 omitted items (mostly hardware such as electrical appliances) which manufacturers could not supply. But the editors stoically admonish, "To make sure that the men who are fighting our battles have the guns and planes and tanks and ships they need, we at home must do without."[4] By 1944, the further reductions of the Sears and Ward's catalogs are partly explainable by the government's wartime paper-saving program.

Technological advancements emerge as the type of merchandise offered changes. The popularity of the sewing machine in the 1890s is one sign of major revolution taking place on the farm. Signs of mechanical progress and the increasing use of electricity in rural areas are the many electrical gadgets offered, such as lamps and irons. Another major step forward is indoor plumbing; in the 1930s Sears recommends the Deluxe Handee Indoor Toilet because "much of the stomach disorders and intestinal ill-health suffered by our adult rural population can often be traced to lack of convenient toilet facilities and the resultant development of the 'deferring habit.' "[5] Another sign of the growing concern for health care is the amount of space Sears devoted to drugs and patent medicines. The 1905 catalog offers such wonder drugs as "Sears' Cure for the Opium and Morphine Habit" and "Injection No. 7" for treatment of gonorrhea. Doctors in this era were few and were not available in many areas, even to those who could afford treatment. Besides, many doctors were illiterate and their methods not entirely trusted. But as the medical profession evolved and the government stepped in to outlaw such quack cures, patent medicines faded from the catalog pages. Automobiles appeared in the 1909 catalog, and though they were dropped after three years because they did not prove profitable through mail order, the number of automobile accessories that occupied more and more pages is a sure sign of the increasing importance of cars in America.

As technology advanced, people found themselves with more leisure time. A few of the most popular items were bicycles and musical instruments, both of which proved early big sellers for Sears. Like most Americans, mail order customers adored moving pictures, and the influence of Hollywood is suggested by the appearance of celebrity names and faces in the catalog. The 1935 edition features a photograph of "Max Factor Supervising Claudette Colbert's Make-up" and includes endorsements of such items as lace panties by Ginger Rogers and Loretta Young.

One of the most obvious ways the catalog reflects change is in fashion. Men's suits become tighter and women's skirts shorter, and corsets give way to girdles. Hairstyles change, too; in 1925, illustrations of bobbed hair accompany offers for the necessary accessories. Cosmetics become increasingly important, and the 1909 catalog instructs women, "There are very few who are hopelessly homely. Because You Are Married Is No Excuse For Neglecting Your Personal Appearance."[6]

Also revealing are the lines of unsuccessful merchandise, those items that tried and failed to entice customers. The rise of grocery store chains saw the discontinuance of groceries in the Ward's catalog, and prefabricated homes bowed out when too many customers could not pay.

The affection felt by so many for mail order catalogs manifested itself in a kind of worshipful folklore. Stories about the importance of Sears, Roebuck and Company to its customers gave the firm and its founder godlike qualities. While campaigning, Eugene Talmadge, a former Georgia governor, told voters that their only three friends were "God Almighty, Sears, Roebuck, and Eugene Talmadge."[7] The most popular story, told in a variety of ways, involves a small boy who, when asked by his Sunday School teacher the origin of the Ten Commandments, confidently replied, "Sears, Roebuck." Other tales involved Richard Sears's integrity and honesty, which took on legendary proportions. The most notorious of these describes an incident on a streetcar, when the conductor dropped and broke his watch. Sears, a passenger, discovered that the watch had been purchased from his company, told the man, "We guarantee our watches not to fall out of people's pockets and break," and promptly sent him a new one.[8]

What quickly became known as "The Farmer's Bible" and "The Great Wish Book" has enjoyed tremendous popularity for many years. During

World War I, the book most often requested by hospitalized soldiers was a Sears catalog. And recently, when Sears sponsored a contest for snapshots of children (the winners to be used as models in the 1981 spring catalog), an overwhelming 50,000 entries flooded their central office.

Today, over one-third of adults in the United States make at least one mail order purchase per year out of the millions of catalogs that go out in the mail. Without mail order and direct mail advertising and selling, the U.S. Post Office would be without a full third of its revenues. Mail order accounts for 18 percent of all U.S. retail sales, and three of the biggest catalog houses (Sears, Montgomery Ward, and Spiegel) use about 118,000 tons of paper annually.

A variety of organizations have recognized the significant niche mail order has carved for itself in American history. In 1946, a New York group of book lovers included the Montgomery Ward catalog in its collection of one hundred American books with the greatest influence on American life. In 1972, the U.S. Postal Service issued a commemorative stamp honoring the "100th Anniversary of Mail Order." Many history books use catalog illustrations and photographs to show how Americans lived, and an American Heritage picture history of America from 1872 to 1972 uses many Montgomery Ward illustrations to show how the mail order industry has affected life-styles.

Thus, the catalog not only shows change but influences it as well. Montgomery Ward and Sears catalogs have been credited with encouraging consumers to purchase newfangled "necessities" they might previously have done without, as in the case of indoor plumbing. The way catalog houses conduct their businesses—offering goods for a single set price—helped to bring an end to the bargaining system. The catalogs are even credited with helping to standardize the language, for items were named in the Chicago dialect and also ordered that way. The habit of ordering clothes instead of making them helped set age-size standards very much in use today. Catalogs also helped advance advertising techniques, as they pioneered in the use of accurate, detailed illustrations of merchandise. And Americans got used to increasingly higher qualities of goods and came to expect a policy that initially shocked local merchants: satisfaction guaranteed or your money back. The use of catalogs in country schools to identify objects unfamiliar to the students was recognized by the U.S. Post Office, which classified mail order publications as aids in the dissemination of knowledge (and thus entitled them to lower second-class rates).

The mail order industry itself has undergone innovations: many orders are now made by phone and charged to credit cards, and more and more items are being displayed on cable television. Compiling the catalog has also become easier as computers reveal which items don't sell well and should be removed. And even though Americans are less dependent on mail order due to the growing number of retail stores and the ease of travel

on highways, mail order and the catalog continue to thrive, for their advantages—great variety, quality, ease, and credit—apparently still appeal to
shoppers.

Today there are three kinds of mail order: big mail order houses, which
offer great variety; novelty houses, which sell gadgets, food gift packs, and
arts and crafts; and small company catalogs, which supply hard to find
items. Sears, Roebuck and Company is still the mail order leader, but
hundreds of other firms have entered the market. (Montgomery Ward
stopped producing its catalog in 1986 for economic reasons.) One can now
buy camping gear from L. L. Bean, tarantulas from a small Arizona firm,
and very exclusive merchandise such as "passports" for pets ($18), an edible
chocolate Monopoly set ($600), and his and hers electricity-generating wind-
mills ($32,000 each) from the famous Neiman-Marcus Christmas catalog.
And perhaps the catalog of catalogs is the *Whole Earth Catalog,* the bible of
the hippie movement in the 1960s and the winner of a National Book Award
in 1971 for one of its later versions. From this mail order manual, one is
directed where to find such items as solar-powered beanies and artificial
insemination for lesbians.

Whether or not the ardent devotion for these books that exist almost
exclusively to sell merchandise is justified, catalogs are historical documents
of popular culture. One writer sees in the Montgomery Ward and Sears
catalogs "the unrefined ore of much of current regionalism. Here is what
Faulkner hopes to startle, and what Lewis once tried to awaken . . . Eden
before the fall."[9] Another lauds the catalog's influence on our culture as
"comparable to that of the cotton gin, the six-shooter, the model-T flivver,
and the million-dollar movie."[10] Or perhaps there is more truth in the
assertion that "mail order catalogs . . . are the greatest invention in the interest of pure fantasy since the discovery of hard-core pornography."[11]
Whatever their proper place in our collective consciousness, they contain
much of American life worth reviewing.

RESEARCH COLLECTIONS

The major sources of catalog collections are the catalog publishers themselves.

Montgomery Ward and Company's Corporate Research Library in Chicago has the only complete set of Montgomery Ward catalogs available for
public use. A partial set (1916–68) is available at Radcliffe College's Schlesinger Library on the History of Women.

Sears, Roebuck and Company has a complete set of catalogs from 1886
to the present at its Merchandise Development and Testing Laboratory
Library and also at its Archives, Business History and Information Center,
both in Chicago. There are over 6,000 volumes. The Library of Congress
has on microfilm every Sears catalog from 1892 to 1956. Sixty-nine rolls

of microfilm containing more than 160 catalogs from 1888 to 1967 have been placed in over one hundred libraries throughout the United States. The Carnegie Library of Pittsburgh has a complete set of Sears catalogs from 1888, classified and indexed.

Another source of Sears catalogs is the Disney Productions Library in Burbank, California. Walt Disney was known for having one of the largest Sears catalog collections on the coast; he used them as a reference tool for period costumes and frequently loaned them to other studios.

A source of both Sears and Ward's catalogs is the Chicago Historical Society Library. It contains catalogs of major mail order houses and many special industries and stores, primarily in Chicago, since the late nineteenth century.

A specialized collection that might be of interest to catalog researchers is a vertical file of mail order ads and pamphlets at the Alfred C. Kinsey Institute for Sex Research at Indiana University.

Collections related to mail order are available at the Dartnell Corporation Publishing-Research Library in Chicago and at the Direct Mail/Marketing Association Information Center in New York.

Finally, anyone interested in starting his or her own catalog collection can select preferences from twenty-four categories by writing to the Direct Mail/Marketing Association, Mail Preference Service, 6 East 43 Street, New York, New York 10017. Ask for the "More Mail" form.

HISTORY AND CRITICISM

Most of the information about the history of catalogs is included in histories of the founders of the mail order firms. By far, the best material can be found on Richard Sears and Sears, Roebuck and Company. The best is Boris Emmet and John E. Jeuck's hefty *Catalogues and Counters: A History of Sears, Roebuck and Company*. It provides a thorough, detailed history of mail order, including Montgomery Ward, and also gives a detailed analysis of merchandise in the Sears catalogs and how it reflects historical and social change. It is especially revealing regarding the initial hatred of mail order houses, the influence that the world wars had on catalog content and design, and the folklore that sprang up around Richard Sears. It also contains an extensive bibliography of related books and articles up to 1948.

Also good, though far less detailed, is Louis E. Asher and Edith Heal's *Send No Money*. Though the book is in some ways a defense of Sears, it also offers some interesting behind-the-scenes information, as Louis Asher was the manager of Sears's advertising and catalog department. For example, Asher warns against reading too much social history into the choice of catalog merchandise; he cites the fact that books offered were often those out of copyright and thus cheaper, rather than apt indicators of popular taste.

And there is David L. Cohn's 1940 *The Good Old Days: A History of American Morals and Manners as Seen Through the Sears, Roebuck Catalogs 1905 to the Present*. This is the only book written solely to gauge the influence of catalogs. It requires some weeding through to get to the useful information, but it is revealing on how the catalogs reflect the evolving stature of women and blacks, for example.

Fewer books have been written about Montgomery Ward, but an excellent—and relatively recent—one is Frank B. Latham's *1872–1972: A Century of Serving Consumers. The Story of Montgomery Ward*. A useful history of mail order, it is especially good in its analysis of the effects current events—especially postal changes—had on mail order, and on the intense advertising war between Ward and Sears. It also provides detailed descriptions of the changes in the Ward catalogs over the years concerning size and design and Montgomery Ward promotional campaigns.

Montgomery Ward is also the focus of Booton Herndon's *Satisfaction Guaranteed: An Unconventional Report to Today's Consumers*. A chapter on "The Wonderful, Wonderful Catalog" is somewhat helpful, but overall the book is too general and the tone is trite.

A well-done history of Spiegel is *The Credit Merchants: A History of Spiegel, Inc.* by Orange A. Smalley and Frederick D. Sturdivant. It offers a great deal of minor information about the Spiegel catalog and mail order in general. It also includes an index with many listings under "Catalogs."

There are other useful histories. Mark Stevens's 1979 *"Like No Other Store in the World": The Inside Story of Bloomingdale's* offers some interesting catalog trivia. Ralph M. Hower's *History of Macy's of New York 1858–1919: Chapters in the Evolution of the Department Store* shows the influence of Montgomery Ward on Macy's use of catalogs, but also shows how the catalog was a flop for a big city store with large operating costs.

J. C. Penney wrote a number of books, but they are very general and written mainly to put forth his Christian beliefs. Somewhat more useful is Norman Beasley's *Main Street Merchant: The Story of the J. C. Penney Company*. It discusses how potential mergers with Montgomery Ward and then with Sears led Penney's into mail order.

There are also many articles available on L. L. Bean, a highly successful catalog pioneer, and the unusual *Whole Earth Catalog*. These include "Using the Old Bean" by John Skow in *Sports Illustrated,* "The L. L. Bean Sublime" by Benjamin DeMott in *Harper's,* and *Newsweek*'s "Whole Earth Revisited" by Lynn Langway and Pamela Abramson. And as new mail order empires are built, articles abound on their founders.

Among the more inclusive books on the mail order houses is Maxwell Sroge's *Inside the Leading Mail Order Houses,* which gives sales statistics on the top 250 mail order houses (which, amazingly, represent only 2 percent of all mail order firms). Godfrey M. Lebhar's *Chain Stores in America 1859–1962* includes a history of Sears and sales figures for Sears and Montgomery

Ward. A useful article is *Time*'s 1982 cover story, "Catalogue Cornucopia," which focuses on the business boom of the growing catalog market.

An increasing number of books are available about mail order, but almost all are how-to's for the entrepreneur, and few devote much attention to catalogs. The best is Richard S. Hodgson's *The Dartnell Direct Mail and Mail Order Handbook,* which has a chapter entitled "Catalogs and Price Lists" that focuses on technical considerations, especially catalog layout, and offers reasons behind the success of some of the biggest catalog companies.

A number of books on advertising include some discussion of catalogs. Frank Spencer Presbrey's *The History and Development of Advertising* offers a concise history of mail order and describes the influence catalogs have had on advertising technique. Daniel Pope's *The Making of Modern Advertising* discusses E. C. Allen and mail order papers. In *The Story of Advertising,* James Playsted Wood focuses on Sears, Roebuck and Company and how magazine ads lured people to examine the catalogs. Allan Marin's *Fifty Years of Advertising as Seen Through the Eyes of Advertising Age 1930–1980* includes partial reprints of some articles on Richard Sears that give a sense of his importance in the first half of the twentieth century.

There are also a number of history books that use catalog covers or pages as illustrations. These include the National Geographic Society's *We Americans,* Alistair Cooke's *America,* Gilman M. Ostrander's *American Civilization in the First Machine Age: 1890–1940,* and Mary Cable and American Heritage's *American Morals and Manners: A Picture History of How We Behaved and Misbehaved.*

There have been few really good articles analyzing the influence of catalogs on American culture. One of the best is Arthur G. Kimball's "Sears-Roebuck and Regional Terms" in a 1963 issue of *American Speech,* which analyzes how the Sears catalog has influenced linguistic changes, especially in rural areas. The author examines catalog indexes over several decades to show changes in speech patterns.

Language is one of the catalog influences discussed in Fred E. H. Schroeder's "Semi-Annual Installment on the American Dream: The Wish Book as Popular Icon" in *Icons of Popular Culture.* Also discussed are the catalog's influence on age-size standards and how the catalog represents a dream of material success for any American, regardless of status.

Also useful are Fred Powledge's "1652 Pages of the American Dream" in *Esquire,* which analyzes life-style changes through the Sears catalogs; George Milburn's "Catalogues and Culture" in *Good Housekeeping,* which discusses how catalogs have helped raise the standard of living by raising expectations; and Lovell Thompson's "Eden in Easy Payments" in a 1937 issue of the *Saturday Review of Literature,* which reviews the contents of that year's Sears catalog. John Garvey's "Dream Books" in *Commonweal* discusses how reprints of Sears catalogs, as well as the L. L. Bean and Whole Earth catalogs, are great for remembering the good old days. Other articles from the *Saturday Review of Literature* include Louis Greenfield's "Trade Winds," which shows the importance of catalogs in bringing literature to rural populations, and Jo Hubbard Chamberlin's "The Big Book," which describes how catalog items have changed over the years (to 1939). The best sources, however, remain the great "wish books" themselves.

NOTES

1. Frank B. Latham, *1872–1972: A Century of Serving Consumers. The Story of Montgomery Ward,* 2nd ed. (Chicago: Montgomery Ward, 1972), p. 96.
2. Ibid., p. 40.
3. David L. Cohn, *The Good Old Days: A History of American Morals and Manners as Seen Through the Sears, Roebuck Catalogs 1905 to the Present* (New York: Simon and Schuster, 1940), p. xxiii.
4. Boris Emmet and John E. Jeuck, *Catalogues and Counters: A History of Sears, Roebuck and Company* (Chicago: University of Chicago Press, 1950), p. 473.
5. Mary Cable and the Editors of American Heritage, *American Manners and Morals: A Picture History of How We Behaved and Misbehaved* (New York: American Heritage, 1969), p. 354.
6. Ibid., p. 339.
7. Emmet and Jeuck, p. 254.
8. Ibid., p. 84.
9. Lovell Thompson, "Eden in Easy Payments," *Saturday Review of Literature,* 15 (April 3, 1937), 15.
10. George Milburn, "Catalogues and Culture," *Good Housekeeping,* 122 (April 1946), 181.
11. Fred Powledge, "1652 Pages of the American Dream," *Esquire,* 74 (December 1970), 190.

BIBLIOGRAPHY

Books and Articles

"America's Wish Book." *Time,* 124 (August 20, 1984), 89.
Ash, Lee. *Subject Collections: A Guide to Book Collections and Subject Emphases as Reported by University, College, Public, and Special Libraries and Museums in the United States and Canada.* 6th ed. New York: R. R. Bowker, 1985.
Asher, Louis E., and Edith Heal. *Send No Money.* Chicago: Argus Books, 1942.
Associated Press. "Mail-Order Catalog Aids World's Needy." *Greenville News,* May 18, 1983, p. 3B.
Beasley, Norman. *Main Street Merchant: The Story of the J. C. Penney Company.* New York: Whittlesey House, 1948.
Bjorncrantz, C. E. "Sears' Big Book: Dinosaur or Phoenix?" *Direct Marketing,* 49 (July 1986), 71.
"Bosom Boards and Buggies." *Time,* 67 (April 16, 1956), 98.
Brann, W. L. *The Romance of Montgomery Ward and Company.* New York: Campbell, Starring, 1929.

"Building the Catalog that Brings in $150,000,000 a Year by Mail." *Printer's Ink,* 100 (July 19, 1917), 3.

Cable, Mary, and the Editors of American Heritage. *American Manners and Morals: A Picture History of How We Behaved and Misbehaved.* New York: American Heritage, 1969.

"Catalog Innovations: Montgomery Ward, Sears, Roebuck, and Chicago Mail Order Company." *Printer's Ink,* 190 (February 2, 1940), 45–46.

"Catalogue Cornucopia." *Time,* 120 (November 8, 1982), 72–73, 75–76, 78–79.

Chamberlin, Jo Hubbard. "The Big Book." *Saturday Review of Literature,* 20 (May 13, 1939), 10–12.

Cohn, David L. *The Good Old Days: A History of American Morals and Manners as Seen Through the Sears, Roebuck Catalogs 1905 to the Present.* New York: Simon and Schuster, 1940.

"A Computerized Catalog of Catalogs." *Newsweek,* 99 (March 8, 1982), 82.

Cooke, Alistair. *Alistair Cooke's America.* New York: Alfred A. Knopf, 1973.

Darnay, Brigitte T., ed. *Directory of Special Libraries and Information Centers.* 8th ed. Detroit: Gale Research, 1981.

De La Iglesia, Maria Elena. *The New Catalogue of Catalogues: The Complete Guide to World-Wide Shopping by Mail.* New York: Random House, 1975.

DeMott, Benjamin. "The L. L. Bean Sublime." *Harper's,* 269 (September 1984), 27.

De Vries, Leonard, and Ilonka van Amstel. *The Wonderful World of American Advertising 1865–1900.* London: John Murray, 1973.

Emmet, Boris, and John E. Jeuck. *Catalogues and Counters: A History of Sears, Roebuck and Company.* Chicago: University of Chicago Press, 1950.

Erbes, P. J., Jr. "Catalog Comeback: Alleged to Have Been on Its Deathbed Ten Years Ago, Mail Order Thrives Today as Never Before." *Printer's Ink,* 191 (April 5, 1940), 11–13.

———. "Catalog No. 126: Ward's 55th Anniversary Book." *Printer's Ink,* 178 (January 28, 1937), 121–22.

———. "Catalog Progress: Study of Current Sears and Ward Books." *Printer's Ink,* 176 (August 6, 1936), 37.

———. "Newest New Catalog: Sears, Roebuck's Latest Offering Drastically Modernized." *Printer's Ink,* 186 (January 26, 1939), 149–53.

Flower, Sidney. *The Mail Order Business.* Chicago: S. Flower, 1902.

Garvey, John. "Dream Books." *Commonweal,* 103 (February 27, 1976), 150–51.

Goldstein, Sue. *The Underground Shopper: A Guide to Discount Mail-Order Shopping.* New York: Andrews and McMeel, 1983.

"Goodbye, Great Wish Book." *Time,* 126 (August 12, 1985), 38.

Greenfield, Louis. "Trade Winds." *Saturday Review of Literature,* 24 (October 18, 1941), 40.

Herndon, Booton. *Satisfaction Guaranteed: An Unconventional Report to Today's Consumers.* New York: McGraw-Hill, 1972.

The History and Progress of Montgomery Ward and Co. . . . the Romance of the Golden Rule and Some Interesting Facts About the Mail Order Business. Chicago: Montgomery Ward, 1925.

Hodgson, Richard S. *The Dartnell Direct Mail and Mail Order Handbook.* 2nd ed. Chicago: Dartnell, 1974.

Holmes, Steven. "In Chicago: A Sears Catalogue of Kids." *Time,* 116 (July 7, 1980), 6.

Hower, Ralph M. *History of Macy's of New York 1858–1919: Chapters in the Evolution of the Department Store.* Cambridge, Mass.: Harvard University Press, 1943.

"Is the Store Becoming Obsolete?" *Time,* 112 (November 27, 1978), 94.

Kent, Rosemary. "King of the Catalogs." *Texas Monthly,* 5 (December 1977), 118–43.

Kimball, Arthur G. "Sears-Roebuck and Regional Terms." *American Speech,* 38 (October 1963), 209–13.

Kurath, Hans. *A Word Geography of the Eastern United States.* Ann Arbor: University of Michigan Press, 1949.

Langway, Lynn, and Pamela Abramson. "Whole Earth Revisited." *Newsweek,* 96 (November 17, 1980), 100, 103.

Latham, Frank B. *1872–1972: A Century of Serving Consumers. The Story of Montgomery Ward.* 2nd ed. Chicago: Montgomery Ward, 1972.

Lebhar, Godfrey M. *Chain Stores in America 1859–1962.* 3rd ed. New York: Chain Store Publishing, 1963.

Lee, James. *Twenty-five Years in the Mail Order Business.* Chicago: A. E. Swett, 1902.

Leypoldt, F., Lynds E. Jones, and R. R. Bowker. *The American Catalogue.* 1880–1911. Reprint. New York: Peter Smith, 1941.

Mahoney, Tom. *The Great Merchants: The Stories of Twenty Famous Retail Operations and the People Who Made Them Great.* New York: Harper and Brothers, 1955.

"Mail-Order Books." *Business Week,* 152 (June 26, 1943), 86–87.

Marin, Allan, ed. *Fifty Years of Advertising as Seen Through the Eyes of Advertising Age 1930–1980.* Chicago: Crain Communications, 1980.

Milburn, George. "Catalogues and Culture." *Good Housekeeping,* 122 (April 1946), 181–84.

"Millions by Mail." *Forbes,* 117 (March 15, 1976), 82.

"One 33J3663F and a 7J4202F: The Buying-by-Catalogue Boom." *Newsweek,* 63 (May 25, 1964), 88–90.

Ostrander, Gilman M. *American Civilization in the First Machine Age: 1890–1940.* New York: Harper and Row, 1970.

Packard, Vance. *The Hidden Persuaders.* New York: David McKay, 1957.

Penney, James Cash. *Fifty Years with the Golden Rule.* New York: Harper, 1950.

———. *View from the Ninth Decade: Jottings from a Merchant's Daybook.* New York: T. Nelson, 1961.

Pope, Daniel. *The Making of Modern Advertising.* New York: Basic Books, 1983.

Powledge, Fred. "1652 Pages of the American Dream." *Esquire,* 74 (December 1970), 190–93, 251–52.

Presbrey, Frank Spencer. *The History and Development of Advertising.* New York: Greenwood Press, 1968.

Reed, J. D. "Magalogs in the Mailbox." *Time,* 126 (September 2, 1985), 73.

Rips, Rae Elizabeth. "An Introductory Study of the Role of the Mail-Order Business in American History, 1872–1914." Master's thesis, University of Chicago, 1938.

Riviere, William A. *The L. L. Bean Guide to the Outdoors.* New York: Random House, 1981.

Roebuck, Alvah C. "Early and Some Later History of Sears, Roebuck and Co." 2 vol. manuscript. Chicago, 1940.

Schell, Frank J. *The Catalog: Yesterday, Today, Tomorrow.* (Pamphlet distributed by Sears, Roebuck and Co., Chicago, n.d.)

Schroeder, Fred E.H. "Semi-Annual Installment on the American Dream: The Wish Book as Popular Icon." In *Icons of Popular Culture.* Edited by Marshall Fishwick and Ray B. Browne. Bowling Green, Ohio: Bowling Green University Press, 1970, pp. 73–86.

Skow, John. "Using the Old Bean." *Sports Illustrated,* 63 (December 2, 1985), 84.

Smalley, Orange A., and Frederick D. Sturdivant. *The Credit Merchants: A History of Spiegel, Inc.* Carbondale: Southern Illinois University Press, 1973.

Sroge, Maxwell, with Bradley Highum. *Inside the Leading Mail Order Houses.* 2nd ed. Colorado Springs: M. Sroge, 1984.

Stevens, Mark. *"Like No Other Store in the World": The Inside Story of Bloomingdale's.* New York: Crowell, 1979.

"The Stores and the Catalogue." *Fortune,* 11 (January 1935), 69–74.

Thompson, Lovell. "Eden in Easy Payments." *Saturday Review of Literature,* 15 (April 3, 1937), 15–16.

Tyler, Poyntz, ed. *Advertising in America.* New York: H. W. Wilson, 1959.

Ulanoff, Stanley M. *Advertising in America: An Introduction to Persuasive Communication.* New York: Hastings House, 1977.

Wathey, Patricia Wogen. *The International Mail-Order Shopping Guide.* Englewood Cliffs, N.J.: Prentice-Hall, 1984.

We Americans. Washington, D.C.: National Geographic Society, 1975.

Wickware, Francis Sill. "Into the Towns and Across the Border: Concluding the Life and Times of Sears, Roebuck." *Collier's,* 124 (December 24, 1949), 30–32, 66–67.

———. "The Life and Times of Sears, Roebuck." *Collier's,* 124 (December 3, 1949), 18–19, 42–43.

———. " 'Please Rush the Gal in the Pink Corset': Continuing the Life and Times of Sears, Roebuck." *Collier's,* 124 (December 17, 1949), 28–29, 48–50.

———. " 'We Like Corn, on or off the Cob': Continuing the Life and Times of Sears, Roebuck." *Collier's,* 124 (December 10, 1949), 20–21, 73–74.

Wood, James Playsted. *The Story of Advertising.* New York: Donald Press, 1958.

Wood, Robert Elkington. *Mail Order Retailing Pioneered in Chicago.* New York: Newcomen Society of England, American Branch, 1948.

Worthy, James. *Shaping an American Institution: Robert E. Wood and Sears, Roebuck.* Urbana: University of Illinois Press, 1984.

Catalogs and Reprints

1897 Sears Roebuck Catalogue. Introduction by S. J. Perelman. Edited by Fred L. Israel. New York: Chelsea House Publishers, 1976.

The Last Whole Earth Catalog: Access to Tools. Menlo Park, Calif.: Portola Institute, 1971.

The 1902 Edition of the Sears, Roebuck Catalogue. New York: Bounty Books, 1969.

1927 Edition of the Sears, Roebuck Catalogue. Edited by Alan Mirken. New York: Bounty Books, 1970.

Sears, Roebuck and Company Catalogs 1888/89-Present. Chicago: Sears, Roebuck (microfilm).

Sears, Roebuck and Co. Consumers Guide: Fall 1900. Northfield, Ill.: DBI Books, 1970.

Sears, Roebuck and Co. 1908 Catalogue No. 117: The Great Price Maker. Edited by Joseph J. Schroeder, Jr. Chicago: Gun Digest, 1969.

Sears, Roebuck and Co. 1908 Solid Comfort Vehicles: Runabouts, Buggies, Phaetons, Surreys, Spring and Delivery Wagons, Pony Rigs, Cutters and Sleighs, Road Carts. Princeton: Pyne Press, 1971.

Whole Earth Epilog. Baltimore: Penguin Books, 1974.

Circus and Outdoor Entertainment

DON B. WILMETH

HISTORIC OUTLINE

Of all forms of early American popular entertainment, excluding popular theater, only the outdoor amusement industry and the circus have managed to survive changing times and tastes, despite noticeable alterations. The traveling tent circus has largely given way to presentation in permanent indoor arenas, and the traditional amusement park, despite the struggling survival of some, has evolved into the "theme" park, such as Disneyland or Six Flags Over Texas. To most observers, the differences between the various forms—be they circus, carnival, fair, or amusement park—are largely irrelevant. The memories evoked from each blur and meld into a single sensory recall. In reality, the various forms are quite different, and myriad examples can be isolated under the general heading of "outdoor entertainment" or, more correctly, "outdoor entertainment and environmental forms." In William F. Mangels's excellent but tentative survey, *The Outdoor Entertainment Business,* a long list of identifiable entertainments is enumerated: circuses, carnivals, amusement parks, carousels, roller coasters, dance halls, shooting galleries, penny arcades, world fairs, menageries, and so on. In this survey chapter, however, I have chosen to deal with only two major categories: (1) the circus and Wild West exhibitions, and (2) outdoor amusements (fairs, exhibitions, pleasure gardens, amusement parks, carnivals, seaside resorts, and theme parks). Although the other public amusements indicated by Mangels are legitimate individual forms, the two areas of concern here represent the major forms of American outdoor entertainment past and present, incorporating a number of the other items mentioned by Mangels.

The Circus

In 1968 Marcello Truzzi, in "The Decline of the American Circus," defined the circus as "a traveling and organized display of animals and skilled performances within one or more circular stages known as 'rings' before an audience encircling these activities." This definition, which provides a workable framework for a study of the circus, includes the traditional circus and the Wild West exhibition under the general category of a circus, but it excludes the carnival, which is socially a very distinct organization and depends, as does the amusement park, on its audience's active participation. The circus, on the other hand, demands a high degree of emotional empathy and passive involvement and thus is more closely related to traditional theater, whereas the carnival and its kin have evolved from the medieval fair tradition. Despite Truzzi's identification of the Wild West as a form of circus, its evolution and form are distinctive enough to be dealt with independently.

In its various forms, the circus is one of the oldest forms of popular entertainment. Historians have rather unsuccessfully attempted to trace the individual circus acts to antiquity, but the modern circus's connection with Rome's Circus Maximus or even earlier traditions is tenuous at best. The circus, as we know it today, more likely dates from the equestrian training circle of a much later period. Its clearest progenitor was Philip Astley who, in 1770, opened what amounted to a one-ring circus in London, featuring horsemanship acts and ultimately developing a form of theater called "hippodrama." The European circuses stayed close to Astley's original form, often in fixed locations, although adding in time clowns, acrobats, jugglers, trapeze artists, trained animals, and other acts. In America the early trend was toward size and movement. In the course of the circus's history, there have been in America, Mexico, and Canada since 1771 (up to the 1950s) over 1,100 circuses and menageries (an even earlier tradition and one of the definite predecessors of the circus in England and America). The peak period of the American circus was in 1903, with approximately ninety-eight circuses and menageries in existence. The pattern since 1903 has been one of steady decline.

The early American circus, then, was virtually transported from England. Although elements of the circus existed prior to 1793 in the form of individual acts, the man who brought the previously disparate elements together in Philadelphia in 1793 was John Bill Ricketts, a Scotsman who arrived in America in 1792. In his permanent building in Philadelphia, Ricketts presented trick riding, a tightrope walker, and a clown. Ricketts had been a pupil of Charles Hughes, whose Royal Circus at Blackfriar's Bridge in

London had been rival to Astley's since 1782. Subsequently, Ricketts's circus made appearances in New York, Boston, and Albany, as well as other cities in the United States and Canada.

The opening of the Erie Canal in 1825 afforded the increasing number of American circuses greater freedom in travel; traveling animal menageries had continued to parallel the increasing number of circuses. By the end of the first quarter of the nineteenth century, efforts were made to merge the menagerie and the circus. The elephant, which was to have a key role in the American circus, was first exhibited in 1796; the second and the most famous early elephant in the new country, Old Bet, was shown by Hackaliah Bailey with great success until 1816. Old Bet has mistakenly been associated by historians with Nathan Howe's circus. Howe and his partner Aaron Turner also have been credited mistakenly with the introduction of the circus tent around 1824. Recent research indicates, however, that the tent was probably not introduced until 1825 or 1826 by J. Purdy Brown.

During the first half of the nineteenth century, distinctive characteristics of the American circus began to evolve. The first circus parade dates from 1837, when a short-lived circus marched through the streets of Albany; in 1838, the circus first used rail travel as transportation (from Forsythe to Macon, Georgia); the first boat circus (under Gilbert Spalding and Charles Rogers), a forerunner of the show boat, dates from 1852. The 1890s and early years of this century saw many small railroad circuses traveling across the country, although wagon shows continued well into the twentieth century. Nevertheless, in time, motorized transportation and the railroad displaced mule power and horsepower. The circus of Tom Mix made the first transcontinental tour of the United States by a motorized circus in 1936.

Among the major changes in the pattern of the American circus, in addition to mobility, was the introduction of multiple rings, in contrast to the European one-ring format. Around 1873, William Cameron Coup added a second ring to the circus, utilizing the name of P. T. Barnum; in 1881, James A. Bailey negotiated the merger of several great circus operations, including Barnum's circus, and opened with the three-ring show. By 1885, virtually all American circuses had adopted the three rings. The circus now incorporated the menagerie, the concert, the side-show, and the street parade as integral ingredients.

The period between 1830 and 1870 saw the emergence of numerous prominent circuses in the history of the American circus, each with colorful and important histories: the George F. Bailey Circus; circuses utilizing the name of the "Lion King" (Isaac Van Amburgh); the several circuses of Seth B. Howes; the Mabie Brothers Circus; the Yankee (Fayette Ludovic) Robinson Circus; the John Robinson Circus; the Spalding and Rogers Circus; the Dan Castello Circus; the Dan Rice Circus (capitalizing on the name of the early American clown); and the W. W. Cole Circus.

The so-called golden age of the American circus—which lasted until about 1917—began in 1871, when W. C. Coup persuaded P. T. Barnum, the showman and museum entrepreneur, to become a partner in a circus enterprise. Barnum lent his name to other shows in addition to Coup's, which ultimately caused a split with Coup in 1875. In 1880, Barnum joined James A. Bailey and James L. Hutchinson in a new operation. This lucrative partnership lasted until 1885 when Barnum refused to deal further with Bailey, and Bailey sold his interest to James Cooper and W. W. Cole. In 1887, after Barnum had experienced a number of setbacks, including the loss of a Madison Square Garden contract to the rival Adam Forepaugh Circus, Barnum gave Bailey full control of the circus and added his name to the new "Barnum & Bailey Greatest Show on Earth." During this golden age, a number of the older circuses continued to compete or operate in their own regional circuits; other new prominent circuses came into their own, including the Sells Brothers Circus, the Great Wallace Circus, and the Lemen Brothers Circus.

The Ringlings, the name most frequently associated with the circus today, were late arrivals on the circus scene. None of the five brothers was involved until 1882. After seeing a traveling circus in their hometown of Baraboo, Wisconsin, they began to do a variety show around Wisconsin. In 1895, after adding more circus acts and animals to their menagerie, they made their first tour outside the Midwest and entered Barnum and Bailey's territory in New England. A year after Bailey's death in 1907, the Ringlings bought the Barnum and Bailey Circus; they finally merged as one in 1919, becoming "Ringling Brothers and Barnum & Bailey Combined Shows."

Various competitors tried to shut out the Ringlings, but the circus had become big business, and their efforts were fruitless; after 1910, the circuses had declined in number and in extravagance. The street parade became obsolete; menageries virtually vanished; and even the big top would practically disappear. Mechanization deprived the circus of its uniqueness and flair; individual initiative became dampened as well. Today, only a dozen or so circuses travel in the United States and they are only a faint reminder of the glories of the traveling tent circus of the turn of the century. During the 1940s and 1950s, the larger circuses—the Clyde Beatty, the King Brothers, and the Ringling shows—experienced a series of disasters. In 1957, "The Greatest Show on Earth" was forced to put away its big top and perform only in permanent facilities, thus depriving the major circus in the United States of one of its great attractions. Ironically, despite the near disappearance of the circus, its total audience continues to grow (thanks in part to television and films) and its revenue to swell. As the modern circus adjusts to modern demands, its age-old appeal apparently continues unabated.

The Wild West Exhibition

The so-called Wild West show is invariably associated with William Frederick "Buffalo Bill" Cody, who found the association of his enterprise with that of the circus or the use of the word "show" anathema. His billing was invariably "Buffalo Bill's Wild West," without the "show," and, if pressed, his general manager John M. Burke would insist that it was an exhibition. In its most ideal form, then, a Wild West show may be defined as an exhibition illustrating scenes and events characteristic of the American Far West frontier.

The exact origin of the Wild West show is difficult to pinpoint. The rodeo is related in part to the Wild West exhibition, insofar as a traveling rodeo with hired contestants would fit a common definition; yet the rodeo is normally a competitive sport in which the contestants pay an entrance fee and receive no pay except prize money. Thus, the kinship between the rodeo and the Wild West show should not be stressed, although, as mentioned below, they share a common beginning in terms of popularity. The Wild West actually evolved in part from the "specs" (or spectacular pageants) of the circus, the old traveling menageries, early exhibitions of cowboy skills and Indians dating from the 1820s, and the numerous plays, novels, and cheap popular literature of the nineteenth century.

Most historians of the Wild West show credit Cody with the consolidation and popularization of this form of entertainment. After ten seasons of performing in mediocre border melodramas built vaguely around his life and exploits as a scout, a buffalo hunter, and a frontiersman, Cody returned to his home of North Platte, Nebraska, in the summer of 1882. Upon his return, he was cajoled into planning the "Old Glory Blow-Out," a Fourth of July celebration of cowboy skill acts climaxed by a buffalo hunt in which Cody demonstrated with blank ammunition his methods of killing buffalo. This date in 1882, then, marks the upsurge of both the Wild West show and the rodeo, although doubtless not the first examples of either. (The rodeo harks back to the byplay and showoffs of early cattle roundups; an early form of the Wild West show was seen in New York by way of Boston in 1843; other elements of Cody's show existed prior to 1882.) What was new in Cody's Wild West exhibition was the combination that spelled success. In its ultimate form, Cody's Wild West became a dominant form of outdoor amusement, reaching its peak of popularity around 1893.

Cody's Wild West was on the upswing in 1883. Initially, his operation was not very successful, although it spawned a host of imitators. With the aid of Nate Salsbury, who joined Cody in 1884, and Dr. William F. Carver, whom he met in 1882–1883 (later, both Carver and Salsbury claimed to be the originator of the Wild West concept), Cody, who was not a consummate showman, began to experience phenomenal success. With the puffed releases of his colorful press agent–manager, "Arizona" or "Major" John M. Burke, Cody's show became the epitome of the romanticized and glamourized American West, particularly in Europe, where Cody made several successful tours. At the beginning of its history, the Wild West appeared to be a representation of the contemporary western scene but, as the old West vanished, it soon transcended the reality and created a legendary West based largely on illusion.

In its first decade, then, the Wild West show had a contemporary interest that began to fade after the turn of the century. The format, which originally had been new and unique, lacked variety, and showmen fell victim to the temptation to combine it with a circus or to add circus acts to its own pageantry. Gordon William Lillie, known as "Major Lillie," "Pawnee Bill," or "the White Chief of the Pawnees" (an early performer with Cody), thought the solution was to restyle his show as "Pawnee Bill's Historic Wild West and Great Far East." The latter included "every type of male and female inhabitant"—Hindu magicians, Singhalese dancers, Madagascar oxen cavalry, Australian bushmen, and so forth. Other shows featured notoriety. "Cummins's Wild West and Indian Congress" featured Red Cloud, Chief Joseph, Geronimo, and Calamity Jane. Despite the changing nature of the Wild West show after the 1890s, the largest number of such entertainments flourished in the early years of the twentieth century. In the course of its history, according to Don Russell, the foremost historian of this phenomenon, there were over one hundred Wild West shows. With the great proliferation of such organizations at the turn of the century, the shows became quite shabby. Cody's last European tour began in 1902 and by 1909 he had to merge his operation with that of Pawnee Bill. By 1908, the "101 Ranch Wild West Show," which began in 1892, became a permanent institution and major competition for the Cody-Pawnee Bill show. World War I marked the end of the golden era of outdoor show business, including the Wild West show. By 1918, there were no major Wild West shows, their popularity having been eclipsed by the increasing popularity of motion pictures and the growing appeal of the more "believable" portrayal of the movie cowboy.

Outdoor Entertainment

The American outdoor amusement industry evolved, as did the circus, from European traditions—the medieval fair and carnival and the seventeenth-century pleasure garden. Indeed, it is possible to trace elements of the carnival, fair, and amusement park back to antiquity. Before the American Revolution, pleasure gardens, modeled on London's most famous gardens, Vauxhall and Ranelagh, appeared in major cities on the East Coast. Like Vauxhall, which was the first internationally famous pleasure garden when it opened in 1661, the American version offered visitors food, drink, music, and free variety acts. As in England and France, the simple pleasure of strolling, eating, and drinking became tiresome, and amusements of a more thrilling and exciting nature were sought.

The end of the nineteenth century saw similar places of amusement develop, however, as a result of improved transportation and technology. With the invention of the trolley came the institution of so-called trolley parks. Dozens of such parks were established by street railways at the end of the line all over the country as an economical method of encouraging weekend riders to use the cars. Initially, these parks offered little that could not have been found at the earlier pleasure garden. During the nineteenth century, however, amusements offered at the gardens and at rural picnic groves and shore resorts began to increase in number and in sophistication. Also, by the 1880s, thanks to new technology, mechanical pleasure rides such as the carousel and a device called "the Ferris wheel" developed.

The most obvious stimulus for the outdoor amusement industry first began when the Vienna World's Fair was held at "The Prater" in Vienna in 1873. A new concept in outdoor entertainment was presented with its large array of amusement "machines" or rides, fun houses, games of chance, and other activities, which created a new and exciting kind of park. Although Jones's Woods, a grove of some 150 acres along the East River, offered New Yorkers in the early nineteenth century a large variety of amusements, it was not until 1893 and the World's Columbian Exposition in Chicago that American showmen sensed the lucrative potential of outdoor amusements.

The true emergence of the American carnival and the exploitation of amusement rides and concessions, then, is usually cited as 1893. Although an area outside the exposition fair proper, called the "Midway Plaisance," began slowly, when the concessionaires hyped its promotion and agreed that the assembled attractions should be moved to various cities, the idea of the street fair or modern carnival had been born. The traveling carnival was fully realized that same year when Frank C. Bostock presented a collection of attractions at Coney Island, the location later of the amusement park's great growth. Bostock's entertainment has been called the first modern carnival in that his efforts mark the first attempt to make portable a group of attractions. Initially these early carnivals were moved by horse-drawn wagons, but by 1914 the "Smith Greater Shows" was moved by truck.

As early as 1883 the more traditional state fairs were invaded by the amusement business, and amusement zones were included at all the world fairs after Chicago in 1893. The trolley companies mentioned above followed suit and patterned a number of the trolley parks after such amusement areas. Today, the carnival business is a large industry. One of the largest of the traveling carnivals, the "Royal American Shows," travels on eighty double-length railroad cars loaded with 145 massive pieces of equipment. Their midway features more than fifty rides and attractions and seven under-canvas shows, illustrating vividly the three distinctive features of the carnival—riding devices, shows or exhibits, and concessions.

The modern concept of the amusement park developed at Coney Island, a beach resort in Brooklyn, New York, which contained a series of parks and independent entertainments. There, beginning in 1895, street railway companies and seaside entertainment entrepreneurs had witnessed the evolution of the ultimate model on which to base their operations. Coney Island's fame began when Billy Boynton built Sea Lion Park in 1895, followed by George C. Tilyou's Steeplechase Park in 1897, and then the purchase in 1903 of Boynton's park by Frederic W. Thompson and Elmer (Skip) Dundy. They rebuilt the Boynton park into a lavish version of the Midway Plaisance—Luna Park—at a cost of nearly $1 million. Luna offered, on a more or less permanent basis, a wildly eclectic environment of attractions, illuminated at night by more than 250,000 incandescent lights. Across Surf Avenue from Luna, a real-estate speculator named William Reynolds quickly countered and spent $3.5 million to build Dreamland Park, where everything was on an even more exuberant scale, all lit by one million bulbs.

The great period of the traditional amusement park dates from Coney Island's spectacular growth at the turn of the century to about World War II, although its decline began, as did that of all outdoor entertainments, around World War I. However, while it lasted, the Coney Island model inspired countless other Luna Parks and Dreamlands all over America, until, by the early years of the new century, the amusement park had become a fixture of most large cities. From World War II to the present, the decline of the traditional amusement park has been slow but steady, with the announcement of the closing of major amusement parks a commonplace event. The lack of needed materials during the war, ultimate patrons' boredom with the aging attractions, natural disasters, and vandalism have all contributed to the traditional amusement park's demise.

A large number of surviving parks represent the latest phase of the outdoor amusement industry. As traditional parks declined in popularity, they were replaced by the "theme" parks, dating from the conception of Disneyland in Anaheim, California, which began in 1954. Apparently, the popularity of the amusement park is not waning. During the summer of 1976, over seventy-five million people attended such parks; more patrons rode roller coasters in 1977 than attended professional football and baseball games combined. Possibly, as Brooks McNamara has suggested, we are now approaching a kind of saturation point for this type of entertainment. If so, definite indications of such a development have yet to materialize fully.

REFERENCE WORKS

This chapter is intended as a companion to my chapter "Stage Entertainment" found elsewhere in the *Handbook of American Popular Culture*. In that essay, the nature of popular entertainment and the study of the major staged forms (dime museum, medicine shows, minstrelsy, vaudeville, burlesque, and popular theater) are discussed and sources provided. In order to conserve space and provide more coverage of those topics germane to this chapter, the overview from that chapter and most of the general sources discussed there are excluded here. This present coverage, however, has been prepared as a separate and complete guide to sources on the circus and outdoor entertainments. It is suggested, nonetheless, that readers consult that chapter for a more thorough guide to American forms of popular entertainment.

To date the most detailed bibliographies or information guides to American popular entertainment are Don B. Wilmeth's *American and English Popular Entertainment: A Guide to Information Sources* and *Variety Entertainment and Outdoor Amusements: A Reference Guide*. These assess most major sources, including unpublished scholarly works, through 1981. This present essay attempts to focus on the standard older sources as well as major published sources since 1981. Other shorter and older bibliographies include John H. Towsen's "Sources on Popular Entertainment" (general sources, basic research tools, libraries and museums, organizations, performer training) and my preliminary, select bibliography, "American Popular Entertainment: A Historical Perspective," which appeared in 1977 and was reprinted in 1979 in *American Popular Entertainment,* edited by Myron Matlaw. Raymond Toole-Stott's four-Volume *Circus and Allied Arts,* a guide to 15,000 sources, is still a standard guide for older sources.

Of the general sources on popular entertainment that put into perspective those forms discussed in this chapter, the most useful are Robert C. Toll's *On with the Show* and the older but still basic *Popular Entertainment Through the Ages* by Samuel McKechnie. Although the latter is limited largely to English forms, it is nonetheless an excellent overview of entertainment and covers most of the European roots of American forms. Joseph and June Bundy Csida's *American Entertainment: A Unique History of Popular Show Business,* an attempt to fashion a history of American entertainments from the files of *Billboard,* though it tries to accomplish too much, provides useful information on outdoor entertainment and the circus. Brooks McNamara's introduction to a special issue of the *Drama Review* on "Popular Entertainments" and Heinrich Richard Falk's "Conventions of Popular Entertainment: Framework for a Methodology" still offer sensible ideas for the study of popular forms. McNamara's "The Scenography of Popular Entertainment" remains a useful framework for studying the architecture and design of popular forms, including the circus and outdoor forms. Maurice Gorham's *Showmen and Suckers: An Excursion on the Crazy Fringe of the Entertainment World* explores the relationship between the showman and the sucker, a condition that prevails in all amusement forms discussed in this chapter. The most thorough exploration of the special language of forms discussed in this chapter, including over 3,000 examples of argot, slang, and terminology, is my *Language of American Popular Entertainment.*

A source that defies classification but surely deserves a place in this chapter is Ricky Jay's *Learned Pigs and Fireproof Women,* a study of the most unique, eccentric, and amazing entertainers to frequent the "show biz" world, many of whom were circus headliners or carnival freaks. Many of the individuals discussed were early itinerant performers, precursors of some of the stranger entertainers later found in more organized forms.

For most of the forms discussed in this chapter, *Amusement Business* is the most significant contemporary trade publication, although the weekly, *Variety,* remains the standard, basic serial for all forms of show business.

The Circus

Of all forms of American popular entertainment, the circus has received the greatest attention, and information is the most plentiful. Still, a great deal of primary material remains in private collections, and many of the published sources are by amateur historians and devoted circus fans who, until recently, have avoided careful documentation. As a result, a comprehensive, reliably researched history of the American circus has yet to be written, although a number of efforts in that direction have recently appeared. In the meantime, students of the circus must refer to those published sources that are most reliable and search for information in circus collections and in the pages of various periodicals and serials. These will be discussed at the conclusion of this section.

The most comprehensive guide to the circus and an indispensable reference for anyone researching the circus is Raymond Toole-Stott's four-volume *Circus and Allied Arts, a World Bibliography* and his more selective list in *A Bibliography of the Books on the Circus in English.* Combined, these major bibliographical volumes contain over 15,000 entries drawn from works in thirteen languages. It should be noted, however, that they are far more useful on foreign antecedents than on the American circus. Robert Sokan's *A Descriptive and Bibliographic Catalog of the Circus and Related Arts Collection at Illinois State University, Normal, Illinois* contains details on 1,373 items and is a useful guide as well. Two of my reference works contain bibliographies of major sources on the circus: *American and English Popular Entertainment* (annotations of 254 sources on the circus) and *Variety Entertainment and Outdoor Amusements* (discussion of over 300 sources). Types of circusiana are discussed in Richard Flint's "A Selected Guide to Source Material on the American Circus."

There are numerous general histories and surveys of the circus. George L. Chindahl's *History of the Circus in America* is especially good on the nineteenth century; John and Alice Durant's *Pictorial History of the American Circus* is sumptuously illustrated and contains a useful list of American circuses; and C. P. Fox and Tom Parkinson's *Circus in America* provides a decent coverage of the circus in its heyday. Isaac. J. Greenwood's *The Circus: Its Origin and Growth Prior to 1835* remains a useful early history, as do R. W. G. Vail's "The Early Circus in America" and "This Way to the Big Top," and John J. Jennings's *Theatrical and Circus Life; or, Secrets of the Stage, Green-Room and Sawdust Arena*. Of all the available surveys, Earl Chapin May's *The Circus from Rome to Ringling* (not to be confused with the less definitive *Circus! From Rome to Ringling* by Marian Murray) is considered by many circus authorities the best single-volume history available. For the uninitiated, Mildred S. and Wolcott Fenner's *The Circus: Lure and Legend* covers the entire gamut of circus literature.

Joe McKennon's *Horse Dung Trail: Saga of American Circus*, although a partially fictionalized history of the American circus from Yankee Robinson (1856) to the end of the horse-drawn circus (1940), is still generally correct in its historical basis. Of the more recent general world histories that place the American circus in international perspective, Rupert Croft-Cooke and Peter Cotes's *Circus: A World History*, Peter Verney's *Here Comes the Circus*, David Jamieson and Sandy Davidson's *The Colorful World of the Circus*, and George Speaight's *A History of the Circus* offer generally reliable accounts, although only Speaight provides some documentation and gives the American circus plentiful coverage. Wilton Eckley's *The American Circus* is the only recent history focusing exclusively on the American circus, although the coverage is limited from the later nineteenth century to the demise of the railroad circus in 1956. Also informative is Robert Toll's coverage of the circus in *On with the Show* and several non-English works, most notably Henry Thetard's *La Merveilleuse Histoire du cirque*; Rolf Lehman's *Circus: Magie der Manege*; and Dominique Jando's *Histoire mondiale du cirque*.

The English prototype of the early American circus is covered with scholarly exactitude in A. H. Saxon's *Enter Foot and Horse* and *The Life and Art of Andrew Ducrow and The Romantic Age of the English Circus*. Less reliable but still recommended are Thomas Frost's *Circus Life and Circus Celebrities*, a classic study of the early English circus, and M. Willson Disher's *Greatest Show on Earth*, which provides an informative and amusing history of Astley's. Recent unpublished scholarly studies include Paul Alexander Daum's "The Royal Circus 1782–1809: An Analysis of Equestrian Entertainments" and George Palliser Tuttle's "The History of the Royal Circus, Equestrian and Philharmonic Academy, 1782–1816, St. George's Fields, Surrey, England."

The early period of the American circus has received careful and documented attention by Stuart Thayer in *Annals of the American Circus 1793–1829*, its sequel, *Annals of the American Circus 1830–1847*, and his earlier small book, *Mudshows and Railers: The American Circus in 1879*. Though not as well documented, Copeland MacAllister's *Uncle Gus and the Circus* focuses on a segment of circus history from 1850 to 1871. Also useful are James S. Moy's "Entertainments at John B. Ricketts's Circus, 1793–1800" and his doctoral dissertation, "John B. Ricketts's Circus 1793–1800"; William W. Clapp, Jr.'s *A Record of the Boston Stage;* Joseph Cowell's *Thirty Years Passed Among the Players in England and America*; John Durang's *The Memoirs of John Durang*, edited by Alan S. Downer; and Chang Reynolds's *Pioneer Circuses of the West*.

Of the plethora of sources on specific circuses or regions, the following offer informative and sometimes insightful accounts: Elbert R. Bowen's *Theatrical Entertainment in Rural Missouri Before the Civil War* and "The Circus in Early Rural Missouri"; Bob Barton's *Old Covered Wagon Show Days,* on the Cole Brothers wagon show in the 1890s; Fred Bradna and Hartzell Spence's *The Big Top: My Forty Years with the Greatest Show on Earth;* Bert J. Chipman's *Hey Rube,* which includes a roster of major circuses (1900–1915); Herb Clement's *The Circus, Bigger and Better Than Ever?*, an account of smaller, contemporary circuses; Richard E. Conover's *The Affairs of James A. Bailey, The Great Forepaugh Show,* and *Give 'Em a John Robinson; This Way to the Big Top: The Life of Dexter Fellows,* the life story of the press agent for Ringling Brothers and Barnum & Bailey, by Dexter W. Fellows and Andrew A. Freeman; Henry Ringling North's *The Circus Kings,* on the Ringling family; the superior *Those Amazing Ringlings and Their Circus* by Gene Plowden; Fred Powledge's *Mud Show: A Circus Season,* a fascinating glimpse of a third-rate traveling circus during the 1974 season; and Gil Robinson's *Old Wagon Show Days,* an account of the John Robinson Circus. Other sources of value include the following: John S. Clarke's *Circus Parade*; Courtney Ryley Cooper's *Under the Big Top* (the circus in the 1920s); W. C. Coup's *Sawdust and Spangles*; Will Delavoye's *Show Life in America*, a not very reliable but unusual source on the illegal methods used by some traveling circuses; *California's Pioneer Circus, Joseph Rowe, Founder. Memoirs and Personal Correspondence Relative to the Circus Business Through the Gold Country in the Fifties* (edited by Albert Dressler); Al G. Field's *Watch Yourself Go By,* circus life in the nineteenth century; Gene Fowler's *Timber Line* (Sells-Floto circus); Alvin F. Harlow's *The Ringlings*; Dean Jensen's beautifully produced *The Biggest, the Smallest, the Longest , the Shortest,* on the Wisconsin circus tradition; F. Beverly Kelley's *It Was Better Than Work,* the memoirs of the late press agent and advance man for Ringling Brothers and Barnum & Bailey; John C. Kunzog's *Tanbark and Tinsel*; Penelope Leavitt and James S. Moy's essay "Spalding and Rogers' Floating Palace, 1852–1859," which explores the architectural features and reasons for success of this unique operation; Esse F. O'Brien's *Circus: Cinders to Sawdust*, a mixture of circus lore and history, yet insightful on the nineteenth-century circus; Gene Plowden's *Circus Press Agent*, the forty-year career of Roland Butler; and Dave Robeson's *Al G. Barnes, Master Showman*.

The circus clown has received superb treatment in John H. Towsen's *Clowns*, the only full survey of the clown in all its various forms with full documentation. Numerous general surveys of clowns have appeared in the last decade or so. Of this group, the following are among the better ones: George Speaight, *The Book of Clowns*; Beryl Hugill, *Bring on the Clowns* (less complete than Towsen or Speaight); Lowell Swortzell, *Here Comes the Clowns: A Cavalcade of Comedy from Antiquity to the Present*; George Bishop, *The World of Clowns*; and Douglas Newton, *Clowns*. Phyllis A. Rogers's scholarly study, "The American Circus Clown," provides a good discussion of the process by which one becomes a clown and gives an ethnographic description of the world from the clown's point of view. Finally, Bill Ballantine's *Clown Alley* vividly recounts the story of Clown College, Ringling Brothers and Barnum & Bailey's training program for clowns.

Various general aspects of the circus, including the parade, circus life, and so forth, have received considerable attention. Among these sources, the following are suggested: Courtney Ryley Cooper's *Circus Day*, impressions of circus life during the first half of this century; Anthony D. Hippisley Coxe's *A Seat at the Circus*, a vivid description of a typical circus performance; the works of Charles Philip Fox, especially *Circus Parades, A Ticket to the Circus, A Pictorial History of Performing Horses, American Circus Posters in Full Color*, and *Old-Time Circus Cuts: A Pictorial Archive of 202 Illustrations*; Jill Freedman's *Circus Days*, a pictorial essay on the Beatty-Cole Circus; Edwin Martin and Don B. Wilmeth's *Mud Show: American Tent Circus Life*, a collection of photographs of seven contemporary traveling tent circuses with an extensive introduction on the history of the circus, its appeal, and decline; Jack Rennert's *100 Years of Circus Posters*; and Marcello Truzzi's "The American Circus as a Source of Folklore: An Introduction" and "Folksongs of the American Circus." The parade has been covered in Richard E. Conover's *Telescoping Tableaux* and *The Fielding Band Chariots*; Fox's *Circus Parades: A Pictorial History of America's Pageant*; Fox and F. Beverly Kelley's *The Great Circus Street Parade in Pictures*; and Gene Plowden's *Singing Wheels and Circus Wagons* and *Merle Evans, Maestro of the Circus*. All aspects of the circus train are covered in Tom Parkinson and Charles Philip Fox's *The Circus Moves by Rail*; less extensive but still good for logistics is Joe McKennon's *Logistics of the American Circus*. The use of Percheron horses in the circus is given extensive coverage in Fox's *Circus Baggage Stock*. The history and nature of circus advertising, extensively illustrated, can be found in Fox and Parkinson's *Billers, Banners and Bombast*. David Lewis Hammarstrom's *Behind the Big Top* contains behind-the-scenes stories about circus performers, owners, and other participants in the circus experience.

P. T. Barnum's ties to the circus are more tenuous than most people realize. The three most reliable biographies of Barnum, however, do include information on his associations with the circus: Neil Harris's *Humbug: The Art of P. T. Barnum*, the best-documented study of Barnum; Irving Wallace's *The Fabulous Showman*, a useful and generally reliable popular study; and M. R. Werner's *Barnum*. Additional sources on Barnum can be found in Nelle Neafie's *A P. T. Barnum Bibliography* and in the chapter entitled "Stage Entertainment" in this handbook.

Because of Barnum's association with the museum, freaks and sideshows are closely related to his contributions to show business. Among the various works on this topic, the following are most comprehensive: Colin Clair's *Human Curiosities;* Frederick Drimmer's *Very Special People;* Leslie Fiedler's *Freaks: Myths and Images of the Secret Self*, the most stimulating and provocative study of the freak; Harry Lewiston, as told to Jerry Holtman, *Freak Show Man;* Daniel Mannix's *We Who Are Not as Others*; and Albert Parry's *Tattoo: Secrets of a Strange Art.*

Sources on performers and animal trainers are too extensive to list in any great number here. Most, however, are chatty autobiographies or biographies and include little that cannot be found in the more reliable general histories and surveys. A few, however, are worthy additions to the literature on the circus. Among these are the following: Bill Ballantine's *Wild Tigers and Tame Fleas;* Clyde Beatty's *The Big Cage;* Frank Bostock's *The Training of Wild Animals,* a good source on early methods of animal training; Courtney Ryley Cooper's *Lion 'N' Tigers 'N' Everything* and *With the Circus;* H. Hediger's *Studies of the Psychology and Behaviour of Captive Animals in Zoos and Circuses;* Lorenz Hagenbeck's *Animals Are My Life;* J. Y. Henderson's *Circus Doctor,* the career of the chief veterinarian of the Ringling Brothers, Barnum & Bailey Circus; Ernest Schlee Millette's *The Circus That Was,* the life of an acrobat; Edwin P. Norwood's *The Other Side of the Circus* and *The Circus Menagerie;* Roman Proske's *Lions, Tigers, and Me;* and Jake Posey's *Last of the Forty Horse Drivers.* Of all recent books on circus animals, the definitive study to date is Joanne Carol Joy's *The Wild Animal Trainer in America,* not only a full history but a perspective investigation of methods of training and the work of modern protection agencies.

A few scholars outside of the immediate area of circus history have shown an interest in the circus from the sociological point of view. Foremost among these is Marcello Truzzi, whose "The Decline of the American Circus" provides a perceptive and penetrating analysis of the circus. He has also edited a special issue of the *Journal of Popular Culture* on "Circuses, Carnivals and Fairs in America," which demonstrates new approaches to circus study. His studies of the carnival, discussed in the section on outdoor entertainment, are even more significant. Paul Bouissac, a linguist and semiotician, has provided a unique method for examining the circus in *Circus and Culture: A Semiotic Approach;* Walter M. Gerson looks at the circus as a social entity in "The Circus: A Mobile Total Institution"; and Robert C. Sweet and Robert W. Habenstein examine significant changes in the circus since 1920 in "Some Perspective on the Circus in Transition."

The unique language of the circus is most thoroughly enumerated in Don B. Wilmeth's *The Language of American Popular Entertainment,* Joe Mc-Kennon's *Circus Lingo,* and, to a lesser extent, in Sherman Louis Sergel's *The Language of Show Biz* and David W. Maurer's "Carnival Cant: A Glossary of Circus and Carnival Slang." Other sources of circus terminology are listed in Wilmeth's glossary.

Necessarily excluded from the bibliography, but of prime significance in the study and research of the circus, are articles from circus periodicals. The circus trade journals, the *New York Clipper* for the latter half of the nineteenth century and *Billboard* for this century, remain the best sources. Although quality and depth of contributions vary, essays in *Bandwagon,* the journal of the Circus Historical Society, provide useful glimpses at specific circuses and at limited time spans of circus history. Especially recommended are the contributions of Stuart Thayer, Fred D. Pfening, Jr., Richard Flint, C. H. Amidon, Joseph T. Bradbury, Gordon M. Carver, John F. Polacsek, Chang Reynolds, Bob Parkinson, and Richard E. Conover. Of less value are essays in *White Tops,* the journal of the Circus Fans Association of America, and in *Little Circus Wagon,* the journal of the Circus Model Builders Association. A superb international journal is *Le Cirque dans l'Univers,* published for the Club de Cirque in France.

The major circus collections are the Circus World Museum Library in Baraboo, Wisconsin, which has a collection especially rich in advertising materials (a helpful brochure on its holdings is available upon request); the Hertzberg Circus Collection in San Antonio, Texas, with extensive holdings of late nineteenth-century material; the Joe E. Ward Collection of circus memorabilia in the Hoblitzelle Theatre Arts Library at the University of Texas in Austin; the Illinois State University Circus and Related Arts Collection in Normal, Illinois, possibly the best balanced collection in the United States; the McCaddon Collection in the Princeton University Library, which houses the working papers of the Barnum and Bailey Circus, ca. 1890 to 1910; the New York Historical Society, which holds the Westervelt Collection of Barnum material, plus some items on the circus; the Ringling Museum of the Circus in Sarasota, Florida, a relatively minor collection; and the Somers, New York, Historical Society, with materials on the early American circus from the area called the "cradle of the American circus."

The Wild West Exhibition

Most general histories of the circus, as well as collections and periodicals listed in the previous section, contain some mention of Wild West shows or house primary materials. There is, however, a growing literature devoted exclusively to this form of entertainment. The most definitive and comprehensive history to date is Don Russell's *The Wild West; or, A History of the Wild West Show*. Also useful are his essays "Cody, Kings, and Coronets," covering the first ten years of Buffalo Bill's Wild West, and "The Golden Age of Wild West Shows." Other studies of the form that provide varying points of view are William Brasmer's "The Wild West Exhibition and the Drama of Civilization," a deprecating view of the phenomenon; Ellsworth Collings and Alma Miller England's *The 101 Ranch*, the definitive source on the Miller brothers; Fred Gipson's *Fabulous Empire: Colonel Zack Miller's Story*, a less reliable history of the 101 Wild West Show; Carolyn Thomas Foreman's *Indians Abroad*, a history of the foreign travel of Indians, including their associations with Wild West shows; Milt Hinkle's "The Kit Carson Wild West Show" and "The Way a Wild West Show Operated"; Madelon B. Katigan's "The Fabulous 101," one of the better brief accounts of this important organization; Ruel McDaniel's "Requiem for the Wild West Shows," the career of Glenn Kischko, who witnessed the glory and death of the spectacles of the Wild West show; Paul E. Mix's *The Life and Legend of Tom Mix;* Fred D. Pfening, Jr.'s *Col. Tim McCoy's Real Wild West and Rough Riders of the World*, the story of a late Wild West enterprise; Joseph Schwartz's "The Wild West Show; 'Everything Genuine,' " a good analysis of the show's appeal; Glenn Shirley's *Pawnee Bill: A Biography of Major Gordon W. Lillie*, which contains an informative history of the Wild West show in general and valuable data on the association between the shows of Cody and Lillie; and Chauncey Yellow Rob's "The Menace of the Wild West Show," a strong attack on the effect of these shows on the American Indian.

As might be expected, most published material on the Wild West concerns Buffalo Bill Cody and his exhibition. Among the dozens of biographies of Cody, a few deal not only with Cody's life before the Wild West but also with the show itself and individuals associated with it. John Burke's *Buffalo Bill, the Noblest Whiteskin*, though not definitive, is readable and essentially correct; Rupert Croft-Cooke and W. S. Meadmore's *Buffalo Bill: The Legend, the Man of Action, the Showman* presents a sympathetic treatment of Cody; William E. Deahl, Jr., in "Nebraska's Unique Contribution to the Entertainment World," deals with the beginnings of the Wild West show in 1883, and his "Buffalo Bill's Wild West Show in New Orleans" examines Cody's appearances at the 1884 World's Industrial and Cotton Exposition; Charles Eldridge Griffin's *Four Years in Europe with Buffalo Bill* reviews the 1903–7 seasons in Europe; Alice J. Hall's "Buffalo Bill and Enduring West" is a serviceable overview with excellent photographs by James L. Amos; Walter Havighurst presents a good popular account of "Little Sure Shot" in *Annie Oakley of the Wild West*.

Albert Johannsen's *The House of Beadle and Adams* is the most complete reference source on the major publisher of dime novels and provides extensive coverage of Cody and stories about him; Jay Monaghan's *The Great Rascal; The Life and Adventures of Ned Buntline* is the best biography of Edward Zane Carroll Judson (Buntline) and provides adequate coverage of his association with Cody; Isabelle S. Sayers's *Annie Oakley and Buffalo Bill's Wild West* contains all the essential facts plus 102 superb illustrations; Raymond W. Thorp's *Spirit Gun of the West: The Story of Doc W. F. Carver* is the definitive biography of Cody's early associate; and Nellie Snyder Yost's *Buffalo Bill: His Family, Friends, Fame, Failures, and Fortune* is the most recent full-length biography, though not necessarily superior in its coverage of the Wild West.

In addition to Cody's numerous autobiographies—none very reliable— a number of biographies were written by Cody's relatives, including the fairly accurate picture of Cody in *Buffalo Bill, King of the Old West* by Elizabeth Jane Leonard and Cody's sister Julia Cody Goodman, and *Last of the Great Scouts* by Helen Cody Wetmore (also Cody's sister), but less reliable than the Goodman account. The two best biographical studies of Cody, however, are Don Russell's *The Lives and Legends of Buffalo Bill* and Henry Blackman Sell and Victor Weybright's *Buffalo Bill and the Wild West;* the latter combining biography with a knowledgeable analysis of the Wild West presentation and the legend of Buffalo Bill. Richard J. Walsh's *The Making of Buffalo Bill,* written in collaboration with Milton S. Salsbury, is a fascinating study of the process by which Cody became a semi-legendary figure and how he was the subject of the deliberate and infinitely skillful use of publicity. A good visual sense of that exploitation can be seen in Jack Rennert's *100 Posters of Buffalo Bill's Wild West.* The most recent and best-documented study of Cody's show is Sarah J. Blackstone's *Buckskins, Bullets, and Business: A History of Buffalo Bill's Wild West.* Also useful is her essay "Scalps, Bullets, and Two Wild Bills," an examination of the treatment of the American Indian based in part on the longer study.

Virtually all the circus collections and periodicals enumerated in the last section contain a great deal on the Wild West show. From time to time, dozens of journals and magazines on the West include essays of interest on the subject of the Wild West show. In addition to the collections already mentioned, the researcher should be familiar with the collections held in the Western History Department of the Denver Public Library, the Nebraska State Historical Society, and the Arizona Pioneers Historical Society. The best-known Buffalo Bill collection can be found at the Buffalo Bill Historical Center in Cody, Wyoming, which includes the Plains Indian Museum, the Buffalo Museum, and the Whitney Gallery of Western Art. Material on the 101 Wild West and Pawnee Bill's Wild West is located in the University of Oklahoma archives in Norman.

Outdoor Entertainment

Fairs, pleasure gardens, expositions, carnivals, amusement parks, and other outdoor amusement forms are closely related to variety shows and the circus, but they have only recently been examined as entertainment vehicles with theatrical elements. Instead of conventional theatrical conventions, these forms depend more on entertainment environments and on a mobile audience. Only the major sources on outdoor entertainment can be mentioned in this chapter; it should be noted, however, that a number of these forms, in particular the American fair (other than world fairs) and the American pleasure garden, have received little serious attention. The special issue of the *Journal of Popular Culture* on "Circuses, Carnivals and Fairs in America," edited by Marcello Truzzi, makes an excellent beginning place for a study of these forms. Patrick C. Easto and Truzzi's "Towards an Ethnography of the Carnival Social System" includes a useful review and evaluation of much of the early available literature.

In order to examine the American forms of outdoor entertainment, background sources are essential. The following items provide an adequate starting place: David Braithwaite's *Fairground Architecture: The World of Amusement Parks, Carnivals, and Fairs;* Thomas Frost's *The Old Showmen and the Old London Fairs,* a standard source; T. F. G. Dexter's *The Pagan Origin of Fairs;* Henry Morley's classic work, *Memoirs of Bartholomew Fair;* Ian Starsmore's *English Fairs;* and H. W. Waters's *History of Fairs and Expositions.* The pleasure garden is best covered in W. S. Scott's *Green Retreats, the Story of Vauxhall Gardens,1661–1859;* James Southworth's *Vauxhall Gardens: A Chapter in the Social History of England;* and Warwick Wroth's *The London Pleasure Gardens in the Eighteenth Century* (with Edgar Arthur) and *Cremorne and the Later London Gardens.* The American equivalent has received little attention, although Joseph Jackson, in "Vauxhall Garden," discusses a Pennsylvania garden (1814–1824); David Ritchey, in "Columbia Garden: Baltimore's First Pleasure Garden," focuses on another early example; and Thomas M. Garrett's "A History of Pleasure Gardens in New York City, 1700–1865" surveys forty-eight such places of amusement. O. G. Sonneck, in *Early Concert Life in America* (1731–1800), devotes much of this study to concerts performed at early pleasure gardens. Major world fairs are surveyed adequately in Edo McCullough's *World's Fair Midway: An Affectionate Account of American Amusement Areas from the Crystal Palace to the Crystal Ball.* David F. Burg's *Chicago White City of 1893* is the most complete history of the World's Columbian Exposition, the major stimulant for the amusement business. The most significant recent study of world fairs in the United States is Robert W. Rydell's *All the World's a Fair,* which examines the "reality behind the utopian visions embodied" in the twelve international expositions organized in major American cities from 1876 to World War I. A quarterly journal, *World's Fair,* provides frequent historical essays.

The best historical surveys of American outdoor entertainment are William F. Mangels's *The Outdoor Entertainment Business* and Joe McKennon's *A Pictorial History of the American Carnival*. Less comprehensive but still useful are Al Griffin's *"Step Right Up Folks!"* and Gary Kyriazi's *The Great American Amusement Parks*. A useful brief historical survey is Richard W. Flint's "Meet Me in Dreamland: The Early Development of Amusement Parks in America," including helpful notes and good illustrations.

Specific sources on the carnival are quite uneven and vary from excellent to extremely mediocre, but they are still informative or revelatory. Among the better sources are Marcello Truzzi and Patrick C. Easto's "The Carnival as a Marginally Legal Work Activity: The Typological Approach to Work Systems"; Easto and Truzzi's "Carnivals, Roadshows and Freaks"; William Lindsay Gresham's *Monster Midway;* Wittold Krassowski's "Social Structure and Professionalization in the Occupation of the Carnival Worker"; John Scarne's "Carnival, Fair, Bazaar, Arcade and Amusement Park Games"; Rollin Lynde Hartt's *The People at Play: Excursions in the Humor and Philosophy of Popular Amusements;* Theodore M. Dembroski's "Hanky Panks and Group Games Versus Alibis and Flats: The Legitimate and Illegitimate of the Carnival's Front End"; Don Boles's *The Midway Showman;* and John F. Cuber's "Patrons of Amusement Parks," a sociological study based on interviews with amusement park patrons in the Cleveland area in 1939.

The writing of Daniel Mannix, a former carnie, provides insights into carnival performers, especially *Step Right Up* and *We Who Are Not as Others,* discussed in the circus section (along with other sources on sideshows and freaks). A number of journalistic writers have captured carnival atmosphere, despite factual weaknesses: good examples are Arthur Lewis's *Carnival,* which makes entertaining reading, and Harry Crews's "Carny," which reveals more of the seamy side of carnival life, as does Susan Meiselas's *Carnival Strippers.* The slang of the carnival is explained in David W. Maurer's "Carnival Cant: A Glossary of Circus and Carnival Slang" and Don B. Wilmeth's *The Language of American Popular Entertainment.*

In addition to the historical surveys of American outdoor entertainment mentioned above (Mangels, McKennon, Griffin, and Kyriazi), Brooks McNamara's "Come on Over: The Rise and Fall of the American Amusement Park" provides a succinct but useful summary of that development. Sylvester Baxter's "The Trolley in Rural Parks" and Day Allen Willey's "The Trolley-Park" provide an understanding of the recreation grounds run by street railway companies.

Coney Island and its amusement parks have been thoroughly studied in Peter Lyon, "The Master Showman of Coney Island" (George Tilyou); Edo McCullough, *Good Old Coney Island;* Robert E. Snow and David E. Wright, "Coney Island: A Case Study in Popular Culture and Technical Change"; and Oliver Pilat and Jo Ranson, *Sodom by the Sea: An Affectionate History of Coney Island.* The study with the greatest perspective and the most effective analysis of the phenomenon, however, is John Kasson's succinct but extremely perceptive study *Amusing the Million: Coney Island at the Turn of the Century*. The most unique investigation of Coney Island is to be found in Rem Koolhaas's *Delirious New York: A Retroactive Manifesto for Manhattan*, in which he looks at the architecture of Coney Island and its symbiotic relationship to the city.

Seaside resorts and amusement areas are discussed in Charles F. Funnell's *By the Beautiful Sea: The Rise and High Times of That Great American Resort, Atlantic City;* Seon and Robert Manley's *Beaches: Their Lives, Legends, and Lore;* and Richmond Barrett's *Good Old Summer Days*. Also useful is Vicki Gold Levi and Lee Eisenberg's *Atlantic City: 125 Years of Ocean Madness*.

In recent years a great deal has been published on the unique art of the amusement park and in particular the carousel. A most stunning and highly recommended work is *Fairground Art* by Geoff Weedon and Richard Ward, full of magnificent illustrations, more than 700 in color. Less extensive in its coverage but still recommended is Frederick and Mary Fried's *America's Forgotten Folk Arts*, with sections on carousel figures and midway show fronts, among other relevant topics. Still standard is Frederick Fried's *Pictorial History of the Carousel*, although several new books include far more visually exciting photographs of carousel animals, most notably Tobin Fraley's *The Carousel Animal*, with photographs by Gary Sinick, Nina Fraley's *The American Carousel*, and William Manns's *Painted Ponies*. An informative source on the design of various outdoor entertainments, including the amusement and theme parks, is Anthony Wylson's *Design for Leisure Entertainment*.

The latest phase of the outdoor amusement industry, the theme park, has received little serious attention other than the coverage in the survey sources listed above and in various guides to amusement parks, representative of which are Tim Onosko's *Fun Land U.S.A.* and Jeff Ulmer's *Amusement Parks of America*, the latter a guide to 319 parks. A more serious analysis of the industry is the special issue of *Theatre Crafts*, "Theme Parks," with ten excellent essays on various aspects of the parks. Typical of the numerous sources on the Walt Disney empire are Richard Beard's *Walt Disney's Epcot*, Richard Schickle's *The Disney Version*, and Christopher Finch's *The Art of Walt Disney from Mickey Mouse to the Magic Kingdoms*.

A study of any aspect of the amusement industry is incomplete without frequent use of *Amusement Business*, the bible of the outdoor amusement business and a spin-off of *Billboard*, another major show business weekly paper. Of special interest is *Amusement Business's* seventy-fifth anniversary issue (December 1969). There are no significant special collections that focus extensively on forms of outdoor entertainment, although several organizations, in particular the International Association of Amusement Parks and Attractions (North Riverside, Illinois) and the Outdoor Amusement Business Association (Minneapolis), promote the interests of the industry.

Finally, although non-print resources, two 1984 documentary films on U.S. world fairs deserve a place in this survey for their excellent insights into the fair's place in our cultural history. Bill Moyers's "A Walk Through the Twentieth Century: Come to the Fairs" provides a vivid overview (available from PBS Video, 1320 Braddock Place, Alexandria, Virginia 22314), and "The World of Tomorrow," produced and directed by Tom Johnson and Lance Bird, is a wonderfully evocative study of how we view our past and is highly recommended (Media Study/Buffalo, 305 E. 21st Street, New York, New York 10011 or Direct Cinema Limited, P.O. Box 69589, Los Angeles, California 90069).

BIBLIOGRAPHY

Books and Articles

General Sources

Csida, Joseph, and June Bundy Csida. *American Entertainment: A Unique History of Popular Show Business*. New York: Billboard/Watson-Guptill, 1978.

Falk, Heinrich Richard. "Conventions of Popular Entertainment: Framework for a Methodology." *Journal of Popular Culture*, 9 (Fall 1975), 480–81.

Gorham, Maurice [Anthony Coneys]. *Showmen and Suckers: An Excursion on the Crazy Fringe of the Entertainment World*. London: Percival Marshall, 1951.

Jay, Ricky. *Learned Pigs and Fireproof Women*. New York: Villard Books, 1987.

McKechnie, Samuel. *Popular Entertainment Through the Ages*. 1931. Reprint. New York: Benjamin Blom, 1969.

McNamara, Brooks. [Introduction]. "Popular Entertainment Issue." *The Drama Review*, 18 (March 1974), 3–4.

———. "The Scenography of Popular Entertainment." *The Drama Review*, 18 (March 1974), 16–25.

Matlaw, Myron, ed. *American Popular Entertainment: Papers and Proceedings on the History of American Popular Entertainment*. Westport, Conn.: Greenwood Press, 1979.

Toll, Robert C. *On with the Show: The First Century of Show Business in America*. New York: Oxford University Press, 1976.

Toole-Stott, Raymond. *Circus and Allied Arts, a World Bibliography*. 4 vols. Derby, England: Harpur, 1958–71.

Towsen, John H. "Sources on Popular Entertainment." *The Drama Review*, 18 (March 1974), 118–22.

Wilmeth, Don B. "American Popular Entertainment: A Historical Perspective." *Choice,* 14 (October 1977), 987–1004. Reprinted in *American Popular Entertainment*. Edited by Myron Matlaw. Westport, Conn.: Greenwood Press, 1979.

———. *The Language of American Popular Entertainment: A Glossary of Argot, Slang, and Terminology*. Westport, Conn.: Greenwood Press, 1981.

———. *Variety Entertainment and Outdoor Amusements: A Reference Guide*. Westport, Conn.: Greenwood Press, 1982.

————, ed. *American and English Popular Entertainment: A Guide to Information Sources.* Detroit: Gale Research, 1980.

The American Circus

Ballantine, Bill. *Clown Alley.* Boston: Little, Brown, 1982.

————. *Wild Tigers and Tame Fleas.* New York: Rinehart, 1958.

Barton, Bob, as told to G. Ernest Thomas. *Old Covered Wagon Show Days.* New York: E.P. Dutton, 1939.

Beatty, Clyde, with Edward Anthony. *The Big Cage.* New York: Century, 1933.

Bishop, George. *The World of Clowns.* Los Angeles: Brooke House, 1976.

Bostock, Frank. *The Training of Wild Animals.* New York: Century, 1903.

Bouissac, Paul. *Circus and Culture: A Semiotic Approach.* Bloomington: Indiana University Press, 1976.

Bowen, Elbert R. "The Circus in Early Rural Missouri." *Missouri Historical Review,* 47 (October 1952), 1–17.

————. *Theatrical Entertainment in Rural Missouri Before the Civil War.* Columbia: University of Missouri Press, 1959.

Bradna, Fred, as told to Hartzell Spence. *The Big Top: My Forty Years with the Greatest Show on Earth.* New York: Simon and Schuster, 1952.

Chindahl, George L. *History of the Circus in America.* Caldwell, Idaho: Caxton Printers, 1959.

Chipman, Bert J. *Hey Rube.* Hollywood: Hollwood Print Shop, 1933.

Clair, Colin. *Human Curiosities.* New York: Abelard-Schuman, 1968.

Clapp, William W., Jr. *A Record of the Boston Stage.* 1853. Reprint. New York: Benjamin Blom, 1968.

Clarke, John S. *Circus Parade.* New York: Scribner's, 1936.

Clement, Herb. *The Circus: Bigger and Better Than Ever?* New York: A. S. Barnes, 1974.

Conover, Richard E. *The Affairs of James A. Bailey.* Xenia, Ohio: Privately printed, 1957.

————. *The Fielding Band Chariots.* Xenia, Ohio: Privately printed, 1969.

————. *Give 'Em a John Robinson.* Xenia, Ohio: Privately printed, 1965.

————. *The Great Forepaugh Show.* Xenia, Ohio: Privately printed, 1959.

————. *Telescoping Tableaux.* Xenia, Ohio: Privately printed, 1956.

Cooper, Courtney Ryley. *Circus Day.* New York: Farrar and Rinehart, 1931.

————. *Lions 'N' Tigers 'N' Everything.* Boston: Little, Brown, 1924.

————. *Under the Big Top.* Boston: Little, Brown, 1929.

————. *With the Circus.* Boston: Little, Brown, 1930.

Coup, W. C. *Sawdust and Spangles: Stories and Secrets of the Circus.* Chicago: H. S. Stone, 1901.

Cowell, Joseph. *Thirty Years Passed Among the Players in England and America.* New York: Harper, 1844.

Coxe, Antony D. Hippisley. *A Seat at the Circus.* London: Evans Brothers, 1951.

Croft-Cooke, Rupert, and Peter Cotes. *Circus: A World History.* New York: Macmillan, 1976.

Daum, Paul Alexander. "The Royal Circus 1782–1809: An Analysis of Equestrian Entertainments." Ph. D. dissertation, Ohio State University, 1973.

Delavoye, Will. *Show Life in America.* East Point, Ga.: Privately printed, 1925.

Disher, M. Willson. *Greatest Show on Earth. Astley's—Afterwards Sanger's—Royal Amphitheatre of Arts, Westminster Bridge Road.* 1937. Reprint. New York: Benjamin Blom, 1969.

Dressler, Albert, ed. *California's Pioneer Circus, Joseph Rowe, Founder.* Memoirs and Personal Correspondence Relative to the Circus Business Through the Gold Country in the Fifties. San Francisco: H. S. Crocker, 1926.

Drimmer, Frederick. *Very Special People: The Struggles, Loves and Triumphs of Human Oddities.* New York: Amjon Publishers, 1973.

Durang, John. *The Memoirs of John Durang (American Actor, 1785–1816).* Edited by Alan S. Downer. Pittsburgh: University of Pittsburgh Press, 1966.

Durant, John, and Alice Durant. *Pictorial History of the American Circus.* New York: A. S. Barnes, 1957.

Eckley, Wilton. *The American Circus.* Boston: Twayne, 1984.

Fellows, Dexter W., and Andrew A. Freeman. *This Way to the Big Top: The Life of Dexter Fellows.* New York: Viking Press, 1936.

Fenner, Mildred S., and Wolcott Fenner, comps. and eds. *The Circus: Lure and Legend.* Englewood Cliffs, N.J.: Prentice-Hall, 1970.

Fiedler, Leslie. *Freaks: Myths and Images of the Secret Self.* New York: Simon and Schuster, 1978.

Field, Al G. *Watch Yourself Go By.* Columbus, Ohio: Spaar and Glenn, 1912.

Flint, Richard W. "A Selected Guide to Source Material on the American Circus." *Journal of Popular Culture,* 6 (Winter 1972), 615–19.

Fowler, Gene. *Timber Line.* New York: Covici Friede, 1933.

Fox, Charles Philip. *Circus Baggage Stock: A Tribute to the Percheron Horse.* Boulder, Colo.: Pruett Publishing, 1983.

———. *Circus Parades: A Pictorial History of America's Pageant.* Watkins Glen, N.Y.: Century House, 1953.

———. *A Pictorial History of Performing Horses.* New York: Bramhall House, 1960.

———. *A Ticket to the Circus.* New York: Bramhall House, 1959.

———, ed. *American Circus Posters in Full Color.* New York: Dover, 1978.

———, ed. *Old-Time Circus Cuts: A Pictorial Archive of 202 Illustrations.* New York: Dover, 1979.

Fox, Charles Philip, and F. Beverly Kelley. *The Great Circus Street Parade in Pictures.* New York: Dover, 1978.

Fox, Charles Philip, and Tom Parkinson. *Billers, Banners and Bombast: The Story of Circus Advertising.* Boulder, Colo.: Pruett Publishing, 1985.

———. *Circus in America.* Waukesha, Wis.: Country Beautiful, 1969.

Freedman, Jill. *Circus Days.* New York: Crown, 1975.

Frost, Thomas. *Circus Life and Circus Celebrities.* 1875. Reprint. Detroit: Singing Tree Press, 1970.

Gerson, Walter M. "The Circus: A Mobile Total Institution." In *Social Problems in a Changing World: A Comparative Reader.* New York: Thomas Y. Crowell, 1969.

Le Grand Livre du cirque. Edited by Monica J. Renevey. 2 vols. Geneva: Edito-Servize, 1977.

Greenwood, Isaac J. *The Circus: Its Origin and Growth Prior to 1835.* 2nd ed. New York: William Abbatt, 1909.

Hagenbeck, Lorenz. *Animals Are My Life*. Translated by Alec Brown. London: The Bodely Head, 1956.

Hammarstrom, David Lewis. *Behind the Big Top*. New York: A. S. Barnes, 1980.

Harlow, Alvin F. *The Ringlings—Wizards of the Circus*. New York: Julian Messner, 1951.

Harris, Neil. *Humbug: The Art of P. T. Barnum*. Boston: Little, Brown, 1973.

Hediger, H[einrich]. *Studies of the Psychology and Behaviour of Captive Animals in Zoos and Circuses*. New York: Criterion Books, 1955.

Henderson, J. Y., as told to Richard Taplinger. *Circus Doctor*. Boston: Little, Brown, 1952.

Hugill, Beryl. *Bring on the Clowns*. Secaucus, N.J.: Chartwell Books, 1980.

Jamieson, David, and Sandy Davidson. *The Colorful World of the Circus*. London: Octopus Books, 1980.

Jando, Dominique. *Histoire mondiale du cirque*. Paris: Jean-Pierre Delange, 1977.

Jennings, John J. *Theatrical and Circus Life; or, Secrets of the Stage, Greenroom and Sawdust Arena*. St. Louis: Herbert and Cole, 1882.

Jensen, Dean. *The Biggest, the Smallest, the Longest, the Shortest*. Madison: Wisconsin House, 1975.

Joys, Joanne Carol. *The Wild Animal Trainer in America*. Boulder, Colo.: Pruett Publishing, 1983.

Kelley, F. Beverly. *It Was Better Than Work*. Gerald, Mo.: Patrice Press, 1982.

Kunzog, John C. *Tanbark and Tinsel*. Jamestown, N.Y.: Privately printed, 1970.

Leavitt, Penelope M., and James S. Moy. "Spalding and Rogers' Floating Palace, 1852–1859." *Theater Survey*, 25 (May 1984), 15–27.

Lehman, Rolf. *Circus: Magie der Manege*. 2 vols. Hamburg: Hoffman und Campe, 1979.

Lewiston, Harry, as told to Jerry Holtman. *Freak Show Man*. Los Angeles: Holloway House, 1968.

MacAllister, Copeland. *Uncle Gus and the Circus*. Framingham, Mass.: Salem House, 1984.

McKennon, Joe. *Circus Lingo*. Sarasota, Fla.: Carnival Publishers, 1980.

———. *Horse Dung Trail: Saga of American Circus*. Sarasota, Fla.: Carnival Publishers, 1975.

———. *Logistics of the American Circus*. Sarasota, Fla.: Carnival Publishers, 1977.

Mannix, Daniel. *We Who Are Not as Others*. New York: Pocket Books, 1976.

Martin, Edwin, and Don B. Wilmeth. *Mud Show: American Tent Circus Life*. Albuquerque: University of New Mexico Press, 1988.

Maurer, David W. "Carnival Cant: A Glossary of Circus and Carnival Slang." *American Speech*, 6 (1931), 327–37.

May, Earl Chapin. *The Circus from Rome to Ringling*. 1932. Reprint. New York: Dover, 1963.

Milburn, George. "Circus Words." *American Mercury*, 24 (November 1931), 351–54.

Millette, Ernest Schlee, as told to Robert Wyndham. *The Circus That Was*. Philadelphia: Dorrance, 1971.

Moy, James S. "Entertainments at John B. Ricketts's Circus, 1793–1800." *Educational Theatre Journal*, 30 (May 1978), 186–202.

———. "John B. Ricketts's Circus 1793–1800." Ph.D. dissertation, University of Illinois, 1977.

Murray, Marian. *Circus! From Rome to Ringling*. New York: Appleton-Century-Crofts, 1956.

Neafie, Nelle. *A P. T. Barnum Bibliography*. Lexington: University of Kentucky Press, 1965.

Newton, Douglas. *Clowns*. New York: Franklin Watts, 1957.

North, Henry Ringling, and Alden Hatch. *The Circus Kings*. Garden City, N.Y.: Doubleday, 1960.

Norwood, Edwin P. *The Circus Menagerie*. Garden City, N.Y.: Doubleday and Page, 1929.

———. *The Other Side of the Circus*. Garden City, N.Y.: Doubleaday and Page, 1926.

O'Brien, Esse F. *Circus: Cinders to Sawdust*. San Antonio: Naylor, 1959.

Parkinson, Tom, and Charles Philip Fox. *The Circus Moves by Rail*. Boulder, Colo.: Pruett Publishing, 1978.

Parry, Albert. *Tattoo: Secrets of a Strange Art*. 1933. Reprint. New York: Macmillan, 1971.

Plowden, Gene. *Circus Press Agent: The Life and Times of Roland Butler*. Caldwell, Idaho: Caxton Printers, 1984.

———. *Merle Evans, Maestro of the Circus*. Miami, Fla.: E. A. Seemann, 1971.

———. *Singing Wheels and Circus Wagons*. Caldwell, Idaho: Caxton Printers, 1977.

———. *Those Amazing Ringlings and Their Circus*. New York: Bonanza Books, 1967.

Posey, Jake. *Last of the Forty Horse Drivers*. New York: Vantage Press, 1959.

Powledge, Fred. *Mud Show: A Circus Season*. New York: Harcourt Brace Jovanovich, 1975.

Proske, Roman. *Lions, Tigers and Me*. New York: Henry Holt, 1956.

Remy, Tristan. *Les Clowns*. Paris: Bernard Grasset, 1945.

———. *Entrees clownesque*. Paris: L'Arche, 1962.

Rennert, Jack. *100 Years of Circus Posters*. New York: Darien House, 1974.

Reynolds, Chang. *Pioneer Circuses of the West*. Los Angeles: Westernlore Press, 1966.

Robeson, Dave, *Al G. Barnes, Master Showman, as Told to Al G. Barnes*. Caldwell, Idaho: Caxton Printers, 1935.

Robinson, Gil. *Old Wagon Show Days*. Cincinnati: Brockwell Publishers, 1925.

Rogers, Phyllis A. "The American Circus Clown." Ph.D. dissertation, Princeton University, 1979.

Saxon, A. H. *Enter Foot and Horse: A History of Hippodrama in England and France*. New Haven: Yale University Press, 1968.

———. *The Life and Art of Andrew Ducrow and The Romantic Age of the English Circus*. Hamden, Conn.: Shoe String Press, 1978.

Sergel, Sherman Louis, ed. *The Language of Show Biz*. Chicago: Dramatic Publishing, 1973.

Sokan, Robert. *A Descriptive and Bibliographic Catalog of the Circus and Related Arts Collection at Illinois State University, Normal, Illinois*. Bloomington, Ill.: Scarlet Ibis Press, 1975.

Speaight, George. *The Book of Clowns*. New York: Macmillan, 1980.

———. *A History of the Circus*. New York: A. S. Barnes, 1980.

Sweet, Robert C., and Robert W. Habenstein. "Some Perspective on the Circus in Transition." *Journal of Popular Culture*, 6 (Winter 1972), 583–90.

Swortzell, Lowell. *Here Comes the Clowns: A Cavalcade of Comedy from Antiquity to the Present*. New York: Viking Press, 1978.

Thayer, Stuart. *Annals of the American Circus 1793–1829*. Manchester, Mich.: Privately printed, 1976.

———. *Annals of the American Circus 1830–1847*. Seattle: Peanut Butter Publishing, 1986.

———. *Mudshows and Railers: The American Circus in 1879*. Ann Arbor, Mich.: Privately printed, 1971.

Thetard, Henry. *La Merveilleuse Histoire du cirque*. 2 vols. Paris: Prisma, 1947.

Toll, Robert C. *On with the Show: The First Century of Show Business in America*. New York: Oxford University Press, 1976.

Toole-Stott, Raymond. *Circus and Allied Arts, a World Bibliography*. 4 vols. Derby, England: Harpur, 1958–71.

———. *A Bibliography of the Books on the Circus in English from 1773 to 1964*. Derby, England: Harpur, 1964.

Towsen, John H. *Clowns*. New York: Hawthorn Books, 1976.

Truzzi, Marcello. "The American Circus as a Source of Folklore: An Introduction." *Southern Folklore Quarterly*, 30 (December 1966), 289–300.

———. "The Decline of the American Circus: The Shrinkage of an Institution." In *Sociology and Everyday Life*. Edited by Marcello Truzzi. Englewood Cliffs, N.J.: Prentice-Hall, 1968.

———. "Folksongs of the American Circus." *New York Folklore Quarterly*, 24 (September 1968), 163–75.

———, ed. "Circuses, Carnivals and Fairs in America." *Journal of Popular Culture*, 6 (Winter 1972), 531–619.

Tuttle, George Palliser. "The History of the Royal Circus, Equestrian and Philharmonic Academy, 1782–1816, St. George's Fields, Surrey, England." Ph.D. dissertation, Tufts University, 1972.

Vail, R[obert] W[illiam] G[lenroie]. "The Early Circus in America." *Proceedings of the American Antiquarian Society*, n.s. 43 (April 1933), 116–85.

———. "This Way to the Big Top." *New York Historical Society Bulletin*, 29 (July 1945), 137–59.

Verney, Peter. *Here Comes the Circus*. New York and London: Paddington Press (Distributed in U.S. by Grosset and Dunlap), 1978.

Wallace, Irving. The Fabulous Showman. New York: Alfred A. Knopf, 1959.

Werner, M. R. *Barnum*. New York: Harcourt, Brace, 1923.

The Wild West Exhibition

Blackstone, Sarah. *Buckskins, Bullets, and Business: A History of Buffalo Bill's Wild West*. Westport, Conn.: Greenwood Press, 1986.

———. "Scalps, Bullets, and Two Wild Bills." *Bandwagon*, 29 (September-October 1985), 18–23.

Brasmer, William. "The Wild West Exhibition and the Drama of Civilization." In *Western Popular Theatre*. Edited by David Mayer and Kenneth Richards. London: Methuen, 1977.

Burke, John. *Buffalo Bill, the Noblest Whiteskin*. New York: G. P. Putnam, 1973.

Collings, Ellsworth, and Alma Miller England. *The 101 Ranch*. Norman: University of Oklahoma Press, 1937.

Croft-Cooke, Rupert, and W. S. Meadmore. *Buffalo Bill: The Legend, the Man of Action, the Showman*. London: Sidgwick and Jackson, 1952.

Deahl, William E., Jr. "Buffalo Bill's Wild West Show in New Orleans." *Louisiana History*, 16 (Summer 1975), 289–98.

———. "Nebraska's Unique Contribution to the Entertainment World." *Nebraska History*, 49 (Autumn 1968), 283–97.

Foreman, Carolyn Thomas. *Indians Abroad*. Norman: University of Oklahoma Press, 1943.

Gipson, Fred. *Fabulous Empire: Colonel Zack Miller's Story*. Boston: Houghton Mifflin, 1946.

Griffin, Charles Eldridge. *Four Years in Europe with Buffalo Bill*. Albia, Iowa: Stage Publishing, 1908.

Hall, Alice J. "Buffalo Bill and the Enduring West." *National Geographic,* 160 (July 1981), 76–103.

Havighurst, Walter. *Annie Oakley of the Wild West*. New York: Macmillan, 1954.

Hinkle, Milt. "The Kit Carson Wild West Show." *Frontier Times*, 38 (May 1964), 6–11, 57–58.

———. "The Way a Wild West Show Operated." *Frontier Times*, 43 (March 1969), 20–23, 50–52.

Johannsen, Albert. *The House of Beadle and Adams*. 3 vols. Norman: University of Oklahoma Press, 1950–62.

Katigan, Madelon B. "The Fabulous 101." *True West*, 8 (September-October 1960), 6–12, 50–51.

Leonard, Elizabeth, Jane, and Julia Cody Goodman. *Buffalo Bill, King of the Old West*. Edited by James William Hoffman. New York: Library Publishers, 1955.

McDaniel, Ruel. "Requiem for the Wild West Shows." *Frontier Times*, 36 (Winter 1961), 22–23, 40.

Mix, Paul E. *The Life and Legend of Tom Mix*. New York: A. S. Barnes, 1972.

Monaghan, Jay. The Great Rascal: The Life and Adventures of Ned Buntline. New York: Bonanza Books, 1951.

Pfening, Fred D., Jr. *Col. Tim McCoys's Real Wild West and Rough Riders of the World*. Columbus: Pfening and Synder, 1955.

Rennert, Jack. 100 Posters of Buffalo Bill's Wild West. New York: Darien House, 1976.

Russell, Don. "Cody, Kings, and Coronets." *The American West*, 7 (July 1970), 4–10, 62.

———. "The Golden Age of Wild West Shows." *The Bandwagon*, 15 (September-October 1971), 21–27.

———*The Lives and Legends of Buffalo Bill*. Norman: University of Oklahoma Press, 1960.

———. *The Wild West; or, A History of the Wild West Show*. Fort Worth: Amon Carter Museum of Western Art, 1970.

Sayers, Isabelle S. *Annie Oakley and Buffalo Bill's Wild West*. New York: Dover, 1981.

Schwartz, Joseph. "The Wild West Show; 'Everything Genuine.'" *Journal of Popular Culture*, 3 (Spring 1970), 656–66.

Sell, Henry Blackman, and Victor Weybright. *Buffalo Bill and the Wild West*. New York: Oxford University Press, 1955.

Shirley, Glenn. *Pawnee Bill: A Biography of Major Gordon W. Lillie*. Lincoln: University of Nebraska Press, 1958.

Thorp, Raymond W. *Spirit Gun of the West: The Story of Doc W. F. Carver*. Glendale, Calif.: Arthur H. Clark, 1957.

Walsh, Richard J., in collaboration with Milton S. Salsbury. *The Making of Buffalo Bill*. Indianapolis: Bobbs-Merrill, 1928.

Wetmore, Helen Cody. *Last of the Great Scouts*. Duluth, Minn.: Duluth Press, 1899.

Yellow Rob, Chauncey. "The Menace of the Wild West Show." *Quarterly Journal of the Society of American Indians*, 2 (July-September 1914), 224–28.

Yost, Nellie Snyder. *Buffalo Bill: His Family, Friends, Fame, Failures, and Fortunes*. Chicago: The Swallow Press, 1979.

Outdoor Amusements

Barret, Richmond. *Good Old Summer Days*. Boston: Houghton Mifflin, 1952.

Baxter, Sylvester. "The Trolley in Rural Parks." *Harper's Monthly*, 97 (June 1898), 60–69.

Beard, Richard. *Walt Disney's Epcot*. New York: Harry N. Abrams, 1982.

Boles, Don. *The Midway Showman*. Atlanta: Pinchpenny Press, 1967.

Braithwaite, David. *Fairground Architecture: The World of Amusement Parks, Carnivals, and Fairs*. New York: Praeger, 1968.

Burg, David F. *Chicago's White City of 1893*. Lexington: University Press of Kentucky, 1976.

Crews, Harry. "Carny." *Playboy*, 23 (September 1976), 96, 98, 195, 196.

Cuber, John F. "Patrons of Amusement Parks." *Sociology and Social Research*, 24 (September-October 1939), 63–68.

Dembroski, Theodore M. "Hanky Panks and Group Games Versus Alibis and Flats: The Legitimate and Illegitimate of the Carnival's Front End." *Journal of Popular Culture*, 6 (Winter 1972), 567–82.

Dexter, T. F. G. *The Pagan Origin of Fairs*. Perranporth, Cornwall, England: New Knowledge Press, 1930.

Easto, Patrick C., and Marcello Truzzi. "Carnivals, Roadshows, and Freaks." *Society*, 9 (March 1972), 26–34.

———. "Towards an Ethnography of the Carnival Social System." *Journal of Popular Culture*, 6 (Winter 1972), 550–66.

Finch, Christopher. *The Art of Walt Disney from Mickey Mouse to the Magic Kingdoms*. New York: Harry N. Abrams, 1975.

Flint, Richard W. "Meet Me in Dreamland: The Early Development of Amusement Parks in America." In *Victorian Resorts and Hotel: Essays from a Victorian Society Autumn Symposium*. Edited by Richard Guy Wilson. Philadelphia: Victorian Society in America, 1982, pp. 99–107.

Fraley, Nina. *The American Carousel*. Berkeley, Calif.: Redbug Workshop, 1979.

Fraley, Tobin. *The Carousel Animal*. Berkeley, Calif.: Zephyr Press, 1983.

Fried, Frederick A. *Pictorial History of the Carousel*. New York: A. S. Barnes, 1964.

Fried, Frederick, A., and Mary Fried. *America's Forgotten Folk Arts*. New York: Pantheon, 1978.

Frost, Thomas. *The Old Showmen and the Old London Fairs*. 1881. Reprint. Ann Arbor: Gryphon Books, 1971.

Funnell, Charles F. *By the Beautiful Sea: The Rise and High Times of That Great American Resort, Atlantic City*. New York: Alfred A. Knopf, 1975.

Garrett, Thomas M. "A History of Pleasure Gardens in New York City, 1700–1865." Ph.D. dissertation, New York University, 1978.

Gresham, William Lindsay. *Monster Midway*. New York: Rienhart, 1953.

Griffin, Al. "*Step Right Up Folks!*" Chicago: Henry Regnery, 1974.

Hart, Rollin Lynde. *The People at Play: Excursions in the Humor and Philosophy of Popular Amusements*. Boston: Houghton Mifflin, 1909.

Jackson, Joseph. "Vauxhall Garden." *Pennsylvania Magazine of History and Biography*, 57 (1933), 289–98.

Kasson, John F. *Amusing the Million: Coney Island at the Turn of the Century*. New York: Hill and Wang, 1978.

Koolhaas, Rem. *Delirious New York: A Retroactive Manifesto for Manhattan*. New York: Oxford University Press, 1978.

Krassowski, Wittold. "Social Structure and Professionalization in the Occupation of the Carnival Worker." Master's thesis, Purdue University, 1954.

Kyriazi, Gary. *The Great American Amusement Parks*. Secaucus, N.J.: Citadel Press, 1976.

Levi, Vicki Gold, and Lee Eisenberg. *Atlantic City: 125 Years of Ocean Madness*. New York: Clarkson N. Potter, 1979.

Lewis, Arthur H. *Carnival*. New York: Trident Press, 1970.

Lyon, Peter. "The Master Showman of Coney Island." *American Heritage*, 9 (June 1985), 14–20, 92–95.

McCullough, Edo. *Good Old Coney Island*. New York: Scribner's, 1957.

———. *World's Fair Midway: An Affectionate Account of American Amusement Areas from the Crystal Palace to the Crystal Ball*. 1966. Reprint. New York: Arno Press, 1976.

McKennon, Joe. *A Pictorial History of the American Carnival*. Sarasota, Fla.: Carnival Publishers, 1972.

McNamara, Brooks. "Come on Over: The Rise and Fall of the American Amusement Park." *Theatre Crafts*, 11 (September 1977), 33, 84–86.

Mangels, William F. *The Outdoor Entertainment Business*. New York: Vantage Press, 1952.

Manley, Seon, and Robert Manley. *Beaches: Their Lives, Legends, and Lore*. Philadelphia: Chilton Book, 1968.

Mannix, Daniel. *Step Right Up*. New York: Harper and Brothers, 1950.

———. *We Who Are Not as Others*. New York: Pocket Books, 1976.

Manns, William. *Painted Ponies*. Millwood, N.Y.: Zon International, 1987.

Maurer, David W. "Carnival Cant: A Glossary of Circus and Carnival Slang." *American Speech*, 6 (June 1931), 327–37.

Meiselas, Susan. *Carnival Strippers*. New York: Farrar, Straus and Giroux, 1976.

Morley, Henry. *Memories of Bartholomew Fair*. 3rd ed. 1880. Reprint. Detroit: Singing Tree Press, 1969.

Onosko, Tim. *Fun Land U.S.A.* New York: Ballantine Books, 1978.

Pilat, Oliver, and Jo Ranson. *Sodom by the Sea: An Affectionate History of Coney Island*. Garden City, N.Y.: Doubleday, Doran, 1941.

Ritchey, David. "Columbia Garden: Baltimore's First Pleasure Garden." *Southern Speech Communication Journal*, 39 (Spring 1974), 241–47.

Rydell, Robert W. *All the World's a Fair: Visions of Empire at American International Expositions, 1876–1916*. Chicago: University of Chicago Press, 1984.

Scarne, John. "Carnival, Fair, Bazaar, Arcade and Amusement Park Games." In *Scarne's Complete Guide to Gambling*. Rev. ed. New York: Simon and Schuster, 1974.

Schickel, Richard. *The Disney Version*. 2nd ed. New York: Simon and Schuster, 1985.

Scott, W. S. *Green Retreats, the Story of Vauxhall Gardens, 1661–1859*. London: Odhams Press, 1955.

Sergel, Sherman Louis, ed. *The Language of Show Biz*. Chicago: Dramatic Publishing, 1973.

Snow, Robert E., and David E. Wright. "Coney Island: A Case Study in Popular Culture and Technical Change." *Journal of Popular Culture*, 9 (Spring 1976), 960–75.

Sonneck, O. G. *Early Concert Life in America (1731–1800)*. Leipzig: Breitkopf and Hartel, 1907.

Southworth, James Granville. *Vauxhall Gardens: A Chapter in the Social History of England*. New York: Columbia University Press, 1944.

Starsmore, Ian. *English Fairs*. Levittown. N.Y.: Transatlantic Arts, 1976.

"Theme Parks." *Theatre Crafts*, 11 (September 1977), 112.

Truzzi, Marcello, ed. "Circuses, Carnivals and Fairs in America." *Journal of Popular Culture*, 6 (Winter 1972), 531-619.

Truzzi, Marcello, and Patrick C. Easto. "The Carnival as a Marginally Legal Work Activity: The Typological Approach to Work Systems." In *Deviant Behavior: Occupational and Organizational Bases*. Edited by Clifton D. Bryant. Chicago: Rand McNally, 1974.

Ulmer, Jeff. *Amusement Parks of America: A Comprehensive Guide*. New York: Dial Press, 1980.

Waters, H. W. *History of Fairs and Expositions*. London, Ont: Reid, 1939.

Weedon, Geoff, and Richard Ward. *Fairground Art*. New York: Abbeville Press, 1981.

Willey, Day Allen. "The Trolley-Park." *The Cosmopolitan*, 33 (July 1902), 265–72.

Wilmeth, Don B. *The Language of American Popular Entertainment: A Glossary of Argot, Slang, and Terminology*. Westport, Conn.: Greenwood Press, 1981.

Wroth, Warwick. *Cremorne and the Later London Gardens*. London: Elliot Stock, 1907.

Wroth, Warwick, and Arthur Edgar. *The London Pleasure Gardens in the Eighteenth Century*. London: Macmillan, 1896.

Wylson, Anthony. *Design for Leisure Entertainment*. London and Boston: Newnes-Butterworths, 1980.

Periodicals

Amusement Business. Nashville, 1961–.

Bandwagon. Columbus, Ohio, 1951–.

Billboard. Los Angeles, 1894–.
Le Cirque dans l'Univers. Vincennes, France, 1950–.
New York Clipper. New York, 1853–1924.
Variety. New York, 1905–.
White Tops. Indianapolis, 1928–.
World's Fair. Corte Madera, Calif. 1981–.

Comic Strips

M. THOMAS INGE

Except for the attention of a few psychologists, sociologists, educationists, and media specialists, American comic art has been the most generally neglected area of popular culture until very recently. What has been written in the past has usually been of a disparaging and condescending nature by critics who at least recognized the broad popular appeal of the comics but who also often viewed them as subversive threats to highbrow culture and social stability. Very few were the writers who found more than ephemeral value in the funnies and comic books, and even fewer who recognized the unique aesthetics of this hybrid form of narrative art.

The daily and Sunday comic strips are part of the reading habits of more than one hundred million people at all educational and social levels in the United States. Any mass medium that plays so heavily on the sensibilities of the populace deserves study purely for sociological reasons, but comic art is important for other reasons as well. While the roots of comic art may be partly European, the comics as we know them today are a distinctively American art form that has contributed heavily to the culture of the world, from Picasso to the pop art movement. They derive from popular patterns, themes, and concepts of world culture—just as Dick Tracy was inspired by Sherlock Holmes (notice the similarity in noses), Flash Gordon and Superman draw on the heroic tradition to which Samson, Beowulf, Davy Crockett, and Paul Bunyan belong. The comics also serve as revealing reflectors of popular attitudes, tastes, and mores, and they speak directly to human desires, needs, and emotions.

Historical studies, biographies, anthologies, and periodicals have begun to proliferate rapidly in this subject area in the past two decades, partly because some publishers have wished to tap the lucrative nostalgia market, but in many cases because others have begun to recognize the importance of documenting this part of our national heritage. Much of the best work has originated in amateur and limited press run publications authored by collectors and devotees of the art form. The study of comics has become a part of high school, college, and university curricula throughout this country and abroad, and annual conventions are held on a national and regional scale for collectors, artists, and fans. This chapter will provide a brief historic summary of the development of the comic strip in particular and a guide to the most useful reference works and resources for those who wish to study the subject. The editorial cartoon is treated in another chapter, while the comic book is given separate treatment in my *Handbook of American Popular Literature* (Greenwood Press, 1988), a companion volume to this handbook.

HISTORIC OUTLINE

While some historians would trace the comic strip to prehistoric cave drawings, the medieval Bayeux tapestry, the eighteenth-century print series of such artists as William Hogarth, the illustrated European broadsheet, the nineteenth-century illustrated novels and children's books, or European and American humorous periodicals, the American comic strip as we know it may have been influenced by all of these antecedents, yet it remains a distinct form of expression unto itself and primarily is an American creation. It may be defined as an open-ended dramatic narrative about a recurring set of characters, told with a balance between narrative text and visual action, often including dialogue in balloons, and published serially in newspapers. The comic strip shares with drama the use of such conventions as dialogue, scene, stage devices, gesture, and compressed time, and it anticipated such film techniques as montage (before Eisenstein), angle shots, panning, close-ups, cutting, and framing. Unlike the play or the film, however, the comic strip is usually the product of one artist (or an artist and a writer) who must be a combined producer-scriptwriter-director-scene designer at once and bring his characters to life on the flat space of a printed page, with respect for the requirements of a daily episode that takes less than a minute's reading time. It is these challenges that make fine comic art difficult to achieve and contribute to its distinct qualities.

Identifying the first comic strip is not easy. Some would suggest James Swinnerton's 1895 feature for the San Francisco *Examiner, Little Bears and Tykes* (often incorrectly identified as *Little Bears and Tigers*), in which bear cubs, who had been used in spot illustrations for the newspaper since 1893, adopted the human postures of small children. Others more commonly suggest Richard Outcault's *The Yellow Kid,* who first appeared in the May 5, 1895, issue of the New York *World,* a street urchin in the middle of riotous activities set in the low-class immigrant sections of the city and identified by the title "Hogan's Alley." Unlike Swinnerton, Outcault developed a central character in his use of the Kid, always clad in a yellow shift on which his dialogue was printed, and by 1896 had moved from a single panel cartoon to the format of a progressive series of panels with balloon dialogue, which would become the definitive form of the comic strip.

Outcault's use of contemporary urban reality in his backgrounds, which had counterparts in the naturalistic novels of Stephen Crane, Frank Norris, and Theodore Dreiser, would not reappear in the comics for over two decades (and even then in the safe Midwestern environment of Sidney Smith's *The Gumps* of 1917, which emphasized the pathos of lower-middle-class life, and Frank King's *Gasoline Alley,* a year later, where the use of chronological time first entered the comics in following the growth of a typical American family). Most of the popular strips that came on the heels of the Kid in the following three decades used humor and fantasy as their major modes, such as Rudolph Dirks's *The Katzenjammer Kids,* one of the longest-running comic strips in existence; Frederick Burr Opper's several wacky creations *Happy Hooligan, Maude the Mule,* and *Alphonse and Gaston;* Richard Outcault's penance for his illiterate outlandish Kid, *Buster Brown;* Winsor McCay's *Little Nemo in Slumberland,* the most technically accomplished and aesthetically beautiful Sunday page ever drawn; Bud Fisher's *Mutt and Jeff,* the first daily comic strip and the first successful comic team in the funnies; George Herriman's classic absurdist fantasy and lyrical love poem *Krazy Kat;* Cliff Sterret's abstractly written and drawn family situation comedy, *Polly and Her Pals;* George McManus's *Bringing Up Father,* whose central characters, Maggie and Jiggs, became a part of American marital folklore; Billy De Beck's tribute to the sporting life, *Barney Google;* Elzie Segar's *Thimble Theater,* which in 1929, after a ten-year run, introduced Popeye to the world; and Frank Willard's boarding house farce, *Moon Mullins.* These were the years when the terms *comics* and *funnies* became inseparably identified with this new form of creative expression, even though comedy and humor were not to remain its primary content.

Although some adventurous continuity and suspense had been used in C. W. Kahles's burlesque of melodrama, *Hairbreadth Harry,* in 1906, Roy Crane's *Wash Tubbs* of 1924 and George Storm's *Phil Hardy* and *Bobby Thatcher* of 1925–27 established the adventure comic strip, and Harold Gray's *Little Orphan Annie,* also of 1924, drew on the picaresque tradition in a successful combination of exotic adventure and homespun right-wing philosophy. The adventure strip would not become a fully developed genre, however, until 1929 and the appearance of the first science fiction strip, *Buck Rogers,* by Richard W. Calkins and Phil Nowlan, and the successful translation of the classic primitive hero from the novels of Edgar Rice Burroughs, *Tarzan* (most beautifully drawn in those years first by Harold Foster and later by Burne Hogarth). The 1930s and 1940s were to be dominated by adventure titles, such as Chester Gould's *Dick Tracy*, Vincent Hamlin's *Alley Oop*, Milton Caniff's *Terry and the Pirates* and his postwar *Steve Canyon*, Alex Raymond's *Flash Gordon*, Lee Falk's *Mandrake the Magician* (drawn by Phil Davis) and *The Phantom* (drawn by Ray Moore), Harold Foster's *Prince Valiant*, Fred Harman's *Red Ryder*, Fran Striker's *The Lone Ranger* (drawn primarily by Charles Flanders), Alfred Andriola's *Charlie Chan* and *Kerry Drake*, Will Eisner's *The Spirit*, and Roy Crane's second contribution to the tradition, *Buzz Sawyer*. Related by the use of the same devices of mystery and suspense and also developed during these years were the soap opera strips, among the best known of which were *Mary Worth*, by Allen Saunders and Dale Connor (a reincarnation of Martha Orr's 1932 antidote for the Depression, *Apple Mary*); writer Nicholas Dallis's *Rex Morgan, M.D.* (drawn by Marvin Bradley and Frank Edgington), followed in 1952 by *Judge Parker* (drawn by Dan Heilman and later by Harold LeDoux), and in 1961 by *Apartment 3-G* (drawn by Alex Kotzky); and Stanley Drake's 1953 collaboration with writer Eliot Caplin on *The Heart of Juliet Jones*.

During the 1950s and 1960s satire flourished and dominated comic strips, although it was consistently present at least from 1930 when Chic Young's *Blondie* satirized at first flappers and playboys of the jazz age and subsequently the institution of marriage in what would prove to be for decades the most popular comic strip in the world. Al Capp's hillbilly comedy of 1934, *Li'l Abner* (with little of the authentic southern humor Billy De Beck had used in *Snuffy Smith*), evolved into an influential forum for ridiculing the hypocrisies and absurdities of the larger social and political trends of the nation. Just as Capp used the denizens of Dogpatch as vehicles for his satire, other artists of postwar America would follow his example and use even more imaginative vehicles, such as the fantasy world of children in *Peanuts* by Charles Schulz, the ancient form of the animal fable by the master of comic mimicry, Walt Kelly, in *Pogo*, an anachronistic military life in the durable *Beetle Bailey* by Mort Walker, an imagined world of prehistoric man by Johnny Hart in *B.C.*, and the absurd world of a medieval kingdom in *The Wizard of Id* by Johnny Hart and Brant Parker. During the 1970s, this trend would continue in such strips as Dik Browne's *Hagar the Horrible*, which relies on a farcical recreation of life among Viking plunderers, but it would also move in interesting new directions. Russel Myers's *Broom Hilda*, a wacky ancient witch, lives in a totally abstract world in the imaginative tradition of Herriman's *Krazy Kat*, while Garry Trudeau's *Doonesbury* moved into the realistic world of the radical student generation of the last decade (but recently updated to follow his characters into their postgraduate lives).

One of the most popular and controversial strips of the 1980s was *Bloom County* by Berke Breathed. Like *Doonesbury*, the satire is often keyed to immediate political and social events, and like *Pogo,* the cast of characters includes several anthropomorphic creatures, including the endearing penguin Opus. Breathed's strip, however, maintains an identity and sense of humor quite its own and unlike any other. Because of their astute commentary on contemporary affairs, both Trudeau and Breathed have been awarded Pulitzer Prizes for editorial cartooning, as has Jules Feiffer, whose weekly cartoon essay has been closer to the comic strip than the political cartoon. Crossing over in the other direction are several political cartoonists who have turned to the comic strip as a more subtle and entertaining way to provide commentary on modern life and mores, such as Doug Marlette's southern-based *Kudzu;* Jeff MacNelly's contribution to the animal fable tradition, *Shoe;* and Mike Peter's combination of cultural satire and nursery rhyme lore, *Mother Goose and Grimm.* Each of these strips in its individual way marks a distinct advance in the form and content of modern satiric comic strips.

The travails of the modern woman, caught between the demands of a profession and traditional female roles, have been treated by several strips in the 1980s, including *Cathy* by Cathy Guisewite, *Sally Forth* by Greg Howard, *On the Fastrack* by Bill Holbrook, and *For Better or For Worse* by Lynn Johnston, except that in the last case the wife has been unable to move fully in the direction of a career in spite of her desire to do so. The fantasy worlds of animals and children and combinations thereof have continued to supply a basis of humor for a number of popular strips, such as *Garfield* by Jim Davis, *Marvin* by Tom Armstrong, and *Calvin and Hobbes* by Bill Watterson, the last one of the most psychologically astute treatments of childhood and the imagination ever to grace the newspaper pages. A new direction in comics humor has been charted by Gary Larson's *The Far Side* and James Unger's *Herman,* both actually single-panel cartoons rather than comic strips and both bringing a sense of the absurd and the bizarre to the funny papers that perhaps is a sign of things to come. The introduction of Bill Griffith's underground Dada fantasy strip, *Zippy the Pinhead,* to mainstream newspapers is an indication of such a trend.

American comic art faces an uncertain future. The space allotted to single comic strips by newspapers has grown increasingly smaller, while syndicate and editorial preference often deters the most creative and therefore possibly unsettling strips, even though such formerly forbidden topics as homosexuality, premarital sex, and abortion have been allowed to enter the funnies. Yet the comic strips remain one of the most singularly attractive features of the newspaper, and even though almost a century old, they have not yet reached their full potential as a powerful form of humanistic expression.

REFERENCE WORKS

The sound bibliographical and reference work that must precede historical and critical research has not been accomplished yet for the comics, but a few tentative efforts have been made, and much good work is in progress. What should be a comprehensive and useful checklist of secondary data— the *International Bibliography of Comics Literature*, by Wolfgang Kempkes— is marred by inaccuracies, incomplete data, and inconvenience. The material is divided into eight general categories, such as histories of the development of comics, structure, readership, etc., and then subdivided by country of origin (Argentina, Australia, Belgium, Brazil, Germany, Finland, France, Great Britain, Italy, Mexico, the Netherlands, Austria, Portugal, Sweden, Switzerland, Spain, South Africa, Czechoslovakia, the USSR, and the United States). A subject cross-index in the first edition was inexplicably deleted in the revised edition, thus making it impossible to locate entries on specific artists or comics, the major use for a checklist. The book is, however, the only readily available source of information on criticism published outside the United States to 1974 and illustrates the extent to which the most comprehensive study of American comics has taken place abroad, especially in Italy, France, and Germany, rather than on native shores. As always, the most significant creators of American culture appear evident to Europe before we seem to be able to perceive them, from Edgar Allan Poe and William Faulkner to Winsor McCay and George Herriman.

Thanks to the efforts of Randall W. Scott, we now have his guide *Comic Books and Strips: An Information Sourcebook,* which lists and describes more than 1,000 publications about the comics including popular anthologies, periodicals, collection catalogs, fan publications, and commentary. A list of 43 libraries with special collections of comics and original art is also provided, along with author, title, and subject indexes. This is an essential reference item in the field of comic art.

The main body of *The World Encyclopedia of Comics,* edited by Maurice Horn, consists of more than 1,200 cross-referenced entries, arranged alphabetically, and devoted either to an artist, a writer, a comic strip title, or a comic book character, and prepared by an international group of contributors. Additional materials include a short history of the development of comic art, a chronology, an original analytic inquiry into the aesthetics of the comics by the editor, a history of newspaper syndication, a glossary, a selected bibliography, and several appendixes and indexes. Unfortunately, there are a number of typographical errors in the text, and the critical comments are often biased. Nevertheless, with corrections, revisions, and updating, this work could be a chief authority among historians and commentators on the comics. Relevant information also will be found in Horn's *The World Encyclopedia of Cartoons,* similar in structure to the above, except that here the almost 1,200 entries deal with cartoonists, animators, editors, and producers, and the works they create in the fields of animation, gag cartoons, syndicated comic panels, editorial cartoons, caricature, and sports cartoons. The entries are supplemented with an overview of caricature and cartoons, a brief history of humor magazines, a world summary of animated cartoons, a chronology, a glossary, and a history of the humor periodicals *Puck, Life,* and *Judge.*

A new reference project initiated by Maurice Horn is the *Contemporary Graphic Artists* series to be issued on a regular basis by Gale Research Company. Each volume will contain biographic, bibliographic, and critical assessments of present and past illustrators, animators, cartoonists, designers, and other graphic artists, but with an emphasis on comic artists. Much of the information has been obtained directly from the artists, many of whom provide comments on their own work. The first volume in 1986 contained an essay, "The Graphic Arts: An Overview," that defined the areas to be covered by the series.

In *Women and the Comics,* Trina Robbins and Catherine Yronwode, a comic book artist and editor, respectively, provide a comprehensive catalog with brief commentary on the work of over 500 women cartoonists and writers in America from 1901 to 1984. In a field thought to have been dominated by men, the authors find that almost from the start comic strips and later comic books have employed feminine talent extensively, although their names were concealed or lost to history. *Great Cartoonists and Their Art* is a collection of personal and biographical essays on comic strip and editorial artists whose work was collected over the years by editorial cartoonist Art Wood. Wood includes quotations from the artists, background on the business, and the technical details of producing cartoons and comics for publication.

Will Eisner, a creator of the comic book and one of the most influential masters of comic art, discusses his ideas and theories on the practice of telling stories in graphic form in *Comics & Sequential Art.* Separate chapters, thoroughly illustrated by examples of his own work, treat imagery, timing, framing, and anatomy, and he discusses comics as a form of reading, learning, and teaching. Eisner views comics as a distinct artistic discipline and a literary/visual form, the development of which has been accelerated by advances in graphic technology and visual communication in this century. This is the best book ever written on the aesthetics of comic art. An engaging and witty overview of the various symbolic devices and shorthand visual images used by cartoonists is *The Lexicon of Comicana* by Mort Walker. While written tongue-in-cheek, the book is a valuable guide to the devices that make comic art distinctive.

Denis Gifford's *Encyclopedia of Comic Characters* contains entries on over 1,200 characters with notes on their creators, place of publication, beginning and ending dates, and description. Most of the characters are British, but quite a few American ones are included. *A Doonesbury Index* by Allan D. Satin is a comprehensive index to the characters, real people, topics, and themes that appeared in G. B. Trudeau's comic strip from 1970 through 1983. Future historians of politics and popular culture in the 1970s will find this extremely valuable.

Teachers wishing to use comics in an educational context will find some useful suggestions in *Cartoons and Comics in the Classroom,* edited by James L. Thomas. It must be used with caution as a reference, however, since it contains some inaccurate information about the history of comics, and since many of the articles are written with a degree of condescension for the art form. *The Art of the Comic Strip* by Shirley Glubok is written mainly for children as an introduction to the history of the art form. It is beautifully illustrated and contains historic sketches on over forty classic comic strips and artists. Bob Bennett's how-to guide, *Collecting Original Cartoon Art,* also contains estimates on the values of original comic strip drawings.

RESEARCH COLLECTIONS

Except for isolated instances, most public and university libraries have made no effort to collect or preserve comic books, comic strips, or related materials. Even the Library of Congress files of comic books were carelessly maintained, and much of the material has disappeared over the years. The best collections, therefore, are those of private collectors, such as the late Woody Gelman of New York, Gordon Campbell of Tennessee, Jim Ivey of Florida, and Murray A. Harris of California, although several of these emphasize original art and artifacts. Such collections are not generally open to the public or are available on an appointment basis only.

A once private collector, Bill Blackbeard, has turned his comprehensive collection of all known comic strips into a nonprofit research center that is open to the public: the San Francisco Academy of Comic Art. The academy can provide copies of sequential runs of comic strips to researchers and institutions for a fee, as well as authoritative information on all aspects of comic art and popular literature. The other major center for research is the Library for Communication and Graphic Arts at Ohio State University in Columbus. Begun with a gift from Milton Caniff of his entire library, papers, and research files, under the direction of Lucy Caswell, the collection has grown rapidly with extensive gifts of papers, publications, and art from other cartoonists and their professional societies. The library also hosts major exhibitions and conferences on the comic arts. The Museum of Cartoon Art was established with the support of several individual artists, led by Mort Walker, and the professional cartoonist societies at the town of Rye, Port Chester, New York. The Cartoon Art Museum in San Francisco is receiving similar support. Both museums emphasize the collection of original art and provide important exhibitions and seminars open to the public.

Another extensive collection is found in the Popular Culture Library, a special division of the Bowling Green State University Library, Bowling Green, Ohio. Also, other large university libraries have begun to develop an interest in this area. Publisher Harry A. Chesler, Jr., gave to Fairleigh

Dickinson University Library in Madison, New Jersey, his collection of materials including 4,000 pieces of original art, the correspondence and records of the Chesler Syndicate, and a body of secondary literature. Comic artist Roy Crane deposited his scrapbooks and original art at the Syracuse University Library in Syracuse, New York. Collections devoted to primary and secondary materials in the areas of comic strips and political cartoons are located at Palomar College Library in San Marcos, California, Kenneth Spencer Research Library at the University of Kansas in Lawrence, James Branch Cabell Library at Virginia Commonwealth University in Richmond, and University of Virginia Library at Charlottesville. The best collection of Walt Disney comic books and strips is found in the Disney Studio Archives in Burbank, California (though not open to the public), but the Anaheim Public Library in California also has an impressive body of Disney material. Undoubtedly other collections exist or are being assembled throughout the country, but the lack of an organized, comprehensive material index to library holdings in popular culture prevents access.

HISTORY AND CRITICISM

It must be noted that because so little of the basic bibliographic and reference work has been completed, as indicated earlier, almost every single book to be discussed in the following pages abounds to one degree or another in errors and mistaken assumptions. Many authors assumed that the beginning date for a daily or Sunday strip was the first appearance in their local newspapers, or the first date on which it was syndicated, whereas it may have begun months earlier. The syndicates themselves have kept very few records and even incomplete files of proof sheets for the strips they distribute. The most knowledgeable and meticulous scholar of the comics, Bill Blackbeard, is writing a history which will establish for the first time much of this factual information, but until his book appears all of the existing histories must be used with great caution. Omitted from discussion here are the many historical and appreciative studies of American comics published abroad in Europe or South America.

A History of American Graphic Humor, by William Murrell, was the first authoritative history of the development of pictorial satire and cartooning in America to include the comics. While he devotes only a few appreciative pages to the comic strip, the work is still valuable as a panorama of the forms of visual art that have influenced the comics. The earliest full-length book entirely devoted to American comic art was Martin Sheridan's *Comics and Their Creators* in 1942. Not actually an organized history, it consisted primarily of biographical sketches and interviews with the artists and writers of over seventy-five of the most popular newspaper comics, copiously illustrated with portraits and reproductions of the strips. It remains a useful resource for some of the primary data on the views and working habits of the cartoonists. The earliest full-scale history was *The Comics,* by Coulton Waugh, a practicing comic artist and devoted scholar of the subject. While many of his facts were faulty, Waugh attempted a comprehensive survey of the important movements and types of comic strips from *The Yellow Kid* through the first decade of the modern comic book. His insights into the reasons for the popularity of certain strips, his comments on the aesthetic principles behind them, and his early effort to define the medium make Waugh's pioneer effort of lasting interest, although he had little appreciation for the comic book as it had developed, and he appeared to accept without question some of the highbrow standards often applied to popular art by the self-appointed guardians of high culture.

The next effort on the part of a single author to chart the history of the medium was Stephen Becker's *Comic Art in America,* although his interests were broader than Waugh's in that he envisioned his book, according to its pretentious subtitle, as "a social history of the funnies, the political cartoons, magazine humor, sporting cartoons, and animated cartoons." Casting his net so broadly led to much superficiality, and his commentary is often derivative, but the volume is a useful storehouse of over 390 illustrations and sample sketches. The text is kept to an absolute minimum and the illustrations are at a maximum in *The Penguin Book of Comics,* by George Perry and Alan Aldridge, aptly described in its subtitle as "a slight history." Originally published in French in conjunction with an exhibition of comic art at the Louvre, and the joint product of six contributors headed by Pierre Couperie, *A History of the Comic Strip* is understandably uneven, yet it contains some of the most provocative comments yet ventured on the aesthetics, structure, symbolism, and themes in comic art. A general survey was undertaken by comic artist Jerry Robinson, *The Comics: An Illustrated History of Comic Strip Art.* Robinson provided a readable and interesting text complemented by thirteen original essays by eminent artists about the theories behind their work.

Though assembled as a catalog for an exhibition at the University of Maryland, Judith O'Sullivan's *The Art of the Comic Strip* contains a brief history with emphases on Winsor McCay, George McManus, George Herriman, and Burne Hogarth, a compilation of short biographies and bibliographic references on 120 comic artists, a chronology of important dates, and a bibliography. *Comics: Anatomy of a Mass Medium,* by Reinhold Reitberger and Wolfgang Fuchs, is a broad effort by two German scholars to relate the comics to their social context and developments in other mass media, but faulty secondary sources and inaccessible primary material led to an inordinate number of factual and other errors, which no one corrected in the process of translation. What appears to be the most ambitious effort yet undertaken to describe the "history of the comic strip" has yielded the first massive volume, *The Early Comic Strip,* by David Kunzle, which reaches the year 1825 before the comic strip as we know it actually begins.

Kunzle traces the full development of narrative art in the European broadsheet, which he sees as an antecedent to the comic strip as he defines it in the introduction. The complete corpus of reproductions of broadsheets in the oversized volume makes it of greater interest to art historians than comic scholars, but it will be interesting to see how this research is brought to bear on the American comic strip in the next volume, if it ever appears.

The short bookshelf of biographies of major comic artists is gradually expanding. Most early efforts took the form of brief personal memoirs or picture books in which the text was incidental to the illustrations. Examples of such promotional books are *Milton Caniff: Rembrandt of the Comic Strip* by John Paul Adams and *Charlie Brown, Snoopy and Me* by Charles M. Schulz and R. Smith Kiliper. As each anniversary of *Peanuts* has passed, Schulz has published volumes interlaced with autobiographical memoirs, such as *Charlie Brown & Charlie Schulz* by Lee Mendelson and Schulz (twentieth anniversary), *Peanuts Jubilee: My Life and Art with Charlie Brown and Others* by Schulz (twenty-fifth), *Happy Birthday, Charlie Brown* by Mendelson and Schulz (thirtieth), and *You Don't Look 35, Charlie Brown* by Schulz (thirty-fifth). Walt Kelly's anthology *Ten Ever-lovin' Blue-eyed Years with Pogo* is another anniversary volume with significant autobiographical content.

Peter Marzio's *Rube Goldberg: His Life and Work* is a full-scale biographical account of Goldberg's versatile career and an interpretation of his art. Marzio achieves a sense of Goldberg's personality and character and provides a model for the kind of treatment other artists deserve. Goldberg's autobiography has been incorporated in Clark Kinnaird's *Rube Goldberg vs. the Machine Age*. Harold Davidson's *Jimmy Swinnerton: The Artist and His Work* is a beautifully designed and printed survey of the career of a major early cartoonist.

In *Krazy Kat: The Comic Art of George Herriman*, Patrick McDonnell, Karen O'Connell, and Georgia Riley de Havenon provide an overview of Herriman's life and career through an assemblage of unpublished letters, documents, photographs, and artwork for friends, as well as an extensive selection of *Krazy Kat* comic strips. There is still a good deal more to be said on Herriman, however. Joseph M. Cahn's *The Teenie Weenies Book: The Life and Art of William Donahey* reports on a little-discussed artist. For more than sixty-five years, Donahey wrote and illustrated a color newspaper feature for the funny pages about a group of Lilliputian characters called *The Teenie Weenies*. The most lavishly produced biographical account we have is John Canemaker's *Winsor McCay: His Life and Art*. In the text, Canemaker emphasizes McCay's importance in American cultural history through his creation of *Little Nemo in Slumberland,* the most beautiful comic strip in the history of the form, and the production of *Gertie the Dinosaur,* which established the potential of the animated film long before Disney. The illustrations are stunning.

Maurice Horn has published several thematic studies of the comics. His *Comics of the American West* is a heavily illustrated survey of the major western comic strips and books and their basic symbolic themes, and his *Women in the Comics* surveys in a similar fashion the images and roles of women as reflected in the comics. A third book, *Sex in the Comics,* is an informal discussion of the presence of sexual behavior in comic strips and books of the mainstream and underground varieties. *Ethnic Images in the Comics,* edited by Charles Hardy and Gail F. Stern, is an exhibition catalog, but it contains more information than is available anywhere else in its seven essays on blacks, Jews, Asians, and other ethnic groups as portrayed in the comics. Another valuable exhibition catalog is *The Comic Art Show,* edited by John Carlin and Sheena Wagstaff, which is a comprehensive look at the influence of cartoons and comics on painting and the fine arts. It contains information not found elsewhere.

The History of Little Orphan Annie by Bruce Smith surveys the history of Harold Gray's famous orphan and her various permutations into a radio show, motion pictures, and the musical stage. Gray's political attitudes and the problems these caused are also discussed. Smith also assembled *The World According to Daddy Warbucks,* appropriately subtitled "Capitalist Quotations from the Richest Man in the World." Most of the quotations supporting free enterprise are culled from others, but occasionally Warbucks is quoted. *The Popeye Story* by Bridget Terry contains some background information on E. C. Segar's comic strip, but its primary concern is the making of the motion picture. Charles Schulz's *Peanuts* is examined from a variety of theoretical perspectives—artistic, cultural, psychological, and political—in *The Graphic Art of Charles Schulz,* edited by Joan Roebuck, with essays by Roebuck, M. Thomas Inge, Elliott Oring, and Umberto Eco, and a memoir by Bill Mauldin. This was the catalog for an exhibition organized to celebrate the strip's thirty-fifth anniversary. The chronology and bibliography are especially useful. Mort Walker speaks out against his critics in *Miss Buxley: Sexism in Beetle Bailey?* with a good deal of disarming humor.

In *Backstage at the Strips,* Mort Walker provides an engaging insider's tour of the world of comic strip artists, how the strips are created, and who the people are who draw and read them. Ron Goulart's *The Adventurous Decade* is an informal and subjective history of the adventure comic strips during the 1930s when the American funnies came of age. The interviews Goulart conducted with living veterans of the period enrich the volume, which tends to adopt a studied controversial view in its critical judgments of the work of classic artists. In the catalog for the Smithsonian Institution's Bicentennial exhibition, *A Nation of Nations,* edited by Peter Marzio, there is an essay by M. Thomas Inge and Bill Blackbeard on the influences of Europe on the development of the comic strip and the later influences of the fully developed American comic strip and book on the culture of the world at large. An offshoot of interest in the comics is the large market for toys and merchandise based on the more popular characters, such as Mickey Mouse, Buck Rogers, Superman, or Little Orphan Annie. An extensive quantity of these mass-produced artifacts have been photographed and cataloged in Robert Lesser's *A Celebration of Comic Art and Memorabilia*.

Throughout the years the popular magazines, newspapers, and journals of commentary have published hundreds of articles and essays on the comics, many worthwhile, others superficial, and still others steeped in disdain for the subject. Much of this material is listed in the Kempkes bibliography. A useful anthology of some of the better essays is *The Funnies: An American Idiom*, edited by David Manning White and Robert H. Abel.

Several critics who have undertaken general assessments of popular culture have devoted portions of their studies to comic art. One of the earliest was Gilbert Seldes in his 1924 pioneer survey of the mass media, *The 7 Lively Arts*. Though somewhat apologetically, Seldes found some virtues in "the 'vulgar' comic strip" in one chapter of that title, but his essay on George Herriman and *Krazy Kat* was one of the first partly to define Herriman's unique genius. In *The Astonished Muse*, Reuel Denney finds the comics deeply rooted in the larger conventions and traditions of art and literature, especially naturalism, and Leo Lowenthal calls for more serious study of the comics in *Literature, Popular Culture, and Society*. One chapter of Charles Beaumont's *Remember? Remember?* praises the daily funnies for their beauty, imagination, communication, and general good to the world. Perhaps some of the most fruitful, provocative, and rational comments are found in Alan Gowans's *The Unchanging Arts*. Gowans recognizes the extent to which the popular visual arts play a functional part in the total context of society and finds the comics one of the century's major art forms. A social scientist who has specialized in writing about the subject is Arthur Asa Berger, whose books include *Li'l Abner: A Study in American Satire*, the first book-length study of a single comic strip; *The Comic-Stripped American*, a series of pieces on the way comics reflect our culture; and *Pop Culture*, a collection of essays with three on the comics.

A special category of interpretive books are the "gospel" studies. Robert L. Short began the trend with *The Gospel According to Peanuts* and followed the phenomenal success of that book with *The Parables of Peanuts*. Then came *The Gospel According to Superman* by John T. Galloway, Jr., *The Gospel According to Andy Capp* by D. P. McGeachy III, and *Good News for Grimy Gulch* by Del Carter (based on Tom K. Ryan's comic strip *Tumbleweeds*). These books basically are sermons or theological disquisitions illustrated by the comics in question and make little commentary of a significant sort on their meaning or value, except insofar as they are all concerned with the problems of human existence. Jeffrey H. Loria's *What's It All About, Charlie Brown?* is a similar kind of book which describes with frequent illustrations the philosophical and psychological meaning of *Peanuts*.

Most serious study of comic art seems to have focused on how it reflects or relates to society and the culture out of which it has grown. Only now are we witnessing the development of a body of writing that attempts to assess the comics on their own terms, by measuring their worth against their own developed standards and aesthetic principles rather than by the irrelevant yardsticks of other related arts. A collection of essays mainly on comic book super-heroes helped initiate this development: *All in Color for a Dime,* edited by Dick Lupoff and Don Thompson. Many of the essays originated in a series of fan magazine articles and still bear the stylistic and judgmental marks of their origin. A second volume, also edited by Thompson and Lupoff, *The Comic-Book Book,* is a marked improvement in this regard. In style and judgment, many of these essays are distinguished. Although most of Maurice Horn's *75 Years of the Comics* is devoted to reprinting sample pages from an exhibition at the New York Cultural Center, his excellent ten-page introduction is one of the best efforts so far to define comic art as it relates to the other narrative arts and on its own internal principles. In *The Art of Humorous Illustration,* Nick Meglin has assembled appreciative, fully illustrated tributes to twelve illustrators, including comic artists Sergio Aragones, Jack Davis, Mort Drucker, Johnny Hart, and Arnold Roth. The purpose of *Moviemaking Illustrated: The Comicbook Filmbook,* by James Morrow and Murray Suid, is to teach the technical principles of filmmaking, but the textbook utilizes nothing but frames from Marvel comic books and thereby makes many valuable points about the complex sound and visual techniques of comic art. *The Art of the Comic Strip,* edited by Walter Herderg and David Pascal, is noteworthy for its excellent choice of illustrations and the perceptive quality of the brief notes and commentary (originally a special issue of *Graphis* magazine). Also of interest is *The Very Large Book of Comical Funnies,* compiled by the staff of the *National Lampoon* as a good-natured satire on the plethora of historic and appreciative books about the comics, but which in its own way displays an appreciative sense of what makes the comics special. In a similar category is *Mad Magazine*'s send-up "The Comics" in *Mad Super Special* Number 36 (Fall 1981), which includes a feature in which several cartoonists—Charles Schulz, Walt Kelly, Ken Ernst and Allen Saunders, Mort Walker, and Mell Lazarus—draw the strip they would really like to do instead of the one they do every day.

Academic criticism of a theoretical kind on the comics has only recently begun. "The Comics as Culture," edited by M. Thomas Inge, is a special issue of the *Journal. of Popular Culture* that includes essays on Walt Kelly, Milton Caniff, and the Tarzan comic strip, and an especially valuable article entitled "The Aesthetics of the Comic Strip," by Robert C. Harvey. Two other articles on the aesthetics of comic art to be recommended, also from the *Journal of Popular Culture,* are "The Funnies, the Movies and Aesthetics" by Earle J. Coleman and "Comic Art: Characteristics and Potentialities of a Narrative Medium" by Lawrence L. Abbott. "Faulkner Reads the Funny Papers" by M. Thomas Inge is an exploration of the possible ways this century's greatest writer was influenced by his reading of comic strips.

The publication of fan magazines and amateur press publications about comic art began in the 1950s and reemerged in the 1960s as a significant development in the history of American magazines. Much of the pioneer scholarship about the comics first appeared in those pages, and extremely useful biographical and bibliographical information can be found there. A history of their development and a listing of titles would require more space than is available for this entire chapter, and it would be almost impossible to assemble a file for back issues on most of them. The comments here will be restricted to only a few of the most professional, informative, and regularly published periodicals to which subscriptions are available.

The most widely circulated and read publication about the world of comic art is *Comics Buyer's Guide,* originated in 1970 by Alan L. Light (under the title *Buyer's Guide for Comics Fandom*). Krause Publications assumed ownership in 1983, and Don and Maggie Thompson became editors. In addition to advertisements for collectors, the weekly includes feature articles, news stories, columns, reviews, and a letters column in which readers vigorously debate issues and controversies with the editors and each other. The second most popular is the *Comics Journal,* a monthly magazine with lengthy essays, in-depth interviews, review columns by leading commentators on the comics, and an aggressive editorial policy that often places the magazine in the center of controversy. Both the *Guide* and the *Journal* make for lively reading, but both contain a good deal more material about comic books than about comic strips. This is not the case with the quarterly *Cartoonist Profiles,* which specializes in interviews with living comic strip artists and profiles on classic artists of the past. A wealth of professional and historic data is found in each issue. A source of reprints of classic strips of the past and ground-breaking essays on major artists is the magazine *Nemo: The Classic Comics Library*. A complete file of issues belongs in any research collection devoted to comic art.

ANTHOLOGIES AND REPRINTS

From the very beginning of the American comic strip in the 1890s, paperback collections of the most widely read titles were popular publications. Thus *The Yellow Kid, Foxy Grandpa, Buster Brown,* and *Mutt and Jeff* appeared in series of reprints, and in 1933 the first comic book, *Funnies on Parade,* was composed of reprints of Sunday and daily strips in color. Over the years various comics would find their way into paperback anthologies and less often into hardcover collections. Usually considered of ephemeral value, few copies survive and are considered collector's items. One of the first substantial anthologies of American cartoons, complete with historical introductions and annotations, was Thomas Craven's *Cartoon Cavalcade* in 1943. Interspersed among the chronologically arranged examples of political and gag cartoons filling over 400 pages were selections from all the popular newspaper comic strips.

The one publisher who first initiated a program of reprinting classic comic strips in the most responsible format, in selected complete runs with authoritative introductions, was the late Woody Gelman of Nostalgia Press. Beginning with Alex Raymond's *Flash Gordon* in 1967, Gelman published one or more volumes a year in his series The Golden Age of Comics. He also issued a series of anthologies of selected daily strips entitled *Nostalgia Comics*. The ultimate result of his program is an extensive bookshelf of handsomely produced collections of the classic comic strips, preserved for convenient reading and future research.

The most ambitious reprint operation undertaken so far was the Classic American Comic Strips series by Hyperion Press of Westport, Connecticut, under the editorship of Bill Blackbeard. Series I contained twenty-two volumes in large format and in hardcover or paperback editions. Drawing on the archives of the San Francisco Academy of Comic Art, each volume contained complete sequential reprints from the first or peak years of selected daily and Sunday strips and an introduction by an authority on the subject of that volume. Unfortunately, the project was discontinued. Blackbeard, in collaboration with Martin Williams, also produced the most lavish general anthology to appear, *The Smithsonian Collection of Newspaper Comics*. This is an essential volume in any library for the general reader and researcher alike.

Several trade and paperback publishers have issued over the years collections of the most popular strips. Among them are Avon Books, Ballantine, Bantam, Dell, Fawcett, Grosset and Dunlap, Holt, Rinehart and Winston, New American Library, Pyramid Books, and Simon and Schuster. Andrews and McMeel specializes in reprint volumes. For a list of available titles, one should consult their catalogs, as the books go in and out of print with unpredictable frequency. There are also a number of specialty publishers now who issue nothing but reprint series and volumes, such as Blackthorne, Dragon Lady Press, Fantagraphics Books, Kitchen Sink Press, and NBM (Nantier-Beall-Minoustchine Publishing Company). The last firm has successfully seen into print a reproduction in twelve hardcover volumes of the complete run of Milton Caniff's *Terry and the Pirates,* the first such reprint project of a major long-run comic strip to reach completion. The series editor, Bill Blackbeard, is now managing a reprinting of Roy Crane's *Wash Tubbs and Captain Easy* in a similar format. Other comic strips which are to be reprinted in complete uniform sets, if the publishers succeed, include E. C. Segar's *Popeye* (Fantagraphics Books), Milton Caniff's *Steve Canyon* (Kitchen Sink Press), Harold Gray's *Little Orphan Annie* (Fantagraphics), Al Capp's *Li'l Abner* (Kitchen Sink), George Herriman's

Krazy Kat (Eclipse Books), and the complete comic strip and comic book work of Charles Crumb (Fantagraphics).

Two reprints of historically important comic strips should receive special note. Since 1926, school children in Texas have been taught their state history through *Texas History Movies,* a comic strip by Jack Patton and John Rosenfield, Jr., first published in the *Dallas Morning News* and later reprinted in numerous collections and textbooks, despite its use of ethnic stereotypes and racial slurs. Even today, *Texas History Movies* is available in a complete oversized reprint volume and in two abbreviated and edited editions (with the racism and offensive language removed). *Han Ola og han Per* was a Norwegian-American comic strip drawn by Peter Julius Rosendahl from 1918 to 1935 for the *Decorah-Posten,* a Norwegian-language newspaper in Iowa. It has continuously been reprinted ever since in various newspapers. The first 223 of the 599 published are collected in a volume available from the Norwegian-American Historical Association with historical and biographical introductions by the editors, Joan N. Buckley and Einar Haugen. The entire anthology is in both Norwegian and English and provides a most unusual source for studying the assimilation of a major ethnic group in the American Midwest.

The number of anthologies of reprinted comic strips is so extensive that they cannot easily be discussed here. Instead the reader will find a list of these in the "Anthologies and Reprints" section of the bibliography at the end of this essay. In most cases those I have selected include introductory appreciations, background essays, biographical notes, or other additional material which will be of interest to the reader and researcher.

BIBLIOGRAPHY

Books and Articles

Abbott, Lawrence L. "Comic Art: Characteristics and Potentialities of a Narrative Medium." *Journal of Popular Culture,* 19 (Spring 1986), 155–76.

Adams, John Paul. *Milton Caniff: Rembrandt of the Comic Strip.* New York: David McKay, 1946.

Beaumont, Charles. *Remember? Remember?* New York: Macmillan, 1963.

Becker, Stephen. *Comic Art in America.* New York: Simon and Schuster, 1959.

Bennett, Bob. *Collecting Original Cartoon Art.* Lombard, Ill.: Wallace-Homestead Book Co., 1987.

Berger, Arthur Asa. *The Comic-Stripped American.* New York: Walker and Co., 1973.

———. *Li'l Abner: A Study in American Satire.* New York: Twayne, 1970.

———. *Pop Culture.* New York: Pflaum/Standard, 1973.

Cahn, Joseph M. *The Teenie Weenies Book: The Life and Art of William Donahey.* La Jolla, Calif.: Green Tiger Press, 1986.

Canemaker, John. *Winsor McCay: His Life and Art.* New York: Abbeville Press, 1987.

Carlin, John, and Sheena Wagstaff, eds. *The Comic Art Show: Cartoons in Painting and Popular Culture.* New York: Fantagraphics Books, 1983.

Carter, Del. *Good News for Grimey Gulch.* Valley Forge, Pa.: Judson Press, 1977.

Coleman, Earle J. "The Funnies, the Movies and Aesthetics." *Journal of Popular Culture,* 18 (Spring 1985), 89–100.

Couperie, Pierre, et al. *A History of the Comic Strip.* Translated by Eileen B. Hennessey. New York: Crown, 1968.

Davidson, Harold. *Jimmy Swinnerton: The Artist and His Work.* New York: Hearst Books, 1985.

Denney, Reuel. *The Astonished Muse.* Chicago: University of Chicago Press, 1957.

Eisner, Will. *Comics & Sequential Art.* Tamarac, Fla.: Poorhouse Press, 1985.

Galloway, John T., Jr. *The Gospel According to Superman.* Philadelphia: Lippincott and A. J. Holman, 1973.

Gifford, Denis. *Encyclopedia of Comic Characters.* Essex, England: Longman, 1987.

Glubok, Shirley. *The Art of the Comic Strip.* New York: Macmillan, 1979.

Goulart, Ron. *The Adventurous Decade.* New Rochelle, N.Y.: Arlington House, 1975.

Gowans, Alan. *The Unchanging Arts.* Philadelphia: J. B. Lippincott, 1971.

Hardy, Charles, and Gail F. Stern, eds. *Ethnic Images in the Comics.* Philadelphia: Balch Institute for Ethnic Studies, 1986.

Harvey, Robert C. "The Aesthetics of the Comic Strip." *Journal of Popular Culture,* 12 (Spring 1979), 640–52.

Herderg, Walter, and David Pascal, eds. *The Art of the Comic Strip.* Zurich: Graphis Press, 1972.

Horn, Maurice. *Comics of the American West.* New York: Winchester Press, 1977.

———. *75 Years of the Comics.* Boston: Boston Book and Art, 1971.

———. *Sex in the Comics.* New York: Chelsea House, 1985.

———. *Women in the Comics.* New York: Chelsea House, 1977.

———, ed. *Contemporary Graphic Artists.* Detroit: Gale Research, 1986-.

———, ed. *The World Encyclopedia of Cartoons.* New York: Chelsea House, 1981.

———, ed. *The World Encyclopedia of Comics.* New York: Chelsea House, 1976.

Inge, M. Thomas. "Faulkner Reads the Funny Papers." In *Faulkner & Humor.* Edited by Doreen Fowler and Ann J. Abadie. Jackson: University Press of Mississippi, 1986, pp. 153–90.

———, ed. "The Comics as Culture." *Journal of Popular Culture,* 12 (Spring 1979), 630–754. Special issue.

Inge, M. Thomas, and Bill Blackbeard. "American Comic Art." In *A Nation of Nations.* Edited by Peter Marzio. New York: Harper and Row, 1976, pp. 600–609.

Kelly. Walt. *Ten Ever-lovin' Blue-eyed Years with Pogo.* New York: Simon and Schuster, 1959.

Kempkes, Wolfgang. *International Bibliography of Comics Literature.* Detroit: Gale Research, 1971. Rev. ed. New York: R. R. Bowker/Verlag Dokumentation, 1974.

Kinnaird, Clark, ed. *Rube Goldberg vs. the Machine Age.* New York: Hastings House, 1968.

Kunzle, David. *The Early Comic Strip*. Vol. 1 of *History of the Comic Strip*. Berkeley: University of California Press, 1973.

Lesser, Robert. *A Celebration of Comic Art and Memorabilia*. New York: Hawthorn Books, 1975.

Loria, Jeffrey H. *What's It All About, Charlie Brown?* New York: Holt, Rinehart and Winston, 1968.

Lowenthal, Leo. *Literature, Popular Culture, and Society*. Englewood Cliffs, N.J.: Prentice-Hall, 1961.

Lupoff, Dick, and Don Thompson, eds. *All in Color for a Dime*. New Rochelle, N.Y.: Arlington House, 1970.

McDonnell, Patrick, Karen O'Connell, and Georgia Riley de Havenon. *Krazy Kat: The Comic Art of George Herriman*. New York: Harry N. Abrams, 1986.

McGeachy, D. P., III. *The Gospel According to Andy Capp*. Richmond, Va.: John Knox Press, 1973.

Mad Magazine. "The Comics." *Mad Super Special*, Number 36 (Fall 1981). New York: E. C. Publications, 1981.

Marzio, Peter. *Rube Goldberg: His Life and Work*. New York: Harper and Row, 1973.

Meglin, Nick. *The Art of Humorous Illustration*. New York: Watson-Guptill, 1973.

Mendelson, Lee. *Charlie Brown and Charlie Schulz*. New York: World, 1970.

Mendelson, Lee, and Charles Schulz. *Happy Birthday, Charlie Brown*. New York: Ballantine Books, 1979.

Morrow, James, and Murray Suid. *Moviemaking Illustrated: The Comicbook Filmbook*. New York: Hayden Book Co., 1973.

Murrell, William. *A History of American Graphic Humor*. 2 vols. New York: Whitney Museum of American Art and Macmillan, 1933, 1938.

National Lampoon. *The Very Large Book of Comical Funnies*. New York: National Lampoon, 1975.

O'Sullivan, Judith. *The Art of the Comic Strip*. College Park, Md.: University of Maryland, Department of Art, 1971.

Perry, George, and Alan Aldridge. *The Penguin Book of Comics*. New York: Penguin Books, 1969. Rev. ed., 1971.

Reitberger, Reinhold, and Wolfgang Fuchs. *Comics: Anatomy of a Mass Medium*. Translated by Nadia Fowler. Boston: Little, Brown, 1972.

Robbins, Trina, and Catherine Yronwode. *Women and the Comics*. Guerneville, Calif.: Eclipse Books, 1985.

Robinson, Jerry. *The Comics: An Illustrated History of the Comic Strip*. New York: Putnam's, 1974.

Roebuck, Joan, ed. *The Graphic Art of Charles Schulz*. Oakland, Calif.: Oakland Museum, 1985.

Satin, Allan D. *A Doonesbury Index: An Index to the Syndicated Daily Newspaper Strip "Doonesbury" by G. B. Trudeau, 1970–1983*. Metuchen, N.J.: Scarecrow Press, 1985.

Schulz, Charles. *Peanuts Jubilee: My Life and Art with Charlie Brown and Others*. New York: Holt, Rinehart and Winston, 1975.

———. *You Don't Look 35, Charlie Brown*. New York: Holt, Rinehart and Winston, 1985.

Schulz, Charles, and R. Smith Kiliper. *Charlie Brown, Snoopy and Me.* Garden City, N.Y.: Doubleday, 1980.

Scott, Randall W. *Comic Books and Strips: An Information Sourcebook.* Phoenix, Arizona: Oryx Press, 1989.

Seldes, Gilbert. *The 7 Lively Arts.* New York: Harper and Brothers, 1924. Rev. ed. Layton, Utah: Peregrine Smith and Sagamore Press, 1957.

Sheridan, Martin. *Comics and Their Creators.* Boston: Hale, Cushman and Flint, 1942.

Short, Robert L. *The Gospel According to Peanuts.* Richmond, Va.: John Knox Press, 1964.

———. *The Parables of Peanuts.* New York: Harper and Row, 1968.

Smith, Bruce. *The History of Little Orphan Annie.* New York: Ballantine Books, 1982.

———. *The World According to Daddy Warbucks: Capitalist Quotations from the Richest Man in the World.* Piscataway, N.J.: New Century, 1982.

Terry, Bridget. *The Popeye Story.* New York: Tom Doherty Associates, 1980.

Thomas, James L., ed. *Cartoons and Comics in the Classroom.* Littleton, Colo.: Libraries Unlimited, 1983.

Thompson, Don, and Dick Lupoff, eds. *The Comic-Book Book.* New Rochelle, N.Y.: Arlington House, 1973.

Walker, Mort. *Backstage at the Strips.* New York: Mason/Charter, 1975.

———. *The Lexicon of Comicana.* Port Chester, N.Y.: Museum of Cartoon Art, 1980.

———. *Miss Buxley: Sexism in Beetle Bailey?* Bedford, N.Y.: Comicana Books, 1982.

Waugh, Coulton. *The Comics.* New York: Macmillan, 1947.

White, David Manning, and Robert H. Abel, eds. *The Funnies: An American Idiom.* New York: Free Press, 1963.

Wood, Art. *Great Cartoonists and Their Art.* Gretna, La.: Pelican Publishing, 1987.

Anthologies and Reprints

Blackbeard, Bill, ed. *Classic American Comic Strips.* 22 vols. Westport, Conn.: Hyperion Press, 1977. (Includes the following titles: Percy Crosby, *Skippy*; Billy De Beck, *Barney Google;* Clare Dwiggins, *School Days;* Harry Fisher, *A. Mutt;* Frank Godwin, *Connie;* Rube Goldberg, *Bobo Baxter;* George Herriman, *Baron Bean;* George Herriman, *The Family Upstairs;* Harry Hershfield, *Abie the Agent;* Harry Hershfield, *Dauntless Durham of the U.S.A;* Clifford McBride, *Napoleon;* Winsor McCay, *Winsor McCay's Dream Days;* George McManus, *Bringing Up Father;* Gus Mager, *Sherlocko the Monk;* Dick Moores, *Jim Hardy;* Frederick Opper, *Happy Hooligan;* Richard Outcault, *Buster Brown;* Elzie C. Segar, *Thimble Theater, Introducing Popeye;* Cliff Sterrett, *Polly and Her Pals;* George Storm, *Bobby Thatcher;* Harry Tuthill, *The Bungle Family;* and Edgar S. Wheelan, *Minute Movies.*)

Blackbeard, Bill, and Malcolm Whyte, eds. *Great Comic Cats.* San Francisco: Troubedor Press, 1981.

Blackbeard, Bill, and Martin Williams, eds. *The Smithsonian Collection of Newspaper Comics*. Washington, D.C.: Smithsonian Institution Press, 1977.

Breathed, Berke. *Billy and the Boingers Bootleg*. Boston: Little, Brown, 1987.

———. *Bloom County*. Boston: Little, Brown, 1983.

———. *Bloom County Babylon*. Boston: Little, Brown, 1986.

———. *Penguin Dreams and Stranger Things*. Boston: Little, Brown, 1985.

———. *Tales Too Ticklish to Tell*. Boston: Little, Brown, 1988.

———. *'Toons for Our Times*. Boston: Little, Brown, 1984.

Briggs, Clare. *When a Feller Needs a Friend and Other Favorite Cartoons*. New York: Dover, 1975.

Browne, Dik. *The Best of Hagar*. Bedford, N.Y.: Comicana Books, 1986.

Bushmiller, Ernie. *The Best of Ernie Bushmiller's Nancy*. Ed. Brian Walker. Bedford, N.Y.: Comicana Books, 1988.

Caniff, Milton. *The Complete Dickie Dare*. Agoura, Calif.: Fantagraphics Books, 1986.

———. *Male Call*. Princeton, Wis.: Kitchen Sink Press, 1987.

———. *Milton Caniff's Steve Canyon*. Princeton, Wis.: Kitchen Sink Press, 1983-.

———. *Terry and the Pirates*. Franklin Square, N.Y.: Nostalgia Press, 1970.

———. *Terry and the Pirates*. 12 vols. New York: Nantier-Beall-Minoustchine Publishing, 1984–87.

Capp, Al. *The Best of Li'l Abner*. New York: Holt, Rinehart and Winston, 1978.

———. *Li'l Abner*. Princeton, Wis.: Kitchen Sink Press, 1988-.

Crane, Roy. *Wash Tubbs and Captain Easy*. New York: Nantier-Beall-Minoustchine Publishing, 1987-.

Craven, Thomas, ed. *Cartoon Cavalcade*. New York: Simon and Schuster, 1943.

Crouch, Bill, ed. *Dick Tracy: America's Most Famous Detective*. Secaucus, N.J.: Citadel Press, 1987.

Crumb, Robert. *The Complete Crumb Comics*. Agoura, Calif.: Fantagraphics Books, 1987-.

———. *Fritz the Cat*. New York: Ballantine Books, 1969.

Davis, Jim. *Garfield Treasury*. New York: Ballantine Books, 1982.

———. *The Second Garfield Treasury*. New York: Ballantine Books, 1983.

Dille, Robert C., ed. *The Collected Works of Buck Rogers in the 25th Century*. New York: Chelsea House, 1969. Rev. ed., 1977.

Dirks, Rudolph. *The Katzenjammer Kids*. New York: Dover, 1974.

Falk, Lee, and Phil Davis. *Mandrake the Magician*. Franklin Square, N.Y.: Nostalgia Press, 1970.

Falk, Lee, and Ray Moore. *The Phantom*. Franklin Square, N.Y.: Nostalgia Press, 1969.

Fleischer, Max. *Betty Boop*. New York: Avon Books, 1975.

Foster, Harold. *Prince Valiant*. 2 vols. Wayne, N.J.: Manuscript Press, 1982–84.

———. *Prince Valiant*. Agoura, Calif.: Fantagraphics Books, 1985-.

———. *Prince Valiant Companions in Adventure*. Franklin Square, N.Y.: Nostalgia Press, 1974.

———. *Prince Valiant in the Days of King Arthur*. Franklin Square, N.Y.: Nostalgia Press, 1974.

Fox, Fontaine. *Toonerville Trolley*. New York: Scribner's, 1972.

Galewitz, Herb, ed. *Great Comics Syndicated by the New York Daily News and Chicago Tribune*. New York: Crown, 1972.

Garner, Philip, ed. *Rube Goldberg: A Retrospective*. New York: Delilah Books, 1983.

Gilmore, Donald H. [pseud.]. *Sex in Comics*. 4 vols. San Diego: Greenleaf Classics, 1971.

Gould, Chester. *The Celebrated Cases of Dick Tracy, 1931–1951*. New York: Chelsea House, 1970.

———. *Dick Tracy, the Thirties, Tommy Guns, and Hard Times*. New York: Chelsea House, 1978.

Gray, Harold. *Arf! The Life and Hard Times of Little Orphan Annie*. New Rochelle, N.Y.: Arlington House, 1970.

———. *Little Orphan Annie*. Agoura, Calif.: Fantagraphic Books, 1987-.

Guisewite, Cathy. *The Cathy Chronicles*. Kansas City, Mo.: Sheed, Andrews, and McMeel, 1978.

Herriman, George. *Krazy and Ignatz: The Complete Kat Comics*. Forestville, Calif.: Eclipse Books, 1988-.

———. *Krazy Kat*. New York: Henry Holt, 1946.

———. *Krazy Kat*. New York: Grosset and Dunlap-Madison Square Press, 1969.

Hogarth, Burne. *Jungle Tales of Tarzan*. New York: Watson-Guptill, 1976.

———. *Tarzan of the Apes*. New York: Watson-Guptill, 1972.

Holbrook, Bill. *On the Fastrack*. New York: Putnam's, 1985.

Howard, Greg. *Sally Forth*. New York: Fawcett Columbine-Ballantine Books, 1987.

Johnson, Crockett [David Johnson Leisk]. *Barnaby*. New York: Henry Holt, 1943.

———. *Barnaby*. 6 vols. New York: Ballantine Books, 1985–86.

Keller, Charles. *The Best of Rube Goldberg*. Englewood Cliffs, N.J.: Prentice-Hall, 1979.

Kelly, Walt. *The Best of Pogo*. Edited by Mrs. Walt Kelly and Bill Crouch. New York: Simon and Schuster, 1982.

———. *Outrageously Pogo*. New York: Simon and Schuster, 1985.

———. *Pluperfect Pogo*. New York: Simon and Schuster, 1987.

———. *Pogo Even Better*. New York: Simon and Schuster, 1984.

Lardner, Ring. *Ring Lardner's You Know Me Al*. New York: Harcourt Brace Jovanovich, 1979.

Larson, Gary. *The Far Side Gallery*. Kansas City, Mo.: Andrews, McMeel and Parker, 1984.

———. *The Far Side Gallery 2*. Kansas City, Mo.: Andrews, McMeel and Parker, 1986.

———. *The Far Side Gallery 3*. Kansas City, Mo.: Andrews and McMeel, 1988.

Lee, Stan. *The Best of Spider-Man*. New York: Ballantine Books, 1986.

McCay, Winsor. *Daydreams and Nightmares: The Fantastic Visions of Winsor McCay*. Ed. Richard Marschall. Westlake Village, Calif.: Fantagraphics Books, 1988.

———. *Dreams of the Rarebit Fiend*. New York: Dover, 1973.

———. *Little Nemo*. Franklin Square, N.Y.: Nostalgia Press, 1972.

———. *Little Nemo in the Palace of Ice and Further Adventures*. New York: Dover, 1976.

———. *Little Nemo—1905–1906*. Franklin Square, N.Y.: Nostalgia Press, 1972.

McManus, George. *Bringing Up Father*. New York: Scribner's, 1973.

———. *Jiggs Is Back*. Berkeley, Calif.: Celtic Book Co., 1986.

MacNelly, Jeff. *The Greatest Shoe on Earth*. New York: Holt, Rinehart and Winston, 1985.

————. *The New Shoe*. New York: Avon Books, 1981.

————. *One Shoe Fits All*. New York: Henry Holt, 1986.

————. *On with the Shoe*. New York: Holt, Rinehart and Winston, 1982.

————. *The Other Shoe*. New York: Avon Books, 1980.

————. *A Shoe for All Seasons*. New York: Holt, Rinehart and Winston, 1983.

————. *The Shoe Must Go On*. New York: Holt, Rinehart and Winston, 1984.

————. *Too Old for Summer Camp and Too Young to Retire*. New York: St. Martin's Press, 1988.

————. *The Very First Shoe Book*. New York: Avon Books, 1978.

Marlette, Doug. *Kudzu*. New York: Ballantine Books, 1982.

Moores, Dick. *Gasoline Alley*. New York: Avon Books, 1976.

Nostalgia Comics. 6 vols. Franklin Square, N.Y.: Nostalgia Press, 1971–74.

Outcault, Richard F. *Buster Brown*. New York: Dover, 1974.

Patton, Jack, and John Rosenfield, Jr. *Texas History Movies*. Collector's Limited Ed. Dallas: Pepper Jones Martinez, 1970.

————. *Texas History Movies*. Abridged and revised. Dallas: Pepper Jones Martinez, 1985.

————. *Texas History Movies*. Abridged and revised. Austin: Texas Historical Association, 1986.

Raymond, Alex. *Flash Gordon*. Franklin Square, N.Y.: Nostalgia Press, 1967.

————. *Flash Gordon in the Planet Mongo*. Franklin Square, N.Y.: Nostalgia Press, 1974.

————. *Flash Gordon in the Underwater World of Mongo*. Franklin Square, N.Y.: Nostalgia Press, 1974.

————. *Flash Gordon into the Water of Mongo*. Franklin Square, N.Y.: Nostalgia Press, 1971.

Ripley, Robert L. *Ripley's Giant Believe It or Not!* New York: Warren Books, 1976.

Rosendahl, Peter J. *Han Ola og han Per*. Edited by Joan N. Buckley and Einar Haugen. Oslo: Universitetsforlaget, 1984.

Schulz, Charles. *Peanuts Treasury*. New York: Holt, Rinehart and Winston, 1968.

————. *The Snoopy Festival*. New York: Holt, Rinehart and Winston, 1974.

Segar, Elzie C. *The Complete E. C. Segar Popeye*. Agoura, Calif.: Fantagraphics Books, 1984–.

Smith, Sidney. *The Gumps*. New York: Scribner's, 1974.

Trudeau, G. B. *The Doonesbury Chronicles*. New York: Holt, Rinehart and Winston, 1975.

————. *Doonesbury Deluxe*. New York: Holt, Rinehart and Winston, 1987.

————. *Doonesbury Dossier*. New York: Holt, Rinehart and Winston, 1984.

————. *Doonesbury's Greatest Hits*. New York: Holt, Rinehart and Winston, 1978.

————. *The People's Doonesbury*. New York: Holt, Rinehart and Winston, 1981.

Unger, Jim. *The 1st Treasury of Herman*. Kansas City, Mo.: Andrews and McMeel, 1979.

————. *Herman, the Fourth Treasury*. Kansas City, Mo.: Andrews, McMeel and Parker, 1984.

————. *Herman, the Third Treasury*. Kansas City, Mo.: Andrews and McMeel, 1982.

————. *Herman Treasury 5*. Kansas City, Mo.: Andrews, McMeel and Parker, 1986.

————. *The Second Herman Treasury*. Kansas City, Mo.: Andrews and McMeel, 1980.

Walker, Mort. *The Best of Beetle Bailey*. Bedford, N.Y.: Comicana Books, 1984.

———. *The Best of Hi and Lois*. Bedford, N.Y.: Comicana Books, 1986.

Watterson, Bill. *Calvin and Hobbes*. Kansas City, Mo.: Andrews, McMeel and Parker, 1985.

———. *The Essential Calvin and Hobbes*. Kansas City, Mo.: Andrews and McMeel, 1988.

———. *Something Under the Bed is Drooling*. Kansas City, Mo.: Andrews and McMeel, 1988.

Willard, Frank. *Moon Mullins: Two Adventures*. New York: Dover, 1976.

Young, Dean, and Rick Marschall. *Blondie and Dagwood's America*. New York: Harper and Row, 1981.

Periodicals

Cartoonist Profiles. Fairfield, Conn.: 1969–.

Comics Buyer's Guide. Iola, Wis.: 1971–.

Comics Journal. Seattle, Wash., 1977–.

Nemo: The Classic Comics Library. Seattle, Wash., 1983–.

Computers

MICHAEL G. WESSELLS

Over the past forty years, the electronic computer has made a meteoric ascent into the lives of millions. Once the rare and sacred objects of the high priests of engineering, computers have become familiar household items and indispensable tools in enterprises such as business, education, government, and medicine. In short, computers have become woven into the daily fabric of Western civilization.

The rapid diffusion of computers in Western society has had a significant impact on popular culture. Superintelligent computers and humanoid robots were popular subjects in both film and literature several decades before computers entered the home. By the late 1970s, computers had become entrenched in the workplace, and many people reported that they were spending as many hours with computers as with other people. By the early 1980s, computer and video games enjoyed soaring popularity, personal computers had become virtually commonplace, and bookstore shelves swelled with popular computer journals and books. This burgeoning popularity led *Time* magazine to designate the personal computer as its "Man of the Year" in 1982, the first time the award had ever been given to a machine. [1]

Being of recent origin, the subject of computers in popular culture has received very little systematic investigation. This is unfortunate since it is an interesting subject in its own right. Furthermore, the study of computers in popular culture could shed light on how the powerful computer technology is transforming people and culture. Without an understanding of these changes, it is all too easy for society to drift imperceptibly away from its moorings and for citizens to find their social system increasingly unintelligible and uncontrollable.

The aims of this chapter are to provide an overview of computers in popular culture and to identify resources and questions that may facilitate research in this area. The achievement of these aims is no easy task, particularly since the subject area has not been defined in even an approximate manner. Although the subject certainly includes popular images of computers from fiction and film, it is important to recognize that computers themselves and the associated popular software, language, and literature have become objects in popular culture. Even the computer industry and the history of computers have captured the attention of general audiences. Because the subject matter is diverse and will undoubtedly change rapidly as computer technology evolves, it is appropriate to avoid narrowing the boundaries of the field prematurely. Accordingly, this chapter examines computers in popular culture with a wide-angle lens, introducing a broad spectrum of topics for future investigations.

At the same time, the subject is so large that it demands some selectivity of coverage. For example, microprocessors have become embedded in many popular products such as automobiles and cameras. Since it would be impossible to consider these diverse applications, a decision has been made to include only computerized games and robots, topics that are very closely associated with computers and that do not fall readily into extant categories in the literature on popular culture.

HISTORIC OUTLINE

Popular fascination with seemingly intelligent automata has ancient origins. In Hellenic Egypt, around 200 B.C., inventors made moving statues that danced and shot out flames in clever religious shows designed to invoke awe of the gods.[2] By the eighteenth century, it was fashionable for noblemen to display life-size automata that, driven by gears and levers, could draw, write, and play musical instruments.[3] Although these devices displayed little of the depth and scope of human intelligence, they introduced into popular culture visions of intelligent machines, anticipating the development of the seemingly intelligent computers of the 1980s.

In the twentieth century, popular images of intelligent computers and robots entered popular culture through science fiction, antedating the construction of the first electronic computers in the mid–1940s. Karl Capek's *R. U. R.,* published in 1921, introduced the word *robot* and painted a dystopian picture in which robots created for work revolted against and ultimately defeated their human makers. In the early 1930s, John W. Campbell published in the pulp magazine *Amazing* several stories that dealt explicitly with computers.[4]

It was the writing of Isaac Asimov, however, that penetrated deeply into popular culture. His 1940 story "Robbie" told of the manufacture of robots as playmates for children and of the heroism of one robot, Robbie, in saving the life of a human child. Despite his voluminous and intriguing cybernetic writings, Asimov is probably best known for his "Three Laws of Robotics," a code of ethical conduct that required robots to protect humans and to remain subservient to them. These laws, which were set forth in *I Robot* and which figured prominently in a dozen stories,[5] embodied and stimulated the public hope for a benign relationship between humans and computers. This was apparent in the late 1970s and early 1980s in the *Star Wars* film series, which involved highly intelligent and friendly robots such as R–2 D–2 and C3PO.

Many science fiction writers, however, have envisioned less benign relationships between people and computers. Arthur Clarke's *2001: A Space Odyssey,* which spawned a popular film of the same title in the late 1960s, depicted a future in which a superintelligent computer seized control over the people who depended upon it for survival. Other writers have explored the possibility that even if the computers themselves are not evil, they will be misused by foolish or evil people. In the popular *War Games* film of the early 1980s, for example, a teenage computer hacker gained illegal access to the NORAD computer system used by the United States to detect missile attacks. By inadvertently activating an intelligent program that plays simulated battle games, he set off a false alarm that nearly triggered an accidental nuclear war. Similarly, in the short-lived "Max Headroom" television series, authoritarian leaders used computers to maximize their own profits while keeping iron-fisted control over the citizens. In film and literature, then, computers have served as a drawing board for the creation of popular images of intelligent machines and of our prospects for living with them.

Images of computers in film and literature, however, were not the only or even the primary vehicles through which computers entered popular culture. The use of computers by the masses undoubtedly played a key role in making computers part of popular culture. In addition, the electronic computer had many precursors, some of which may have influenced popular culture in earlier periods. Recently, the development of the computer industry has itself become a topic of popular interest and entrepreneurial folklore. For these reasons, it is appropriate to sketch briefly the historical development of computing by the masses.

The origins of computers may be traced back to ancient events such as the development of the concept of numbers and of devices such as the counting board and the abacus. But it was not until the seventeenth century that mechanical calculating devices were built by mathematicians such as Blaise Pascal, a Frenchman, after whom the contemporary programming language Pascal was named. In 1804, the French inventor Joseph Marie Jacquard built a weaving machine that used holes punched into cards as a means of programming a loom to weave specific patterns. By 1812, over

10,000 Jacquard looms were in use in France, one of the earlier mass exposures to programmable devices.[6]

The nineteenth century witnessed the development of a number of more complex calculating machines. Prominent among these were the difference engine and the analytical engine of Charles Babbage and the card-punching machine of Herman Hollerith, whose Tabulating Machine Company merged with another company that eventually evolved into IBM.[7]

The first digital computers evolved in the 1940s out of projects associated with World War II. At Harvard, Howard Aiken developed the Mark I, an electromechanical relay computer. In England, a special purpose electronic computer called Colossus was built in 1943 by Alan M. Turing in order to decipher the secret German code.[8] The first general purpose electronic computer, ENIAC, was developed at the University of Pennsylvania by J. Presper Eckert, Jr., and John Mauchly. ENIAC was a mammoth machine that stretched over one hundred feet, weighed thirty tons, and contained 18,000 vacuum tubes that failed at an alarming rate. For obvious reasons, it never found its way into the home.

In the 1950s, the Census Bureau and several business corporations began using large computers, and companies such as Sperry and IBM began their competition for the mainframe market. Although the large mainframes were too expensive to be used widely by the public, they enabled the development of ideas about artifical intelligence that gradually diffused into popular culture. In 1957, John McCarthy coined the term *artificial intelligence,* and by 1958, Herbert Simon and Allen Newell had developed an inference system that solved difficult mathematical problems. Excited by this accomplishment, Simon wrote: "There are now in the world machines that think, that learn and that create. Moreover, their ability to do these things is going to increase rapidly until—in the visible future—the range of problems they can handle will be coextensive with the range to which the human mind has been applied."[9] The era of intelligent machines seemed to have arrived.

From the 1960s to the middle of the 1970s, mainframe computers became much more widespread because of signficant reductions in cost and size, increases in reliability, the development of time sharing, and the creation of programming languages such as BASIC, FORTRAN, COBOL, and Pascal that used English words as commands. Nevertheless, computers remained too large and expensive for home use, and computing was too highly technical to attract substantial public attention. In fact, public involvement in computing was often thwarted by the chauvinistic culture of computer centers, which at universities were populated by hackers. These virtuoso programmers and technicians spoke in arcane languages unintelligible to the masses. Aside from a few rare exceptions, they viewed amateur or popular computing with disdain, making beginners feel as if they had entered a foreign land whose inhabitants delighted in flaunting their intellectual superiority.

Nevertheless, computers came increasingly into the public eye during this period. Herbert Simon brought the idea of artificial intelligence to the business community in his 1960 book, *The New Science of Management Decision*. In 1964, *U.S. News and World Report* carried an article entitled "Is the Computer Running Wild?" In 1966, NBC introduced its "Star Trek" series, in which characters routinely spoke and posed difficult questions to a highly intelligent computer. In 1968, Arthur Clarke published *2001: A Space Odyssey,* and in 1970, *National Geographic* featured an article entitled "Behold the Computer Revolution." By the early 1970s, computers had become standard scientific instruments and had penetrated deeply into the workplace. Talk of the computer revolution had become commonplace, and books such as William H. Desmonde's *Computers and Their Uses* and J. Newman's *The Computer: How It's Changing Our Lives* had begun to appear regularly. In addition, books such as D. Parker's *Crime by Computer* called public attention to the social problems associated with computer use.

The age of popular computing, however, awaited the development of a personal computer that was relatively inexpensive and easy to use. In 1973, the prerequisite technical breakthrough occurred when the Intel Corporation introduced the chip, a fingernail-size integrated circuit that contained thousands of components. Because it was small and suitable for mass production, the chip touched off a wave of size and cost reductions that set the stage for the emergence of the microcomputer or personal computer. In 1973, MITS, Inc., introduced the Altair 8800, a personal computer that came in kit form for hobbyists and that was featured on the cover of *Popular Electronics* in January 1975. Tandy Corporation introduced its first Radio Shack microcomputer in 1976. A year later, Commodore entered the market with the popular PET computer, which was followed by the VIC–20.

Yet it was the Apple that made the personal computer a household item. In 1976, Steven Jobs and Stephen Wozniak, the founders of Apple Computer, built an Apple I in Jobs's home garage and introduced it at the Homebrew Club, a group of computer enthusiasts in California.[10] Apple introduced its highly successfuly Apple II in 1977, and it rapidly became the standard in many elementary and secondary schools. By 1982, Apple had reached the Fortune 500, and Jobs and Wozniak had become folk heroes.

Realizing the immense size of the personal computer market, IBM entered the field in 1981 with its IBM PC and captured over 20 percent of the market in its first year. The battle between industry giants such as IBM and small enterprises such as Apple had the popular appeal of a struggle between David and Goliath, making industry watching a popular pastime. Moreover, computers and accessories were changing at a dizzying pace, and users needed information in order to keep up. The result was an explosive growth in popular trade journals such as *PC Week* and *Infoworld* and popular magazines such as *Byte, Datamation,* and *PC Magazine*. In addition, books about computer engineering, hackers, and the inner workings of computer corporations attracted a large audience. Most notable among these were Tracy Kidder's *Soul of a New Machine,* Frederick Brooks's *The Mythical Man-Month,* Steven Levy's *Hackers: Heroes of the Computer Revolution,* Michael Moritz's *The Little Kingdom: The Private Story of Apple Computer,* Katherine Davis Fishman's *The Computer Establishment,* and Robert Sobel's *IBM: Colossus in Transition.*

The popular appeal of computers in the 1980s stemmed not only from reductions in size and cost but also from the development of learnable, user friendly software. Systems software such as the CP/M and MS-DOS operating systems enjoyed soaring popularity. And software companies such as Microsoft, Ashton-Tate, and Lotus Development Corporation marketed large numbers of prepackaged application programs that were easily used even by computer novices. Before long, software stores cropped up, offering computer owners an expanding array of popular word-processing packages such as *Wordstar, Word Perfect,* and *Volkswriter,* spreadsheets such as *Visicalc* and *Supercalc,* and data base management programs such as *dBase II.* The situation for consumers grew even brighter with the appearance of software packages such as *Lotus 1–2–3* and *Symphony* that combined word processing, spreadsheets, and data base management. The movement toward user friendly software was so successful that it stimulated the production of user friendly systems, notably Apple's Macintosh, which was introduced in 1984 and was followed by its own line of journals such as *Macworld,* and of integrated software packages such as *Jazz.*

Starting in the late 1970s, computers became a major source of recreation. In shopping malls, bars, and universities across the nation, computerized shooting and chasing games such as *Space Invaders, Asteroids, Defenders,* and *Pacman* became familiar social magnets that attracted throngs of children and adults. Video game arcades cropped up, replacing the older pinball arcades. At the same time, large numbers of people used mainframe computers to play games such as *Adventure* in which players explored imaginary underworlds, fighting monsters, casting spells, and collecting treasures.

The popularity of video games soon declined as personal computers moved into homes. Initially, home games had been simple affairs such as *Pong,* in which opponents used game paddles to swat an electronic tennis ball back and forth on a television screen. But as microcomputers became more powerful and as software producers recognized the size of the game market, sophisticated home computer games proliferated and came to include chess games such as *Sargon,* search games such as *King's Quest,* shooting games such as *Marauder* and *Star Trek,* and Nintendo games like *Mario Brothers.* Books that listed and identified games, such as Brian Murphy's *Sorcerers and Soldiers: Computer Wargames, Fantasies and Adventures,* enjoyed increasing popularity.

Games, however, were only part of the recreational appeal of computers. In 1983, *Scientific American* began a regular article entitled "Computer Recreations." By the mid–1980s, personal computer clubs, computer camps, and electronic bulletin boards had become significant centers of recreation for adults and children. In addition, computers had become frequent objects of humor in comic strips such as *Doonesbury* and in books such as Richard L. Diddays's *Computers—Caricatures and Cartoons* and S. Harris's *What's So Funny About Computers?* And bookstores and computer stores began carrying humorous posters such as "Murphy's Computer Law" by Celestial Arts and "Rick Meyerowitz's Digital Deli Map of Personal Computer America" by Workman Publishing.

The advent of the personal computer created a vast public curiosity about how to operate computers, what kinds of computers to buy, and how to use computers in business and education. By the early 1980s, popular books such as B. Albrecht's *What to Do After You Hit Return* and R. L. Albrecht's *BASIC: A Self Teaching Guide*, Charles P. Holtzman's *What to Do When You Get Your Hands on a Microcomputer*, and Tom Logsdon's *How to Cope with Computers* had appeared in many bookstores. Whereas many of the early popular books on computing emphasized programming, these have given way to books too numerous to list on specialized packages such as *Lotus 1–2–3* and *Word Perfect*.

Increased public awareness of the power of the computer as an intellectual tool, coupled with the spread of personal computers throughout society, created the public perception that it would be a handicap to remain uninformed about computers. Computer literacy became a national obsession in the schools, and bookstores sold large numbers of dictionaries of computer technology such as Alan Freedman's *The Computer Glossary* and John Prenis's *The Computer Dictionary*. There were also sharp increases in the numbers of popular and educational books that surveyed the diverse applications of computers. Representative items include Michael Arbib's *Computers and the Cybernetic Society*, J. David Bolter's *Turing's Man: Western Culture in the Computer Age*, Harvey and Barbara Deitel's *Computers and Data Processing*, Jeffrey Frates and William Moldrup's *Computers and Life*, Neill Graham's *The Mind Tool*, Grace Hopper and Steven Mandell's *Understanding Computers*, H. D. Lechner's *The Computer Chronicles*, Tom Logsdon's *Computers Today and Tomorrow*, Patrick McKeown's *Living with Computers*, Daniel Slotnick et al.'s *Computers and Applications: An Introduction to Data Processing*, and Robert and Nancy Stern's *Computers and Information Processing*.

As rhetoric about a computer revolution gained currency and as people experienced firsthand problems such as privacy invasion, incorrect computer billing, and broken Anytime Teller Machines, they became interested in the social impact of computers. This led to the rapid expansion of a literature best described as popular social commentary, which blended futurology with popular social science in equal amounts. In contrast to the small amount of attention received by the earliest social commentaries, such as N. Wiener's *The Human Use of Human Beings,* large audiences were attracted to Alvin Toffler's *The Third Wave,* John Naisbitt's *Megatrends: Ten New Directions Transforming Our Lives,* and Daniel Bell's *The Coming of Post-Industrial Society,* all of which suggested that we are increasingly becoming an information society in which computers play a prominent role.

Some of the social commentaries, such as Christopher Evans's *The Micro Millennium,* were optimistic and predicted that, aside from problems such as rising unemployment among unskilled workers, the computer would usher in a new era of increased productivity and of human–machine partnership. Others, such as Ian Reineke's *Electronic Illusions: A Skeptic's View of Our High-Tech Future,* took a pessimistic view, proclaiming that computers are instruments of dehumanization and disempowerment.

The computer boom also stimulated interest in artificial intelligence, creating a sizable audience for popular books such as Richard Bellman's *An Introduction to Artificial Intelligence: Can Computers Think?,* Bertram Raphael's *The Thinking Computer: Mind Inside Matter,* F. David Peat's *Artificial Intelligence: How Machines Think,* and Lawrence Stevens's *Artificial Intelligence: The Search for the Perfect Machine.* Public interest in artificial intelligence skyrocketed in the early 1980s as expert systems entered the business place, stimulating the public appetite for books on expert systems such as Richard Forsyth's *Expert Systems: Principles and Case Studies.* The book that captivated the public attention more than any other, however, was Edward Feigenbaum and Pamela McCorduck's *The Fifth Generation: Artificial Intelligence and Japan's Computer Challenge to the World.* An alarmist description of Japan's long-range plan to develop a new generation of intelligent computers that could talk and solve intricate problems, this book fueled the growing national concern over Japan's technological prowess. It also convinced many that America's economic fate rests on its ability to develop and use computers effectively.

Aside from economic issues, the prospect of cohabiting the planet with intelligent machines raised provocative and ancient questions such as What is man? and How do people differ from machines? In his 1969 book *The Sciences of the Artificial,* Herbert A. Simon called public attention to the intimate linkage between computers and psychology and to the possibility that the human mind is a system for information processing. This theme has been explored subsequently in many books written for general audiences, such as Margaret Boden's *Artificial Intelligence and Natural Man,* Daniel Dennett's *Brainstorms: Philosophical Essays on Mind and Psychology,* Douglas Hofstadter's *Godel, Escher, Bach,* Hofstadter and Dennett's *The Mind's I: Fantasies and Reflections on Self and Soul,* and Stephen Michael Kosslyn's *Ghosts in the Mind's Machine: Creating and Using Images in the Brain.*

The advances in artificial intelligence, coupled with the increased public awareness of the use of specialized robots in manufacturing, have helped to introduce real robots into popular culture. In 1983, Heath, Inc., marketed

Hero–1, a mobile, talking robot that was less than practical since it cost $2,500 and could lift no more than one pound. Several years later, RB Robot Corporation began marketing the RB5X Intelligent Robot, which used sonar and tactile sensors to move around while avoiding obstacles. Similar in shape to the fictional R–2 D–2 robot from the *Star Wars* film series, it could be programmed to vacuum the house and to carry messages and light objects. Because of the high cost of robots that will do work around the home, it is safe to predict that small recreational droids will be the most popular home robots over the next ten or so years. Already popular is the Tomy line of toy robots, which includes OMNIBOT, a small droid that can be controlled by a remote transmitter and can deliver messages and snacks on a small serving tray. It will be a long time before truly useful robots become common household items.

Communication via computer has become one of the most popular facets of home computing in the 1980s, creating a substantial market for practical guides such as Alfred Glossbrenner's *The Complete Handbook of Personal Computer Communications* and J. Deken's *The Electronic Cottage,* and also for policy analyses such as Wilson P. Dizard, Jr.'s *The Coming Information Age: An Overview of Technology, Economics, and Politics.* Using modems that connect to standard telephone lines, increasing numbers of users send and receive messages via electronic mail, participate in computer conferences, read and post messages on electronic bulletin boards, search through electronic data bases such as DIALOG, and shop and bank electronically. Millions use information utilities such as CompuServe and The Source, which enable users to monitor events on Wall Street, scan AP or UPI news reports, check airline schedules, or read abstracts from popular magazines.

An increasingly popular form of computerized information service called videotex, which combines text with color video images, appeared in the late 1970s. In 1979, the British Post Office installed the Prestel videotex service, which failed because of its high price. Elsewhere, videotex initiatives fared better. In 1981, the French postal, telegraph, and telephone authorities (PTT) gave away small terminals intended for use as telephone directories. But private businesses quickly recognized the potential of the terminals and began offering services such as stock prices, games, medical advice, and even wife swapping.[11] Use of the videotex services in France has become something of a craze, which has been called "Le Phénomène Minitel." Videotex has yet to catch on in the United States, although corporate giants such as Sears and IBM are exploring the possibility of a cooperative videotex venture.[12]

The effects of computers on popular communications can also be seen in the entry of new terms into the popular lexicon. Words such as "hacker," "floppy disk," "software," and "chip" have become staples in the popular vocabulary, and they all stem from the development of computers. A subtler but transformative effect of computers on language, however, lies in the development of new terms to talk about people, particularly about human cognitive activity. It has become commonplace to conceptualize memory in terms of the "storage" and "retrieval" of information and to describe thinking as "information processing."[13] Talk of intelligent computers, electronic brains, and expert systems has been prominent in popular magazines and books. In addition to being powerful tools, computers have become shapers of our social reality and our image of ourselves.

REFERENCE WORKS

No reference works focus specifically on computers in popular culture. Nevertheless, researchers in this area will find a number of useful resources, including some excellent general introductions to sources of information about computers. Darlene Myers Hildebrandt's *Computer Information Directory* serves as an overview of periodicals, reviews, indexes, encyclopedias, handbooks, and international listings of hardware and software. Although it is relatively comprehensive, this directory provides little in the way of detailed evaluations to guide the user. In contrast, Sayre Van Young's *Microsource: Where to Find Answers to Questions About Microcomputers* is more selective, but it provides substantive descriptions and evaluations of information sources concerning microcomputers. Particularly useful for the study of popular culture are his guides to software directories and computer camps. A third, although somewhat dated, general resource is Ciel Michele Carter's *Guide to Reference Sources in the Computer Sciences*.

General sources of information also include numerous encyclopedias and dictionaries. The *McGraw-Hill Encyclopedia of Science and Technology* provides a very brief, nonanalytical introduction to computers, how they work, and what they can do. Robert A. Edmunds's *The Prentice-Hall Encyclopedia of Information Technology,* which is intended primarily for businesspeople, contains 150 essays for general audiences on computers and their applications and issues associated with their use. Anthony Ralston's *Encyclopedia of Computer Science and Engineering* provides a comprehensive but relatively nontechnical introduction to computers. A more technical discussion is provided by the sixteen-volume *Encyclopedia of Computer Science and Technology,* edited by Jack Belzer, Albert G. Holzman, and Allen Kent. Of the dictionaries that may be useful in the study of the impact of computers on popular language, Laura Darcy and Louise Boston's *Webster's New World Dictionary of Computer Terms* is the most comprehensive, but a more recent and relatively nontechnical work is the *Dictionary of Computing & Information Technology* by A. J. Meadows et al. In the analysis of computer terminology and different languages, Alan Isaacs's *The Multilingual Computer Dictionary* is a useful listing, although it does not include explanations of the derivations of the terms. In the study of acronyms, a useful resource is the *Dictionary of New Information Technology Acronyms* by M. Gordon, A. Singleton, and C. Rickards.

Of the numerous guides to the books and periodicals on computers, the most comprehensive are the periodical *ACM Guide to Computing Literature,* the *Current Index of Computer Literature,* and *Computer Books and Serials in Print.* These works are lists rather than guides that contain detailed reviews, and, although they cover some nontechnical works, their primary emphasis is technical. Other sources on relatively technical material are *Computing Reviews* and Darlene Myers's *Computer Science Resources: A Guide to Professional Literature.*

Microcomputing is the area that contains most of the literature pertaining directly to popular culture. The periodical *Microcomputer Index* provides a relatively comprehensive listing of works in this area, and Michael Nicita and Ronald Petrusha's *The Reader's Guide to Microcomputer Books* provides a useful guide to the literature. Unusually substantive and pointed reviews of books and articles may be found in *LAMP: Literature Analysis of Microcomputer Publications,* which includes a section on video and computer games.

In the area of the history of computers, an essential resource is James W. Cortada's *An Annotated Bibliography of the History of Data Processing.* Although it lacks a subject index, it provides information about nearly 1,500 books and articles arranged into three appropriate historical periods. Cortada's *Historical Dictionary of Data Processing* includes both definitions and interpretive essays on many subjects, some of which concern popular culture. The most useful, although technical, primary source on the evolution of computing is *Annals of the History of Computing.* This periodical published the most extensive bibliography in this area, Brian Randall's "An Annotated Bibliography on the Origins of Computers."

There is an increasing number of software indexes and reviews available. *The Software Encyclopedia* is analogous to *Books in Print* and lists over 23,000 pieces of software of all varieties. Relatively comprehensive listings are also provided by two works of three volumes each: the *Datapro Directory of Microcomputer Software* and *The Software Catalog.* The latter source is particularly useful for its large number of game listings. A more specialized reference concerning data bases is Owen Davies and Mike Edelhart's *Omni Online Database Directory.* For reviews on software, the periodical *Software Reviews on File* provides reviews from numerous sources on both popular and technical software. A popular but less comprehensive source of software reviews is Stewart Brand's *Whole Earth Software Catalog.* Much of the most popular software, particularly in the area of games, was developed for the early Atari and Commodore home computers. This software is listed and reviewed in *The Blue Book for the Atari Computer* and *The Blue Book for the Commodore Computer,* respectively.

The impact of computers on popular social activity is evident in the development of computer camps, computer clubs, and the associated electronic bulletin boards and free software exchange systems. Mike Benton's *The Complete Guide to Computer Camps and Workshops* includes an introductory discussion of computer camps and also identifies the more prominent camps and workshops given in the United States. Robert Froelich's *The IBM PC (and Compatibles) Free Software Catalog and Directory* provides a comprehensive listing of clubs, bulletin boards, and free software as well. Gary Phillips's *IBM PC Public Domain Software*, although less comprehensive than Froelich's volume, provides more detailed evaluations of free software, a desirable feature since the quality of public domain software is highly variable.

Few of the reference tools on science fiction concentrate specifically on computers, although several general resources are available. Donald Tuck's three-volume work, *The Encyclopedia of Science Fiction and Fantasy*, is the most thorough treatment of authors and subjects. Curtis Smith's *Twentieth Century Science-Fiction Writers* offers a brief historical survey of the primary works and the development of the major science fiction authors. William Contento's *Index to Science Fiction Anthologies and Collections* and *Index to Science Fiction Anthologies and Collections 1977–1983* provides a comprehensive listing of works by author and by title. Thoughtful essays on the origins and the development of science fiction are provided by Neil Barron's *Anatomy of Wonder: A Critical Guide to Science Fiction*, which includes numerous annotated bibliographies, a discussion of children's science fiction, and a guide to science fiction in foreign languages.

The science fiction magazines are indexed, by period, in Donald Day's *Index to the Science Fiction Magazines, 1926–1950*, Erwin Strauss's *The MIT Science Fiction Society Index to the S-F Magazines, 1951–1965*, and the *Index to the Science Fiction Magazines, 1966–1970*. Interpretive essays on science fiction magazines are provided by Marshall Tymn and M. Ashley in *Science Fiction, Fantasy, and Weird Fiction Magazines*.

There is only one bibliography available on social commentary on computers. This is Gary Abshire's *The Impact of Computers on Society and Ethics: A Bibliography*. Unfortunately, this bibliography was published in 1980 and has become dated since the literature has expanded so rapidly.

RESEARCH COLLECTIONS

There are no research collections devoted specifically to computers in popular culture. The Digital Museum in Boston and the Charles Babbage Institute at the University of Minnesota have libraries containing information on the history of computing. The libraries associated with the Smithsonian Institution also have libraries concerning computers and the history of technology.

Many of the best libraries concerning computers, however, are found at universities that have become major centers for computer science and artificial intelligence. Harvard University, Carnegie-Mellon University, Stanford University, and the Massachusetts Institute of Technology all have expansive collections that are rather technical but that nevertheless contain many books concerning computers and culture. Until the study of computers in popular culture has advanced farther, researchers will have to rely mostly on general research collections and film archives.

HISTORY AND CRITICISM

Science fiction has been one of the primary vehicles through which computers have entered popular culture. In *The Cybernetic Imagination in Science Fiction,* Patricia S. Warrick provides a historical survey of computers in science fiction, tracing the development of the images of hope, fear, and dehumanization that are prominent in the literature. She also develops a tripartite system for classifying the models of the universe and of human-machine relationships that are expressed in science fiction works involving computers. Her classification into closed-system models, open-system models, and isolated-system models adds structure to a sprawling literature and is more flexible and multidimensional than the traditional categories of utopian and dystopian literature. In addition to providing a wealth of information about computers in science fiction, Warrick offers many insights into the complex relationships among technology, society, and literary imagination.

Very little work has been done on the history of computers in popular culture. This is understandable since the widespread use of computers is so recent a phenomenon and since the technology and its applications change daily. But it is also regrettable since studies of this subject could elucidate the cultural changes produced by the computer revolution.

Numerous historical works examine the evolution of computers per se. Herman Goldstein's *The Computer from Pascal to von Neumann* traces the history of computers back several hundred years, while S. H. Lovington's *Early British Computers: The Story of Vintage Computers and the People Who Built Them,* N. Metropolis's *A History of Computing in the Twentieth Century,* and Nancy Stern's *From ENIAC to UNIVAC* focus on events in this century. Several book-length studies of pioneers in computing have been published, including Geoffrey Austrian's *Herman Hollerith,* Andrew Hodges's *Alan Turing: The Enigma,* and Morrison and Morrison's *Charles Babbage and His Calculating Engines: Selected Writings by Charles Babbage and Others.* The history of programming is featured in Richard Wexelblatt's *History of Programming Languages.* The development of the microcomputer has received attention in *Fire in the Valley: The Making of the Personal Computer* by Paul Freiberger and Michael Swaine.

With so much material available on the history of computing, the time is ripe for studies of how developments in computing have influenced popular culture and vice versa. A first step in this direction is Pamela Mc-Corduck's *Machines Who Think,* which sketches the history of artificial intelligence. Although this book presents an excessively optimistic assessment of the prospects of artificial intelligence, it provides an insider's view of the artificial intelligentsia and of the connections between popular and technical culture. It is also one of the few books that recognize the reciprocal nature of the relationship between popular and technical culture.

Book-length studies of computers in culture have leaned toward social philosophy, policy analysis, and futurology rather than popular culture. The chief exception is Sherry Turkle's widely read *The Second Self: Computers and the Human Spirit.* Interpreting hundreds of hours of personal observations and interviews, Turkle shows that the computer is an evocative object that stimulates ordinary people to think about the differences between machines and people, life and death, and self and others. Taking the reader into the worlds of young children playing with computerized talking machines and of adolescents captivated by the world of computer games, she sketches the richness of the everyday interactions between humans and computers. She also dispels such common misconceptions as the idea that playing computer games is a mindless activity. Drawing upon her training in both psychology and sociology, she shows that the computer has become both a social magnet and a medium through which ordinary people establish and explore their identity. Although her analyses are speculative, they raise many productive questions and hint at the fruitfulness of studying computers in popular culture from a psychological perspective.

Several books have examined the role of computers in subcultures, particularly the hacker subculture, which has received extensive popular attention. In *Hackers: Heroes of the Computer Revolution,* Steven Levy describes hacker communities as grounded in the values of freedom of information and technical aesthetics. Levy dispels the common stereotypes of hackers as either villains or heroes, showing that there are many different varieties of hackers and that most hackers are more concerned with technical virtuosity than with power or material gain. Levy, however, gives too little attention to the psychological hazards of hacking. The hazards and also the psychology of hackers are depicted by Neil Frude in *The Intimate Machine: Close Encounters with the New Computers.* Frude proposes that hackers develop through three stages, the last of which is characterized by extreme social withdrawal and isolation from everyone but other hackers.

Turkle's *The Second Self: Computers and the Human Spirit* also explores hacker subculture, concentrating on the artificial intelligence community at MIT. Although she points out the contributions of these cultures in developing new views of mind, she also describes individuals who prefer computers over sex and who reject the world of heterosexual relationships as too irrational and uncontrollable. Turkle also shows how new ideas from technical subcultures diffuse into mass society, a topic that merits attention in studies of popular culture.

Of the many books written for general audiences that examine how computers are changing society, the most comprehensive is Tom Forester's *High-Tech Society: The Story of the Information Technology Revolution,* which surveys a wide array of topics, particularly in the areas of business, work, and communication. Whereas many studies merely mention the global nature of the computer revolution and then move on, this volume examines computers and society within an intercultural perspective, discussing a wealth of material on computers in British and European societies. Forester also gives an admirably balanced presentation of a literature adrift in conflicting ideological biases and unsupported claims.

Balance, however, is not the norm in the literature on technology and society, which has long been polarized into the camps of technological optimism and technological pessimism. Optimists such as Lynn White, author of *Medieval Technology and Social Change,* and Melvin Kranzberg, editor of the periodical *Technology and Culture,* have tended to argue that technology itself is neither good nor evil and that people have the power to choose to use computers in beneficial or harmful ways. In contrast, technological pessimists such as Jacques Ellul (*The Technological Society*), Lewis Mumford (*The Myth of the Machine: The Pentagon of Power,*) and Langdon Winner (*Autonomous Technology: Technics-out-of-Control as a Theme in Political Thought*) have argued passionately that the machine is out of control, that technology is destiny, and that people in fact have little control over the evolution of technology and society.

These currents of optimism and pessimism also run through the literature on computers and culture. In *Beyond the Gutenberg Galaxy: Microcomputers and the Emergence of Post-Typographic Culture,* Eugene Provenzo identifies numerous social problems associated with the widespread use of computers but then suggests that we have the ability to manage these problems by making appropriate choices. Optimism is also found in government reports and formal policy analyses. In *The Computerization of Society,* a report commissioned by the French government, Simon Nora and Alan Minc argue that the uncontrolled penetration of computer giants such as IBM into France could weaken the French economy, lead to a loss of control over information, and erode French culture. They then make suggestions about how societies may formulate policies that enable them to constrain and direct the use of computers. Of course, it remains to be seen whether the computer revolution is as controllable as Nora and Minc suggest.

Primary among the educational optimists is Seymour Papert, author of *Mindstorms: Children, Computers, and Powerful Ideas,* who contends that the computer has the potential to revolutionize education by allowing children to learn through discovery, particularly in areas such as mathematics. Papert argues that teachers will remain important, but that children learn best when they use their own curiosity to explore microworlds with intellectual tools of their making. That Papert's view is too highly optimistic is made clear in Douglas Sloan's *The Computer in Education: A Critical Perspective,* which restores balance by showing that Papert barely mentions the attendant problems of radically transforming the curriculum, of centering learning around computers rather than people, and of accepting the tacit ideology behind the mainstream uses of computers.

The voice of pessimism sounds loudly in Theodore Roszak's *The Cult of Information: The Folklore of Computers and the True Art of Thinking.* Roszak contends that computers are having adverse effects on American culture, undermining education and ushering in an era of dependency and of misguided worship of data processing over creative, artistic thought. Despite his excessive pessimism, he provides excellent analyses of the media hype and language changes that have shaped popular thinking about computers. More strident critiques of the computer revolution include Michael Shallis's *The Silicon Idol: The Micro Revolution and Its Social Implications,* Ian Reinecke's *Electronic Illusions: A Skeptic's View of Our High-Tech Future,* and Tony Solomonides and Les Levidow's *Compulsive Technology: Computers as Culture,* which argue that computers are tools of ideological subjugation used by the many for the benefit of the few. These books resort too often to simplistic computer bashing, overlooking the real choices that exist about how to use computers within the social order. Nevertheless, they serve as an antidote to the naive utopianism and elitism that runs through many popular computing magazines and books on computer applications.

Pessimism and alarmism also abound in studies that focus more narrowly on a particular issue, such as labor-management relations. In *Techno Stress: The Human Cost of the Computer Revolution,* Craig Brod argues that computers are increasing stress in the workplace by increasing health risks, decreasing human interaction, and allowing management to monitor productivity closely. Managerial abuse of computers is also the theme in Mike Cooley's *Architect or Bee? The Human/Technology Relationship* and in Harley Shaiken's *Work Transformed: Automation and Labor in the Computer Age.* Both argue that the widespread use of computers in manufacturing has increased unemployment, deskilled jobs, reduced workers' pride in craftsmanship, and strengthened their feelings of alienation. Management, on the other hand, has used computers not only to increase productivity but also to tighten control over workers and to undermine the power of labor unions. Although these works lack balance and rely on oversimplified stereotypes of labor and management, they increase social awareness of specific misuses of computers, helping to prepare an informed citizenry that can make wiser decisions about how to use computers. They also point out the need for careful analyses of how to construct human-machine systems that increase both worker satisfaction and productivity. Research in this area, called human factors, is in its infancy and is reviewed capably by Raymond Nickerson in *Using Computers: Human Factors in Information Systems* and by Ben Schneiderman in *Software Psychology: Human Factors in Computer and Information Systems*.

Because computers are powerful tools for acquiring and processing information and because, as Bacon stated, knowledge is power, many popular social commentaries have examined the challenge to privacy associated with the widespread and poorly regulated use of computers. A. F. Westin's *Privacy and Freedom* identified privacy as a prerequisite for personal freedom and for the maintenance of democratic society, and it also pointed out the need for balance between the needs of the state for information and the needs of the citizen for privacy. The erosion of this balance is the subject of Milton Wessel's *Freedom's Edge: The Computer Threat to Society* and David Burnham's *The Rise of the Computer State: The Threat to Our Freedoms, Our Ethics and Our Democratic Process,* both of which present an alarmist picture of how government agencies and corporations are misusing millions of computer records on everything from personal medical records to information on financial transactions. Both of these works, however, rely excessively on case histories rather than on thorough statistical analysis. In contrast, Kenneth Laudon's *Dossier Society: Value Choices in the Design of National Information Systems* presents voluminous data in support of the thesis that the privacy of citizens is being abused and that computers are tipping the balance of power away from the individual toward large corporations and government agencies. Appropriately, Laudon shows that computers themselves do not challenge privacy. Rather, it is people and institutions that challenge privacy by using computers in inappropriate ways.

All of these books on privacy serve to clarify the values that ought to inform public debate about a national information policy. Nevertheless, they all suffer by assuming too readily that there is a right to privacy that has been philosophically justified and legally established. As pointed out in Ferdinand Schoeman's *Philosophical Dimensions of Privacy: An Anthology,* some philosophers have argued that privacy is not a separate right and that it may be subsumed under the rights to property and freedom. Furthermore, the legal status of the right to privacy has not been resolved, as Warren Freedman has documented carefully in *The Right of Privacy in the Computer Age.*

Of all the areas in which computers have aroused popular hope and fear, artificial intelligence has been the most prominent, the most controversial, and the least understood. Early promises, most of which never materialized, increased the public belief that thinking computers were just around the corner, if not already in existence. By 1971, a time at which it had become apparent to most researchers that powerful thinking machines were not imminent, nearly 40 percent of the public believed that the computer was either an electronic brain or a thinking machine.[14] Popular visions of intelligent computers are now apparent in popular business literature on expert systems, in public debate about a space-based missile defense system driven by computers, and in cartoon series such as "Transformers." These visions have been encouraged by a host of recent books such as McCorduck's *Machines Who Think,* Feigenbaum and McCorduck's *The Fifth Generation: Artificial Intelligence and Japan's Computer Challenge to the World,* R. Jastrow's *The Enchanted Loom—Mind in the Universe,* Marvin Minsky's *The Society of Mind,* and Lawrence Stevens's *Artificial Intelligence: The Search for the Perfect Machine.* All of these works, which reflect missionary zeal rather than the sober, cautious attitude of science, appeal too frequently to faith rather than to reasoned argument and careful analysis.

Critics of artificial intelligence have pointed out that a substantial gap exists between promise and reality in the field of artificial intelligence. An unusually balanced view of the current state of artificial intelligence is provided by Margaret Boden's *Artificial Intelligence and Natural Man,* which makes it very clear that superintelligent computers remain a distant hope. Joseph Weizenbaum, in *Computer Power and Human Reason: From Judgment to Calculation,* demythologizes artificial intelligence by explaining how computers work and by identifying a rather long list of inflated claims and unfilfilled promises in the field. In addition, he shows how readily people fall into the trap of attributing intelligence to demonstrably stupid systems such as his ELIZA program, which mimicked only superficially a form of psychotherapy but that many people nonetheless talked to as if it were human.

Critics have also been quick to point out the hazards of relying heavily on artificial intelligence systems to protect national security. In David Bellin and Gary Chapman's *Computers in Battle: Will They Work?,* members of Computer Professionals for Social Responsibility, many of whom have extensive experience in working on national security projects, point out that computerized weapons systems have a high failure rate and that problems such as hardware and software reliability are merely the tip of the iceberg. More severe problems stem from the difficulties of testing computerized military systems under combat conditions and of designing them in ways that minimize human error. The greatest problem, however, is that preprogrammed systems take into account only the situations that the designers of the systems have foreseen. As the authors note, war is inherently unpredictable, and a computer that is reliable in neutralizing one kind of attack may prove to be ineffective in handling unusual attacks. By making these and many other points, this book contributes important information to the public debate over issues of national defense. The main weakness of this book is that it gives too little attention to the possible advantages of using smart, low-impact weapons rather than devastating nuclear bombs to defend heavily populated areas such as Europe, an idea that Frank Barnaby develops well in *The Automated Battlefield*.

Proponents of artificial intelligence have often suggested that artificial intelligence systems are minds and that the human mind can be viewed as a program that processes information. Skeptics, however, have argued that this idea solves one part of the traditional mind-body problem at the expense of amplifying another part. As discussed in J. Haugeland's *Mind Design: Philosophy, Psychology, Artificial Intelligence* and *Artificial Intelligence: The Very Idea*, in Paul Churchland's *Matter and Consciousness*, and in Daniel Dennett's *Brainstorms: Philosophical Essays on Mind and Psychology*, the relationship between brains and programs is anything but clear. Furthermore, it is utterly mysterious as to how programs can exhibit consciousness in the sense that humans do.

Other critics have pointed out that human minds cannot be equated with computer programs and that we stand to lose our humanity by accepting the mind-program analogy prematurely. In the controversial *What Computers Can't Do*, Hubert Dreyfus states that computers are limited because they lack the phenomenological context that grounds and constrains human thought and consciousness. In *Mind over Machine: The Power of Human Intuition and Expertise in the Era of the Computer*, both Hubert and Stuart Dreyfus contend that many people exhibit unconscious, intuitive skill that cannot be described by the kinds of rules that guide computers. In *The Mind's New Science: A History of the Cognitive Revolution*, Howard Gardner points out that there is now substantial evidence that people can perform many tasks simultaneously, whereas current computers are serial processors that process only one item at a time. Similarly, Gardner's *Frames of Mind: The Theory of Multiple Intelligences* identifies several different kinds of human intelligence, some of which are not the strictly logical variety that is best suited to computers. Joseph Weizenbaum, in *Computer Power and Human Reason: From Judgment to Calculation*, cautions that uncritical acceptance of the view that the mind is like a computer deemphasizes our capacity to link thought with emotions such as love while overemphasizing the rational side of human nature. Although some of these criticisms may fall by the wayside as new generations of computers evolve, it seems wise not be too hasty in remaking ourselves in the image of the machine.

The entry of artificial intelligence systems into fields such as business, law, and medicine has also stimulated controversy over the ethics of decision making by computers. Weizenbaum is reluctant to turn over complex decisions to computers because they lack moral judgment and the full scope of human intelligence and because people need to make their own choices in order to maintain and develop their moral capacity. A wider range of both positive and negative opinions on this issue is presented in M. Yazdani and A. Narayanan's *Artificial Intelligence: Human Effects* and Karamjit Gill's

Artificial Intelligence for Society. But the most comprehensive and scholarly treatment of ethical and legal issues associated with computer use is Deborah Johnson and John Snapper's *Ethical Issues in the Use of Computers.*

ANTHOLOGIES AND REPRINTS

Although there is little material regarding computers in popular culture per se, numerous anthologies bring together prominent science fiction stories on computers and robots. The better anthologies of early stories include Groff Conklin's *Science Fiction Thinking Machines,* Roger Elwood's *Invasion of the Robots,* Harry Harrison's *War with the Robots,* Anthony Lewis's *Of Men and Machines,* Sam Mescowitz's *The Coming of the Robots,* Eric Frank Russell's *Men, Mountains and Machines,* and Robert Silverberg's *Men and Machines.* An unusual and particularly engaging anthology is Leslie Katz's *Fairy Tales for Computers,* which, by including selections from Thoreau, Butler, Einstein, and the Bible, creates a broad historical and philosophical context for the study of computers in science fiction. Anthologies of more recent material include Michael Ashley's *Souls in Metal,* Isaac Asimov's *Thinking Machines,* Abbe Moshowitz's *Inside Information: Computers in Fiction,* and Dennie Van Tassel's *Computers, Computers, Computers: In Fiction and in Verse.* An anthology on cyborgs, which are part human and part machine, is T. N. Scortia and G. Zebrowski's *Human Machines: An Anthology of Stories About Cyborgs.*

Numerous anthologies assemble popular social commentaries regarding the computer revolution. An early anthology was Z. Pylyshyn's *Perspectives on the Computer Revolution,* which was published in 1970. Although this volume is now of interest primarily for historical reasons, it may be useful to researchers who wish to link popular social forecasts to their social contexts and to determine how well or how poorly the early forecasts have fared. A more contemporary volume is M. L. Dertouzos and J. Moses's *The Computer Age: A Twenty-Year View,* which includes papers that examine the influence of computers in the home, in the workplace, and in government. This volume, however, is excessively optimistic, and it is also dated since it was published before 1980 and the personal computer boom. A volume that is better balanced but that is also somewhat dated is C. C. Gottlieb and A. Borodin's *Social Issues in Computing.*

The most comprehensive and current anthologies on the social implications of computers are Tom Forester's *The Microelectronics Revolution* and *The Information Technology Revolution.* These include popular articles on topics such as the microelectronics industry, telecommunications, the post-industrial society, the role of computers in business and manufacturing, and the implications of the new technology for labor and management. Both volumes are organized topically, and the papers within each section express conflicting points of view, providing a balanced perspective. Although some of the articles are either too general or too polemic to be of lasting value, they nevertheless illustrate the popular rhetoric and propaganda surrounding computers. Popular rhetoric about computers is also captured well in Douglas Flaherty's *Humanizing the Computer: A Cure for the Deadly Embrace,* which develops a highly optimistic perspective by incorporating material from a wide variety of popular magazines.

In thinking about computers and culture, it is important to reflect upon the situation of Third World countries that seek to import or develop computer technology as a means of increasing their wealth and standard of living. Guenter Friedrichs and Adam Schaff's *Microelectronics and Society: A Report to the Club of Rome* puts the computer revolution in global, if pessimistic, perspective and examines the impact of computers on wealth, employment, and power in developing nations. Similarly, Alan Burns's *New Information Technology* sketches the international changes produced by the widespread use of computers and examines issues of power and wealth. While both volumes suffer from a paucity of concrete evidence and from excessive reliance on case studies, they increase awareness of how the widespread use of computers can erode traditional Third World cultures and promote dependency upon technologically advanced societies. These volumes serve as a poignant reminder that the study of computers in popular culture must look beyond the Western horizon.

NOTES

1. Otto Friedrich, "Machine of the Year," *Time,* 121 (January 1983), 14–24.
2. Pamela McCorduck, *Machines Who Think* (San Francisco: Freeman, 1979), p. 6.
3. F. David Peat, *Artificial Intelligence: How Machines Think* (New York: Simon and Schuster, 1985), p. 238.
4. Patricia S. Warrick, *The Cybernetic Imagination in Science Fiction* (Cambridge, Mass.: MIT Press, 1980), p. 53.
5. Ibid., p. 65.
6. Robert A. Stern and Nancy Stern, *An Introduction to Computers and Information Processing* (New York: Wiley, 1985), p. 83.
7. Ibid., p. 86.
8. Tom Forester, *High-Tech Society* (Cambridge, Mass.: MIT Press, 1987), p. 17.
9. Herbert Simon and Alan Newell, "Heuristic Problem Solving: The Next Advance in Operations Research," *Operations Research,* 6 (1958), 450.
10. Forester, *High-Tech Society,* p. 132.
11. Ibid., p. 127.
12. Patrick G. McKeown, *Living with Computers* (New York: Harcourt Brace Jovanovich, 1987), p. 380.
13. Michael G. Wessells, *Cognitive Psychology* (New York: Harper and Row, 1982), p. 30.
14. C. Schiller and B. Gilchrist, *A National Survey of the Public's Attitudes Toward Computers* (New York: AFIPS/Time, 1971).

BIBLIOGRAPHY

Books and Articles

Abshire, Gary M., ed. *The Impact of Computers on Society and Ethics: A Bibliography*. Morristown, N.J.: Creative Computing, 1980.

Albrecht, B. *What to Do After You Hit Return*. Menlo Park, Calif.: People's Press, 1975.

Albrecht, R. L. *BASIC: A Self Teaching Guide*. 2nd ed. New York: Wiley, 1978.

Arbib, Michael A. *Computers and the Cybernetic Society*. 2nd ed. New York: Academic Press, 1984.

Ashley, Michael, ed. *Souls in Metal*. New York: St. Martin's Press, 1977.

Asimov, Isaac. *I Robot*. New York: Gnome Press, 1950.

———. "Robbie." In *Science Fiction Thinking Machines*. Edited by Groff Conklin. New York: Vanguard, 1954.

———. *Thinking Machines*. Milwaukee: Raintree, 1981.

Austrian, Geoffrey. *Herman Hollerith*. New York: Columbia University Press, 1982.

Barnaby, Frank. *The Automated Battlefield*. New York: Free Press, 1986.

Barron, Neil, ed. *Anatomy of Wonder: A Critical Guide to Science Fiction*. 2nd ed. New York: R. R. Bowker, 1981.

"Behold the Computer Revolution." *National Geographic,* 138 (November 1970), 36–48.

Bell, Daniel. *The Coming of Post-Industrial Society*. New York: Basic Books, 1973.

Bellin, David, and Gary Chapman, eds. *Computers in Battle: Will They Work?* New York: Harcourt Brace Jovanovich, 1987.

Bellman, Richard. *An Introduction to Artificial Intelligence: Can Computers Think?* San Francisco: Boyd and Fraser, 1978.

Belzer, Jack, Albert G. Holzman, and Allen Kent, eds. *Encyclopedia of Computer Science and Technology*. 16 vols. New York: Marcel Dekker, 1975–81.

Benton, Mike. *The Complete Guide to Computer Camps and Workshops*. Indianapolis: Bobbs-Merrill, 1984.

The Blue Book for the Atari Computer. Chicago: WIDL Video Publications, 1983.

The Blue Book for the Commodore Computer. Chicago: WIDL Video Publications, 1983.

Boden, Margaret. *Artificial Intelligence and Natural Man*. New York: Basic Books, 1977.

Bolter, J. David. *Turing's Man: Western Culture in the Computer Age*. Chapel Hill: University of North Carolina Press, 1984.

Bork, Alfred. *Personal Computers for Education*. New York: Harper and Row, 1984.

Brand, Stewart, ed. *Whole Earth Software Catalog for 1986*. Garden City, N.Y.: Doubleday, 1985.

Brod, Craig. *Techno Stress: The Human Cost of the Computer Revolution*. Reading, Mass.: Addison-Wesley, 1984.

Brooks, Frederick P. *The Mythical Man-Month*. Reading, Mass.: Addison-Wesley, 1975.

Burnham, David. *The Rise of the Computer State: The Threat to Our Freedoms, Our Ethics and Our Democratic Process*. New York: Random House, 1980.

Burns, Alan. *New Information Technology*. New York: Wiley, 1984.

Capek, Karel. *R. U. R.* New York: Doubleday, 1923.

Carter, Ciel Michele. *Guide to Reference Sources in the Computer Sciences*. New York: Macmillan, 1974.

Churchland, Paul M. *Matter and Consciousness*. Cambridge, Mass.: MIT Press, 1984.

Clarke, Arthur C. *2001: A Space Odyssey*. New York: New American Library, 1968.

Cohen, John. *Human Robots in Myth and Science*. Cranbury, N.J.: A. S. Barnes, 1967.

Computer Books and Serials in Print. New York: R. R. Bowker, 1985.

Conklin, Groff, ed. *Science Fiction Thinking Machines*. New York: Vanguard, 1954.

Contento, William. *Index to Science Fiction Anthologies and Collections*. Boston: G. K. Hall, 1978.

———. *Index to Science Fiction Anthologies and Collections 1977–1983*. Boston: G. K. Hall, 1978.

Cooley, Mike. *Architect or Bee? The Human/Technology Relationship*. Boston: South End Press, 1980.

Cortada, James W. *An Annotated Bibliography of the History of Data Processing*. Westport, Conn.: Greenwood Press, 1983.

———. *Historical Dictionary of Data Processing*. Westport, Conn.: Greenwood Press, 1987.

Current Index of Computer Literature. Bala-Cynwyd, Pa.: Information Research Institute, 1985.

Darcy, Laura, and Louise Boston. *Webster's New World Dictionary of Computer Terms*. New York: Simon and Schuster, 1983.

Datapro Directory of Microcomputer Software. 3 vols. Delran, New Jersey: Datapro Research Corporation, 1987.

Davies, Owen, and Mike Edelhart. *Omni Online Database Directory 1985*. New York: Macmillan, 1984.

Day, Donald B. *Index to the Science Fiction Magazines, 1926–1950*. Portland, Ore.: Perri Press, 1952.

Deitel, Harvey M., and Barbara Deitel. *Computers and Data Processing*. New York: Academic Press, 1985.

Deken, J. *The Electronic Cottage*. New York: William Morrow, 1981.

Dennett, Daniel C. *Brainstorms: Philosophical Essays on Mind and Psychology*. Montgomery, Vt.: Bradford, 1981.

Dertouzos, M. L., and J. Moses, eds. *The Computer Age: A Twenty-Year View*. Cambridge, Mass.: MIT Press, 1980.

Desmonde, William H. *Computers and Their Uses*. Englewood Cliffs, N.J.: Prentice-Hall, 1964.

Didday, Richard L. *Computers—Caricatures and Cartoons*. Champaign, Ill.: Matrix, 1976.

Dizard, Wilson P., Jr. *The Coming Information Age: An Overview of Technology, Economics, and Politics*. New York: Longman, 1982.

Dreyfus, Hubert L. *What Computers Can't Do*. New York: Harper and Row, 1972.

Dreyfus, Hubert L., and Stuart E. Dreyfus. *Mind over Machine: The Power of Human Intuition and Expertise in the Era of the Computer*. New York: Free Press, 1986.

Edmunds, Robert A., ed. *The Prentice-Hall Encyclopedia of Information Technology*. Englewood Cliffs, N.J.: Prentice-Hall, 1987.

Ellul, Jacques. *The Technological Society*. Translated by John Wilkinson. New York: Alfred A. Knopf, 1964.

Elwood, Roger, ed. *Invasion of the Robots*. New York: Paperback Library, 1965.

Evans, Christopher. *The Micro Millennium*. New York: Viking Press, 1979.

Feigenbaum, Edward A., and Pamela A., McCorduck. *The Fifth Generation: Artificial Intelligence and Japan's Challenge to the World*. Reading, Mass.: Addison-Wesley, 1983.

Fishman, Katherine Davis. *The Computer Establishment*. New York: Harper and Row, 1981.

Flaherty, Douglas. *Humanizing the Computer: A Cure for the Deadly Embrace*. Belmont, Calif.: Wadsworth, 1986.

Forester, Tom. *High-Tech Society: The Story of the Information Technology Revolution*. Cambridge, Mass.: MIT Press, 1987.

———, ed. *The Information Technology Revolution*. Cambridge, Mass.: MIT Press, 1985.

———, ed. *The Microelectronics Revolution: The Complete Guide to the New Technology and Its Impact on Society*. Cambridge, Mass.: MIT Press, 1980.

Forsyth, Richard, ed. *Expert Systems: Principles and Case Studies*. New York: Chapman and Hall, 1984.

Frates, Jeffrey, and William Moldrup. *Computers and Life*. Englewood Cliffs, N.J.: Prentice-Hall, 1983.

Freedman, Alan. *The Computer Glossary*. New York: Computer Language Co., 1983.

Freedman, Warren. *The Right to Privacy in the Computer Age*. New York: Quorum Books, 1987.

Freiberger, Paul, and Michael Swaine. *Fire in the Valley: The Making of the Personal Computer*. Berkeley, Calif.: Osborne/McGraw-Hill, 1984.

Friedrichs, Guenter, and Adam Schaff, eds. *Microelectronics and Society: A Report to the Club of Rome*. New York: New American Library, 1982.

Froelich, Robert A. *The IBM PC (and Compatibles) Free Software Catalog and Directory*. New York: Dilithium, 1986.

Frude, Neil. *The Intimate Machine: Close Encounters with the New Computers*. London: Century, 1983.

Gardner, Howard. *Frames of Mind: The Theory of Multiple Intelligences*. New York: Basic Books, 1983.

———. *The Mind's New Science: A History of the Cognitive Revolution*. New York: Basic Books, 1985.

Gill, Karamjit S., ed. *Artificial Intelligence for Society*. New York: Wiley, 1986.

Glossbrenner, Alfred. *The Complete Handbook of Personal Computer Communications*. New York: St. Martin's Press, 1983.

Goldstein, Herman H. *The Computer from Pascal to von Neumann*. Princeton, N.J.: Princeton University Press, 1972.

Gordon, M., A. Singleton, and C. Rickards, *Dictionary of New Information Technology Acronyms*. 2nd ed. London: Kogan Page, 1986.

Gottlieb, C. C., and A. Borodin, eds. *Social Issues in Computing*. New York: Academic Press, 1974.

Graham, Neill. *The Mind Tool*. 3rd ed. St. Paul: West, 1983.

Harris, S. *What's So Funny About Computers?* Los Altos, Calif.: Kaufmann, 1982.

Harrison, Harry, ed. *War with the Robots*. New York: Pyramid Books, 1962.

Haugeland, J. *Artificial Intelligence: The Very Idea*. Cambridge, Mass.: MIT Press, 1985.

———, ed. *Mind Design: Philosophy, Psychology, Artificial Intelligence*. Cambridge, Mass.: MIT Press, 1981.

Hildebrandt, Darlene Myers, ed. *Computer Information Directory*. 4th ed. Federal Way, Wash.: Pedaro, 1987.

Hodges, Andrew. *Alan Turing: The Enigma*. London: Burnett Books, 1983.

Hofstadter, Douglas R. *Godel, Escher, Bach: An Eternal Golden Braid*. New York: Basic Books, 1978.

Hofstadter, Douglas R., and Dennett, Daniel C. *The Mind's I: Fantasies and Reflections on Self and Soul*. New York: Basic Books, 1981.

Holtzman, Charles P. *What to Do When You Get Your Hands on a Microcomputer*. Blue Ridge Summit, Pa.: TAB Books, 1982.

Hopper, Grace, and Steven L. Mandell. *Understanding Computers*. St. Paul: West, 1984.

Index to the Science Fiction Magazines, 1966–1970. Cambridge, Mass.: New England Science Fiction Association, 1971.

Isaacs, Alan, ed. *The Multilingual Computer Dictionary*. New York: Facts on File, 1981.

"Is the Computer Running Wild?" *U.S. News and World Report* (February 24, 1964), 18–20.

Jastrow, R. *The Enchanted Loom—Mind in the Universe*. New York: Simon and Schuster, 1982.

Johnson, Deborah G., and John W. Snapper, eds. *Ethical Issues in the Use of Computers*. Belmont, Calif.: Wadsworth, 1985.

Katz, Leslie, ed. *Fairy Tales for Computers*. Boston: Nonpareil Books, 1969.

Kidder, Tracy. *Soul of a New Machine*. Boston: Little, Brown, 1981.

Kosslyn, Stephen Michael. *Ghosts in the Mind's Machine: Creating and Using Images in the Brain*. New York: W. W. Norton, 1983.

LAMP: Literature Analysis of Microcomputer Publications. Mahwah, N.J.: Soft Images, 1986.

Laudon, Kenneth C. *Dossier Society: Value Choices in the Design of National Information Systems*. New York: Columbia University Press, 1986.

Lechner, H. D. *The Computer Chronicles*. Belmont, Calif.: Wadsworth, 1984.

Levy, Steven. *Hackers: Heroes of the Computer Revolution*. New York: Dell, 1984.

Lewis, Anthony O., Jr., ed. *Of Men and Machines*. London: E. P. Dutton, 1963.

Logsdon, Tom. *Computers Today and Tomorrow: The Microcomputer Explosion*. Rockville, Md.: Computer Science Press, 1985.

———. *How to Cope with Computers*. Rochelle Park, N.J.: Hayden, 1982.

Lovington, S. H. *Early British Computers: The Story of Vintage Computers and the People Who Built Them*. Bedford, Mass.: Digital, 1980.

McCorduck, Pamela. *Machines Who Think*. San Francisco: Freeman, 1979.

McGraw-Hill Encyclopedia of Science and Technology. 4th ed. 14 vols. New York: McGraw-Hill, 1977.

McKeown, Patrick G. *Living with Computers*. New York: Harcourt Brace Jovanovich, 1987.

Meadows, A. J., M. Gordon, A. Singleton, and M. Feeney. *Dictionary of Computing and Information Technology*. 3rd ed. New York: Nichols, 1987.

Mescowitz, Sam, ed. *The Coming of the Robots*. New York: Collier, 1963.

Metropolis, N., ed. *A History of Computing in the Twentieth Century*. New York: Academic Press, 1980.

Minsky, Marvin. *The Society of Mind*. New York: Simon and Schuster, 1985.

Moritz, Michael. *The Little Kingdom: The Private Story of Apple Computer*. New York: William Morrow, 1984.

Morrison, P., and E. Morrison, eds. *Charles Babbage and His Calculating Engines: Selected Writings by Charles Babbage and Others*. New York: Dover, 1961.

Moshowitz, Abbe, ed. *Inside Information: Computers in Fiction*. Reading, Mass. Addison-Wesley, 1977.

Mumford, Lewis. *The Myth of the Machine: The Pentagon of Power*. New York: Harcourt Brace Jovanovich, 1964.

Murphy, Brian. *Sorcerers and Soldiers: Computer Wargames, Fantasies and Adventures*. Norris Plains, N.J.: Creative Computing Press, 1984.

Myers, Darlene. *Computer Science Resources: A Guide to Professional Literature*. White Plains, N.Y.: Knowledge Industry Publications, 1981.

Naisbitt, John. *Megatrends: Ten New Directions Transforming Our Lives*. New York: Warner, 1982.

Newman, J. *The Computer: How It's Changing Our Lives*. Washington, D.C.: U.S. News and World Report, 1972.

Nicita, Michael, and Ronald Petrusha. *The Reader's Guide to Microcomputer Books*. New York: Golden-Lee, 1984.

Nickerson, Raymond S. *Using Computers: Human Factors in Information Systems*. Cambridge, Mass.: MIT Press, 1986.

Nora, Simon, and Alan Minc. *The Computerization of Society: A Report to the President of France*. Cambridge, Mass.: MIT Press, 1980.

Papert, Seymour. *Mindstorms: Children, Computers, and Powerful Ideas*. New York: Basic Books, 1980.

Parker, D. *Crime by Computer*. New York: Scribner's, 1976.

Peat, F. David. *Artificial Intelligence: How Machines Think*. New York: Simon and Schuster, 1985.

Phillips, Gary. *IBM PC Public Domain Software*. Culver City, Calif.: Ashton-Tate, 1984.

Prenis, John. *The Computer Dictionary*. Philadelphia: Running Press, 1983.

Provenzo, Eugene F., Jr. *Beyond the Gutenberg Galaxy: Microcomputers and the Emergence of Post-Typographic Culture*. New York: Teachers College Press, 1986.

Pylyshyn, Z., ed. *Perspectives on the Computer Revolution*. Englewood Cliffs, N.J.: Prentice-Hall, 1970.

Ralston, Anthony, ed. *Encyclopedia of Computer Science and Engineering*. 2nd ed. New York: Van Nostrand Reinhold, 1983.

Randall, Brian. "An Annotated Bibliography on the Origins of Computers." *Annals of the History of Computing*, 1 (October 1979), 1–73.

Raphael, Bertram. *The Thinking Computer: Mind Inside Matter*. San Francisco: Freeman, 1976.

Reinecke, Ian. *Electronic Illusions: A Skeptic's View of Our High-Tech Future*. New York: Penguin Books, 1984.

Roszak, Theodore. *The Cult of Information: The Folklore of Computers and the True Art of Thinking*. New York: Pantheon, 1986.

Russell, Eric Frank, ed. *Men, Mountains and Machines*. New York: Dobson, 1955.

Schneiderman, Ben. *Software Psychology: Human Factors in Computer and Information Systems*. Cambridge, Mass.: Winthrop, 1980.

Schoeman, Ferdinand D., ed. *Philosophical Dimensions of Privacy: An Anthology*. Cambridge, England: Cambridge University Press, 1984.

Scortia, T. N., and G. Zebrowski, eds. *Human Machines: An Anthology of Stories About Cyborgs*. New York: Vintage, 1975.

Shaiken, Harley. *Work Transformed: Automation and Labor in the Computer Age*. New York: Holt, Rinehart and Winston, 1984.

Shallis, Michael. *The Silicon Idol: The Micro Revolution and Its Social Implications*. New York: Schocken Books, 1984.

Silverberg, Robert, ed. *Men and Machines*. New York: Meredith Press, 1968.

Simon, Herbert A. *The New Science of Management Decision*. New York: Harper and Row, 1960.

———. *The Sciences of the Artificial*. 2nd ed. Cambridge, Mass.: MIT Press, 1969.

Sloan, Douglas, ed. *The Computer in Education: A Critical Perspective*. New York: Teachers College Press, 1984.

Slotnick, Daniel L., Evan M. Butterfield, Ernest S. Colantonio, Daniel J. Kopetzky, and Joan K. Slotnick. *Computers and Applications: An Introduction to Data Processing*. Lexington, Mass. D. C. Heath, 1986.

Smith, Curtis C., ed. *Twentieth Century Science-Fiction Writers*. 2nd ed. Chicago: St. James Press, 1986.

Sobel, Robert. *IBM: Colossus in Transition*. New York: Times Books, 1981.

The Software Catalog. 3 vols. New York: Elsevier, 1987.

The Software Encyclopedia. 2 vols. New York: R. R. Bowker, 1985.

Solomonides, Tony, and Les Levidow, eds. *Compulsive Technology: Computers as Culture*. London: Free Association Books, 1985.

Stern, Nancy. *From ENIAC to UNIVAC*. Bedford, Mass.: Digital Press, 1981.

Stern, Robert A., and Nancy Stern. *An Introduction to Computers and Information Processing*. 2nd ed. New York: Wiley, 1985.

Stevens, Lawrence. *Artificial Intelligence: The Search for the Perfect Machine*. Hasbrouck Heights, N.J.: Hayden, 1985.

Strauss, Erwin S., ed. *The MIT Science Fiction Society Index to the S-F Magazines, 1951–1965*. Cambridge, Mass.: MIT Press, 1966.

Toffler, Alvin. *The Third Wave*. New York: William Morrow, 1980.

Tuck, Donald H. *The Encyclopedia of Science Fiction and Fantasy*. 3 vols. Chicago: Advent, 1974–87.

Turkle, Sherry. *The Second Self: Computers and the Human Spirit*. New York: Simon and Schuster, 1984.

Tymn, Marshall B., and M. Ashley, eds. *Science Fiction, Fantasy, and Weird Fiction Magazines*. Westport, Conn.: Greenwood Press, 1985.

Van Tassel, Dennie L., ed. *Computers, Computers, Computers: In Fiction and in Verse*. New York: Thomas Nelson, 1977.

Van Young, Sayre. *Microsource: Where to Find Answers to Questions About Microcomputers*. Littleton, Colo.: Libraries Unlimited, 1986.

Warrick, Patricia S. *The Cybernetic Imagination in Science Fiction*. Cambridge, Mass.: MIT Press, 1980.

Weizenbaum, Joseph. *Computer Power and Human Reason: From Judgment to Calculation*. San Francisco: Freeman, 1976.

Wessel, Milton R. *Freedom's Edge: The Computer Threat to Society*. Reading, Mass.: Addison-Wesley, 1974.

Westin, A. F. *Privacy and Freedom*. New York: Atheneum, 1967.

Wexelblatt, Richard, ed. *History of Programming Languages*. New York: Academic Press, 1982.

White, Lynn. *Medieval Technology and Social Change*. New York: Oxford University Press, 1966.

Wiener, N. *The Human Use of Human Beings*. New York: Avon, 1950.

Winner, Langdon. *Autonomous Technology: Technics-out-of-Control as a Theme in Political Thought*. Cambridge, Mass.: MIT Press, 1977.

Yazdani, M., and A. Narayanan, eds. *Artificial Intelligence: Human Effects*. New York: Wiley, 1984.

PERIODICALS

Abacus. New York, 1983-.

ACM Guide to Computing Literature. New York, 1973-.

Acorn User. London, 1982-.

AI and Society. New York, 1987-.

Annals of the History of Computing. Arlington, Va., 1979-.

Apple User. Stockport, England, 1981-.

Australian Personal Computer. Sydney, Australia, 1980-

Bits and Bytes. Christchurch, New Zealand, 1982-.

Business Computer Digest and Software Review. Washington, D.C., 1983-.

Business Week. New York, 1929-.

Byte. Peterborough, N.H., 1975-.

Calico. Provo, Utah, 1983-.

CALL A.P.P.L.E. Renton, Wash., 1978-.

Commodore Computer Club. Vancouver, B.C., 1979-.

Communications of the ACM. New York, 1958-.

Compute! Greensboro, N.C., 1979-.

Computers and Video Games. London, 1981-.

Computer Bookbase. Cerritas, Calif., 1982-.

Computer Entertainer. North Hollywood, Calif., 1982-.

Computers and People. Newtonville, Mass., 1967-.

Computers and Society. New York, 1973-.

Computers and the Humanities. Sarasota, Fla., 1966-.

Computers in Human Behavior. New York, 1985-.

Computerworld. Framingham, Mass., 1967-.

Computing Reviews. New York, 1960-.

Creative Computing. Morristown, N.J., 1974–85.

Datamation. New York, 1957-.

Dr. Dobb's Journal of Computer Calisthenics and Orthodontia. Redwood City, Calif., 1976-.
Educational Technology. Englewood Cliffs, N.J., 1967-.
Family Computing. New York, 1983-.
Forbes. New York, 1917-.
Fortune. Chicago, 1930-.
Futurist. Bethesda, Md., 1967-.
Harvard Business Systems. Boston, 1922-.
High Technology. Boston, 1984-.
Home Computing Journal. Eugene, Ore., 1986-.
Impact of Science on Society. Paris, 1950-.
InCider. Peterborough, N.H., 1983-.
Infosystems. Wheaton, Ill., 1960-.
Infoworld. Framingham, Mass., 1979-.
Interface. Santa Cruz, Calif., 1971-.
International Computer Chess Association Newsletter. Naperville, Ill., 1978-.
LOGO Exchange. Westport, Conn., 1982-.
Lotus. Cambridge, Mass., 1985-.
Macworld. San Francisco, 1984-.
Management Review. Saranac Lake, N.Y., 1914-.
Microcomputer Index. Mountain View, Calif., 1981-.
Omni Magazine. New York, 1978-.
Online Today. Columbus, Ohio, 1981-.
PC Magazine. New York, 1982-.
PC Week. New York, 1983-.
PC World. San Francisco, 1983-.
Personal Computers Today. Bethesda, Md., 1982-.
Personal Computing. Rochelle Park, N.J., 1977-.
Popular Computing. New York, 1981–85.
Psychology Today. New York, 1967-.
Recreational Computing. Menlo Park, Calif., 1972–81.
Science. Washington, D.C., 1883-.
Science Digest. New York, 1937-.
Science News. Philadelphia, 1978-.
Scientific American. New York, 1845-.
Sloan Management Review. Cambridge, Mass., 1958-.
Softalk. North Hollywood, Calif., 1980–84.
Software Reviews on File. New York, 1985-.
Technology Review. Cambridge, Mass., 1899-.
T.H.E. Journal. Santa Anna, Calif., 1974-.
Whole Earth Review. Sausalito, Calif., 1984-.

Dance

LORETTA CARRILLO

Dance at its most popular level in America has served as a form of social, participational recreation. Country or folk dancing and city or social dancing together describe the major patterns. The history of recreational dance in this country, moreover, parallels the development of dance as a form of popular stage entertainment and testifies to the great influence each form has had upon the other. Nineteenth-century minstrels borrowed jigs and clog dances from white and black folk dancers who performed at city and plantation festivities, much as the spectacular Broadway musicals of the 1920s and 1930s borrowed from social dance of the time. What the history of dance in America clearly shows is that Americans have not only enjoyed watching dance, but they have also nurtured a rich and varied tradition of dance as a form of popular social recreation.

HISTORIC OUTLINE

In early America, as in all lands, dance initially played a purely ceremonial role as part of religious observances. Ritualistic Indian circle dances, replete with complex formations and incantations, constituted the only form of dance European settlers in the New World encountered. The Puritans were strongly discouraged from engaging in couple dancing. Increase Mather preferred "unmixed" dancing, and his condemnation of "promiscuous" couple dances dates from the 1680s in the pamphlet "An Arrow Against Profane and Promiscuous Dancing Drawn Out of the Quiver of Scriptures." Dance historian Nancy Chalfa Ruyter, however, has corrected the popular misconception that the Puritans disapproved of all dancing. She asserts, rather, that by and large, dancing was considered not only pleasant recreation, but was an important element of a cultivated life-style. Couple dancing along with Maypole and other festival dancing was certainly frowned upon, but formation dances were the popularly accepted form of Puritan dance activity. A later, more tolerant, religious sect living in Albany, New York, the Shakers or "Shaking Quakers"of Revolutionary days, actually incorporated step and round dances into their religious ceremonies. The Shakers believed that dancing was an angelic activity that helped rid them of sin and bring them closer to an ecstatic, ideal communion with God.

Other English, French,and Spanish colonists brought rich native traditions of folk dancing that included hornpipes and jigs in addition to stately court dances such as the minuet and gavotte. In England, John Playford's *The English Dancing Master or Plaine and Easie Rules for the Dancing of Country Dances, with the Tune to Each Dance,* published in the 1650s, became a standard country dancing manual for English and European dancing masters. The publication of *The English Dancing Master* began the standardization of country dances, which made their way into society circles and challenged for the first time, according to historian Richard Nevell, the popularity of fancy drawing room dances of the wealthy.

Despite the railings of Puritan ecclesiastics such as Mather, good numbers of New England Puritans and other colonists continued to dance. By 1716 Boston claimed two dancing masters, one of whom was forced to move to New York when the rivalry for authority and for students became too keen. John Griffith, the most famous of the colonial dancing masters, is said to have traveled along the eastern seaboard from Rhode Island as far south as Charleston, South Carolina, renting space, advertising in newspapers, and giving instructions in the popular dances of the day. By the mid 1700s, Virginians were dancing the court gavotte as well as the country reels outlined in Playford's manual. George Washington was reported to have especially enjoyed dancing the Sir Roger de Coverly, later known as the Virginia reel. In Philadelphia, the first "Assembly" or ball was held in 1748, establishing a tradition of a yearly social gathering with dancing as the main activity. By the days of the American Revolution, city people and country folk in all the colonies were performing traditional contra dances as well as new occasional ones with names such as Jefferson and Liberty and the Washington Quickstep. Moreover, the wealthy classes in all regions of the country continued the tradition of court dances.

In the late eighteenth century, French entertainers and dancing masters such as the Alexander Placide family, who came to America to escape the terrors of the French Revolution, greatly influenced the course of theater as well as social dancing in America. Having the greatest influence in high society circles of Newport, New Hampshire, New York, and Philadelphia, the French dancing masters brought sophisticated versions of country dances which they renamed *les contredanses*. So widespread was the French influence that the French quadrille, a slowed-down version of the minuet, became the forerunner of the American square dance. Also quite important was the effect French and all dancing masters in America had well into the late nineteenth century upon improvising and complicating the country dance steps, and upon standardizing their execution as well as developing dance rules of etiquette.

Anti-British sentiment in America in the late eighteenth and nineteenth centuries fostered general preference for the French quadrille over English contra dances, although rural areas of New England kept alive the English folk dancing tradition. In the southern Appalachian Mountains of Kentucky, West Virginia, North Carolina, and Tennessee, the Scottish and Irish settlers and their descendants continued to jig and clog, which eventually became the trademark of southern country dancing. Using native African rhythms and dances such as the "Giouba," which used figures of the court dances with hip movements of the Congo, the black slaves on southern plantations during this period incorporated the jig footwork rhythms into their own peculiar dance styles. This early black dance tradition was later perfected by the nineteenth-century jig and clog dancers or "buckdancers" such as William Henry Lane, known as Master Juba (derived from the "Giouba" dance), who gained wide popularity in America and Europe. Southern regional black dance in America, in addition, eventually blossomed in the early twentieth century into the tap and jazz forms perfected by black professional dancers. In another region of the country, western settlers and cowboy dancers of the period favored the cotillion with the "caller" who shouted out the dance formations. Western square dancers of the day danced the Wagon Wheel and the Texas Star.

In the city, social dancing became increasingly refined and adapted rules of etiquette under the guidance of the dancing masters. Hundreds of manuals such as *Dick's Quadrille Book* (1878) were published during the 1800s dictating correct placement and deportment. Couple dancing had been popularized in the first half of the nineteenth century by the waltz and the polka, European country dances which were both integrated into the quadrilles of the day. Initially considered scandalous because of the close contact of the couple, the waltz grew so popular that the dancing masters were forced to accept a refined version of it. However, the extent to which social dance in America was breaking away from the control of dancing masters was seen when in 1883, fearful that dance would become vulgar without proper instruction, they formed the American National Association of Masters of Dancing to preserve the genteel way of dancing.

In a further attempt to exert control over social dance of the day, Allen Dodworth, New York's leading dancing master, published a manual in 1885 designed to show the proper, refined way to execute ballroom dancing. The manual, *Dancing and Its Relation to Education and Social Life,* placed importance on dancing as a form of cultivated behavior and contained a system of teaching with diagrams and musical scores. Also contributing to the effort to keep social dancing refined were regular articles in popular periodicals such as *Godey's Lady's Book,* which contained rules on proper dance deportment.

By the early 1900s, the waltz, the polka, and the schottische were the favorite social dances. Mrs. Cornelius Vanderbilt II was staging balls as the most important social events of the season, and "correct" dancing was fully accepted as a cultivated activity for high society. Social dancing was also established as a fixed feature of American social life at all levels. Around the time, however, the rich musical and dance traditions of southern blacks, which had been nurtured in New Orleans, were being seen and heard more frequently and were to change permanently the face of social dance in America by introducing a new sense of rhythm. New Orleans saloon music known as "ragtime,"with its "ragged" or syncopated rhythm, gave rise to the turkey trot, grizzly bear, bunny hug, and the kangaroo dip. So popular did these dances become that they set off a dance craze that lasted well into the late 1920s. Far more daring than the tame waltz had been, these new dances allowed couples to hang on to each other and dance cheek to cheek.

Society matrons now thundered that deportment and etiquette had been completely lost in the new dances. Irene and Vernon Castle came to society's rescue, however, when between 1912 and 1919 they did much to popularize a refined way of performing the popular social dances of the period. The Castles performed the turkey trot, the tango, and the hesitation waltz with equal grace and elegance. Performing at afternoon *thés dansants* or "tea dances" held at ballrooms and cabarets, the Castles gave rise to a new emphasis on refined social dancing. The Castles even created new dances such as the Castle walk and gained wide popularity touring the United States and Europe giving demonstrations. Other dance demonstrators quickly followed the Castles' lead and performed in halls and ball-dining rooms in major cities all across America. Maurice and Walton, Joan Sawyer and Jack Jarret, and Arthur Murray and Irene Hammond were all dance demonstrators during the period 1910–20.

Given the immense popularity of social dancing during this period, popular music began to concentrate on music to dance by. Irving Berlin's "Alexander's Ragtime Band" was extremely popular, as was the "jazz" music of black musicians, which was now a more familiar sound to the white American public. The black bottom, the shimmy, and the varsity drag, dances adapted from the black tradition, were all summarily denounced as immoral. Paying no attention to pulpit preachers, however, the enthusiastic dancers of the 1920s continued to perform all of the new dances in public halls all over the country. The Charleston, appearing in the 1923 black performers' review *Running Wild,* along with Harry Fox's improvised routine in the Ziegfeld Follies, the foxtrot, quickly became the dances of the 1920s.

The public dance arena gained wide popularity during the 1920s when hundreds of dance halls sprang up in San Francisco's Barbary Coast, New Orleans's French Quarter, Chicago's South Side, and New York's Bowery and Tenderloin District. Several types of halls catering to different clienteles and social classes developed. Municipal districts and civic groups such as clubs and lodges sponsored dances at public halls. Another type of public dance arena, the "taxi-dance" ballrooms, were for men only and offered dance partners for the price of a ticket. More elaborate dance palaces, complete with chandeliers and gilt drapes, could be found in major cities. The Roseland and the Savoy in New York, the Trianon and Aragon in Chicago, the Hollywood Paladium in Los Angeles, and similar arenas in Detroit, Cleveland, Cincinnati, and Denver entertained millions of dancers throughout the 1920s and 1930s.

The decade of the 1930s is perhaps best known as the classic period of the Broadway musical and the Hollywood musical film, both of which featured dancing. Musicians such as George Gershwin, Irving Berlin, and Cole Porter were composing music for Broadway shows, and Fred Astaire and Ginger Rogers reigned as the dance couple of Hollywood dance film. James Cagney, Shirley Temple, Bill "Bojangles" Robinson, George Raft, and Buddy Ebsen all performed routines and also contributed toward making dance the center of stage and film entertainment during the decade. In the social dance arena, Arthur Murray's mail order dance instruction business was flourishing, and the lindy hop, created on the occasion of Charles Lindbergh's 1927 cross-Atlantic flight, became a very popular dance that incorporated the energetic movements of the Charleston and the black bottom. Young people were increasingly becoming the biggest followers of dance fads, particularly when the big dance bands and swing music along with jitterbugging became popular during the closing years of the decade.

Benny Goodman, Tommy Dorsey, Duke Ellington, Glenn Miller, and swing music became the rage in the 1940s. Jitterbugging quickly became the favorite dance of American servicemen and their dance partners in entertainment centers and canteens. The jitterbug was unquestionably perfected at Harlem's Savoy Ballroom, where dancers incorporated gymnastic feats such as airborne turns and tosses into the dance, and the best performers became dance demonstrators in their own right. The second feature of social dance during this period was the rage for Latin music and dances. Cesar Romero and Carmen Miranda performed the samba, rumba, conga, and mambo to music by Xavier Cugat, Tito Puente, and Perez Prado for an American dance public who diligently tried to learn the syncopated rhythm and hip movements. Generally, they settled for less complicated versions of Latin dances; however, the interest in the Latin rhythm never died. The resurgence of interest in social dance in the 1970s, in fact, was due to a great extent to the popularity of the hustle, a New York City Hispanic youth dance that required complex timing and an acute sense of rhythm.

With the decade of the 1950s came Elvis Presley and rock-and-roll music and dancing. In 1956 "American Bandstand," a television program developed in Philadelphia and hosted by Dick Clark, provided an arena for teenagers to dance to the new music. Adults still preferred the fox trot and the cha-cha and vocal hits by Frank Sinatra and Rosemary Clooney. The younger generation, on the other hand, danced the stroll and listened to music by Jerry Lee Lewis, Bill Haley and the Comets, the Everley Brothers, and the Platters.

Chubby Checker and the twist, a dance that both adults and teenagers found easy to perform, dominated the rock-and- roll dance scene in the early 1960s. The period also produced such fad dances as the mashed potatoes and the jerk, which, like the twist, separated the dancing couple and stressed the ingenuity of individual styles and movements. The French discotheque became popular in America during this time and developed as the night spot where one could dance amid strobe lights and glittering decor. Black music and dance of the period came to be called the "Motown Sound" (the record label under which much of the music was produced). Such stars as Diana Ross and the Supremes, the Temptations, and Smokey Robinson and the Miracles were Motown celebrities. Social dancing in the mid-and late 1960s waned, however, as the Beatles began to revolutionize rock music. The rock concert replaced dancing as the popular social entertainment pastime when young people preferred listening to popular singers Jimi Hendrix, Janis Joplin, and Jefferson Airplane sing at rock festivals such as Woodstock and the Monterey Pop Festival. By the late 1960s, the drug culture had inspired and produced "acid rock," the ultimate in undanceable music.

In the 1970s, a return to dancing brought back the discos and a new, updated version of "American Bandstand." The 1971 show "Soul Train" featured black dances such as the breakdown and the scooby doo, which incorporated variations of the "lock step" and showed once again black dance's emphasis on complicated rhythm and timing. The hustle, a dance originating in Hispanic *barrios* of New York City, was at the center of the dance craze of the 1970s and is credited with bringing back technique to social dancing. The New York City disco Studio 54 became the fashionable dancing spot for such celebrities as Liza Minelli and ballet superstar Mikhail Baryshnikov. In addition, the 1977 movie *Saturday Night Fever* gave the dance craze of the 1970s new life. Studios and instructors once again became popular, and television came up with programs such as "Dance Fever," where dancing couples from across the country competed for prize money. The period also witnessed a nostalgic yearning for the good old days of dancing, and afternoon tea dances, held at hotels and clubs, featured programs of music from the 1930s and 1940s while couples glided across dance floors.

In more recent times, the popularity of new wave and punk rock music of the late 1970s and early 1980s attests to a new breed of dancers. Sporting Mohawk hairdos dyed pink, purple, or blue, and wearing leather clothing, these dancers reject recent stylized movement. Their dancing is characterized by ritualistic-like jumping up and down while shivering and shaking the body. Breakdancing has been the most recent influence upon American social dance in the mid 1980s. Performed on the sidewalks and street corners of New York City and other large urban centers, breakdancing, with its emphasis on athletic improvisation in the breakdance idiom, has been perfected by black ghetto youth who have earned the status of exhibition performance dancers. The contemporary cult of punk rock and new wave music and the influence of breakdancing provide the latest evidence that popular music and dancing are so closely connected that one inevitably influences and shapes the other.

While social dance developed in the late nineteenth and early twentieth centuries as the most popular form of recreational dance in America, country dancing remained popular in isolated regions and changed much less drastically than did social dance, particularly in the twentieth century. City dancing, as has been shown, responded to the innovations in popular music. Country dance, on the other hand, retained the patterns and innovations developed prior to the Civil War. Although such movement innovations as the "swing" and "waltz" steps were integrated, for example, into the square dances of the 1880s and 1890s, country dancing in America remained essentially unchanged through the nineteenth century. Country dancing and folk culture, however, experienced a revival with the 1918 publication of Elizabeth Burchenal's *Twenty-eight Contra Dances, Largely from the New England States*. Country dances from Maine to Massachusetts were rediscovered, and a sense of their historical value and that of folk life-styles as well inspired the founding of centers committed to preserving and studying American folk cultures. In addition, western country dance was kept alive by Dorothy and Lloyd Shaw in Denver, Colorado. Lloyd Shaw's *Cowboy Dances,* first published in 1939, renewed interest in western square dance, as did his troupe of demonstration dancers who toured the United States and Europe.

The last category of dance developed in America as a form of popular culture is defined as "national" or "ethnic" folk dance. While the English, Irish, and Scottish country dance traditions have had the greatest influence on the development of American country dance, other ethnic groups have kept alive national dances that reflect the mother country's culture. Defined more as demonstration rather than participational dances, ethnic folk dances such as the Israeli *hora* dance, the Mexican *el jarabe* courtship dance, the Scottish Highland fling, and the Italian *tarantella* have symbolic value in and of themselves. Though they can be and very often are performed by untrained dancers, their fullest expression is usually given by trained dancers in demonstrations at celebrations, festivities or especially staged performances. An example can be seen in the Spanish *flamenco* dancers who have not only mastered the intricate footwork but who can also execute the stylized body movements that suggest the sensuality at the heart of *flamenco* dance. Moreover, national or ethnic folk dances usually express a facet of the culture's history or are meant to show themes—love, death, war—common to all ethnic folk dances. Lastly, American ethnic folk dances express this country's heterogeneous cultural makeup and the influence all folk cultures have had upon shaping a popular American dance tradition.

REFERENCE WORKS

Reference materials devoted solely to social, folk, and ethnic dance are almost non-existent. The researcher must make use of general dance reference materials, searching for sections within general reference works. The major reference work for all dance studies is the ten-volume *Dictionary Catalogue of the Dance Collection* housed at Lincoln Center, which catalogs all materials in the collection up to 1973. Entries on social, folk, and ethnic dance are included in the over 300,000 entries. The annual *Bibliographic Guide to Dance* continues where the *Dictionary Catalogue* leaves off and lists materials for the Lincoln Center collection since 1973.

Another, older, standard dance reference tool which lists works on American dance forms is Paul D. Magriel's *A Bibliography of Dancing: A List of Books and Articles on the Dance and Related Subjects,* with its supplement covering 1936–40. Mary H. Kaprelian's *Aesthetics for Dancers: A Selected Annotated Bibliography,* published by the American Alliance for Health, Physical Education and Recreation, lists books and journal articles arranged by topic. Useful general dance dictionaries include Barbara Naomi Cohen-Stratyner's *Biographical Dictionary of Dance,* which profiles dance figures spanning the last four centuries of dance history in Europe and America. Walter G. Raffe's *Dictionary of the Dance* is another general reference work, providing historical, critical, and technical information on dance through the ages. Among useful encyclopedias and handbooks are Anatole Chujoy's *The Dance Encyclopedia* and Agnes de Mille's *The Book of the Dance.* While mainly a ballet encyclopedia, Chujoy's book contains lengthy, authoritative articles on various forms of dance and is a standard reference work in the area. Much more pertinent to the American dance scene and, more precisely, to the development of social dance, de Mille's book offers a well-illustrated treatment of American dance history by a major American dance pioneer. The *Guide to Dance Periodicals, 1959–63* indexes articles devoted to dance alphabetically by author and subject. Other general indexes and abstracts which dance researchers find helpful tools include the *Arts and Humanities Citation*

Index, the *Humanities Index,* and the *Reader's Guide to Periodical Literature.* Two other quite useful indexes are the *Music Index* and the *Art Index.* Specific compilations of dance research, notably dissertations, published by the American Association for Health, Physical Education, Recreation and Dance include Esther Pease's *Compilation of Dance Research, 1901–1964; Research in Dance I,* a 1968 supplement to the previous volume; *Research in Dance II,* which covers research completed and in progress from 1967 through 1972; *Research in Dance III,* a listing of theses and dissertations for advanced degrees from 1971 to 1982; and *Completed Research in Health, Physical Education, Recreation and Dance,* an annual listing of research since 1959. Lastly, a major project under way is *The International Encyclopedia of Dance,* edited by Selma Jeanne Cohen, which intends to cover the entire field of dance and is forthcoming from Charles Scribner.

RESEARCH COLLECTIONS

The Dance Collection of the New York Public Library at Lincoln Center is the most comprehensive dance library in the United States and probably in the world. The collection covers all aspects of dance and features all manner of manuscripts, films, playbills, and special collections. The Harvard Theatre Collection has extensive rare materials on early American dance, as do the Hoblitzelle Theatre Arts and Perry Castaneda Libraries at the University of Texas at Austin. Major university libraries, including the University of California at Los Angeles, Yale, Cornell, the University of Chicago, the Indiana University School of Music, and the University of Michigan, all have quite respectable general collections of dance materials adequate for the researcher interested in topics in dance as a form of popular culture.

HISTORY AND CRITICISM

General Books and Articles

A good place to begin researching the history of popular dance in America is in general histories that attempt to place the development of America's popular dance forms in a broad context of dance as a performance art. A newcomer to the field would find Curt Sachs's classic 1937 *World History of Dance* a comprehensive and scholarly history of the dance through the ages. Evelyn Porter's *Music Through Dance* is still a valuable early general history; it devotes the last two chapters to the development of nineteenth and twentieth century social dances, and, in addition, includes a valuable treatment of the jazz age and the close relationship between the music and dance of the ragtime era.

An invaluable general introductory text is Paul D. Magriel's *Chronicles of the American Dance*. Although the collection's main focus is on dance as a performance art, it has three very important articles: "Juba and American Minstrelsy," "The Dodworth Family and Ballroom Dance in New York," and "Dance in Shaker Ritual." All are examples of early dance history scholarship and give the dance researcher an excellent introduction to dance in the development of American culture. Agnes de Mille's *The Dance in America* devotes sections to parallel developments in American music halls, the history of the social dance scene, and the far-ranging influence of Negro minstrel and folk dance groups. A companion volume is Walter Terry's classic text, *The Dance in America,* which attempts to trace performance as well as social dance in America. The text has very useful chapters on dance in colonial America, on black dance, and on ethnic dance. Doris Hering's *Twenty-Five Years of American Dance* is another invaluable classic introductory history with chapters on social dance, ballroom, and exhibition and ethnic dance. Arthur Todd's "Four Centuries of American Dance" is an excellent series of eight *Dancemagazine* articles which begins with the dance of the American Indian and traces developments through pioneer dances, Negro folk dance, and pertinent trends in theatre dance from 1734 to 1900. The scholarship presented in these articles is solid and insightful. A very useful introductory text which takes an anthropological approach to the development of dance in America is Jamake Highwater's *Dance: Rituals of Experience*. The work is useful for its discussion of American society's values as they have shaped the country's dance forms. One of the most pertinent studies in this field is Nancy Lee Chalfa Ruyter's excellent book *Reformers and Visionaries: The Americanization of the Art of Dance,* which traces America's turn–of-the-century acceptance of performance dance as a respectable, serious artistic pursuit. Several general studies of the early history of America's cultural life should be read as background material providing a context for specific treatments of dance history. Several extremely useful works are Russel B. Nye's *The Cultural Life of the New Nation, 1776–1830;* Percy A. Scholes's *The Puritans and Music in England and New England;* Louis B. Wright's *The Cultural Life of the American Colonies, 1607–1763;* and *The Arts in America: The Colonial Period* by Louis B. Wright et al.

Folk and Ethnic Dance

Among general sources in this area, Cecil J. Sharp's *The Dance: An Historical Survey of Dancing in Europe* is still must reading since the treatment is one of the earliest modern scholarly discussions of Western folk dance and its applications to American trends. Other valuable general texts are La Meri's early *Dance as an Art Form* and her recent work, *Total Education in Ethnic Dance*. Both accounts present definitions of ethnic dance by country, with some attention to American ethnic dances. A lesser-known but valuable general historical work is J. Tillman Hall's *Folk Dance,* which provides insights into folk dancing as an avenue for social integration and as an educational tool in learning about other American ethnic cultures. Betty Casey's recent *International Folk Dancing U.S.A.* is an extremely handsome book, complete with a brief history of American folk dancing, descriptions of dance leaders, selected camps and organizations, and dance groups and institutions for various ethnic folk dancers from around the world. A last general source, Richard Nevell's *A Time to Dance: American Country Dancing from Hornpipes to Hot Hash,* is perhaps the most valuable, with its extensive bibliography of contra, round, western square, and southern Appalachian square dancing forms.

A sampling of book-length sources that treat regional dance developments and that also provide historical material as well as instructions includes Betty Casey's *Dance Across Texas* and Lucile K. Czarnowski's *Dances of Early California Days.* Two other valuable books are Beth Tolman and Ralph Page's *The Country Dance Book* and Frank Smith's *The Appalachian Square Dance.* Several excellent shorter-length articles are Lee Ellen Friedland's "Traditional Folkdance in Kentucky," Jennifer P. Winstead's "Tripping the Light Fantastic Toe: Popular Dance of Early Portland, Oregon, 1800–1864," and Gretchen Schneider's "Pidgeon Wings and Polkas: The Dance of the California Miners." All are well-documented, scholarly treatments.

Square Dance

Two standard works in this area are Samual Foster Damon's *The History of Square Dancing,* which critics have labeled the definitive work, and Martin Rossoff's *Hoedown Heritage: The Evolution of Modern Square Dancing.* Ralph Page's "A History of Square Dancing in America" is an authoritative work by a prominent scholar in the area. Western square dance is treated in *Cowboy Dances* by Lloyd Shaw, the man responsible for reviving interest in western square dancing in the 1930s.

Social Dance

Social dancing, which developed in the urban centers and distinguished itself from country dance forms, is taken up in the classic work of 1888, *Dancing and Its Relation to Education and Social Life* by Allen Dodworth. Rosetta O'Neill's treatment of Dodworth's control over turn-of-the-century social dance in New York is especially valuable. Other classic defenses of dancing are Edward Lawson's *On Dancing and Its Refining Influence in Social Life* of 1884 and the Rev. J. B. Gross's *The Parson on Dancing* of 1879, which relies on a careful use of the Bible to defend the art of fair Terpsichore. These apologies for dance must be read in conjunction with the classic treatises against dancing written by Increase and Cotton Mather, which are very well edited and discussed by Joseph E. Marks III in *The*

Mathers on Dancing. Arthur Cole's 1942 account of social dance history in "The Puritan and Fair Terpsichore" is a most valuable piece, especially for its attention to the early development of dancing in education at Harvard and Yale.

The influence of Europe's dance tradition in this country transmitted via dancing masters is the topic of a most useful scholarly article by Ann Barzel, "European Dance Teachers in the United States." A group of well-researched seminal articles on social dance forms in the seventeenth and eighteenth centuries are Chrystelle T. Bond's "A Chronicle of Dance in Baltimore: 1780–1814"; Joy Van Cleef's "Rural Felicity: Social Dance in Eighteenth Century Connecticut"; and Shirley Wynne's "From Ballet to Ballroom: Dance in the Revolutionary Era." In addition, Paul Nettle's discussion of the waltz in "Birth of the Waltz" lets us see precisely how that dance paved the way for a new liberal attitude in social dance forms.

A short but excellent study of dance in education is Joseph E. Marks's *America Learns to Dance,* which emphasizes the important place dance increasingly held in the cultural and educational life of the new country. Arthur Franks takes a scholarly approach in *Social Dance: A Short History,* as does Belinda Quirey in *May I Have the Pleasure? The Story of Popular Dancing.* Popular but nonetheless very useful introductory histories are found in Peter Buckman's *Let's Dance: Social, Ballroom and Folk Dancing* and Don McDonagh's *Dance Fever.* A very recent book published by the Metropolitan Museum of Art is *Dance: A Very Social History* by Carol McD. Wallace and others, which nicely brings together discussions of the evolution of social dance, its corresponding costumes or clothing fashions, and the iconography of dance.

Albert McCarthy's *The Dance Band Era: The Dancing Decades from Ragtime to Swing, 1910–1950* traces popular dance forms through the concurrent developments in popular music. A very interesting sociological account of the popularity of the taxi dance hall and dancer is found in Paul Cressey's *The Taxi-Dance Hall.* A later excellent study of the same topic is Russel B. Nye's "Saturday Night at the Paradise Ballroom or Dance Halls in the Twenties." Nye also presents a brief but useful treatment of popular dance in the 1930s and 1940s in "The Big Band Era" in *The Unembarrassed Muse.* Frank Calabria very nicely researches the dance marathon phenomenon in "The Dance Marathon Craze," which adds to our knowledge of 1920s dance behavior. No bibliography of social dance would be complete without mentioning *Castles in the Air,* Irene Castle's story of her and her husband Vernon's role in popularizing social dance by making it acceptable in high society during the years 1900–1930.

Musical Theatre

Any story of American social dance history must take into consideration the early and consistently intimate connections between popular theatrical dance and the social dance taking place in dance schools and balls or "assemblies" across the country. An examination of general histories of American popular musical theatre yields valuable insights into the earliest of forms which were the foundation for later social dance developments. Julian Mates's excellent work on early stage entertainments in *The American Musical Stage Before 1800* and *America's Musical Stage: Two Hundred Years of Musical Theatre* describes the pantomime ballets and comic operas that set the stage for the later vaudeville and musical comedy developments that became the signature forms of the American musical stage. Of the valuable general histories of the entire American musical theater, several well serve the dance researcher in providing a basic framework into which dance history properly fits. Stanley Green's *The World of Musical Comedy*, David Ewen's *The Story of America's Musical Theatre*, Tom Vallance's *The American Musical Theatre*, and Richard Kislan's *The Musical: A Look at the American Musical Theatre* and *Hoofing on Broadway: A History of Show Dancing* together cover all phases and developments of American stage dance. Two very important and valuable collections of essays are *American Popular Entertainment*, edited by Myron Matlaw, and *Musical Theatre in America*, edited by Glenn Loney. Pertinent articles in the first volume deal with the popularity of pantomime, minstrel shows, burlesque, and blacks in vaudeville, in addition to treating the influence of Ruth St. Denis on the development of dance as a high art form in the early twentieth century. Two particularly useful articles from the second volume trace the tremendous influence of black dance on choreography in the American musical theater.

The one dance figure whose career greatly influenced developments in social dance is Fred Astaire. Three volumes provide ample information about Astaire's influence and career. Arlene Croce's *Fred Astaire and Ginger Rogers Book* traces Astaire's approach to dance on film and his creation of a classic American dance style on stage and in film. Croce's valuable insights also target Astaire's profound effect upon popular dance, as he inserted elements of class and elegance only the best could come near to imitating. Bob Thomas's *Astaire: The Man, the Dancer, the Life of Fred Astaire* is a chatty biography written by a friend of forty years and is most useful when read in conjunction with Astaire's own autobiography, *Steps in Time*.

Another major dance performer whose career has had a great impact upon American popular dance forms is Agnes de Mille. Besides her very useful dance histories mentioned earlier, her series of dance autobiographies gives a full account of her response to dance currents in her own time and ways in which she has emerged as a seminal figure in shaping modern American dance forms. The three pertinent de Mille autobiographies are *Dance to the Piper, And Promenade Home,* and *Speak to Me, Dance with Me*.

In the area of jazz dance, two books worth mention as general histories are *Anthology of American Jazz Dance*, edited by Gus Giordano, the dean of American jazz dance, and John Shepherd's *Tin Pan Alley*. The Giordano volume offers a fine collection of essays that trace the history of jazz dance as well as developments in performance dance seen in Jerome Robbins's jazz ballets and social dance developments in the popular swing dance period. A brief but useful text, *Tin Pan Alley* chronicles the close development between the period's popular music and dance, a phenomenon we take for granted today.

Black Dance

So powerful an influence has black dance been upon modern American social dance that historians regard it as the true, indigenous precursor of present-day social dance. Two absolutely essential texts covering the entire field are Marshall and Jean Stearns's *Jazz Dance: The Story of American Vernacular Dance* and Lynne Fauley Emery's *Black Dance in the United States from 1619 to 1970.* The Stearns volume draws on extensive field work to document the native African roots of America's vernacular dance forms. Each chapter deals thoroughly with developments, records contributions of particular artists, and puts all information into a larger historical, social context. The book has an extensive bibliography and is an overall scholarly treatment of the highest caliber. Likewise, *Black Dance in the United States* traces African dance roots and influences, and ties them to developments in music, poetry, and oral literature. Emery's scholarly approach is impressive yet highly readable and useful. A good companion article to Emery's studies is Helen Armstead-Johnson's "Blacks in Vaudeville: Broadway and Beyond" in *American Popular Entertainment,* along with the much earlier Marian Hannah Winter article "Juba and American Minstrelsy" in *Chronicles of the American Dance.* Hans Nathan's *Dan Emmett and the Rise of Early Negro Minstrelsy* is a solid treatment of the subject and should be read in conjunction with Edith J. Issacs' *The Negro in American Theatre* and Tom Fletcher's *One Hundred Years of the Negro in Show Business.* James Haskins's *The Cotton Club* chronicles the significant 1920s and 1930s era of Harlem's influence upon the development of black music and dance performance.

The life stories of important black performers should also be taken into account in the history of black dance in America. Several performers are seminal, influential figures. The legendary Josephine Baker tells her story in *Josephine,* while Katherine Dunham's *A Touch of Innocence* chronicles her own important life in the development of American black dance forms. Two other important works tracing Dunham's influence are *Kaiso! Katherine Dunham: An Anthology of Writings,* edited by VeVe A. Clarke and Margaret B. Wilkerson, and *Katherine Dunham: Reflections on the Social and Political Contexts of Afro-American Dance,* edited by Joyce Aschenbrenner. The last volume is an excellent monograph which traces Dunham's place at the forefront of the attempt to pioneer a respectful and rightful place for Afro-American dance in America. The last great performance artist whose career should be taken into account is Judith Jamison. Olga Maynard's biography, *Judith Jamison: Aspects of a Dancer,* details Jamison's rise in the Alvin Ailey company. Maynard nicely portrays Jamison's goals, trials, and accomplishments along with those of Ailey's troupe as they chart the hazards and fortunes of black dancers in the contemporary American dance scene.

Periodicals

Periodical literature devoted to popular dance can be found in major scholarly journals and in popular dance magazines. The oldest journals are *Dance Index* and *Dance Perspectives* (later superseded by *Dance Chronicle: Studies in Dance and the Related Arts*). The *Dance Research Journal,* published by the Congress on Research in Dance, is another excellent publication focusing on scholarly dance research in all areas. *Dance Observer* contains useful material and includes book reviews, while *Dance Scope* covers the field of dance education. The *Journal of Physical Education, Recreation and Dance* is an excellent publication that features research on social as well as folk and ethnic dance; it also includes book reviews. A more popular but extremely useful publication is *Dancemagazine,* which attempts to cover all dance forms in practice in the United States today, from classical ballet to street breakdancing. Several useful journals can be found on folk dancing. *English Dance and Song, The English Folk Dance Society Journal,* and *Folk Music Journal* are three successive titles of the major journal covering the folk dance field; they contain reviews, scholarly articles, and notes on research. *American Squares* and *Square Dance* are other magazines covering club and association news and square dance news.

BIBLIOGRAPHY

Books and Articles

Andrews, E. D. "The Dance in Shaker Ritual." In *Chronicles of the American Dance.* Edited by Paul D. Magriel. New York: Da Capo Press, 1978, p. 3–14.
Armstead-Johnson, Helen. "Blacks in Vaudeville: Broadway and Beyond." In *American Popular Entertainment.* Edited by Myron Matlaw. Westports Conn.: Greenwood Press, 1979, pp. 77–86.
Art Index. New York: H. W. Wilson, 1929–.
Arts and Humanities Citation Index. Philadelphia: Institute for Scientific Information, 1975–.
Aschenbrenner, Joyce, ed. *Katherine Dunham: Reflections on the Social and Political Contexts of Afro-American Dance. Dance Research Annual XII.* New York: Congress on Research in Dance, 1981.
Astaire, Fred. *Steps in Time.* New York: Da Capo Press, 1979.
Baker, Josephine. *Josephine.* New York: Harper and Row, 1977.

Barzel, Ann. "European Dance Teachers in the United States." *Dance Index,* 3 (1944); 56–100.

Bibliographic Guide to Dance. New York: G. K. Hall, 1976–.

Bond, Chrystelle T. "A Chronicle of Dance in Baltimore: 1780–1814." *Dance Perspectives,* 17 (Summer 1976), 4–49.

Burchenal, Elizabeth. *Twenty-eight Contra Dances, Largely from the New England States.* New York: G. Schirmer, 1918.

Buckman, Peter. *Let's Dance: Social, Ballroom and Folk Dancing.* New York: Penguin Books, 1979.

Calabria, Frank. "The Dance Marathon Craze."*Journal of Popular Culture,* 10 (1976), 54–69.

Casey, Betty. *Dance Across Texas.* Austin: University of Texas Press, 1985.

———. *International Folk Dancing U.S.A.* New York: Doubleday, 1981.

Castle, Irene. *Castles in the Air.* New York: Da Capo Press, 1958.

Chujoy, Anatole, ed. *The Dance Encyclopedia.* New York: Simon and Schuster, 1976.

Clarke, VeVe A., and Margaret B. Wilkerson. *Kaiso! Katherine Dunham: An Anthology of Writings.* Berkeley: Institute for Study of Social Change, Women's Center, University of California, 1978.

Cohen, Selma Jeanne, ed. *The International Encyclopedia of Dance.* New York: Scribner's, forthcoming.

Cohen-Stratyner, Barbara Naomi. *Biographical Dictionary of Dance.* New York: Schirmer Books, 1982.

Cole, Arthur. "The Puritan and Fair Terpsichore." *Mississippi Valley Historical Review* 29 (1942). New York: Dance Horizons, 1942.

Completed Research in Health, Physical Education, Recreation and Dance. Washington, D.C.: American Alliance for Health, Physical Education, Recreation and Dance 1981.

Cressey, Paul. *The Taxi-Dance Hall.* New York: Greenwood Press, 1968.

Croce, Arlene. *The Fred Astaire and Ginger Rogers Book.* New York: Vintage Books, 1972.

Czarnowski, Lucile K. *Dances of Early California Days.* Palo Alto, Calif.: Pacific Books, 1950.

Damon, Samuel Foster. *The History of Square Dancing.* Barre, Mass.: Barre Gazette, 1957.

de Mille, Agnes. *And Promenade Home.* Boston: Little, Brown, 1958.

———. *The Book of the Dance.* New York: Golden Press, 1963.

———. *The Dance in America.* Washington, D.C.: United States Information Service, 1971.

———. *Dance to the Piper.* Boston: Little, Brown, 1951.

———. *Speak to Me, Dance with Me.* Boston: Little, Brown, 1972.

Dick's Quadrille Book. New York: Dick and Fitzgerald, 1878.

Dictionary Catalogue of the Dance Collection. 10 vols. New York: New York Public Library and G. K. Hall, 1974.

Dodworth, Allen. *Dancing and Its Relation to Education and Social Life.* New York: N.p., 1885.

Dunham, Katherine. *A Touch of Innocence.* New York: Books for Libraries, 1980.

Emery, Lynne Fauley. *Black Dance in the United States from 1619 to 1970*. New York: Dance Horizons, 1980.

Ewen, David. *The Story of America's Musical Theatre*. Philadelphia: Chilton Book, 1968.

Fletcher, Tom. *One Hundred Years of the Negro in Show Business*. New York: Burdge, 1967.

Franks, Arthur. *Social Dance: A Short History*. London: Routledge and Kegan Paul, 1963.

Friedland, Lee Ellen. "Traditional Folkdance in Kentucky." *Country Dance and Song*, 10 (1979), 5–19.

Giordano, Gus, ed. *Anthology of Jazz Dance*. Evanston, Ill.: Orion Publishing, 1975.

Green, Stanley. *The World of Musical Comedy*. New York: Da Capo Press, 1980.

Gross, Rev. J. B. *The Parson on Dancing*. Philadelphia: J. B. Lippincott, 1879. New York: Dance Horizons, 1979.

Guide to Dance Periodicals. Vols. 1–10. New York: Belknap Press, 1931–62.

Hall, J. Tillman. *Folk Dance*. Pacific Palisades, Calif.: Goodyear Publishing, 1969.

Haskins, James. *The Cotton Club*. New York: Goodyear Publishing, 1969.

Hering, Doris, ed. *Twenty-five Years of American Dance*. New York: Rudolf Orthwine, 1951.

Highwater, Jamake. *Dance: Rituals of Experience*. New York: A and W, 1978.

Humanities Index. New York: H. W. Wilson, 1975-.

Isaacs, Edith J. *The Negro in American Theatre*. New York: Theatre Arts, 1947.

Kaprelian, Mary H. *Aesthetics for Dancers: A Selected Annotated Bibliography*. Washington, D.C.: American Alliance for Health, Physical Education and Recreation, 1976.

Kislan, Richard. *Hoofing on Broadway: A History of Show Dancing*. New York: Prentice-Hall, 1987.

———. *The Musical: A Look at the American Musical Theatre*. Englewood Cliffs, N.J.: Prentice-Hall, 1980.

La Meri. *Dance as an Art Form*. New York: Scribners, 1933.

———. *Total Education in Ethnic Dance*. New York: Marcel Dekker, 1977.

Lawson, Edward. *On Dancing and Its Refining Influence in Social Life*. London: N.p., 1884.

Loney, Glenn, ed. *Musical Theatre in America*. Westport, Conn.: Greenwood Press, 1984.

McCarthy, Albert. *The Dance Band Era: The Dancing Decades from Ragtime to Swing, 1910–1950*. Radnor, Pa.: Chilton Book, 1971.

McDonagh, Don. *Dance Fever*. New York: Random House, 1979.

Magriel, Paul D. *A Bibliography of Dancing: A List of Books and Articles on the Dance and Related Subjects*. New York: H. W. Wilson, 1936.

———. *A Bibliography of Dancing: A List of Books and Articles on the Dance and Related Subjects, 4th Cumulated Supplement*. New York: H. W. Wilson, 1936–40.

———. *Chronicles of the American Dance from the Shakers to Martha Graham*. New York: Da Capo Press, 1978.

Marks, Joseph, III, ed. *America Learns to Dance: A Historical Study of Dance Education in America Before 1900*. New York: Dance Horizons, 1957.

———, ed. *The Mathers on Dancing*. New York: Dance Horizons, 1975.

Mates, Julian. *The American Musical Stage Before 1800*. New Brunswick, N.J.: Rutgers University Press, 1962.

———. *America's Musical Stage: Two Hundred Years of Musical Theatre*. Westport, Conn.: Greenwood Press, 1985.

Matlaw, Myron, ed. *American Popular Entertainment*. Westport, Conn.: Greenwood Press, 1979.

Maynard, Olga. *Judith Jamison: Aspects of a Dancer*. New York: Doubleday, 1982.

Music Index. Detroit: Information Service, 1949–.

Nathan, Hans. *Dan Emmett and the Rise of Early Negro Minstrelsy*. Norman: University of Oklahoma Press, 1962.

Nettle, Paul. "Birth of the Waltz." *Dance Index*, 5 (1946), 208–28.

Nevell, Richard. *A Time to Dance: American Country Dancing from Hornpipes to Hot Hash*. New York: St. Martin's Press, 1977.

Nye, Russel B. "The Big Band Era." In *The Unembarrassed Muse: The Popular Arts in America*. New York: Dial Press, 1970, pp. 326–40.

———. *The Cultural Life of the New Nation, 1776–1830*. New York: Harper and Row, 1960.

———. "Saturday Night at the Paradise Ballroom or Dance Halls in the Twenties." *Journal of Popular Culture*, 7 (1974), 14–22.

———. *Society and Culture in America, 1830–1860*. New York: Harper and Row, 1974.

O'Neill, Rosetta. "The Dodworth Family and Ballroom Dance in New York." In *Chronicles of American Dance*. Edited by Paul Magriel. New York: Da Capo Press, 1948, pp. 81–100.

Page, Ralph. "A History of Square Dancing in America." In *Focus on Dance: Dance Heritage*. Washington, D.C.: American Association for Health, Physical Education and Recreation, 1977.

Pease, Esther, ed. *Compilation of Dance Research, 1901–1964*. Washington, D.C.: American Association for Health, Physical Education and Recreation, Dance Division, 1964.

Playford, John. *The English Dancing Master or, Plaine and Easie Rules for the Dancing of Country Dances, with the Tune to Each Dance*. Edited by Hugh Mellor and Leslie Bridgewater. London: Dance Books, 1984.

Porter, Evelyn. *Music Through Dance*. London: B. T. Batsford, 1937.

Quirey, Belinda. *May I Have the Pleasure? The Story of Popular Dancing*. London: British Broadcasting Co., 1976.

Raffe, Walter G. *Dictionary of the Dance*. New York: A. S. Barnes, 1964.

Readers' Guide to Periodical Literature. New York: H. W. Wilson, 1890–.

Research in Dance I: A Supplement to Compilation of Dance Research 1901–1966. Washington, D.C.: American Association for Health, Physical Education and Recreation, Dance Division, 1968.

Research in Dance II: Research Completed and in Progress from 1967–1972. Washington, D.C.: American Association for Health, Physical Education and Recreation, Dance Division, 1973.

Research in Dance III. Washington, D.C.: American Association for Health, Physical Education and Recreation, Dance Division, 1982.

Rossoff, Martin. *Hoedown Heritage: The Evolution of Modern Square Dancing*. Sandusky, Ohio: American Squaredance Magazine, 1977.

Ruyter, Nancy Lee Chalfa. *Reformers and Visionaries: The Americanization of the Art of Dance.* New York: Dance Horizons, 1979.

Sachs, Curt. *World History of Dance.* New York: W. W. Norton, 1937.

Schneider, Gretchen. "Pidgeon Wings and Polkas: The Dance of the California Miners." *Dance Perspectives,* No.39 (1969), 1–57.

Scholes, Percy. *The Puritans and Music in England and New England.* London: Oxford University Press, 1934.

Sharp, Cecil J. *The Dance: An Historical Survey of Dancing in Europe.* London: Haltox and Truscott Smith, 1924.

Shaw, Lloyd. *Cowboy Dances.* Caldwell, Ohio: Caxton Printers, 1952.

Shepherd, John. *Tin Pan Alley.* London: Routledge and Kegan Paul, 1982.

Smith, Frank. *The Appalachian Square Dance.* Berea, Ky.: Berea College, 1955.

Stearns, Marshall, and Jean Stearns. *Jazz Dance: The Story of American Vernacular Dance.* New York: Schirmer Books, 1968.

Terry, Walter. *The Dance in America.* New York: Harper and Row, 1971.

Thomas, Bob. *Astaire: The Man, the Dancer, the Life of Fred Astaire.* New York: St. Martin's Press, 1984.

Todd, Arthur. "The Dance of the American Indian." *Dancemagazine,* 23 (September 1949), 18–19.

———. "Folk Dance of Our Pioneers." *Dancemagazine,* 23 (November 1949), 20–21, 34–35.

———. "Negro American Theatre Dance, 1840–1900." *Dancemagazine,* 24 (November 1950), 20–21, 33–34.

———. "The Negro Folk Dance in America." *Dancemagazine,* 24 (January 1950), 14–15.

———. "The Rise of Musical Comedy Dance." *Dancemagazine,* 24 (December 1950), 23–25, 38–39.

———. "Theatre Dance in America, 1784–1812." *Dancemagazine,* 24 (April 1950), 24–25, 40.

———. "Theatre Dance in America, 1820–35." *Dancemagazine,* 24 (May 1950), 22–24.

———. "Theatrical Dancing in America Before the Revolution, 1734–1775." *Dancemagazine,* 24 (March 1950), 20–21, 35.

Tolman, Beth, and Ralph Page. *The Country Dance Book.* Guilford, Vt.: Countryman Press, 1937.

Vallance, Tom. *The American Musical Theatre.* New York: Castle Books, 1970.

Van Cleef, Joy. "Rural Felicity: Social Dance in Eighteenth Century Connecticut." *Dance Perspectives,* No. 65 (1976), 1–44.

Wallace, Carol McD., et al. *Dance: A Very Social History.* New York: Metropolitan Museum of Art, 1986.

Winstead, Jennifer P. "Tripping the Light Fantastic Toe: Popular Dance of Early Portland, Oregon, 1800–1864." In *American Popular Entertainment.* Edited by Myron Matlaw. Westport, Conn.: Greenwood Press, 1979, pp. 229–240.

Winter, Marian Hannah. "Juba and American Minstrelsy." In *Chronicles of the American Dance.* Edited by Paul Magriel. New York: Da Capo Press, pp. 39–63.

Wright, Louis B. *The Cultural Life of the American Colonies, 1607–1763.* New York: Harper and Row, 1957.

Wright, Louis B., et al. *The Arts in America: The Colonial Period.* New York: Scribner's, 1966.

Wynne, Shirley. "Form Ballet to Ballroom: Dance in the Revolutionary Era." *Dance Scope,* 10 (1975–76), 65–73.

Periodicals

American Squares. New York, 1945–65.

Dance Chronicle: Studies in Dance and the Related Arts. New York, 1977-.

Dance Index. New York, 1942–48.

Dancemagazine. New York, 1927-.

Dance Observer. New York: 1936–64.

Dance Perspectives. New York, 1959–77.

Dance Research Journal. New York, 1974-.

Dance Scope. New York, 1965–81.

English Dance and Song. London, 1899–1931.

The English Folk Dance Society Journal. London, 1927–31.

Folk Music Journal. London, 1931-.

Journal of Physical Education, Recreation and Dance. Washington, D.C., 1975-.

Square Dance. Glenview, Ill., 1966-.

Death

ROBERT A. ARMOUR
and J. CAROL WILLIAMS

HISTORIC OUTLINE

Throughout American history, popular customs have reflected general American attitudes toward death. From the seventeenth-century folk art of tombstone carving, to the more elaborate nineteenth-century monuments, to this century's reproductions of Michelangelo's masterpieces in famous Forest Lawn Cemetery, the art that has adorned our cemeteries has made visible the values we have placed on death. Likewise, the rituals associated with death also represent popular values: hiring an *aanspreecker* in colonial Dutch American communities to visit the homes of friends of the deceased to announce the death; the quick burial in mass graves of the soldiers killed on Civil War battlefields; or the sight of an entire nation in mourning as it watches the riderless horse lead the body of a slain president to its resting place. The purpose of this introduction is to give an overview of popular attitudes toward death in America. Because of the many ethnic and religious variations that have existed side by side in this land, it is impossible to make generalizations about the attitudes toward death, which have varied with culture and time, but we can pinpoint some writers and events that were typical of their day.

One of the first books published in the Old World about America was an illustrated version of Thomas Hariot's *A Briefe and True Report of the New Found Land of Virginia* (1588). This book, written by a fine scientist sent over by Sir Walter Raleigh to record the history of the new colony at Roanoke Island, was one of the earliest accounts of the customs of the people native to this land. Among the illustrations by John White is a drawing of an Indian burying ground, which consisted of a platform on high wooden columns inside a thatched hut of considerable size. The skin of a dead chief was stripped from the body, tanned, and then replaced over the skeleton so that the figure of the chief was preserved. Then, according to the caption that accompanies the drawing, the body was placed on the platform, where one of the priests in charge of the dead murmured prayers day and night. This, the earliest example of published writing about death in North America, demonstrates that the Indians had concerns for their dead that are similiar to those still held by a large segment of the population: interest in the preservation of the body, reverence for the dead, and acceptance of the role of the clergy.

As the Europeans began to populate the eastern seaboard, they brought with them, along with their political, economic, and artistic attitudes, ideas about death. Those ideas found quick expression. During the first winter in the new land, 52 of the original 102 settlers at the Plymouth colony died before spring. And in Virginia, of the roughly 1,650 people who had come to the colony by 1625, approximately 1,000 had died; over 300 had been killed in the Indian massacre of 1622. The deaths in Virginia were accepted as expected events; John Smith, in his *History of Virginia* (1624), simply refers to the deaths and rails at the leaders whose stupidity caused them. God is given credit for the good things that happened at Jamestown, but He is not blamed for the suffering. This attitude established a pattern that was carried on in the southern colonies throughout the colonial period. The writings of William Byrd II discuss sicknesses and deaths, but there is only brief mention of the dying process and no doubt of the afterlife. Even deists such as Thomas Jefferson believed without much question in a future state of rewards and punishment, and the words of Philip Vickers Fithian, the tutor for the family of Robert Carter of Virginia just before the Revolution, typify the concern for the afterlife during the Enlightenment. When he thought he might be dying during a serious illness, he resigned "myself body and soul and Employment to god who has the hearts of all in his hand, and who I am persuaded, if he has anything for me to do in Life, will preserve, and in a measure fit it me for it, if not, I am in his hand, let him do as seems good in his eyes."

However, the attitude in the colonies controlled by the Puritans was by no means so accepting or passive. These people began early in the education of their children to establish a healthy respect for death. Two of the most popular books of Puritan New England were intended to instill in children their parents' fears. James Janeway, in *A Token for Children* (1676), taught them about the ever nearness of death, and *The New England Primer* used thoughts about death to illustrate some of the letters of the alphabet: "T-*Time* cuts down all/Both Great and Small" and "X-Xerxes the great did die/So must you and I," among others.

Life was viewed by the Puritan as a pilgrimage, a difficult trip whose ultimate goal is heaven. American Puritans were greatly influenced by John Bunyan's *Pilgrim's Progress* (1678), and their expectations for life and death followed closely Christian's pilgrimage through the temptations of life. The goal is the Celestial City, which can be reached only through death. This attitude led to a duality in the Puritan's ideas about death. One side of the Puritan said that death would bring relief from the travails of life and would bring the traveler into the presence of God. This side welcomed death, perhaps even longed for it. The other side of the Puritan realized that the dying person may not be among those chosen to be saved by God and therefore may well be damned to an eternity without the presence of God. In this manner the Puritan at once both glorified death and feared its consequences.

The words of the Puritan preacher Jonathan Edwards expressed this duality. In his *Personal Narrative* (ca. 1740) he wrote: "The heaven I desired was a heaven of holiness; to be with God, and to spend my eternity in divine love. . . . Heaven appeared exceedingly delightful, as a world of love; and that all happiness consisted in living in pure, humble, heavenly, divine love." Yet in his famous sermon, "Sinners in the Hands of an Angry God" (1741), he describes hell in such terms as to make death a frightening prospect: ". . . it is a great furnace of wrath, a wide and bottomless pit, full of the fire of wrath, that you are held over by in the hand of that God, whose wrath is provoked and incensed as much against you, as against many of the damned in hell. . . ."

The popular image of parsimonious and socially dull Puritans is put to the lie by a description of their funerals. Historical records demonstrate that substantial parts of estates were spent for the funeral of the deceased. In addition to the expected expenses for a coffin, winding sheet, and grave, large amounts of money were spent on gloves and rings for the invited guests at the funeral and for extensive amounts of spices, cider, and rum. The costs of the alcoholic beverages became one of the largest single expenses in a Puritan funeral. The practice, of course, was not restricted to the Puritan colonies, and people in other colonies also began to complain about the high cost of dying, especially the costs of providing gifts and drinks for the guests.

The importation of the romantic movement from Europe as the eighteenth century turned into the nineteenth led to a different attitude toward death in America. The romantics were fascinated with death, and thoughts of death dominated the "graveyard" writers who were central to the movement. Many writers in the early romantic period, such as Philip Freneau and William Cullen Bryant, meditated on the meaning of death; but perhaps the American writer best known for his compulsion about death was Edgar Allan Poe. Many of his poems and stories about death demonstrate a duality of horror and longing, but none illustrates the point better than some verses from "Annabel Lee" (1849), which describes the death of the narrator's girlfriend:

> And this was the reason that, long ago,
>   In this kingdom by the sea,
> A wind blew out of a cloud by night
>   Chilling my Annabel Lee;
> So that her highborn kinsmen came
>   And bore her away from me,
> To shut her up in a sepulchre
>   In this kingdom by the sea.
>
> The angels, not half so happy in Heaven,
>   Went envying her and me—
> Yes!—that was the reason (as all men know,
>   In this kingdom by the sea)
> That the wind came out of the cloud chilling
>   And killing my Annabel Lee.

Some of the nineteenth-century theologians continued the Puritan concepts even though the Puritan movement itself had died out. John Owen, writing in Philadelphia in 1827, made an impassioned plea for the Calvinistic view of the afterlife. In *The Death of Death in the Death of Christ,* which was endorsed by thirteen other ministers from the city, Owen reinforced and restated the basic tenets of Calvinism: "... let these doctrines, of God's eternal *election,* the free grace of *conversion, perseverance,* and their *necessary* consequences, be asserted." In other words, salvation depended on God's determination to save a particular soul. This was not an uncommon view of death at the time, but one that was to be given less credence as the nineteenth century passed.

A few years later, another book, *The Tree and its Fruits or, The Last Hours of Infidels & Christians Contrasted* (1839), coming out of the same city but written by the American Sunday-School Union, focused on the last hours of the dying. The effort was to show that the good died easily and the evil died with difficulty. "It is a fact," the Union writes, "which appears worthy of being more prominently held up to the view of all whose minds are in any degree interested in the great concerns of eternity, that nearly all those who have been conspicuous in the ranks of infidelity, have left this world in a tempest of horror and dismay, as though the anathema maranatha, pronounced against all who love not the Lord Jesus, had withered them before their time; whilst it is notoriously true, that those who meet death with the greatest composure, and who triumpht over all his terrors, are the men whose lives have adorned the gospel of God their Saviour."

A more moderate and eloquent view of death was presented in the dedication speech for Hollywood Cemetery in Richmond, Virginia, in June

1849. Oliver Baldwin's view of death was no less traditional than those of Owen or the Union, but his ideas were more tempered with charity: "The Grave, the Grave, how simply but powerfully it speaks through the eye of the soul, and bids it meditate upon itself and its destiny. An ancient writer has said that man was taken from the dust of the earth to prompt him to humility. But a still stronger incentive to humility is the fact which he daily witnesses that to dust he must return." Dust, according to Baldwin, is the fate of all, not just those who are elected by God for salvation or those who have lived without sin and can expect an easy death. Baldwin went on to discuss at some length the value of a fine cemetery, both to those who expect to reside there shortly and to those who visit old friends and relatives there.

In 1859 Charles Darwin published *The Origin of Species,* which eventually changed the attitudes of many Americans toward death. Darwin, of course, challenged the historical accuracy of the Bible, but, in one way, his method was more of a challenge than his content. He had used science to arrive at conclusions that affected religion, and humankind was forced to decide between science and religion or to find a way to reconcile the two. Among the first to try the latter was William Rounseville Alger in *A Critical History of the Doctrine of Future Life* (1867). Alger was by no means a scientist, but he did view humankind as living in a scientific cycle in which all plants and animals have a place and a role: "The individual man dies . . . for the good of the species, and that he may furnish the conditions for the development of a higher life elsewhere. It is quite obvious that, if individuals did not die, new individuals could not live, because there would not be room. It is also equally evident that, if individuals did not die, they could never have any other life than the present." Alger claimed that this consideration made death a "necessity and benignity," rather than a horror; and he maintained that "the noble purpose of self-sacrifice enables us to smile upon the grave."

By the end of the century, writers were more consciously trying to reconcile Darwin with their own views of death. John Fiske, in *The Destiny of Man* (1892), attempted to show that his own Christian faith was not at odds with the theory of evolution. In his last chapter, he considered the afterlife, which is after all, he suggested, a religious matter not to be considered scientifically but accepted as a point of faith. Fiske put limits on the use of science and maintained that one must go beyond science to discover the truth about death. William James engaged himself in the same debate but used science to arrive at his conclusions in *Human Immortality* (1898). James wanted to show that the scientific assumption that life ends when the brain is dead is too limited. He argued that the brain has several functions: " . . . our soul's life, as we here know it, would none the less in literal strictness be the function of the brain. The brain would be the individual variable, the mind would vary dependently on it. But such dependence on the brain for this natural life would in no wise make immortal life impossible,—it might be quite compatible with supernatural life behind the veil hereafter."

While the intellectuals were trying to decide how to deal with the scientific problems raised during the century, others were finding different expressions of their ideas about death. Well-known writers, such as Henry Wadsworth Longfellow and Oliver Wendell Holmes, wrote poems that sought the solace of death; and writers less well known at the time, such as Walt Whitman and Emily Dickinson, adopted death as a major theme. Among the popular writers, however, death remained uncomplicated by theories of evolution and scientific methods. The elegiac and funeral verses of some sentimental poets received wide circulation and represented an altogether different attitude toward death than did the theories of ministers and psychologists or the poetry of Whitman and Dickinson. Julia A. Moore, the "Sweet Singer of Michigan," was renowned for her crude poetry inspired by the deaths of children:

LITTLE ANDREW

Andrew was a little infant,
And his life was two years old;
He was his parent's eldest boy,
And he was drowned, I was told.
His parents never more can see him
In this world of grief and pain,
And Oh! they will not forget him
While on earth they do remain.

One bright and pleasant morning
His uncle thought it would be nice
To take his dear little nephew
Down to play upon the raft,
Where he was to work upon it,
And this little child would company be—
The raft the water rushed around it,
Yet he the danger did not see.

This little child knew no danger—
Its little soul was free from sin—
He was looking in the water,
When, alas, the child fell in.
Beneath the raft the water took him,
For the current was so strong,
And before they could rescue him
He was drowned and was gone.

Oh! how sad were his kind parents
When they saw their drowned child,
As they brought him from the water,

It almost made their hearts grow wild.
Oh! how mournful was the parting
From that little infant son.
Friends, I pray you, all take warning,
Be careful of your little ones.

In the first decades of the twentieth century, the attitudes toward death did not change radically from those at the end of the previous one. Samuel McChord Crothers ended his *The Endless Life* (1905) with the allegory of Mr. Honest, who dies peacefully: "Our doubts and fears vanish when we see Mr. Honest standing by the river's bank talking with happy earnestness with his friend Good-conscience. . . . Those who share that faith recognize, in all humility, their own limitations." And G. Lowes Dickinson in *Is Immortality Desirable?* decides, to no one's surprise, that it is: "To sum up, then, the immortality which I hold to be desirable, and which I suggest to you as desirable, is one in which a continuity of experience analogous to that which we are aware of here is carried on into a life after death, the essence of that life being continuous unfolding no doubt through stress and conflict, of those potentialities of Good of which we are aware here as the most significant part of ourselves."

Such attitudes remained typical through the middle part of the twentieth century; and indeed, it is possible to find some writers even in the seventh decade who claim to hold such traditional views. However, the growing importance of science, including the science of trying to understand the mind, and the diminishing importance of religion have changed attitudes. But some of the most significant changes in the attitudes toward death have resulted from other societal changes. The concept of the family has changed from one in which there were several generations of one family living under the same roof to one in which there are normally only two generations within a household—and then only until the children are old enough to move out on their own. This change, coupled with the growth of homes for the elderly and with increased mobility, means that children are less likely to see their grandparents die.

Another factor influencing that phenomenon is the growth of modern hospital facilities and the tendency for the aging to spend their last weeks in a hospital, both benefiting and suffering from life-prolonging treatment. The result is that very few people die at home now, as people did a century ago. If a person does not die accidentally on a highway, the likelihood is that he or she will die in the unfamiliar surroundings of a hospital room. The entire family probably will not be present, and surely the youngest children will be absent. One result of these changes is that children are likely to reach adulthood before they are in the presence of a dying person; the act of death becomes a mystery only to be described by older persons, or perhaps never even discussed at all.

Another change in our society that has influenced our attitudes concerns the growing dependence on the funeral home for its services. Early in this century, the undertaker would come to the home of the deceased and embalm the body there. It would be laid out in the parlor until it was time for the services, and the body would then probably have been taken to a church for the religious service and from there to the grave site for burial. Many changes began to alter this procedure. First, the process of embalming was moved to the facilities of the undertaker, where the family was not bothered with the unpleasantness of it and where the risks of spreading contagious diseases were diminished. Then, many people found that rising building costs were forcing them to forego the luxury of a parlor, which formerly had been little used except for Sunday afternoon visits from the preacher and for funerals. Some houses were built without parlors, and, in others, the television set was moved in and the room became the family room or den, hardly places suitable for the display of a body. To complicate matters more, the size of the front door was reduced for architectural reasons, and the caskets would no longer fit through. The result was that the undertaker began to provide space in his building for the display of the body and for visitation by family and friends. The presence of death was taken from the home and moved to this other place, significantly called a "funeral home," and the room set aside for visitation was called the "parlor." The person who operated such an establishment no longer simply performed the basic services of an undertaker, but became a professional overseeing the entire process of the funeral. He, and even today he is almost always a man, gave himself a new title—"funeral director." He added a chapel to the building so that the body did not have to be taken to a church for services, and ultimately he relieved the family of much of the organizational responsibility for arranging for the disposition of a relative's body.

These changes mean that the presence of death is physically removed from the household and that some of the trauma of dealing with a death is passed from the hands of the family to those of a professional who is paid for his services. Those in the colonial period who complained about the high costs of funerals would be astounded by the bills presented today by hospitals, rest homes, and funeral directors for services rendered during a person's last days and the funeral that follows. But these professionals provide services that have become accepted by the large part of Americans at mid-twentieth century.

For many Americans, death has become an unfamiliar event, made mysterious and frightening by the fact that so few people experience its presence during their formative years. But there have been intellectual challenges to this system that have been influential. In 1963 Jessica Mitford wrote *The American Way of Death*, which was an exposé of the funeral industry. This book, and others like it, became the impetus for a more careful look at the funeral practices that had become so widely accepted. It challenged the necessity for embalming, expensive caskets, and elaborate cemetery plots; and some people began asking if the high expenses of a funeral were justified. The most pointed attack, however, was directed at the funeral directors themselves, who were accused of creating a myth about the value of their services. Mitford's book was sensational, and she used isolated cases, in some instances, to support her points; but the overall message of the book was accurate and led many people to question the methods of the American way of death.

Then, in 1969, Elizabeth Kubler-Ross wrote *On Death and Dying,* which became a major challenge to the way we have been treating our dying patients. Kubler-Ross, herself a medical doctor, demonstrated that often the dying patient is given good medical treatment but poor death counseling by medical professionals whose primary goal is the saving of life. Few physicians are trained to deal with the traumas of death and are not capable of assisting their patients with the problems of dying. Kubler-Ross has interviewed hundreds of dying patients and listened to their tales, and this book is in part a record of what they have told her and in part a plea for a better understanding and for more sensible treatment of the dying patient. It, like Mitford's book, has forced the American public to reconsider its attitude toward death.

These influences have led to mixed attitudes toward death in contemporary America. While the majority of Americans still insist on what they think of as a traditional view of death and funerals, there are signs that Mitford, Kubler-Ross, and others have had their impact. That attitudes have been changed somewhat is reflected in the general acceptance of college courses and church seminars on death, newspaper and magazine articles on the costs of funerals, memorial societies that discuss alternative means of disposing of the body, and television shows that even bring the presence of death into situation comedies. Suggestions for reform, however, meet with widespread resistance, and demonstrate that attitudes toward death are deep seated in our society.

In the 1980s death and dying have remained strong in American popular consciousness as a result of the AIDS epidemic, drought conditions in Africa, and conflict in Lebanon, Ireland, Afghanistan, and Central America. The popular media have done much to heighten public awareness of these events and to make death headline news.

REFERENCE WORKS

Death may be a personal concern, a philosophical issue, the subject of religious dogma, the source of emotional difficulties, a disruptive force in society, and the source of the demand for one's services. To claim that every academic discipline is interested in death from some perspective and that most everyday activities are touched by some aspect of death is not an exaggeration. Although the omnipresence of death and the varied interest in the topic have resulted in diverse materials on death, they have also complicated the task of the researcher. The researcher must locate within larger disciplines and areas of interest those works that apply rather specialized approaches to death.

Both general and specialized bibliographies on death and dying are now available to assist in researching the topic of death, but these rapidly become outdated as new books and articles appear. Robert Fulton, director of the Center for Death Education and Research at the University of Minnesota, has updated an earlier bibliography, *Death, Grief and Bereavement: A Bibliography 1845–1975,* which contains nearly 4,000 entries that approach death primarily from an empirical perspective. Books dealing with suicide, literary works, and theological studies are excluded. The emphasis is on issues of contemporary concern such as terminal care, the definition of death, euthanasia, and sudden infant death syndrome. The bibliography is indexed by subject, and numbered entries are listed alphabetically by author.

A Bibliography of Books on Death, Bereavement, Loss, and Grief: 1935–1968 by Austin H. Kutscher, Jr., and Austin H. Kutscher, together with *Supplement 1, 1968–1972* by Austin H. Kutscher, Jr., and Martin Kutscher, is an uncritical bibliography, indexed by author, of approximately 2,400 books published in the United States. These titles are grouped in forty categories, ranging from ancestor worship to undertaking and widows' allowances. In another general bibliography, *Death: A Bibliographic Guide,* Albert Jay Miller and Michael Acri classify nearly 4,000 entries under seven headings, such as religion, theology, science, and nursing experiences. Citations are to professional journals, to books, and to articles in popular magazines. These entries are described briefly or not at all, but a very useful section on audiovisual media contains nearly 200 references to films, filmstrips, microfilms, recordings and tapes, slides, transparencies, photographs and prints, and kits. Martin L. Kutscher has two recent helpful works, *A Comprehensive Bibliography of Thanatology Literature* and *A Cross-Index of Indices of Books on Thanatology.* A brief description of over 200 of the leading fall and winter books on death from more than one hundred publishers can be found in *Publishers Weekly,* September 25, 1978.

Several specialized bibliographies are available. The National Institute of Mental Health published *Bibliography on Suicide and Suicide Prevention,* edited by Norman L. Farberow, which covered literature from 1897 to 1970. A partial survey of literature on suicide since 1975 can be found in *Bioethical Perspectives on Death and Dying: Summaries of the Literature,* edited by Madeline M. Nevins. *Research on Suicide: A Bibliography,* by John L. McIntosh, is a useful and well-organized reference source. It is more recent than the other bibliographies cited here.

A good specialized bibliography focusing on difficulties encountered by survivors of the deceased is *Adjustments to Widowhood and Some Related Prob-*

lems: A Selective and Annotated Bibliography by Cecile Strugnell. Approximately 450 entries are grouped in three major sections, the largest of which, "bereavement," is subdivided into bereavement of children, bereavement of the elderly widowed, and cross-cultural studies of bereavement. The entries are not indexed by either author or subject; however, the citations under each subheading are listed alphabetically by author, and each entry is carefully described.

Funeral Service: A Bibliography of Literature on Its Past, Present and Future, the Various Means of Disposition and Memorialization, edited by Barbara K. Harrah and David F. Harrah, contains approximately 2,000 entries on aspects of the funeral industry. The entries are briefly described and are indexed by subject and author. The section of references to audiovisual materials and the section listing cemetery associations, memorial societies, and other funeral related organizations are most useful.

There is one reference book that provides general information on death studies. *Death Education: An Annotated Resource Guide,* by Hannelore Wass and a number of other scholars, is a valuable tool. It contains discussions of books on death and dying, articles, bibliographies, audiovisual materials, organizations that offer help to those in need, and community resources.

RESEARCH COLLECTIONS

The scarcity of special collections on death and the highly specialized nature of those that do exist is in part a function of the nature of the topic of death. Although the Columbia University Library is recognized as the repository for materials of the Foundation of Thanatology, the library reports that its works on death are dispersed through the main collection and catalogued under broader headings in its different libraries.

Existing special collections are specialized and limited in scope. The American Antiquarian Society in Worcester, Massachusetts, for instance, houses pamphlet and book collections containing the texts of approximately 1,200 funeral sermons delivered between 1656 and 1830. Also housed there are three collections of photographs of New England gravestones. These collections, one by Harriette Marifield Forbes and the others by Daniel Farber, present photographs of entire stones, as well as details of sculptured aspects of stones, and are usually indexed by stone cutter and graveyard.

Several organizations interested in life after death have collections of literature on death, but these are usually limited to works dealing with communication with the dead and the survival of death. The Eileen J. Garrette Library of Parapsychology Foundation in New York City contains a reference collection of about 10,000 volumes, which includes such topics as survival of death, reincarnation, communication with the dead, and descriptions of deathbed out-of-body experiences. These materials are available for use only in the library. The Parapsychology Library at the Physical

Research Foundation in Durham, North Carolina, houses 600 books, 300 bound periodical volumes, 200 journals, and an annotated bibliography of "out-of-body experiences" sheets on file there. The materials are also available to the public for reference use only.

The Association for Research and Enlightenment, Virginia Beach, Virginia, has a collection of more than 25,000 books that focus on psychic phenomena and spiritual growth. Among these are 250 titles on future life, 350 titles on reincarnation, and 250 titles on death and dying. Members of the association may borrow by mail, but nonmembers are permitted to use these resources at the center. The Theosophical Society in America, with its headquarters at Wheaton, Illinois, houses a 15,000-volume collection of works in occultism, mysticism, and theosophy. Books may be borrowed personally or by mail, and to assist study in certain areas, the society compiles a representative reading list on some subjects. The reading list on life after death, for example, contains over seventy entries briefly described, many of which are by Theosophical students.

Works on funeral customs and the funeral industry are collected at the San Francisco College of Mortuary Science and at the Beryl L. Boyen Library of the National Foundation of Funeral Service in Evanston, Illinois. Over 500 books and bound periodical volumes on embalming, restorative art, funeral directing and management, and a special collection of color films on the burial customs of foreign countries are housed at the library of the San Francisco College of Mortuary Science. The holdings at the Boyen Library are considerably larger. Two hundred fifty thousand books, 300 bound periodical volumes, and 300 prints and pamphlets on bereavement, funeral and burial customs, and the funeral service are available for reference use only.

Other libraries that house specialized collections on death include the National Cancer Foundation Library of Cancer Cure, Inc., in New York City, which contains 400 books, ninety bound periodical volumes, a number of archives items, articles, and documents on thanatology, gerontology, and counseling of advanced cancer patients. These materials are not available to the general public. The Gerontology Learning Resources Center of the Institute of Gerontology in Detroit, which is open to the public for reference use, has over 650 books and 140 periodical volumes, approximately 750 government documents, and clippings, pamphlets, bibliographies, and tapes on all aspects of gerontology, including death and aging.

Folk tales and superstitions transmitted orally from generation to generation that come close to the heart of the ordinary individual's concern with death are preserved at two universities. The Center of Intercultural and Folk Studies at Western Kentucky University at Bowling Green estimates that the Folklore and Folklife Archives there have at least 200 tapes and perhaps 2,000 manuscripts pertaining to death that have been gathered from various parts of Kentucky and adjoining states. Tapes and manuscripts of these collections are individually indexed, usually by area, informant, collector, and subject.

The William R. Perkins Library at Duke University contains the Frank Clyde Brown Papers. Between 1912 and 1948, Brown collected about 38,000 folktales and notes on folklore, 1,400 songs vocally recorded, and 650 musical scores from people in North Carolina and surrounding areas. Much of the folklore has been published in a seven-volume work entitled *The Frank C. Brown Collection of North Carolina Folklore,* edited by Newman Ivey White. Volume 6 contains material on death, superstitions, and the afterlife.

Journals

Although this is changing, journal materials available on death have reflected the same tendency toward specialization within existing fields that is found in special collections. Prior to 1970, a number of different magazines and professional journals had devoted single issues to the treatment of death, but no journals were available that dealt exclusively with the varied aspects of death and dying. The Fall 1968 issue of *Sociology Symposium* is primarily a collection of articles on various aspects of the funeral industry. The lead articles are followed by a bibliography of the sociology of death and six extensive book reviews. A publication of the American Psychotherapy Association, *Voices: The Art and Science of Psychotherapy* (Spring/Summer 1969), combines short articles with poems and cartoons to present a broad, readable, and personal perspective on the process of dying. Perhaps the most widely circulated of these magazines and journals that devoted a single issue for death and dying is *Psychology Today* (August 1969). That issue of *Psychology Today* (which describes itself as the magazine about psychology, society, and human behavior) contained six main articles on death in addition to the well-known *"Psychology Today* Questionnaire on You and Death" designed by Edwin Shneidman.

Other specialized journals have followed this pattern. *Prism,* a monthly magazine published by the American Medical Association for the discussion of nonclinical issues facing medicine, devoted its June 1975 issue to death. Most articles deal with the physician's confrontation with death in the medical profession, although several articles do discuss funeral practices and cemeteries. *Humanitas,* the journal of the Center for the Study of Human Development at the Institute of Man in Pittsburgh, covered death in its February 1975 issue. Articles are by authorities such as Elizabeth Kubler-Ross and sociologist Gordon M. Vernon, and the topics range from a discussion of the language of the dying patient to a discussion of death and the imagination. *Monist,* an international journal of general philosophical inquiry, explored philosophical problems of death in its April 1976 issue. Articles are written by professional philosophers on such topics as rationality and the fear of death and voluntary and nonvoluntary euthanasia. These articles are more limited in scope and are more academic than those previously mentioned.

As the first journal to deal exclusively with the many aspects of death, *Omega: Journal of Death and Dying,* emphasizes the impact of death on the human being and on the human community. Although it is largely a psychological journal, the articles are nontechnical and are generally of popular appeal. Several books in death and dying literature are reviewed in each issue. *Advances in Thanatology* began publication the following year and publishes short articles that are quite diverse in content, ranging from guides to interviewing the bereaved to a consideration of the Jewish view of organ transplants. *Death Studies* is the newest of the journals focusing on death. It includes papers on the scope and history of death education, model death courses, and new counseling techniques. The journal is interdisciplinary and reports on programmatic research and available resources, as well as on educationally related topics.

Suicide and Life-Threatening Behavior, the official publication of the American Association of Suicidology, has a multidisciplinary approach to self-destructive and other destructive behaviors. Although the emphasis is on suicide, articles on topics such as sudden infant death and battered children appear. A special supplement to *Death Studies* for February 1985 was devoted to suicide: *Suicide: Practical, Developmental, and Speculative Issues,* edited by Judith M. Stillion. Articles deal with the effects of suicide among patients on mental health professionals, suicide among children and adolescents, and legal and sociological concerns for suicide.

The *Journal of Medical Humanities and Bioethics,* formerly the *Journal of Bioethics,* is intended for the practitioner, but students and others interested in the ethics of treating dying patients will find it useful.

Two newer journals have appeared that promise to be valuable. The *Euthanasia Review* is published by the Hemlock Society and permits an open discussion of euthanasia. It encourages scholarly debate over active and passive euthanasia, the right to die, living wills, etc. The *Journal of Near-Death Studies,* sponsored by the Institute for the Advancement of Near Death Studies, explores topics such as clinical death, out-of-the-body experiences, and so on.

HISTORY AND CRITICISM

Analyses of the past and present impact of death on American culture are found in most disciplines. Surveys of the history of the funeral industry, philosophical debates on death with dignity, and current psychological studies of bereavement in children all spotlight part of that impact. The materials available to the researcher are numerous and, to stress again, varied. Clearly, all such analyses cannot be covered in this short space, and, unfortunately, not even all the different approaches to the cultural impact of death can be covered. The discussion that follows centers on four major themes: American culture and death, which includes history, funerals, and the family; religion and the afterlife; ethical and medical issues; and psychological and sociological issues. This will provide a general, but limited, survey of those works that explore the impact of death on American society.

American Culture

Perhaps the most neglected aspect of the American experience in the flood of death and dying literature is the historical backdrop for current beliefs and attitudes. A few recent essay collections begin to fill this gap. *Death in America,* edited by David E. Stannard, includes articles on the attitude toward death in pre-Civil War America, death in the American folk culture, and death and the Puritan child. Stannard expands his essay, which appears in this volume on death and the Puritan child, in *The Puritan Way of Death* and provides a detailed and exhaustive look at death and the Puritan way of life. *Death in the American Experience,* edited by Arien Mack, deals with death in the counterculture, in American poetry, and in the Christian and Judaic traditions. *Passing: The Vision of Death in America,* edited by Charles O. Jackson, represents the best of the volumes that treat death from a historical perspective. Jackson's aim is to explore the historical dimension of death and the responses to death. By organizing his material chronologically and by including essays that discuss attitudes in each century toward death, death rituals, and burial techniques, Jackson provides an excellent historical perspective on death in American culture. The major historical overview of death in our culture does not limit itself to American attitudes. Philip Aries's *The Hour of Our Death* is a major study of worldwide societies. It is a history of man's changing attitudes toward death over the past 1,000 years. This French historian has combined cultural studies with psychology and theology in his book.

Elizabeth Kubler-Ross's publication of *On Death and Dying* in 1969 was a turning point in death and dying literature and preceded an outpouring of works on death. Her now-famous volume described the highly technological situation in which we all must die and described five stages that dying patients often experience. The fear of death and dying surfaced, and talk began about what now was referred to as "the taboo topic"—the event we all deny will occur to us. Ernest Becker argues for the universality of this fear of death, not just for Americans, but for all human beings, in his Pulitzer Prize winner, *The Denial of Death.* The fear of death, the denial of death, and the taboo nature of death were echoed in a variety of works, especially in introductions to works on death and dying. Richard G. Dumont and Dennis C. Foss examine this aspect of America's view of death in *The American View of Death: Acceptance or Denial.* The authors see their primary contribution as providing a clear articulation of the acceptance-denial controversy and as providing a survey of the current social and scientific knowledge concerning Americans' attitudes toward death. Perhaps the most complete study available of the death attitudes of Americans in the late 1960s is Gordon M. Vernon's *Sociology of Death: An Analysis of Death Related Behavior*. From a sociological point of view, Vernon discusses the meaning of death in society, bereavement, fear of death, humor, and childhood experiences. *Death and Ethnicity: A Psychocultural Study* by Richard A. Kalish and David K. Reynolds provides a cross-ethnic comparison of death attitudes in America. Their study, which concentrates on black Americans, Japanese Americans, and Mexican Americans, is one of the very few cross-ethnic studies available.

The American funeral and the funeral industry have become an integral part of the American death. Robert W. Habenstein and William Lamers chart the development of the funeral industry from its earliest beginnings to its present status as a nearly indispensable service to survivors of the deceased in *The History of American Funeral Directing*. But not everyone is comfortable with the role the industry now plays, and the industry has been the subject of intense criticism. Jessica Mitford's *The American Way of Death* is the best known of a series of sharp criticisms of American funeral customs and the commercial exploitation associated with those customs. Ruth Mulvey Harmer's *The High Cost of Dying* and Leroy Bowman's *The American Funeral: A Study in Guilt, Extravagance, and Sublimity* both sound the same notes as does Mitford's work. In each, the value of the costly funeral customs of Americans and the practices by the industry that reinforce these customs are viewed with a highly critical eye.

In the decades since the publication of these works, changes have occurred in the industry, motivated in part by these criticisms. But the criticism continues, as is evidenced by the 1978 final staff report to the Federal Trade Commission, *Funeral Industry Practices*. The most thorough examination of current funeral practices and customs, however, is *Funerals: Consumers' Last Rights* by the editors of *Consumer Reports*. This objective examination presents an overview of the American funeral, details on arranging for a funeral and burial, alternatives to the American funeral, and suggestions of how to plan one's own funeral. An appendix provides extremely useful information regarding embalming and pre-need laws and gives full descriptions of embalming, restoration, and autopsy procedures. Another useful source is *A Manual of Death Education and Simple Burial* by Ernest Morgan, which has the advantage of being very compact yet comprehensive. This small booklet is distributed by most memorial societies and provides economical alternatives to the typical American funeral. The addresses are provided of donor clearinghouses, eyebanks, tissue banks, and medical and dental schools that need body donations.

The manner in which a society buries its dead betrays much about its citizens' attitudes toward life and death. Cemeteries are extremely revealing. The gravestone carving of early cemeteries was probably the first, and certainly the most extensive, artistic expression of the view of death of early Americans. *Graven Images: New England Stonecarving and Its Symbols, 1650–1815* by Allan I. Ludwig and *Memorials for Children of Change: The Art of Early New England Stonecarving* by Dickran and Ann Tashjian combine fine photographs of grave carvings with commentary on the significance of and the development of the details of these carvings. Emily Wasserman's *Gravestone Designs: Rubbings and Photographs from Early New York and New Jersey* and Peter Benes's *The Masks of Orthodoxy: Folk Gravestone Carving in Plymouth County, Massachusetts, 1689–1805* provide similar analyses of more specific geographic areas. Not only the carvings, but also the Epitaphs inscribed on the stones reveal attitudes toward death. *A Collection of American Epitaphs and Inscriptions with Occasional Notes* by Timothy Alden is a five-volume work indexed by names mentioned, making access to this collection less cumbersome.

The physical layout of the cemetery is also telling. *Famous and Curious Cemeteries: A Pictorial, Historical, and Anecdotal View of American and European Cemeteries and the Famous and Infamous People Who Are Buried There* by John Francis Marion spotlights thirty-five cemeteries in the United States, including Forest Lawn Memorial Park in Glendale, California. Forest Lawn is the best known of the American cemeteries; its promotional booklet, *Pictorial Forest Lawn,* through color photographs and narrative provides a tour of the architecture, sculptural reproductions, and original artworks on the grounds of Forest Lawn.

Psychological and Sociological Issues

Many argue that the function of the funeral ceremony is to help the family through the period of grief over the deceased. *Acute Grief and the Funeral,* edited by Vanderlyn R. Pine, contains about thirty-five short essays by funeral directors, doctors, chaplains, and sociologist. Despite the title, the establishment of the role of the funeral industry in the grief process is the primary subject; and the articles reflect the position that the funeral is an invaluable ceremony for overcoming grief. Acute grief is given no extended analysis. Rabbinical Assembly published *The Bond of Life: A Guide Book for Mourners* by Rabbi Jules Harlow, which details the proper Jewish procedure for mourning. *The Bond of Life* is extremely valuable in helping one to understand the place of the funeral and death in the Jewish religion and in providing a framework within which one can grieve.

The funeral and the period of mourning are often the beginning rather than the end of the grief process. Many books deal with the topic of bereavement, but to list a few will suggest the types of studies available. *Bereavement: Its Psychosocial Aspects,* edited by Bernard Schoenberg, is a good collection of sociological studies of bereavement as it relates to the family and to the health professional. The process of bereavement and the role of bereavement in human experience are also explored. Eric Bermann's *Scapegoat: The Impact of Death-Fear on an American Family* comes very near the core of the effects of death on American families. A close-up of a single family involved in an extended death watch reveals the impact of death and the death-fear on the daily routines, social roles, and values. *Scapegoat* is an excellent mirror of American culture. *Widow to Widow* is for women who have lost their husbands. Written by Phyllis R. Silverman, it suggests that women can deal effectively with their grief if they have as a role model some other woman who has been successful in accepting grief.

Many important works on bereavement deal with children. *A Child's Parent Dies: Studies in Childhood Bereavement* by Erna Furman and *The Child in His Family: The Impact of Disease and Death,* edited by James E. Anthony and Cyrille Koupernik, are both scholarly and well-written studies. The theoretical chapters on grief, mourning, and the effects of early parental death on child development in *A Child's Parent Dies* are balanced by case studies taken from a three-year project sponsored by the Cleveland Center for Research in Child Development. *The Child in His Family* is a collection of articles by recognized authorities and ties death to the cultural context in which it occurs. The problems we experience in coping with death are viewed as a result of our cultural values.

For those interested in how to talk with children about death, a small volume, *Talking About Death: A Dialogue Between Parent and Child* by Earl Grollman, is excellent. Grollman provides a context in which parents and children can discuss death as a real event in life. His presentation presumes that the parent is reluctant to discuss death and aims to break down that reluctance while focusing on the importance of the dialogue to the child. Very useful sections give descriptions and addresses of organizations that may be of help to the survivors, and describe and group by ages children's books, films, and cassettes that deal with death.

Hannelore Wass and Charles A. Corr have edited two recent books that are especially helpful in dealing with children and death. The more important is *Helping Children Cope with Death: Guidelines and Resources.* Now in its second edition, it considers children's thought about death; pastoral counseling; and parents, teachers, and health professionals as helpers. It also lists helpful books and audiovisual materials. Their second book is *Children and Death.*

Death of a student or death of a student's relative is a special problem for teachers. J. L. Thomas has edited a volume, *Death and Dying in the Classroom: Readings for Reference.* For the most part the essays are written by teachers and other educators. Some discuss the experience of dealing with the death of a student or someone close to a student; other essays deal with death education.

Religion and the Afterlife

The most urgent religious and philosophical question raised by death is whether anything survives the death of the body and, if so, what the after death experience is like. Although the question seems universal and urgent, it has yet to be answered to everyone's satisfaction. Different major religious sects have each taken their stand on the place of death in their religions and on the possibility for future life. This belief in a future life is carefully and thoroughly examined in William Alger's *A Critical History of the Doctrine of Future Life*. This scholarly history covers, among other aspects, the rabbinical doctrine, the Hebrew doctrine, and the grounds for the belief itself. *Christian Beliefs About Life After Death* by Paul Badham is a more contemporary study that seeks to show the development of these beliefs and how they might be defended by an examination of first-century thought and the New Testament. *Death: Meaning and Mortality in Christian Thought and Contemporary Culture* by Milton Gatch not only details the history of the idea of death in the Judeo-Christian tradition but also studies religious and cultural attempts by Western societies to deal meaningfully with death.

The smaller sects that diverge from traditional paths usually have their own positions on death and the afterlife. Any information regarding the positions of such groups is best sought directly from their national headquarters. Several do publish books or pamphlets that specifically outline the sect's position on death and the afterlife. The Watchtower Bible and Tract Society distributes *Is This Life All There Is?*, which presents an interpretation of the Bible accounting for the presence of death in the world and describing the resurrection of the dead. The Church of Scientology has published *Have You Lived Before This Life?* by the church's founder, L. Ron Hubbard.

Oddly, several sects with a decidedly Eastern emphasis distribute publications on death and the afterlife. The Sanatana Dharma Foundation issues a modern-day interpretation of *The Tibetan Book of the Dead* called *A Manual for Guiding a Person Through the After Death Experience,* by H. Charles Berner, while the Vedanta Society of California distributes *Life After Death* by Swami Vivekananda, and the Ramakrishna-Vivedananda Center offers *Man in Search of Immortality* by Swami Nikhilananda.

By far, the best evidence for life after death comes from spiritualism, psychic phenomena, and deathbed experiences, but such evidence is neither ample nor widely accepted. A good historical account of spiritualism and its impact on American literature is Howard Kerr's *Mediums, and Spirit-Rappers and Roaring Radicals: Spiritualism in American Literature 1850–1900.* Kerr surveys alleged communications between the living and the dead between 1845 and 1860 and analyzes the satiric and humorous literary response to spiritualism and its impact on occult fiction. The history of the movement and its impact is then extended to 1900. A good index makes this a helpful source on spiritualism. Deathbed experiences of members of the medical profession and the dying are often cited as evidence for life after death since the descriptions of these experiences bear striking similarity to each other and to those experiences described in *The Tibetan Book of the Dead*. The most well known of the recent reports of deathbed experiences, *Life After Life* by Ralph Moody, Jr., is primarily a report of case studies of those who have come very close to dying. A more empirical forerunner of Moody's work focusing on those attending the dying is *Deathbed Observations by Physicians and Nurses* by Karlis Osis. This survey of the observations of 9,000 nurses and doctors reveals similarities in their observations of the dying and near dying that are very similar to those reported by Moody.

The surprising and widespread popularity of Moody's book has led to considerable recent scholarly interest in near-death experiences. The first major book on the topic was *Life at Death: A Scientific Investigation of the Near-Death Experience* by Kenneth Ring. This respected study is an important contribution to the subject. *The Near-Death Experience,* edited by Bruce Greyson and Charles P. Flynn, is an anthology of essays that make a good general introduction to the topic, but they do not break much new ground.

Ethical and Medical Issues

Whether anything survives the death of the body is only one of the crucial issues raised by death. Death in our world of increasing medical knowledge and medical technology raises some extremely difficult medical and ethical issues. We no longer agree, for example, on an issue so fundamental as what criteria should be used to determine when a person is dead. Old issues such as euthanasia have again surfaced and have become the subject of intense debate. Several general anthologies have recently appeared that isolate some of these medical and ethical issues. Two good collections have exactly the same unimaginative, yet descriptive, title. *Ethical Issues in Death and Dying,* edited by Robert F. Weir, concentrates on the problems of determining when someone is dead, on whether we should allow someone to die, and on suicide. Verdicts of a number of recent court cases are included, and articles are written by lawyers, physicians, theologians, and psychologists. *Ethical issues in Death and Dying,* edited by Tom L. Beauchamp and Seymor Perlin, covers similar issues, but it does so from a decidedly philosophical perspective. A section on the significance of life and death, containing excerpts from philosophical works, distinguishes this collection from Weir's in yet another way. F. P. Herter et al. have edited an anthology intended for physicians, but of more general value: *Human and Ethical Issues in the Surgical Care of Patients with Life-Threatening Disease*. Supported by the Foundation of Thanatology, it has value for all those interested in ethical dilemmas.

Euthanasia and death with dignity debates have immense personal and economic impact in our present society. Although the most celebrated patient in America in this regard is Karen Ann Quinlan (see, for example, *Karen Ann Quinlan: Dying in the Age of Eternal Life* by B. D. Colen and *Karen Ann: The Quinlans Tell Their Story* by Joseph and Julia Quinlan), the debate over euthanasia and death with dignity began many years earlier. *The Right to Die,* published by the Group for the Advancement of Psychiatry, contains fourteen articles resulting from a 1971 symposium on the question of when and under what circumstances a person may choose to terminate his or her life. *Death by Choice* by Daniel C. Maguire continues the debate by emphasizing changes in medical technology that make the issue crucial and by criticizing the tardiness of the body of law in dealing with the issue. Jerry B. Wilson's *Death by Decision: The Medical, Moral, and Legal Dilemmas of Euthanasia* follows its historical account of euthanasia and its survey of religious views with a strong advocacy of mercy in caring for dying patients. One of the most useful single works on euthanasia is O. Ruth Russel's *Freedom to Die: Moral and Legal Aspects of Euthanasia.* The body of the text discusses changing attitudes toward death and dying and gives a historical review of both thought and action on euthanasia, as well as arguments and proposals for its legalization. The appendix contains petitions submitted to legislatures and to the United Nations, legislative proposals and bills, a list of societies promoting euthanasia, a discussion of the definition of death, living wills, and a list of articles, books, and relevant court cases. A recent book on euthanasia is *Euthanasia and Religion: A Survey of the Attitudes of World Religions of the Right-to-Die* by Gerald A. Larue. It briefly sketches teachings on euthanasia of Christianity, Judaism, Islam, and other major faiths.

Suicide has recently attracted considerable attention in the media, especially concerning adolescents. Several books and countless magazine articles have appeared on the topic. Of general value is *Family Therapy for Suicidal People* by Joseph Richman. The book gives practical advice for family members who have to deal with a suicide attempt, or at least a potential one. Richman combines clinical advice with theory and exploration of the important issues.

The hospice movement has come into its own in the 1980s. Many books on the subject seem to be guides for those who wish to open and operate such a facility, such as *Hospice: Complete Care for the Terminally Ill,* edited by Jack M. Zimmerman. Other books on hospices are of more general interest. The reader should especially consult two books edited by Charles and Donna Corr: *Hospice Care: Principles and Practice* and *Hospice Approaches to Pediatric Care. Hospice USA,* edited by Austin Kutscher, is a useful general introduction to the concept. As popular as the concept of the hospice has become, there still are those who prefer to care for their own ill and dying patients. For them books such as *Coming Home: A Guide to the Home Care of the Terminally Ill* are valuable. This book, by D. Duda, discusses the personal side of caring for the ill at home, but it also gives practical advice.

General Attitudes

Although aspects of death are usually discussed by a specialized discipline, general anthologies that cover a variety of topics are numerous. Some are extremely valuable; others are too superficial in their treatment of death and dying to be useful. *Man's Concern with Death* by Arnold Toynbee et al., one of the valuable collections, includes articles by Toynbee, Eric Rhocle, Niniam Smart, and others on attitudes toward death and dying. Another helpful anthology is *Death: Current Perspectives,* edited by Edwin Shneidman. His approach to death from societal, personal, cultural, and interpersonal perspectives is useful in getting a broad overview of death. The articles are generally well written and highly readable. *Death Inside Out,* edited by Peter Steinfels and Robert Veatch, centers on the possibility and concept of "a good death," while *A Book of Readings and Sources: Death and Society,* edited by James P. Carse and Arlene B. Dallery, uses articles on recent court cases, religious positions, and philosophical arguments to cover a variety of topics ranging from abortion to aging. Robert Fulton's *Death and Identity,* which was first published in 1965, has been revised and contains useful and interesting theoretical discussions of death as well as discussions of grief and of death in society. *The Meaning of Death* by Herman Feifel was one of the first general anthologies on death and, even though it has not been revised, it is still useful in providing an overview of death and dying. It also contains essays on several subjects—for example, death in modern art—that are neglected in more recent works.

The Last Dance by Lynne DeSpelder and Albert Strickland was designed as a general textbook for college classes on death and dying, but it is readable, informative, and interesting. It presents an overview of the subject as seen in art and literature, as well as through experiential data. Recent scholarship has focused on the differences between the sexes in their response to death. Judith Stillion's *Death and the Sexes: An Examination of Differential, Attitude, Behavior, and Coping Skills* looks at these differences and is an important study of gender's impact on our culture. Finally, *Death Anxiety* by Richard Lonetto and Donald Templer is a review of research into death anxiety and a summary of the literature on the subject. It is of help especially to psychologists.

Three projects that are under way to reprint, collect, and distribute materials on death and dying should be mentioned. The Arno Press series, "Literature of Death and Dying," is a collection of approximately forty titles, including reprints of classical works on death and original anthologies. Although the project does not focus on American literature, it does include historical works that have been influential in America, as well as some American works. The Center for Death Education and Research in Minneapolis, Minnesota, has established a cassette library of lectures, interviews, discussions, and dialogues on death-related topics. Twenty-four titles are presently available. The center has compiled a fourth edition of Robert Fulton's *Death, Grief and Bereavement: A Bibliography, 1845–1975,* containing nearly 4,000 references. In addition, a number of publications and films can be obtained through the center. Finally, Educational Perspectives Associates in DeKalb, Illinois, issues a multimedia catalog in their death and dying series, which is primarily designed for educational purposes. Filmstrips of cemeteries and funeral customs and cassettes on death in art, music, and literature are part of this series.

The books mentioned here have been selected from the vast amount of material available on death and should be considered no more than good places to begin one's own research on a specific aspect of death. The works cited here are also limited in being unrepresentative of the varied functions and manifestations of death in our culture. Death is a major theme in the visual and performing arts, and its image is of major significance in popular culture. The lyrics of popular songs consistently reflect its darker side; the threat of death lurks behind the advertising of life insurance companies and the American Cancer Society. Death is a theme in literature, and more and more frequently it is being integrated as a theme into television programming. Very little has been written on the role death plays in these aspects of our culture. But, as discussion of death continues and as we continue to become increasingly aware of the presence of death in every part of our culture, analyses of these roles will no doubt contribute to the already large body of literature on the subject. we will then be much closer to an understanding of the popular cultural expression of and representation of death in America.

BIBLIOGRAPHY

Books and Articles

Alden, Timothy. *A Collection of American Epitaphs and Inscriptions with Occasional Notes.* New York: Ayer, 1977.

Alger, William Rounseville. *A Critical History of the Doctrine of Future Life.* New York: W.J. Widdleton, 1867.

American Sunday-School Union. *The Tree and Its Fruits; or, The Last Hours of Infidels and Christians Contrasted.* Philadelphia: American Sunday School Union, 1839.

Anthony, James E., and Cyrille Koupernik, eds. *The Child in His Family: The Impact of Disease and Death.* Vol. 2. New York: John Wiley and Sons, 1973.

Aries, Philip. *The Hour of Our Death.* New York: Alfred A. Knopf, 1981.

Badham, Paul. *Christian Beliefs About Life After Death.* New York: Barnes and Noble, 1976.

Baldwin, Oliver P. *Address Delivered at the Dedication of the Hollywood Cemetery*. Richmond: Macfarlane and Fergusson, 1849.

Beauchamp, Tom L., and Seymor Perlin. *Ethical Issues in Death and Dying*. Englewood Cliffs, N.J.: Prentice-Hall, 1978.

Becker, Ernest. *The Denial of Death*. New York: Free Press, 1973.

Benes, Peter. *The Masks of Orthodoxy: Folk Gravestone Carving in Plymouth County, Massachusetts, 1689–1805*. Amherst: University of Massachusetts Press, 1977.

Bermann, Eric. *Scapegoat: The Impact of Death-Fear on an American Family*. Ann Arbor: University of Michigan Press, 1973.

Berner, H. Charles. *A Manual for Guiding a Person Through the After Death Experience: A Modern Day Interpretation Based upon "The Tibetan Book of the Dead."* Lucerne Valley, Calif.: Causation Press, 1967.

Bowman, Leroy. *The American Funeral: A Study in Guilt, Extravagance, and Sublimity*. Westport, Conn.: Greenwood Press, 1973.

Bunyan, John. *Pilgrim's Progress*. New York: New American Library, 1972.

Carse, James P., and Arlene B. Dallery. *A Book of Readings and Sources: Death and Society*. New York: Harcourt Brace Jovanovich, 1977.

Colen, B. D. *Karen Ann Quinlan: Dying in the Age of Eternal Life*. New York: Nash Publishing, 1976.

Corr, Charles A., and Donna M. Corr, eds. *Hospice Approaches to Pediatric Care*. New York: Springer, 1985.

———, eds. *Hospice Care: Principles and Practice*. New York: Springer, 1983.

Crothers, Samuel McChord. *The Endless Life*. Boston: Houghton Mifflin, 1905.

Darwin, Charles. *The Origin of Species*. New York: AMS Press, 1972.

"Death, Dying and Life After Life: A Lively Marketplace." *Publishers Weekly*, 214 (September 25, 1978), 92–98.

DeSpelder, Lynne, and Albert Strickland. *The Last Dance*. Palo Alto, Calif.: Mayfield, 1983.

Dickinson, G. Lowes. *Is Immortality Desirable?* Boston: Houghton Mifflin, 1909.

Duda, D. *Coming Home: A Guide to the Home Care of the Terminally Ill*. Santa Fe: John Muir, 1984.

Dumont, Richard G., and Dennis C. Foss. *The American View of Death: Acceptance or Denial*. Cambridge, Mass.: Schenkman Publishing, 1972.

Edwards, Jonathan. *Representative Selections*. Edited by Clarence H. Faust and Thomas H. Johnson. New York: Hill and Wang, 1962.

Farberow, Norman L., ed. *Bibliography on Suicide and Suicide Prevention: 1897–1957* and *1958–1970*. Rockville, Md.: National Institute of Mental Health, 1972.

Feifel, Herman, ed. *The Meaning of Death*. New York: McGraw-Hill, 1965.

Fiske, John. *The Destiny of Man*. Boston: Houghton Mifflin, 1892.

Fithian, Philip Vickers. *Journal and Letters of Philip Vickers Fithian*. Edited by Hunter Dickinson Farish. Charlottesville, Va.: Dominion Books, 1968.

Fulton, Robert, ed. *Death and Identity*. Bowie, Md.: The Charles Press, 1976.

———, ed. *Death, Grief and Bereavement: A Bibliography 1845–1975*. New York: Ayer, 1976.

Funeral Industry Practices. Washington, D.C.: Bureau of Consumer Protection, Federal Trade Commission, 1978.

Funerals: Consumers' Last Rights. Mount Vernon, N.Y.: Consumers Union, 1977.

Furman, Erna. *A Child's Parent Dies: Studies in Childhood Bereavement*. New Haven: Yale University Press, 1974.

Gatch, Milton McC. Death: *Meaning and Mortality in Christian Thought and Contemporary Culture*. New York: Seabury Press, 1969.

Greyson, Bruce, and Charles P. Flynn, eds. *The Near-Death Experience*. Springfield, Ill.: Charles C. Thomas, 1984.

Grollman, Earl A. *Talking About Death: A Dialogue Between Parent and Child*. Boston: Beacon Press, 1970.

Group for the Advancement of Psychiatry. *The Right to Die*. New York: Jason Aronson, 1974.

Habenstein, Robert W., and William Lamers. *The History of American Funeral Directing*. Milwaukee: Bulfin Printers, 1962.

Hariot, Thomas. *A Briefe and True Report of the New Found Land of Virginia . . . , 1588,* as reprinted in *Virginia: Four Personal Narratives*. New York: Arno Press, 1972.

Harlow, Rabbi Jules, ed. *The Bond of Life: A Book for Mourners*. New York: Rabbinical Assembly, 1975.

Harmer, Ruth Mulvey. *The High Cost of Dying*. New York: Collier Books, 1963.

Harrah, Barbara K., and David F. Harrah. *Funeral Service: A Bibliography of Literature on Its Past, Present and Future, the Various Means of Disposition and Memorialization*. Metuchen, N.J.: Scarecrow Press, 1976.

Herter, F. P., K. Ford, L. C. Mark, et al., eds. *Human and Ethical Issues in the Surgical Care of Patients with Life-Threatening Disease*. Springfield, Ill: Charles C. Thomas, 1986.

Hubbard, L. Ron. *Have You Lived Before This Life?* Los Angeles: Church of Scientology Publications Organization, 1959.

Is This Life All There Is? New York: Watchtower Bible and Tract Society of New York, 1974.

Jackson, Charles O., ed. *Passing: The Vision of Death in America*. Westport, Conn.: Greenwood Press, 1977.

James, William. *Human Immortality*. Boston: Houghton Mifflin, 1898.

Janeway, James. *A Token for Children*. New York: Garland, 1976.

Kalish, Richard A., and David K. Reynolds. *Death and Ethnicity: A Psychocultural Study*. Los Angeles: University of Southern California Press, 1976.

Kerr, Howard. *Mediums, and Spirit-Rappers and Roaring Radicals: Spiritualism in American Literature 1850–1900*. Chicago: University of Illinois Press, 1972.

Kubler-Ross, Elizabeth. *On Death and Dying*. New York: Macmillan, 1969.

Kutscher, Austin, ed. *Hospice USA*. New York: Columbia University Press, 1983.

Kutscher, Austin H., Jr., and Austin H. Kutscher, eds. *A Bibliography of Books on Death, Bereavement, Loss, and Grief: 1935–1968*. New York: Health Science Publishing, 1969.

Kutscher, Austin H., Jr., and Martin Kutscher. *A Bibliography of Books on Death, Bereavement, Loss, and Grief: Supplement 1, 1968–1972*. New York: Health Science Publishing, 1974.

Kutscher, M. L., et al., eds. *A Comprehensive Bibliography of Thanatology Literature*. New York: MSS Information, 1976.

———, eds. *A Cross-Index of Indices of Books on Thanatology*. New York: MSS Information, 1976.

Larue, Gerald A. *Euthanasia and Religion: A Survey of the Attitudes of World Religions of the Right-to-Die.* Los Angeles: Hemlock Society, 1985.

Lonetto, Richard, and Donald I. Templer. *Death Anxiety.* Washington, D.C.: Hemisphere, 1986.

Ludwig, Allan I. *Graven Images: New England Stonecarving and Its Symbols, 1650–1815.* Middletown, Conn.: Wesleyan University Press, 1966.

McIntosh, John L. *Research on Suicide: A Bibliography.* Westport, Conn.: Greenwood Press, 1985.

Mack, Arien, ed. *Death in the American Experience.* New York: Schocken Books, 1974.

Maguire, Daniel C. *Death by Choice.* Garden City, N.Y.: Doubleday, 1974.

Marion, John Francis. *Famous and Curious Cemeteries: A Pictorial, Historical, and Anecdotal View of American and European Cemeteries and the Famous and Infamous People Who are Buried There.* New York: Crown, 1977.

Miller, Albert Jay, and Michael James Acri. *Death: A Bibliographic Guide.* Metuchen, N.J.: Scarecrow Press, 1977.

Mitford, Jessica. *The American Way of Death.* New York: Simon and Schuster, 1963.

Moody, Ralph, Jr. *Life After Life.* New York: Bantam Books, 1975.

Moore, Julia A. "Little Andrew," as quoted in *Adventures of Huckleberry Finn,* by Mark Twain. Edited by Sculley Bradley, Richmond Croom Beatty, and E. Hudson Long. New York: W .W. Norton, 1962.

Morgan, Ernest. *A Manual of Death Education and Simple Burial.* Burnsville, N.C.: Celo Press, 1980.

Nevins, Madeline M., ed. *Bioethical Perspectives on Death and Dying: Summaries of the Literature.* Rockville, Md.: Information Planning Associates, 1977.

The New England Primer. New York: Dodd, Mead, 1899.

Nikhilananda, Swami. *Man in Search of Immortality.* Kent, England: George Allen and Unwin, 1968.

Osis, Karlis. *Deathbed Observations by Physicians and Nurses.* New York: Parapsychology Foundation, 1961.

Owen, John. *The Death of Death in the Death of Christ. A Treatise of the Redemption and Reconciliation That Is in the Blood of Christ.* Philadelphia: Green and M'Laughlin, 1827.

Pictorial Forest Lawn. Glendale, Calif.: Forest Lawn Memorial-Park Association, 1970.

Pine, Vanderlyn R., et al., eds. *Acute Grief and the Funeral.* Springfield, Ill.: Charles C. Thomas, 1976.

Poe, Edgar Allan. *Selected Prose and Poetry.* Edited by W. H. Auden. New York: Holt, Rinehart and Winston, 1950.

Quinlan, Joseph, and Julia Quinlan, with Phyliss Battelle. *Karen Ann: The Quinlans Tell Their Story.* Garden City, N.Y.: Doubleday, 1977.

Richman, Joseph. *Family Therapy for Suicidal People.* New York: Springer, 1986.

Ring, Kenneth. *Life at Death: A Scientific Investigation of the Near-Death Experience.* New York: Coward, McCann and Geoghegan, 1980.

Russell, O. Ruth. *Freedom to Die: Moral and Legal Aspects of Euthanasia.* New York: Human Sciences Press, 1977.

Schoenberg, Bernard, et al., eds. *Bereavement: Its Psychosocial Aspects.* New York: Columbia University Press, 1975.

Shneidman, Edwin, ed. *Death: Current Perspectives.* Palo Alto, Calif.: Mayfield Publishing, 1976.

Silverman, Phyllis R. *Widow to Widow.* New York: Springer, 1986.

Smith, John. *The General History of Virginia, New England, and the Summer Isles.* Cleveland: World, 1966.

Stannard David E. *The Puritan Way of Death: A Study in Religion, Culture,and Social Change.* New York: Oxford University Press, 1977.

Stannard, David E., ed. *Death in America.* Philadelphia: University of Pennsylvania Press, 1975.

Steinfels, Peter, and Robert M. Veatch, eds. *Death Inside Out.* New York: Harper and Row, 1974.

Stillion, Judith M. *Death and the Sexes: An Examination of Differential, Attitude, Behavior, and Coping Skills.* New York: Hemisphere, 1985.

———. ed. *Suicide: Practical, Developmental, and Speculative Issues.* Supplement to *Death Education,* February 1985.

Strugnell, Cecile. *Adjustment to Widowhood and Some Related Problems: A Selective and Annotated Bibliography.* New York: Health Sciences Publishing, 1974.

Tashjian, Dickran, and Ann Tashjian. *Memorials for Children of Change: The Art of Early New England Stonecarving.* Middletown, Conn.: Wesleyan University Press, 1974.

Thomas, J. L., ed. *Death and Dying in the Classroom: Readings for Reference.* Phoenix: Oryx Press, 1984.

Toynbee, Arnold, et al. *Man's Concern with Death.* New York: McGraw-Hill, 1968.

Vernon, Gordon M. *Sociology of Death: An Analysis of Death Related Behavior.* New York: Krieger, 1970.

Vivekananda, Swami. *Life After Death.* Mayavati, Pithoragarh, Himalayas: Advita Ashrama, 1975.

Wass, Hannelore, et al. *Death Education: An Annotated Resource Guide.* Washington, D.C.: Hemisphere, 1980.

Wass, Hannelore, and Charles A. Corr, eds. *Children and Death.* Washington, D.C. Hemisphere, 1984.

———, eds. *Helping Children Cope with Death: Guidelines and Resources.* Washington, D.C.: Hemisphere, 1984.

Wasserman, Emily. *Gravestone Designs: Rubbings and Photographs from Early New York and New Jersey.* New York: Dover, 1972.

Weir, Robert F., ed. *Ethical Issues in Death and Dying.* New York: Columbia University Press, 1977.

White, Newman Ivey, ed. *The Frank C. Brown Collection of North Carolina Folklore.* 7 vols. Durham, N.C.: Duke University Press, 1964.

Wilson, Jerry B. *Death by Decision: The Medical, Moral, and Legal Dilemmas of Euthanasia.* Philadelphia: Westminister Press, 1975.

Zimmerman, Jack M., ed. *Hospice: Complete care for the Terminally Ill.* Baltimore: Urban and Schwarzenberg, 1986.

Periodicals

Advances in Thanatology. New York, 1971–.

Death Studies. New York, 1977–.

The Euthanasia Review. New York, 1987–.

Humanitas, Pittsburgh, 1965–.

Journal of Medical Humanities and Bioethics. New York, 1976–.

Journal of Near-Death Studies. New York, 1981–.

Monist. La Salle, Ill., 1890–.

Omega: Journal of Death and Dying. Farmingdale, N.Y., 1970–.

Prism. Chicago, 1973–76.

Psychology Today. New York, 1967–.

Publishers Weekly. New York, 1872–.

Sociology Symposium. Bowling Green, Ky., 1968–.

Suicide and Life-Threatening Behavior. New York, 1971–.

Voices: The Art and Science of Psychotherapy. Orlando, Fla., 1965–.

Debate and Public Address

ROBERT H. JANKE

Debate and public address in the United States are two distinct but related areas within the academic discipline of speech communication. The study of debate is frequently grouped with argumentation or included as a component of forensics, whereas the study of public address is often coupled with rhetoric. In this chapter, however, debate and public address are generally considered as a single area of inquiry, although the section dealing with reference works also treats educational debate and public speaking as separate skills in communication.

Culture in the United States is perceived as a matter of taste, with many factors, primarily economics and education, influencing each individual's preferences. It is pluralistic, ranging from the high to the low, with boundaries loose and ever changing. A treatment of debate and public address as an element of American popular culture could appropriately begin with a frequently quoted statement by William Norwood Brigance from the preface to his celebrated work, *A History and Criticism of American Public Address:* "Most of the mighty movements affecting the destiny of the American nation have gathered strength in obscure places from the talk of nameless men, and gained final momentum from leaders who could state in common words the needs and hopes of common people."[1] This momentum might come from the sophisticated inaugural address of a patrician president or from the outspoken words of an uneducated civil rights worker. Great speakers through the centuries have shared the ability to move their listeners to action, whether at a political meeting, a religious assembly, or an outdoor rally or through broadcasts on radio and television. In the democratic American process, the people, responding either directly or indirectly to these speakers, take action that determines the course of historical events.

This chapter deals with such speakers. It is a survey whose scope is necessarily wide; however, it does not include such related areas as mass communication, interpersonal communication, group discussion, parliamentary procedure, or the issues of freedom of speech or the right to communicate. Space allotted here is limited. The references and bibliographic items are therefore selective and the descriptions brief. The major criterion is usefulness. The intent is to offer a concise guide for the student or general reader to important and practical source material.

HISTORIC OUTLINE

The history of debate and public address in the United States is, in essence, the religious, political, and social history of the nation. Therefore, an outline of value to the reader should include, in chronological order, a selection of the most significant speakers, popular issues, and contemporary events that have contributed to this history.

The most significant speakers of early New England were the preachers, who exerted considerable influence, for they were also leaders and teachers whose sermons adapted the established theology to everyday application. What many consider to be the first notable speech delivered in America is John Winthrop's speech on liberty. Winthrop, who was chosen the first governor of the Massachusetts Bay Colony, opposed broad democracy. In 1635, he argued that man was not free to do simply as he wished but must submit to civil and lawful authority, an authority which encompassed a moral covenant between God and man, an authority which was looked upon as the "ecclesiastical elect."

This theological approach, known as theocracy, was upheld by four generations of the Mather family, who were predominant in shaping the lives of the colonists during the later seventeenth and early eighteenth centuries. Richard Mather advocated the liberalizing of the means to attain church membership; his son, Increase Mather, assuming the pastorate of Boston's North Church, upheld the Puritan views of church and state. Increase's son, Cotton Mather, became recognized as New England's leading Puritan preacher. He spoke out on the vital issues of the time, for example, advocating the inoculation against smallpox; but he is known today largely for his part in the Salem witch trials of 1692. Cotton's son, Samuel Mather, the fourth generation of what is referred to as America's first dynasty, succeeded his father and grandfather as pastor of North Church but was less influential than his illustrious predecessors.

Changing concepts in religion gradually spread throughout the colonies. Soloman Stoddard, a liberal preacher in Northampton, Massachusetts, espoused a doctrine of predestination. In 1727, he was succeeded in the pulpit by his grandson, Jonathan Edwards. From among Edwards's hundreds of sermons, the best known is "Sinners in the Hands of an Angry God," preached in 1741, which epitomized his theme that all men were sinners facing damnation and could be saved only through God's arbitrary, pre-destined choice. Traveling evangelist George Whitefield preached more than 18,000 sermons, primarily on New Calvinism, which offered personal salvation through the acceptance of Christ and sanctioned a sense of freedom previously unknown to the colonists.

During this same period the seeds of freedom were also developing in the political sphere. The concept of the town meeting, which took many forms throughout the colonies, gave the colonists the opportunity to air grievances and discuss issues in a democratic manner. Increasingly these issues centered on British rule and the union of the colonies. As early as 1754, addressing the representatives to the congress at Albany, Benjamin Franklin of Philadelphia advocated a confederation. In Boston, Samuel Adams, a highly effective orator, aroused the citizens to the cause with his fiery speeches, one in particular delivered in Faneuil Hall in 1770 following the massacre of five colonists by British soldiers; at a meeting three years later his heated oratory triggered the dumping of tea into Boston harbor.

While such men as Samuel Adams and his compatriot James Otis were addressing assemblies for the revolutionary cause in Boston, Patrick Henry was arguing for American independence in Virginia. His speech in that state's House of Burgesses in opposition to King George III's Stamp Act of 1765, delivered to shouts of "Treason!," is recognized as a triumph in American oratory. Henry's statement delivered before the second Virginia Convention on March 23, 1775, at St. John's Church in Richmond, is now part of American folklore: "Is life so dear, or peace so sweet, as to be purchased at the price of chains and slavery? Forbid it, Almighty God! I know not what course others may take; but as for me, give me liberty or give me death!"[2] Henry became known as the Voice of the Revolution.

Some of the most intense and significant debates of this period in American history took place in 1787 and 1788 as the various states deliberated the proposed federal constitution. In Virginia, the opponents were evenly matched. The Anti-federalists, led by Patrick Henry, who thought that Virginia should refrain from immediate ratification, lost by a narrow margin to the Federalists, led by James Madison, who cogently refuted the points made by Henry. In a similar dispute in New York, Alexander Hamilton's oratory in favor of the Federalist cause defeated the Anti-federalists under the leadership of Governor George Clinton. Eventually the Constitution was ratified, and the fledgling government was launched as George Washington assumed the presidency in 1789. Washington's statement from his "Farewell Address" of 1797 is frequently quoted in political debate: " 'Tis our true policy to steer clear of permanent alliances with any portion of the foreign world."[3]

The popular issues treated in the debates and public addresses during the first half of the nineteenth century included such matters as tariffs, New England manufacturing, foreign interests, centralization of government, expansion, internal improvements, sectionalism, slavery, nullification, and secession. These issues were debated at thousands of rallies, platforms, and "stumps" across the country, as well as in the famed halls of the nation's capitol.

Three of America's most distinguished orators, known as the Great Triumvirate, emerged during this early national period referred to as America's Golden Age of Oratory: Henry Clay from the West, the North's Daniel Webster, and the South's John C. Calhoun. Clay's eloquent speech on the New Army bill, delivered before the House in 1813, rallied the forces necessary to bring the War of 1812 to a successful conclusion. Clay was popularly called the Great Pacificator during the Missouri controversy of 1820 and continued to play this role throughout his long career. Daniel Webster, considered America's foremost public speaker, was known equally for his political, legal, and platform or special occasion speaking. He is best remembered for his debate in the Senate in 1830 with Robert Y. Hayne of South Carolina, who argued for the states' right of nullification, the right to put liberty first and union afterward. Webster's famous reply, concluding with the statement, "Liberty *and* Union, now and forever, one and inseparable!" has ever since been identified with popular American oratory.[4] Calhoun was the most effective orator from the South, a leading spokesman for states' rights and slavery. But in the final speech of his career, on the Clay Compromise Measures of 1850, he could not persuade his fellow senators to support his stand against Clay and Webster in their combined efforts to preserve the Union.

Other prominent public speakers of the early nineteenth century included John Quincy Adams, known for his compromises on the Treaty of Ghent and arguments for the Monroe Doctrine; Thomas Hart Benton, longtime senator from Missouri whose oratorical skills were directed at western expansion; and Thomas Corwin, political leader from Ohio whose speech "Against War with Mexico," delivered to the Senate in 1847, caused him to be burned in effigy as a traitor.

Some twenty years earlier had begun an era of what was called platform speaking, reflected in the emergence and development of professional orators who addressed themselves, either voluntarily or for a fee, to specific issues, usually concerned with some demand for social reform, such as abolition, women's rights, or prohibition.

Antislavery spokesmen included William Lloyd Garrison of Massachusetts, who agitated against slavery through the New England Antislavery Society, the American Antislavery Society, and numerous other abolitionist societies which he helped to establish; Wendell Phillips, public orator noted for his speech delivered in 1837 to an overflowing crowd in Boston's Faneuil

Hall on the murder of abolitionist Elijah Lovejoy; and Charles Sumner, who is best known for his offensive "Crimes Against Kansas" speech, delivered to the Senate in 1856 in opposition to the Kansas-Nebraska bill. (This speech resulted in Sumner's being severely assaulted by his opponents and left unconscious on the floor of the Senate.) Edward Everett was a well-known and highly skilled orator of the time who, as circumstances evolved, was the principal speaker at the ceremony dedicating the cemetery on the battlefield at Gettysburg, Pennsylvania, in 1863, an occasion made famous by the brief address of Abraham Lincoln.

Numerous blacks also spoke in public on the slavery question. Chief among these was Frederick Douglass, an ex-slave whose greatest speeches include "The Meaning of July Fourth for the Negro," delivered in Corinthian Hall, Rochester, New York, on July 5, 1852, and the "West India Emancipation" speech delivered at Canandaigua, New York, on August 4, 1857. Other black speakers prominent during this period were Charles Lennox Remond, Henry Highland Garnet, Samuel Ringgold Ward, James McCune Smith, and Robert Purvis. Some decades later, Booker T. Washington became recognized as the national spokesman for the Negro, largely as a result of his oration before the Cotton States and International Exposition in Atlanta, Georgia. This speech, delivered on September 18, 1895, became known as the "Atlanta Compromise Address." Favoring greater economic opportunity at this time rather than broader societal changes, Washington declared, "In all things that are purely social we can be as separate as the fingers, yet one as the hand in all things essential to mutual progress."[5]

Abraham Lincoln was among the most effective popular orators of the mid-century period. Upon accepting the Republican nomination in Illinois for the U.S. Senate in 1858, he stated: " 'A house divided against itself cannot stand.' I believe this government cannot endure, permanently half *slave* and half *free*."[6] His opponent, Stephen A. Douglas, the Little Giant, refuted Lincoln's statement several weeks later by arguing that the people should have the right to decide for themselves. The stage was thus set for a series of seven debates that attracted audiences numbering into the thousands across the prairies of Illinois. These debates are still the best known in American history. Although Douglas won the Senate seat, the debates provided the path to the presidency for Lincoln only two years later. Lincoln's masterpiece, the "Gettysburg Address," delivered on November 19, 1863, and since memorized by millions of school children, ranks among the world's great speeches.[7] Also considered a special work of oratorical literature is his "Second Inaugural Address," delivered March 4, 1865, famed for the words: "With malice toward none, with charity for all, with firmness in the right as God gives us to see the right, let us strive on to finish the work we are in."[8]

Following the Civil War the issues facing the nation were new and varied, but no popular debate topic was more crucial than that dealing with the reconstruction of the Southern states. Robert G. Ingersoll was known for his verbal brilliance while defending the cause of the Northern Republicans. Georgia's Henry Grady became known as the spokesman for the new South.

A distinctive feature of this era of platform speaking, a period when the role of women in American society was universally acknowledged as being inferior to that of men, was that women, despite resistance and sometimes ridicule, emerged as public speakers on popular issues. With an address on July 4, 1828, in New Harmony, Indiana, Frances Wright was a forerunner among early American women orators, appealing for reforms in education. Other women orators followed, such as Angelina Grimké, a southerner who moved northern audiences to the anti-slavery cause, and Abbey Kelley Foster, who spoke out fiercely on the issues of women's rights and temperance, often denouncing her audiences and frequently meeting with public disapproval. The speaking career of Ernestine L. Rose was largely concerned with human rights, particularly the rights of women; and Lucy Stone traveled and spoke extensively for women's rights. In 1848 in Seneca Falls, New York, Elizabeth Cady Stanton addressed the first Women's Rights Convention, which she and Lucretia Mott had promoted. A leading advocate for the cause of prohibition was Frances E. Willard, who crusaded widely for temperance, presiding over the National Women's Christian Temperance Union and eventually broadening her advocacy to include labor reform and women's liberation. Pioneer black women orators, concerned mainly with anti-slavery and women's rights, included Sojourner Truth, Frances Ellen Watkins Harper, and Sarah P. Remond.

Susan B. Anthony was foremost in the women's movement as a speaker and organizer. She lectured for more than forty-five years, and her influence on popular culture was reflected in 1979 when her likeness was sculptured for the obverse of the one dollar coin.

During the nineteenth century two uniquely American media concerned with public address were the "lyceums" and the "Chautauquas." Thousands of lyceums, organized and staffed by civic-minded volunteers, flourished in cities across the nation at this time, operating mainly in auditoriums during the winter months. Originally intended to provide a platform for a series of educational lectures by local specialists, the lyceums soon attracted the nation's leading statesmen and scholars. The long list of traveling speakers, who drew large crowds and earned large fees, included such prominent personalities as Henry Ward Beecher, Ralph Waldo Emerson, Horace Greeley, Oliver Wendell Holmes, James Russell Lowell, Theodore Parker, and Daniel Webster. Wendell Phillips's "The Lost Arts," delivered some 2,000 times over a period of forty years, was a major attraction.

The Chautauquas originated and operated in a different manner. At Lake Chautauqua, New York, during the summer of 1874, John H. Vincent offered a program of lecture courses. Based on the success and growth of his project, he acquired a partner, Keith Vawter, and in 1904 organized what became known as "traveling Chautauquas." The Chautauquas, traveling with tents mostly through the rural areas during the summer months, were particularly popular with the masses, and their programs featuring distinguished speakers on appealing topics catered to mass tastes. William Jennings Bryan and Russell H. Conwell were audience favorites. Conwell presented his lecture, "Acres of Diamonds," to over 6,000 audiences during a period of more than fifty years and with his huge profits founded Temple University. It is estimated that during a single year Chautauqua programs were offered in some 10,000 communities, with a total audience of four million.[9]

As the various lyceums either disappeared or merged to form literary societies during the period after the Civil War, newly formed lecture bureaus supplied speakers who gave audiences what they wanted to hear, utilizing local facilities for public address and providing eminent speakers for substantial fees. James B. Pond became a major entrepreneur whose contracted speakers included the best that money could attract: Henry Ward Beecher, Chauncey M. Depew, John B. Gough, Robert G. Ingersoll, and Wendell Phillips, to name only a few. Mark Twain was extremely successful on the lecture circuit, reportedly earning more money from public address than from publication. With the coming of the economic depression of 1929, the traveling Chautauqua phenomenon waned, but through the 1930s and 1940s lecture bureaus continued to supply large and enthusiastic audiences with such speakers as Richard Halliburton, Eleanor Roosevelt, and Lowell Thomas.

From the early days of colonial "theocracy" through the expansion into the many different denominations existing today, the clergy wielded considerable persuasive power. Some of these individuals made significant contributions to American popular culture. Theodore Parker's noteworthy sermon, "The Transient and the Permanent in Christianity," delivered in a South Boston church in 1841, established him as an advocate of modernist doctrines and aroused wide criticism. He became known for his sermons against slavery, the most noted being his denunciation of Webster for his speech of March 7, 1850. Henry Ward Beecher, like his father, Lyman Beecher, was a powerful orator for many causes, including the antislavery movement, and is recognized as the greatest American preacher of the nineteenth century. His "Memorial Sermon on Abraham Lincoln," delivered April 23, 1865, is a sublime example of oratorical tribute.

Skillfully organized revivalism became big business during the latter half of the nineteenth century, and the best-known revivalist was Dwight L. Moody. Not ordained, Moody preached in convention halls, warehouses, and theaters to audiences numbering well into the thousands. Following Moody by a generation and addressing audiences into the early decades of the twentieth century, Billy (William A.) Sunday, a former baseball player with the Chicago White Sox, also not ordained, continued in the tradition of Moody in "saving souls." Sunday was an energetic preacher who put sawdust on the floor so that sinners would not make a noise as they walked down the aisle to the foot of his speaking platform, a ritual known as "hitting the sawdust trail." Later, Archbishop Fulton J. Sheen, a Roman Catholic traditionalist with a commanding presence and a sharp intellect, brought his evangelism to a radio and television audience estimated at thirty million at its peak. His television program, "Life Is Worth Living," won an Emmy Award in 1952. Currently, eminent Protestant evangelist Billy (William F.) Graham attracts large audiences in major cities largely through his "crusades," some of which are televised. Other popular evangelists, however, rely on television to attract millions of viewers and millions of dollars, mixing religion with social and political issues. The most successful of these preachers include Jerry Falwell, founder of the Moral Majority; Oral Roberts, head of Oral Roberts University; Pat Robertson, former chief of the Christian Broadcasting Network and a U.S. presidential candidate in 1988; and Robert Schuller, builder of the Crystal Cathedral.

As the nineteenth century drew to a close, the Populists were advocating free coinage of silver, agrarian reform, and a graduated federal income tax. Involved in these issues was the most prominent speaker of the period, William Jennings Bryan, a Democrat of Nebraska with Jeffersonian principles. His address to the Democratic convention in Chicago in 1896, "The Cross of Gold," advocating the cause of labor and the farmer, is considered a high point of convention oratory. Bryan had a long and popular career as a proponent for humanity, democracy, and religious orthodoxy, which culminated in 1924 in the world-famous Scopes "Monkey Trial" in Dayton, Tennessee, where he argued eloquently for the cause of the divine creation of man against Clarence S. Darrow, the lawyer for the defense of the theory of evolution.

The popular hero of the Spanish-American War, New York Republican Theodore Roosevelt, as Vice President of the United States, addressed an audience at the Minnesota State Fair, Minneapolis, on September 2, 1901, in which he made a vigorous plea that this nation maintain the principles of the Monroe Doctrine. He illustrated his attitude:

A good many of you are probably acquainted with the old proverb: "Speak softly and carry a big stick—you will go far." If a man continually blusters, if he lacks civility, a big stick will not save him from trouble; and neither will speaking softly avail, if back of the softness there does not lie strength, power. . . . So it is with the nation.[10]

Assuming the presidency upon the assassination of William McKinley less than two weeks later, Roosevelt spoke extensively and successfully to break the trusts of big business and the railroads and to promote conservation.

Roosevelt's well-known speech calling for decency in government, "The Man with the Muck-Rake," delivered in Washington, D.C., in 1906, reflected the tenor of the time. Other progressives noted for public address were also campaigning for reform, including Albert J. Beveridge, Robert M. La Follette, and William E. Borah.

In the early years of the twentieth century, issues of war and peace, as well as reform, engulfed Democratic President Woodrow Wilson, a crusading, intellectual speaker. Wilson's "Peace Without Victory" speech delivered to the Senate on January 21, 1917, intended to convince the warring European powers to resolve their conflict, was to no avail: three months later, on April 2, Wilson had to appear before a joint session of Congress to ask for a declaration of war. This momentous "War Message" was enthusiastically endorsed, and the nation embarked on its first world war. In an address before a joint session of Congress on January 8, 1918, Wilson proposed his famous Fourteen Points as a basis for a peace treaty. Following the conclusion of this war, against strong opposition from the Senate led by Henry Cabot Lodge, Wilson traveled to Versailles, and on January 25, 1919, appealed to the international delegates for the formation of a League of Nations as a means to render justice and maintain peace. Although the world was not then ready for Wilson's idealistic vision, his concepts would find realistic expression a generation later in the formation of the United Nations.

Faced with the darkest depression known in this country, Democrat Franklin D. Roosevelt assumed the presidency on March 4, 1933, and the era of the New Deal was launched. His inaugural address, transmitted by radio, was heard by more people than any previous public address, and his words brought a renewal of hope and confidence:

This great Nation will endure as it has endured, will revive and prosper. So, first of all, let me assert my firm belief that the only thing we have to fear is fear itself— nameless, unreasoning, unjustified terror which paralyzes needed efforts to convert retreat into advance.[11]

A week later, on March 12, Roosevelt gave his first radio "fireside chat," in which he personalized the workings of government. The success of the fireside chat was immediate. Roosevelt continued to bring the problems and solutions of government directly to the people through some thirty of these chats, and the people responded by backing him in his programs for recovery and reform.

Following the Japanese attack on Pearl Harbor in the Hawaiian Islands, Roosevelt addressed a joint session of Congress on December 8, 1941:

Yesterday, December 7, 1941—A date which will live in infamy—the United States of America was suddenly and deliberately attacked by naval and air forces of the

Empire of Japan. . . . With confidence in our armed forces—with the unbounding determination of our people—we will gain the inevitable triumph—so help us God.[12]

The peace that came with the "inevitable triumph" ushered in an era known as the Cold War. An "iron curtain," a term employed by Winston Churchill in a speech delivered at Westminster College in Fulton, Missouri, on March 5, 1946, was drawn between the forces of communism and the free peoples of the Western world. Democratic President Harry Truman, confronted with a major crisis when the communist army of North Korea invaded South Korea in June 1950, used a radio address to declare a national emergency. Less than a year later, in a historic controversy over military policy, Truman relieved General of the Army Douglas MacArthur of his command of the United Nations Forces in the Far East, and MacArthur was honored with an invitation to address a joint session of Congress. On April 19, 1951, the respected World War II hero, receiving a tremendous ovation, stated his position and bid goodbye:

But I still remember the refrain of one of the most popular barrack ballads of that day which proclaimed most proudly that "Old soldiers never die; they just fade away." And like the old soldier of that ballad, I now close my military career and just fade away—an old soldier who tried to do his duty as God gave him the light to see that duty.[13]

A new type of participatory government, made possible by electronics, was introduced with the debates and public addresses of the two national political conventions and the succeeding presidential campaigns in 1952, when for the first time these proceedings were brought directly to the people coast to coast via television. Never before had so many people witnessed history in the making. The Republicans nominated General of the Army Dwight D. Eisenhower; the Democrats nominated the articulate governor of Illinois, Adlai E. Stevenson. Eisenhower was elected by the largest popular vote ever cast for a presidential candidate, and his inaugural address, televised on January 20, 1953, was the first to be seen and heard by millions of people throughout the country.[14]

The power of television as an element in determining the course of political events was dramatically emphasized during the fall of 1960, when the Republican candidate for the presidency, Vice President Richard M. Nixon, confronted the Democratic nominee, Senator John F. Kennedy of Massachussetts, in a series of four debates. Although the original impression of the electorate was that the candidates were equally qualified, Kennedy's fluency and charisma, transmitted to millions of viewers through the medium of television, carried the debates and, ultimately, the election. Kennedy's eloquent inaugural address, telecast on January 20, 1961, noted for its epigram, "Ask not what your country can do for you—ask what you can do for your country," sought to inspire a new beginning, a New Frontier, in attempts to solve problems both at home and abroad.[15]

The major domestic problem facing the nation during this period was civil rights. In the forefront of black protest was the Rev. Martin Luther King, Jr., who delivered hundreds of speeches and organized marches, boycotts, and sit-ins to achieve his vision of nonviolent integration. King's "I Have a Dream" speech, delivered on August 28, 1963, from the steps of the Lincoln Memorial to a crowd of more than 200,000 blacks and whites who had marched on Washington, is the most renowned public address of the civil rights movement. Advocating an opposing point of view was Malcolm X (Malcolm Little), whose address, "The Ballot or the Bullet," delivered on April 3, 1964, in Cleveland, pressed for black nationalism. Black rhetoric became more militant with Stokely Carmichael, who coined the slogan "Black Power," and H. Rap Brown, who threatened armed confrontation. The revolutionary public statements of Black Panthers Huey P. Newton, Eldridge Cleaver, and Bobby Seale expressed the ideology of Marx and Lenin. As the struggle continued into the 1970s, the debate and public address of black revolution became less inflammatory.

Concurrent with black agitation as a vital oratorical issue was the complex problem of the war in Vietnam. The question of how to achieve a permanent peace divided the nation. President Kennedy's commencement address at American University, delivered on June 10, 1963, calling for peaceful solutions to international problems, led to the Nuclear Test Ban Treaty and detente with the Soviet Union. Outspoken against appeasement with the Soviet Union was conservative Republican Senator Barry M. Goldwater, whose speech delivered at a rally sponsored by the Detroit Economic Club on March 25, 1964, urged peace through strength. As the Vietnam War continued, prominent vocal advocates of peace included Senators J. William Fulbright, George McGovern, Eugene McCarthy, and Robert F. Kennedy. The administration's Vietnam policy was openly probed on television by the Senate Foreign Relations Committee. Amid great dissension within the leadership of his own party, Democratic President Lyndon B. Johnson in a historic nationally televised address on March 31, 1968, announced both the cessation of bombing in Vietnam and his decision not to seek reelection. Unrest in the country was strong. Educators, clergymen, and other groups addressed themselves to the war issue, but young people across the nation became the most potent voice for peace. Hundreds of student demonstrations and protests on college and university campuses, some peaceful, others violent, emphatically expressed opposition to the war. Such public expression undoubtedly contributed greatly to the ceasefire agreement, effective January 28, 1973, with which the Nixon administration brought U.S. involvement in Vietnam to a close.

During this same period, the Space Age became a popular issue of debate and public address. Astronaut John H. Glenn, Jr., following his orbital flight around the earth, declared before a joint session of Congress on February 26, 1962, that "what we have done so far are but small building blocks in a huge pyramid to come."[16] Seven years later, on July 20, 1969, Neil Armstrong became the first human being to set foot on the moon. Millions of people all over the world watched and listened as Armstrong, the first person to address the planet Earth from another planetary body, proclaimed: "That's one small step for a man, one giant leap for mankind."[17]

During the 1970s, one of the popular issues debated at length was women's rights, including a proposed Equal Rights Amendment to the Constitution. This issue was exemplified by the public addresses and activities of Representative Shirley Chisholm, the first black woman elected to Congress, who in 1972 actively sought the Democratic presidential nomination. Other prominent issues of the decade included the energy crisis, culminating in an antinuclear rally in Washington, D.C., in 1979; and homosexual or "gay" rights, whose activists also marched on Washington during that year. In addition, the debate and public address centering on two historic events of the 1970s had great impact on popular culture. First, as part of the aftermath of the Watergate incident, the American public witnessed the televised debate of the Committee on the Judiciary of the House of Representatives in 1974, as members considered the possible impeachment of President Nixon. Less than two weeks later, in an address unprecedented in American history, speaking to the nation via television from the White House, Nixon announced his resignation. The other historic event of major oratorical importance during this period was the celebration of the U.S. Bicentennial during 1976. Students from more than 8,500 high schools, colleges, and universities argued pertinent topics as part of the Bicentennial Youth Debate program, and ceremonial speech activities across the nation involved many thousands.

The 1976 presidential campaign was distinguished by three televised debates between Republican President Gerald R. Ford and Democratic candidate Jimmy Carter of Georgia, marking the first such confrontation since the Kennedy-Nixon debates of 1960. The vice presidential candidates, Democratic Senator Walter F. Mondale of Minnesota and Republican Senator Robert J. Dole of Kansas, met face-to-face in a single debate, establishing the first such televised encounter. Four years later, in the fall of 1980, presidential candidate John B. Anderson, Illinois Republican congressman turned Independent, faced Republican presidential candidate Ronald Reagan of California in a single debate; and Reagan confronted President Carter, also in a single debate. The 1984 campaign saw President Reagan, dubbed the Great Communicator by the press, meet opponent Mondale in two debates and Vice President George Bush face Democratic vice presidential candidate Geraldine A. Ferraro, New York congresswoman, in one debate. Attracting millions of viewers, these debates, complex in structure and difficult to assess, afforded maximum nationwide mass involvement in debate and public address.

The 1980s witnessed two of the largest peaceful assemblies ever to take place in this country, reflecting two paramount issues which American speakers have repeatedly addressed during recent decades. On June 12, 1982, a crowd estimated to be more than 500,000 marched through Manhattan and rallied at Central Park to protest the proliferation of nuclear arms. Among the dozens of diverse speakers who exhorted the audience to press for worldwide disarmament were the Rev. William Sloane Coffin, Jr., Coretta Scott King, and Orson Welles. On August 27, 1983, a crowd of about 250,000 gathered to observe the twentieth anniversary of the Rev. Martin Luther King, Jr.'s "I Have a Dream" speech at the original site, the steps of the Lincoln Memorial in Washington. Some five hours of speeches delivered by Coretta Scott King, Benjamin Hooks, the Rev. Jesse Jackson, and Andrew Young, among others, called for jobs, peace, freedom, and a rebirth of the civil rights movement.

What must be considered a preeminent address delivered by an American in modern times was not the work of a great orator, but that of a great writer. William Faulkner, on accepting the 1949 Nobel Prize for literature at the awards ceremony in Stockholm, Sweden, held December 10, 1950, spoke to the world at a time when the fear of atomic annihilation cast a pall:

I decline to accept the end of man. It is easy enough to say that man is immortal simply because he will endure: that when the last ding-dong of doom has clanged and faded from the last worthless rock hanging tideless in the last red and dying evening, that even then there will still be one more sound: that of his puny inexhaustible voice, still talking. I refuse to accept this. I believe that man will not merely endure: he will prevail.[18]

From the town meeting to the march on Washington, debate and public address, stimulated and magnified in modern times by radio and television, has been an integral part of American popular culture. Through the power of public speaking the American people have reached the crucial decisions that have governed the country as well as the personal choices by which they have lived. Essentially, the debate and public address of America's past not only has served the immediacy of particular occasions but also has provided a rich heritage of permanent and popular literature.

REFERENCE WORKS

The reference works in debate and public address noted below include not only resources for scholarly inquiry but also means through which communication skills can be learned. There is as yet no comprehensive reference work specifically designated as an encyclopedia of American debate and public address. For information pertaining to a particular orator, a great debate, a controversial issue, or a historical movement, a library's indexing system is an appropriate first reference. The standard familiar encyclopedias frequently offer a concise overview. (As of this writing, the Annenberg School of Communications and Oxford University Press have announced the forthcoming publication of a four-volume reference, *International Encyclopedia of Communications*.)

The following three references are practical introductory works designed to prepare students who are embarking on research projects in speech communication. *Communication Research: Strategies and Sources,* by Rebecca B. Rubin, Alan M. Rubin, and Linda J. Piele, is an elementary guide to the literature available in the major areas of communication, including speech communication. This reference offers basic information on the library research process, design of the research project, and the use of computer search of on-line data bases. *Research in Speech Communication,* by Raymond K. Tucker, Richard L. Weaver II, and Cynthia Berryman-Fink, is comprehensive in its coverage. It gives an overview of research procedures and then introduces the three basic methods of problem solving: historical-critical, descriptive, and experimental. Chapters dealing with generating quantitative data and statistical models are clearly presented, and bibliographic listings are extensive. *Communication Research Methods,* by John Waite Bowers and John A. Courtright, is intended for upper-division undergraduate and beginning graduate students. It combines a social science research methods approach with data analysis and statistical concepts. The detailed application of statistics, using case studies and examples, is a major strength of this reference.

The federal government is a principal source of reference material. The U.S. Congress's *Congressional Record* is of inestimable value because it routinely prints more debates and speeches than any other U.S. publication. From the First Congress to the present, the proceedings have been reported in four series of publications: *Annals of Congress* (1789–1824); *Register of Debates* (1824–37); *Congressional Globe* (1833–73); and *Congressional Record* (1873 to date), issued daily and biweekly, and also permanently bound and indexed. Although not a verbatim or complete account of daily congressional proceedings, the *Record* is the official and most authoritative publication of the words spoken on the floor of the two houses.

The presidential papers, including public messages, speeches, and statements, as well as transcripts of news conferences, can be found in the U.S. General Services Administration's *Weekly Compilation of Presidential Documents* and annual *Public Papers of the Presidents of the United States*. References have been published for each year of office for Presidents Hoover, Truman, Eisenhower, Kennedy, Johnson, Nixon, Ford, Carter, and Reagan. The

Department of State Bulletin, issued monthly by the U.S. Department of State's Bureau of Public Affairs, is the official record of this country's foreign policy and includes major addresses and news conferences of the president and the secretary of state as well as statements made before congressional committees by the secretary and other senior Department of State officials.

The federal government produces additional publications numbering annually into the thousands. These publications cover almost every conceivable subject and can be especially useful as a source for factual data in the preparation of a speech. Since 1895, the Superintendent of Documents, U.S. Government Printing Office, has issued a monthly catalog, under various titles, listing current publications. This catalog is indexed annually by author, title, title keyword, and subject. Moreover, through various sources, there is bibliographic access to publications dating back to 1774.

Joe Morehead's *Introduction to United States Public Documents* presents a contemporary overview of accessing federal government information, including on-line data bases and microform collections. This work examines the publications, reports, and materials of the legislative, executive, and judicial branches of the government, the independent agencies with regulatory powers, and the advisory committees and commissions. Although the materials cited are not exhaustive, this reference is an appropriate starting point for gaining information from federal publications. *Government Reference Books: A Biennial Guide to U.S. Government Publications,* compiled by LeRoy C. Schwarzkopf, is an annotated guide to bibliographies, catalogs, dictionaries, indexes, and other reference works issued by agencies of the U.S. government. Also of great value as a research tool is *Index to U.S. Government Periodicals: A Computer-Generated Guide to 183 Selected Titles by Author and Subject.* This work provides access to substantive articles published in the periodicals produced by more than one hundred federal agencies.

The Speech Communication Association (SCA), 5105 Backlick Road, Bldg. E, Annandale, Virginia 22003, is a national organization that serves those who are concerned with the principles of communication, particularly speech communication. Its annual *Speech Communication Directory* provides useful current information pertaining to debate and public address. This reference is published in cooperation with the SCA's four regional organizations: Central States Speech Association, Eastern Communication Association, Southern Speech Communication Association, and Western Speech Communication Association. Listed are the names and addresses of the officers of the national association and its divisions, boards, commissions, and committees as well as those heading the regional, state, and various affiliated and related speech organizations, and the editorial staffs of the several publications. Alphabetical and geographical listings of the membership, totaling more than 6,000, are a virtual "Who's Who" in the field of speech communication. Also included is a roster of institutions of higher education that offer programs in speech and the names of appropriate administrative officers. The Speech Communication Association, in addition, publishes a separate directory of graduate programs in the speech communication arts and sciences.

Abstracts provide a convenient form for surveying contemporary scholarship: *Communication Abstracts,* a quarterly international information service edited by Thomas F. Gordon, presents current summaries of communications related literature in the various subfields of communication. These abstracts are drawn from close to 200 professional periodicals, including *International Popular Culture* and *Journal of Popular Culture,* as well as recent books and book chapters. *Dissertation Abstracts International: The Humanities and Social Sciences,* compiled monthly, publishes abstracts of doctoral dissertations offering insight into contemporary research and thought in debate and public address. These abstracts are grouped under the subheading "Speech Communication" in the "Communications and the Arts" section. More than 7,000 doctoral dissertations in communication and theater are listed in *A Guide to Doctoral Dissertations in Communication Studies and Theater,* edited by Richard Leo Enos and Jeanne L. McClaran. This guide includes dissertations filed through 1977, and among its divisions are "Forensics," "Public Address and Rhetorical Criticism," and "Rhetoric." University Microfilms International, Ann Arbor, Michigan, issues a catalog of doctoral dissertations in the broad field of communications. Citations pertinent to debate and public address can be found under the headings "Argumentation/Persuasion," "Rhetoric," and "Theory/Methods/Research."

The major bibliographies and indexes in the area of debate and public address include the following: *Bibliography of Speech Education,* compiled by Lester Thonssen and Elizabeth Fatherson in 1939, and *Bibliography of Speech Education: Supplement, 1939–1948,* compiled by Thonssen, Mary Margaret Robb, and Dorothea Thonssen, comprise an authoritative reference of articles, books, and advanced degree theses from the nineteenth century through 1948. These listings are indexed by the various areas of speech and dramatic art, including public speaking, debate, radio speaking, after-dinner speaking, and pulpit speaking. *Rhetoric and Public Address: A Bibliography, 1947–1961,,* compiled and edited by James W. Cleary and Frederick W. Haberman, is a comprehensive and clearly organized listing of articles, books, monographs, and doctoral dissertations that appeared during the period. *Bibliography of Speech and Allied Areas, 1950–1960,* by Dorothy I. Mulgrave, Clark S. Marlor, and Elmer E. Baker, Jr., is a selective compilation of doctoral dissertations and books. A major division of the work on public address includes subheadings for debate, history, orators, public speaking, and rhetoric. "A Bibliography of Rhetoric and Public Address for the Year [1947–1969]," compiled by Frederick W. Haberman and others from 1948 through 1969, which appeared initially in *Quarterly Journal of Speech* and subsequently in *Speech Monographs* (now *Communication Monographs*), offers a comprehensive bibliography of contemporary studies in the history, theory, and criticism of public address. From 1970 through 1975, this bibliography was published, together with other selective bibliographies and listings of graduate theses and dissertations in the various areas of speech communication, in *Bibliographic Annual in Speech Communication,* edited successively by Ned A. Shearer and Patrick C. Kennicott. This bibliography was discontinued with the 1975 edition. "A Bibliography of Speech and Theatre in the South for the Year [1954–1982]" (title varies), compiled by Ralph T. Eubanks, V. L. Baker, and others over the years, appeared annually in *Southern Speech Communication Journal.* Significant material relevant to communication literature of the South is listed. This bibliography was discontinued with the 1982 compilation.

Three specialized bibliographies are applicable reference works for research in debate and public address: *Political Campaign Communication: A Bibliography and Guide to the Literature, 1973–1982,* by Lynda Lee Kaid and Anne Johnston Wadsworth, cites more than 2,400 interdisciplinary entries from books, pamphlets, journal articles, dissertations, and theses relevant to American political campaign processes. *Religious Broadcasting, 1920–1983: A Selectively Annotated Bibliography,* by George H. Hill and Lenwood Davis, is a compilation of books, dissertations, theses, and articles. Subject and author indexing includes religious affiliations, networks, organizations, and personalities. The coverage in this reference is mostly of Christian radio and television broadcasting, but includes as well Baha'i, Jewish, ecumenical, and interfaith broadcasts. *Women Speaking: An Annotated Bibliography of Verbal and Nonverbal Communication, 1970–1980,* by Mary E. W. Jarrard and Phyllis R. Randall, is an interdisciplinary guide to published empirical and scholarly research on women's communication during the 1970s. Entries are organized into three divisions of communication: settings, characteristics, and means. A comprehensive subject index that lists works by specific topics, including rhetorical analysis, sex differences, sex role stereotyping, and style of speaking, is most useful.

The Speech Communication Association publishes more than forty annotated bibliographies covering various aspects of communication and distributes them for the cost of the postage. Titles include "Argumentation and Debate," "Argumentation Theory," "Black American Rhetorical Studies," "Coaching Debate and Forensics," "Communication and Gender," "Communication and Politics," "Feminist Rhetoric," "Health Communication," "Persuasion," "Political Campaign Debating," "Resources for Public Speaking," "Rhetoric of Gay Liberation," "Video Tape Resources in Speech Communication," and "Voice and Articulation."

A reference highly useful to researchers in debate and public address is *Index to Journals in Communication Studies Through 1985,* edited by Ronald J. Matlon. This publication lists primary articles, volume by volume, of fifteen major journals in communication from their inception through 1985. Works are also indexed by contributor and subject matter. *Speech Index: An Index to 259 Collections of World Famous Orations and Speeches for Various*

Occasions, composed by Roberta Briggs Sutton in 1966, and a 1966–80 supplement composed by Charity Mitchell provide a guide to speeches of famous orators from the earliest times to the present. Entries are arranged and cross-referenced by speaker, subject, and type of speech. *Index to American Women Speakers, 1828–1978,* compiled by Beverley Manning, is intended to aid in locating women's speeches, past and present. Indexed by author, subject, and title, the work encompasses the full range of women's interests but concentrates heavily on women's rights and struggles.

Audio and video recordings are a valuable primary reference. The yearly output of recordings, however, is prolific, and it is difficult to obtain a "complete" directory. *On Cassette, 1986/1987: A Comprehensive Bibliography of Spoken Word Audiocassettes* offers over 20,000 annotated and cross-referenced entries. Indexed by title, author, reader/performer, subject, producer-distributor/title, and producer/distributor, this work is current, thorough, and practical. Also useful is Gerald McKee's *Directory of Spoken-Word Audio Cassettes,* which lists offerings of nearly 700 producers of spoken-word audio cassettes. Among these listings can be found tapes dealing with speaking skills. Such titles as "Effective Public Speaking," "Speak for Success," and "How to Enter the World of Paid Speaking" illustrate available resources. This work includes the names and addresses of the producers/distributors and a subject index. *Video Source Book,* published annually since 1979, contains more than 40,000 video cassette programs available from 850 sources. Entries are classified by title, subject, and wholesaler. Titles listed in the subject index under "Communication" include "How to Make a More Effective Speech" and "Speaking Before a Group"; titles listed under "Speech" include "Preparing to Speak" and "Public Speaking." The producers or distributors indexed in the above directories will usually fill a request free of charge for their brochure or catalog.

Professional speakers who are stimulating or entertaining are always in demand, and prospective audiences can find assistance in locating them. *Speakers and Lecturers: How to Find Them. A Directory of Booking Agents, Lecture Bureaus, Companies, Professional and Trade Associations, Universities, and Other Groups Which Organize and Schedule Engagements for Lecturers and Public Speakers on All Subjects, with Information on Speakers, Subjects, and Arrangements, and Biographical Details on over 2,000 Individuals,* edited by Paul Wasserman, is of considerable use in bringing together speakers and audiences. Howard J. Langer's *Directory of Speakers* contains an alphabetical listing of about 1,300 available speakers. This work is indexed by both geographical area and subject and includes a short biographical sketch of each speaker. The International Platform Association, with executive offices in Winnetka, Illinois, is a nonprofit organization that promotes the professional speaking interests of its approximately 5,000 members. This organization is the successor to the International Lyceum Association, established in 1903, and traces its origins to the American Lyceum Association, which was founded by Daniel Webster and Josiah Holbrook in 1831. Its members are professional lecturers and others who appear before live audiences to inform and entertain, as well as program chairmen, booking agents, and men and women of various fields who are interested in oratory and the power of the spoken word. The International Platform Association sponsors an Orator's Hall of Fame, whose members are such renowned speakers as William Jennings Bryan, John F. Kennedy, Martin Luther King, Jr., Abraham Lincoln, Douglas MacArthur, Franklin D. Roosevelt, Adlai Stevenson, and Daniel Webster.

Debating and public speaking is not only an area of interest to the critic or historian but also a skill that can be acquired. Skill in debating and public speaking is probably best learned in the classroom under the guidance of an instructor with the aid of a suitable textbook selected from an abundant supply on the market. Several of the more widely recognized books and sources that offer instruction in speaking in public are presented first; then publications that treat educational or academic debate are considered. Many textbooks, of course, are written so that a person of average intelligence and discipline can use them as references for self-study. *Principles and Types of Speech Communication,* by Douglas Ehninger, Bruce E. Gronbeck, Ray E. McKerrow, and Alan H. Monroe, used on college campuses for more than fifty years and now in its tenth edition, is a leading basic textbook. The authors are noted for their organizational pattern for persuasive speeches known as the "motivated sequence." Included are chapters detailing the adapting of a speech to an audience, outlining a speech, and the use of visual aids, as well as sample speeches for study and analysis. *The Art of Public Speaking,* by Stephen E. Lucas, is a second widely used basic textbook, and here, too, the public speaking process is explicated step by step from preparation through delivery. Rudolph F. Verderber's *The Challenge of Effective Speaking* is a third significant textbook. Chapters treating descriptive speeches, speeches of definition, expository speeches, persuasive speeches, speeches of conviction, speeches to actuate, and speeches of refutation are clearly presented. A somewhat different format from the above textbooks is offered in *The Speaker's Handbook,* by Jo Sprague and Douglas Stuart. Using a prescriptive approach, this work is cross-referenced, with endpapers, a subject index, and tabbed and numbered running heads. *The Communication Handbook: A Dictionary,* by Joseph A. DeVito, is a practical supplemental guide. Terms are defined either briefly or in essay form to make them understandable and useable; and for some entries, sources for further reference are offered.

In addition to traditional textbooks, there are numerous books designed for do-it-yourself popular use. These works frequently are written by well-known persons and are anecdotal in format. Current examples include Steve

Allen's *How to Make a Speech,* Ed McMahon's *The Art of Public Speaking,* and Jack Valenti's *Speak Up with Confidence: How to Prepare, Learn, and Deliver Effective Speeches.* A popular offering of this sort, also, is Dale Carnegie's *The Quick and Easy Way to Effective Speaking.* Collections of humorous stories, quotations, epigrams, and unusual facts and illustrations for the speaker are readily available. *The Public Speaker's Treasure Chest* and a companion volume, *The Toastmaster's Treasure Chest,* by Herbert V. Prochnow and Herbert V. Prochnow, Jr., are examples of this type of reference.

Instruction in public speaking is offered by both commercial and noncommercial organizations in communities throughout the country. Listings of commercial organizations can be obtained by consulting the classified pages of the local telephone directory under such headings as "Public Speaking Instruction." Probably the most widely known commercial organization engaged in the teaching of public speaking is Dale Carnegie, which is international in scope. The Carnegie method has proven successful for hundreds of thousands of students since 1912. Other commercial programs are competitive.

Among the noncommercial organizations that provide opportunities to develop skills in public speaking is Toastmasters International. The first Toastmasters club was established in 1924; and local Toastmasters groups now number more than 5,600, with a membership of approximately 120,000 in over forty-seven countries. Each local group consists of about twenty to forty persons who meet regularly to learn and practice techniques of public speaking and constructive evaluation. Included in the organization's annual activities are the sponsorship of the World Championship of Public Speaking and the bestowal of the Golden Gavel Award to a prominent communicator. *Toastmaster Magazine,* a monthly publication, is devoted to relevant news and articles. Toastmasters International is affiliated with Gavel Clubs, an organization of sixty local groups with about 2,500 members who cannot participate in the complete Toastmasters club program. Both of the above organizations are headquartered in Santa Ana, California. International Training in Communication, formerly International Toastmistress Club, founded in 1938, is an organization of over 1,400 local groups with headquarters in Anaheim, California. This is an association of approximately 27,000 adults who are interested in speech improvement and communication.

Educational debate in this country is conducted under the guidance of both secondary and collegiate institutions. Several formats for educational debating are officially recognized, and each is organized in accordance with established rules and procedures applicable to competitive tournament debating. Austin J. Freeley's *Argumentation and Debate: Critical Thinking for Reasoned Decision Making* is a comprehensive textbook that has been used for the typical undergraduate course in argumentation and debate for a quarter of a century. Chapters dealing with evidence, reasoning, case construction, evaluation, and tournament procedures are clear and authoritative. This work covers national intercollegiate debate practices for the American Forensic Association's National Debate Tournament (NDT) as well as for the programs of the Cross Examination Debate Association (CEDA). Appendixes include the second Reagan-Mondale debate of 1984, a transcript of an intercollegiate debate of 1984, a listing of the NDT national intercollegiate debate propositions from the academic year 1920–21 through 1985–86, and a listing of the CEDA national debate propositions from the academic year 1971–72 through 1985–86. *Contemporary Debate,* by J. W. Patterson and David Zarefsky, offers an introduction to argumentation and debate theory. The text makes extensive use of hypothetical illustrations in discussing the decision-making process, with a solid explanation of testing hypotheses, and also serves as a handbook for the academic debater. *Introduction to Debate,* edited by Carolyn Keefe, Thomas B. Harte, and Laurence E. Norton, is a basic text for undergraduate debating students. Of special relevance for contemporary reference is Keefe's chapter, "Debate Ethics and Morality." The revised edition of *The Debater's Guide,* by Jon M. Ericson and James J. Murphy, with Raymond Bud Zeuschner, is both thorough in coverage and concise in format. Appropriate for either collegiate or secondary use, this volume treats the underlying concepts of building the debate case, constructing affirmative and negative cases, refutation, cross-examination, and delivery style. For the experienced debater, *Advanced Debate: Readings in Theory, Practice and Teaching,* edited by David A. Thomas and Jack Hart, presents fifty-two readings contributed by authorities in all areas of debate. Appendixes include a guide to reference works, a selected bibliography, and a glossary. *Basic Debate,* by Maridell Fryar, David A. Thomas, and Lynn Goodnight, is intended for the novice high school debater. This beginning text deals with basic forensic skills; principles of affirmative case, negative case, and cross-examination; and mechanics, preparation, and strategies for student congress. *Student Congress and Lincoln-Douglas Debate,* by Maridell Fryar and David A. Thomas, offers insight into the theory and practice of these two specialized high school forensic events. An additional reference of interest to academic debaters is the "Opposing Viewpoints" series published by Greenhaven Press, St. Paul, Minnesota. Available in three separate categories—books, pamphlets, and sources—this series offers diverse points of view on a broad spectrum of contemporary issues.

Resource materials pertaining to the annual debate topics are available from various sources: governmental, institutional, and commercial. The Superintendent of Documents, U.S. Government Printing Office, annually publishes a bibliography applicable to the topics: *Subject Bibliography 043,* which furnishes an annotated listing of government publications relating to the national high school debate topic; and *Subject Bibliography 176,* which furnishes an annotated listing of government publications relating to the college debate topic. Among the leading sources that offer materials on the high school topic are the Speech Communication Association, Annandale, Virginia; the National Forensic League, Ripon, Wisconsin; the American Enterprise Institute for Public Policy Research, Washington, D.C.; and the National Textbook Company, Lincolnwood, Illinois. Sources offering handbooks and other materials relating to the college topic include the Study Group of the Alan Company, Clayton, Missouri, and Springboards, Inc., St. Louis, Missouri. The above list is only a sampling. Additional information on debating and debate resources may be obtained by writing to the Secretary of the American Forensic Association, University of Wisconsin-River Falls, River Falls, Wisconsin 54022, or by consulting the *Speech Communication Directory,* referred to above.

An appropriate first reference in researching the area of educational debate is Arthur N. Kruger's *Argumentation and Debate: A Classified Bibliography*. This work contains approximately 6,000 entries, of which about 650 are listings of doctoral dissertations and master's theses. With an emphasis on studies published in the United States during the twentieth century, this bibliography is subdivided into the various areas of debate, including history, ethics, debate organizations, forms of debate, high school forensics, collections, and bibliographies, and is indexed by both author and subject.

Compilations of intercollegiate debates provide useful reference tools for many aspects of debating. Among these compilations are the following two series: *Intercollegiate Debates: Being Briefs and Reports of Many Intercollegiate Debates,* a work of twenty-two volumes edited successively by Paul M. Pearson and Egbert Ray Nichols, presents selective affirmative and negative debates on important topics of the day as argued by various college debate teams from 1909 to 1941. A compilation of thirty-seven volumes, *University Debaters' Annual: Constructive and Rebuttal Speeches Delivered in Debates of American Colleges and Universities During the College Year,* edited successively by Edward Charles Mabie, Edith M. Phelps, and Ruth Ulman, offers representative intercollegiate debates and other forensic activities presented on American campuses from the academic year 1914–15 through 1950–51. Selected bibliography and briefs accompany each debate. Debates from these two series as well as numerous other debates, arguments, and briefs are listed by subject in *Debate Index,* compiled by Edith M. Phelps; *Debate Index Supplement,* compiled by Julia E. Johnsen; and *Debate Index Second Supplement,* compiled by Joseph R. Dunlap and Martin A. Kuhn.

Championship Debating—West Point National Debate Tournament Final-Round Debates and Critiques, 1949–60, together with a second volume published six years later, both edited by Russel R. Windes and Arthur N. Kruger, provides a record of the annual National Debate Tournament from its inception at the U.S. Military Academy in 1947 through 1966, when the American Forensic Association assumed responsibility for conducting the tournament. For the years 1967 through 1985, transcripts of the final round of the National Debate Tournament appeared in the *Journal of the American Forensic Association*. The debates of 1986 have been published in the first volume of a new annual series sponsored by the Speech Communication Association and the American Forensic Association with the cooperation of the Cross Examination Debate Association and the National Forensic Association. *Championship Debates and Speeches,* edited by John K. Boaz and James R. Brey, presents the 1986 National Debate Tournament Final Debate, sponsored by the American Forensic Association; the 1986 National CEDA Tournament Final Debate, sponsored by the Cross Examination Debate Association; the 1986 National Individual Events Tournament: Winning Speeches in Original Events, sponsored by the American Forensic Association; and the 1986 National Championship Tournament in Individual Speaking Events: Winning Speeches in Original Events, sponsored by the National Forensic Association. Critiques of the judges of each event add greatly to the use of these transcripts as a reference work.

An international debate program between teams from the United States and those of foreign countries has been established since the early part of the twentieth century. *Fifty Years of International Debate, 1922–1972,* by Robert N. Hall and Jack L. Rhodes, is a brief documentation beginning with the visit of the Oxford University debating team to Bates College, Lewiston, Maine, in 1922, and concluding with the visit on American campuses of a team from the Soviet Union in the spring of 1972. Current information about international debating can be obtained from the program's sponsor, the Committee on International Discussion and Debate of the Speech Communication Association.

RESEARCH COLLECTIONS

The researcher in American debate and public address will find it difficult to locate specific collections so designated. Collections are more easily located by the name of the speaker, occasion, or issue.

A logical first reference to research collections is *Research Centers Directory,* edited by Mary Michelle Watkins. The several indexes in this work are of considerable aid to the researcher; but there are no listings in the subject index for debate, public address, or oratory. References to general collections, however, can be found in the subject index under "Communication Arts," "Communication in Management," and "Communication in Organizations."

A second comprehensive reference is Lee Ash and William G. Miller's computerized compilation, *Subject Collections: A Guide to Special Book Collections and Subject Emphases as Reported by University, College, Public, and Special Libraries and Museums in the United States and Canada.* This work presents an alphabetical listing of subjects and persons for whom collections have been established. Again, no listings are offered for debate, public address, or oratory. The only listing under "Public Speaking and Speakers" is that of the Chauncey Mitchell Depew Collection in the library of George Washington University. Entries are included, however, for presidential collections as well as for many individuals well known for their oratory.

A third guide of considerable scope is *Directory of Special Libraries and Information Centers: A Guide to More Than 18,000 Special Libraries, Research Libraries, Information Centers, Archives, and Data Centers Maintained by Government Agencies, Business, Industry, Newspapers, Educational Institutions, Nonprofit Organizations, and Societies in the Fields of Science and Technology, Medicine, Law, Art, Religion, the Social Sciences, and Humanistic Studies*, edited by Brigitte T. Darnay. There are no listings for debate, public address, or oratory; and the listings under "Speech" are a combination of speech communication and speech science. Among the research collections in speech communication described in this work are those at the following centers: ERIC Clearinghouse on Reading and Communication Skills, National Council of Teachers of English, Urbana, Illinois (annotated below); Humanities Division Library, Southern Illinois University, Carbondale; Emerson College Library, Boston; and Sciences-Engineering Library, University of California, Santa Barbara. This directory also describes numerous collections of sound recordings.

A fourth major source of information pertaining to research collections is the annual *American Library Directory*. The collections of more than 37,000 libraries are listed by geographical communities within each state, the regions administered by the United States, and the provinces of Canada. Among the listings are the libraries and archives of ABC, CBS, and NBC in New York, where each of the three major commercial radio and television networks maintains collections dealing, in part, with current issues and events; and Thirteen Research Library of the Educational Broadcasting Corporation in New York, which holds audiovisual materials and videotapes of public interest.

Special Collections in Libraries of the Southeast, edited by J. B. Howell, smaller in scope than the above guides, includes annotations of relevant collections in all types of libraries in the ten states comprising the southeastern part of the country. These collections are listed by person or subject under geographical communities for each state. This guide is especially useful for researching prominent local citizens and regional history. *Library and Reference Facilities in the Area of the District of Columbia*, edited by Margaret S. Jennings, lists holdings in the Washington area. Included are those of the Democratic National Committee Research/Issues Library and the Republican National Committee Library, both of political interest.

Complementing the above directories as a valuable source for researchers of debate and public address in popular culture is the *National Union Catalogue of Manuscript Collections*, compiled by the U.S. Library of Congress. The first twenty-two issues in this ongoing series, which cover the years

1959 through 1984, describe approximately 54,799 collections located in 1,297 repositories in the United States. The cumulative indexes categorize approximately 597,000 references to topical subjects and personal, family, corporate, and geographical names.

1988 Directory of Communication Research Centers in North American Universities, compiled by Barry S. Sapolsky, Jodi S. Hale, and Jayme Harpring, tabulates pertinent data for fifty-two communication research centers and institutes affiliated with universities in the United States and Canada. This spiral-bound guide includes the governance structure, staffing, facilities, funding, publications, methodologies, and research pursuits for each listing.

The Educational Resources Information Center (ERIC), sponsored by the Office of Educational Research and Improvement of the U.S. Department of Education, offers access to education-related journal articles as well as hard-to-find unpublished, noncopyrighted documents. ERIC, formed in 1966, consists of a national network of sixteen clearinghouses, each representing a broad educational subject area, integrated through a central computerized facility. Materials related to debate and public address are processed through the ERIC Clearinghouse on Reading and Communication Skills (ERIC/RCS), which is located at the headquarters of the National Council of Teachers of English (NCTE), 1111 Kenyon Road, Urbana, Illinois 61801. Three guides facilitate a search for information from ERIC's bibliographic data base: *Thesaurus of ERIC Descriptors* is the source of subject headings and vocabulary for information retrieval from the ERIC collections. The U.S. Department of Education's monthly *Resources in Education,* originated as *Research in Education,* indexes such "fugitive literature" as speeches, position papers, and research reports. Microfiche or paper copies of most of the listed documents are available from ERIC Document Reproduction Service, Alexandria, Virginia. *Current Index to Journals in Education* (CIJE) is an annotated index to articles from more than 760 publications in the field of education and peripherally related areas, including the major speech journals. Reprints of many of the journal articles can be ordered from University Microfilms International, Article Clearinghouse, Ann Arbor, Michigan. Options for searching the ERIC data base also include three on-line vendors: BRS Information Technologies, Latham, New York; DIALOG Information Services, Palo Alto, California; and SDC Information Services, Santa Monica, California.

The presidential libraries and museums, which are maintained by the National Archives and Records Administration, Washington, D.C., are a primary source for rhetorical research. These collections, listed below, house official public papers pertaining to all aspects of the presidency and include presidential speech texts and voice recordings of speeches: Herbert Hoover Library, West Branch, Iowa (some papers being filed at Stanford University); Franklin D. Roosevelt Library, Hyde Park, New York; Harry S. Truman Library, Independence, Missouri; Dwight D. Eisenhower Library,

Abilene, Kansas; John F. Kennedy Library, Boston, Massachusetts; Lyndon Baines Johnson Presidential Library, Austin, Texas; Gerald R. Ford Library, Ann Arbor, Michigan (the Ford Museum being located in Grand Rapids); and Jimmy Carter Library, Atlanta, Georgia. As of this writing, the site for Richard M. Nixon's library and the plans for a library for Ronald Reagan's papers are still in the process of negotiation. Together these collections span a time period of more than the past fifty years.

Collections of audio and video recordings have reflected the growth of the recording and broadcasting industries as well as the increased recognition of recordings as a primary research source. Most sound collections concentrate on music of all types; however, the researcher will find spoken-word recordings in abundance, including recordings of addresses, debates, newscasts, readings, lectures, and oral history. "Recorded Sound Collections: New Materials to Explore the Past," an article by Ellen Reid Gold, describes the country's leading sound collections of interest to the researcher in debate and public address.

Two national archives housed in Washington, D.C., are of major importance. The collection of the Motion Picture, Broadcasting, and Recorded Sound Division of the Library of Congress encompasses some 1.5 million sound recordings on disc, tape, wire, and cylinder. Holdings include radio programs from 1924 to the present and television programs on tape and film from 1948 to the present, as well as recordings of the National Press Club luncheon speakers and NBC Radio broadcasts. A substantial collection of recorded sound is also held by the Motion Picture, Sound, and Video Branch of the National Archives and Records Administration. Recordings of speeches, panel discussions, press conferences, court and conference proceedings, interviews, entertainment programs, and news broadcasts have been gathered largely from the various federal agencies but include as well many from private and other sources. Thus, the holdings in this collection are mostly unpublished or not commercially available. These recordings date from the 1890s and include the voices of Presidents Theodore Roosevelt, William Howard Taft, Woodrow Wilson, Warren G. Harding, and Calvin Coolidge. Also included are the special collections of ABC Radio, American Town Meeting of the Air, League of Nations, and National Public Radio.

Among the major collections of sound recordings throughout the country of interest to researchers in debate and public address are the following: Stanford Archive of Recorded Sound, Braun Music Center, Stanford University, Stanford, California; Yale Collection of Historical Sound Recordings, Sterling Memorial Library, Yale University, New Haven, Connecticut, which contains recordings of historical interest in the fields of drama, politics, literature, and documentary from the end of the nineteenth century to the present, with an emphasis on the history of performance practice in the arts; G. Robert Vincent Voice Library, Michigan State University, East Lansing, Michigan, which houses historical sound recordings of voices and events in all fields of human endeavor; Record Collection of the Donnell Library Center, New York Public Library, New York City, which includes recordings of speeches and documentaries; Rodgers and Hammerstein Archives of Recorded Sound, Performing Arts Research Center, New York Public Library, New York City, which holds materials dealing with the performing arts as well as literary, historical, and political events; Audio Archives of the George Arents Research Library for Special Collections, E. S. Bird Library, Syracuse University, Syracuse, New York, which includes among its 250,000 items sound recordings of political leaders, poets, theatrical personalities, singers, and transcriptions of audio broadcasts dating from the earliest of the Thomas Edison cylinder recordings to the present; and the Phonoarchive at the University of Washington, School of Communication, Seattle, Washington. Holdings in the recorded sound collections listed above are indexed or described in various catalogs, brochures, and articles which are available through the archivists.

A collection of particular interest is Arnold's Archives, 1106 Eastwood, S.E., East Grand Rapids, Michigan 49506, which offers spoken-word recordings by hundreds of figures associated with American popular culture. Available are the recorded voices of such varied personalities as P. T. Barnum, Roberto Clemente, Jack Dempsey, Amelia Earhart, Helen Keller, Fiorello LaGuardia, Joe Louis, Joseph R. McCarthy, Jacqueline Kennedy Onassis, Babe Ruth, Norman Thomas, and Walter Winchell.

A fascinating archive of taped radio and television programs spanning a period from the 1920s to the present is housed in the Museum of Broadcasting, New York City. This collection's audiotapes and videotapes, which can be monitored in console booths, preserve a wide variety of broadcasts, including presidential oratory beginning with Warren G. Harding as well as addresses of the World War II era. The museum issues a subject guide to its collection.

The Vanderbilt Television News Archive, Nashville, Tennessee, contains videotapes of the evening news telecasts of the three major networks as seen in Nashville. This collection dates from August 5, 1968, and now consists of more than 11,000 hours of news tapes. In addition, this archive houses approximately 3,600 hours of tapes of special newscasts of such events as presidential speeches and press conferences, and presidential and vice presidential debates. These holdings, which are readily accessible and rapidly expanding, include coverage of the Democratic and Republican national conventions of 1968, 1972, 1976, 1980, and 1984, as well as such diverse historical events as the Nixon impeachment debates of 1974 and the reopening celebration of the Statue of Liberty of July 4, 1986. These tapes are indexed by subject and date in *Television News Index and Abstracts: A Guide to the Videotape Collection of the Network Evening News Programs in the Vanderbilt Television News Archive.*

HISTORY AND CRITICISM

American debate and public address emerged as a discrete area of scholarly inquiry in higher education in this country during the early part of the twentieth century. Any contemporary approach to the study of the history and criticism of American debate and public address, however, has its roots in the rhetorical theory of philosophers and scholars dating back to the ancient Greeks.

Among the preeminent classical works that modern critics embrace are Plato's *Gorgias* and *Phaedrus;* Aristotle's *The Rhetoric,* considered to this day the single most thorough and influential philosophical analysis of the art of speaking; Cicero's *De Oratore* (55 B.C.); Quintilian's *Institutio Oratoria* (Education of an Orator, ca. A.D. 93); Longinus's *On the Sublime* (ca. first half of the first century); Francis Bacon's *The Advancement of Learning* (1605); George Campbell's *The Philosophy of Rhetoric* (1776); Hugh Blair's *Lectures on Rhetoric and Belles Lettres* (1783); and Richard Whately's *Elements of Rhetoric* (1828). Complete translations and reprints of these works are readily available. Pertinent excerpts from the writings named above of Plato, Aristotle, Cicero, Quintilian, and Longinus may be found in translation in *Readings in Classical Rhetoric,* edited by Thomas W. Benson and Michael H. Prosser; and *The Rhetoric of Blair, Campbell, and Whately,* by James L. Golden and Edward P. J. Corbett, offers substantial selections from the works of these three theorists. *The Rhetoric of Western Thought,* by James L. Golden, Goodwin F. Berquist, and William E. Coleman, surveys major theory through the three great periods: the classical period of Greece and Rome, the British period of the seventeenth to the nineteenth century, and the contemporary period of the twentieth century. Dividing contemporary rhetorical theory into four areas, "Rhetoric as Meaning," "Rhetoric as Value," "Rhetoric as Motive," and "Rhetoric as a Way of Knowing," the authors explore works of renowned theorists I. A. Richards, Marshall McLuhan, Richard Weaver, Kenneth Burke, Stephen Toulmin, and Chaim Perelman.

An overview recounting the study and practice of rhetorical criticism from the early twentieth century through its development into the 1970s can be found in Charles J. Stewart's "Historical Survey: Rhetorical Criticism in Twentieth Century America," the lead essay in *Explorations in Rhetorical Criticism,* edited by G. P. Mohrmann, Charles J. Stewart, and Donovan J. Ochs. The following two works serve well as an introduction to rhetorical theory and criticism: *Contemporary Theories of Rhetoric: Selected Readings,* edited by Richard L. Johannesen, which offers relevant essays and selections from the works of contemporary theorists Burke, McLuhan, Perelman, Richards, Toulmin, and Weaver; and Douglas Ehninger's *Contemporary Rhetoric: A Reader's Coursebook,* an anthology of twenty-seven essays, which presents an overview of contemporary rhetorical scholarship grouped by subject areas. A more recent work, *Contemporary Perspectives on Rhetoric,* by

Sonja K. Foss, Karen A. Foss, and Robert Trapp, also functions as an introduction to contemporary rhetoric, treating the works of Richards, Weaver, Toulmin, Perelman, and Burke, as well as Ernesto Grassi, Michel Foucault, and Jürgen Habermas. Worthy of note are the synthesis in the final chapter and the well-organized bibliography.

Historical Studies of Rhetoric and Rhetoricians, edited by Raymond F. Howes, offers twenty-two essays by distinguished scholars, including Carroll C. Arnold, Hoyt H. Hudson, Everett Lee Hunt, Wayland Maxfield Parrish, Karl R. Wallace, Herbert A. Wichelns, and James A. Winans. In a work sponsored by the Speech Communication Association and edited by Lloyd F. Bitzer and Edwin Black, *The Prospect of Rhetoric: Report of the National Developmental Project,* leading rhetoricians attempt to answer the question, What is the essential outline of a conception of rhetoric useful in the second half of the twentieth century? This report concludes in part that, because modern technology has created new channels and techniques of communication, the scope of rhetorical studies should be broadened to explore such contemporary phenomena as popular music, news reporting and interpretation, and film, which have become increasingly influential in American culture. A collection of essays, *Form and Genre: Shaping Rhetorical Action,* edited by Karlyn Kohrs Campbell and Kathleen Hall Jamieson, was published as a result of the 1976 conference on " 'Significant Form' in Rhetorical Criticism," under the auspices of the Speech Communication Association. The contributors, who include Herbert Simons, Edwin Black, Michael Halloran, Ronald Carpenter, Bruce E. Gronbeck, Ernest G. Bormann, and the editors, explore theoretical perspectives and their possible application to new rhetorical understanding.

Among the many significant essays published during this century of interest to the modern student of rhetorical history and critical theory, three are paramount. "The Literary Criticism of Oratory" (1925) by Herbert A. Wichelns sets forth the neo-Aristotelian approach, which established the standard for much of the criticism that followed in the 1930s and 1940s. "Public Address: A Study in Social and Intellectual History" (1947) by Ernest J. Wrage urges an idea-centered critical orientation as an alternative to the traditional speaker-centered approach. Both of these essays have been reprinted in *Methods of Rhetorical Criticism: A Twentieth-Century Perspective,* a solid introductory textbook edited by Bernard L. Brock and Robert L. Scott. The third essay, "Rhetoric: Its Function and Its Scope" (1953) by Donald C. Bryant, discusses aspects of rhetoric as instrumental, critical, philosophical, and social disciplines. Bryant's essay has been reexamined in his more recent *Rhetorical Dimensions in Criticism.*

Distinguished collections of essays published in honor of an esteemed colleague, used as textbooks or for reference, have contributed greatly to the whole of speech history and criticism. Several are briefly listed: *Studies in Rhetoric and Public Speaking in Honor of James Albert Winans,* edited by

A. M. Drummond, is a volume of eleven scholarly papers including the aforementioned "The Literary Criticism of Oratory." The seventeen studies offered in *The Rhetorical Idiom: Essays in Rhetoric, Oratory, Language, and Drama Presented to Herbert August Wichelns with a Reprinting of His "Literary Criticism of Oratory"* (1925), edited by Donald C. Bryant, include Karl R. Wallace's "Rhetoric, Politics, and Education of the Ready Man," of political interest, and Bryant's " 'A Peece of a Logician': The Critical Essayist as Rhetorician," of literary interest. *American Public Address: Studies in Honor of Albert Craig Baird,* edited by Loren Reid, presents fifteen critical essays on such speakers as Oliver Wendell Holmes, Clarence Darrow, Ralph J. Bunche, and Edward R. Murrow. *Rhetoric in Transition: Studies in the Nature and Uses of Rhetoric,* edited by Eugene E. White and presented as a tribute to Carroll C. Arnold, offers ten essays by leading scholars, including Lloyd F. Bitzer, Robert L. Scott, Edwin Black, and Douglas Ehninger. The essays included in *Explorations in Rhetoric: Studies in Honor of Douglas Ehninger,* edited by Ray E. McKerrow, provide insights into areas of classical rhetoric.

Textbooks published during the last several decades on the theory and practice of rhetorical criticism offer various theoretical definitions and critical methodologies. These different approaches are not mutually exclusive. In the critical evaluation of debate and public address, it is frequently sound not to rely solely on the work of one critic or one method. Five widely accepted works are discussed here. *Speech Criticism,* by Lester Thonssen, A. Craig Baird, and Waldo W. Braden, is a comprehensive introductory treatise that is grounded in the classics. The authors deal with the nature of rhetorical criticism, development of theory, methods of the critics, and standards of judgment, and provide extensive bibliographies for further study. Carroll C. Arnold's introductory textbook, *Criticism of Oral Rhetoric,* clearly written and practical, uses a traditionalist approach to analysis. The beginning student may also wish to peruse an earlier work, Anthony Hillbruner's *Critical Dimensions: The Art of Public Address Criticism,* in which the author cogently and concisely treats the standard extrinsic and intrinsic factors of public address. Also intended for the beginning student is a slim paperback which approaches the criticism and evaluation of public address from a traditional rhetorical point of view: Robert S. Cathcart's *Post-Communication: Critical Analysis and Evaluation.* Edwin Black's provocative and controversial work, *Rhetorical Criticism: A Study in Method,* is written for the advanced or graduate student and the professional audience. Black attacks the shortcomings of the various approaches to rhetorical criticism, particularly the neo-Aristotelian, as he considers the entire genre of the argumentative process.

Other works deal forthrightly with the process and practice of critical analysis by providing applicable examples of important speeches and by illuminating a particular means by which "to do criticism." Lionel Crocker's *Rhetorical Analysis of Speeches* offers a paragraph-by-paragraph rhetorical analysis of eleven speeches by such orators as Franklin D. Roosevelt, Harry Emerson Fosdick, Wendell L. Willkie, and Lyndon B. Johnson, as well as the famous persuasive speeches of Brutus and Antony in Shakespeare's *Julius Caesar* (III, ii). L. Patrick Devlin's *Contemporary Political Speaking,* in analyzing the nature of oral politics, presents thirteen topics and speakers of political significance in the 1960s and 1970s, including verbatim transcripts of their speeches. *Critiques of Contemporary Rhetoric,* by Karlyn Kohrs Campbell, discusses the rhetorical process and the traditional, psychological, and dramatistic systems of criticism and includes nine speeches by such leaders as Richard M. Nixon, George Wald, Spiro T. Agnew, Eldridge Cleaver, Jo Freeman, and Emmet John Hughes. In *A Choice of Worlds: The Practice and Criticism of Public Discourse,* assuming that the student of public address is both a producer and a consumer, James R. Andrews presents six basic principles of rhetoric as guides for both the speaker and the critic and for illustration selects twelve speeches on historical and contemporary issues. Andrews's more recent work, *The Practice of Rhetorical Criticism,* is also intended for undergraduate courses in rhetorical criticism. The first part of this sourcebook submits an overview of the nature of criticism, context and audience, speaker, and analysis; the second part reprints Richard M. Nixon's "Address to the Nation on the War in Vietnam, November 3, 1969," and offers critical analysis of it by Robert P. Newman, Hermann G. Stelzner, Karlyn Kohrs Campbell, and Forbes Hill; and the third part presents studies by contemporary scholars illustrating a variety of critical approaches.

Great Speeches for Criticism and Analysis, by Lloyd E. Rohler and Roger Cook, groups transcripts of speeches, mostly well-known, into the two broad categories of deliberative speeches and ceremonial speeches. The initial chapter describes critical theories, and critical examinations accompany some of the speeches. Of particular interest is Lois J. Einhorn's essay, which addresses the issue of ghostwriting. The speeches range chronologically from Franklin D. Roosevelt's "First Inaugural Address" (1933) through Ronald Reagan's "Tribute to the *Challenger* Astronauts" (1986). Videotapes of most of the speeches included in this collection are available in a series of four volumes, each with five speakers, making this work an especially valuable learning instrument.

History of American Oratory, by Warren Choate Shaw, published in 1928, is recognized as the first comprehensive history of American oratory. Shaw presents descriptive studies of twenty-one representative orators from Patrick Henry to Woodrow Wilson and includes a pertinent bibliography for each. Of greater influence today, however, is *A History and Criticism of American Public Address,* a seminal study published in two volumes in 1943, edited by William Norwood Brigance, and followed twelve years later by a third volume, edited by Marie Kathryn Hochmuth. Brigance's work is divided into two parts: Part 1 presents a historical background of public address from the colonial period through 1930; Part 2 offers twenty-nine analytical studies of leaders from the fields of religion, reform, law, general culture, education, labor, and statecraft, ranging chronologically from Jonathan Edwards to Woodrow Wilson. The analyses vary in style and scope but are uniformly sound. Hochmuth introduces the third volume with a significant essay, "The Criticism of Rhetoric," and presents critical studies of such orators as Alexander Hamilton, Susan B. Anthony, Clarence Darrow, Theodore Roosevelt, William E. Borah, Harry Emerson Fosdick, and Franklin D. Roosevelt. The extensive footnotes, bibliographies, and indexes contribute to the usefulness of these three volumes.

The Rhetoric of Protest and Reform: 1878–1898, edited by Paul H. Boase, presents thirteen essays divided into five parts that deal with labor protest, the agrarian revolt, women speakers, religious issues, and the efforts of intellectuals in the reform movement. Primarily historical or neo-Aristotelian in their critical approach, the essayists together offer a survey of public address from the "Gilded Age" through the "Gay Nineties" as orators spoke out against injustice and corruption in their struggle toward democratic reform.

Robert T. Oliver's *History of Public Speaking in America* is an evaluative work of broad scope, which illuminates the influence of public address on the flow of history from the earliest period through the era of Woodrow Wilson. Oliver's style is anecdotal, and the work includes extensive bibliographies. A volume as insightful and utilitarian as Oliver's, and more current in coverage, is *America in Controversy: History of American Public Address,* edited by DeWitte Holland. While Oliver concentrates largely on individual orators and their contributions, Holland presents an idea- and issue-centered study, an analytic work which traces twenty-four significant debates, beginning with evangelism among the Indians in the Massachusetts Bay Colony through the peace movement and the Vietnam War. The rhetoric of the polarity of views is developed and supported for such major controversies as the separation of church and state, the Constitution, slavery, imperialism, the agrarian issue, socialism, suffrage and prohibition, the New Deal, internal communism, the black revolution, and freedom of speech in the 1960s. A different approach is taken by Barnet Baskerville in *The People's Voice: The Orator in American Society.* Baskerville examines the changing role of the orator and attitudes toward oratory throughout periods of American history from "The Revolutionary Period: The Orator as Hero" to "The Contemporary Scene: The Decline of Eloquence." This lively work elucidates America's political, social, and intellectual history.

American Orators Before 1900: Critical Studies and Sources and its companion volume, *American Orators of the Twentieth Century: Critical Studies and Sources,* both edited by Bernard K. Duffy and Halford R. Ryan, offer critical essays treating public speakers from various fields of endeavor, including presidents, congressional leaders, diverse individuals largely known for their oratory, and significant religious figures. Each essay follows the same format: an introduction which places the speaker in historical perspective, a critical examination of the oratory, information sources (research collections and collected speeches, selected critical studies, and selected biographies), and a chronology of major speeches. Among the fifty-five orators discussed in the work on the earlier period are Susan B. Anthony, John Cotton, Jefferson Davis, Abraham Lincoln, Red Jacket, Sojourner Truth, Booker T. Washington, and George Washington; among the fifty-eight orators discussed in the work on the twentieth century are Cesar Chavez, Clarence S. Darrow, Everett M. Dirksen, Jesse Jackson, Barbara Jordan, Martin Luther King, Jr., Ronald Reagan, and Eleanor Roosevelt.

More than 200 debates, beginning with those pertaining to the Stamp Act and concluding with those dealing with the repeal of the Silver Purchase Act, are presented chronologically in the fourteen volumes of *Great Debates in American History: From the Debates in the British Parliament on the Colonial Stamp Act (1764–1765) to the Debates in Congress at the Close of the Taft Administration (1912–1913),* edited by Marion Mills Miller. This is an estimable source containing explanations, the debates themselves, and summaries of how decisions and compromises were reached by the leaders who forged this country. Miller's work discusses the relevant debates leading up to the Revolutionary War as well as the popular Lincoln-Douglas debates of 1858, which prefigured the outbreak of the Civil War. Both of these periods of American history have been treated by contemporary rhetorical scholars. Three monographs sponsored on the occasion of the nation's Bicentennial by the Speech Communication Association as part of its series entitled "The Continuing American Revolution" offer scholarly research and thought treating the American Revolution as an ongoing process of communication symbolizing the American experience. Barbara A. Larson's *Prologue to Revolution: The War Sermons of the Reverend Samuel Davies, A Rhetorical Study* provides critical insights into the religious and secular events and issues of the late 1750s, which formed a frame of reference for the revolution that followed. Ronald F. Reid's *The American Revolution and the Rhetoric of History* presents a study of the relationships between rhetoric and history, arguing that the past must be seen as it actually was. *The American Ideology: Reflections of the Revolution in American Rhetoric,* by Kurt W. Ritter and James R. Andrews, critically illuminates the rhetorical process that shaped and reflected American ideology through ceremonial discourse from the period of the American Revolution and continuing to the contemporary civil rights struggle. Strong documentation contributes to the value of all three works. In addition, Richard Allen Heckman's *Lincoln vs. Douglas: The Great Debates Campaign* assesses the role of the Lincoln-Douglas debates in the history of American oratory. The reader is also referred to Lionel Crocker's *An Analysis of Lincoln and Douglas as Public Speakers and Debaters,* which offers the texts of the debates as well as a number of studies reflecting on the speaking effectiveness of the two political leaders. *Anti-Slavery and Dis-*

union, 1858–1861: Studies in the Rhetoric of Compromise and Conflict, edited by J. Jeffery Auer, presents a solid integration of historical analysis and rhetorical criticism in twenty-three essays relating to the central issues preceding the Civil War.

No series of debates since the Lincoln-Douglas debates has captured the imagination of the American public and the attention of scholars of debate and public address as completely as that between John F. Kennedy and Richard M. Nixon during the presidential campaign of 1960. The foremost book dealing with this clash is *The Great Debates: Background—Perspective—Effects,* edited by Sidney Kraus, later reissued as *The Great Debates: Kennedy vs. Nixon, 1960.* This work is an overview that presents the texts of the four debates as well as insights of various communications experts. Interesting to read, also, is Nixon's account of these debates in his book *Six Crises.* (He writes here, too, about his "Checkers" speech and his debate with Khrushchev.)

The campaign debates in the fall of 1976 between Gerald R. Ford and Jimmy Carter mark the second such series of face-to-face exchanges between presidential candidates, and these debates have been duly described and analyzed. Three relevant efforts are here listed: *The Great Debates: Carter vs. Ford, 1976,* edited by Sidney Kraus, presents studies contributed by a wide range of authorities on the background, perspectives, and analyses of the debates. *The Presidential Debates: Media, Electoral, and Policy Perspectives,* edited by George F. Bishop, Robert G. Meadow, and Marilyn Jackson-Beeck, offers essays dealing with the campaign setting, communications context, and cognitive and behavioral consequences of the debates. *Carter vs. Ford: The Counterfeit Debates of 1976,* by Lloyd Bitzer and Theodore Rueter, treats campaign context, argumentation, and format. All three works include transcripts of the debates.

A straightforward foundation for the study of modern political rhetoric is presented in *Handbook of Political Communication,* edited by Dan D. Nimmo and Keith R. Sanders. This work is a collection of twenty-two essays that cover theoretical approaches, modes and means of persuasive communication, political communication settings, and methods of study. Contemporary works of note examine presidential rhetoric: *Essays in Presidential Rhetoric,* edited by Theodore Windt with Beth Ingold, analyzes the rhetoric of six presidents, from John F. Kennedy to Ronald Reagan. A companion volume, *Presidential Rhetoric: 1961 to the Present,* also edited by Windt, presents selected texts of public addresses delivered by these same presidents. (This collection is noted under "Anthologies and Reprints" below.) Dante Germino's *The Inaugural Addresses of American Presidents: The Public Philosophy and Rhetoric* is a brief study in which the author contends that a public philosophy espousing God and nation is expressed through presidential inaugural addresses.

Critical and historical works of so-called regional oratory illuminate the debate and public address of a particular geographical area and serve as a means of placing it within a meaningful context. Southern oratory from 1828 to 1970 is analyzed and evaluated in Waldo W. Braden's trilogy. *Oratory in the Old South, 1828–1860* presents nine essays ranging from "The Rhetoric of the Nullifiers" to "The Southern Unionist, 1850–1860" and concludes that there is no genre of southern oratory, thereby destroying the myth of the southern orator. Dealing with the post-Civil War years, 1870–1910, in *Oratory in the New South,* Braden refers to the public address of these decades as oratory of "accommodation." The eight essays in this volume include Danny Chapman's "Booker T. Washington Versus W. E. B. Du Bois: A Study in Rhetorical Contrasts" and Annette Shelby's "The Southern Lady Becomes an Advocate." Both of these volumes contain useful bibliographies. Completing this definitive trilogy, *The Oral Tradition in the South* presents six essays that include studies of southern demagoguery and the segregationist rhetoric of white supremacy. *The Oratory of Southern Demagogues,* edited by Cal M. Logue and Howard Dorgan, is a collection of nine critical essays, each treating a southern political figure prominent during the first half of the twentieth century. *Landmarks in Western Oratory,* edited by David H. Grover, brings together criticism of the oration of the Plains Indians, the Mormons, Henry Spalding, Thomas Starr King, and Upton Sinclair, among others, and suggests that western oratory has an indigenous quality of its own.

Oratory from the pulpit is an integral part of the whole of American debate and public address. *Preaching in American History: Selected Issues in the American Pulpit, 1630–1967,* edited by DeWitte Holland, is a collection of twenty essays which describe and analyze significant issues debated by America's religious leaders over a span of more than three centuries. Much of this work is devoted to modern preaching and issues that are important today. A companion volume, *Sermons in American History: Selected Issues in the American Pulpit, 1630–1967,* also edited by Holland, presents representative sermons on those issues covered in the critical work. (This second collection is noted under "Anthologies and Reprints" below.) Henry H. Mitchell's *Black Preaching* provides a history of black preaching and insights into the black sermon and the role of the black preacher. *Prime Time Preachers: The Rising Power of Televangelism,* by Jeffrey K. Hadden and Charles E. Swann, and *Religious Television: The American Experience,* by Peter G. Horsfield, are thought-provoking studies that examine the increasing influence of television evangelism and the power of religious rhetoric. They are of particular value to those interested in the study of religious communication as well as political and social movements. *Religious Communication Today,* the annual journal published by the Religious Speech Communication Association, offers articles and resources pertinent to the field.

The first history of black oratory in the United States during the twentieth century is Marcus H. Boulware's *The Oratory of Negro Leaders, 1900–1968.*

Boulware presents a survey, largely biographical, of prominent black speakers from Booker T. Washington to Martin Luther King, Jr., and includes chapters on public addresses of black women, fraternal oratory, and church and pulpit oratory, as well as radio and television speaking. Although the work is not critical, it offers a vital description of black oratory during the period. *The Rhetoric of Black Americans,* a critical study written by James L. Golden and Richard D. Rieke, explores the role of persuasive black rhetoric in achieving the goal of the "good life." Interweaving more than fifty complete texts of addresses, debates, sermons, interviews, essays, and letters from the early period of the struggle to 1970, the work offers a rhetorical analysis by theme. The history and criticism of black oratory is supplemented by two books that offer perspectives and source materials on debate and public address of the 1960s. *The Rhetoric of Black Power,* by Robert L. Scott and Wayne Brockriede, presents public speeches and critical essays on the issues of black power. Included are two different interpretations by Stokely Carmichael, "Stokely Carmichael Explains Black Power to a Black Audience in Detroit" and "Stokely Carmichael Explains Black Power to a White Audience in Whitewater, Wisconsin," in addition to a description of black power by Charles V. Hamilton. *The Black Panthers Speak,* edited by Philip S. Foner, sets forth primary source materials, including official documents of the Panthers and selected essays and speeches of Huey P. Newton, Bobby Seale, Eldridge Cleaver, David Hilliard, Fred Hampton, and some of the Panther women. Foner's work does not offer a critical analysis but serves as a basis for further research in Black Panther rhetoric. A readable study in social and intellectual history that provides background material for an exploration of the contemporary black movement can be found in *Forerunners of Black Power: The Rhetoric of Abolition,* edited by Ernest G. Bormann. This work includes essays in speech criticism and a diverse collection of abolition speeches.

A vast majority of the published work in the history and criticism of debate and public address pertains to eminent persons of the past or present, their orations, and the issues they debated, whereas comparatively little has been published in readily accessible form about "unknown" or lesser-known speakers and their addresses. *Rhetoric of the People: Is There Any Better or Equal Hope in the World?,* edited by Harold Barrett, contains fourteen essays concerning the oral discourse of the ordinary citizen's involvement in public life. These clearly written, analytical essays range from "Every Man His Own Orator: The Impact of the Frontier on American Public Address" to "Student Campaign Speaking for Eugene McCarthy in the Presidential Primary Contest of 1968." J. Jeffrey Auer's *The Rhetoric of Our Times* presents forty-two articles, speeches, and analyses dealing with the "gut issues" of the 1960s. Included among the socially relevant topics are "Student Protests: From Dissent to Defiance?," "The Rhetoric of the Streets: Some Legal and Ethical Considerations," "American Public Address and the Mass Media," and "The Ku Klux Klan Presents Its Case to the Public, 1960."

The following three volumes deal with the academic field of speech communication and were produced within a context of self-study proposed by its leading scholars. The first (1954) was prepared under the auspices of the Speech Association of America (now Speech Communication Association), the second (1959) was sponsored by the Speech Association of the Eastern States (now Eastern Communication Association), and the third (1985) was commissioned by the Eastern Communication Association as it celebrated its seventy-fifth anniversary. *A History of Speech Education in America: Background Studies,* edited by Karl R. Wallace, is an authoritative examination of the development of rhetoric and speech education in this country, covering a span from colonial times to the mid–1920s. Included are chapters pertaining to the elocutionary movement, the Delsartian tradition, intercollegiate debating, private schools of speech, and the national speech organizations. *Re-establishing the Speech Profession: The First Fifty Years,* edited by Robert T. Oliver and Marvin G. Bauer, surveys for the "non-expert" the historic developments in the field of speech. Conceived as a successor to these two volumes is *Speech Communication in the Twentieth Century,* edited by Thomas W. Benson. The seventeen essays in this work are divided into two parts, the first reviewing theory and research in the various areas of speech communication, and the second offering overviews of organizational and conceptual issues of communication studies.

Several diverse studies explore a specific aspect of American debate and public address and are of wide general interest. *Aboriginal American Oratory: The Tradition of Eloquence Among the Indians of the United States,* by Louis Thomas Jones, records a descriptive appreciation of the inherent eloquence of Indian oratory. This work is interesting, illustrated, and, although not a definitive study, includes notes and references. Lillian O'Connor's *Pioneer Women Orators: Rhetoric in the Ante-bellum Reform Movement* is a study of the women orators of the mid-nineteenth century who crusaded on the issues of slavery, temperance, and women's rights. A strength of this work is its presentation of a historical setting and biographical data for the first women to be recognized from a public platform. *American Demagogues: Twentieth Century,* by Reinhard H. Luthin, discusses the public career of ten "masters of the masses" who lusted for power during the first half of this century. Easily readable essays with extensive bibliographic notes are devoted to such popular leaders as James M. Curley, Frank Hague, Eugene Talmadge, Huey P. Long, and Joseph R. McCarthy, all highly skilled in the art of political oratory. Donald E. Phillips's *Student Protest, 1960–1970: An Analysis of the Issues and Speeches* functions as an interdisciplinary summary and guide to the student movement, beginning with the sit-in demonstrations in Greensboro, North Carolina, in 1960 and climaxing with the events at Kent

State University, Kent, Ohio, in 1970. Its bibliography is particularly comprehensive and well organized. *A War of Words: Chicano Protest in the 1960s and 1970s,* by John C. Hammerback, Richard J. Jensen, and Jose Angel Gutierrez, analyzes the rhetorical discourse of four principal leaders: Reies Lopez Tijerina, Cesar Chavez, Rodolfo "Corky" Gonzales, and Jose Angel Gutierrez. Included is a bibliographic essay that surveys Mexican-American rhetoric. *Hispanic Voices,* edited by Robert W. Mullen, offers a collection of thirteen essays as an introduction to the role of Hispanic protest rhetoric as it attempts to encompass a greater concern for global issues. *Gayspeak: Gay Male and Lesbian Communication,* edited by James W. Chesebro under the auspices of the Caucus on Gay Male and Lesbian Concerns of the Speech Communication Association, presents twenty-five essays treating homosexuality as a social issue, or, more specifically, as a communication phenomenon. The chapters entitled "Gay Liberation as a Rhetorical Movement" (Part V) and "Gay Rights and the Political Campaigns" (Part VI) are relevant to debate and public address.

Finally, the various professional journals are an indispensable source of contemporary scholarship in debate and public address. Two prestigious journals published by the Speech Communication Association are relevant: *Quarterly Journal of Speech* offers historical, critical, empirical, and theoretical investigations into all areas of human communication. Each issue contains in-depth essays as well as critical reviews of books that have been recently published in the several areas of speech. *Communication Monographs,* issued quarterly, is devoted to all modes of inquiry into communication theory, broadly defined. In addition, journals of a similar nature are also published quarterly by each of the four regional divisions of the Speech Communication Association: *Communication Quarterly* (Eastern Communication Association), *Southern Speech Communication Journal* (Southern Speech Communication Association), *Central States Speech Journal* (Central States Speech Association), and *Western Journal of Speech Communication* (Western Speech Communication Association).

Journal of the American Forensic Association, published quarterly by the American Forensic Association, presents scholarly studies in argumentation, persuasion, discussion, debate, and other types of forensic activities. *National Forensic Journal* is a biannual publication of the National Forensic Association, an organization that focuses on intercollegiate individual speaking events. This journal offers scholarly inquiry into all aspects of forensics. Additional publications that offer articles, reviews, and commentary relating to forensics include *Speaker and Gavel,* a quarterly publication of Delta Sigma Rho-Tau Kappa Alpha, a national honorary forensic society for college students; *Forensic,* a quarterly publication of Pi Kappa Delta, a national honorary fraternal organization also for those involved in forensic speaking at the college level; and *Rostrum,* published monthly by the National Forensic League, an honorary society for high school students.

Association for Recorded Sound Collections Journal, issued three times a year by the Association for Recorded Sound Collections, is of interest to the collector or researcher concerned with historical-discographic matters in recorded sound. Although the articles and reviews in this journal are devoted largely to music, information can be found about all sound recordings, including spoken-word recordings.

ANTHOLOGIES AND REPRINTS

Anthologies of speeches are numerous and are infinitely organized and categorized. In addition to pure anthologies, some volumes dealing with the history or criticism of public address and some designated primarily as speech textbooks contain noteworthy speeches. Many collections have been published, moreover, of the addresses of a well-known individual speaker, for example, Mark Twain, W.E.B. Du Bois, Adlai E. Stevenson, Robert F. Kennedy, Norman Vincent Peale, Billy Graham, Malcolm X, and Ronald Reagan, to name only a few. These are best located by checking the indexing system of any good-sized library, particularly college and university libraries, under the name of the speaker. Some anthologies attempt to give complete and authoritative texts of speeches; others for quite legitimate reasons present edited or abridged versions.

Among those sources which are particularly concerned with contemporary oration, a most respected anthology is *Representative American Speeches,* an annual series compiled since 1938 successively by A. Craig Baird, Lester Thonssen, and Waldo W. Braden, and presently by Owen Peterson. Each volume contains about twenty speeches, not necessarily the "best" speeches of each year but rather those most representative. Many of these speeches are from the political arena. A cumulative speaker index for the years 1937–38 through 1959–60 appears in the 1959–60 volume, for the years 1960–61 through 1969–70 in the 1969–70 volume, and for the years 1970–71 through 1979–80 in the 1979–80 volume. The 1985–86 volume contains a cumulative speaker index for the years 1980–81 through 1985–86. A second highly regarded source of contemporary speeches is the semimonthly publication *Vital Speeches of the Day.* These speeches, delivered by leaders from all fields of endeavor on current problems of national interest, are impartially selected to present both sides of public questions. This periodical is indexed annually in November. A third source of contemporary speeches is the *New York Times;* its *Index: A Book of Record* is complete from September 1851 to the present.

The turn of the twentieth century brought several multivolume anthologies that became standard references and are still highly regarded by scholars and students of oratory. Among them are David J. Brewer's ten-volume compilation, *The World's Best Orations from the Earliest Period to the Present Time,* which gives prominence to English and American orators. More than 620 speeches delivered by 383 speakers from the time of Pericles to the late nineteenth century are included. The series is arranged alphabetically by orator, for each of whom a short biographical sketch is given, and is scrupulously indexed in Volume 10. Guy Carleton Lee's ten-volume work, *The World's Orators: Comprising the Great Orations of the World's History with Introductory Essays, Biographical Sketches and Critical Notes,* is exactly what its title implies, the final three volumes dealing exclusively with orators of America. Volume 8 covers the secular oratory of the eighteenth century, Volume 9 presents the classical oratory of the first half of the nineteenth century, and Volume 10 is concerned largely with the period of the Civil War and includes a general index. William Jennings Bryan's *The World's Famous Orations* is also a ten-volume work whose last three volumes are devoted to American oratory. These volumes cover public speaking in America for the years 1774 to 1905; Volume 10 also contains an index to the series.

Ashley H. Thorndike's work of fifteen volumes, *Modern Eloquence: A Library of the World's Best Spoken Thought,* published in 1928, is, indeed, almost a library in itself. The various volumes are devoted to specialized areas: after-dinner speeches, of which more than 300 are presented; speeches dealing with such commercial and professional interests as banking, economics, railroads, law, medicine, engineering, labor, journalism, theater, ministry, and science; public affairs, including citizenship, government, and education; the standard historical masterpieces, one volume being devoted to American history; speeches concerning World War I; plus humorous, inspirational, and scientific lectures. A general index in Volume 15 guides by speaker, speech, occasion, subject, or quotation. A diversified collection of speeches delivered by prominent Americans from the colonial period through the 1960s is included in *The World's Great Speeches,* a comprehensive single-volume anthology edited by Lewis Copeland and Lawrence W. Lamm. A section devoted to domestic affairs contains speeches by Fiorello H. LaGuardia, John L. Lewis, Thomas E. Dewey, and Herbert Hoover; a section dealing with World War II presents addresses by Franklin D. Roosevelt, Wendell L. Willkie, Charles A. Lindbergh, Fulton J. Sheen, Dorothy Thompson, Henry A. Wallace, and Norman Thomas; and a section of informal speeches includes those of Ralph Waldo Emerson, Edward Everett Hale, Mark Twain, Irvin S. Cobb, Will Rogers, and John D. Rockefeller, Jr. Also included are speeches delivered by Harry S. Truman, Adlai E. Stevenson, Dwight D. Eisenhower, John F. Kennedy, Richard M. Nixon, Martin Luther King, Jr., and Malcolm X. *The Voices of History: Great Speeches of the English Language,* selected and introduced by Lord George-Brown of Great Britain's House of Lords, is a compilation of oratory of ninety-five well-known speakers, organized chronologically beginning with Sir Thomas More and concluding with President Jimmy Carter. This work is comprised largely of excerpts from speeches, and it is of interest for those who enjoy reading eloquent discourse.

Companion anthologies edited by Ernest J. Wrage and Barnet Baskerville, *American Forum: Speeches on Historic Issues, 1788–1900* and *Contemporary Forum: American Speeches on Twentieth-Century Issues,* present an issue-centered history of significantly relevant oration. Each issue is illuminated with speeches representing competing points of view, a historical context, and biographical sketches of the speakers. The first compilation contains twenty-six speeches arranged chronologically in relation to basic historic issues, beginning with the speeches of Patrick Henry and James Madison on the ratification of the federal constitution and concluding with the speeches of Albert J. Beveridge and William Jennings Bryan on U.S. imperialism. The thirty-two speeches of the second anthology deal with issues of the twentieth century: the Progressive era, the League of Nations debate, the question of modernism versus fundamentalism in religion, the polemics of the New Deal, issues in higher education and social change, isolationism, the Cold War, and desegregation. Especially useful are the bibliographical notes indicating supplementary information and other speeches on the topic. Also issue-centered is *Selected American Speeches on Basic Issues (1850–1950),* edited by Carl G. Brandt and Edward M. Shafter, Jr. Complete texts of nineteen noteworthy public addresses with appropriate background information are presented in three parts: "Time of Civil Strife: Slavery and States' Rights," "The Dawn of the Twentieth Century: American Nationalism and Expansion," and "World Wars I and II: Crises and Controversies."

Several works that have been compiled primarily for use as textbooks also function as research tools. Glenn R. Capp's *Famous Speeches in American History* contains the eighteen speeches that professors of public address voted the most significant. The speeches range chronologically from Patrick Henry's "Liberty or Death" to John F. Kennedy's "Inaugural Address" and include orations by George Washington, Daniel Webster, Ralph Waldo Emerson, Abraham Lincoln, Henry W. Grady, Booker T. Washington, William Jennings Bryan, Theodore Roosevelt, Woodrow Wilson, Franklin D. Roosevelt, Douglas MacArthur, and Adlai E. Stevenson. *American Speeches,* edited by Wayland Maxfield Parrish and Marie Hochmuth, presents twenty-eight classic speeches beginning chronologically with Jonathan Edwards's "Sinners in the Hands of an Angry God" and concluding with Franklin D. Roosevelt's "America Has Not Been Disappointed," in addition to an introductory essay on rhetorical criticism and a thorough analysis of Abraham Lincoln's "First Inaugural Address." *Selected Speeches from American History,* edited by Robert T. Oliver and Eugene E. White, presents twenty-two distinguished speeches as case studies in persuasion, ranging from George Whitefield's "Abraham's Offering Up His Son Isaac" to Pope Paul VI's "Address at the United Nations." *Contemporary American Speeches: A Sourcebook of Speech Forms and Principles,* edited by Wil A. Linkugel, R. R. Allen, and Richard L. Johannesen, offers forty-two speeches delivered during the 1960s, 1970s, and 1980s. They are an uncommon mixture of the well known and the little known, selected to illustrate speech forms and principles and to guide the student in speech analysis. Included are Martin Luther King, Jr.'s "Love, Law, and Civil Disobedience," Douglas MacArthur's "Farewell to the Cadets," and Barbara C. Jordan's "Democratic Convention Keynote Address," as well as seven outstanding speeches presented by college students. Halford Ross Ryan's *American Rhetoric from Roosevelt to Reagan: A Collection of Speeches and Critical Essays* contains thirty-three speeches and ten critical essays. Covering a fifty-year period of American history, the public addresses printed in this anthology center attention on diverse national issues. Included are speeches of, among others, Huey P. Long, Father (Charles E.) Coughlin, Eleanor Roosevelt, Douglas MacArthur, Richard M. Nixon, Adlai E. Stevenson, Shirley Chisholm, Barbara C. Jordan, and Jerry Falwell.

John Graham's *Great American Speeches, 1898–1963: Texts and Studies* presents twenty-four significant speeches beginning with William Jennings Bryan's "Naboth's Vineyard" and concluding with Adlai E. Stevenson's "Eulogy: John Fitzgerald Kennedy." The volume includes headnotes and offers critical studies centering on Franklin D. Roosevelt, Douglas MacArthur, and John F. Kennedy. This anthology is singular in that the texts of the speeches are available on recordings edited by Graham and published by Caedmon as part of its series of Great American Speeches. (Caedmon also offers recordings of great women's speeches, black speeches, and American Indian speeches, as well as the Hamilton vs. Jefferson debates and the Lincoln vs. Douglas debates.) A thematic collection of interest to the history and criticism of public address is Charles W. Lomas's *The Agitator in American Society,* which presents thirteen representative speeches illustrating the rhetoric of violence, socialism and social reform, civil rights, and anti-communism. Two anthologies dealing with the public address of the 1960s exemplify the rhetoric and illuminate the issues of the period. *The Great Society: A Sourcebook of Speeches,* edited by Glenn R. Capp, traces the evolution and analyzes the basic concept of the Great Society in addition to the specific issues of civil rights, education, and poverty. Twenty speeches are included by such leaders as John F. Kennedy, Lyndon B. Johnson, Hubert H. Humphrey, Dwight D. Eisenhower, George W. Romney, Ronald Reagan, Ralph J. Bunche, and Richard M. Nixon. *In Pursuit of Peace: Speeches of the Sixties,* edited by Donald W. Zacharias, offers an informative introduction and ten key speeches, each with headnotes, paired so as to present opposing points of view in five areas: "Scientists and Politics," "Peace and Security," "Religion and War," "Soldiers and Peace," and "Dissent and Vietnam."

Three paperbound anthologies designed for popular reference and enjoyment are Houston Peterson's *A Treasury of the World's Great Speeches,* George W. Hibbitt's *The Dolphin Book of Speeches,* and Stewart H. Benedict's *Famous American Speeches.* Peterson's collection dates from Biblical times to the mid–1960s and includes for each speech a foreword and an afterword which give details of the speaker, the setting, and the effect of the speech on the audience. Among the speeches are Elizabeth Cady Stanton's keynote address in 1848 to the first women's rights convention as well as the Sacco and Vanzetti claims of innocence in 1927. Hibbitt's collection is also comprehensive in scope, dating from the Greeks to the mid–1960s. Included are Clare Boothe Luce's "American Morality and Nuclear Diplomacy," John H. Glenn, Jr.'s "A New Era," and several eulogies rendered upon the assassination of John F. Kennedy. Benedict's collection, a slim volume of twenty-three important speeches, includes William Faulkner's "Nobel Prize Speech" and Douglas MacArthur's "Old Soldiers Never Die." Charles Hurd's *A Treasury of Great American Speeches* is also styled for popular taste. A palatable newspaper format presents the "who, what, when, where, and why" as an introduction to each speech. Running a gamut from John Winthrop's "Liberty is the proper end and object of authority" to Richard M. Nixon's "We cannot learn from one another until we stop shouting at one another," this anthology contains addresses delivered by almost one hundred speakers, including Alfred E. Smith, Robert C. Benchley, John L. Lewis, George S. Patton, Cornelia Otis Skinner, and Carl Sandburg.

Two recently published anthologies offer an overview of the role of American women speakers in affecting the course of social, cultural, and political history. *We Shall Be Heard: Women Speakers in America, 1828-Present,* by Patricia Scileppi Kennedy and Gloria Hartmann O'Shields, presents twenty-eight speeches arranged chronologically into three periods: "Early Period Pioneers—Pre-Civil War," "Civil War—Turn-of-the-Century," and "World War I—Contemporary." A photograph of the speaker, a bibliographic essay, and a list of references amplify each speech. *Outspoken Women: Speeches by American Women Reformers, 1635–1935,* by Judith Anderson, is a compilation of forty speech texts presented in alphabetical order by the name of the speaker, each accompanied by an abbreviated biographical sketch. This work begins chronologically with Anne Hutchinson's testimony of 1637 and concludes with the speeches of notable reformers of the early twentieth century: Emily Greene Balch, Mary McLeod Bethune, Carrie Chapman Catt, Crystal Eastman, Elizabeth Gurley Flynn, Charlotte Perkins Gilman, Emma Goldman, Mary Harris "Mother" Jones, Florence Kelley, Carry Nation, Kate Richards O'Hare, Leonora O'Reilly, Alice Paul, Margaret Sanger, Rose Schneiderman, Ida Tarbell, Mary Church Terrell, and Lillian Wald.

Compilations of presidential rhetoric are important sources for debaters, speakers, and those concerned with political communication. *The President Speaks: The Inaugural Addresses of the American Presidents from Washington to Nixon,* edited by Davis Newton Lott, offers for each speech a capsule description of "The President," "The Nation," and "The World," as well as a perspective on the speaking occasion, but does not attempt to analyze the addresses. Michael J. Lax's *The Inaugural Addresses of the Presidents of the United States, 1789–1985,* published in celebration of the fiftieth inaugural, is an impressive-looking volume which presents the speeches without description or comment. *The State of the Union Messages of the Presidents, 1790–1966* is a three-volume work edited by Fred L. Israel. The addresses are not annotated, but the usefulness of the anthology is enhanced by the inclusion of a comprehensive index of significant events and policy in U.S. history. *Presidential Rhetoric: 1961 to the Present,* edited by Theodore Windt, covers the period of the six presidencies from John F. Kennedy to Ronald Reagan. Presented are texts of important speeches, together with a very brief description of the term in office and a bibliography. (This work is a companion volume to Windt's *Essays in Presidential Rhetoric,* noted under "History and Criticism" above.)

Public address from the pulpit has played a significant role in the evolution of American history and culture and has been duly anthologized. A comprehensive anthology encompassing Christian preaching in America from the early period of Jonathan Edwards to the modern era of Billy Graham and Martin Luther King, Jr., can be found in the thirteen volumes of *Twenty Centuries of Great Preaching: An Encyclopedia of Preaching,* edited by Clyde E. Fant, Jr., and William M. Pinson, Jr. Among other preachers whose sermons the editors considered relevant to the issues and needs of their day are George Whitefield, Lyman Beecher, John Jasper, Henry Ward Beecher, John A. Broadus, Phillips Brooks, Dwight L. Moody, Sam Jones, Billy Sunday, Henry Sloane Coffin, Harry Emerson Fosdick, Walter Maier, Fulton J. Sheen, Norman Vincent Peale, and Peter Marshall. This work includes biographies of the preachers and is thoroughly indexed in Volume 13. *Sermons in American History: Selected Issues in the American Pulpit, 1630–1967,* edited by DeWitte Holland, presents brief analyses of twenty selected issues and sermons representing various points of view on these issues. Included are the sermons of noted preachers as well as those not well known, speaking on such topics as "The Ecumenical Movement," "The Thrust of the Radical Right," and "The Pulpit and Race Relations, 1954–1966." (This work is a companion volume to Holland's *Preaching in American History: Selected Issues in the American Pulpit, 1630–1967,* noted under "History and Criticism" above.) Contemporary sermons are published in *Pulpit Digest,* an ecumenical bimonthly periodical devoted to religious issues, and in *Master Sermon Series,* a monthly periodical. A three-volume collection, *Outstanding Black Sermons,* edited in order by J. Alfred Smith, Sr., Walter B. Hoard, and Milton E. Owens, Jr., offers the work of prominent Christian preachers of the present-day black community. Volume 3 includes additional resources for sermons and preaching.

Greater public awareness of minority oratory came with the civil rights issues and the arousing of black consciousness during the past several decades. The most comprehensive of the anthologies devoted exclusively to the black speaker is Philip S. Foner's *The Voice of Black America: Major Speeches by Negroes in the United States, 1797–1971*. Divided into six chronological sections beginning with "The Antebellum Period, 1797–1860" and concluding with "Civil Rights to Black Power, September 1963–1971," Foner presents scores of important speeches, many of which have never appeared in book form, each with a brief historical setting. Among the more contemporary speeches are "The Third World and the Ghetto" by H. Rap Brown, "It's Time for a Change" by Shirley Chisholm, and "The Legacy of George Jackson" by Angela Davis. Other voices include those of Paul Robeson, Langston Hughes, Martin Luther King, Jr., Lorraine Hansberry, Dick Gregory, Malcolm X, Ossie Davis, Adam Clayton Powell, Jr., Kenneth B. Clark, Eldridge Cleaver, Julian Bond, and Huey P. Newton. Not as broad in scope as Foner's work are three anthologies worth noting: *Rhetoric of Racial Revolt,* by Roy L. Hill; *The Negro Speaks: The Rhetoric of Contemporary Black Leaders,* edited by Jamye Coleman Williams and McDonald Williams; and *The Voice of Black Rhetoric: Selections,* edited by Arthur L. Smith and Stephen Robb. Hill's work is a collection of almost fifty speeches dealing with racial relations, the speeches ranging from those of Booker T. Washington to Malcolm X and including those of Elijah Muhammad, Marian Anderson, James Baldwin, Martin Luther King, Jr., Thurgood Marshall, and A. Philip Randolph. This study provides biographical sketches, introductions, commentaries, and some analyses, but these are brief and at random. The Williamses' book reprints a cross-section of twenty-three speeches, many of them abridged, beginning with William L. Dawson's "Race Is Not a Limitation" in 1945, and extending chronologically to Edward W. Brooke's "Address to the National Convention of the NAACP" in 1967. Other speakers include Patricia Roberts Harris, Ralph J. Bunche, Carl T. Rowan, Roy Wilkins, Sadie T. M. Alexander, Whitney M. Young, Jr., Constance Baker Motley, Edith S. Sampson, and Howard Thurman. A portrait of each speaker brightens the text. Smith and Robb present an anthology of significant speeches of twenty orators spanning in time from David Walker (1828) to H. Rap Brown (1967). This work includes an appropriate introduction, headnotes, and a pertinent bibliography.

Two vintage anthologies, historically significant and readily available, are Alice Moore Dunbar's *Masterpieces of Negro Eloquence: The Best Speeches Delivered by the Negro from the Days of Slavery to the Present Time,* published in 1914 on the occasion of the fiftieth anniversary of the Proclamation of Emancipation and reissued in 1970 as part of the Basic Afro-American Reprint Library; and Carter G. Woodson's *Negro Orators and Their Orations,* published in 1925 and reprinted in 1969. Dunbar presents without introduction or commentary the public addresses of forty-nine speakers ranging from Prince Saunders to W.E.B. Du Bois. Woodson's work is wider in scope and includes early protest speeches by such pseudonymous orators as "Othello" and "A Free Negro," as well as "The Negro's First Speech in Congress" by John Willis Menard and orations by Frederick Douglass and Booker T. Washington. A short sketch of each orator is presented, and an effort is made to publish the complete unaltered text.

Popular interest in minority oration encompasses a sympathetic understanding of the American Indian. W. C. Vanderwerth's *Indian Oratory: Famous Speeches by Noted Indian Chieftains* offers an interesting, illustrated collection with authoritative headnotes. The speeches range from Teedyuscung's "I Gave the Halloo" in 1758 to Quanah Parker's "Some White People Do That, Too" in 1910. Chief Joseph's "An Indian's Views of Indian Affairs," one of the most widely quoted speeches delivered by an American Indian, is reprinted in full. Four centuries of Indian oratory, arranged chronologically, can be found in *I Have Spoken: American History Through the Voices of the Indians,* compiled by Virginia Irving Armstrong. A total of 251 speeches, parts of speeches, and statements, each with a very brief introduction, together with notes on the original sources of the speeches, are presented in a simple, highly readable format. Both collections include sizable bibliographies of works pertaining to the Indian. These two anthologies offer valuable insight into the events of American history and the contribution of Indian oratory to the whole of American debate and public address.

In conclusion, it should be remembered that a debate or public address is delivered orally to a specific audience at a particular time and place. The message is *heard*. Part of the joy and satisfaction that comes from analyzing and evaluating a debate or pondering a speech is in hearing the sound of the words. Debate and public address should be read aloud to appreciate its full impact and beauty.

NOTES

1. William Norwood Brigance, ed., *A History and Criticism of American Public Address,* 2 vols. (New York: McGraw-Hill, 1943; reprint, New York: Russell and Russell, 1960), 1: vii.

2. Patrick Henry, "Liberty or Death," in Wayland Maxfield Parrish and Marie Hochmuth, eds., *American Speeches* (New York: Longmans, Green, 1954), p. 94. Many of the popular speeches from which brief passages are quoted in this chapter can be found in more than one of the sources cited below.

3. George Washington, "Farewell Address," in Glenn R. Capp, ed., *Famous Speeches in American History* (Indianapolis: Bobbs-Merrill, 1963), p. 40.

4. Daniel Webster, "Second Speech on Foote's Resolution—Reply to Hayne," in Parrish and Hochmuth, *American Speeches,* p. 229.

5. Booker T. Washington, "Atlanta Exposition Address," in Philip S. Foner, ed., *The Voice of Black America: Major Speeches by Negroes in the United States, 1797–1971* (New York: Simon and Schuster, 1972), p. 581.

6. Abraham Lincoln, "A House Divided," Ernest J. Wrage and Barnet Basketville, eds., *American Forum: Speeches on Historic Issues, 1788–1900* (New York:

Harper and Brothers, 1960; reprint, Seattle: University of Washington Press, 1967), p. 180.

7. On the occasion of its 150th anniversary, the International Platform Association conducted a survey among more than 200 members of congress, journalists, speakers, and speech professionals to determine "What Is the Best Speech Given in the English Language During the 150 Years' Existence of the IPA?" Lincoln's "Gettysburg Address" was the first choice, followed in order by Winston Churchill's "Blood, Toil, Tears and Sweat" and Martin Luther King, Jr.'s "I Have a Dream."

8. Abraham Lincoln, "Second Inaugural Address," in Capp, *Famous Speeches in American History,* p. 94.

9. The Chautauqua concept is now more than one hundred years old. Information pertaining to current programs in the arts, education, religion, social and political affairs, and recreation can be obtained by writing to Chautauqua Institution, Chautauqua, New York 14722.

10. Theodore Roosevelt, "National Duties: Address at Minnesota State Fair, September 2, 1901," in *The Strenuous Life: Essays and Addresses* (New York: Century, 1901, 1928), p 288.

11. Franklin D. Roosevelt, "First Inaugural Address," in Ernest J. Wrage and Barnet Baskerville, eds., *Contemporary Forum: American Speeches on Twentieth-Century Issues* (New York: Harper and Brothers, 1962; reprint, Seattle: University of Washington Press, 1969), p. 157.

12. Franklin D. Roosevelt, "The President's War Address: We Will Gain the Inevitable Triumph—So Help Us God," in *Vital Speeches of the Day,* VIII; 5, p. 130.

13. Douglas MacArthur, "American Policy in the Pacific," in A. Craig Baird, ed., *Representative American Speeches: 1951–1952,* Vol. 24, No. 3 of the Reference Shelf series (New York: H. W. Wilson, 1952), p. 30.

14. There had been a limited television coverage for Harry Truman's inaugural address on January 20, 1949. For a brief historical overview of radio and television broadcasting in presidential campaigns from 1924 through 1960, see Samuel L. Becker and Elmer W. Lower, "Broadcasting in Presidential Campaigns," in Sidney Kraus, ed., *The Great Debates: Kennedy vs. Nixon, 1960,* reissued, (Bloomington: Indiana University Press, 1977), pp. 25–55; and updated by the same authors in "Broadcasting in Presidential Campaigns, 1960–1976," in Sidney Kraus, ed., *The Great Debates: Carter vs. Ford, 1976,* (Bloomington: Indiana University Press, 1979), pp. 11–40.

15. John F. Kennedy, "Inaugural Address," in Lester Thonssen, ed., *Representative American Speeches: 1960–1961,* Vol. 33, No. 3 of the Reference Shelf series (New York: H. W. Wilson, 1961), p. 39.

16. John H. Glenn, Jr., "Address Before the Joint Meeting of Congress" in Lester Thonssen, ed., *Representative American Speeches: 1961–1962,* Vol. 34, No. 4 of the Reference Shelf series (New York: H. W. Wilson, 1962), p. 206.

17. Neil Armstrong, quoted by John Noble Wilford, "Astronauts Land on Plain; Collect Rocks, Plant Flag,"*New York Times,* July 21, 1969, p. 1. See also Wernher Von Braun and Frederick I. Ordway III, "The First Men on the Moon," in *Encyclopedia Americana,* International ed., Vol. 25 (Danbury, Conn.: Grolier, 1982), pp. 357–63.

18. William Faulkner, "Address upon Receiving the Nobel Prize for Literature,"

in *William Faulkner: Essays, Speeches and Public Letters,* ed. James B. Meriwether (New York: Random House, 1965), p. 120.

BIBLIOGRAPHY

Books and Articles

Allen, Steve. *How to Make a Speech.* New York: McGraw-Hill, 1986.

American Library Directory. 39th ed. 2 vols. New York: R. R. Bowker, 1986.

Andrews, James R. *A Choice of Worlds: The Practice and Criticism of Public Discourse.* New York: Harper and Row, 1973.

———. *The Practice of Rhetorical Criticism.* New York: Macmillan, 1983.

Arnold, Carroll C. *Criticism of Oral Rhetoric.* Columbus, Ohio: Charles E. Merrill, 1974.

Ash, Lee, and William G. Miller, comps. *Subject Collections: A Guide to Special Book Collections and Subject Emphases as Reported by University, College, Public, and Special Libraries and Museums in the United States and Canada.* 6th ed., rev. and enl. 2 vols. New York: R. R. Bowker, 1985.

Auer, J. Jeffery, ed. *Anti-slavery and Disunion, 1858–1861: Studies in the Rhetoric of Compromise and Conflict.* New York: Harper and Row, 1963.

———, ed. *The Rhetoric of Our Times.* New York: Appleton-Century-Crofts, 1969.

Barrett, Harold, ed. *Rhetoric of the People: Is There Any Better or Equal Hope in the World?* Amsterdam: Rodopi N.Y., 1974.

Baskerville, Barnet. *The People's Voice: The Orator in American Society.* Lexington: University Press of Kentucky, 1979.

Benson, Thomas W., ed. *Speech Communication in the Twentieth Century.* Carbondale: Southern Illinois University Press, 1985.

Benson, Thomas W., and Michael H. Prosser, eds. *Readings in Classical Rhetoric.* Boston: Allyn and Bacon, 1969.

Bishop, George F., Robert G. Meadow, and Marilyn Jackson-Beeck, eds. *The Presidential Debates: Media, Electoral, and Policy Perspectives.* New York: Praeger, 1980.

Bitzer, Lloyd F., and Edwin Black, eds. *The Prospect of Rhetoric: Report of the National Developmental Project.* Englewood Cliffs, N.J.: Prentice-Hall, 1971.

Bitzer, Lloyd F., and Theodore Rueter. *Carter vs. Ford: The Counterfeit Debates of 1976.* Madison: University of Wisconsin Press, 1980.

Black, Edwin. *Rhetorical Criticism: A Study in Method.* New York: Macmillan, 1965. Reprint. Madison: University of Wisconsin Press, 1978.

Boase, Paul H., ed. *The Rhetoric of Protest and Reform: 1878–1898.* Athens, Ohio: Ohio University Press, 1980.

Boaz, John K., and James R. Brey, eds. *Championship Debates and Speeches.* Vol. 1-. Annandale, Va.: Speech Communication Association and American Forensic Association, 1986-.

Bormann, Ernest G., ed. *Forerunners of Black Power: The Rhetoric of Abolition.* Englewood Cliffs N.J.: Prentice-Hall, 1971.

Boulware, Marcus H. *The Oratory of Negro Leaders, 1900–1968.* Foreword by Alex

Haley. Contributions in Afro-American and African Studies, No. 1. West-port, Conn.: Negro Universities Press, 1969.

Bowers, John Waite, and John A. Courtright. *Communication Research Methods.* Glenview, Ill.: Scott, Foresman, 1984.

Braden, Waldo W. *The Oral Tradition in the South.* Baton Rouge: Louisiana State University Press, 1983.

———, ed. *Oratory in the New South.* Baton Rouge: Louisiana State University Press, 1979.

———, ed. *Oratory in the Old South, 1828–1860.* Baton Rouge: Louisiana State University Press, 1970.

Brigance, William Norwood, ed. *A History and Criticism of American Public Address.* 2 vols. New York: McGraw-Hill, 1943. Reprint. New York: Russell and Russell, 1960. See also Marie Kathryn Hochmuth, ed., below.

Brock, Bernard L., and Robert L. Scott, eds. *Methods of Rhetorical Criticism: A Twentieth-Century Perspective.* 2nd ed., rev. Detroit: Wayne State University Press, 1980.

Bryant, Donald C. *Rhetorical Dimensions in Criticism.* Baton Rouge: Louisiana State University Press, 1973.

———. "Rhetoric: Its Function and Its Scope."*Quarterly Journal of Speech,* 39 (December 1953), 401–24. In Walter R. Fisher, ed., *Rhetoric: A Tradition in Transition. In Honor of Donald C. Bryant.* East Lansing: Michigan State University Press, 1974, pp. 195–246.

———, ed. *The Rhetorical Idiom: Essays in Rhetoric, Oratory, Language, and Drama Presented to Herbert August Wichelns with a Reprinting of His "Literary Criticism of Oratory" (1925).* Ithaca, N.Y.: Cornell University Press, 1958. Reprint. New York: Russell and Russell, 1966.

Campbell, Karlyn Kohrs. *Critiques of Contemporary Rhetoric.* Belmont, Calif.: Wadsworth, 1972.

Campbell, Karlyn Kohrs, and Kathleen Hall Jamieson, eds. *Form and Genre: Shaping Rhetorical Action.* Falls Church, Va.: Speech Communication Association, 1978.

Carnegie, Dale. *The Quick and Easy Way to Effective Speaking.* Revision by Dorothy Carnegie of *Public Speaking and Influencing Men in Business,* by Dale Carnegie (1962). New York: Pocket Books/Simon and Schuster, 1977.

Cathcart, Robert S. *Post-Communication: Critical Analysis and Evaluation.* 2nd ed. Indianapolis: Bobbs-Merrill, 1981.

Chesebro, James W., ed. *Gayspeak: Gay Male and Lesbian Communication.* New York: Pilgrim Press, 1981.

Cleary, James W., and Frederick W. Haberman, comps. and eds. *Rhetoric and Public Address: A Bibliography, 1947–1961.* Madison: University of Wisconsin Press, 1964.

Crocker, Lionel. *An Analysis of Lincoln and Douglas as Public Speakers and Debaters.* Springfield, Ill.: Charles C. Thomas, 1968.

———. *Rhetorical Analysis of Speeches.* Boston: Allyn and Bacon, 1967.

Current Index to Journals in Education. Vols. 1–11, No. 2. New York: Macmillan Information, January 1969-February 1979; Vol. 11, No. 3-. Phoenix: Oryx Press, March 1979-.

Darnay, Brigitte T., ed. *Directory of Special Libraries and Information Centers: A Guide to More Than 18,000 Special Libraries, Research Libraries, Information Centers, Archives, and Data Centers Maintained by Government Agencies, Business, Industry, Newspapers, Educational Institutions, Nonprofit Organizations, and Societies in the Fields of Science and Technology, Medicine, Law, Art, Religion, the Social Sciences, and Humanistic Studies.* 10th ed. 3 vols. Detroit: Gale Research, 1987.

DeVito, Joseph A. *The Communication Handbook: A Dictionary.* New York: Harper and Row, 1986.

Devlin, L. Patrick. *Contemporary Political Speaking.* Belmont, Calif.: Wadsworth, 1971.

Dissertation Abstracts International: The Humanities and Social Sciences. Ann Arbor, Mich.: University Microfilms International, 1938-.

Drummond, A. M., ed. *Studies in Rhetoric and Public Speaking in Honor of James Albert Winans.* By pupils and colleagues. New York: Century, 1925. Reprint. New York: Russell and Russell, 1962.

Duffy, Bernard K., and Halford R. Ryan, eds. *American Orators Before 1900: Critical Studies and Sources.* Westport, Conn.: Greenwood Press, 1987.

————, eds. *American Orators of the Twentieth Century: Critical Studies and Sources.* Westport, Conn.: Greenwood Press, 1987.

Dunlap, Joseph R., and Martin A. Kuhn, comps. *Debate Index Second Supplement.* Vol. 36, No. 3 of the Reference Shelf series. New York: H. W. Wilson, 1964. See also Julia E. Johnsen, comp.; and Edith M. Phelps, comp., below.

Ehninger, Douglas. *Contemporary Rhetoric: A Reader's Coursebook.* Glenview, Ill: Scott, Foresman, 1972.

Ehninger, Douglas, Bruce E. Gronbeck, Ray E. McKerrow, and Alan H. Monroe. *Principles and Types of Speech Communication.* 10th ed. Glenview, Ill.: Scott, Foresman, 1986.

Enos, Richard Leo, and Jeanne L. McClaran, eds. *A Guide to Doctoral Dissertations in Communication Studies and Theater.* Ann Arbor, Mich.: University Microfilms International, 1978.

Ericson, Jon M., and James J. Murphy, with Raymond Bud Zeuschner. *The Debater's Guide.* Rev. ed. Carbondale: Southern Illinois University Press, 1987.

Eubanks, Ralph T., et al. "A Bibliography of Speech and Theatre in the South for the Year [1954–1982]." Title varies. *Southern Speech Communication Journal* (formerly *Southern Speech Journal*), vols. 20–49 (1955–84).

Foner, Philip S., ed. *The Black Panthers Speak.* Preface by Julian Bond. Philadelphia: J. B. Lippincott, 1970.

Foss, Sonja K., Karen A. Foss, and Robert Trapp. *Contemporary Perspectives on Rhetoric.* Prospect Heights, Ill.: Waveland Press, 1985.

Freeley, Austin J. *Argumentation and Debate: Critical Thinking for Reasoned Decision Making.* 6th ed. Belmont, Calif.: Wadsworth, 1986.

Fryar, Maridell, and David A. Thomas. *Student Congress and Lincoln-Douglas Debate.* Skokie, Ill.: National Textbook, 1981.

Fryar, Maridell, David A. Thomas, and Lynn Goodnight. *Basic Debate.* 2nd ed. Lincolnwood, Ill.: National Textbook, 1986.

Germino, Dante. *The Inaugural Addresses of American Presidents: The Public Philosophy and Rhetoric.* Preface and Introduction by Kenneth W. Thompson. Vol. 7,

White Burkett Miller Center Series on the Presidency and the Press. Lanham, Md.: University Press of America, 1984.

Gold, Ellen Reid. "Recorded Sound Collections: New Materials to Explore the Past."*Central States Speech Journal,* 31 (Summer 1980), 143–51. "Errata."*Central States Speech Journal,* 31 (Fall 1980), n.p.

Golden, James L., Goodwin F. Berquist, and William E. Coleman. *The Rhetoric of Western Thought.* 3rd ed. Dubuque: Iowa: Kendall/Hunt, 1983.

Golden, James L., and Edward P. J. Corbett. *The Rhetoric of Blair, Campbell, and Whately.* New York: Holt, Rinehart and Winston, 1968.

Golden, James L., and Richard D. Rieke. *The Rhetoric of Black Americans.* Columbus, Ohio: Charles E. Merrill, 1971.

Gordon, Thomas F., ed. *Communication Abstracts.* Beverly Hills, Calif.: Sage, 1978–.

Grover, David H., ed. *Landmarks in Western Oratory.* Laramie: University of Wyoming and Western Speech Association, 1968.

Haberman, Frederick W., et al. "A Bibliography of Rhetoric and Public Address for the Year [1947–1969]."*Quarterly Journal of Speech.* Vols. 34–36 (1948–50); *Communication Monographs* (formerly *Speech Monographs*). Vols. 18–36 (1951–69), Falls Church, Va.: Speech Communication Association, 1948–69.

Hadden, Jeffrey K., and Charles E. Swann. *Prime Time Preachers: The Rising Power of Televangelism.* Introduction by T. George Harris. Reading, Mass.: Addison-Wesley, 1981.

Hall, Robert N., and Jack L. Rhodes. *Fifty Years of International Debate, 1922–1972.* New York: Speech Communication Association, 1972.

Hammerback, John C., Richard J. Jensen, and Jose Angel Gutierrez. *A War of Words: Chicano Protest in the 1960s and 1970s.* Westport, Conn.: Greenwood Press, 1985.

Heckman, Richard Allen. *Lincoln vs. Douglas: The Great Debates Campaign.* Washington, D.C.: Public Affairs Press, 1967.

Hill, George H., and Lenwood Davis. *Religious Broadcasting, 1920–1983: A Selectively Annotated Bibliography.* New York: Garland, 1984.

Hillbruner, Anthony. *Critical Dimensions: The Art of Public Address Criticism.* New York: Random House, 1966.

Hochmuth, Marie Kathryn, ed. *A History and Criticism of American Public Address.* Vol. 3. New York: Longmans, Green, 1955. Reprint. New York: Russell and Russell, 1965. See also William Norwood Brigance, ed., above.

Holland, DeWitte, ed. *America in Controversy: History of American Public Address.* Dubuque: Iowa: William C. Brown, 1973.

———, ed. *Preaching in American History: Selected Issues in the American Pulpit, 1630–1967.* Nashville, Tenn.: Abingdon Press, 1969.

Horsfield, Peter G. *Religious Television: The American Experience.* New York: Longman, 1984.

Howell, J. B., ed. *Special Collections in Libraries of the Southeast.* Introduction by Frances Neel Cheney. Jackson, Miss.: Howick House, 1978.

Howes, Raymond F., ed. *Historical Studies of Rhetoric and Rhetoricians.* Ithaca, N.Y.: Cornell University Press, 1961.

Index to U.S. Government Periodicals: A Computer-Generated Guide to 183 Selected Titles by Author and Subject. Chicago: Infordata International, 1970–.

Jarrard, Mary E. W., and Phyllis R. Randall. *Women Speaking: An Annotated Bibliography of Verbal and Nonverbal Communication, 1970–1980*. New York: Garland, 1982.

Jennings, Margaret S., ed. *Library and Reference Facilities in the Area of the District of Columbia*. 11th ed. White Plains, N.Y.: Knowledge Industry Publications, 1983.

Johannesen, Richard L., ed. *Contemporary Theories of Rhetoric: Selected Readings*. New York: Harper and Row, 1971.

Johnsen, Julia E., comp. *Debate Index Supplement*. Vol. 14, No. 9 of the Reference Shelf Series. New York: H. W. Wilson, 1941. See also Joseph R. Dunlap, and Martin A. Kuhn, comps., above; and Edith M. Phelps, comp., below.

Jones, Louis Thomas. *Aboriginal American Oratory: The Tradition of Eloquence Among the Indians of the United States*. Los Angeles: Southwest Museum, 1965.

Kaid, Lynda Lee, and Anne Johnston Wadsworth. *Political Campaign Communication: A Bibliography and Guide to the Literature, 1973–1982*. Metuchen, N.J.: Scarecrow Press, 1985.

Keefe, Carolyn, Thomas B. Harte, and Laurence E. Norton, eds. *Introduction to Debate*. Foreword by Gerald H. Sanders. New York: Macmillan, 1982.

Kennicott, Patrick C., ed. *Bibliographic Annual in Speech Communication*. Falls Church, Va.: Speech Communication Association, 1973–75.

Kraus, Sidney, ed. *The Great Debates: Background—Perspective—Effects*. Introduction by Harold D. Lasswell. Bloomington: Indiana University Press, 1962. Reprint. Gloucester, Mass.: Peter Smith, 1968. Rev. ed. *The Great Debates: Kennedy vs. Nixon, 1960*. Bloomington: Indiana University Press, 1977.

———, ed. *The Great Debates: Carter vs. Ford, 1976*. Bloomington: Indiana University Press, 1979.

Kruger, Arthur N. *Argumentation and Debate: A Classified Bibliography*. 2nd ed. Metuchen, N.J.: Scarecrow Press, 1975.

Langer, Howard J., ed. *Directory of Speakers*. Phoenix: Oryx Press, 1981.

Larson, Barbara A. *Prologue to Revolution: The War Sermons of the Reverend Samuel Davies, A Rhetorical Study*. Bicentennial Monographs. Edited by Robert S. Cathcart. Falls Church, Va.: Speech Communication Association, 1978.

Logue, Cal M., and Howard Dorgan, eds. *The Oratory of Southern Demagogues*. Baton Rouge: Louisiana State University Press, 1981.

Lucas, Stephen E. *The Art of Public Speaking*. 2nd ed. New York: Random House, 1986.

Luthin, Reinhard H. *American Demagogues: Twentieth Century*. Introduction by Allan Nevins. Boston: Beacon Press, 1954. Reprint. Gloucester, Mass.: Peter Smith, 1959.

Mabie, Edward Charles, ed. *University Debaters' Annual: Constructive and Rebuttal Speeches Delivered in Debates of American Colleges and Universities During the College Year*. Vols. 1–2 (1914/15–1915/16). New York: H. W. Wilson, 1915–16. See also Edith M. Phelps, ed.; and Ruth Ulman, ed., below.

McKee, Gerald. *Directory of Spoken-Word Audio Cassettes*. New York: Jeffrey Norton, 1983.

McKerrow, Ray E., ed. *Explorations in Rhetoric: Studies in Honor of Douglas Ehninger*. Glenview, Ill.: Scott, Foresman, 1982.

McMahon, Ed. *The Art of Public Speaking*. New York: Putnam's, 1986.

Manning, Beverley. *Index to American Women Speakers, 1828–1978.* Metuchen, N.J.: Scarecrow Press, 1980.

Matlon, Ronald J., ed. *Index to Journals in Communication Studies Through 1985.* Annandale, Va.: Speech Communication Association, 1987.

Miller, Marion Mills., ed. *Great Debates in American History: From the Debates in the British Parliament on the Colonial Stamp Act (1764–1765) to the Debates in Congress at the Close of the Taft Administration (1912–1913).* 14 vols. New York: Current Literature, 1913. Reprint. 3 vols. Metuchen, N.J.: Mini-Print, 1970.

Mitchell, Charity. *Speech Index: An Index to Collections of World Famous Orations and Speeches for Various Occasions, Fourth Edition Supplement, 1966–1980.* Metuchen, N.J.: Scarecrow Press, 1982. See also Roberta Briggs Sutton, below.

Mitchell, Henry H. *Black Preaching.* Philadelphia: J. B. Lippincott, 1970.

Mohrmann, G. P., Charles J. Stewart, and Donovan J. Ochs, eds. *Explorations in Rhetorical Criticism.* University Park: Pennsylvania State University Press, 1973.

Morehead, Joe. *Introduction to United States Public Documents.* 3rd ed. Littleton, Colo.: Libraries Unlimited, 1983.

Mulgrave, Dorothy I., Clark S. Marlor, and Elmer E. Baker, Jr. *Bibliography of Speech and Allied Areas, 1950–1960.* Philadelphia: Chilton, 1962. Reprint. Westport, Conn.: Greenwood Press, 1972.

Mullen, Robert W., ed. *Hispanic Voices.* Lexington, Mass.: Ginn Custom Publishing, 1984.

New York Times Index: A Book of Record. New York: New York Times, 1851-.

Nichols, Egbert Ray, ed. *Intercollegiate Debates.* Subtitle varies. Vols. 2–22. New York: Noble and Noble, 1910–41. See also Paul M. Pearson, ed., below.

Nimmo, Dan D., and Keith R. Sanders, eds. *Handbook of Political Communication.* Beverly Hills, Calif.: Sage, 1981.

Nixon, Richard M. *Six Crises.* New York: Doubleday, 1962.

O'Connor, Lillian. *Pioneer Women Orators: Rhetoric in the Ante-bellum Reform Movement.* New York: Columbia University Press, 1954.

Oliver, Robert T. *History of Public Speaking in America.* Boston: Allyn and Bacon, 1965. Reprint. Westport, Conn.: Greenwood Press, 1978.

Oliver, Robert T., and Marvin G. Bauer, eds. *Re-establishing the Speech Profession: The First Fifty Years.* New York: Speech Association of the Eastern States, 1959.

On Cassette, 1986/1987: A Comprehensive Bibliography of Spoken Word Audiocassettes. New York: R. R. Bowker, 1986.

Patterson, J. W., and David Zarefsky. *Contemporary Debate.* Boston: Houghton Mifflin, 1983.

Pearson, Paul M., ed. *Intercollegiate Debates: Being Briefs and Reports of Many Intercollegiate Debates.* Vol. 1. New York: Hinds, Hayden and Eldredge, 1909. See also Egbert Ray Nichols, ed., above.

Phelps, Edith M., comp. *Debate Index.* Rev. ed. Vol. 12, No. 9 of the Reference Shelf Series. New York: H. W. Wilson, 1939. See also Joseph R. Dunlap and Martin A. Kuhn, comps.; and Julia E. Johnsen, comp., above.

———, ed. *University Debaters' Annual: Constructive and Rebuttal Speeches Delivered in Debates of American Colleges and Universities During the College Year.* Vols.

3–33 (1916/17–1946/47). New York: H. W. Wilson, 1917–47. See also Edward Charles Mabie, ed., above; and Ruth Ulman, ed., below.

Phillips, Donald E. *Student Protest, 1960–1970: An Analysis of the Issues and Speeches. Revised Edition with a Comprehensive Bibliography*. Lanham, Md.: University Press of America, 1985.

Prochnow, Herbert V., and Herbert V. Prochnow, Jr. *The Public Speaker's Treasure Chest*. 4th ed. New York: Harper and Row, 1986.

———. *The Toastmaster's Treasure Chest*. New York: Harper and Row, 1979.

Reid, Loren, ed. *American Public Address: Studies in Honor of Albert Craig Baird*. Columbia: University of Missouri Press, 1961.

Reid, Ronald F. *The American Revolution and the Rhetoric of History*. Bicentennial Monographs. Edited by Robert S. Cathcart. Falls Church, Va.: Speech Communication Association, 1978.

Ritter, Kurt W., and James R. Andrews. *The American Ideology: Reflections of the Revolution in American Rhetoric*. Bicentennial Monographs. Edited by Robert S. Cathcart. Falls Church, Va.: Speech Communication Association, 1978.

Rohler, Lloyd E., and Roger Cook. *Great Speeches for Criticism and Analysis*. Greenwood, Ind.: Alistair Press, Educational Video Group, 1988.

Rubin, Rebecca B., Alan M. Rubin, and Linda J. Piele. *Communication Research: Strategies and Sources*. Belmont, Calif.: Wadsworth, 1986.

Sapolsky, Barry S., Jodi S. Hale, and Jayme Harpring, comps. *1988 Directory of Communication Research Centers in North American Universities*. Tallahassee, Fla.: Communication Research Center, Florida State University, 1988.

Schwarzkopf, LeRoy C., comp. *Government Reference Books 84/85: A Biennial Guide to U.S. Government Publications*. 9th biennial vol. Littleton, Colo.: Libraries Unlimited, 1986.

Scott, Robert L., and Wayne Brockriede. *The Rhetoric of Black Power*. New York: Harper and Row, 1969.

Shaw, Warren Choate. *History of American Oratory*. Indianapolis: Bobbs-Merrill, 1928.

Shearer, Ned A., ed. *Bibliographic Annual in Speech Communication*. Falls Church, Va.: Speech Communication Association, 1970–72.

Speech Communication Directory, [1935–] (formerly *Speech Association of America Directory* and *Speech Communication Association Directory*). Annandale, Va.: Speech Communication Association, 1935–.

Sprague, Jo, and Douglas Stuart. *The Speaker's Handbook*. 2nd ed. San Diego: Harcourt Brace Jovanovich, 1988.

Superintendent of Documents. *Monthly Catalogue of United States Government Publications*. Washington, D.C.: Government Printing Office, 1895–.

———. *Subject Bibliography 043: Publications Relating to the [1975/76–] National High School Debate Topic*. Washington, D.C.: Government Printing Office, 1975–.

———. *Subject Bibliography 176: Publications Relating to the [1975/76–] College Debate Topic*. Washington, D.C.: Government Printing Office, 1975–.

Sutton, Roberta Briggs. *Speech Index: An Index to 259 Collections of World Famous Orations and Speeches for Various Occasions*. 4th ed., rev. and enl. New York: Scarecrow Press, 1966. See also Charity Mitchell, above.

Television News Index and Abstracts: A Guide to the Videotape Collection of the Network

Evening News Programs in the Vanderbilt Television News Archive. Nashville, Tenn.: Jean and Alexander Heard Library, Vanderbilt University, 1972-.

Thesaurus of ERIC Descriptors. 11th ed., 1987. Phoenix: Oryx Press, 1986.

Thomas, David A., and Jack Hart, eds. *Advanced Debate: Readings in Theory, Practice and Teaching.* Foreword by Donn W. Parson. 3rd ed. Lincolnwood, Ill.: National Textbook, 1987.

Thonssen, Lester, A. Craig Baird, and Waldo W. Braden. *Speech Criticism.* 2nd ed. New York: Ronald Press, 1970. Reprint. Melbourne, Fla.: Krieger Publishing, 1981.

Thonssen, Lester, and Elizabeth Fatherson, comps. *Bibliography of Speech Education.* New York: H. W. Wilson, 1939.

Thonssen, Lester, Mary Margaret Robb, and Dorothea Thonssen, comps. *Bibliography of Speech Education: Supplement, 1939–1948.* New York: H. W. Wilson, 1950.

Tucker, Raymond K., Richard L. Weaver II, and Cynthia Berryman-Fink. *Research in Speech Communication.* Englewood Cliffs, N.J.: Prentice-Hall, 1981.

Ulman, Ruth, ed. *University Debaters' Annual: Reports of Debates and Other Forensic Activities of American Colleges and Universities During the Academic Year.* Vols. 34–37 (1947/48–1950/51). New York: H. W. Wilson, 1948–51. See also Edward Charles Mabie, ed.; and Edith M., Phelps, ed., above.

U.S. Congress. *Annals of Congress.* 1st–18th Cong., 1st sess., 1789–1824. Washington, D.C.: Gales and Seaton, 1834–56.

———. *Congressional Globe.* 23rd–42nd Cong., 1833–73. Washington, D.C.: Globe Office, 1834–73.

———. *Congressional Record: Containing the Proceedings and Debates of the 43rd-Congress 1873-.* Washington, D.C.: Government Printing Office, 1874–.

———. *Register of Debates.* 18th Cong., 2nd sess.–25th Cong., 1st sess., 1824–37. Washington, D.C.: Gales and Seaton, 1825–37.

U.S. Department of Education. Office of Educational Research and Improvement. *Resources in Education.* Washington, D.C.: Government Printing Office, 1966–.

U.S. Department of State. Bureau of Public Affairs. *Department of State Bulletin.* Washington, D.C.: Government Printing Office, 1939–.

U.S. General Services Administration. *Public Papers of the Presidents of the United States.* Washington, D.C.: Government Printing Office, 1958–.

———. *Weekly Compilation of Presidential Documents.* Washington, D.C.: Government Printing Office, 1965–.

U.S. Library of Congress. *National Union Catalogue of Manuscript Collections.* Washington, D.C.: Library of Congress, 1962–.

Valenti, Jack. *Speak Up with Confidence: How to Prepare, Learn, and Deliver Effective Speeches.* New York: William Morrow, 1982.

Verderber, Rudolph F. *The Challenge of Effective Speaking.* 6th ed. Belmont, Calif.: Wadsworth, 1985.

Video Source Book. 7th ed. Syosset, N.Y.: National Video Clearinghouse, 1985.

Wallace, Karl R., ed. *History of Speech Education in America: Background Studies.* New York: Appleton-Century-Crofts, 1954.

Wasserman, Paul, ed. *Speakers and Lecturers: How to Find Them. A Directory of Booking Agents, Lecture Bureaus, Companies, Professional and Trade Associations, Uni-*

versities, and Other Groups Which Organize and Schedule Engagements for Lecturers and Public Speakers on All Subjects, with Information on Speakers, Subjects, and Arrangements, and Biographical Details on over 2,000 Individuals. 2nd ed. 2 vols. Detroit: Gale Research, 1981.

Watkins, Mary Michelle, ed. *Research Centers Directory.* Foreword by Erich Bloch. 11th ed. 2 vols. Detroit: Gale Research, 1987.

White, Eugene E., ed. *Rhetoric in Transition: Studies in the Nature and Uses of Rhetoric.* University Park: Pennsylvania State University Press, 1980.

Wichelns, Herbert A. "The Literary Criticism of Oratory." In A. M. Drummond, ed., *Studies in Rhetoric and Public Speaking in Honor of James Albert Winans.* By pupils and colleagues. New York: Century, 1925, pp. 181–216. Reprint. New York: Russell and Russell, 1962. In Donald C. Bryant, ed., *The Rhetorical Idiom: Essays in Rhetoric, Oratory, Language, and Drama Presented to Herbert August Wichelns with a Reprinting of His "Literary Criticism of Oratory" (1925).* Ithaca, N.Y.: Cornell University Press, 1958, pp. 5–42. Reprint. New York: Russell and Russell, 1966. Also in Bernard L. Brock and Robert L. Scott, eds., *Methods of Rhetorical Criticism: A Twentieth-Century Perspective.* 2nd ed., rev. Detroit: Wayne State University Press, 1980, pp. 40–73.

Windes, Russel R., and Arthur N. Kruger, eds. *Championship Debating—West Point National Debate Tournament Final-Round Debates and Critiques, 1949–60.* Portland, Me.: J. Weston Walch, 1961.

————, eds. *Championship Debating.* Vol. 2 (1961–66). Portland, Me.: J. Weston Walch, 1967.

Windt, Theodore, ed., with Beth Ingold. *Essays in Presidential Rhetoric.* Rev. printing. Dubuque, Iowa: Kendall/Hunt, 1984.

Wrage, Ernest J. "Public Address: A Study in Social and Intellectual History."*Quarterly Journal of Speech,* 33 (December 1947), 451–57. In Bernard L. Brock and Robert L. Scott, eds., *Methods of Rhetorical Criticism: A Twentieth-Century Perspective.* 2nd ed., rev. Detroit: Wayne State University Press, 1980, pp. 116–24.

Anthologies and Reprints

Anderson, Judith. *Outspoken Women: Speeches by American Women Reformers, 1635–1935.* Dubuque, Iowa: Kendall/Hunt, 1984.

Armstrong, Virginia Irving, comp. *I Have Spoken: American History Through the Voices of the Indians.* Introduction by Frederick W. Turner III. Chicago: Sage Books/Swallow Press, 1971.

Baird, A. Craig, ed. *Representative American Speeches.* Vols. 11–31 (1937/38–1958/59) of the Reference Shelf series. New York: H. W. Wilson, 1938–59. See also Waldo W. Braden, ed.; Owen Peterson, ed.; and Lester Thonssen, ed., below.

Benedict, Stewart H., ed. *Famous American Speeches.* New York: Laurel/Dell, 1967.

Braden, Waldo W., ed. *Representative American Speeches.* Vols. 43–52 (1970/71–1979/80) of the Reference Shelf series. New York: H. W. Wilson, 1971–80. See also A. Craig Baird, ed., above; and Owen Peterson, ed.; and Lester Thonssen, ed., below.

Brandt, Carl G., and Edward M. Shafter, Jr., eds. *Selected American Speeches on Basic Issues (1850–1950)*. Boston: Houghton Mifflin/Riverside Press, 1960.

Brewer, David J., ed. *The World's Best Orations from the Earliest Period to the Present Time*. 10 vols. St. Louis: Ferd. P. Kaiser, 1900. Reprint. 2 vols. Metuchen, N.J.: Scarecrow Press, 1970.

Bryan, William Jennings, ed. *The World's Famous Orations*. Vols. 8–10. New York: Funk and Wagnalls, 1906.

Capp, Glenn R. *Famous Speeches in American History*. Indianapolis: Bobbs-Merrill, 1963.

———, ed. *The Great Society: A Sourcebook of Speeches*. Belmont, Calif.: Dickenson, 1967.

Copeland, Lewis, and Lawrence W. Lamm, eds. *The World's Great Speeches*. 3rd enl. ed. New York: Dover, 1973.

Dunbar, Alice Moore, ed. *Masterpieces of Negro Eloquence: The Best Speeches Delivered by the Negro from the Days of Slavery to the Present Time*. New York: Bookery, 1914. Reprint. New York: Johnson Reprint, 1970.

Fant, Clyde E., Jr., and William M. Pinson, Jr., eds. *Twenty Centuries of Great Preaching: An Encyclopedia of Preaching*. 13 vols. Waco, Tex.: Word Books, 1971.

Foner, Philip S., ed. *The Voice of Black America: Major Speeches by Negroes in the United States, 1797–1971*. New York: Simon and Schuster, 1972. Reprint. 2 vols. New York: Capricorn Books, 1975.

George-Brown, George Alfred Brown, Baron, ed. *The Voices of History: Great Speeches of the English Language*. New York: Stein and Day, 1980. Orig. pub. as *The Voice of History: Great Speeches of the English Language*. London: Sidgwick and Jackson, 1979.

Graham, John, ed. *Great American Speeches, 1898–1963: Texts and Studies*. New York: Appleton-Century-Crofts, 1970.

Hibbitt, George W., ed. *The Dolphin Book of Speeches*. Garden City, N.Y.: Dolphin/Doubleday, 1965.

Hill, Roy L. *Rhetoric of Racial Revolt*. Denver: Golden Bell Press, 1964.

Hoard, Walter B., ed. *Outstanding Black Sermons*. Vol. 2. Valley Forge, Pa.: Judson Press, 1979. See also Milton E. Owens, Jr., ed.; and J. Alfred Smith, Sr., ed., below.

Holland, DeWitte, ed. *Sermons in American History: Selected Issues in the American Pulpit, 1630–1967*. Nashville, Tenn.: Abingdon Press, 1971.

Hurd, Charles, comp. *A Treasury of Great American Speeches*. New and rev. ed. by Andrew Bauer. New York: Hawthorn Books, 1970.

Israel, Fred L., ed. *The State of the Union Messages of the Presidents, 1790–1966*. Introduction by Arthur M. Schlesinger. 3 vols. New York: R. R. Bowker and Chelsea House, 1967.

Kennedy, Patricia Scileppi, and Gloria Hartmann O'Shields. *We Shall Be Heard: Women Speakers in America, 1828-Present*. Dubuque: Iowa: Kendall/Hunt, 1983.

Lax, Michael J., ed. *The Inaugural Addresses of the Presidents of the United States, 1789–1985*. Atlantic City, N.J.: American Inheritance Press, 1985.

Lee, Guy Carleton, ed. *The World's Orators: Comprising the Great Orations of the*

World's History with Introductory Essays, Biographical Sketches and Critical Notes. Vols. 8–10. New York: Putnam's/Knickerbocker Press, 1900–1901.

Linkugel, Wil A., R. R. Allen, and Richard L. Johannesen. *Contemporary American Speeches: A Sourcebook of Speech Forms and Principles.* 5th ed. Dubuque, Iowa: Kendall/Hunt, 1982.

Lomas, Charles W. *The Agitator in American Society.* Englewood Cliffs, N.J.: Prentice-Hall, 1968.

Lott, Davis Newton, ed. *The President Speaks: The Inaugural Addresses of the American Presidents from Washington to Nixon.* 3rd ed. New York: Holt, Rinehart and Winston, 1969.

Oliver, Robert T., and Eugene E. White, eds. *Selected Speeches from American History.* Boston: Allyn and Bacon, 1966.

Owens, Milton E., Jr., ed. *Outstanding Black Sermons.* Vol. 3. Valley Forge, Pa.: Judson Press, 1982. See also Walter B. Hoard, ed., above; and J. Alfred Smith, Sr., ed., below.

Parrish, Wayland Maxfield, and Marie Hochmuth, eds. *American Speeches.* New York: Longmans, Green, 1954.

Peterson, Houston, ed. *A Treasury of the World's Great Speeches.* Rev. and enl. ed. New York: Fireside/Simon and Schuster, 1965.

Peterson, Owen, ed. *Representative American Speeches.* Vols. 53– (1980/81–) of the Reference Shelf series. New York: H. W. Wilson, 1981–. See also A. Craig Baird, ed.; and Waldo W. Braden, ed., above; and Lester Thonssen, ed., below.

Ryan, Halford Ross. *American Rhetoric from Roosevelt to Reagan: A Collection of Speeches and Critical Essays.* 2nd ed. Prospect Heights, Ill.: Waveland Press, 1987.   .

Smith, Arthur L., and Stephen Robb, eds. *The Voice of Black Rhetoric: Selections.* Boston: Allyn and Bacon, 1971.

Smith, J. Alfred, Sr., ed. *Outstanding Black Sermons.* Vol. 1. Valley Forge, Pa.: Judson Press, 1976. See also Walter B. Hoard ed.; and Milton E. Owens Jr., ed., above.

Thonssen, Lester, ed. *Representative American Speeches.* Vols. 32–42 (1959/60–1969/70) of the Reference Shelf Series. New York: H. W. Wilson, 1960–70. See also A. Craig Baird, ed.; Waldo W. Braden, ed.; and Owen Peterson, ed.,above.

Thorndike, Ashley H., ed. *Modern Eloquence: A Library of the World's Best Spoken Thought.* 15 vols. New York: Modern Eloquence, 1928.

Vanderwerth, W. C. *Indian Oratory: Famous Speeches by Noted Indian Chieftains.* Foreword by William R. Carmack. Norman: University of Oklahoma Press, 1971.

Williams, Jamye Coleman, and McDonald Williams, eds. *The Negro Speaks: The Rhetoric of Contemporary Black Leaders.* New York: Noble and Noble, 1970.

Windt, Theodore, ed. *Presidential Rhetoric: 1961 to the Present.* 3rd ed. Dubuque, Iowa: Kendall/Hunt, 1983.

Woodson, Carter G., ed. *Negro Orators and Their Orations.* Washington, D.C.: Associated, 1925. Reprint. New York: Russell and Russell, 1969.

Wrage, Ernest J., and Barnet Baskerville, eds. *American Forum: Speeches on Historic*

Issues, 1788–1900. New York: Harper and Brothers, 1960. Reprint. Seattle: University of Washington Press, 1967.

————, eds. *Contemporary Forum: American Speeches on Twentieth-Century Issues.* New York: Harper and Brothers, 1962. Reprint. Seattle: University of Washington Press, 1969.

Zacharias, Donald W., ed. *In Pursuit of Peace: Speeches of the Sixties.* New York: Random House, 1970.

Periodicals

Association for Recorded Sound Collections Journal. Washington, D.C., 1968–.

Central States Speech Journal. Detroit, 1949–.

Communication Monographs (formerly *Speech Monographs*). Annandale, Va., 1934–.

Communication Quarterly (formerly *Today's Speech*). Upper Montclair, N.J., 1953–.

Forensic. Portales, N.M., 1915–.

Journal of the American Forensic Association (formerly *The Register*). Falls River, Wis., 1964–.

Master Sermom Series. Royal Oak, Mich., 1970–.

National Forensic Journal. Mansfield, Pa., 1983–.

Pulpit Digest (formerly *New Pulpit Digest,* a merger of *Pulpit Digest* and *Pulpit Preaching*). Louisville, Ky., 1972–.

Quarterly Journal of Speech (formerly *Quarterly Journal of Public Speaking* and *Quarterly Journal of Speech Education*). Annandale, Va., 1915–.

Religious Communication Today. Manhattan, Kans., 1978–.

Rostrum (formerly *Bulletin*). Ripon, Wis., 1934–.

Southern Speech Communication Journal (Formerly *Southern Speech Bulletin* and *Southern Speech Journal*). Boone, N.C., 1935–.

Speaker and Gavel (merger of *Speaker* and *Gavel*). Lawrence, Kans., 1964–.

Toastmaster Magazine. Santa Ana, Calif., 1932–.

Vital Speeches of the Day. Mount Pleasant, S.C., 1934–.

Western Journal of Speech Communication (formerly *Western Speech* and *Western Speech Communication*). Pullman, Wash., 1937–.

Editorial Cartoons

NANCY POGEL
and PAUL SOMERS, JR.

Although editorial cartooning has a long history in the United States, it originated in Europe. The key words–"cartoon" and "caricature" -derive from the Italian *cartone,* "a large sheet of paper," and *caricare,* "to exaggerate, change, or overload." The Englishman William Hogarth, whose moral indignation led him from fine art to satirical engravings denouncing the evils of his society, may be considered the first cartoonist. His successors, Thomas Rowlandson, George Cruikshank, and, especially, James Gillray, inspired emulation. Since that time, other Englishmen such as John Tenniel, David Low, and Ronald Searle, along with the Frenchmen Honoré Daumier and Jean Louis Forain, have influenced American artists. In recent years, the Australian Patrick Oliphant and the Canadian Paul Szep have become quite popular here. For the most part, however, the American editorial cartoonists have reflected the political and social moods of the nation, refining and simplifying their work to insure the maximum impact on a public with little time to ponder the complex drawings and lengthy captions of earlier times.

Herbert Block (Herblock) has defined the editorial cartoonist as "the kid who points out that the Emperor is without his clothes." From Ben Franklin to Jeff MacNelly, America has produced a long line of artists–left, right, and center–idealists and cynics whose work has tried to keep politics honest. Unfortunately, the political or editorial cartoonists who have not also been accepted by "high culture" enthusiasts as painters, printmakers, or major illustrators have been relegated to secondary or backseat positions, as have so many artists in a variety of popular culture categories.

Thus, although early editorial cartoons or drawings by the most famous have been collected and celebrated, research into late nineteenth-and twentieth-century editorial cartooning has only begun to become a legitimate concern for scholars and collectors in the last few decades. Indexes are incomplete; independent bibliographical and biographical guides appear in limited numbers; and serious critical analysis of editorial cartooning and cartoonists—stylistic, political, historical—remains in its infancy. The field is ripe for the energetic scholar who is patient and willing to break new ground.

HISTORIC OUTLINE

The editorial cartoon has been around much longer than the comic strip, and it was taken seriously at an earlier date. No matter how poorly it was drawn or how tasteless it might have been, a widely distributed cartoon attacking a king or, in the United States, a president, could not be ignored.

American editorial cartooning probably began in 1747 with "Non Votis" or "The Wagoner and Hercules," the designing and/or drawing of which are attributed to Benjamin Franklin. Franklin is also associated with the second oldest extant political cartoon, "Join or Die," the representation of the colonies as a disjointed snake, which appeared in his *Pennsylvania Gazette* for May 9, 1754. The engraver was Paul Revere, whose 1770 engraving "The Boston Massacre" was widely circulated for its propaganda value. Revere had copied a drawing by Henry Pelham, stepbrother of John Singleton Copley.

Shortly before the Revolution, Franklin supposedly designed the cartoon "Magna Britannia: her Colonies Reduced" for distribution in England, hoping the symbolic representation of Britannia fallen from her place of eminence at the top of the globe, her limbs (each bearing the name of a North American colony) severed, would help sway England toward a more lenient colonial policy. Indeed, up to the point at which the French entered the war, mezzotints and engravings in London supported the colonists.

Few cartoons appeared during this period: Frank Weitenkampf has located a mere seventy-eight produced before 1828. An exception to the busy cartoons of the day-and one that seems almost modern in its simplicity-was drawn by Elkanah Tisdale in 1812. Gilbert Stuart has traditionally received the credit, but it was Tisdale who added a few pencil strokes to the map of Governor Elbridge Gerry's ingeniously contrived Essex County senatorial district, thus creating the dragonlike "gerrymander" and adding a word to our language.

Given the bitterness of partisan politics that characterized the early-not to mention the later-years of the Republic, it is surprising that there are so few cartoons of George Washington, who was scurrilously derided by his foes. William Murrell surmises that "too ardent" patriots have destroyed unflattering cartoons of the Father of Our Country. Thomas Jefferson was not so fortunate, and several cartoons survive that mock his Gallic and democratic proclivities. In fact, the first American cartoon designed for newspaper reproduction in the *New York Evening Post* (1814) dealt with Jefferson's highly unpopular Embargo Act.

Although Franklin, Tisdale, and others were well known, Edinburgh-born William Charles was the first to become famous here primarily as a political cartoonist. Charles drew heavily upon the works of English cartoonists Gillray and Rowlandson and left no disciples after his death in 1820, but he deserves to be remembered, nevertheless, for popularizing the political cartoon.

The next phase in the history of American editorial cartoons was initiated by the development of lithography, a process that was much faster than woodcuts and engravings. The first lithographed cartoon appeared in 1829; thereafter, lithographed cartoons flourished. Most of them were produced by the firms of Henry R. Robinson and Currier & Ives. Robinson's company produced many political lithographs between 1831 and 1849, and some were superior to those by Currier & Ives, a name that has become synonymous with lithography. The Currier & Ives firm produced over 7,000 different titles between 1840 and 1890 and sold some ten million copies, only 80 of which titles were political cartoons. They were realistic: faces were copied from photographs; and numerous balloons filled with finely printed dialogue floated over the stiff figures. As the Civil War approached, the firm often marketed cartoons, sometimes drawn to order, on both sides of a controversial issue. It is precisely the drawn-to-order nature of these cartoons that makes them seem so woodenly quaint today.

Although Currier & Ives documented the mid-century discord with their lithographs, especially those dealing with the campaigns of 1856 and 1860, the Civil War, and Abraham Lincoln, there were other media germinating that would soon leave the lithographers in the shade and would begin another phase in American editorial cartooning. Englishman Henry Carter arrived here in 1848, changed his name to Frank Leslie, and, by the mid–1850s, was embarked on a series of magazine ventures, the most successful of which was *Frank Leslie's Illustrated Newspaper* (later *Frank Leslie's Illustrated Weekly*). Other Leslie publications included *The Jolly Joker, The Cartoon, Chatterbox,* and *Phunny Phellow.* An impressive list of artists was employed by Leslie, as well as by *Vanity Fair, Harper's Weekly,* and the scores of other publications that appeared and disappeared abruptly: the Anglo-Irishman Frank Bellew, who was popular before the war and whose elongated caricature of Lincoln is still remembered, and many others, most notably the German Thomas Nast and the Viennese Joseph Keppler.

Born in Landau, Germany, in 1840, Thomas Nast came to New York City at the age of six. He became deeply interested in art, especially in the great English cartoonists Leech, Tenniel, and Gilbert. Nast said that he was indebted to Tenniel for his striking use of animals as symbols. At fifteen, he won a job with *Frank Leslie's Illustrated Weekly*. During the Civil War, his illustrations for *Harper's Weekly* were extremely popular. He soon turned to a more emblematic, less reportorial style, which was sometimes allegorical, nearly always emotionally powerful. So effective a voice for the Union did he become that Lincoln called him "our best recruiting sergeant."

The South had its own German-born artist, Adalbert J. Volck, a Baltimore dentist who produced a few excellent caricatures, most notably twenty-nine "Confederate War Etchings" (1863). He scathingly portrayed Lincoln as a clown, a Negro, a woman, and an oriental dancer. Apparently, he gave up cartooning after the war.

Nast, however, continued to draw, and his style evolved into caricature. Eventually, it was through his battle against the Tweed Ring that he made his mark as one of America's most powerful editorial cartoonists. Incensed by the corruption of Boss Tweed, Nast began to fire his volleys from the pages of *Harper's Weekly*. He took Tammany Hall's own tiger and made it into a fearful symbol of marauding lawlessness, to be used against Tweed in the election of 1871. Tweed lost and went to jail in 1873. He escaped, only to be identified and arrested again in Spain because an official recognized him from one of Nast's cartoons. Unfortunately for Nast, right and wrong were never again so plainly distinguishable. His attacks remained formidable, but he was sometimes at a loss for a target, as his own Republican party proved itself susceptible to corruption. He quit *Harper's* in 1887 and lost much of his effectiveness. His investments failed, and by 1902 he had no choice but to accept the post of U.S. Consul to Guayaquil, Equador, where he died in December of the same year. But he left behind him such long-lasting symbols as the Tammany tiger and the Republican elephant, the less durable rag baby of inflation, and the Democratic donkey, which he did not create but did popularize. By his influence on public opinion, he demonstrated that a popular, forceful editorial cartoonist was someone to be reckoned with.

The passing of Nast did not leave a vacuum, however, for there arose the comic weeklies. Joseph Keppler, who came to St. Louis from Vienna in late 1867 or early 1868, started two German-language comic weeklies, both of which failed. In 1872, he went to New York and worked for Frank Leslie. He founded a German-language weekly, *Puck,* in 1876 and an English version in 1877. The magazine thrived and in less than ten years had a circulation of 80,000. An excellent cartoonist himself, Keppler employed many of the best artists of the time.

Puck's heyday partly overlapped Nast's decline. In 1884, Nast was disgruntled by the Republicans' nomination of the tainted James G. Blaine and expressed himself in a cartoon. The Democratic *Puck* joined in and revived an idea Keppler had used against Grant: the tattooed man. Bernard Gillam drew the scandalous series, depicting the husky Blaine in his undershorts, covered with tattoos representing his opponents' allegations of "corruption." The Republicans responded with Frank Beard's cartoon in *Judge,* dramatizing a rumor that Grover Cleveland was the father of an illegitimate child. Perhaps the most telling shot in the cartoon war was "The Royal Feast of Belshazzar Blaine and the Money Kings," drawn by Walt McDougall for the New York *World.* In the drawing, patterned after the *Last Supper,* Blaine, Jay Gould, and other New York financiers feast on such dishes as "patronage." Displayed on billboards around the state, the cartoon contributed to Blaine's defeat in New York and in the national election. According to Charles Press, this marked the real beginning of daily editorial cartooning as a profession.

One of *Puck's* two great rivals, *Judge,* was founded in 1881 by a dissatisfied *Puck* cartoonist, James A. Wales. Perhaps *Judge's* most famous symbol was the "Full Dinner Pail," cartoonist Grant Hamilton's embodiment of the prosperity of Republican William McKinley's first administration. As Stephen Becker points out, these "Full Dinner Pail" cartoons drawn by Hamilton and by Victor Gillam represented an advance in cartooning technique because of their greater simplicity and, therefore, immediacy, as compared to the crowded panel cartoons of the late nineteenth century. The third great comic weekly of the period was *Life,* founded in 1883 by *Harvard Lampoon* graduates led by J. A. Mitchell. Much, although not all, of its satire was social rather than political.

The development of newspaper cartooning was gradual; James Gordon Bennett had started the New York *Telegram* in 1867 and had used sensationalism to boost sales. In the first regular use of cartoons in a newspaper, he printed a front-page cartoon every Friday. Joseph Pulitzer, who bought the New York *World* in 1883, made an even bigger impression with editorial cartoons such as the devastating "Feast of Belshazzar." William Randolph Hearst took over the New York *Journal* in 1895 and began the great circulation war. He brought with him from San Francisco Homer Davenport, who is perhaps best remembered for his caricatures of Republican National Chairman Mark Hanna as smug and bloated, his suit decorated with dollar signs. Hearst snatched Frederick Burr Opper from *Puck* in 1899. Although critics have been condescending toward his technique, Opper was a cartoonist of great versatility and popularity, with a successful comic strip, *Happy Hooligan,* and several telling series of political cartoons, such as "Alice in Plunderland" and "Willie and His Papa." His career was unusual because of its variety and length and also because he was one of the few cartoonists able to make the changeover from the comic magazines, with their complicated, multifigured cartoons, to the daily newspapers, whose deadlines necessitated a more direct style and simpler designs.

By the turn of the century, editorial cartoons were featured regularly in newspapers all over the country. This proliferation so alarmed the politicians who were the target of these drawings that between 1897 and 1915 the legislatures of California, Pennsylvania, Alabama, and New York formulated anti-cartoon legislation. Only two states passed anti-cartoon bills: California's 1897 law was widely ridiculed and never enforced, but Pennsylvania's 1903 law was more formidable. Cartoonist Charles Nelan drew gubernatorial candidate Samuel Pennypacker as a parrot in Philadelphia *North American* cartoons. Upon winning, Pennypacker pushed through the Pennsylvania legislature a law prohibiting the drawing or publishing of any caricature or cartoon for the purpose of exposing a person to ridicule. Nelan and the *North American* immediately violated the law with a series of front-page caricatures. The outraged Pennypacker branded Nelan a "hired outcast." Nelan in turn threatened to sue Pennypacker for libel and forced the governor to apologize. Although there were a few subsequent cases filed under the anti-cartoon law after that, its back was broken, and it was repealed in 1907. Not until the late twentieth century would there be another such concerted legal assault on political cartooning.

The war with Spain provided cartoonists with inspiration for a while, but Theodore Roosevelt literally sustained them for years. His teeth, mustache, and glasses made him easy to draw. He was a favorite subject for two of the early twentieth century's best-known cartoonists: John T. McCutcheon and Jay N. (Ding) Darling. Charles Press has put them at the head of a group of cartoonists he labels "bucolic."

John Tinney McCutcheon was one of the most notable of a large group of outstanding midwestern cartoonists active around the turn of the century. He drew editorial cartoons and nostalgic panels, and illustrated books, such as his famous *Boys in Springtime*. Of his political cartoons for the Chicago *Tribune*, perhaps the best known are his 1932 Pulitzer Prize winner, "A Wise Economist Asks a Question," and "The Mysterious Stranger" (1904), which shows Missouri standing in line with states of the Republican column after it deserted the solid South to vote for Roosevelt.

Another durable midwesterner was Jay N. (Ding) Darling of Iowa. His "The Long, Long Trail," a 1919 tribute to Teddy Roosevelt, has often been reproduced. The duration of his career is shown by the dates of his Pulitzer Prizes—1924 and 1943; he received his last award when he was sixty-six. According to Stephen Becker, however, by that time he was "almost a throwback" to the less sophisticated days of the early part of the century.

In approximately the middle of these men's careers came the next major event in American history: World War I. During the three years of war before the American entry, major U.S. newspaper cartoonists, all but one of whom favored intervention on behalf of the French and English, were busy drawing German atrocities. The interventionist artists included W. A. Rogers and Nelson Harding of the Brooklyn *Eagle*. Dutch artist Louis Raemaekers, whose work appeared in the Hearst papers, is generally considered to be better than the Americans who drew for the Allied cause. The lone pen wielded in defense of neutrality belonged to Luther D. Bradley of the Chicago *Daily News* He died early in 1917, before his antiwar convictions were tested. With the United States in the war, a Bureau of Cartoons, set up under the direction of George J. Hecht, successfully channeled cartoonists' work into the war effort by suggesting topics and otherwise maximizing the propaganda value of cartoons.

Luther Bradley was the only cartoonist for an important newspaper to oppose the war, but the radical cartoonists also opposed it and became prominent in the development of modern political cartooning. Much of their work appeared in *Masses* (1911–17) and *Liberator* (1918–24), because their uncompromising political views were unacceptable to the mainstream. They did not put their shoulders to the wheel of the Allied cause, but instead produced cartoons such as Robert Minor's in 1915, which presented the army medical examiner's idea of the "perfect soldier": a muscular giant with no head.

Three of the radical cartoonists who were most important and most satisfied to be called cartoonists were Boardman Robinson, Art Young, and Robert Minor. Boardman Robinson was the most influential in terms of his effect on subsequent generations of political cartoonists, partly by virtue of his pioneering technique using crayon on grained paper, as Daumier and Forain did before him, and partly because of his position as an instructor at the Art Students League in New York from 1919 to 1930. Among those he influenced may be listed his fellow radical cartoonists Robert Minor and Clive Weed, as well as Oscar Cesare, Rollin Kirby, and Edmund Duffy.

Robert Minor gave up his successful career as a mainstream artist to draw cartoons that reflected his socialist and antiwar beliefs. He simplified his style to increase the impact of the intensely political cartoons he drew for *Masses*.

Art Young probably received the widest distribution of any of the radical cartoonists, partly because he came to socialism relatively late in life, after he had been on the staffs of several major newspapers. With *Masses* editor Max Eastman, Young was also sued unsuccessfully by the Associated Press for libel and was prosecuted in vain by the government under the Espionage Act for obstructing recruitment into the armed forces. In spite of government suppression, *Masses,* in its various forms, provided a forum for some of the best cartoonists of the period. Indeed, art editor John Sloan, along with George Bellows and George Luks, were acclaimed artists of the Ashcan school. It is precisely this exceptional degree of talent, coupled with a technique perfectly suited to the expression of moral outrage, that has made the names and influence of the radical cartoonists last longer than their more moderate contemporaries.

In 1922, the first Pulitzer Prize for editorial cartooning was awarded; it went to Roland Kirby of the New York *World.* If winning prizes is any indication, he was the dominant editorial cartoonist of the 1920s, winning again in 1925 and in 1929 (Nelson Harding won in 1927 and 1928). Kirby is considered to be a transitional figure between the early multifigure cartooning and the modern single-figure panels.

Many of the best comic artists of the 1930s drew social rather than political cartoons for magazines such as *The New Yorker, Vanity Fair,* and *Time*. The Depression, however, along with FDR and his NRA eagle, gave editorial cartoonists plenty of inspiration. As it happened, most cartoonists and most publishers were against Roosevelt. Notable exceptions were C. D. Batchelor, D. R. Fitzpatrick, and, at first, John T. McCutcheon.

Edmund Duffy, who has been called Kirby's heir, won three Pulitzer Prizes in the next decade: 1931, 1934, and 1940. Just as Rollin Kirby's famous "Mr. Dry" was not represented in any of his prize-winning cartoons, so Duffy's chinless little Ku Klux Klansman was also overlooked by the judges. Like Kirby, Duffy was influenced by Boardman Robinson, and he is credited by Stephen Becker with continuing Kirby's move away from the crowded panels of the nineteenth century and toward the single-figure cartoon of those dominant figures of the mid-twentieth century, Herblock and Bill Mauldin.

The 1930s also gave cartoonists the slant-eyed figure of Japanese militarism and the easily caricatured Mussolini and Hitler. The St. Louis *Post-Dispatch's* Daniel R. Fitzpatrick, in a style reminiscent of Boardman Robinson, made effective use of the swastika as a symbol of oppression. Fitzpatrick, who had won a Pulitzer Prize in 1926, would win another in 1955.

During World War II, Bill Mauldin's work in *The Stars and Stripes* provided a welcome relief from patriotic propaganda. He was a combat veteran himself, and his characters, Willie and Joe, were survivors, not heroes. The public took to them immediately. In 1945, Mauldin won the Pulitzer Prize. His popularity continued after the war, with some diminution: his style and the savagery behind it were too grating for a public that wanted amusement, not a crusade. When he returned to cartooning in 1958 with the St. Louis *Post-Dispatch,* he had switched to a lighter grease pencil and opened up his cartoons. And, as his Pulitzer Prize in 1959 for an anti-Russian cartoon showed, the targets were fatter. The civil rights struggles of the 1960s provided him with the southern redneck to ridicule. Overall, Mauldin may be said to have moved in the same general direction as his liberal counterpart, Herbert Block.

By his own testimony uncomfortable with the "liberal" label, Herbert L. Block ("Herblock") was an active cartoonist throughout the 1930s. He was awarded the Pulitzer Prize in 1942, but his preeminence generally begins after the war. He was one of the first cartoonists to oppose the anticommunist hysteria, and he courageously assailed Senator Joseph McCarthy. "Mr. Atom," his sinister personification of the bomb, ranks among the most effective cartoon symbols of the mid-twentieth century. Along with Mauldin, he continues to be a force into the eighties, winning a Pulitzer again in 1979.

Among the younger men who challenged the dominance of Herblock and Mauldin is Patrick Oliphant, who came from Australia in 1964 to work for the Denver *Post*. As the story goes, he and his wife studied the past Pulitzer Prize-winning drawings, and he won one in 1966. Influenced by British cartoonist Ronald Searle, Oliphant has in turn influenced other artists with his fine, exuberant line and emphasis on sheer humor. Oliphant is considered by some to be the preeminent editorial cartoonist drawing in America today. A true satirist, he gets his laughs at the expense of the foolish, no matter what party or profession they belong to. Formerly with the Washington *Star*, he, like Mauldin, has no local newspaper affiliation, instead drawing directly for syndication.

Another comparatively recent addition to the top echelon actually pre-dates Pat Oliphant. An Iowa devotee of Ding Darling, Paul Conrad left the Denver *Post* in 1964 for the Los Angeles *Times*. Lawsuits filed by Mayor Sam Yorty and the Union Oil Company attest to Conrad's effectiveness there. Stephen Hess and Milton Kaplan's 1975 inclusion of Conrad in the "big four" with Herblock, Mauldin, and Oliphant was not universally accepted, but he is unarguably one of the very top cartoonists today. He may be accused of lack of subtlety, for he sometimes breaks bones in the process of drawing blood, but the sheer wildness of his concepts and his skill in executing them with fine and intricate lines make him deadly when he is on target. Conrad won Pulitzer Prizes in 1964, 1971, and 1984.

The other important cartoonists drawing today are too numerous even to list here. Furthermore, any attempt to classify them is bound to be unsatisfactory, for cartoonists resist being categorized just as adamantly as do writers. Keeping these caveats in mind, it is convenient to begin with the so-called new wave, a term used in the early 1960s to include Hugh Haynie of the Louisville *Courier-Journal;* Bill Sanders of the Milwaukee *Journal;* the resurgent Bill Mauldin, whose *Let's Declare Ourselves Winners* (1985) represents his first collection in twenty years; and other, generally liberal cartoonists such as Tony Auth of the Philadelphia *Inquirer*. Especially hard-hitting and somewhat younger, at least in terms of national promi-nence, are Tom Darcy of *Newsday*, Bill Shore of the Los Angeles *Herald Examiner*, and Paul Szep of the Boston *Globe*. Hill is also a leading American authority on the history of the editorial cartoon. Texan Ben Sargent of the Austin *American Statesman* (Pulitzer, 1982) admits to being "probably un-ashamedly liberal." A "second beach head" was established by Don Wright of the Miami *News* (Pulitzer, 1980), who has influenced Mike Peters of the Dayton *Daily News* (Pulitzer, 1981), Doug Marlette of the Atlanta *Consti-tution*, (Pulitzer, 1988) Bob Englehart of the Hartford *Courant*, and Duane Powell of the Raleigh *News Observer*.

Conservative cartoonists include Don Hesse of the St. Louis *Globe Dem-ocrat*, Charles Werner of the Indianapolis *Star*, Tom Curtis of the *National Review*, Wayne Stayskal of the Tampa *Tribune*, Dick Wright of the Providence *Journal,* Dick Locher of the Chicago *Tribune* (Pulitzer, 1983), and Steve Benson of the Arizona *Republic.*

Jeff MacNelly, formerly of the Richmond *News Leader,* now of the Chicago *Tribune,* winner of three Pulitzer Prizes, comes closer than any of the other conservatives to the free-swinging hilarity of Oliphant. Indeed, so popular is MacNelly, vying with Oliphant for the lead in the number of syndicated subscribers, that his numerous imitators have earned the title of "the new school," or the sobriquet "MacNelly clones," depending on who is calling the names.

Jim Borgman of the Cincinnati *Enquirer* defies classification. "I don't really want to be a bumper-sticker orator. . . . I'm more interested in keeping the debate alive than in crusading for a certain ideology." While drawing for a fairly conservative paper, he did not coddle President Reagan. A humane cartoonist who often attains high impact is Draper Hill of the Detroit *News.* Hill is also a leading American authority on the history of the editorial cartoon.

There was once disagreement as to whether or not Garry Trudeau and Jules Feiffer's use of the strip medium instead of the single panel disqualified them as editorial cartoonists, although the winning of the Pulitzer Prize by Trudeau in 1975 and by Feiffer in 1986 is strong evidence on their behalf. At any rate, it is impossible to deny Trudeau's popularity among young people and liberals. Feiffer has been effective since the late 1950s, not only in his merciless forays against the liberals' nemeses, but also in his equally merciless exposure of the self-deception and hypocrisy to which so many liberals fall prey.

Anti-strip cartoonists to the contrary, the 1987 Pulitzer Prize was awarded to relative newcomer Berke Breathed, creator of *Bloom County.* With a cast featuring children and a penguin, Breathed primarily satirizes social issues. On occasion, however, such as the time Bill the schizophrenic cat ran for president with the campaign slogan "This time, why not the worst?," he lashed out at political absurdity as well. Breathed at least partly supplanted Trudeau on campus.

Absurd is the word for *Washingtoon,* the world of yet another strip cartoonist, Mark Alan Stamaty, of the *Village Voice* and the Washington *Post,* and his style exemplifies his attitude: crude drawings with rules of perspective deliberately ignored. A panel might well show a large head surrounded by tiny figures. He often packs his panels with lengthy captions— in and out of balloons—which almost crowd the figures off the page. Although he is uncompromisingly liberal and attacks the Reagan administration's policies and the gutless gullibility of the voters without devoting space to liberal foibles, his barbs are not without empathy.

A small but growing number of women are active in the profession. Etta Hulme of the Fort Worth *Star-Telegram* has served as president of the Association of American Editorial Cartoonists. Kate Salley Palmer is syndicated and has worked for newspapers in South Carolina. Of the younger women editorial cartoonists, Signee Wilkinson graduated from the University of Denver in 1972 and moved from the San Jose *Mercury* to the Philadelphia *Daily News* in 1985. M. G. Lord studied under Garry B. Trudeau at Yale and went with *Newsday* in 1981 at the age of twenty-four.

In the early 1980s syndication, both by individual artists and by groups of artists "packaged" together, became widespread. Cartoonists just out of—or still in—college were suddenly exposed to mass audiences. While no one denies the importance of this phenomenon, critics disagree as to its effect. On one hand, it does enable cartoonists to reach a larger audience. Also, it helps some to make more money while letting the syndicates take care of business details. Among the drawbacks is the fact that young artists may be thrust into national prominence before they are ready. Apprentice mistakes may be made, if not before a national readership, at least under the unforgiving eye of editors who subscribe to the syndicate. Insofar as the profession of editorial cartooning is concerned, the availability of inexpensive syndicated packages makes it less likely that mid-sized newspapers will be willing to hire a beginning artist, even at a low salary. Also, a syndicated cartoonist is likely to look increasingly to a national audience, at the expense of local issues.

In spite of this trend away from the local cartoon, several artists continue to deal heavily with local issues alongside national and international concerns and in spite of the greater money and fame available outside their own backyards. Some of the more prominent of these include George Fisher of the *Arkansas Gazette,* Draper Hill of the Detroit *News,* Paul Rigby of the New York *Daily News,* and Ben Sargent of the Austin *American Statesman.* Only Sargent was syndicated at the time of this writing.

A national cartoonist can turn a local issue into a national one, as the community of Palm Beach found out during two weeks in 1985 when Garry Trudeau spotlighted their law requiring non-residents to carry an identification card. A national outcry and local lawsuits ensued, and the ordinance was subsequently struck down by the courts.

In the litigious 1980s, the shadow of libel suits has fallen across the editorial cartoonist's drawing board. Although no editorial cartoonist to date has lost a libel suit, the mere frequency of their filing is becoming a factor for both editors and cartoonists to consider.

Referring to the inclusion of "malicious intent" in the legal definition of libel, Mike Peters of the Dayton *Daily News* says: "Of course a cartoonist is trying to inflict with malice. There's no doubt a cartoonist is trying to get the politician with malice." And a Philadelphia *Inquirer* editor was quoted on a "Donahue" show as responding to a politician's suing because a cartoonist had held him up to ridicule: "My goodness, a political cartoonist holding up a politician to ridicule. That's not libel, that's a job description."

A list of unsuccessful suers and their suees in recent years would include

Los Angeles Mayor Sam Yorty and Paul Conrad, Massachussetts Governor Edward King and Paul Szep, and former Ohio Supreme Court Justice James Celebreze and Milt Priggee.

Political evangelist Jerry Falwell sued *Hustler* publisher Larry Flynt over an ad parody depicting the evangelist committing incest with his mother in an outhouse. A jury awarded Falwell $200,000 for "emotional distress," but the decision was reversed by the Supreme Court. Although this was not an editorial cartoon, *Hustler* was attacking Falwell on political grounds, and the "emotional distress" precedent could have had far-reaching effects on cartoonists' First Amendment protection.

These developments continue to be worrisome to editors and cartoonists, as the time and expense of defending against even the most far-fetched of libel suits may intimidate all but the most fearless—or deep-pocketed— publishers.

In recent years several editorial cartoonists have branched out and begun drawing comic strips. One of the earliest of these was Jeff MacNelly's apolitical *Shoe* in 1977. Others include Mike Peters's *Mother Goose and Grimm*, Wayne Stayskal's *Balderdash*, and Bill Watterson's *Calvin and Hobbes*. Pat Oliphant's *Sunday Punk*, which ran briefly in 1984, often dealt with social or political issues. Doug Marlette's *Kudzu* features the hypocritical evangelist Rev. Will B. Dunn, star of "There's No Business Like Soul Business."

If some editorial cartoonists have sought artistic outlet (and increased earnings) in less biting political expression, others have expanded the comic art form more in the direction of the novel, while retaining elements of social and/or political criticism. Jules Feiffer wrote the cartoon novel *Tantrum* about a forty-two-year-old man who wills himself back to the age of two yet retains all the desires and knowledge of an adult. Art Spiegelman, who with Françoise Mouly edits *Raw*, "The Comics Magazine for Damned Intellectuals," has taken "Maus" from the pages of *Raw* to the book-length *Maus: A Survivor's Tale*. In this black-and-white story of the Holocaust as Spiegelman's parents lived it, Jews are depicted as mice and the Nazis as cats. The resulting incongruous hybrid is as close to literature as it is to comics. Ralph Steadman has combined drawings and text for the grotesque biography *Sigmund Freud* and *I. Leonardo*.

In general, the early 1980s saw a trend toward originality of style, with an increasing emphasis on humor for its own sake, perhaps a by-product of the political "honeymoon" of the early Reagan years. By the mid-eighties, however, a backlash set in, with some cartoonists launching cartoon barbs at the president and his oft-indicted associates. Among the critics of the new geniality was Bill Sanders of the Milwaukee *Journal*. While praising the talented new artists entering the profession and seeing a "quantum leap in the quality of humor and the use of the gag motif," he warned that "this new infusion carries an ominous quality that threatens the integrity of political cartooning. It is, quite simply, a lack of substance and ideology. Too many gag groupies are serving up sugar-coated placebos. . . . These gag-a-day efforts have about as much passion as a Doris Day movie, dovetailing nicely with the moderate nature of today's editorial pages."[1]

Although the debate over humor versus message continues, American editorial cartoonists tend to be concerned with a combination of comic effect, artistic skill, originality, and substantive issues.

REFERENCE WORKS

Although general encyclopedias, art reference works, and journalism indexes and bibliographies lend some help with the best-known figures in the field—especially those who also have "high culture" reputations—few indexes, bibliographies, or biographical dictionaries deal exclusively or comprehensively with editorial cartooning or political cartoonists.

The most comprehensive bibliographies that deal primarily with editorial cartooning appear in the major history and criticism books, such as Stephen Hess and Milton Kaplan's *The Ungentlemanly Art*. Researchers should be sure to consult the revised edition of Hess and Kaplan (1975), which has a longer bibliography. Even in this, the best bibliography, there are no page numbers in periodical entries, and the items are not annotated.

Another useful bibliography appears in Roy Nelson's *Cartooning*. Nelson deals with social and strip as well as editorial cartooning, and there is some annotation. The Fort Worth exhibition publication, *The Image of America in Caricature and Cartoons,* also contains an extensive bibliography, but it is not annotated. A number of items are American history references that have only indirect bearing on editorial cartooning.

Researchers may find the bibliography at the end of Ralph E. Shikes's *The Indignant Eye* more useful. The annotated list for the chapter on recent and American cartooning is especially valuable. More specialized history and criticism books about individual cartoonists, such as Morton Keller's *The Art and Politics of Thomas Nast,* deserve attention as well. The Keller book includes brief annotations for a number of significant Nast studies.

Although it does not deal exclusively with American editorial cartooning, a recently published and soon to be expanded bibliography by Dr. John A. Lent, *Comic Art: An International Bibliography,* deserves attention. The 156-page compilation includes 1,197 bibliography entries broken down alphabetically and by continent and country. Books, journal articles, monographs, and conference reports, as well as seminar papers and fugitive materials, are included. Almost half of the entries deal with American materials, and according to Lent, editorial cartoonists are strongly represented in the selection. The materials are also well indexed by author and by subject under three categories: general, cartoonists, and cartoons and comics titles. The bibliography is available only from the author, Dr. John A. Lent (669

Ferne Blvd., Drexel Hill, Pennsylvania 19026), who is also the journals reviewer for *Witty World*.

Among the standard references in journalism, *An Annotated Journalism Bibliography* should be consulted. Compiled by Warren C. Price and Calder M. Pickett, the bibliography lists forty-eight items under the "Cartoons, Cartooning" heading. J. Brander Matthews also wrote a bibliographical essay on comic periodicals in 1875 that is still of value today. Some other bibliographies look promising but turn out to be disappointing. Wolfgang Kempkes's *The International Bibliography of Comics Literature* deals almost entirely with strips and contains only a few items on editorial cartooning.

It is also profitable to review reprints of the subject catalogs of major libraries with fine arts holdings, such as the Harvard University's Fogg Library Catalog, the Metropolitan Museum of Art Library Catalog, and the Catalog of the Museum of Modern Art Library.

For periodical items, students may wish to go beyond the standard guides to look at the *Art Index,* which lists by subject as well as by artist. In addition, the Ryerson Library Index of the Art Institute of Chicago includes only periodical article references and thus serves a special function among art library catalogs. The search for books and articles about major figures in the field usually requires cartoonists' names, since the subject indexes are not entirely trustworthy.

For annotated references to recent major books, festschriften, periodical articles, and exhibition catalogs, *RILA: Repértoire international de la littérature de l'art* (International Repertory of the Literature of Art) is a good reference because *RILA* often includes items not listed elsewhere and because reviews are substantial. *RILA* indexes political cartooning under the Library of Congress heading "Caricatures and Cartoons."

For recent bibliography, students will want to consult not only the standard library references and on-line data bases, but the "Reviews" sections of cartooning journals such as *Target, Witty World,* and *AAEC Notebook*. A more complete description of their importance as bibliographical sources appears in the "Periodicals" subsection of this chapter.

There are also only a few sources that provide shortcuts for researchers seeking biographical data on individual cartoonists, and none of these is both up to date and comprehensive. It is wise to use several to cross-check.

Maurice Horn, well known for *The World Encyclopedia of Comics,* has edited *The World Encyclopedia of Cartoons,* a much-needed two-volume reference guide that includes a significant amount of material on U.S. editorial cartoonists. With the help of twenty-two contributors, Horn's book includes an overview of caricature and cartooning with a section on "The Editorial Cartoon," a brief history of humor magazines, "A World Chronology" of important dates in cartoon art from the Renaissance to the present, alphabetical entries which include among the 1,200 cross-referenced entries a liberal assortment of biographical/critical descriptions of major editorial cartoonists as well as contextual items relevant to editorial cartooning. In Horn's appendixes, he lists Pulitzer Prize winners through 1979 and Sigma Delta Chi Award winners through 1977. He also includes a helpful glossary of cartooning terms and a short selected bibliography which includes several major books and journal articles on editorial cartooning. The book is indexed by proper names, subject, illustration titles, and country. The final entry in Volume 2 is a brief history of *Puck, Judge,* and *Life,* with illustrations.

Horn is also editing the continuing edition of *Contemporary Graphic Artists* for Gale Research Company. Each volume features bibliographies and critical articles on more than one hundred graphic artists; many editorial cartoonists such as Hill, Borgman, Locher, and Sargent are included. The book is cross-indexed by artists' names, occupation, and subjects.

Masters of Caricature, edited by Ann Gould with commentary and introduction by William Feaver, is a series of brief biographies and artwork examples of 243 caricaturists of historical and current importance; it provides some basic introductions to many important figures in the field. Art critic for the London *Observer,* Feaver provides a helpful background essay on the art, but the biographical entries, written by a number of different contributors, are uneven and contain enough occasional errors so that researchers should seek additional verification. The chronological organization is creditable and invites comparisons and contrasts across international lines, but a number of significant caricaturists are missing or omitted because of a limited definition of the term *caricaturist,* and the selected bibliography will not be of great help to serious students.

The *Encyclopedia of Twentieth-Century Journalists* by William H. Taft includes more than 1,000 biographical sketches of journalists but is of limited value to students of editorial cartooning. Although most of the book is devoted to editors, reporters, photographers, and publishers, some major editorial cartoonists are included.

Over 300 editorial cartoonists' photos and biographies (many prepared by the cartoonists themselves) appear in the *National Cartoonists' Society Album,* edited by Mort Walker. The book's disadvantage is that editorial cartoonists are intermixed with magazine artists and strip cartoonists who are members of the society.

John Chase's *Today's Cartoon,* published in 1962, is a yearbook of 139 editorial cartoonists. It includes photos, biographical data, and informal commentary for each entry. Biographical sketches of some major cartoonists, together with photos of the artists, also appear in Lynne Deur's *Political Cartoonists.* Although this simple book can be categorized as history and criticism, the sketches are so brief that it is more helpful as a reference guide if depth is not a requirement.

Deur's book, like most of the other reference works, reprints representative cartoons for most of the cartoonists included. In addition, *The Image of America in Caricature and Cartoon* has a valuable appendix of 132 biograph- ical sketches of figures involved in the Fort Worth exhibition. Although sketches are brief and not current, historical as well as contemporary figures are represented. A number of how-to books, such as Chuck Thorndike's *The Business of Cartooning,* also provide thumbnail sketches of a few political cartoonists of an earlier period. Thorndike includes C. D. Batchelor, "Ding" Darling, and John McCutcheon.

Some well-established editorial cartoonists are listed in *Who's Who in America* or *Who's Who in American Art.* To find out about a living editorial cartoonist currently working in the field, researchers may wish to consult the membership list of the Association of American Editorial Cartoonists, which is updated annually. The list is not available to the general public, but the association may respond to serious researchers. This list or a similar membership roster from the National Cartoonists' Society may omit several major figures who are not members. Biographical descriptions of well- known deceased cartoonists appear in the *Dictionary of American Biography.*

Although there are no recently published indexes, Frank Weitenkampf's *Political Caricature in the United States, in Separately Published Cartoons . . . an Annotated List* indexes some of the most important editorial cartoons. The index is chronological, so that the book also serves as a history of editorial cartooning in the United States. Weitenkampf provides locations as well as descriptions for 1,158 cartoon entries. Bernard Reilly of the Library of Congress Prints and Photographs Division reports that indexes of several of the library's cartoon collections will soon be published.

RESEARCH COLLECTIONS

Traditionally, research collections of editorial cartoons were hard to locate because such collections were not fully reported or cataloged. Although specific holdings of editorial and political cartoons are often still not fully reported within a general cartoon collection, progress has been made within the last decade.

With the appearance of *The Image of America in Caricature and Cartoon* in 1976 and the newest edition of Lee Ash's *Subject Collections: A Guide to Special Book Collections and Subject Emphases as Reported by University, College, Public and Special Libraries and Museums in the United States and Canada* (1985), more complete lists of editorial cartoon collections in the United States, Canada, and Great Britain are available.

The Image of America in Caricature and Cartoon concentrates on U.S. col- lections; the Canadian and British references are included primarily where there are holdings directly related to U.S. history and culture. The list of private collectors is necessarily incomplete. The alphabetized inventory of collections, arranged by state, was compiled through the use of 2,000 ques- tionnaires and through personal contacts; in some cases, the library or personal collector has reported specifically what period or what cartoonists his collection covers and what has been cataloged. In other instances, however, and especially with regard to large collections, the information is too vague or too general and requires verification.

The 1985 edition of Lee Ash's *Subject Collections* lists three pages of cartoon collections under the headings "Caricatures and Cartoons" and "Caricaturists and Cartoonists." Some collections are described more fully than others, but approximately three-quarters of the listings are of interest to students of American editorial cartooning.

The largest collection of caricatures and cartoons is probably to be found in the Library of Congress. Bernard Reilly, head curator of the Prints and Photographs Division, reports that the Library of Congress has four major collections of political cartoons. The most extensive of the four is the Caroline and Erwin Swann Collection of nineteenth-and twentieth-century drawings, which includes approximately 2,500 editorial cartoons, comic strips, and single caricatures. Use of the collection is restricted because of the delicate state of preservation of many of the items, but cataloging of the items is now complete, and an edited manuscript of cataloged items is in progress and will soon be published. The Cartoon Drawings Collection is a group of about 2,200 early twentieth-century drawings by American artists primarily for political cartoons. A large portion of the collection was originally drawn for American newspapers and journals and was collected by George T. Maxwell and donated to the library. That collection is now on video disc, and the collection has been described on data base. About 600 American cartoons from 1798 to 1900 are also collected in the library's Political Cartoon Print Collection, which is international in scope. The American portion of the collection has been cataloged, and a published catalog of items up to 1876 is being prepared.

In addition, the Cabinet of American Illustration, which is primarily a set of drawings for American magazine and book illustrations, contains approximately 200 editorial and political cartoons, including work by Thomas Nast and Joseph Keppler. According to Reilly, a major preservation program is in progress to restore these drawings. This collection is also available to researchers on video disc, and a data base catalog is available at the Library of Congress. The Prints and Photographs Division is continually enlarging its editorial cartoon holdings. Among its several important acquisitions since 1980 are several hundred Rollin Kirby drawings and about one hundred original Luther Bradley drawings for cartoons.

A relatively new and important repository for editorial cartoons is the Library of Communication and Graphic Arts at the Ohio State University. The library is only ten years old, but it has as a primary long-term goal the development of comprehensive collections (published works, manuscript materials, and original cartoons) in the history of American cartoon art. Comic artist Milton Caniff, a 1930 graduate of the Ohio State University, contributed his papers in 1973 to establish the nucleus of the collection. Since these initial contributions, the library's collection has grown rapidly. According to Professor Lucy Caswell, curator, the library has editorial cartoons by hundreds of people. The library has 25 cartoons or more (for some more than 1,000) from the following cartoonists: Brian Basset, Ned Beard, Eugene Craig, Bill Crawford, Edwina Dumm, Billy Ireland, Ed Kuekes, Jim Larrick, Winsor McCay, Ray Osrin, Eugene Payne, Mike Peters, Art Poinier, Milt Priggee, Jeff Stahler, L. D. Warren, Charles Werner, Ned White, and Scott Willis. The Woody Gelman Collection contains over sixty original comic strips and editorial cartoons by Winsor McCay. The Ned White Collection has almost 400 of his editorial cartoons plus the work of ninety-three other cartoonists including Vaughn Shoemaker, Rollin Kirby, and Herblock. The G. T. Maxwell Collection has examples of his original cartoons and cartoons by Louis M. Glackens, Frederick Burr Opper, Michael Angelo Wolfe, Eugene Zimmerman (Zim), and several other early cartoonists.

The business aspects of cartooning are documented in the Ohio State Library's Toni Mendez Collection, the records of her many years as a licensing agent representing cartoonists. United Feature Syndicate has donated a very large collection of United and NEA syndicate proofs. The library became the permanent archive for the Association of American Editorial Cartoonists in 1984; the National Cartoonists Society named the library as its archival depository in 1985. Recently, *Target,* the political cartooning quarterly, also named the library as its archive. Every few years the library sponsors "A Festival of Cartoon Art," featuring panel discussions by working cartoonists and scholars as well as historical exhibits and original artwork by current cartoonists.

While the library provides a carefully controlled environment and a special security system to ensure the safety of its collection, the library's brochures emphasize that "the purpose of the Library for Communication and Graphic Arts is not to collect curiosities or to function as a museum but to encourage scholarly examination of the mass media arts which both reflect and change life." According to Professor Caswell, materials in the library are available to qualified researchers upon request following their registration as users. Inventory lists and other finding aids are available for each collection. Researchers are encouraged to make advance arrangements prior to coming to the library. The Library for Communication and Graphic Arts of the Ohio State University is located at 242 West 18th Avenue, Room 147, Columbus, Ohio 43210–1107.

In addition, major editorial cartoon collections cited in *The Image of America in Caricature and Cartoon* or in Lee Ash's *Subject Collections* include the collections of the New York Public Library; the Smithsonian Institution; the Boston Public Library; the Lilly Library of the University of Indiana; the Hal Coffman Collection of the Fort Worth (Texas) Public Library; the

New York Historical Society; the Syracuse University Library; the Chesler Collection of the Library of Fairleigh Dickinson University, Florham-Madison, New Jersey; the Free Library of Philadelphia; and the Philadelphia Museum of Art. Other noteworthy collections of American political or editorial cartoons and drawings can be found at the Fogg Art Museum of Harvard University; the John Hay Library of Brown University; the Princeton University Library; the American Antiquarian Society Library, Worcester, Massachusetts; the Butler Institute of American Art in the Kenneth Spencer Research Library of the University of Kansas at Lawrence; the Ablah Library at Wichita State University; the University of Southern Mississippi's William David McCain Graduate Library at Hattiesburg; and the University of Virginia's Alderman Library.

Specialized libraries, whose collections are limited to work concerned with a single public figure, often have political or editorial cartoons, but usually in relatively small numbers. Libraries and memorials such as Woodrow Wilson House, Washington D.C.; the Herbert Hoover Presidential Library, West Branch, Texas; the Dwight D. Eisenhower Presidential Library, Abilene, Kansas; the Calvin Coolidge Memorial Room, Northhampton, Massachusetts; the Franklin D. Roosevelt Presidential Library, Hyde Park, New York; the Lyndon B. Johnson Presidential Library, Austin, Texas; the Woodrow Wilson Birthplace Foundation, Staunton, Virginia; and the Gerald Ford Presidential Museum, Grand Rapids, Michigan, all have some collections of cartoons and caricatures relating to their special interests.

While the works of significant editorial cartoonists are frequently scattered among the major collections across the country, some libraries report substantial holdings of a particular cartoonist's works. The Bancroft Library of the University of California, Berkeley, has a collection of Rube Goldberg original drawings for editorial cartoons and comic strips. Pat Oliphant's cartoons for the Denver *Post* between 1965 and 1968 are in the library of the University of Colorado, Boulder. Some Paul Conrad original cartoons are held by the Syracuse University Library collection in New York. A larger number can be found in the Paul F. Conrad Collection at the Central University Library of the University of California at San Diego. Clifford K. Berryman's cartoons may be seen at the Idaho State Historical Society in Boise. Louis Raemaekers's drawings and cartoons are at the Hoover Institution on War, Revolution, and Peace at Stanford University.

There is a collection of John T. McCutcheon cartoons in the Illinois Historical Society Library and at Northern Illinois University, DeKalb; a larger number of several hundred McCutcheon works drawn from 1916 to 1945 are at the Northwestern University Library, Evanston, Illinois; and the largest group of McCutcheon drawings is at the Purdue University libraries in West Lafayette, Indiana. McCutcheon, a Purdue alumnus, is represented by 800 cartoons in his alma mater's collection.

Thomas Nast cartoons are held in a number of different collections, including the Library of Congress and the New York Public Library, which has a large group of mounted Nast drawings and checklists of his cartoons and the books that he illustrated. Other collections of Nast cartoons are reported by Columbia University Library, New York; the Art Institute of Chicago; Boston Public Library's print collection; Hopkins Center Art Galleries, Dartmouth College, Hanover, New Hampshire; the Cincinnati Art Museum; and the University of Rochester Library and Memorial Art Gallery. There are also smaller collections at Hamilton College, Clinton, New York, and at the Rutgers University Art Gallery, New Brunswick, New Jersey.

A major group of J. N. "Ding" Darling cartoons may be found at Drake University, Des Moines, Iowa, and in special collections at the University of Iowa Library, Iowa City. According to Lee Ash, the University of Iowa collection includes 600 cartoons and four file drawers of manuscript material. There is an extensive subject index.

A major source for twentieth-century cartoons is the Albert Reid Collection at the University of Kansas in the Kenneth Spencer Research Library at Lawrence. To Reid's personal collection of cartoons were added the works of later cartoonists like Bill Mauldin, Rollin Kirby, and Daniel B. Dowling. That group also contains some of Nast's work.

Some Daniel J. Fitzpatrick cartoons are in general collections. One major reported collection of Fitzpatrick's work is held by the Missouri Historical Society, St. Louis. David Levine's caricatures and cartoons are collected by the Brooklyn Museum, New York, and Frederick Burr Opper cartoons are to be found in the Lake County Historical Society of Mentor, Ohio. The Brooks Memorial Art Gallery, Memphis, Tennessee, has cartoons by J. P. Alley, and the Oregon Historical Society has a small collection of Homer Davenport's work. John Chase's cartoons are in the New Orleans Public Library and the Tulane University Library.

The social protest cartoons of Boardman Robinson are located in a number of major collections and also at the Munson-Williams Proctor Institute, Utica, New York, and at St. Bonaventure University, St. Bonaventure, New York. The Munson-Williams Proctor Institute also holds cartoons of Reginald Marsh and John Sloan, whose works are widely disseminated among important collections as well. The State Historical Society of Wisconsin has the H. T. Webster Collection, which contains cartoons from the Progressive era through the 1950s.

Other cartoonists, such as Fred O. Seibel of the Richmond *Times-Dispatch*, are collected at the University of Virginia Library, Charlottesville, and the James Branch Cabell Library of Virginia Commonwealth University, Richmond. Tom Little of the Nashville *Tennesseean* has cartoons in the collections of the Joint University Libraries, Nashville, Tennessee. Adalbert J. Volck, the Confederate Civil War cartoonist and illustrator, is collected in several libraries, notably in the Virginia Historical Society, Richmond; the Chicago Public Library; and the Peabody Institute, Baltimore.

Radical political and/or editorial cartoons have not been carefully indexed or reported nationally, and there exists a need for more research in that area; however, Jannette Fiore, curator of special collections at Michigan State University, East Lansing, reports that the Michigan State Library Alternative Press Collection contains a number of such cartoons and caricatures of interest to students of radical political cartooning on both the right and the left.

In addition to library collections, *The Image of America in Caricature and Cartoon* cites several private collectors, such as cartoonist-historian Draper Hill of the Detroit *News*. Other nonlibrary collectors, such as the Museum of Cartoon Art in Rye Town, Port Chester, New York, report well over 1,000 original political or editorial cartoons. According to museum curator Sherman Krisher, the collection includes cartoons by Nast, Trudeau, and MacNelly as well as a substantial number of books on the history of editorial cartooning; the museum's major emphasis, however, remains social and strip cartooning.

A rule of thumb for locating unrecorded or unreported collections, especially for cartoonists who did not acquire major or national reputations, is to consult the newspaper libraries where they worked and the libraries in the locales where they were best known.

HISTORY AND CRITICISM

The first real historian of the subject was Philadelphia-born James P. Malcolm, a fierce loyalist whose 1813 book, *An Historical Sketch of the Art of Caricaturing,* describes a very few caricatures dealing with the American war, while touching on Asian and European caricatures but emphasizing the British.

In 1862, Richard Grant White provided for *Harper's New Monthly Magazine* a survey of caricature from the time of the Egyptians up to the present in France and England, concluding with a plea for caricaturists to exercise restraint. In "The Limits of Caricature" in 1866, *The Nation* pointed out technical weaknesses in American caricature and concluded that "upon the whole, we can hardly esteem caricature as an agreeable or particularly useful art; for fairness and good nature are almost impossible in the practice."

American scholarly consideration of editorial cartooning may be said to have begun in 1878, with James Parton's *Caricature and Other Comic Art.* Parton traced the history of caricature from Roman times to his own, devoting the final thirty-odd pages to early and later American caricature from Franklin to Nast. The study is still worthwhile and includes 203 illustrations.

A few years later, Arthur Penn noted "The Growth of Caricature" in *The Critic,* citing Parton as a source. He commented on the failure of American imitations of *Punch* and on the success of *Puck,* while criticizing it for weakness in pictorial social commentary. Writing in *The Century* in 1892, Joseph Bucklin Bishop dated political caricature in the United States from the first administration of Andrew Jackson. His scholarly interest in dating various cartoons is noteworthy.

Frederick Taylor Cooper and Arthur Bartlett Maurice's *The History of the Nineteenth Century in Caricature* is another valuable full-length early study. Over 250 illustrations, many of them full-page, are a strong point of this book; it emphasizes French and British caricature but devotes considerable attention to the American forms, including Currier & Ives, Nast, *Puck,* and *Judge,* and to the rise of the daily newspaper cartoon at the close of the century.

Another scholarly milestone is Frank Weitenkampf's *American Graphic Art,* which appeared in 1912, was revised and enlarged in 1924, and was reprinted in 1970. In a solid work that was a source for many subsequent researchers, Weitenkampf devoted some of the fifteen chapters to etching, lithography, and so on, and examines caricature from Franklin up to the newspaper cartoonists of his own time, with extensive discussion of early comic periodicals, beginning with *Yankee Doodle* in 1856. Weitenkampf continued his consideration of editorial cartooning as a serious art form in 1913 with his illustrated article "American Cartoonists of Today," which appeared in *Century.* Evaluating several contemporary cartoonists, he wrote that a review of the best of them "discloses an admirable average of elevated endeavor and intention."

Twenty years later came the first volume of William Murrell's indispensable *A History of American Graphic Humor,* which ranges from the earliest wood engravings through the Civil War. In addition to an extensive background, the book provides 237 illustrations, listing the source or location of each. Murrell's comments, necessarily brief, are nevertheless historically and aesthetically worthwhile. Published in 1938, Volume 2 uses 242 illustrations in taking us up through the presidential campaign of 1936. Between these two publication dates, Murrell's concise and useful "The Rise and Fall of Cartoon Symbols" appeared in *The American Scholar.*

Thomas Craven's *Cartoon Cavalcade* presents strip and humorous cartoons as well as editorial ones, spanning from 1883 to 1943. Copiously illustrated, the book also includes several essays by Craven relating the graphic humor of various periods to events and attitudes of the time.

The next year, 1944, saw the publication of Allan Nevins and Frank Weitenkampf's *A Century of Political Cartoons.* In addition to an excellent nine-page introductory essay on caricature and cartoon, it provides generalizations on the artistic merits of the cartoons and their artists, as well as a history of American political cartooning until 1900. Many of the one hundred cartoons are accompanied by an explanatory one-page note, with sidelights on the artist.

Journalism professors have commented on editorial cartoons. Frank Luther Mott mentioned some historical highlights of the subject in *American Journalism*. Professor Henry Ladd Smith documented "The Rise and Fall of the Political Cartoon" in the *Saturday Review* in 1954, labeling the first quarter of this century the "golden age of the political cartoonists."

Stephen Becker's *Comic Art in America* is an important work, even though it devotes only one chapter (fifty-five pages) to editorial cartooning. Its strengths include the numerous illustrations and detailed coverage of the Pulitzer Prize years, 1922–58. Becker's editorial comments are occasionally hyperbolic, but he provides an excellent overview, and his judgments are sharper here than in some of the other chapters in this book, which critics have treated none too kindly.

The best book on American editorial cartooning is Stephen Hess and Milton Kaplan's *The Ungentlemanly Art* because of its comprehensiveness and its documentation of both print and graphic sources. Perhaps the authors lose some of the advantage of currency by devoting only 54 of the book's 173 pages to the chapter on "Newspapers, 1884–1975," even in the revised edition. After the introduction, subsequent chapters are arranged according to media: "Copper Engraving and Woodcut," "Lithography and Early Magazines," "Magazines," and "Newspapers." The thematic-topical organization of the newspaper chapter is quite effective. The revised edition of 1975 is only slightly revised, adding a dozen or so new bibliographical references and some current cartoons.

Other works, more restricted in subject matter, include Kenneth M. Johnson's *The Sting of the Wasp*, which has as its subject the San Francisco humor magazine *The Wasp*, which has unfortunately received far less attention than its contemporaries, *Puck* and *Judge*. Also specialized is Ralph E. Shikes's *The Indignant Eye*, subtitled "The Artist as Social Critic in Prints and Drawings from the Fifteenth Century to Picasso." In addition to providing an illustrated history of European protest art, Shikes devotes a seventy-page chapter to "The United States Since 1870," beginning with Nast, but doubling back to touch upon some early engravers and cartoonists. He deals with the major cartoonists from Keppler and Davenport up through the radical cartoonists, predictably ignoring more amiable artists such as Darling and McCutcheon. The remainder of the chapter is concerned primarily with printmakers, but he credits Herblock with doing much to keep dissent alive during the McCarthy years and reproduces two of his cartoons. In spite of its concentration on protest art, Shikes's work is helpful, not only for its consideration of some important cartoonists, but also because it provides artistic yardsticks for us to measure them by.

A book that is even more specialized than Shikes's is Richard Fitzgerald's *Art and Politics*, which tells the story of *Masses* and *Liberator* in the first chapter and devotes a chapter each to Art Young, Robert Minor, John Sloan, K. R. Chamberlain, and Maurice Becker. The thesis of this excellent study is, "While their [radical cartoonists'] greatest successes were in capturing the ferment of artistic and political dissent, their most significant failure was their continual inability to provide a deeper analysis of the role of art and politics in the culture." Fitzgerald includes an extensive bibliography of the art and politics of the period and sixty full-page illustrations.

The Masses has inspired another fine work, Rebecca Zurier's Art for the Masses (1911–1917): A Radical Magazine and Its Graphics. This catalog is a retrospective of the artwork from The Masses. Zurier's animated essays chronicle the magazine's brief but tumultuous life and place the graphics in their social and historical context.

Restricted chronologically is Mary and Gordon Campbell's The Pen, Not the Sword, which is an extensively illustrated anthology of the period of Nast, Keppler, Gillam, Opper, and other artists of the end of the nineteenth century, and is accompanied by some confusing background essays.

The Cartoon History of California Politics by Ed Salzman and Ann Leigh Brown grew out of a bicentennial exhibit at the University of California Museum of Art. Short essays provide background for the cartoons, which range from 1949 to 1977. Similarly, The Image of America in Caricature and Cartoon reproduces the exhibition presented at the Amon Carter Museum in Fort Worth, Texas. Ron Taylor, the Amon Carter Museum's curator of history, provides an introduction devoting two pages to an overview of American cartoons and caricatures, followed by thirty-seven pages of American history related to cartoons, especially some of those reprinted later in the book. Further, each of the 263 cartoons is accompanied by a brief paragraph that analyzes its background and point of view.

Syd Hoff, known for his New Yorker cartoons, is the author and editor of Editorial and Political Cartooning, which is divided into three sections: "The Old Masters," "The Moderns: U.S. and Canada," and "The Moderns: The World." Although it is unscholarly, the book is extensive and ecumenical in its inclusion of 700 cartoons by 165 cartoonists. Hoff provides informal background and sometimes makes instructive aesthetic judgments.

Especially valuable as a reference work and a source of illustrations is Michael Wynn Jones's 1975 book, The Cartoon History of the American Revolution, although the reader is sometimes at a loss to determine on which side of the Atlantic a particular cartoon originated.

Charles Press's The Political Cartoon was published in 1979. Written from a political scientist's point of view, this extensively illustrated book emphasizes the role of editorial cartoonists in a democracy. Press devotes several chapters to an anecdotal history of American editorial cartooning. The chapter "Since World War II" is especially welcome for its coverage of today's cartoonists. The author is critical of some of the "new wave" cartoonists (Conrad, Darcy, Don Wright, Szep) and drops Conrad from

Hess's "big four," leaving Herblock, Mauldin, and Oliphant. The chapter on politics in the strips is useful, as is the book overall, filling in background omitted by other studies. Roy Paul Nelson's history, *Comic Art and Caricature,* a valuable modern reference, appeared in 1978.

Another group of books deals primarily with world cartooning, but several merit our attention because they devote some space to Americans. Michael Wynn Jones's *The Cartoon History of Great Britain* provides good background on British cartoonists, as well as a chapter entitled "World War I-America to the Front." Draper Hill's three books, *Mr. Gillray, the Caricaturist; Fashionable Contrasts: 100 Caricatures by James Gillray;* and *The Satirical Etchings of James Gillray,* shed light on an English artist who had great influence on Americans.

Wider in scope but shorter in length, Clifford K. Berryman's booklet, *Development of the Cartoon,* is interesting primarily because its author was a well-known cartoonist. Most of its nineteen pages are concerned with an informal history of world cartooning and caricature, with some sketches of famous caricatures apparently drawn by Berryman himself. After a paragraph on Nast, he explains that lack of space prevents him from discussing modern cartoonists. H. R. Westwood's *Modern Caricaturists,* with an introduction by David Low, has a chapter on Rollin Kirby and one on D. R. Fitzpatrick. More recently, *Mightier Than the Sword* by W. G. Rogers surveys important European cartoonists and caricaturists. Its discussion of the relationship between British and early American cartoonists is helpful, and it treats Mauldin, Herblock, and Feiffer in the last chapter. The book has surprisingly few illustrations. While it provides more illustrations, Bevis Hillier's *Cartoons and Caricatures* touches only briefly on American cartoonists. *The Cartoon* by John Geipel, however, has fifteen pages on Americans, eclectically mixing editorial with social cartoonists as it goes from Revere to Herblock and Oliphant, touching on Charles Dana Gibson, Peter Arno, James Thurber, and others along the way. Other chapters deal with strip and animated cartoons.

Although Ralph Shikes and Steven Heller's *The Art of Satire: Painters as Caricaturists from Delacroix to Picasso* deals primarily with the satirical drawings of thirty-four painters of the nineteenth to mid-twentieth centuries, especially the French, it does include works of Americans George Grosz, John Sloan, and Ad Reinhardt. Folio-sized with 154 black-and-white illustrations, it is well annotated and has a useful bibliography. *Political Graphics: Art as a Weapon* by French historian and medievalist Robert Philippe is heavily continental in its emphasis and lavishly illustrated with poster and cartoon art, some of it in color, from the past 500 years. Post–1930 works are slighted, and those that are reproduced are mostly poster art. Philippe does include works by John Fischetti, Pat Oliphant, Don Wright, Gerald Scarfe, and others. A sixteen-page afterword by Steven Heller, art director for the *New York Times Book Review,* comments on selections by David

Levine, Edward Sorel, Fritz Eichenberg, Brad Holland, and others. Brief biographical sketches of "Fifty Names in Political Graphics" are appended. Similar to Philippe's book in its emphasis is *The Art of Caricature* by British art historian Edward Lucie-Smith. Although David Levine's "Nixon and Brezhnev" is included, the rest of the meager American representation includes Charles Addams, Peter Arno, Al Capp, and James Thurber.

A study of Victorian taste valuable to students of caricature is Roy T. Matthews and Peter Mellini's *In Vanity Fair*. Thoroughly cataloged and indexed, it includes caricatures of American politicians by Thomas Nast and others probably by James Montgomery Flagg. Colin Seymour-Ure and Jim Schoff's *David Low* makes it clear why the English cartoonist was so important and so influential for those to follow.

There are several book-length studies of individual editorial cartoonists, including, from the early period, William A. Beardsley's *An Old New Haven Engraver and His Work: Amos Doolittle* and Harry B. Weiss's *William Charles, Early Caricaturist, Engraver and Publisher of Children's Books*. About Currier & Ives are the books *Mr. Currier and Mr. Ives* by Russell Crouse, *Currier and Ives* by F. A. Conningham, and *Currier and Ives, Printmakers to the American People* by Harry T. Peters.

Not surprisingly, Thomas Nast is also well represented. The definitive biography is Albert Bigelow Paine's *Th. Nast: His Period and His Pictures,* warmly written with a wealth of personal details. Paine includes rare early drawings and sketches among the 450 illustrations he reproduces, and treats Nast, whom he had met, with contagious admiration and affection. An antidote to this subjectivity is Morton Keller's *The Art and Politics of Thomas Nast,* which sees bigotry as much as altruism behind Nast's campaign against the Irish-Catholic Tweed. The large-format book reproduces 241 cartoons and illustrations, mostly full-page. A third book on Nast—and the scholar would be wise to consult all three—is *Thomas Nast: Political Cartoonist* by J. Chal Vinson, which emphasizes in its forty-page text the events of Nast's life more than his personality and reproduces 154 drawings. Joseph Keppler is the subject of "Keppler and Political Cartooning" by Frank Weitenkampf in the *Bulletin of the New York Public Library* and of Draper Hill's excellent Harvard A.B. thesis, "What Fools These Mortals Be! A Study of the Work of Joseph Keppler, Founder of Puck." *Satire on Stone: The Political Cartoons of Joseph Keppler* by Richard Samuel West was published in 1988.

In addition to Hill's, there are several unpublished theses and dissertations that contribute to the study of editorial cartooning: J. H. Bender, Jr.'s "Editorial Cartoonists: Development/Philosophy Today," Joseph Anthony Gahn's "The American of William Gropper, Radical Cartoonist," and Charles N. Faerber's "An Examination of the Career Patterns and Editorial Roles of a Number of Staff Editorial Cartoonists on Contemporary American English-Language Newspapers."

Of the books about single cartoonists, several deal with the radical cartoonists, two of which are titled *John Sloan*, one by Albert E. Gallatin and the other by Lloyd Goodrich. Albert Christ-Janer is the author of *Boardman Robinson*. Peter Marzio's *Rube Goldberg: His Life and Work* is at once biographical and critical. David L. Lendt's *Ding: The Life of Jay Norwood Darling* is primarily a biography, with little attention paid to Darling's cartoons.

Also, there are some autobiographies: *Art Young: His Life and Times;* John T. McCutcheon's *Drawn from Memory;* Walt McDougall's *This Is the Life!;* and Rube Goldberg's which may be found in *Rube Goldberg vs. the Machine Age,* edited by Clark Kinnaird. Bill Mauldin's *A Sort of Saga* deals only with the artist's boyhood years.

Often overlooked, the how-to books sometime incorporate history, criticism, and strong illustrations in the course of their instruction. Noteworthy examples are Mort Gerberg's *The Arbor House Book of Cartooning,* which includes drawings by Feiffer, MacNelly, Oliphant, and others; Roy Paul Nelson's *Humorous Illustration and Cartooning,* which expands on Nelson's earlier book, *Cartooning;* Grant Wright's *The Art of Caricature;* Dick Spencer III's *Editorial Cartooning;* and Rube Goldberg's "Lesson #19" in the *Famous Artists Cartoon Course.* Other how-to books include Mike Peters's *The World of Cartooning with Mike Peters,* Gene Byrnes's *The Complete Guide to Cartooning,* and Clare Briggs's *How to Draw Cartoons.* Especially valuable is *Ye Madde Designer* by the influential British caricaturist David Low. Between March 1973 and March 1976, a series of instructive articles on cartoons and cartooning by Jack Markow also appeared in *Writer's Digest.*

Periodicals

There are a number of mainstream periodicals of historical importance for students of editorial cartooning (*Puck, Judge, Harper's Weekly, Caricature, Cartoons Magazine,* and so on), but only a few current periodicals deal exclusively with the subject, and one of the most useful has recently ceased publication. In some of the remaining periodicals, editorial cartooning shares space with strip and social cartooning.

Until Richard Samuel West began publishing the *Puck Papers* in the late 1970s, there was no single reliable periodical devoted exclusively to American political cartooning. In 1981 West turned the *Puck Papers* into a quarterly, *Target,* which was even more impressive than its predecessor. Unfortunately, *Target* ceased publication with the Winter 1987 issue.

Between 1981 and 1987, however, *Target* captured a picture of the field that was multidimensional. It offered probing interviews with working cartoonists; it provided accurate historical and astute critical articles written in a clear style that made them accessible to academics and collectors, to professionals in the field, and to interested lay readers. This publication (now in the Ohio State University Library Archives) remains a valuable research tool. The exceptional layout permitted an appreciation of pictorial as well as written work; *Target* regularly included clean, clear cartoon reproductions to accompany articles and to introduce readers to the work of new and experienced political cartoonists; the format was never crowded and always professional. It was one of the few publications that reviewed new books in depth; its editors were not afraid to deal with controversy; indeed, it remains one of the best sources for understanding major concerns and trends in the field from both inside and outside the political cartoon industry. It also includes American, Canadian, and British "Drawing Boards," columns that provide information about movement in the field, awards, and so on. Indeed, there is not enough that can be said about the contribution that this much-needed quarterly made. The writers of this chapter mourn the departure of *Target*, but we look forward to a new cartoon publication that West promises in about a year. If West's new publication approaches the quality of *Target*, then it deserves support from everyone interested in editorial cartooning.

Cartoonist PROfiles, edited by cartoonist Jud Hurd, is one of the remaining current quarterly publications that interviews living artists and also contains features about important cartoonists of the past. Editorial cartoonists are frequently included, and each issue is regarded by collectors as a valuable item. *Cartoonist PROfiles* reproduces several cartoons by the featured artists as well as photographs of the cartoonists. Subscription correspondence should be addressed to *Cartoonist PROfiles*, P.O. Box 325, Fairfield, Connecticut 06430.

A new publication as of summer 1987 is *Witty World*, an enterprising international cartoon quarterly with a glossy format. It is published by Joseph George Szabo with an advisory board consisting of Maurice Horn, Richard LaPalme, and Richard Samuel West. Its audience is "professional and aspiring cartoonists; professionals in related fields of graphics, advertising, illustration, animation and commercial arts; students and academicians; art, communication and cultural programs and cartoon fans and collectors." In its first issue, *Witty World* announced that it would feature the work of great cartoonists around the world as well as lesser known and newer cartoonists. The aim of the magazine is "to serve as a forum for all those involved in comic/cartoon art, listening to local and global professional problems, debating over them, and perhaps developing some useful solutions." The intention of the staff, according to Szabo, is to "keep our readers updated on important international events, and the latest cartoonist techniques, equipment and materials available." The first two issues of the magazine include exemplary articles on censorship; interviews with international editorial cartoonists; a section entitled "Witty Wire," which deals with brief announcements, competitions, and conferences; "Focus," a cartoon section devoted to internationally sensitive topics; interpretive articles on international styles and cartoon genres; regular articles on "Law" and

"Syndicate"; and a healthy review section that deals with both books and journals of importance to those interested in cartooning generally and editorial cartooning more specifically. In its "Calendar" section are included cartoon competitions and exhibitions.

Although *Witty World* does not focus exclusively on American editorial cartoons, the inclusion in the second issue of a fine article by Richard Samuel West, "Poison Penmen: Two Centuries of American Political Cartooning," suggests its value for those interested especially in editorial cartooning in the United States. While its advertisements and classified sections tend to make the format rather too busy, even they provide an up-to-date aid for students and researchers interested in new reference guides, conferences, exhibitions, employment and movement within the industry, collectors, and collections. Subscriptions are available from Witty World Publications, P.O. Box 1458, North Wales, Pennsylvania 19454.

The Museum of Cartoon Art and Hall of Fame of Rye Town, Port Chester, New York, has also published *Inklings* somewhat irregularly. *Inklings* reports on events and exhibits at the museum and elsewhere; it also includes some special features about cartoonists and cartooning. In 1978, *Inklings* was merged with *Cartoonist PROfiles* and was distributed under its own name, but as an insert in the older periodical.

The National Cartoonists' Society, 9 Ebony Court, Brooklyn, New York 11229, produces the *American Cartoonist,* an annual, which became a quarterly publication in the late 1970s. Mail relating to the *American Cartoonist* should be sent to the editors, Box 2322, Bridgeport, Connecticut 06608. Similarly, the American Association of Editorial Cartoonists publishes the *AAEC Notebook* monthly. It includes reviews of new books and is also a treasurehouse of interesting behind-the-scenes information. The association's publications are generally distributed only to members, but special requests are usually honored. The Library of Communication and Graphic Arts at Ohio State University holds a complete run of this publication, which began in August 1959 as *AAEC News*. The AAEC's address is 475 School Street, S.W., Washington, D.C. 20024.

Of additional help are the journalism and media periodicals, such as *Editor and Publishers, Journalism Quarterly, Washington Journalism Review,* or Northwestern University's *Byline,* which are specialized sources for articles on political cartooning and its relationship to editorial policy, ethics in the profession, and other phases of newspaper work.

Similarly, the *Masthead* is published quarterly by the National Conference of Editorial Writers, 6223 Executive Boulevard, Rockville, Maryland 20852. The periodical occasionally publishes significant articles about editorial cartooning such as Draper Hill's "Cartoonists Are Younger—and Better" (Fall 1986). In fall 1985, *Media History Digest* devoted an entire nine-article issue to cartoons and comics, including articles on caricature history, Thomas

Nast, and political cartooning. *Newspaper Research Journal* also sometimes publishes relevant articles such as James Best's recent contribution, "Editorial Cartoonists: A Descriptive Survey" (Winter 1986).

Periodically, more general scholarly periodicals such as the *Journal of Popular Culture* and the *Journal of American Culture,* published at Bowling Green University under the able direction of Professor Ray Browne, include scholarly articles of interest to editorial cartoon students, and the annual meetings of the Popular Culture Association and the American Culture Association frequently include an interesting selection of papers on American editorial cartooning.

For additional new articles appearing in journals, readers are advised to consult the "Reviews" section in the new *Witty World,* which promises to provide, if the first issues are any indication, up-to-date references to editorial cartooning articles not only in the journals already mentioned here, but in other journals of general interest, trade journals, newspapers, and news magazines.

ANTHOLOGIES AND REPRINTS

Anthologies and published collections of editorial cartoons fall roughly into three categories: those that are arranged around a specific historical period; those that are concerned with a particular historical event, topic, or significant political figure; and those that collect a single political cartoonist's work.

In the first category, Jerry Robinson's *The 1970s: Best Political Cartoons of the Decade* and Richard B. Freeman and Richard Samuel West's *The Best Political Cartoons of 1978* deserve prominent mention. Robinson's anthology is arranged chronologically by year. Freeman and West's well-selected anthology features the work of major editorial cartoonists such as Oliphant, MacNelly, Feiffer, Levine, and Auth. Also among the better recent anthologies in this group is *The Gang of Eight,* in which eight of America's most important cartoonists have selected their favorite cartoons "for a collection that reveals two decades of American history through the eyes of our most perceptive and candid observers." The emphasis is on the 1980s, and the book contains essays by each cartoonist and an introduction by Tom Brokaw. The eight are Auth, Conrad, Feiffer, MacNelly, Marlette, Peters, Szep, and Wright.

Less satisfying to recent reviewers is Charles Brooks's annual *Best Editorial Cartoons* of the year series. Published annually since 1973, it reprints cartoons by a number of editorial cartoonists; however, the collection depends on submissions from the artists, and in some recent editions a number of important cartoonists such as Oliphant, Levine, MacNelly, and Herblock, who create some of the "best cartoons," have not been represented. Brooks has been faulted for including too many cartoons in a crowded format and for not including work by the "major" cartoonists the anthology claims to gather. Cartoons are arranged according to categories, which vary with each year. Although there is no text accompanying individual cartoons, forewords in the last decade by Karl Hubenthal, Mike Peters, Tip O'Neill, Daniel Moynihan, Jack Kemp, James Watt, and others are interesting commentaries on the state of the nation and the state of political cartooning. In addition, Brooks lists winners of the Pulitzer Prize, the National Headliners' Club Awards, the National Newspaper Awards of Canada, and the Sigma Delta Chi Awards; however, Brooks' Pulitzer Prize list has not always been entirely reliable. One year the Pulitzer was awarded to a cartoonist who did not contribute to Brooks' book, so Brooks substituted another name in the winner's slot.

The International Salon of Cartoons publishes an anthology in conjunction with an international exhibition and judging held annually since 1964. Typical of these collections is *The Thirteenth International Salon of Cartoons,* a 690-page, 1976 version from the Montreal World's Fair exhibition. Cartoons are gathered by country of origin, and there are 70 pages of U.S. entries. Although a general introduction precedes them, no commentary accompanies specific cartoons.

Many other exhibitions have produced printed anthologies or exhibition catalogs. One of the most ambitious is Blaisdell and Selz's *The American Presidency in Political Cartoons: 1776–1976,* which reprints cartoons selected from the University of California (Berkeley) Art Museum's bicentennial exhibition. Professor Peter Selz, director of the museum, and Professor Emeritus Thomas Blaisdell of the political science department each contribute an introductory essay. The book collects 113 cartoons, and the accompanying text provides background to each cartoon. Earlier exhibition catalogs, such as that for Syracuse University's Martin H. Bush Exhibition of June 1966, *American Political Cartoons (1865–1965),* gathered work by Thomas Nast, John T. McCutcheon, Homer Davenport, Clifford K. Berryman, Frederick Burr Opper, Jay "Ding" Darling, Carey C. Orr, Clarence D. Batchelor, Karl Hubenthal, Ray B. Justus, Don Wright, Richard Q. Yardley, and others. The Ohio State University Libraries also published an exhibition catalog in conjunction with the 1983 "Festival of Cartoon Art," which includes an introductory essay by Alan Gowens.

Jews in American Graphic Satire and Humor is a catalog of a number of ethnic editorial/political cartoons selected from an exhibit of the John and Selma Appel Collection. It includes an informative running text by the Appels which places the cartoons in context. The project was produced in 1984 by the American Jewish Archives on the campus of the Hebrew Union College-Jewish Institute of Religion, Cincinnati.

Among the anthologists dealing with early years in American history, Joan D. Dolmetsch has edited *Rebellion and Reconciliation,* which is a collection of satirical prints about the revolution, including one hundred political satires from the Colonial Williamsburg collection. Gary L. Bunker and Davis Bitton's *The Mormon Graphic Image, 1834–1914* is a collection of cartoons, caricatures, and illustrations with a detailed running text to accompany 129 cartoon reproductions. *A Cartoon History of U.S. Foreign Policy 1776–1976* is a lively publication by the editors of the Foreign Policy Association and has an introduction by Daniel P. Moynihan. The book includes 196 prints, engravings, lithographs, and newspaper cartoons. An earlier book by the Foreign Policy Association published in 1968, *A Cartoon History of U.S. Foreign Policy Since World War I,* reprints the work of ninety editorial cartoonists and includes 250 reproductions. Special emphasis is on work by John Fischetti, Herblock, and Mauldin. Rollin Kirby's *Highlights: A Cartoon History of the Nineteen Twenties* is a chronologically arranged anthology of sixty full-page cartoons Kirby did for the New York *World.*

A number of anthologies specialize in war cartoons. *American Caricatures Pertaining to the Civil War* is one of several important Civil War collections. Published in 1918, it reproduces primarily Currier & Ives lithographs from the originals published between 1856 and 1872. Another significant collection is *The American War Cartoons* by Matt Morgan and others. Spanish-American War cartoons are found in Charles L. Bartholomew's *Cartoons of the Spanish-American War by Bart* and in Charles Nelan's *Cartoons of Our War with Spain;* World War I is the subject of George Hecht's *The War in Cartoons,* Louis Raemaekers's *America in the War* and *Raemakers' Cartoon History of the War,* and Boardman Robinson's *Cartoons on the War.*

Several anti-war and specifically anti-nuclear weapons anthologies also appeared in the 1980s. Most noteworthy are Steven Heller's *Warheads: Cartoonists Draw the Line,* which samples political and editorial cartoons that deal with the nuclear threat. Sponsored by the Nuclear Weapons Freeze Campaign, the ninety-drawing collection anthologizes Oliphant, Feiffer, Osborn, Searle, M. G. Lord, R. O. Blechman, Herb Gardner, and others. In *Art Against War,* D. J. R. Bruckner, Seymour Chwast, and Steven Heller collect antiwar art from the last 400 years. The collection is organized chronologically, and it includes a helpful accompanying text.

The Statue of Liberty's centennial celebration was the occasion for Dani Aguila's anthology *Taking Liberty with the Lady,* which collects close to 500 Statue of Liberty cartoons. Originally conceived as part of the centennial's fundraising campaign, the anthology was refused official sanction because the cartoons were not all clearly laudatory and did not all lend "dignity and prestige to the national symbol of freedom and liberty." Aguila, a cartoonist for the *Filipino Reporter,* managed to have the volume published despite the official rejection. The collection includes both recent and older Statue of Liberty cartoons. About 200 American cartoons and 100 cartoons from over forty foreign countries are included.

Political campaigns have inspired a number of published cartoon collections as well. Pierce G. Fredericks edited *The People's Choice: The Issues of the 1956 Campaign as Seen by the Nation's Best Political Cartoonists.* The book contains 102 reproductions of works by political cartoonists working in the mid-1950s. Earlier anthologies of campaign cartoons include *The Political Campaign of 1912 in Cartoons* by Nelson Harding, and Bib Crockett and Jim Berryman's cartoons in the Washington *Evening Star* anthologies for the campaigns of 1948, 1952, and 1956. Jeff MacNelly's *The Election That Was—MacNelly at His Best* is fifty-six pages of MacNelly cartoons from the 1976 campaign.

Still other anthologies collect reprints of cartoons pertaining to a particular political figure. "Ding" Darling's *As Ding Saw Hoover* and Clarence Batchelor's *Truman Scrapbook* fall into this category. James N. Giglio and Greg G. Thielen edited *Truman in Cartoon and Caricature,* which includes cartoons by Berryman, Fitzpatrick, Herblock, Darling, Orr, and S. J. Ray of the Kansas City *Star.* The cartoons are arranged around major events during the Truman years, and each section is introduced with a chapter of text that puts the cartoons that follow in context.

Yet another important collection in this category is *LBJ Lampooned,* edited by Charles Antin and Sig Rosenblum, which contains cartoon criticism of Lyndon B. Johnson by forty cartoonists including Mauldin, Feiffer, Oliphant, and Haynie. The book's six chapters are preceded by a classic commentary by Feiffer, which defines the position of many cartoonists on the Vietnam War and LBJ.

Several books of individual cartoonists' work have also been devoted to Watergate and the Nixon years. Jules Feiffer's *Feiffer on Nixon: The Cartoon Presidency,* Gary Trudeau's *Guilty, Guilty, Guilty!,* Paul Conrad's *The King and Us,* Paul Szep's *At This Point in Time,* Mike Peters's *The Nixon Chronicles,* Ranan Lurie's *Nixon Rated Cartoons,* Bill Sanders's *Run for the Oval Room . . . They Can't Corner Us There!,* and Herbert Block's *Herblock's Special Report* are only a few among the best of these collections.

A recent striking anthology of Ronald Reagan cartoons is *Reagancomics.* The one cartoon or panel per page format helps strengthen this collection's impact. Steven Heller's anthology of Feiffer cartoons, *Jules Feiffer's America: From Eisenhower to Reagan,* contains 400 strong cartoons from twenty-five years of Feiffer's work arranged by chapters that are devoted to seven presidents. Brief introductions head the chapters. The 1980s also produced anthologies that concentrated on lesser lights than presidents. *100 Watts: The James Watt Memorial Cartoon Collection,* edited by Carew Papritz, is a strong anthology that includes one hundred cartoons by thirty-six American editorial cartoonists. All "100 Watts" are critical of Watt.

A much earlier anthology built around a single political figure is Albert Shaw's *A Cartoon History of [Teddy] Roosevelt's Career,* published in 1910. Included are 630 cartoons and drawings, as well as other pictures to accompany a biographical text. Shaw also authored a two-volume cartoon history of Lincoln. Other Lincoln cartoons appear in Rufus Rockwell Wilson's

Lincoln in Caricature and in an earlier collection that contains John Tenniel drawings, William S. Walsh's *Abraham Lincoln and the London Punch.*

Some other collections pertaining to particular figures or historical periods that are more difficult to categorize include *Red Cartoons from the Daily Worker,* edited by Walt Carmon and published in 1926 and 1928. The books are folio size, with fifty full-page cartoons in each folio. Those included read like a *Who's Who* among radical cartoonists. A more recent anthology of note is Steven Heller's *Man Bites Man,* which collects two decades of satiric art (since 1960). This international anthology features a sampling of twenty-two artists' work, including Blechman, Gahan Wilson, Osborn, Feiffer, Levine, Searle, and others. Tom Wolfe writes the introduction. *Getting Angry Six Times a Week,* "a portfolio of political cartoons" by fourteen major cartoonists, and edited by Alan F. Westin, is an anthology of civil liberties cartoon "galleries" originally planned or published by *The Civil Liberties Review,* a bimonthly magazine of the American Civil Liberties Union. The magazine ceased publication in 1979 after publishing ten sets of "galleries." And *Pulling Our Own Strings,* edited by Gloria Kaufman and Mary Kay Blakely, is a collection of feminist humor. Although the selection of essays and other written text outweighs the selection of drawings, the anthology does contain feminist issue cartoons by Etta Hulme, Jules Feiffer, Garry Trudeau, Mike Peters, Ellen Levine, Martha F. Campbell, Tony Auth, and Betty Swords.

In *Great Cartoonists and Their Art,* cartoonist-collector Art Wood reproduces 120 cartoons from his collection, which features comic strip artists but includes a number of editorial cartoons. The accompanying text contains a number of Wood's personal anecdotes and experiences with cartoonists whose work he has collected. Interesting observations are mixed with gossip. *The Sting of the Bee* is an anthology built around cartoonists' work for a single newspaper, *The Sacramento Bee.* The loosely arranged collection features the work of Arthur Buel, cartoonist from 1910 to 1938, Newton Pratt, cartoonist from 1938 to 1971, and Dennis Renault, 1972 to the present. Pratt's work receives the greatest emphasis. *The Art of the Dart: Nine Masters of Visual Satire* is a catalog for the exhibition held at the Gryphon Gallery in Michigan. The catalog collects cartoons by Conrad, Feiffer, Guindon, Hill, Levine, MacNelly, Mauldin, Oliphant, and Peters, and concludes with a historical essay by Hill. The exhibition included both historically significant caricatures and cartoons and samples of the work of the nine contemporary artists.

Pulitzer Prize cartoonists are reprinted in several anthologies, most notably in John Hohenberg's *The Pulitzer Prize Story.* Hohenberg reproduces cartoons along with prize-winning features and editorials. An earlier anthology, Dick Spencer III's *Pulitzer Prize Cartoons,* reproduces on full pages the Pulitzer winners from 1922 through 1950 and includes not only capsule summaries of the year's events, but also informal biographical sketches and commentary to accompany each reproduction. Gerald W. Johnson's *The Lines Are Drawn*, like Hohenberg's book, is more current than Spencer's. It includes Pulitzer Prize-winning cartoons for the years 1922–58, accompanied by essays based on the cartoons' historical contexts.

By far the largest category of anthologies is the one that includes collections of work by specific cartoonists. In the case of Mauldin or Herblock, who excel with a typewriter as well as a brush and pen, the accompanying commentary may also be by the cartoonist himself. Among Herblock's more recent efforts are *Herblock Through the Looking Glass*, Block's ninth book, which is organized by themes and includes 130 pages of written text. Some recent collections combine the work of a columnist and a cartoonist. Cal Thomas, columnist, and Wayne Stayskal, cartoonist, teamed up to produce *Liberals for Lunch*, a set of well right-of-center commentaries about controversies on which conservatives hold strong opinions. *The Mood of America* is a collection from *The* Cincinnati *Inquirer* featuring cartoons by Jim Borgman and text by James F. McCarty. The book is primarily a set of social observations with some political implications by the columnist and cartoonist, who travel the country and send their responses back to *The Inquirer* from fourteen cities or towns; their journey ends in New York City at the refurbished Statue of Liberty dedication ceremonies. It includes 165 Borgman drawings.

Many of the best-known cartoonists from Nast to Oliphant have published a number of personal collections: Darling, McCutcheon, Mauldin, Herblock, Lurie, Trudeau, and Feiffer have been prolific. In the 1980s, Oliphant produced a collection a year, including *The Jellybean Society, Ban This Book, . . . But Seriously Folks!, The Year of Living Perilously, Between a Rock and Hard Place*, and *Make My Day*. Other established cartoonists have produced several collections in the last decade. Paul Conrad created strong collections in *Pro and Conrad* and *Drawn and Quartered*. Mike Peters produced *Win One for the Geezer* and *Peters: On the Brink*. Paul Szep gathered his controversial work for the Boston *Globe* into *To a Different Drummer* and *The Next Szep Book*. Doug Marlette's fourth collection, *It's a Dirty Job . . . But Somebody Has to Do It*, appeared in 1984, and *There's No Business Like Soul Business*, which showcases parody television evangelist Rev. Will B. Dunn from Marlette's *Kudzu* strip, was published in 1987. Simon and Schuster published Don Wright's second collection, *Wright Side Up*, in 1981. Draper Hill of the Detroit *News* has produced three collections of Detroit mayor Coleman Young cartoons, the latest of which is *A View from the Top*. Hill's local cartoons are mixed with national and international theme drawings in *Political Asylum*, an exhibition catalog featuring two decades of his work. Typically, many of the 115 cartoons feature cartoonist-historian Hill's cartoons that reference earlier cartoons, paintings, and literature. Hill's commentary accompanies the drawings. George Fisher, also famous for regional and local cartoons with broader significance, collected his views of Arkansas in *Old Guard Rest Home* and *God Would Have Done It If He'd Had the Money*.

A newer, offbeat cartoonist, Mark Alan Stamaty, creator of the psuedo-comic strip parody of Washington and power politics, published his work for the *Village Voice* and the Washington *Post* in *Washingtoon* and *More Washingtoons*. Other relatively new cartoonists include Mike Keefe of the Denver *Post*, who created *KeefeKeebab*; female cartoonist M. G. Lord, who draws for New York's *Newsday* and who published *Mean Sheets*; and Pulitzer Prize winner Berke Breathed, who produced *Toons for the Times* and *Bloom County Babylon: Five Years of Basic Naughtiness*. Ben Sargent created one of the favorite offerings of the 1980s, *Big Brother Blues*, the second collection of Sargent cartoons. Sargent creates a narrator, Big Brother, who takes the reader through the book and brings unity to Sargent's treatment of local, national, and international politics. Tom Toles's *The Taxpayer's New Clothes* is a first collection marked by a distinctive style.

Hugh Haynie's *Hugh Haynie: Perspective*, Jeff MacNelly's *MacNelly: The Pulitzer Prize Winning Cartoonist*, Don Wright's *Wright On!*, David Levine's *No Known Survivors*, Doug Marlette's *The Emperor Has No Clothes*, and Pat Oliphant's *An Informal Gathering* are all strong personal collections published in the 1970s.

NOTES

1. Bill Saunders, "Using the Knife," *Target* (Spring 1982), 13.

BIBLIOGRAPHY

Books And Articles

Aguila, Dani, ed. *Taking Liberty with the Lady*. Nashville, Tenn.: Eaglenest Publishing, 1986.
The *"All American" Art—Cartooning*. Brooklyn: Higgins Ink, 1944.
Allen, Edison. *Of Time and Chase*. New Orleans: Habersham, 1969.
American Caricatures Pertaining to the Civil War. New York: Brentano's, 1918.
American Political Cartoons (1865–1965). Martin H. Bush Exhibition. Syracuse: Syracuse University, June 1966.
Antin, Charles, and Sig Rosenblum, eds. *LBJ Lampooned: Cartoon Criticism of Lyndon B. Johnson*. New York: Cobble Hill Press, 1968.
Appel, John, and Selma Appel. *Jews in American Graphic Satire and Humor*. Cincinnati: American Jewish Archives, 1984.
The *Art Index*. New York: H. W. Wilson, 1933–.
Ash, Lee. *Subject Collections: A Guide to Special Book Collections and Subject Emphases as Reported by University, College, Public and Special Libraries and Museums in the United States and Canada*. 6th ed. New York: R. R. Bowker, 1985.

Attwood, Francis G. *Attwood's Pictures: An Artist's History of the Last Ten Years of the Nineteenth Century*. New York: Life Publishing, 1900.

Auth, Tony. *Behind the Lines*. Boston: Houghton Mifflin, 1977.

Bartholomew, Charles L. *Bart's Cartoons for 1902 from the Minneapolis Journal*. Minneapolis: Journal Printing, 1903.

———. *Cartoons of the Spanish-American War by Bart*. Minneapolis: Journal Printing, 1899.

Batchelor, Clarence. *Truman Scrapbook: Washington Story in Cartoons and Text*. Deep River, Conn.: Kelsey Hill Publishing, 1951.

Beard, Frank. *Fifty Great Cartoons*. Chicago: Ram's Horn, 1899.

Beardsley, William A. "An Old New Haven Engraver and His Work: Amos Doolittle." 1910. Photostat in the Library of Congress.

Becker, Stephen. *Comic Art in America*. New York: Simon and Schuster, 1959.

Bender, J. H., Jr. "Editorial Cartoonists: Development/Philosophy Today." Master's thesis, University of Missouri, 1962.

Benson, Steve. *Fencin' with Benson*. Phoenix: Arizona Republic, 1984.

Berkowitz, Herb B. "Political Cartooning's Southern Revival." *Art Voices/South*, 1 (July/August 1978), 65–70.

Berryman, Clifford K. *Berryman Cartoons*. Washington, D.C.: Saks, 1900.

———. *Berryman's Cartoons of the Fifty-eighth House*. Washington, D.C.: C. K. Berryman, 1903.

———. *The Bunk Book*. Washington, D.C.: Gridiron Club, Menu Committee, 1925.

———. *Development of the Cartoon*. Columbia: University of Missouri Bulletin, 1926.

Bishop, Joseph Bucklin. "Early Political Caricature in America." *The Century*, 44 (June 1892), 219–31.

Blaisdell, Thomas C., Jr., and Peter Selz. *The American Presidency in Political Cartoons: 1776–1976*. Santa Barbara: Peregrine Smith, 1976.

Blake, W. B. "The American Cartoon." *The Independent*, 74 (January 23, 1913), 214–17.

Block, Herbert. *The Herblock Book*. Boston: Beacon Press, 1952.

———. *The Herblock Gallery*. New York: Simon and Schuster, 1968.

———. *Herblock on All Fronts*. New York: New American Library, 1980.

———. *Herblock's Here and Now*. New York: Simon and Schuster, 1955.

———. *Herblock's Special for Today*. New York: Simon and Schuster, 1958.

———. *Herblock's Special Report*. New York: W. W. Norton, 1974.

———. *Herblock's State of the Union*. New York: Simon and Schuster, 1972.

———. *Herblock Through the Looking Glass*. New York: W. W. Norton, 1984.

———. *Straight Herblock*. New York: Simon and Schuster, 1964.

Borgman, Jim. *The Great Communicator*. Cincinnati: Colloquial Books, 1985.

———. *Smorgasborgman*. Cincinnati: Armadillo Press, 1982.

Bowman, Bowland Claude. *The Tribune Cartoon Book for 1901*. Minneapolis: Tribune Printing, 1901.

———. *The Tribune Cartoon Book for 1902*. Minneapolis: Tribune Printing, 1902.

Bradley, Luther. *Cartoons by Bradley*. Chicago: Rand McNally, 1971.

Bramhall, William. *The Great American Misfit*. New York: Clarkson N. Potter, 1982.

Branch, John. *Would You Buy a Used Cartoon from This Man?* Chapel Hill, N.C.: 1979.

Breathed, Berke. *Bloom County Babylon: Five Years of Basic Naughtiness*. Boston: Little, Brown, 1986.

——. *'Toons for the Times*. Boston: Little, N.P., Brown, 1984.

Briggs, Clare A. *How to Draw Cartoons*. New York: Harper and Brothers, 1926. 2nd ed., Garden City, N.Y.: Garden City Publishing, 1937.

Brigham, Clarence S. *Paul Revere's Engraving*. Worcester, Mass.: American Antiquarian Society, 1954.

Brooks, Charles, ed. *Best Editorial Cartoons of 1972*. Gretna, La.: Pelican Publishing, 1973–. Annual.

Bruckner, D.J.R., Seymour Chwast, and Steven Heller. *Art Against War*. New York: Abbeville Press, 1984.

Bunker, Gary L., and Davis Bitton. *The Mormon Graphic Image, 1834–1914*. Salt Lake City: University of Utah Press, 1983.

Burck, Jacob. *Hunger and Revolt*. New York: Daily *Worker*, 1935.

——. *Our 34th President*. Chicago: Chicago Sun-Times, 1953.

Byrnes, Gene. *The Complete Guide to Cartooning*. New York: Grossett and Dunlap, 1950.

The Campaign of '48 in Star Cartoons. Washington, D.C.: Evening Star, 1948. Also by the same publisher: *The Campaign of '52* and *The Campaign of '56*.

Campbell, Bill. *The Last Cartoons*. Little York, Ill.: Privately printed, 1980.

Campbell, Mary, and Gordon Campbell. *The Pen, Not the Sword: A Collection of Great Political Cartoons from 1879 to 1898*. Nashville, Tenn.: Aurora, 1970.

Caricature and Its Role in Graphic Satire. Exhibit by the Department of Art. Providence, R.I.: Brown University, 1971.

"Caricature, Cartoon, and Comic Strip."*Encyclopaedia Britannica*. 15th ed. Vol. 3, 909–22.

Carl, Leroy Maurice. "Meanings Evoked in Population Groups by Editorial Cartoons." Ph.D. dissertation, Syracuse University, 1967.

Carmon, Walt, ed. *The Case of Sacco and Vanzetti in Cartoons from the Daily Worker*. New York: The Daily Worker, 1927.

——, ed. *Red Cartoons from the Daily Worker*. 2 vols. Chicago: The Daily Worker and Workers Monthly, 1927 and 1928.

"The Cartoon as a Means of Artistic Expression."*Current Literature,* 53 (October 1912), 461–64.

Cartoons of the War of 1898 with Spain. Chicago: Belford, Middlebrook, 1898.

Casswell, Lucy Shelton, and George H. Loomis, Jr. *Billy Ireland*. Columbus: Ohio State Library Publications Committee, 1980.

Catalog of the Library of the Museum of Modern Art. 14 vols. Boston: G. K. Hall, 1976.

Catalogue of the Harvard University Fine Arts Library, the Fogg Art Museum. 15 vols. Boston: G. K. Hall, 1971. *First Supplement*. 3 vols. Boston: G. K. Hall, 1976.

Cesare, Oscar. *One Hundred Cartoons*. Boston: Small, Maynard, 1916.

Chase, John, ed. *Today's Cartoon*. New Orleans: Hauser Press, 1962.

Christ-Janer, Albert. *Boardman Robinson*. Chicago: University of Chicago Press, 1946.

Cobb, Ron. *My Fellow Americans*. Los Angeles: Price, Stern, Sloan, 1970.

——. *Raw Sewage*. Los Angeles: Price, Stern, Sloan, 1970.

Conningham, F. A. *Currier & Ives*. New York: World, 1950.

Conrad, Paul. *The King and Us: Editorial Cartoons by Conrad*. Los Angeles: Clymer Publications, 1974.

Conrad, Paul, and Malcolm Boyd. *Drawn and Quartered*. New York: Harry N. Abrams, 1985.

————. *Pro and Conrad*. San Rafael, Calif.: Los Angeles Herald Examiner, 1979.

————. *When in the Course of Human Events*. New York: Sheed and Ward, 1973.

Contemporary Cartoons: An Exhibition of Original Drawings. San Marino, Calif.: Huntington Library, 1937.

Cooper, Frederick Taylor, and Arthur Bartlett Maurice. *The History of the Nineteenth Century in Caricature*. New York: Dodd, Mead, 1904. Reissued Detroit: Tower Books, 1971.

Craven, Thomas, ed. *Cartoon Cavalcade*. New York: Simon and Schuster, 1943.

Crawford, Charles, ed. *Cal Alley*. Memphis: Memphis State Press, 1973.

Crouse, Russell. *Mr. Currier and Mr. Ives*. Garden City, N.Y.: Doubleday, Doran, 1930.

Dahl, Francis. *Dahl's Boston*. Boston: Little, Brown, 1946.

————. *What! More Dahl?* Boston: Hale, 1944.

Darcy, Tom. *The Good Life*. New York: Avon, 1970.

Darling, Jay N. *As Ding Saw Hoover*. Edited by John M. Henry. Ames: Iowa State College Press, 1954.

————. *Cartoons from the Files of the Register and Leader*. Des Moines: Register and Leader, 1908.

————. *Ding Goes to Russia*. New York: McGraw-Hill, 1932.

————. *Ding's Half Century*. Edited by John M. Henry. New York: Duell, Sloan and Pearce, 1962.

————. *The Education of Alonzo Applegate and Other Cartoons*. Des Moines: Register and Leader, 1910.

————. *Midwest Farming as Portrayed by a Selection from Ding's Cartoons*. Des Moines: Pioneer Hi-Bred Corn, 1960.

Davenport, Homer. *Cartoons*. New York: DeWitt, 1898.

————. *The Dollar or the Man? The Issue of Today*. Boston: Small, Maynard, 1900.

Deur, Lynne. *Political Cartoonists*. Minneapolis: Lerner Publications, 1972.

Diggs, R. *Great Diggs of 77*. San Francisco: Rip Off Press, 1977.

Dobbins, Jim. *Dobbins' History of the New Frontier*. Boston: Humphries, 1964.

Dolmetsch, Joan D. *Rebellion and Reconciliation*. Charlottesville: University Press of Virginia, 1976.

Donahey, James H. *Cartoons by Donahey*. Cleveland: Vinson and Korner, 1900.

Doyle, Jerry. *According to Doyle: A Cartoon History of World War II*. New York: Putnam's, 1943.

Drepperd, Carl. *Early American Prints*. New York: Century, 1930.

Eastman, Joel. *The Maine Thing, Some of My Best Friends Are Republicans*. Freeport, Me.: Bond Wheelright, 1964.

Englehart, Bob. *Never Let Facts Get in the Way of a Good Cartoon*. Dayton, Ohio: Dayton Journal Herald, 1979.

Faerber, Charles N. "An Examination of the Career Patterns and Editorial Roles of a Number of Staff Editorial Cartoonists on Contemporary American English-Language Newspapers." M.A. thesis, San Diego State University, 1977.

Fearing, Jerry. *Fearing Revisited*. St. Paul: St. Paul Dispatch and Pioneer, 1981.

Feaver, William. *Masters of Caricature*. New York: Alfred A. Knopf, 1981.

Feiffer, Jules. *Feiffer on Civil Rights*. New York: Anti-Defamation League of B'nai B'rith, 1966.

————. *Feiffer on Nixon: The Cartoon Presidency*. New York: Random House, 1974.

————. *Feiffer's Album*. New York: Random House, 1963.

————. *Feiffer's Children*. Kansas City, Mo.: Andrews, McMeel and Parker, 1986.

————. *The Great Comic Book Heroes*. New York: Random House, 1965.

————. *Hold Me*. New York: Random House, 1962.

————. *Jules Feiffer's America: From Eisenhower to Reagan*. Edited by Steven Heller. New York: Alfred A. Knopf, 1982.

————. *Marriage Is an Invasion of Privacy and Other Dangerous Views*. Kansas City, Mo.: Andrews, McMeel and Parker, 1984.

————. *Tantrum*. New York: Alfred A. Knopf, 1980.

Fischetti, John. *Zinga Zinga Za!* Chicago: Follett, 1973.

Fisher, George. *Fisher*. Little Rock, Ark.: Rose Publishing, 1978.

————. *Fisher's Gallery*. Little Rock, Ark.: Rose Publishing, 1973.

————. *God Would Have Done It If He'd Had the Money*. Little Rock, Ark.: Rose Publishing, 1983.

————. *Old Guard Rest Home*. Little Rock, Ark.: Rose Publishing, 1983.

Fitzgerald, Richard. *Art and Politics*. Westport, Conn.: Greenwood Press, 1973.

Fitzpatrick, Daniel R. *As I Saw It*. New York: Simon and Schuster, 1953.

————. *Cartoons by Fitzpatrick*. St. Louis: St. Louis Post Dispatch, 1947.

Fleming, E. McClury. "Symbols of the United States from Indian Queen to Uncle Sam." In Ray Brown et al., eds., *Frontiers of American Culture*. West Lafayette, Ind.: Purdue University Press, 1968.

Foreign Policy Association. *A Cartoon History of U.S. Foreign Policy 1776–1976*. New York: William Morrow, 1975.

————. *A Cartoon History of U.S. Foreign Policy Since World War I*. New York: Vintage, 1968.

Fredericks, Pierce, ed. *The People's Choice: The Issues of the 1956 Campaign as Seen by the Nation's Best Political Cartoonists*. New York: Dodd, Mead, 1956.

The Freedom Fighter's Manual. New York: Grove Press, 1985.

Freeman, Richard B. *Watergate: The Unmaking of a President*. Lexington: University Press of Kentucky, 1975.

Freeman, Richard B., and Richard Samuel West. *The Best Political Cartoons of 1978*. Lansdale, Pa.: Puck Press, 1979.

Gahn, Joseph Anthony. "The America of William Gropper, Radical Cartoonist." Ph.D. dissertation, Syracuse University, 1966.

Gallatin, Albert E. *John Sloan*. New York: E. P. Dutton, 1925.

Garrett, William R. *The Early Political Caricature in America and The History of the United States*. N.p.: American Classical Printers, 1929.

Geipel, John. *The Cartoon: A Short History of Graphic Comedy and Satire*. New York: A. S. Barnes, 1972.

Gerberg, Mort. *The Arbor House Book of Cartooning*. New York: Arbor House, 1983.

Getlein, Frank. *The Bite of the Print*. New York: Clarkson N. Potter, 1963.

Giglio, James N., and Greg G. Thielen. *Truman in Cartoon and Caricature*. Ames: Iowa State University Press, 1984.

Goldberg, Rube. "Lesson #19."*Famous Artists Cartoon Course*. Westport, Conn.: Famous Artists, 1956.

Goodrich, Lloyd. *Five Paintings from Thomas Nast's Grand Caricaturama*. New York: Swann Collection of Caricature and Cartoon, 1970.

———. *John Sloan*. New York: Macmillan, 1952.

Gould, Ann, ed. *Masters of Caricature*. New York: Alfred A. Knopf, 1981.

Graham, Bill. *"A Little Drum Roll Please . . . "* Little Rock: Arkansas Gazette, 1974.

Gros, Raymond, ed. *T. R. in Cartoon*. New York: Saalfield Publishing, 1910.

Grove, Lloyd. "Trudeau on Reagan, Bush, Sinatra, Breathed, and Fatherhood."*Target* (Spring 1987), 13–21.

Hancock, La Touche. "American Caricature and Comic Art." *The Bookman,* 16 (October 1902), 120–21; (November 1902), 263–74.

Harding, Nelson. *The Political Campaign of 1912 in Cartoons*. Brooklyn, N.Y.: Daily Eagle, 1912.

Haynie, Hugh. *Graphics '75: Watergate, the Unmaking of a President*. Lexington, Ky.: University of Kentucky Printing Services, 1975.

———. *Hugh Haynie: Perspective*. Louisville, Ky.: Courier Journal and Louisville Times, 1974.

Hecht, George, ed. *The War in Cartoons*. New York: E. P. Dutton, 1919.

Heller, Steven. *Man Bites Man*. New York: A and W, 1981.

———, ed. *Jules Feiffer's America: From Eisenhower to Reagan*. New York: Alfred A. Knopf, 1982.

———, ed. *Warheads: Cartoonists Draw the Line*. New York: Penguin Books, 1983.

Hess, Stephen, and Milton Kaplan. *The Ungentlemanly Art*. New York: Macmillan, 1968. Rev. ed., 1975.

Hill, Draper. "Editorial Cartoons." In *Encyclopedia of Collectibles*. New York: Time-Life, 1978.

———. *The Lively Art of J. P. Alley*. Memphis, Tenn.: Brooks Memorial Art Gallery, 1973.

———. *Political Asylum*. Text by John Silverstein. Windsor, Ontario: Art Gallery of Windsor, 1985.

———. *A View from the Top: The Young Years 1982–1985*. Detroit: Detroit News, 1986.

———. "What Fools These Mortals Be! A Study of the Work of Joseph Keppler, Founder of Puck." A.B. thesis, Harvard College, 1957.

———, ed. *Fashionable Contrasts: 100 Caricatures by James Gillray*. London: Phaidon, 1966.

———, ed. "Illingworth on Target." Exhibition of the cartoons and drawings of Leslie Illingworth. Littleton, N.H.: Littleton Courier, 1970.

———, ed. *Mr. Gillray, the Caricaturist*. London: Phaidon, 1965.

———, ed. *The Satirical Etchings of James Gillray*. New York: Dover, 1976.

Hillier, Bevis. *Cartoons and Caricatures*. New York: E. P. Dutton, 1970.

Hoff, Syd. *Editorial and Political Cartooning*. New York: Stravon Educational Press, 1976.

Hofmekler, Ori. *Hofmekler's People*. New York: Holt, Rinehart and Winston, 1982.

Hohenberg, John, ed. *The Pulitzer Prize Story*. New York: Columbia University Press, 1959.

Horn, Maurice. *Contemporary Graphic Artists*. Detroit: Gale Research, 1986-.

————. *The World Encyclopedia of Cartoons.* 2 vols. New York: Chelsea House, 1980.

Horsey, David. *Horsey's Rude Awakenings.* Seattle: Madrona, 1981.

Huck, Gary, and Mike Konopacki. *Bye! American.* Chicago: Charles H. Kerr, 1987.

Huot, Leland, and Alfred Powers. *Homer Davenport of Silverton.* Bingen, Wash.: West Shore Press, 1973.

The Image of America in Caricature and Cartoons. Fort Worth, Tex.: Amon Carter Museum of Western Art, Swann Collection and Lincoln National Corp. of Fort Wayne, 1976.

Index to Art Periodicals (Ryerson Library of Chicago Art Institute). Boston: G. K. Hall, 1962. 11 vols. *First Supplement.* Boston: G. K. Hall, 1975.

Johnson, Gerald W. *The Lines Are Drawn.* New York: J. B. Lippincott, 1958.

Johnson, Herbert. *Cartoons.* Philadelphia: J. B. Lippincott, 1936.

Johnson, John J. *Latin America in Caricature.* Austin: University of Texas Press, 1980.

Johnson, Kenneth M. *The Sting of the Wasp.* San Francisco: Book Club of California, 1967.

Johnson, Malcolm, ed. *David Claypool Johnston.* Exhibition catalog of exhibition held by the American Antiquarian Society, Boston College, the Boston Public Library, and the Worcester Art Museum, Boston, March 1970.

Jones, Taylor. *Add-Verse to Presidents.* New York: Dembner Books, 1982.

Kaufman, Gloria, and Mary Kay Blakely. *Pulling Our Own Strings.* Bloomington: Indiana University Press, 1980.

Keefe, Mike. *KeefeKeebab.* Denver: Denver Post, 1984.

Keen, Sam. *Faces of the Enemy.* San Francisco: Harper and Row, 1986.

Keller, Morton. *The Art and Politics of Thomas Nast.* New York: Oxford University Press, 1968.

Kelly, Walt. *The Jack Acid Society Black Book.* New York: Simon and Schuster, 1957, 1961, 1962.

Kempkes, Wolfgang. *The International Bibliography of Comics Literature.* Detroit: Gale Research, 1971. 2nd rev. ed. New York: R. R. Bowker/Verlag Dokumentation, 1974.

Kenner, Hugh. "The Exploding Duck and Other Primal Tales." *National Review,* 30 (October 13, 1978), 1287–91.

Keppler, Joseph. *A Selection of Cartoons from Puck.* New York: Keppler and Schwarzman, 1893.

Ketchum, Alton. *Uncle Sam, the Man in the Legend.* New York: Hill and Wang, 1959.

Kinnaird, Clark, ed. *Rube Goldberg vs. the Machine Age.* New York: Hastings House, 1968.

Kirby, Rollin. *Highlights: A Cartoon History of the Nineteen Twenties.* New York: William Farquhar Payson, 1931.

Konopacki, Mike. *Beware Konopacki.* Madison, Wis.: Press Connection, 1979.

Krumbhaar, E. B. *Isaac Cruikshank.* Philadelphia: University of Pennsylvania Press, 1966.

Lamb, Chris. "Cartoonists on Trial: *The Masses* and Freedom of the Press." *Target* (Summer 1987), 18–22.

————. "With Malicious Intent: Libel and the Political Cartoonist." *Target* (Autumn 1985), 15–21.

Langsam, Walter C., and L. D. Warren. *The World and Warren's Cartoons*. Hicksville, N.Y.: Exposition Press, 1976.

Larkin, Oliver W. *Daumier, Man of His Time*. New York: McGraw-Hill, 1966.

Lendt, David L. *Ding: The Life of Jay Norwood Darling*. Ames, Iowa: Iowa State University Press, 1979.

Lent, John A. *Comic Art: An International Bibliography*. Drexel Hill, Pa.: Privately printed, 1987.

Levine, David. *Artists, Authors, and Others: Drawings by David Levine*. Washington, D.C.: Smithsonian Institution, 1976.

———. *The Arts of David Levine*. New York: Alfred A. Knopf, 1978.

———. *The Man from M.A.L.I.C.E.* New York: E. P. Dutton, 1966.

———. *No Known Survivors: David Levine's Political Plank*. Boston: Gambit, 1970.

———. *Pens and Needles*. Boston: Gambit, 1969.

Lewis, Ross. *Cartoons of R. A. Lewis*. Milwaukee: Milwaukee Journal, 1968.

Library Catalog (Metropolitan Museum of Art). 25 vols. Boston: G. K. Hall, 1960.

"The Limits of Caricature." *The Nation*, 7 (July 19, 1866), 55.

Locher, Richard. *Dick Locher Draws Fire*. Chicago: Tribune Services, 1980.

Locher, Richard. *Send in the Clowns: Chicago Tribune Editorial Cartoons by Locher*. Chicago: Chicago Tribune, 1982.

Long, Scott. *Hey! Hey! LBJ! or, He Went Away and Left the Faucet Running*. Minneapolis: Ken Sorenson Printing, 1969.

Lord, M. G. *Mean Sheets*. Boston: Little, Brown, 1982.

Low, David. *A Cartoon History of Our Times*. New York: Simon and Schuster, 1939.

———. *Ye Madde Designer*. London: The Studio, 1935.

Lucie-Smith, Edward. *The Art of Caricature*. Ithaca: Cornell University Press, 1981.

Lurie, Ranan R. *Lurie's Almanac*. Kansas City, Kans.: Andrews and McMeel, 1981, 1982, 1983.

———. *Lurie's World*. Honolulu: University Press of Hawaii, 1980.

———. *Nixon Rated Cartoons*. New York: Quadrangle New York Times Books, 1973.

———. *Pardon Me, Mr. President*. New York: Quadrangle New York Times Books, 1975.

Lynch, John Gilbert Bohun. *A History of Caricature*. London: Faber and Gwyer, 1926.

McCarty, James F., and Jim Borgman. *The Mood of America*. Cincinnati: Cincinnati Enquirer, 1986.

McCutcheon, John T. *Cartoons by McCutcheon*. Chicago: McClurg, 1903.

———. *The Cartoons that Made Prince Henry Famous*. Chicago: Chicago Herald Record, 1903.

———. *Congressman Pumphrey, the People's Friend*. Indianapolis: Bobbs-Merrill, 1907.

———. *Drawn from Memory*. Indianapolis: Bobbs-Merrill, 1950.

———. *John McCutcheon Book*. Selections by Franklin J. Meine and John Maryweather. New York: Caxton Club, 1948.

———. *The Mysterious Stranger and Other Cartoons*. New York: McClure, Phillips, 1905.

———. *T. R. in Cartoons*. Chicago: McClurg, 1903.

McCutcheon, John, et al. *History of World War II in Cartoon*. Chicago: Chicago Tribune, 1943.

McDougall, Walt. *This Is the Life!* New York: Alfred A. Knopf, 1926.

MacNelly, Jeff. *The Election That Was—MacNelly at His Best*. New York: Newspaper-books, 1976.

———. *MacNelly: The Pulitzer Prize Winning Cartoonist*. Richmond, Va.: Westover Publishing, 1972.

Malcolm, James P. *An Historical Sketch of the Art of Caricaturing*. London: Longman, Hurst, Rees, Orme, and Brown, 1813.

Manning, Reg. *Little Itchy Itchy and Other Cartoons*. New York: J. J. Augustin, 1944.

Markow, Jack. "Artists and Cartoonists Q's. Roads to Cartooning, Part I." *Writer's Digest* (March 1973), 36–39.

———. "Artists and Cartoonists Q's. Roads to Cartooning, Part II." *Writer's Digest* (April 1973), 36–38.

———. "Cartooning." *Writer's Digest* (October 1974), 50.

———. "Cartooning." *Writer's Digest* (December 1974), 47.

———. "Cartooning. Cartoon Schools." *Writer's Digest* (July 1974), 50–52.

———. "Cartooning. Oliphant for President." *Writer's Digest* (March 1976), 48.

———. "Cartooning. Woman, Where Art Thou?" *Writer's Digest* (February 1974), 48.

Marlette, Doug. *The Emperor Has No Clothes*. Washington, D.C.: Graphic Press, 1976.

———. *It's a Dirty Job . . . But Somebody Has to Do It*. Charlotte N.C.: Willnotdee Press, 1984.

———. *There's No Business Like Soul Business*. Atlanta: Peachtree, 1987.

Marzio, Peter C. *Do It the Hard Way: Rube Goldberg and Modern Times*. Washington, D.C.: Smithsonian Institution, 1970.

———. *Rube Goldberg: His Life and Work*. New York: Harper and Row, 1973.

Matthews, Albert. *Brother Jonathan*. Cambridge, Mass.: Wilson, 1902.

———. *Uncle Sam*. Worcester, Mass.: Davis Press, 1908.

Matthews, J. Brander. "The Comic Periodical Literature of the United States." *The American Biblioplast*, 7 (August 1875), 199–201.

Matthews, Roy T., and Peter Mellini. *In Vanity Fair*. Berkeley: University of California Press, 1982.

Mauldin, William. *Back Home*. New York: William Sloane Associates, 1947.

———. *Bill Mauldin's Army*. Novato, Calif.: Presidio Press, 1983.

———. *The Brass Ring*. New York: W. W. Norton, 1971.

———. *I've Decided I Want My Seat Back*. New York: Harper and Brothers, 1965.

———. *Let's Declare Ourselves Winners*. Novato, Calif.: Presidio Press, 1985.

———. *Mud and Guts*. A Look at the Common Soldier of the American Revolution. Published on the Occasion of the 200th Anniversary of the Encampment at Valley Forge. Division of Publications, National Park Service, U.S. Department of the Interior, 1978.

———. *A Sort of a Saga*. New York: Sloan, 1949. Reprint New York: W. W. Norton, 1973.

———. *Up Front*. New York: World, 1945.

———. *What's Got Your Back Up?* New York: Harper and Row, 1961.

Morgan, Matt, et al. *The American War Cartoons*. London: Chatto and Windus, 1874.

Morris, William C. *Spokesman—Review Cartoons*. Spokane: Review Publishing, 1908.

Mott, Frank Luther. *American Journalism*. New York: Macmillan, 1941. Rev. ed., 1950.

Murrell, William. *A History of American Graphic Humor*. 2 vols. New York: Whitney Museum, 1933, 1938. Reissued. New York: Cooper Square, 1967.

———. "The Rise and Fall of Cartoon Symbols." *The American Scholar,* 4 (Summer 1935), 206–13.

Nelan, Charles. *Cartoons of Our War with Spain*. New York: Stokes, 1898.

Nelson, Roy Paul. *Cartooning*. Chicago: Henry Regnery, 1975.

———. *Comic Art and Caricature*. Chicago: Contemporary Books, 1978.

———. *Fell's Guide to the Art of Cartooning*. New York: Frederick Fell, 1962.

———. *Humorous Illustration and Cartooning*. Englewood Cliffs, N.J.: Prentice-Hall, 1984.

Nevins, Allan, and Frank Weitenkampf. *A Century of Political Cartoons*. New York: Scribner's, 1944. Reprint. New York: Farrar, Straus and Giroux, 1975.

Ohman, Jack. *Back to the 80's: A Deja View of the 1980's in Cartoons and Essays*. New York: Simon and Schuster, 1986.

Oliphant, Pat. *Ban This Book*. Kansas City, Mo.: Andrews and McMeel, 1982.

———. *Between a Rock and a Hard Place*. Kansas City, Mo.: Andrews, McMeel and Parker, 1986.

———. *. . . But Seriously Folks!* Kansas City, Mo.: Andrews and McMeel, 1983.

———. *Four More Years*. New York: Simon and Schuster, 1969.

———. *An Informal Gathering*. New York: Simon and Schuster, 1978.

———. *The Jellybean Society*. Kansas City, Mo.: Andrews and McMeel, 1981.

———. *Make My Day*. Kansas City, Mo.: Andrews, McMeel and Parker, 1985.

———. *The Oliphant Book*. New York: Simon and Schuster, 1969.

———. *The Year of Living Perilously*. Kansas City, Mo.: Andrews, McMeel, and Parker, 1984.

Opper, Frederick Burr. *John, Jonathan, and Mr. Opper*. London: Grant Richards, 1903.

———. *Willie and His Papa*. New York: Grossett and Dunlap, 1901.

Osborn, R. *War Is No Damn Good*. Garden City, N.Y: Doubleday, 1946.

Osborn, Ralph. *Osborn on Osborn*. New Haven, Conn.: Ticknor and Fields, 1982.

Paine, Albert Bigelow. *Th. Nast: His Period and His Pictures*. New York: Pearson Publishing, 1904. Reissued. Gloucester, Mass.: Peter Smith, 1967. Reprint. New York: Benjamin Blom, 1971.

Papritz, Carew, ed. *100 Watts: The James Watt Memorial Cartoon Collection*. Auburn, Wash.: Khyber Press, 1984.

Papritz, Carew, and Russ Tremayne. *Reagancomics*. Seattle: Khyber Press, 1984.

Parton, James. *Caricature and Other Comic Art*. New York: Harper and Brothers, 1878. Reprint. New York: Harper and Row, 1969.

Penn, Arthur. "The Growth of Caricature." *The Critic* (February 25, 1882), 49–50.

Peters, Harry T. *Currier & Ives, Printmakers to the American People*. 2 vols. Garden City, N.Y.: Doubleday, Doran, 1929, 1931.

Peters, Mike. *The Nixon Chronicles*. Dayton, Ohio: Lorentz Press, 1976.

———. *Peters: On the Brink*. New York: Pharos Books, 1986.

———. *Win One for the Geezer*. New York: Bantam Books, 1982.

———. *The World of Cartooning with Mike Peters: How Caricatures Develop.* Dayton, Ohio: Landfall Press, 1985.

Peterson, William, ed. "A Treasury of Ding." *The Palimpsest* (monthly journal of the State Historical Society of Iowa) (March 1972), 81–177.

Pett, Joel. *Pett Peeves.* Bloomington, Ind.: Herald-Times Publication, 1982.

Philippe, Robert. *Political Graphics: Art as a Weapon.* New York: Abbeville Press, 1982.

Powell, Dwane. *Surely Someone Can Still Sing Bass!* Raleigh, N.C.: News and Observer, 1981.

Press, Charles. "The Georgian Political Cartoon and Democratic Government." *Comparative Studies in Society and History,* 19 (April 1977), 216–38.

———. *The Political Cartoon.* Madison, N.J.: Fairleigh Dickinson Press, 1979.

Price, Warren C., and Calder M. Pickett. *An Annotated Journalism Bibliography, 1958–1968.* Minneapolis: University of Minnesota Press, 1970.

"The Pulitzer War." *Target* (Summer 1987), 12–15.

Punch. *Cartoons from Punch.* 4 vols. London: Bradbury and Agnew, 1906.

Raemaekers, Louis. *America in the War.* New York: Century, 1918.

———. *Raemaekers' Cartoon History of the War.* New York: Century, 1918–19.

———. *Raemaekers' Cartoons.* Garden City, N.Y.: Doubleday, Page, 1917.

Rajski, Raymond B., ed. *A Nation Grieved: The Kennedy Assassination in Editorial Cartoons.* Rutland, Vt.: Charles E. Tuttle, 1967.

Reid, Albert Turner. *Albert T. Reid's Sketchbook.* Compiled by John W. Ripley and Robert W. Richmond. Topeka, Kans.: Shawnee County Historical Society, 1971.

Rigby, Paul. *Rigby's New York and Beyond.* New York: Andor Publishing, 1984.

RILA: *Repértoire international de la littérature de l'art* (International Repertory of the Literature of Art). New York: College Art Association of America, 1975.

Robinson, Boardman. *Cartoons on the War.* New York: Dutton, 1915.

———. *Ninety-three Drawings.* Colorado Springs: Colorado Springs Fine Art Center, 1937.

Robinson, Jerry. *The 1970s: Best Political Cartoons of the Decade.* New York: McGraw-Hill, 1980.

Rogers, W. G. *Mightier Than the Sword.* New York: Harcourt, Brace and World, 1969.

Rogers, William A. *America's Black and White Book.* New York: Cupples and Leon, 1917.

———. *Hits at Politics.* New York: R. H. Russell, 1896.

———. *A World Worth While.* New York: Harper, 1922.

St. Hill, Thomas Nast. *Thomas Nast's Christmas Drawings for the Human Race.* New York: Harper and Row, 1971.

Salzman, Ed, and Ann Leigh Brown. *The Cartoon History of California Politics.* Sacramento, Calif.: Journal Press, 1978.

Sanders, Bill. *Run for the Oval Room . . . They Can't Corner Us There!* Milwaukee: Alpha Press, 1974.

———. "Using the Knife." *Target* (Spring 1982), 13.

Sargent, Ben. *Big Brother Blues.* Austin: Texas Monthly Press, 1984.

Scarfe, Gerald. *Gerald Scarfe.* New York: Thames and Hudson, 1982.

Seymour-Ure, Colin, and Jim Schoff. *David Low*. London: Secker and Warburg, 1985.

Shaw, Albert. *Abraham Lincoln*. 2 vols. New York: Review of Reviews, 1929.

———. *A Cartoon History of Roosevelt's Career*. New York: Review of Reviews, 1910.

Shikes, Ralph E. *The Indignant Eye: The Artist as Social Critic in Prints and Drawings from the Fifteenth Century to Picasso*. Boston: Beacon Press, 1969.

Shikes, Ralph E., and Steven Heller. *The Art of Satire: Painters as Caricaturists from Delacroix to Picasso*. New York: Pratt Graphics Center and Horizon Press, 1984.

Shoemaker, Vaughn. *1938 A.D., 1939 A.D., 1940 A.D., '41 and '42 A.D., '43 and '44 A.D., and '45 and '46 A.D*. Chicago: *Chicago Daily News*, 1939, 1940, 1941, 1943, 1945 and 1947. (A series of volumes.)

———. *Shoemaker*. Chicago: Chicago American, 1966.

Smith, Dorman H. *One Hundred and One Cartoons*. Chicago: Ring, 1936.

Smith, Henry Ladd. "The Rise and Fall of the Political Cartoon."*Saturday Review*, 37 (May 29, 1954), 708ff.

Spencer, Dick, III. *Editorial Cartooning*. Ames: Iowa State College Press, 1949.

———. *Pulitzer Prize Cartoons*. Ames: Iowa State College Press, 1951.

Spiegelman, Art. *Maus: A Survivor's Tale*. New York: Pantheon, 1986.

Stamaty, Mark Alan. *More Washingtoons*. New York: Prentice-Hall, 1986.

———. *Washingtoon*. New York: Congdon and Weed, 1983.

Stanley, Don, and Frank McCullough. *The Sting of the Bee*. Sacramento, Calif.: Sacramento Bee, 1982.

Steadman, Ralph. *Between the Eyes*. London: Jonathan Cape, 1984.

———. *I, Leonardo*. New York: Summit Books, 1983.

———. *Sigmund Freud*. New York: Paddington Press, 1979.

Stein, Ed. *Stein's Way*. Denver: Denver Publishing, 1983.

Suter, David. *Suterisms*. New York: Ballantine Books, 1986.

Swearington, Rodger. *What's So Funny Comrade?* New York: Praeger, 1961.

Szep, Paul. *At This Point in Time*. Boston: Boston Globe, 1974.

———. *The Harder They Fall*. Boston: Boston Globe, 1975.

———. *In Search of Sacred Cows*. Boston: Boston Globe, 1968.

———. *Keep Your Left Hand High*. Boston: Boston Globe, 1969.

———. *The Next Szep Book*. Winchester, Mass.: Faber and Faber, 1985.

———. *Them Damned Pictures*. Boston: Boston Globe, 1978.

———. *To a Different Drummer*. Brattleboro, Vt.: Lewis Publishing, 1983.

Taft, William H. *Encyclopedia of Twentieth-Century Journalists*. New York: Garland, 1986.

The Thirteenth International Salon of Cartoons. Montreal: International Pavilion of Humour, 1976.

Thomas, Cal, and Wayne Stayskal. *Liberals for Lunch*. Westchester, Ill.: Crossway Books, 1986.

Thorndike, Chuck. *The Business of Cartooning*. New York: House of Little Books, 1939.

Toles, Tom. *The Taxpayer's New Clothes*. Kansas City, Mo.: Andrews, McMeel, and Parker, 1985.

Trever, John. *Trever's First Strike.* Andover, Mass.: Brick House Publishing, 1983.

Trinidad, Corky. *Marcos: The Rise and Fall of the Regime: A Cartoon Biography.* Honolulu: Arthouse, 1986.

Trudeau, Gary B. *Ask for May, Settle for June.* New York: Holt, Rinehart and Winston, 1982.

———. *Guilty, Guilty, Guilty!* New York: Holt, Rinehart and Winston, 1973.

———. *Unfortunately, She Was Also Wired for Sound.* New York: Holt, Rinehart and Winston, 1983.

———. *The Wreck of the "Rusty Nail."* New York: Holt, Rinehart and Winston, 1983.

Vincent, Howard P. *Daumier and His World.* Evanston,: Ill.: Northwestern University Press, 1968.

Vinson, J. Chal. *Thomas Nast: Political Cartoonist.* Athens: University of Georgia Press, 1967.

Walker, Mort. "The Museum of Cartoon Art."*Witty World* (Autumn 1987), 26–27.

———, ed. *National Cartoonists' Society Album, 1972–77.* New York: National Cartoonists' Society, 1977.

Walsh, William S. *Abraham Lincoln and the London Punch.* New York: Moffat, Yard, 1909.

Washington Evening Star. *The Campaign of '48.* Washington, D.C.: Washington Star, 1949. Also *The Campaign of '52* (1953), and *Campaigns of '56* (1957).

Webster, H. T. *The Best of H. T. Webster.* New York: Simon and Schuster, 1953.

Weiss, Harry B. *William Charles, Early Caricaturist, Engraver and Publisher of Children's Books.* New York: Public Library, 1932.

Weitenkampf, Frank. "American Cartoonists of Today," *Century,* 85 (February 1913), 540–52.

Weitenkampf, Frank. *American Graphic Art.* New York: Holt, 1912. Rev. ed. New York: Macmillan, 1924. Reprint. New York: Johnson Reprint, 1970.

———. "Keppler and Political Cartooning."*Bulletin of the New York Public Library,* 42 (December 1938), 906–8.

———. *Political Caricature in the United States, in Separately Published Cartoons ... An Annotated List.* New York: New York Public Library, 1953. Reissued. New York: Arno Press, 1971.

West, Richard Samuel. "Cartoons and Comments: On the Syndication Glut."*Puck* (Winter 1981), 11.

———. "Poison Penmen: Two Centuries of American Political Cartooning."*Witty World* (Autumn 1987), 4–7.

———. *Satire on Stone: The Political Cartoons of Joseph Keppler.* Urbana: University of Illinois Press, 1988.

———. "Yankee Doodle Dirge: Being an Examination into the Untimely Deaths of Mid-Nineteenth Century American Humor Magazines."*Target* (Spring 1987), 4–8.

Westin, Alan F. *Getting Angry Six Times a Week.* Boston: Beacon Press, 1979.

Westwood, H. R. *Modern Caricaturists.* London: Lovat Dickinson, 1932.

What America Thinks: Editorials and Cartoons. Chicago: What America Thinks Inc., 1941.

White, Richard Grant. "Caricature and Caricaturists." *Harper's Monthly Magazine,* 24 (April 1862), 586–607.

Whitman, Bert. *Here's How: About the Newspaper Cartoon. A Collection of Editorial Cartoons from the Past Decade.* Lodi, Calif.: Lodi Publishing, 1968.

Who's Who in America. 39th ed. 2 vols. Chicago: Marquis Who's Who, Inc., 1976.

Williams, R. E. "Humorous Cartoon."*Encyclopedia Americana,* 1976 ed. Vol. 5, 734–39.

Wilson, Rufus Rockwell. *Lincoln in Caricature.* New York: Horizon Press, 1953.

Wood, Art. *Great Cartoonists and their Art.* Gretna, La.: Pelican Publishing, 1987.

Wright, Don. *Wright On! A Collection of Political Cartoons.* New York: Simon and Schuster, 1971.

———. *Wright Side Up.* New York: Simon and Schuster, 1981.

Wright, Grant. *The Art of Caricature.* New York: Privately printed, 1904.

Wynn Jones, Michael. *The Cartoon History of Great Britain.* New York: Macmillan, 1971.

———. *The Cartoon History of the American Revolution.* New York: Putnam's, 1975.

Young, Art. *Art Young: His Life and Times.* New York: Sheridan House, 1939.

———. *The Best of Art Young.* New York: Vanguard, 1936.

———. *On My Way.* New York: Liveright, 1928.

———. *Thomas Rowlandson.* New York: Wiley, 1938.

Zimmerman, Eugene. *Cartoons and Caricatures.* Scranton. Pa.: Correspondence Institute of America, 1910.

———. *This and That About Caricature.* New York: Syndicate Press, 1905.

Zurier, Rebecca. *Art for the Masses (1911–1917): A Radical Magazine and Its Graphics.* New Haven: Yale University Art Gallery, 1985.

Periodicals

American Association of Editorial Cartoonists [AAEC] Notebook. Washington, D.C., 1973-.

American Cartoonist (formerly an annual, *The Cartoonist*). Bridgeport, Conn., 1977-.

Byline. Evanston, Ill., 1975—.

Cartoonews. Orlando, Fla., 1975–.

Cartoonist PROfiles. Fairfield, Conn., 1969–.

Crimmer's: The Harvard Journal of Pictorial Fiction. Cambridge, Mass., 1974–76.

Editor and Publisher. New York, 1901–.

Inklings. Rye Town, Port Chester, N.Y., 1976–.

Journalism Quarterly. Athens, Ohio, 1924–.

The Journal of American Culture. Bowling Green, Ohio, 1978–.

The Journal of Popular Culture. Bowling Green, Ohio, 1967–.

The Masthead. Rockville, Md., 1948–.

Media History Digest. New York, 1980–.

Newspaper Research Journal. Memphis, Tenn., 1979–.

The Puck Papers. Narberth, PA., 1978–81.

Target. Wayne, Pa., 1981–87.

Washington Journalism Review, Washington, D.C., 1977-.

Witty World. North Wales, Pa. 1987-.

Fashion

VICKI L. BERGER

The rag business . . . the garment industry . . . ready-to-wear . . . clothing or apparel . . . the second skin . . . the near environment . . . fashion. Critics denounce it. Philosophers scrutinize it. In a broad sense, the industry includes fiber and fabric manufacturers, apparel designers and manufacturers, wholesalers, retailers, and a host of auxiliary enterprises such as fashion periodicals, resident buying offices, and advertising agencies. It is the complex, dynamic, and fascinating industry that produces and delivers "fashion."

The term *fashion* is derived from the Latin *factio,* a making, and in its pure definition refers to the make, form, or shape of a thing or the current style or mode of speech, conduct, apparel, and so on. A few basic fashion terms are presented in the context of "apparel," but the same concepts apply to many other components of the environment such as furniture, appliances, wall coverings, window treatments, decorative accessories, and automobiles. First, there is the concept of "style." In relation to apparel, a style refers to a garment with particular features or characteristics that distinguish it from other garments of the same type. A style may or may not be popular at any given time, and its distinctive features do not change. For example, bell-bottom jeans may or may not be popular at a given time, but the shape of the flared legs distinguishes the bell-bottom style from pegged or tapered jeans. The style or styles that are accepted or popular at a particular time in a particular place are called "fashions." Acceptance or nonacceptance implies change, and the way in which fashion changes is explained as the "fashion cycle." The life span of a fashion, usually portrayed graphically as a bell curve, begins with introduction of the design, followed by rise to the peak of popularity or general acceptance, followed by decline in popularity and abandonment or rejection. The very new and expensive styles adopted by fashion leaders are called "high fashions," while those worn by the majority of people are called "mass fashions." When a style remains "in fashion" for an extended period of time, perhaps for years, it is called a "classic." Examples include a Chanel suit, a long-sleeved crew neck sweater, a Chesterfield coat, or a shirtwaist dress. Short-lived fashions are called "fads." They come and go quickly and have a very compressed fashion cycle. These basic concepts provide a foundation for investigating the dynamics of fashion—an integral part of the near environment and a cultural mirror reflecting the taste, technology, and spirit of the times. The intent of this chapter is to provide an introduction to the concept of fashion as it applies to apparel and, in concert with other chapters in this book, to present basic bibliographic information needed to begin the study of fashion.

HISTORIC OUTLINE

The beginnings of the ready-to-wear industry in the United States can be traced to early nineteenth-century East Coast port cities such as New Bedford, New York, Boston, Philadelphia, and Baltimore. Here, enterprising custom tailors responded to the needs of visiting sailors by offering for sale ready-made pants, shirts, and jackets. Inexpensive and poorly made, the garments became known as "slops" and the firms that produced and sold them as "slop shops." In spite of the low quality of this early ready-made clothing, the idea caught on and expanded to provide garments for bachelors who had no wives to sew for them and for plantation owners who needed inexpensive work clothes for their slaves. As cities increased in population and as the American pioneers pushed the frontier westward, new markets emerged for ready-made garments—higher quality clothing for the middle-class city dwellers and sturdy work clothes for laborers. One of the most famous stories of the manufacture of ready-made clothes for laborers is that of Levi Strauss and his denim trousers. Levi set out for California in 1850 to seek his fortune in the gold rush. He arrived with a roll of sturdy sailcloth from which he planned to make tents, but he soon found that the "forty-niners" needed trousers more than tents. Levi responded by using the cloth to make double-stitched pants for the miners. When the supply of sailcloth was depleted, he switched to a cotton fabric imported from France called *serge de Nimes*. His San Francisco manufacturing business prospered, and his denim trousers became one of the most famous and versatile ready-made garments ever created.

By the mid-nineteenth century the demand for ready-to-wear clothing was well established. Machinery capable of producing fabric in large quantity was already available, a legacy of eighteenth-century English inventors.

Soon, three innovations crucial in the history of the American fashion business emerged—the sewing machine, graded paper patterns, and standardized sizes. An early one-thread, chain stitch sewing machine was patented by Barthelemy Thimonnier in 1830. This was followed by a two-thread machine invented by American Walter Hunt and a hand-run machine by Elias Howe patented in 1846. Isaac Singer developed the foot treadle in 1859 and began to produce sewing machines. Soon they were used in the home by seamstresses, in the production of military uniforms, and in the mass production of men's apparel. Graded or sized paper patterns appeared in the 1860s in two rival fashion magazines. Mr. and Mrs. Ebenezer Butterick introduced paper patterns in 1863 in their magazine *Metropolitan* (later the *Delineator*). Rival Ellen Demorest published her line of paper patterns in the *Mirror of Fashion*. Both Madame Demorest and the Buttericks enjoyed tremendous success. Patterns were used not only by individual homemakers but also by clothing manufacturers. The need for army uniforms during the Civil War stimulated development of mass production in another way. Clothing factories were founded to produce uniforms, and specifications for standardization of sizes were adopted. The elements of customer demand, fabric supply, sewing machines, graded patterns, and standardized sizes were now in place.

During the early nineteenth century, most women's clothes were custom-made, that is, constructed to the exact measurements of the wearer. The manufacture of ready-made clothes for women did not grow as rapidly as men's, but by 1860, the U.S. Census mentioned ninety-six manufacturers of hoopskirts, cloaks, and mantillas. The garments left much to be desired in quality and design. Although the industry grew, home dressmaking continued to fill a need.

As the middle class prospered, more people had the income and leisure time to become interested in fashionable clothing. Although dolls dressed in Paris fashions were sent to the United States as early as the mid-eighteenth century, it was the proliferation of nineteenth-century popular magazines that introduced American consumers to the latest fashions. In addition to black-and-white or color fashion plates, these magazines included needlework, knitting, and crocheting instructions as well as house plans, fiction, music, editorials, society news, and advice. Three early publications were *Graham's Magazine* (1826–58), *Godey's Lady's Book* (1830–98), and *Peterson's Magazine* (1842–98). To these were added the *Metropolitan* (the *Delineator*), *Mirror of Fashion*, the *Woman's Home Companion*, *Pictorial Review*, *Queen of Fashion* (*McCall's*), and *Burton's Gentlemen's Magazine*. Several fashion magazines started in the nineteenth century are still providing American consumers with fashion ideas—*McCall's*, *Ladies' Home Journal*, *Harper's Bazaar*, and *Vogue*.

In addition to the increase in fashion communication, three other nineteenth-century fashion industry trends must be mentioned—the recognition of individual European fashion designers, the rise of department and specialty retail stores, and the prevalence of "sweatshop" conditions, which led to the establishment of apparel industry unions. Since the thirteenth century, French royalty had been the fashion trend setters for Europe. Fashions were created by anonymous tailors and dressmakers, known as the *couture,* whose identities were carefully guarded by their wealthy clients. The first recognized designer was Rose Bertin, dressmaker to Queen Marie Antoinette. A second early designer was Louis Hippolyte Leroy, official dressmaker to Napoleon's wives, Josephine and then Marie-Louise. The nineteenth century brought the decline of royal fashion dominance and the rise of modern couture, founded by Charles Frederick Worth. Worth, who is considered the first successful independent fashion designer, established his own business in Paris in 1860 and attracted many prominent, wealthy clients, including Empress Eugenie and her court. His success inspired others such as Paquin, Madame Cheruit, Jacques Doucet, Redfern, the Callot sisters, and Jeanne Lanvin, and by the end of the century, Paris couture was a well-established industry.

The nineteenth century also brought changes in the way fashion goods reached final consumers in the United States. Retailing by means of the barter system, trading posts, general stores, and itinerant peddlers dominated the colonial period. Increasing population and growth of cities led entrepreneurs to establish department and specialty stores such as Lord and Taylor, Bloomingdale's, and Macy's. Needs of the rural population, coupled with the development of the postal system of rural free delivery, created an opportunity to sell merchandise by mail. The general merchandise firms of Montgomery Ward and Sears, Roebuck responded by providing mail order retailing for farm and rural populations.

In contrast to the positive changes occurring in fashion retailing, the situation in the manufacturing sector was dismal. Immigrant workers collected cut garment pieces at the factory and took them home to sew or worked long hours in unhealthy, unsafe sweatshops. Although the ready-to-wear industry was growing, products were considered to be for the lower-class population who could not afford a seamstress or custom-made clothes. As conditions worsened, unrest among workers grew. Some federal and state laws were passed to improve industry standards, and in 1900 the International Ladies' Garment Workers Union was founded. Representing the men's clothing workers, the Amalgamated Clothing Workers of America was founded in 1914. Both unions worked for improved labor-management relations; cooperation in research, education, and industry development; and social welfare services for members.

Two highlights of the early twentieth-century fashion industry were the public acceptance of ready-to-wear clothing and the recognition of individual American fashion designers. As improvements were made in textile and apparel manufacturing technology, the quality of ready-to-wear garments improved, and slowly ready-made clothing overcame its lower-class stigma. Consumers, especially women working outside the home, recognized ready-to-wear clothing as a great convenience. Increased demand and acceptance followed. American manufacturers and retailers, however, were still looking toward French couture for designs provided by Paul Poiret, Gabrielle "Coco" Chanel, Vionnet, Patou, Molyneux, and others. This continued until World War II, when access to Paris couture was curtailed. Shoes and fabric were rationed, and Americans were forced to buy American ready-to-wear, replenish wardrobes by sewing at home, or "make do." During the war,

Dorothy Shaver, then president of Lord & Taylor, and an outstanding fashion merchant, smashed the tradition of idolizing Paris designers. Her store, for the first time in retail history, advertised clothes designed by Americans and featured their names: Elizabeth Hawes, Clare Potter, Vera Maxwell, Tom Brigance, and Claire McCardell, the last considered by many to have been the first true sportswear designer. The rule that only French-inspired clothes could be smart had been broken.[1]

American designers were no longer anonymous entities identified only by a store label. Until the 1950s, the ready-to-wear industry was comprised mainly of small, privately owned, single-product businesses. In the late 1950s and 1960s, mergers and acquisitions created huge, publicly owned multiproduct corporations in the textile and apparel industry. This trend has reversed in the 1980s, and many firms are now reverting to private ownership. Present and future fashion industry concerns include import/export balances, quality control, automation, mergers and the use of established brand names, and declining employment levels. Fashion of the 1980s is truly internationally inspired by a multitude of French, Japanese, American, English, and Italian designers whose fashions permeate all levels and ages of society from youngsters wearing colorful McKids clothes from Sears, Roebuck to grandmothers wearing stonewashed Guess jeans by Georges Marciano.

REFERENCE WORKS

A systematic, organized search will uncover vast amounts of information and will, no doubt, cut across a broad spectrum of subject matter, each source approaching the study of fashion with methods and terminology specific to the particular discipline's point of view. Starting points for subject searching are the *Dewey Decimal Classification and Relative Index* or the *Library of Congress Subject Headings* to determine the fashion terms or phrases that best describe the subtopic. Researchers using libraries operating under the Dewey system will find fashion headings under Social Sciences, Technology, and Arts. Social Sciences classification "Customs and Folklore" includes number 391, "Costume," with holdings pertaining to garments, hair styles, body contours, bathing, tattooing, use of cosmetics, perfume, jewelry, and fashion. Under Technology (Applied Sciences), classification number 646, "Clothing and Care of the Body," researchers will find works on clothing for climatic zones, sewing, patternmaking, cutting, fitting, clothing care, hairdressing, facial care, manicuring, and so on. Works on clothing and art are classified under the Arts, number 746, " Drawing and Decorative Arts."

A similar search of the *Library of Congress Subject Headings* reference volumes will determine other key words and related subjects. Two major categories are "Clothing and Dress" and "Costume." Under "Clothing and Dress" (GT 500–2350, TX 340, GN 418–419, RA 779, TT 507) researchers will find works on clothing from the standpoint of utility as a covering for the body and works on the art of dress. Works on clothing of particular places or periods, as well as on costume for the theater, movies, or special occasions are listed under "Costume" (GT 500–2370). Many key phrases beginning with "fashion" are cross-referenced to "Clothing and Dress," "Costume," or other Library of Congress headings.

Armed with terms and phrases that best identify the fashion topic, the researcher is prepared to examine the library subject card catalog. Manual searching may be augmented by using a computer searching service. Useful electronic data base systems for fashion (apparel, clothing, costume, dress) include InfoTrac (merchandising, retailing, business, technology, social science), DIALOG (art-related topics), ERIC (education, social science), and *Psychological Abstracts.*

Researchers should consult four basic categories of reference tools: encyclopedias of fashion, costume, and textiles; indexes; bibliographies; and dictionaries. The works described below will be useful ready references for designer biographies, historic and current fashions, and fashion terminology, and for identifying additional book and periodical literature.

Three encyclopedias provide illustrated, alphabetically organized collections of fashion terms. Most recent is Georgina O'Hara's *The Encyclopaedia of Fashion,* covering fashion topics from the 1840s to the 1980s. Apparel terminology and biographies of designers, fashion celebrities, publication editors, art directors, photographers, and illustrators are included. Catherine Houck's *The Fashion Encyclopedia: An Essential Guide to Everything You Need to Know About Clothes* includes fiber names, designers, style feature terms, and fashion retailers. *The Encyclopedia of World Costume* by Doreen Yarwood features both Western and non-Western terminology and a valuable bibliography.

For more detailed biographical sketches of designers, illustrators, photographers, and editors, consult *McDowell's Directory of Twentieth Century Fashion.* This reference also features guides to fashion design schools, professional organizations, and chronological lists of British and American fashion award winners. The international fashion perspective is covered by Eleanor Lambert's *World of Fashion: People, Places, Resources.* For each geographical area (Africa, Asia, Australia, Europe, the Americas), this resource describes manufacturing centers, exports, fashion schools, costume collections, trade associations, honors, and awards. Biographical sketches of designers and names of Coty Award winners are included.

Devoted exclusively to men's wear, O. E. Schoeffler and William Gale's *Esquire's Encyclopedia of 20th Century Men's Fashions* is truly comprehensive in scope. Concise histories of articles of dress (e.g., sports jackets, dress shirts, beachwear) are illustrated with color plates, line drawings, reprints from *Esquire,* and advertisements. Biographical sketches of designers, an excellent glossary, and several chapters on textile and apparel manufacturing contribute to the worth of this specialized reference tool.

Answers to questions concerning textiles used in the fashion industry will be found in the *American Fabrics Encyclopedia of Textiles,* published by the editors of *American Fabrics and Fashions Magazine.* Illustrated chapters cover man-made and natural fibers, historic textiles, textile inventors and inventions, and manufacturing processes. Especially useful for fashion research are origins of fabric names (e.g., shantung, oxford, batiste, denim, calico) and a more than 3,000-word dictionary.

Two sets of indexes and several standard indexing tools will provide leads for articles, illustrations, and books. *The Clothing Index: An Index to Periodical Literature, January 1970-December 1979,* edited by Sandra S. Hutton, surveys fifteen other indexes and abstracts plus twenty-one journals. From a computerized data base of 4,319 articles, 3,619 are included and are well organized by headings (e.g., fashion merchandising and marketing) and subheadings (e.g., advertising, fads, fashion acceptance). Her 1986 edition, *The Clothing and Textile Arts Index: An Index to Periodical Literature, 1980–1984,* reviews eighteen indexes and abstracts, thirty-five journals, and bibliographies from other books and articles, bringing the total number of citations in both editions to 11,684. These indexes provide an excellent starting point for locating articles.

Standard indexing tools should be selected according to the specific fashion topic. Researchers may wish to consult *Business Periodicals Index, Art Index, Artbibliographies Modern, RILA: International Repertory of the Literature of Art, Readers' Guide to Periodical Literature, Social Sciences Index, Arts and Humanities Citation Index, Humanities Index, New York Times Index,* and/or the *National Geographic Index.*

Older indexes that are useful as guides to visual sources and illustrated texts are the *Costume Index: A Subject Guide to Plates and to Illustrated Text* by Isabel Monro and Dorothy Cook and the 1957 *Costume Index Supplement* by Isabel Monro and Kate Monro. These works provide a guide to full-page and small illustrations and patterns. Topics are organized alphabetically and are keyed to 962 books and one periodical, *National Geographic.*

Sources will quickly multiply when researchers combine leads from indexes with sources listed in specialized bibliographies discussed below. Annotations in three bibliographies provide brief summaries of books and articles.

The Costume Society of America Bibliography: 1983 by Polly Willman and *The Costume Society of America Bibliography: 1974/1979* by Adele Filene and Willman list over 1,500 works on fashion alphabetized by author. Some are annotated and others give a citation of a review of the work. Helpful appendixes include lists of publishers, museums and associations, colleges and universities, key word index, and a time period index.

For information on fashion expenditures, consumption, marketing, advertising, and promotion as well as production of textiles and clothing, researchers should consult T. Geitel Winakor's *Economics of Textiles and Clothing: A Bibliography*. This reference lists journal articles, books, and bulletins readily available in major libraries. The section on "Fashion" includes sixty-eight sources relating to theories of fashion and its transmission and the relationship of fashion change to costs, output, and consumer welfare. Also available are a 1982 edition and a 1987 supplement.

Two English bibliographies broaden the scope of books and articles on fashion. *The Select Bibliography of Clothing Sources,* published by the Clothing and Footwear Institute, is a reading list containing sections on fashion design, social aspects of fashion and clothing, history of costume, and clothes and the body. Pegaret Anthony and Janet Arnold's *Costume: A General Bibliography* is a joint project of the Costume Society of England and the Victoria and Albert Museum. Over 500 annotated articles, books, and journals are organized in sections devoted to reference works, guides to collections, journals, social history, theory and psychology, thirteen countries, specific fashion topics, and textiles.

In 1972, the American Home Economics Association published *Aesthetics and Clothing: An Annotated Bibliography,* an interdisciplinary guide to approximately 1,600 books and articles. The search included fifteen years (1955–70) for books and five years (1965–70) for periodicals. Sources are organized topically (e.g., aesthetic theory; process of design; and women's, men's, and children's fashion). Annotations are helpful and indicate presence of fashion illustrations. For works on functional clothing design, see *Clothing for Handicapped People: An Annotated Bibliography and Resource List* by Naomi Reich, Patricia Otten, and Marie Carver.

Useful for older, international, or foreign-language works is Hilaire Hiler and Meyer Hiler's *Bibliography of Costume: A Dictionary Catalog of About Eight Thousand Books and Periodicals*. This 1939 classic covers books, periodicals, and portfolios of plates dealing with dress, jewelry, decoration of the body, and general and special occasion clothing of "all countries, times, and people." Like Monro's 1937 *Costume Index,* this legacy from the Great Depression era should not be overlooked.

Every discipline develops its own jargon or terminology, enabling practitioners to communicate in the special language of the field. Newcomers to the "language of fashion" as well as veterans trying to sort out double meanings and fine nuances of words can refer to several fashion/apparel/costume dictionaries. Because of the visual nature of fashion, illustrations are especially helpful and are noted when included.

Begin with Charlotte Calasibetta's *Essential Terms of Fashion: A Collection of Definitions* "to more accurately define current apparel and accessories." This illustrated dictionary presents an overall term and then explains many variations or styles, for example, "robe" followed by twenty-three styles of robes. It provides a quick reference for writing fashion show commentary or ad copy or any other project calling for descriptions of 1980s fashion looks. Follow *Essential Terms of Fashion* with Calasibetta's *Fairchild's Dictionary of Fashion* and Mary Brooks Picken's classic *The Fashion Dictionary: Fabric, Sewing, and Apparel as Expressed in the Language of Fashion*. Both are illustrated.

For apparel and textile terminology, consult four standard references. *Clothing Terms and Definitions,* published by the Clothing and Footwear Institute, is apparel production–oriented. Isabel Wingate's *Fairchild's Dictionary of Textiles* explains textile terms, professional and trade associations, inventors, needlework and embroidery terms, brand names, and obsolete fabric terms (a boon for fashion historians). This illustrated dictionary is the ideal bookshelf companion for *Fairchild's Dictionary of Fashion* by Calasibetta.

Fashion Production Terms by Debbie Gioello and Beverly Berke presents garment industry terminology organized by the flow of the production process or by the route the garment takes from its origin through development to completion. Each term or phrase is illustrated with line drawings or photographs. For example, the entry "Apparel Silhouette" includes a definition, a three-part outline of silhouette styles, plus nine line drawings. *Fashion Production Terms* is one in a series of works entitled *The Language of Fashion,* which will appear in its final form as a seven-volume illustrated encyclopedia.

George Linton's illustrated *Modern Textile and Apparel Dictionary* includes trade association names, fibers, fabric names, processes, weaves, and job titles. A special section, "Fashion and Style," is a dictionary within the dictionary, especially useful for fashion writers and department store advertising staff.

When a research project involves the history of fashion, folk costume, or specialized dress (e.g., academic, ecclesiastical, military), refer to Ruth Turner Wilcox's *The Dictionary of Costume*. This work is profusely illustrated with individual line drawings and full-page, collage-style plates. As an example, the entry for "hat" includes forty-five definitions and eighty-two line drawings of hat styles. Another illustrated history of fashion reference is *A Dictionary of English Costume: 900–1900* by Cecil and Phillis Cunnington and Charles Beard. Extra features are an extensive glossary of fabric names and a list of obsolete color names.

For an unconventional look at early twentieth-century men's fashion terminology, see *A Dictionary of Men's Wear* by William Baker. Baker's purpose is to make the book comprehensive (covering almost everything about men's wear of use and interest) as well as interesting. This is an example from the "Z" section:

Zouave cap—a sort of fez

Zouave jacket—a short j. or blouse reaching about to the waist, and cut away in front

Zouave trousers—bloomers

Zouave uniform—you've just read it!

Two reference tools will lead the researcher to organizations and agencies that provide data on the textile and apparel industry. A 1981 United States Department of Commerce publication, *Sources of Statistical Data: Textiles and Apparel, 1980,* names 186 national and international sources of economic information. *Information Sources on the Clothing Industry,* published by the United Nations Industrial Development Organization in 1974, is an international guide to professional and trade organizations, directories, handbooks, textbooks, monographs, periodicals, United Nations proceedings, reference tools, films, marketing, exporting, and purchasing. Addresses for 876 sources are provided.

RESEARCH COLLECTIONS

For pure viewing pleasure, watch for announcements of costume exhibitions at local historical societies, museums, and colleges or universities. Persistence will be rewarded with exhibits ranging from silk kimonos and calico sunbonnets to designer collections. For serious research, begin by identifying specific collections pertinent to the fashion project. For addresses of museums containing costume collections, consult *The Costume Society of America Membership Directory: 1987, The Costume Society of America Bibliography: 1983,* and Pieter Bach's *Textile, Costume, and Doll Collections in the United States and Canada.* For brief descriptions of collection contents, three sources will be helpful. Eleanor Lambert's *World of Fashion: People, Places, Resources* contains a "Costume and Fashion Archive" section for each country listed, including twenty-six collections in the United States. More detailed descriptions are found in Cecil Lubell's *Textile Collections of the World, Volume 1: United States and Canada.* This illustrated guide is organized alphabetically by city and includes addresses, collection descriptions, information on research facilities, and museum publications. Although concentrating on textile collections, many entries include a section on costume collections. Volume 2 describes collections in the United Kingdom and Ireland; volume 3 describes French collections. *International Directory of Historical Clothing* by Irene Huenefeld identifies collections and contents in the United States, Canada, and twenty-four European countries. Institutions are cross-referenced by location, category (e.g., accessory, formal and casual clothing, historical clothing, jewelry), and century.

Additional collection information for the United Kingdom is found in Naomi Tarrant's *Collecting Costumes: The Care and Display of Clothes and Accessories,* Pegaret Anthony and Janet Arnold's *Costume: A General Bibliography,* and Janet Arnold's *A Handbook of Costume.* Currently being compiled by Elizabeth Ann Coleman and Suman Shenoi of the Costume Society of America is a directory of costume/textile collections located in museums, historical societies, galleries, and libraries around the world. This directory will provide descriptions based on eleven categories: costumes, accessories, shawls, ethnic—North and South America, ethnic—other, uniforms, ecclesiastical, laces, theater costumes and sketches, fashion periodicals and prints, and textiles related to apparel. The recent call for information has yielded approximately 3,500 entries.

From the many North American costume collections described in these guides, a few are listed here as examples: the Brooklyn Museum; Chicago Historical Society; Cincinnati Art Museum; the Colonial Williamsburg Foundation; Denver Art Museum; Fashion Institute of Technology, New York City; Indianapolis Museum of Art; Los Angeles County Museum of Art; McCord Museum, Montreal; Metropolitan Museum of Art-Costume Institute, New York City; Mint Museum, Charlotte; Museum of Fine Arts, Boston; North Carolina Museum of History, Raleigh Old Sturbridge Village; Phoenix Art Museum, Arizona Costume Institute; Smithsonian Institution, Washington, D.C.; Valentine Museum, Richmond; University of Washington, Seattle; and the Wadsworth Atheneum, Hartford.

For in-depth study, a tentative list of museums may be compiled from the guides listed above. A mail or telephone survey may then be conducted to determine the presence or absence of desired costumes, textiles, photographs, fashion plates, silhouettes, and so on. Inquire about research facilities and museum policies and ask permission to examine specific items. Some museums permit costumes to be photographed; others do not. Assemble all materials that might be needed: camera, film, sketch pad, pencils (no ink pens), erasers, tape measure, magnifying glass, data collection sheets, white cotton photographer's gloves, and so on. Should questions arise during the visit, do not hesitate to ask the curator of costumes.

Illustrated commentaries describing specific collections or exhibits are often available. Examples are Dilys Blum's *Illusion and Reality: Fashion in France, 1700–1900* from the Houston Museum of Fine Arts; *An Elegant Art:*

Fashion and Fantasy in the Eighteenth Century from the Los Angeles County Museum of Art; and Elizabeth Jackimowicz's *Eight Chicago Women and Their Fashions, 1860–1929* from the Chicago Historical Society. "A Century of Fashion 1865–1965" is a traveling museum exhibition presented by Encyclopedia Britannica. Designed and created by Donald Stowell and Erin Wertenberger, the twelve-showcase exhibit presents accurate representations of women's, men's, and children's clothes. "A Century of Fashion" will tour the United States through 1992.

HISTORY AND CRITICISM

Fashion history and theory are such broad topics and have been approached from so many perspectives that a formidable body of literature has developed. The following discussion covers history, social/psychological aspects, design, marketing, and fashion periodicals, each with a few selected examples. Many more sources are listed in the bibliography at the end of this chapter.

One approach is the survey of Western civilization method, typically an illustrated fashion history beginning with Egyptian dress and ending at the beginning or middle of the twentieth century. Examples of this genre are Lucy Barton's *Historic Costume for the Stage*, Michael and Ariane Batterberry's *Mirror, Mirror: A Social History of Fashion*, François Boucher's *20,000 Years of Fashion: The History of Costume and Personal Adornment*, Millia Davenport's *The Book of Costume*, James Laver's *Costume and Fashion: A Concise History*, and R. Turner Wilcox's *The Mode in Costume*. An added feature in Blanche Payne's *History of Costume from the Ancient Egyptians of the Twentieth Century* is a collection of forty-three 1/8-inch scale pattern drafts ranging from a fourteenth-century pourpoint to an 1895 black serge raincoat. These surveys provide a comprehensive starting point for historic research, and their bibliographies and illustration captions will lead the researcher to additional secondary and primary sources. Specialization in a time period, geographical area, or style feature provides other approaches used in works such as James Laver's *Costume in Antiquity*, Peter Copeland's *Working Dress in Colonial and Revolutionary America*, Alison Gernsheim's *Victorian and Edwardian Fashion: A Photographic Survey*, Barbara Bernard's *Fashion in the Sixties*, and R. Turner Wilcox's *The Mode in Hats and Headdress*.

Several reprint editions have rescued classic historic costume books and made them readily available for researchers. Thomas Hope's *Costumes of the Greeks and Romans* was originally published in 1812 and contains a brief text and 300 costume plates. Also valuable for its costume plates is *Historic Costume in Pictures*, a collection of 125 illustrations issued by publishers Braun and Schneider in Munich between 1861 and 1890. Providing both illustrations and patterns are Karl Kohler's *A History of Costume* and Juan de Alcega's *Tailor's Pattern Book, 1589*, translated and reproduced from the

Spanish original in 1979. Another late sixteenth-century source is *Vecellio's Renaissance Costume Book,* 500 woodcut illustrations of world costumes reprinted by Dover in 1977. For research on American costume consult Dover's 1970 reprint of Alice Morse Earle's *Two Centuries of Costume in America: 1620–1820,* originally published in 1903, and Tudor's 1969 one-volume reprint of Elisabeth McClellan's *History of American Costume: 1607–1870,* originally published in 1904 and 1910.

Discussions of the social psychology of dress typically address the concepts of origins and functions of clothes, clothing as nonverbal communication, clothing behavior (self-concept, role, status, life-style), and physical appearance. Early theorists and their works include Frank Parsons's *The Psychology of Dress,* Hilaire Hiler's *From Nudity to Raiment,* and John Flugel's *The Psychology of Clothes.* Follow these early writers with another trio: Lawrence Langner, *The Importance of Wearing Clothes;* Mary Ryan, *Clothing: A Study in Human Behavior;* and Mary Rosencranz, *Clothing Concepts: A Social-Psychological Approach.* To investigate the combination of sociology and psychology with semiology, consult *The Fashion System* by Roland Barthes. Four recent survey textbooks provide the researcher with an overview of social/psychological aspects of clothing and with bibliographies for further reading: Marilyn Horn and Lois Gurel, *The Second Skin: An Interdisciplinary Study of Clothing;* Susan Kaiser, *The Social Psychology of Clothing and Personal Behavior;* Mary Kefgen and Phyllis Touchie-Specht, *Individuality in Clothing Selection and Personal Appearance: A Guide for the Consumer;* and Penny Storm, *Functions of Dress: Tool of Culture and the Individual.*

Included within the scope of fashion design are works on elements and principles of design, fashion illustration and photography, and biographies of designers. Begin with Sharon Tate's *Inside Fashion Design,* an illustrated guide to apparel manufacturing, the role of the designer, organizing and fabricating a line, sources of inspiration, and elements and principles of design. Follow with *Visual Design in Dress* by Marian Davis for a more in-depth analysis of the framework of design, elements and principles, glossary of design terms, and bibliography. To understand the actual process of creating the pattern or the design in three-dimensional form, refer to works on "flat pattern" or "draping." The flat pattern technique (dart manipulation to create a paper pattern) is explained in Helen Armstrong's *Pattern Making for Fashion Design,* Norma Hollen and Carolyn Kundel's *Pattern Making by the Flat-Pattern Method,* Jeanne Powell and Carol Foley's *Pattern Making,* and Ernestine Kopp et al.'s *Designing Apparel Through the Flat Pattern.* The draping method (manipulating fabric on a dress form to create a garment) is described in Hilde Jaffe and Nurie Relis's *Draping for Fashion Design* and Martha Shelden's *Design Through Draping.* A 1948 book by Marion Hillhouse and Evelyn Mansfield, *Dress Design: Draping and Flat Pattern Making,* is valuable for design techniques as well as styles of the 1940s. Helpful sources for basic fashion illustration and photography are *The Complete Book of Fashion Illustration* by Sharon Tate and Mona Edwards, *Drawing Fashion* by Bill Thames, *Fashion Photography: A Guide for the Beginner* by Robert Randall, and *Professional Fashion Photography* by Robert Farber. For brief information on specific fashion designers, consult *Who's Who in Fashion* by Anne Stegemeyer and the general encyclopedias mentioned above. For further study, turn to autobiographies such as Pierre Balmain's *My Years and Seasons,* Elizabeth Hawes's *Fashion Is Spinach,* and Paul Poiret's *My First Fifty Years,* or to biographies such as Edmonde Charles-Roux's *Chanel and Her World,* Sara Lee's *American Fashion: The Life and Lines of Adrian, Mainbocher, McCardell, Norell, and Trigere,* or Caroline Milbank's *Couture: The Great Designers.*

For an introduction to the dynamics of fashion marketing, the researcher should consult Sidney Packard and Abraham Raine's *Consumer Behavior and Fashion Marketing* and Kathryn Greenwood and Mary Murphy's *Fashion Innovation and Marketing.* Then, for discussions of international and domestic fashion centers, wholesale markets and distribution, types of retail stores, merchandising procedures, and auxiliary fashion enterprises, select one of three comparable works: *Fashion from Concept to Consumer* by Gini Frings, *Inside the Fashion Business: Text and Readings* by Jeannette Jarnow, Miriam Guerreiro, and Beatrice Judelle, or *Fashion Buying and Merchandising* by Sidney Packard, Arthur Winters, and Nathan Axelrod. Fashion promotion (including style shows, visual merchandising, advertising, and public relations) is covered in Pamela Phillips, Ellye Bloom, and John Mattingly's *Fashion Sales Promotion: The Selling Behind the Selling,* Arthur Winters and Stanley Goodman's *Fashion Advertising and Promotion,* and Susan Goschie's *Fashion Direction and Coordination.* Pros and cons of careers in the fashion industry are offered in *The Fashion Directors: What They Do and How to Be One* by Elaine Jabenis, *The Fashion Business: Dynamics and Careers* by Sidney Packard and Abraham Raine, and *Fashion Business: It's All Yours* by Estelle Hamburger.

Trade publications are fashion magazines and newspapers published specifically for professionals in the textile and apparel industry. Contents are aimed at the manufacturer, wholesaler, retail buyer, retail store manager, or visual merchandiser rather than the consumer, and include market research, trends, industry news, and classified ads. Two Fairchild Publications newspapers, *Women's Wear Daily* and *Daily News Record* for menswear, are considered the most important, comprehensive fashion industry trade papers. Serving industry segments are specialized trade publications such as *Accessories, Advertising Age, Chain Store Age, Footwear News, Hosiery News, Stores,* and *Visual Merchandising and Store Design.* For names and addresses of trade associations and over seventy trade publications, consult Jarnow, Guerreiro, and Judelle's *Inside the Fashion Business: Text and Readings.*

In contrast to trade publications, popular magazines report and interpret fashion news and trends to the ultimate consumer. Some cover a broad spectrum of topics including fashion; others are geared toward a specialized audience. For women's fashions, *Vogue* and *Harper's Bazaar* cover high fashion for the sophisticated, mature, higher-income consumer. *Elle, Mademoiselle,* and *Glamour* target the college-age and young career woman, while *New Ingenue* and *Seventeen* focus on fashions for teens. Some fashion articles may be found in other popular magazines such as *Ladies' Home Journal, Town and Country, Redbook, Cosmopolitan, Woman's Day, Family Circle, Good Housekeeping,* and *McCall's.* Examples of magazines designed for special interest audiences are *Ebony* and *Essence* for the black readership and *Bride's Magazine* and *Modern Bride* for the bride-to-be. Newspaper coverage includes the *New York Times Magazine* and *W,* fashion and life-style articles from *Women's Wear Daily.* For menswear, *Gentlemen's Quarterly* and *M: The Civilized Man* provide coverage of high-fashion trends. *Playboy* and *Esquire* offer fashion trend articles and ads, while magazines such as *Bicycling* and *Sports Illustrated* present special interest sportswear articles.

For fashion history projects involving nineteenth-century clothing, see library collections of *Graham's Magazine, Godey's Lady's Book, Peterson's Magazine, Harper's Bazaar,* or *Burton's Gentlemen's Magazine.* Collections of articles and illustrations from periodicals also provide sources for historic costume research. *The Changing American Woman: 200 Years of American Fashion* is a reprint of a special supplement of *Women's Wear Daily,* originally issued on July 26, 1976. Collections from *Harper's Bazaar* include Jane Trahey's *Harper's Bazaar: 100 Years of the American Female* and Stella Blum's *Victorian Fashions and Costumes from Harper's Bazar [sic]: 1867–1898.* Assembled from *Vogue* are *In Vogue: Sixty Years of International Celebrities and Fashion from British Vogue* by Georgina Howell, *Fashion Drawing in Vogue* by William Packer, and *The Art of Vogue Photographic Covers: Fifty Years of Fashion and Design* by Valerie Lloyd.

Mail order catalogs, past and present, provide valuable fashion illustrations and descriptions. A prime example is the *Sears, Roebuck and Co. Catalogue,* available on microfilm, in reprint editions, and in collections such as Stella Blum's *Everyday Fashions of the Thirties as Pictured in Sears Catalogs.*

Four journals containing scholarly research articles on fashion are *Dress, Costume, Clothing and Textiles Research Journal,* and the *Home Economics Research Journal. Dress,* the journal of the Costume Society of America, began publication in 1975. Examples of its contents are Patricia Cunningham's "Eighteenth Century Nightgowns: The Gentleman's Robe in Art and Fashion," Jo Paoletti's "Clothes Make the Boy, 1869–1910," and Robert Hillestad's "The Underlying Structure of Appearance." The journal of the Costume Society of England, *Costume,* includes articles such as Elizabeth Sanderson's "The Edinburgh Milliners, 1720–1820" and Margaret Swain's "The Patchwork Dressing Gown." The Association of College Professors of Textiles and Clothing publishes the *Clothing and Textiles Research Journal,* which includes a number of articles on the fashion industry. Two examples are Barbara Nordquist's "International Trade in Textiles and Clothing: Implications for the Future" and Rita Kean's "Perceived Importance of Selected Skills to a Group of Discount Store Buyers." The *Home Economics Research Journal* is a quarterly publication of the American Home Economics Association. Its fashion articles have included "Store Status and Country of Origin as Information Cues: Consumer's Perception of Sweater Price and Quality" by Brenda Sternquist and Bonnie Davis and "Imported Versus U.S.-produced Apparel: Consumer Views and Buying Patterns" by Kitty Dickerson.

ANTHOLOGIES AND REPRINTS

Few anthologies exist. The seven described in this section contain reprints or collections of articles from a variety of sources, and most are designed as textbooks.

Most recent is Jeannette Jarnow, Miriam Guerreiro, and Beatrice Judelle's *Inside the Fashion Business: Text and Readings.* This fashion marketing text covers principles of fashion merchandising, an overview of the domestic apparel market, foreign producers, and auxiliary fashion enterprises. Each chapter includes several readings (fifty in all) reprinted from sources such as *Apparel World, Women's Wear Daily, Bobbin, Daily News Record, Stores,* and *Advertising Age.* For an up-to-date survey of the fashion industry, begin with this collection of readings.

Twenty-three reprints on the subjects fashion marketing, planning, selling, and fashion trends are presented in Sidney Packard's *Strategies and Tactics in Fashion Marketing: Selected Readings.* The readings, all by Packard, are selected from *Knitting Times, Apparel World,* and books and manuscripts by the same author.

From his "Feminine Fashions" column in the *New Yorker,* Kennedy Fraser has assembled *The Fashionable Mind: Reflections on Fashion 1970–1981.* Thirty articles chronicle topics ranging from hot pants to hats, fitness to fall collections, and the executive woman to electronic shopping. Two anthologies by Patrick Cash and Irene Kleeberg focus on fashion merchandising: *The Buyer's Manual* and *The Management of Fashion Merchandising: A Symposium.* Both were published by the National Retail Merchants Association and contain articles on the role and future of fashion retailing, buying techniques, advertising, visual merchandising, assortment planning, trends, and careers in fashion.

For an overview of the subdisciplines of clothing and fashion, consult Lois Gurel and Marianne Beeson's *Dimensions of Dress and Adornment: A Book of Readings.* This collection includes fifty-four articles on origins and functions of dress, anthropological perspectives, historical influences, social and psychological aspects, and apparel economics.

And last, devoted entirely to cross-cultural subjects, the researcher may refer to *Traditional Folk Textiles and Dress: Selected Readings and Bibliography* by Barbara Nordquist, Jean Mettam, and Kathy Jansen. Thirty-nine articles from scholarly, trade, or craft journals are divided into eight sections (Africa, Middle East, Europe, Indian subcontinent, Asia, Oceania, North America, and South America), each with introduction, several readings, and bibliography.

Several reprinted books have been identified in the preceding sections to which they belong by subject. Among publishers, Dover Publications must be recognized for reprinting a number of valuable fashion and costume books.

NOTE

1. Jeannette A. Jarnow, Miriam Guerreiro, and Beatrice Judelle, *Inside the Fashion Business: Text and Readings,* 4th ed. (New York: Macmillan, 1987), p. 133.

BIBLIOGRAPHY

Books and Articles

Alcega, Juan de. *Tailor's Pattern Book, 1589*. Bedford, England: Ruth Bean, 1979.

American Fabrics and Fashions Magazine, eds. *American Fabrics Encyclopedia of Textiles*. 3rd ed. Englewood Cliffs, N.J.: Prentice-Hall, 1980.

American Home Economics Association. *Aesthetics and Clothing: An Annotated Bibliography*. Washington, D.C.: American Home Economics Association, 1972.

Anthony, Pegaret, and Janet Arnold. *Costume: A General Bibliography*. London: Costume Society of England, 1977.

Armstrong, Helen Joseph. *Pattern Making for Fashion Design*. New York: Harper and Row, 1987.

Arnold, Janet. *A Handbook of Costume*. London: Macmillan, 1973.

———. *Patterns of Fashion: Englishwomen's Dresses and Their Construction*. New York: Drama Book, 1977.

Artbibliographies Modern. Santa Barbara, Calif.: American Bibliographical Center, 1969-.

Art Index. New York: H. W. Wilson, 1930-.

Arts and Humanities Citation Index. Philadelphia: Institute for Scientific Information, 1976-.

Avedon, Richard. *Avedon—Photographs, 1947–1977*. New York: Farrar, Straus and Giroux, 1978.

Bach, Pieter, ed. *Textile, Costume, and Doll Collections in the United States and Canada*. Lopez, Wash.: R. L. Shep, 1981.

Bailey, David, and Martin Harrison. *Shots of Style: Great Fashion Photographs*. London: Victoria and Albert Museum, 1985.

Baker, Lillian. *100 Years of Collectible Jewelry, 1850–1950*. Paducah, Ky.: Collector Books, 1978.

Baker, William Henry. *A Dictionary of Men's Wear*. Cleveland: W. H. Baker, 1908.

Balmain, Pierre. *My Years and Seasons*. London: Cassell, 1964.

Barthes, Roland. *The Fashion System*. New York: Hill and Wang, 1983.

Barton, Lucy. *Historic Costume for the Stage*. Boston: Walter H. Baker, 1938.

Batterberry, Michael, and Ariane Batterberry. *Mirror, Mirror: A Social History of Fashion*. New York: Holt, Rinehart and Winston, 1977.

Bernard, Barbara. *Fashion in the Sixties*. New York: St. Martin's Press, 1978.

Berstein, Leonard S. *"How's Business?" "Don't Ask" : Tales from the Garment Center*. New York: Saturday Review Press, 1974.

Black, J. Anderson, and Madge Garland. *A History of Fashion*. New York: William Morrow, 1975.

Blum, Dilys. *Illusion and Reality: Fashion in France, 1700–1900*. Houston: Museum of Fine Arts, 1986.

Blum, Stella, ed. *Everyday Fashions of the Thirties as Pictured in Sears Catalogs*. New York: Dover, 1986.

———, ed. *Everyday Fashions of the Twenties as Pictured in Sears and Other Catalogs*. New York: Dover, 1981.

———, ed. *Paris Fashions of the 1890's: A Picture Source Book*. New York: Dover, 1984.

———, ed. *Victorian Fashions and Costumes from Harper's Bazar: 1867–1898*. New York: Dover, 1974.

Boucher, François. *20,000 Years of Fashion: The History of Costume and Personal Adornment*. New York: Harry N. Abrams, 1967.

Brockman, Helen L. *The Theory of Fashion Design*. New York: Wiley, 1965.

Buck, Anne. "Clothes in Fact and Fiction, 1825–1865." *Costume,* 17 (1983), 89–104.

———. *Victorian Costume and Costume Accessories*. New York: Thomas Nelson, 1961.

Business Periodicals Index. New York: W. H. Wilson, 1958-.

Calasibetta, Charlotte. *Essential Terms of Fashion: A Collection of Definitions*. New York: Fairchild, 1986.

———. *Fairchild's Dictionary of Fashion*. New York: Fairchild, 1975.

Carillo, Loretta. "Fashion." In *Concise Histories of American Popular Culture*. Edited by M. Thomas Inge. Westport, Conn.: Greenwood Press, 1982, pp. 129–35.

Cash, Patrick, and Irene Cumming Kleeberg, eds. *The Buyer's Manual*. New York: National Retail Merchants Association, 1979.

Charles-Roux, Edmonde. *Chanel and Her World*. London: Weidenfeld and Nicolson, 1981.

Clothing Terms and Definitions. 3rd ed. London: Clothing and Footwear Institute, 1983.

Cobrin, Harry A. *The Men's Clothing Industry: Colonial Through Modern Times*. New York: Fairchild, 1970.

Cohn, David Lewis. *The Good Old Days: A History of American Morals and Manners as Seen Through the Sears, Roebuck Catalogs 1905 to the Present*. New York: Simon and Schuster, 1940.

Coleman, Dorothy Smith. "Fashion Dolls/Fashionable Dolls." *Dress,* 3 (1977), 1–8.

Coleman, Elizabeth Ann, and Suman Shenoi, eds. *Directory of Costume/Textile Collections*. Earleville, Md.: Costume Society of America, forthcoming.

Contini, Mila. *Fashion: From Ancient Egypt to the Present Day*. New York: Odyssey Press, 1965.

Copeland, Peter F. *Working Dress in Colonial and Revolutionary America*. Westport, Conn.: Greenwood Press, 1977.

The Costume Society of America Membership Directory: 1987. Earleville, Md.: Costume Society of America, 1987.

Crawford, Morris De Camp. *One World of Fashion*. New York: Fairchild, 1946.

———. *The Ways of Fashion*. New York: Fairchild, 1948.

Cunningham, Patricia A. "Eighteenth Century Nightgowns: The Gentleman's Robe in Art and Fashion."*Dress,* 10 (1984), 2–11.

Cunnington, Cecil Willett, Phillis Cunnington, and Charles Beard. *A Dictionary of English Costume: 900–1900*. London: Adam and Charles Black, 1960.

Davenport, Millia. *The Book of Costume*. New York: Crown, 1948.

Davis, Marian L. *Visual Design in Dress*. 2nd ed. Englewood Cliffs, N. J.: Prentice-Hall, 1987.

DeLong, Marilyn Revell. *The Way We Look: A Framework for Visual Analysis of Dress*. Ames: Iowa State University Press, 1987.

DePaola, Helena, and Carol Stewart Mueller. *Marketing Today's Fashion*. 2nd ed. Englewood Cliffs, N. J.: Prentice-Hall, 1986.

Dewey, Melvil. *Dewey Decimal Classification and Relative Index*. 9th ed. New York: Forest Press, 1965.

Dickerson, Kitty G. "Imported Versus U.S.-Produced Apparel: Consumer Views and Buying Patterns." *Home Economics Research Journal,* 10 (March 1982), 241–52.

Dillon, Linda S. "Business Dress for Women Corporate Professionals." *Home Economics Research Journal,* 9 (December 1980), 124–29.

Dolan, Maryanne. *Vintage Clothing, 1880–1960: Identification and Value Guide*. Florence, Ala.: Books Americana, 1984.

Earle, Alice Morse. *Two Centuries of Costume in America: 1620–1820*. 1903. Reprint. 2 vols. New York: Dover, 1970.

Etherington-Smith, Meredith. *Patou*. New York: St. Martin's/Marek, 1983.

Ewing, Elizabeth. *History of Twentieth Century Fashion*. Totowa, N.J.: Barnes and Noble, 1986.

Ewing, William A. *The Photographic Art of Hoyningen-Huene*. New York: Rizzoli, 1986.

Fairchild, John. *The Fashionable Savages*. Garden City, N.Y.: Doubleday, 1965.

Farber, Robert. *Professional Fashion Photography*. Garden City, N.Y.: American Photographic Book, 1978.

Fetterman, Nelma Irene. "A Bibliometric Analysis of Clothing Literature with Implications for Information Storage and Retrieval." Ph.D. dissertation, Ohio State University, 1977.

Filene, Adele, and Polly Willman. *The Costume Society of America Bibliography: 1974/1979*. N.p.: Costume Society of America, n.d.

Flugel, John Carl. *The Psychology of Clothes*. London: Hogarth Press, 1930.

Folse, Nancy McCarthy, and Marilyn Henrion. *Careers in the Fashion Industry: What the Jobs Are and How to Get Them*. New York: Harper and Row, 1981.

Fraser, Kennedy. *The Fashionable Mind: Reflections on Fashion 1970–1981*. New York: Alfred A. Knopf, 1981.

Frings, Gini Stephens. *Fashion from Concept to Consumer*. 2nd ed. Englewood Cliffs, N.J.: Prentice-Hall, 1987.

Gernsheim, Alison. *Victorian and Edwardian Fashion: A Photographic Survey*. New York: Dover, 1981.

Gioello, Debbie Ann, and Beverly Berke. *Fashion Production Terms*. New York: Fairchild, 1979.

Goschie, Susan. *Fashion Direction and Coordination*. Indianapolis: Bobbs-Merrill, 1980.

Greenwood, Kathryn Moore, and Mary Fox Murphy. *Fashion Innovation and Marketing*. New York: Macmillan, 1978.

Gurel, Lois M., and Marianne S. Beeson. *Dimensions of Dress and Adornment: A Book of Readings*. Dubuque, Iowa: Kendall/Hunt, 1979.

Hamburger, Estelle. *Fashion Business: It's All Yours*. San Francisco: Canfield Press, 1976.

Hawes, Elizabeth. *Fashion Is Spinach*. New York: Random House, 1938.

Hiler, Hilaire. *From Nudity to Raiment*. London: Foyle, 1929.

Hiler, Hilaire, and Meyer Hiler. *Bibliography of Costume: A Dictionary Catalog of About Eight Thousand Books and Periodicals*. New York: H. W. Wilson, 1939.

Hillestad, Robert. "The Underlying Structure of Appearance." *Dress*, 5 (1980), 117–25.

Hillhouse, Marion S., and Evelyn A. Mansfield. *Dress Design: Draping and Flat Pattern Making*. Boston: Houghton Mifflin, 1948.

Historic Costume in Pictures. New York: Dover, 1975.

Hollander, Anne. *Seeing Through Clothes*. New York: Viking Press, 1978.

Hollen, Norma R., and Carolyn J. Kundel. *Pattern Making by the Flat-Pattern Method*. 6th ed. New York: Macmillan, 1987.

Hope, Thomas. *Costumes of the Greeks and Romans*. 1812. Reprint. New York: Dover, 1962.

Horn, Marilyn J., and Lois M. Gurel. *The Second Skin: An Interdisciplinary Study of Clothing*. 3rd ed. Boston: Houghton Mifflin, 1981.

Houck, Catherine. *The Fashion Encyclopedia: An Essential Guide to Everything You Need to Know About Clothes*. New York: St. Martin's Press, 1982.

Howell, Georgina. *In Vogue: Sixty Years of International Celebrities and Fashion from British Vogue*. New York: Schocken Books, 1976.

Hudson, Kenneth, and Ann Nicholls. *The Directory of Museums and Living Displays*. 3rd ed. New York: Stockton Press, 1985.

Huenefeld, Irene Pennington. *International Directory of Historical Clothing*. Metuchen, N.J.: Scarecrow Press, 1967.

Humanities Index. New York: H. W. Wilson, 1975–.

Hutton, Sandra S., ed. *The Clothing and Textiles Arts Index: An Index to Periodical Literature, 1980–1984*. Monument, Colo.: Sandra S. Hutton, 1986.

———, *The Clothing Index: An Index to Periodical Literature, January 1970-December 1979*. Lincoln, Nebr.: Micro Control Systems, 1982.

Jabenis, Elaine. *The Fashion Directors: What They Do and How to Be One*. New York: Wiley, 1983.

Jackimowicz, Elizabeth. *Eight Chicago Women and Their Fashions, 1860–1929*. Chicago: Chicago Historical Society, 1978.

Jackson, Carole. *Color Me Beautiful*. New York: Ballantine, 1981.

Jaffe, Hilde, and Nurie Relis. *Draping for Fashion Design*. Reston, Va.: Reston, 1973.

Jarnow, Jeannette A., Miriam Guerreiro, and Beatrice Judelle. *Inside the Fashion Business: Text and Readings*. 4th ed. New York: Macmillan, 1987.

Joseph, Nathan. *Uniforms and Nonuniforms: Communication Through Clothing*. New York: Greenwood Press, 1986.

Judelle, Beatrice. *The Fashion Buyer's Job*. New York: National Retail Merchants Association, 1971.

Kaiser, Susan B. *The Social Psychology of Clothing and Personal Behavior*. New York: Macmillan, 1985.

Kean, Rita C. "Perceived Importance of Selected Skills to a Group of Discount Store Buyers." *Clothing and Textiles Research Journal*, 4 (Fall 1985), 31–37.

Kefgen, Mary, and Phyllis Touchie-Specht. *Individuality in Clothing Selection and Personal Appearance: A Guide for the Consumer*. 4th ed. New York: Macmillan, 1986.

Kelley, Eleanor, David Blouin, Rose Glee, Sarah Sweat, and Lydia Arledge. "Career Appearance: Perceptions of University Students and Recruiters Who Visit Their Campuses." *Home Economics Research Journal*, 10 (March 1982), 253–63.

Kennett, Frances. *The Collector's Book of Fashion*. New York: Crown, 1983.

Kidwell, Claudia B. *Cutting a Fashionable Fit: Dressmakers' Drafting Systems in the United States*. Washington, D.C.: Smithsonian Institution Press, 1979.

———. *Women's Bathing and Swimming Costume in the United States*. Washington, D.C.: Smithsonian Institution Press, 1968.

Kim, Minja, and Holly Schrank. "Fashion Leadership Among Korean Women." *Home Economics Research Journal*, 10 (March 1982), 227–34.

Kleeberg, Irene C., and Patrick Cash, eds. *The Management of Fashion Merchandising: A Symposium*. New York: National Retail Merchants Association, 1977.

Kohler, Karl. *A History of Costume*. London: G. G. Harrap, 1928.

Kopp, Ernestine, Vittorina Rolfo, Beatrice Zelin, and Lee Gross. *Designing Apparel Through the Flat Pattern*. Rev. 5th ed. New York: Fairchild, 1982.

Koren, Leonard. *New Fashion Japan*. New York: Kodansha International, 1984.

Lambert, Eleanor. *World of Fashion: People, Places, Resources*. New York: R. R. Bowker, 1976.

Langner, Lawrence. *The Importance of Wearing Clothes*. New York: Hastings House, 1959.

Laver, James. *Costume and Fashion: A Concise History*. New York: Oxford University Press, 1983.

———. *Costume in Antiquity*. New York: Clarkson N. Potter, 1964.

———. *Modesty in Dress: An Inquiry into the Fundamentals of Fashion*. Boston: Houghton Mifflin, 1969.

Lawford, Valentine. *Horst: His Work and His World*. New York: Alfred A. Knopf, 1984.

Lee, Sara Tomerlin. *American Fashion: The Life and Lines of Adrian, Mainbocher, McCardell, Morell, and Trigere*. New York: Quadrangle/New York Times, 1975.

Ley, Sandra. *Fashion for Everyone: The Story of Ready-to-Wear, 1870–1970's*. New York: Scribner's, 1975.

Library of Congress Subject Headings. 10th ed. Washington, D.C.: Library of Congress, 1986.

Linton, George Edward. *The Modern Textile and Apparel Dictionary.* 4th ed. Plainfield, N.J.: Textile Book Service, 1973.

Lloyd, Valerie. *The Art of Vogue Photographic Covers: Fifty Years of Fashion and Design.* New York: Harmony Books, 1986.

Los Angeles County Museum of Art. *An Elegant Art: Fashion and Fantasy in the Eighteenth Century.* New York: Harry N. Abrams, 1983.

———. *Fabric and Fashion: Twenty Years of Costume Council Gifts.* Los Angeles: Los Angeles County Museum of Art, 1974.

Lubell, Cecil. *Textile Collections of the World, Volume 1: United States and Canada.* New York: Van Nostrand Reinhold, 1976.

———. *Textile Collections of the World, Volume 2: United Kingdom and Ireland.* New York: Van Nostrand Reinhold, 1976.

———. *Textile Collections of the World, Volume 3: France.* New York: Van Nostrand Reinhold, 1976.

Lurie, Alison. *The Language of Clothes.* New York: Random House, 1981.

Lynam, Ruth. *Couture: An Illustrated History of the Great Paris Designers and Their Creations.* Garden City, N.Y.: Doubleday, 1972.

McClellan, Elisabeth. *History of American Costume: 1607–1870.* New York: Tudor, 1969.

McDowell, Colin. *A Hundred Years of Royal Style.* London: Muller, Blond, and White, 1985.

———. *McDowell's Directory of Twentieth Century Fashion.* Englewood Cliffs, N.J.: Prentice-Hall, 1985.

Madsen, Axel. *Living for Design: The Yves Saint Laurent Story.* New York: Delacorte Press, 1979.

Milbank, Caroline Rennolds. *Couture: The Great Designers.* New York: Stewart, Tabori and Chang, 1985.

Molloy, John T. *Dress for Success.* New York: Warner Books, 1975.

———. *The Woman's Dress for Success Book.* New York: Warner Books, 1977.

Monro, Isabel Stevenson, and Dorothy E. Cook. *Costume Index: A Subject Guide to Plates and to Illustrated Text.* New York: H. W. Wilson, 1937.

Monroe, Isabel Stevenson, and Kate M. Monro. *Costume Index Supplement.* New York: H. W. Wilson, 1957.

National Geographic Society. *National Geographic Index: 1888–1946.* Washington, D.C.:National Geographic Society, 1967.

———. *National Geographic Index: 1947–1976.* Washington, D.C.: National Geographic Society, 1977.

Nevinson, John Lea. *Origin and Early History of Fashion Plate.* Washington, D.C.: Smithsonian Institution Press, 1967.

Newton, Stella Mary. *Health, Art and Reason: Dress Reformers of the Nineteenth Century.* London: J. Murray, 1974.

A New Wave in Fashion: Three Japanese Designers. Phoenix: Arizona Costume Institute of the Phoenix Art Museum, 1983.

New York Times Index. New York: New York Times, 1851-.

Nordquist, Barbara K. "International Trade in Textiles and Clothing: Implications for the Future." *Clothing and Textiles Research Journal* 3 (Spring 1985), 35–39.

Nordquist, Barbara K., Jean E. Mettam, and Kathy Jansen. *Traditional Folk Textiles and Dress: Selected Readings and Bibliography*. Dubuque, Iowa: Kendall/Hunt, 1986.

Nystrom, Paul Henry. *Economics in Fashion*. New York: Ronald Press, 1928.

O'Hara, Georgina. *The Encyclopedia of Fashion*. New York: Harry N. Abrams, 1986.

Olian, Jo Anne. *The House of Worth: The Gilded Age, 1860–1918*. New York: Museum of the City of New York, 1982.

Packard, Sidney. *The Fashion Business: Dynamics and Careers*. New York: Holt, Rinehart and Winston, 1983.

———. *Strategies and Tactics in Fashion Marketing: Selected Readings*. New York: Fairchild, 1982.

Packard, Sidney, and Abraham Raine. *Consumer Behavior and Fashion Marketing*. 2nd ed. Dubuque, Iowa: Kendall/Hunt, 1979.

Packard, Sidney, Arthur A. Winters, and Nathan Axelrod. *Fashion Buying and Merchandising*. 2nd ed. New York: Fairchild, 1983.

Packer, William. *Fashion Drawing in Vogue*. New York: Coward-McCann, 1983.

Paoletti, Jo B. "Clothes Make the Boy, 1869–1910." *Dress*, 9 (1983), 16–20.

Parsons, Frank Alvah. *The Psychology of Dress*. New York: Doubleday, 1920.

Payne, Blanche. *History of Costume from the Ancient Egyptians to the Twentieth Century*. New York: Harper and Row, 1965.

Penn, Irving. *Inventive Paris Clothes, 1909–1939: A Photographic Essay*. New York: Viking Press, 1977.

Phillips, Pamela M., Ellye Bloom, and John D. Mattingly. *Fashion Sales Promotion: The Selling Behind the Selling*. New York: Wiley, 1985.

Picken, Mary Brooks. *The Fashion Dictionary: Fabric, Sewing, and Apparel as Expressed in the Language of Fashion*. New York: Funk and Wagnalls, 1973.

Poiret, Paul. *My First Fifty Years*. London: V. Gollancz, 1931.

Polhemus, Ted, and Lynn Procter. *Fashion and Anti-fashion: An Anthropology of Clothing and Adornment*. London: Thames and Hudson, 1978.

Powell, Jeanne, and Carol Foley. *Pattern Making*. Englewood Cliffs, N.J.: Prentice-Hall, 1987.

Psychological Abstracts. Lancaster, Pa.: American Psychological Association, 1927-.

Randall, Robert. *Fashion Photography: A Guide for the Beginner*. Englewood Cliffs, N.J.: Prentice-Hall, 1984.

Readers' Guide to Periodical Literature. New York: H. W. Wilson, 1900-.

Reich, Naomi, Patricia Otten, and Marie Negri Carver. *Clothing for Handicapped People: An Annotated Bibliography and Resource List*. Washington, D.C.: President's Committee on Employment of the Handicapped, 1979.

Rhodes, Zandra, and Anne Knight. *The Art of Zandra Rhodes*. Boston: Houghton Mifflin, 1985.

Ribeiro, Aileen. *Dress and Morality*. New York: Holmes and Meier, 1986.

RILA: International Repertory of the Literature of Art. Williamston, Me.: Clark Art Institute, 1973-.

Riley, Robert. *The Fashion Makers*. New York: Crown, 1968.

Roach, Mary Ellen, and Joanne B. Eicher. *The Visible Self: Perspectives on Dress*. Englewood Cliffs, N.J.: Prentice-Hall, 1973.

Robertson, Helie. *Esprit, the Making of an Image*. San Francisco: Esprit, 1985.

Rogers, Dorothy S., and Lynda R. Gamans. *Fashion: A Marketing Approach.* New York: Holt, Rinehart and Winston, 1983.

Rosencranz, Mary Lou. *Clothing Concepts: A Social-Psychological Approach.* New York: Macmillan, 1972.

Roshco, Bernard. *The Rag Race.* New York: Funk and Wagnalls, 1963.

Rudofsky, Bernard. *Are Clothes Modern? An Essay on Contemporary Apparel.* Chicago: P. Theobald, 1947.

Ryan, Mary Shaw. *Clothing: A Study in Human Behavior.* New York: Holt, Rinehart and Winston, 1966.

Sanderson, Elizabeth. "The Edinburgh Milliners, 1720–1820." *Costume,* 20 (1986), 18–28.

Schoeffler, O. E., and William Gale. *Esquire's Encyclopedia of Twentieth Century Men's Fashions.* New York: McGraw-Hill, 1973.

Schrank, Holly L., Alan I. Sugawara, and Minja Kim. "Comparison of Korean and American Fashion Leaders." *Home Economics Research Journal,* 10 (March 1982), 235–40.

Sears, Roebuck and Co. *The 1897 Sears, Roebuck Catalogue.* New York: Chelsea House, 1968.

––––––. *The 1902 Sears, Roebuck Catalogue.* New York: Bounty Books, 1969.

Segal, Marvin E. *From Rags to Riches: Success in Apparel Retailing.* New York: Wiley, 1982.

The Select Bibliography of Clothing Sources: Compiled According to the Structure of the Clothing Examinations of the Clothing Footwear Institute. London: Clothing and Footwear Institute, 1980.

Severn, Bill. *The Long and Short of It: Five Thousand Years of Fun and Fury over Hair.* New York: David McKay, 1971.

Shelden, Martha G. *Design Through Draping.* Minneapolis: Burgess, 1967.

Social Sciences Index. New York: H. W. Wilson, 1975-.

Solomon, Michael, ed. *The Psychology of Fashion.* Lexington, Mass.: Lexington Books, 1985.

Spitzer, Harry, and F. Richard Schwartz. *Inside Retail Sales Promotion and Advertising.* New York: Harper and Row, 1982.

Stamper, Anita A., Sue H. Sharp, and Linda B. Donnell. *Evaluating Apparel Quality.* New York: Fairchild, 1986.

Stegemeyer, Anne. *Who's Who in Fashion.* New York: Fairchild, 1986.

Sternquist, Brenda, and Bonnie Davis. "Store Status and Country of Origin as Information Cues: Consumer's Perception of Sweater Price and Quality." *Home Economics Research Journal,* 15 (December 1986), 124–31.

Storm, Penny. *Functions of Dress: Tool of Culture and the Individual.* Englewood Cliffs, N.J.: Prentice-Hall, 1987.

Stowell, Donald, and Erin Wertenberger. *A Century of Fashion 1865–1965.* Chicago: Encyclopedia Britannica, 1987.

Swain, Margaret. "The Patchwork Dressing Gown." *Costume,* 18 (1984), 59–65.

Tarrant, Naomi. *Collecting Costumes: The Care and Display of Clothes and Accessories.* London: George Allen and Unwin, 1983.

Tate, Sharon Lee. *Inside Fashion Design.* 2nd ed. New York: Harper and Row, 1984.

Tate, Sharon Lee, and Mona Shafer Edwards. *The Complete Book of Fashion Illustration.* 2nd ed. New York: Harper and Row, 1987.

————. *The Fashion Coloring Book*. New York: Harper and Row, 1984.

Thames, Bill. *Drawing Fashion*. New York: McGraw-Hill, 1985.

Trahey, Jane, ed. *Harper's Bazaar: 100 Years of the American Female*. New York: Random House, 1967.

Trautman, Patricia. *Clothing America: A Bibliography and Location Index of Nineteenth Century American Pattern Drafting Systems*. Brooklyn: Costume Society of America, 1987.

United Nations Industrial Development Organization. *Information Sources on the Clothing Industry*. New York: United Nations, 1974.

U.S. Department of Commerce. International Trade Administration. *Sources of Statistical Data: Textiles and Apparel, 1980*. Washington, DC: Government Printing Office, July 1981.

Vecchio, Walter, and Robert Riley. *The Fashion Makers: A Photographic Record*. New York: Crown, 1968.

Vecellio, Cesare. *Vecellio's Renaissance Costume Book*. New York: Dover, 1977.

Wallach, Anne. "Fashions and Underfashions: Two Hundred Years of Attitudes and Underwear as Seen in Contemporary Paper Dolls." *Dress*, 5 (1979), 49–62.

Warwick, Edward, Henry C. Pitz, and Alexander Wyckoff. *Early American Dress: The Colonial and Revolutionary Periods*. New York: Bonanza, 1965.

Watkins, Susan M. *Clothing: The Portable Environment*. Ames: Iowa State University Press, 1984.

Westby, Barbara M. *Sears List of Subject Headings*. 10th ed. New York: H. W. Wilson, 1972.

White, Palmer. *Elsa Schiaparelli: Empress of Paris Fashion*. New York: Rizzoli, 1986.

Wilcox, R. Turner. *The Dictionary of Costume*. New York: Scribner's, 1969.

————. *Five Centuries of American Costume*. New York: Scribner's, 1963.

————. *The Mode in Costume*. New York: Scribner's, 1958.

————. *The Mode in Hats and Headdress*. New York: Scribner's, 1948.

Willman, Polly. *The Costume Society of America Bibliography: 1983*. 3rd ed. New York: Costume Society of America, n.d.

Winakor, T. Geitel. *Economics of Textiles and Clothing: A Bibliography*. Ames: Iowa State University, 1980.

Winakor, T. Geitel, and Jacqueline Lubner-Rupert. "Dress Style Variation Related to Perceived Economic Risk." *Home Economics Research Journal*, 11 (June 1983), 343–51.

Wingate, Isabel B., ed. *Fairchild's Dictionary of Textiles*. 6th ed. New York: Fairchild, 1979.

Winters, Arthur A., and Stanley Goodman. *Fashion Advertising and Promotion*. 6th ed. New York: Fairchild, 1984.

Women's Wear Daily. *The Changing American Woman: 200 Years of American Fashion*. New York: Fairchild, 1976.

Wood, Barry James. *Show Windows: Seventy-five Years of the Art of Display*. New York: Congdon and Weed, 1982.

Worrell, Estelle Ansley. *Children's Costume in America 1607–1910*. New York: Scribner's, 1980.

————. *Early American Costume*. Harrisburg, Pa.: Stackpole, 1975.

Yarwood, Doreen. *The Encyclopedia of World Costume*. New York: Scribner's, 1978.

Periodicals

Accessories. Norwalk, Conn., 1908–.
Advertising Age. Chicago, 1930–.
American Fabrics and Fashions. New York, 1946–.
Apparel Executive. New York, 1964–72.
Bicycling. Emmaus, Pa., 1962–.
Bobbin Magazine. Columbia, S.C., 1959–.
Bride's Magazine. New York, 1934–.
The Burton's Gentlemen's Magazine. Philadelphia, 1837–40.
California Apparel News. Los Angeles, 1945–.
Chain Store Age: General Merchandise Trends. New York, 1925–.
Clothing and Textiles Research Journal. Monument, Colo., 1982–.
Connoisseur. New York, 1901–.
Cosmopolitan. New York, 1886–.
Costume. London, 1967/68–.
Daily News Record. New York, 1892–.
Delineator. New York, 1873–1937.
Dress. Englishtown, N.J., 1975–.
Ebony. Chicago, 1945–.
Elle. New York, 1985–.
Esquire. New York, 1933–.
Essence. New York, 1970–.
Family Circle. New York, 1932–.
FemmeLines. New York, 1957–.
Footwear News. New York, 1945–.
Gentlemen's Quarterly. New York, 1957–.
Glamour. New York, 1939–.
Godey's Lady's Book. Philadelphia, New York, 1830–98.
Good Housekeeping. New York, 1885–.
Graham's Magazine. Philadelphia, 1826–58.
Harper's Bazaar. New York, 1867–.
Home Economics Research Journal. Washington, D.C., 1972–.
Hosiery News. Charlotte, N.C., 1921–.
Ingenue. Dunellen, N.J., 1959–73.
Journal of Popular Culture. Bowling Green, Ohio, 1967–.
Knitting Times. New York, 1833–.
Ladies' Home Journal. Des Moines, Iowa, 1983–.
M: The Civilized Man. New York, 1983–.
Mademoiselle. New York, 1935–.
MascuLines. New York, 1957–.
McCall's. New York, 1870–.
Metropolitan. New York, 1868–75.
Metropolitan Fashions. New York, 1873–1901.
Mirror of Fashion. New York, 1840–50, 1853–55.
Modern Bride. New York, 1949–.
New Ingenue. New York, 1973–.

New York Times Magazine. New York, 1896–.
Peterson's Magazine. Philadelphia, 1842–98.
Pictorial Review. New York, 1899–1939.
Playboy. Chicago, 1953–.
Queen of Fashion. New York, 1870–79.
Redbook. New York, 1903–.
Sears, Roebuck Catalog. Chicago, 1891–.
Seventeen. New York, 1944–.
Sports Illustrated. New York, 1954–.
Stores. New York, 1912–.
Town and Country. New York, 1846–.
Visual Merchandising and Store Design. Cincinnati, 1922–.
Vogue. New York, 1892–.
W. New York, 1971–.
Woman's Day. New York, 1937–.
Woman's Home Companion. Springfield, Ohio, 1873–1957.
Women's Wear Daily. New York, 1892–.

Data Base Systems

DIALOG. Palo Alto, Calif., Dialog Information Services, 1972–.
ERIC. Washington, D.C., U.S. Department of Education, 1966–.
InfoTrac. Belmont, Calif., Information Access Co., 1982–.

Film

ROBERT A. ARMOUR

Despite the drop in the number of people going to the movies each week, the interest in the study of the history and appreciation of film has increased greatly in the past decade. The number of books and articles on film has kept pace with the increase in the demand for study at both the secondary school and college levels. The explosion of books on the subject that occurred in the mid–1960s has waned, but the publication of solid—and in some cases, not so solid—books has continued. Now the problem becomes one of wading through the mass of material to find good scholarly help when studying film. Students and others interested in film sometimes have serious problems trying to find film study materials beyond that of reviews in the daily paper or monthly magazine.

As with any other area of popular culture, the books published on film appeal to a wide variety of audiences. Many of these books are intended for the popular audience and are written quickly without much film analysis. This chapter will focus on the more serious type whose facts and judgments can more generally be considered reliable; occasional reference will be made to more popular books when they have proved to be especially well done or unique. In this brief survey of film study materials, only books have been included. There are, of course, thousands of useful articles, but in this limited space all that can be done is to direct the reader to indexes of journals. The emphasis here—by limitation of space and purpose—is on American film and on books readily available in this country in English.

HISTORIC OUTLINE

The date was December 28, 1895. The place was the basement of a cafe in Paris. The audience was the first public one to pay its way to watch movies, paying to be fascinated by moving images of a baby eating his meal, workers leaving a factory, and a train rushing into a station. The scenes were taken from ordinary life, but the experience was far from ordinary. This event was produced by the Lumière brothers, but the technology that led to this moment had been the result of the imagination and persistence of many inventors, both in Europe and America.

Eadweard Muybridge in 1877 had discovered that sequential still photographs of a horse running could be placed in a series and "projected" in such a manner as to make the photographic image of the horse appear to be running. In New Jersey in the late 1880s Thomas Edison and his crew led by William Dickson developed the idea of putting photographs on a single piece of continuous film, and George Eastman supplied the film. For projection Edison decided on the Kinetoscope, a peephole machine through which the film could be shown to one person at a time. Several creative inventors worked on the idea of a projector, but it was finally the Lumière brothers who were able to adapt Edison's ideas and develop the first practical means of allowing many people to view a movie simultaneously. The history of this new art form was then to be written in light.

Once the photographic technology had been developed, the next stage was to decide what to do with it. Obviously audiences could not long be enthralled by shots of a baby eating and would demand more. The Lumières, Edison, rivals at American Mutoscope and Biograph Co., as well as others, attempted to expand the cinematic subject matter; but it was another Frenchman, George Melies, who first achieved any success at telling a story with film. He was a magician who used the medium as part of his act, but in the process he began to depict plot as well as action. His most famous film was *A Trip to the Moon* (1902), which described a fanciful space voyage.

In order to develop a narrative process for film, the filmmaker had to learn to manipulate both space and time, to change them, and to move characters and action within them much as a novelist does. What Melies had begun, Edison and his new director of production continued. Edwin S. Porter learned how to use dissolves and cuts between shots to indicate changes in time or space, or both; the result was films such as *The Great Train Robbery* (1903). This Western, shot in the wilds of New Jersey, told the complete story of a train robbery, the chase of the bandits, and their eventual defeat in a gunfight with the posse. Cross-cutting allowed Porter to show in sequence activities of both the posse and the bandits that were supposed to take place at the same time.

Businessmen began to realize the financial potential for movies. While movies were first shown as part of vaudeville and other forms of entertainment, they soon became the featured attraction themselves. By 1905 the first nickelodeon had opened in Pittsburgh, where customers each paid a nickel to see a full program of a half dozen short films. The opening of theaters completed the elements necessary for an industry: product, technology, producer, purchaser, and distributor.

In 1907, a would-be playwright came to Edison with a filmscript for sale. Edison did not like the script, but he hired its author, David Wark Griffith, as an actor. Griffith needed money and accepted the job. Thus began the career of the man who would turn this entertainment into an art. He began making films himself shortly. His tastes in plots were melodramatic, but his interests in technique were both innovative and scientific. Guided by his cameraman, Billy Bitzer, he began to experiment with editing and shots, finding many ideas for cinematic technique in the sentimental novels and poems of nineteenth-century literature. Gradually he persuaded both audiences and company bosses to accept the idea of a more complicated plot told in a lengthy movie. The result was the first major, long film. In 1915, after unheard-of amounts of time in production, Griffith released *The Birth of a Nation,* a story of the South during the Civil War and Reconstruction. The racial overtones of the film caused considerable controversy, but the power of the images and the timing of the editing created a work of art whose aesthetic excellence is not questioned. In response to the criticism of his racial views, the next year Griffith directed *Intolerance,* which interwove four stories of intolerance into a single film. Griffith was to continue as one of America's leading directors until audiences began to lose their taste for melodrama, and other directors had learned his methods. He had been responsible for launching the careers of several directors, such as Raoul Walsh, and numerous actors, such as Lillian and Dorothy Gish, Mary Pickford, and H. B. Walthall.

While Griffith was learning how to get the most from screen actors, Thomas Ince was polishing the art of telling a story efficiently. In the early 1900s, he directed a few films (*Civilization,* 1916, is the best known), but he quickly turned his attention to production, leaving the details of directing to others under his close supervision. His talent was for organization, and today he is credited with perfecting the studio system. Film is actually a collaborative art, and Ince learned how to bring the talents of many different people into a system that produced polished films, without the individualizing touches found in those films of Griffith or others who work outside the strict studio system.

One man who learned his trade from Griffith was Mack Sennett. Sennett worked for Griffith for a few years as a director and writer, but his interests were more in comedy than in melodrama. In 1912 he broke away and began to work for an independent company, Keystone. Here he learned to merge the methods of stage slapstick comedy with the techniques of film; the results were the Keystone Kops, Ben Turpin, and Charlie Chaplin. Sennett's films used only the barest plot outline as a frame for comic gags that were improvised and shot quickly. From the Sennett method, Charlie Chaplin developed his own technique and character. He began making shorts under the direction of Sennett, but in 1915 he left and joined with Essenay, which agreed to let him write and direct his own films at an unprecedented salary. Here he fleshed out his tramp character; one of his first films for Essenay was *The Tramp* (1915). He continued making films that combined his own comic sense and acrobatic movements with social commentary and along with Mary Pickford became one of the first "stars." Later he made features, such as *The Gold Rush* (1925) and *Modern Times* (1936). Sennett and Chaplin began a period of great film comedy. Buster Keaton combined a deadpan look with remarkable physical ability and timing. He too began making shorts, but soon was directing and starring in features, such as *The General* (1926). Harold Lloyd (*The Freshman*, 1925) and Harry Langdon (*The Strong Man*, 1926) also created comic characters that demonstrated their individuality and imagination.

From these ingredients came the studio system and the star system. Moviegoing audiences created a need for a great number of films, and small companies were unable to meet the demand. Adolph Zukor at Paramount and Marcus Loew, Louis B. Mayer, and Irvin Thalberg at Metro-Goldwyn-Mayer quickly learned the means of applying American business methods to this new industry. They bought out their competition and eventually controlled film production, distribution, and exhibition. Even the actors and directors got into the act as Chaplin, Griffith, Pickford, and Douglas Fairbanks joined together to create United Artists, intended at first to distribute the various productions of its founders. Later it too became a studio force, along with Columbia, Fox, Warners, and others.

With the studios came the stars. The public hungered for new heroes and new love objects, and the studios were quick to give the public what it wanted. Along with the stars who had been established in the early 1900s came the new generation of the 1920s: Rudolph Valentino, Gloria Swanson, Clara Bow. The stars soon became the nucleus of American myth, and the public followed their affairs, marriages, and extravagant lives with keen interest. This was the stuff Hollywood was made of. Fortunately there were behind these stars creative directors, such as Cecil B. DeMille, Eric Von Stroheim, and Henry King, who were able to mold the talents of the stars into movies.

During the 1920s American films dominated the worldwide industry, but they were greatly influenced and enhanced by developments and personalities from Europe. The Russians Sergei Eisenstein (*Potemkin*, 1925) and V. I. Pudovkin (*Mother*, 1926) were especially influential in their understanding of montage (the relationship of the images to each other and the meaning that results). American interest in fantasy was influenced both directly and indirectly by *The Cabinet of Dr. Caligari* (1919), directed by the

German Robert Wiene, and *Destiny* (1921), directed by an Austrian working in Germany, Fritz Lang.

Some Europeans came to America to make films: Ernst Lubitsch, Victor Seastrom, and F. W. Murnau, for example. The influence on American film of these films and filmmakers was profound; they left their strong impression on what came to be known as the Hollywood movie.

The story surrounding the coming of sound to movies is a complex and complicated one. The idea of connecting sound to the visuals was an old one; Edison had in fact entered the movie business because he was searching for visuals to go with the phonograph he was already marketing. To convert the movie technology to sound was expensive. Despite development of the necessary technology (most notably in this country by Lee de Forest), the industry was reluctant to invest in the change. In the mid–1920s Western Electric developed a method for putting the sound on a disk that could be roughly synchronized with the film. None of the big studios could be convinced to try it, but Warner Brothers was about to be forced out of business by the other, larger companies. It had little to lose and decided to take the risk. For a year Warners distributed a program with short sound films of slight interest, but on October 6, 1927, it premiered *The Jazz Singer* with Al Jolson. Sound was used to help tell the story, and the public loved it. Quickly, Warners established its financial base, and other studios rushed to emulate it; but problems developed. Studios had to reequip themselves. The camera, which had been struggling to free itself and discover new methods of expression, found itself confined to a large box and immobile. Actors had to learn to speak to their audiences, and exhibitors had to invest in sound projectors and speakers. Once the problems were overcome, however, the marriage of sound to the visuals became a natural extension of the art.

The period between the coming of sound and World War II was dominated by the studios. They controlled the production—including story, the role of the directors, and the selection of actors—distribution, and exhibition (they owned their own theaters). In the 1930s America went to the movies; by the end of the decade some eighty million people saw a movie every week. The studios provided them with the means to live out their fantasies, find heroes, and escape from the Depression.

One factor directly affecting the films of the 1930s was censorship. Hollywood movies in the late 1920s and early 1930s had become rather open in their use of sex, and the scandals in the private lives of the stars shocked the public even as it hungered for vicarious living. Fear of government intervention and of the Depression forced the studios to censor themselves. They established the Hays Office under the directorship of Will Hays, former postmaster-general, and this office published a strict moral code for on-screen activities and language. The results stifled creativity, but the new moral tastes of the public were satisfied.

The stars captured the public's imagination as in no other time in American popular culture: Fred Astaire and Ginger Rogers, Jean Harlow, Clark Gable and Vivian Leigh, Edward G. Robinson, and Marlene Dietrich. The comics maintained the traditions of the silent comedians: Charlie Chaplin continued to make movies and was joined by the Marx Brothers, Mae West, and W. C. Fields.

At the same time, the directors had to find a path through the maze created by the studios, the Hays Office, and the stars. They had to bring all these divergent elements together to make movies. Men such as John Ford and Howard Hawks created their own visions of America and discovered methods of capturing the American myth on film. Many of the directors of the period were immigrants: Josef von Sternberg, Alfred Hitchcock, Fritz Lang, Otto Preminger, and Frank Capra. Each discovered for himself the essence of this country and its people. Perhaps that essence was most fittingly expressed in a film that came at the end of the prewar period, *Citizen Kane* (1941), the first film Orson Welles directed.

The war changed the industry. Many residents of Hollywood took time off to participate in the war effort. Some, like John Ford and Frank Capra, made films for the government. Others, like Fritz Lang, continued to make commercial films, but they were propaganda-oriented and helped build morale. The stars went to the battle areas to entertain the troops. Even studio space was commandeered to produce war documentaries, and war films became a dominant fictional genre.

After the war the rate of change accelerated. Anti-trust suits broke up the large companies and forced them to sell their theaters. And television began to keep the public at home. The movie industry responded with attempts at expanding the medium to attract new interests: 3-D, Cinema-Scope, Technicolor; and it continues to experiment: quadraphonic sound, sensurround, holographic images, and giant leaps in special effects have been tried.

However, in responding to competition from television, the use and type of subject matter have taken precedence over the development of technology. The movie makers have thought it necessary to give the public something that television cannot do as well. The result has been increasingly explicit depiction of sex and violence. Both sex and violence have been staples of the movies since the beginning, but the contemporary cinema has found new methods of enticing the public with them.

As the major Hollywood studios began to lose their domination of the American movie industry and turned their attention to television production, the leadership was taken up by independent producers and directors, making their own films and then distributing them through the networks originally established by the Hollywood companies. Stanley Kubrick, Robert Altman, Arthur Penn, Peter Bogdanovich, and Francis Ford Coppola have provided America with a new group of filmmakers, men who have demonstrated a certain independence of subject and method. Part of the void left by the diminishing importance of Hollywood has been filled by foreign filmmakers whose films have been greeted with enthusiasm by American audiences. Ingmar Bergman, François Truffaut, and Federico Fellini have dominated, but for the first time countries outside of Europe have begun to leave their mark. Japan has been especially productive.

Perhaps, however, the most important change in movies in recent years has been in the audience. By no means the number of people who went to the movies in the late 1930s still do, but those who do go are younger and more knowledgeable about film. They read the books, subscribe to film journals, watch filmed interviews with movie people on television, and read daily reviews. Many in today's audience are college-educated and have taken film courses while in school; they can talk intelligently about montage, jump cuts, and fade-outs.

Films in the 1980s have seen diverse trends. Directors such as Stephen Speilberg and George Lucas have brought the old-fashioned adventure film back to popularity. As a result of their work special effects have become one of the stars of the decade. The American film industry has always imitated success, and this has never been truer than in the 1980s; most successful films have had sequels, which use the same characters and similar plots. In order to attract the teenage audience, which now dominates the moviegoing population, horror films have become more grotesque, language less imaginative and more earthy, and sex scenes more obvious. Films for teens have also developed into their own genre, with stock characters, plots, and a recognizable attitude toward life. As the decade comes to a close, films about the Vietnam War have become a major vehicle for both entertainment and political analysis.

REFERENCE WORKS

A valuable collection of general reference books that cover a great number of film topics has been published. None is complete in itself, and all contain numerous errors, but they can be used for quick and easy reference as long as detailed criticism or analysis is not needed.

Four books compete as encyclopedias of film. The oldest is Roger Manvell's *The International Encyclopedia of Film*. It contains brief essays on film directors, important films, significant actors, and recurring cinematic themes. Where possible, a book or two on the entry will be mentioned as bibliography. *The Filmgoer's Companion,* edited by Leslie Halliwell, is updated periodically, but, aside from the occasional brief discussion of a theme, consists almost entirely of filmographies of film figures. *The Oxford Companion to Film,* edited by Liz-Anne Bawden, is flawed, but it can be perceptive and generally accurate. Perhaps its most disappointing feature is its limited filmographies of the major figures. Ephraim Katz's *The Film En-*

cyclopedia keeps its errors to a minimum. It gives brief entries on directors, actors, and others, and its definitions of film terms are quite useful.

One important general reference is the annual *International Film Guide* published in London under the general editorship of Peter Cowie. This book is an odd collection of film information from reviews to lists of film societies to a survey of film production in countries around the world. It is sometimes difficult to find what one is looking for, but the search will be fun because the reader may well find something else he or she was not looking for.

One of the most serious problems in film study is finding the factual data necessary for accuracy. Knowing when a film was released and who deserves credit for it is important, but often the information is hard to uncover. If the film is not available for firsthand checking, the researcher will have to turn to one of the reference guides. Richard Dimmitt began a list called *A Title Guide to the Talkies,* which has been continued by Andrew Aros. These men list title, date, distributor, and source of the story, but little else. In a series of volumes the Library of Congress has published a complete list of all the films that have been copyrighted. These volumes also list the dates, length, and producer. One nice feature of this work is that it includes television commercials and short films, which are often difficult to date from other sources. Eventually this work will be replaced by one coming out under the sponsorship of the AFI, called *The American Film Institute Catalogue of Motion Pictures.* A separate volume will cover each decade, and every film produced during the decade will be listed with credits, date, and plot summary. The indexes will be extensive. So far only two volumes of this valuable book have been released (1921–30, edited by Kenneth W. Munden, and 1961–70, edited by Richard Krasfur), but other volumes are in production and will eventually include short films and newsreels as well as features.

A useful series of reference books has been undertaken by Frank N. Magill. Each volume of his series follows roughly the same format: credits, plot summary, and analysis of individual films. Each film usually is given several pages, so the information, while not voluminous, is neither superficial nor spotty. The level of the series is appropriate for secondary school and undergraduate students and for the general public. The books are intended to be general guides to the films, so the scholarship is sound and reliable, but it avoids controversy. He has published two volumes on films in the English language and another on films in other languages. He is now publishing an annual which covers prominent films of each previous year. It also includes brief descriptions of books on film published during the year and interviews with filmmakers who have made their mark recently.

An important aspect of film study is locating the films themselves for rental or purchase. James Limbacher's *Feature Films on 8mm and 16mm* lists the renter or seller, running time, and brief credits.

Bibliographies of published material about film are central to film study as they lead the researcher to articles and books on film. Finding magazine articles is one of the most serious problems for the film researcher, but now there are a number of bibliographic guides to help. Unfortunately none is so good or so complete as to make all the rest unnecessary, and they must be cross-checked if the researcher wishes to be complete. Peter Bukalski's *Film Research* is of a general nature. This is a selected, critical bibliography, with limited annotation. Similar is *The Film Book Bibliography, 1940–1975* by Jack C. Ellis, Charles Derry, and Sharon Kern. Robert Armour in *Film: A Reference Guide* does not cover as many books as the others, but his bibliography is in essay form and somewhat more descriptive. The most recent, and probably most exhaustive, is George Rehrauer's *The Macmillan Film Bibliography*. In two volumes he makes his annotations on thousands of books on film and recommends the best.

In 1941 Harold Leonard published *The Film Index,* which existed for years as the main bibliography of film articles in English. It covers chiefly the silent period, but it mentions some articles to about 1936. To fill in the gap between Leonard and the present time, three different bibliographies have appeared. Perhaps the most valuable is *The New Film Index,* edited by Richard Dyer MacCann and Edward W. Perry. They have included the articles listed in standard annual journal indexes, such as *The Readers' Guide,* and then in addition have fully indexed thirty-eight of the major film journals in English. MacCann and Perry have brought their bibliography to 1970, at which point several annual bibliographies have begun. The *Humanities Index* and *Readers' Guide to Periodical Literature* both list numerous articles on film; in each the reader must look under "moving pictures" to find the bulk of the entries. They are especially valuable in locating reviews.

Two major annual indexes to periodical articles are now being published. Vincent Aceto, Jane Graves, and Fred Silva have begun their annual bibliography *Film Literature Index,* which covers 126 journals fully and another 150 nonfilm journals selectively. Unfortunately there is no annotation of the entries. Karen Jones is the general editor of the *International Index to Film Periodicals,* which covers fewer journals than the *Film Literature Index* but does include a few journals not indexed by the latter. The *International Index's* brief annotations are helpful. The researcher would do well to consult both indexes.

The most convenient guide to the numerous periodicals containing articles on film is a recent publication of the American Film Institute called *Factfile: Film and Television Periodicals in English,* edited by Diana Elsas. (It can be purchased by writing to the AFI.) This volume lists eighty-two journals that deal primarily with film, or television, or both, and gives a brief annotation of each. The list includes the scholarly journals, such as *Film Quarterly* or *Cinema Journal,* technical ones, such as *American Cinematographer,* and popular ones, such as *American Film,* the organ of the AFI.

The researcher should be aware that while many of the journals are of general interest, others appeal to the special interests of readers. For instance, *Literature/Film Quarterly* devotes its space to articles on feature films that have some connection with works of literature. *Media and Methods* is directed at the secondary school teacher, and *Film Culture* is concerned with the independent filmmaker.

The list in *Factfile* is not complete and does not include the many periodicals that, though not primarily film journals, frequently publish articles on film, but it contains the basic journals and is an excellent checklist.

Other checklists may be found in the bibliographies mentioned earlier in this Chapter, but unlike the AFI *Factfile*, they all lack annotation and do not include subscription information.

One final reference book will prove valuable for the film fan, the student, and the scholar alike. *Film Facts* by Cobbett Steinberg is a collection of useful and not so useful information about the movies. It covers the economics of the industry, lists of popular films and stars, ten-best lists from numerous sources, and catalogs of awards and festivals.

RESEARCH COLLECTIONS

In dealing with archives that house film materials, the researcher is faced with some libraries that collect films and others that collect film related materials. Locating the film itself may be one of the most difficult problems for the researcher. Most of the early nitrate films have been destroyed for one reason or another, often because the film stock itself is unstable. The researcher can depend on only five centers in this country for major—and expensive—efforts to preserve the early films: the Library of Congress and the American Film Institute in Washington, the Museum of Modern Art in New York, Eastman House in Rochester, and the University of California at Los Angeles Film and Television Archive. Each of these archives is collecting, preserving and holding films and does a first-rate job of maintaining our film heritage, but there are problems. The work is costly and time-consuming. Not all films are held in viewable prints, and the archives have not yet been able to publish an index of their holdings. There are additionally several other libraries with sizable collections of films, and the researcher should not overlook local sources.

Aside from the films themselves, film related material might include film scripts, stills, journals, books, costumes, and fugitive materials, such as letters and posters. All of the archives mentioned with film collections also have some film related material, but the best collections of related material are at the Library and Museum of the Performing Arts (a branch of the New York Public Library at Lincoln Center) and the Theater Arts Library at the University of California at Los Angeles.

Whether the researcher is looking for films or film related materials, he or she would do best to write to the archives to inquire whether they have the necessary material before making the effort to visit the archives themselves. Security is understandably tight at these centers, and the researcher should take proper identification and should be prepared to demonstrate the seriousness of his or her research.

The best general survey of libraries that house film collections and service film scholars is *Film Study Collections* by Nancy Allen. This book is a guide to the development of the collections by librarians and their use by researchers. For the librarian, Allen describes collection development—both retrospective and current, selecting periodicals, and evaluating both published materials and nonprint materials. For the scholar and film fan, Allen describes the use and location of film scripts, bookstores and film memorabilia dealers, major U.S. archives, reference services, and the holdings in film study of many important libraries. She even provides a chapter of basic library instruction for those who do not know how to use a library. This important book should be in every private and public collection.

A general guide to the archives can be found in the *North American Film and Video Directory,* by Olga S. Weber. This guide lists the archives and their locations and approximate sizes, but its value is limited. It lists only archives with film collections and does not describe the holdings or distinguish between significant holdings and minor ones.

Finally, it might be noted that while the distributors of films do not maintain research collections, they are usually most helpful to the researcher. Most are happy to work with researchers. Some of their better catalogs are useful sources of information, and the people in charge of collections for the companies are often knowledgeable and helpful.

HISTORY AND CRITICISM

One of the most popular aspects of film study is concerned with the personalities of the people involved in the industry. Perhaps the actors and actresses attract the most attention, but directors and other members of the production team have their devoted followers too. In a guide as short as this one, it is impossible to list individually all the books that have appeared on movie people. The researcher can consult the card catalog in almost any good library for these books, but there is a sizable list of reference works that pertain to the people. These works may well lead the researcher to hard-to-find or obscure data about them.

Mel Schuster has written two books, *Motion Picture Performers* and *Motion Picture Directors,* that list magazine and periodical articles. These guides list articles on both the personalities and their cinematic contributions from the turn of the century to the early 1970s.

David Thomson's book, *A Biographical Dictionary of Film,* also covers both directors and actors, but he gives different information. His book consists of short essays on the major figures. Most essays include a filmography, a brief critical comment, and a highly selected bibliography.

Information about the actors can be found in other works. Richard Dimmitt has edited *An Actor Guide to the Talkies,* which covers movies between 1949 and 1964. He surveys some 8,000 features and lists the actors for each, but he does not list the role played by each actor, a serious handicap. Evelyn Mack Truitt has also listed actors in *Who Was Who on Screen.* Arranged by actor rather than by film, this guide gives all of an actor's films and dates.

David Quinland has published two useful guides to actors. His *Illustrated Directory of Film Stars* and *The Illustrated Directory of Film Character Actors* include capsule descriptions as well as evaluations and filmographies.

Directors are the subjects of several research guides. James Robert Parish and Michael R. Pitts have edited *Film Directors: A Guide to Their American Films.* Included are the feature films, with dates and company, for approximately 520 directors. Georges Sadoul's *Dictionary of Filmmakers* is even more inclusive. This book contains about 1,000 entries for directors, screenwriters, and others on the production side of the industry, but no actors.

A valuable collection of critical essays on numerous directors serves as a good general introduction to directors' work. *Great Film Directors: A Critical Anthology* is edited by Leo Braudy and Morris Dickstein. They have included three or four scholarly essays each on Bergman, Capra, Lang, Griffith, and nineteen more. A second book, in two volumes, with essays on major directors is *American Directors* by Jean-Pierre Coursodon and Pierre Sauvage. In this case they have only a single essay on each director, but the essays are informative and interesting.

A reference guide to screenwriters has been published jointly by the Academy of Motion Pictures and the Writers' Guild of America. *Who Wrote the Movie and What Else Did He Write?* is extensive for the period 1936 through 1969. Included are both film title and writer's indexes. Larry Langman's *A Guide to American Screenwriters: The Sound Era, 1929–1982* lists the complete works of American screenwriters. Its two volumes cover over 5,000 writers and their films

There are now a number of variations of the generic screenplay being published. A shooting script is written before the film is shot and is the outline for what is going to happen. The cutting continuity is the written record of what has been shot and is obviously made after the film is finished. The shooting script tells what the screenwriter felt should be included. The cutting continuity tells what the director and the editor actually left in. And, finally, a shot analysis is a more detailed cutting continuity. The researcher needs to know which he is dealing with since a shooting script may indicate a scene that was never included in the final film and a cutting continuity may not demonstrate the screenwriter's intentions at all.

There are two checklists of published screenplays in print. Both are needed, as neither is inclusive, and neither makes a distinction between shooting scripts, cutting continuities, and shot analysis. Howard Poteet's *Published Radio, Television and Film Scripts: A Bibliography* lists some 668 film scripts (some are different versions of the same film script). Clifford McCarty's *Published Screenplays: A Checklist* lists the scripts for only 388 films, but he gives slightly more information than does Poteet about each entry. McCarty includes production company, date, director, author of the screenplay, original source, and the bibliographical data for the published screenplay. Through both of these sources the researcher can locate most of the screenplays that have so far been published.

There is another variation of the screenplay which is gaining in popularity: the frame blowup continuity. These books give a frame enlargement for every shot in the film, and the researcher can almost "read a film." Perhaps the most impressive of these works is *The Complete Greed,* by Herman Weinberg, which combines frame blowups with the screen-play.

The definitive history of film is yet to be written, but there are numerous books that contribute to that history, and they do make fascinating reading. Despite the fact that no other art has its history so well documented, there remains much confusion about many of the details in the early development of film, in part because at the beginning so few people took this new form of entertainment seriously.

One of the earliest attempts at writing the history of the medium came from an Englishman, Paul Rotha, in what is now a respected classic, *The Film Till Now*. The book first was published in 1930, but in the mid–1960s Richard Griffith brought it up to date. It is thorough, complete, and long; it was written by a man who could write about film critically and theoretically, as well as historically. It is by no means a popular history, but the researcher will find it very useful. Later is the same decade Lewis Jacobs wrote the first general history of real importance to deal primarily with the American cinema. *The Rise of the American Film* emphasizes the industry but manages to cover a great number of films and their makers.

In the post-World War II period, Arthur Knight contributed *The Liveliest Art: A Panoramic History of the Movies,* which first came out in 1957. Though dated now, the book is still readable and reliable. It is valuable but too short to make any claim at completeness.

Most recently there have been several attempts at writing a good general history. Highly regarded and now in its fourth edition is Gerald Mast's *A Short History of the Movies*. This balanced and perceptive book is perhaps the most useful history on the market so far. His format is rather standard for one-volume histories of film, but his research is thorough and his writing reasonably lively.

Thomas Bohn and Richard Stromgren have written *Light and Shadows,* which is also a solid general history. Their book is valuable, especially in the modern period, on which they have an excellent chapter on the influence of television on movies. John Fell's *A History of Film's* and David Cook's

A History of Narrative Film are also solid and valuable brief histories. All of these books are written by competent scholars and provide basic histories of the American film.

And finally, Eric Rhode's massive book, *A History of the Cinema from Its Origins to 1970,* is a large-scale effort at writing a world history of the movies. Both Mast and Bohn and Stromgren devote chapters to the European cinematic contributions and developments, but Rhode's focus is far more international than theirs. The book is not as readable as Mast's, but on the international scene it is unsurpassed.

Then there are books that do not record a general history, but do focus on a particular period, such as the silent era. One of the nicest aspects of the silent era is that its history can still be told by the people who were part of it. Firsthand accounts, such as *When the Movies Were Young,* by Linda Arvidson, who was Mrs. D. W. Griffith, and *The Movies, Mr. Griffith, and Me,* by Lillian Gish, have the natural flaws of any history written by the subjective participants, but the freshness and familiarity make such books excellent places to begin a study of the early days of the art.

Kevin Brownlow's *The Parade's Gone By* makes a similar contribution. In this case a scholar has interviewed the most important directors of the silent era and has intermingled their remarks with his own deliberate insights. This is oral history interpreted by a scholar without the biases of participation in the events that become that history. While Brownlow intermingled his thoughts with the words of the directors, George Pratt has written his history of the era, *Spellbound in Darkness,* by combining his commentary with reviews of the films as they were seen by critics contemporary with the films. The book is at times hard to follow, but Pratt is a competent scholar, and the reviews chronicle an art form and the culture that spawned it.

Naturally, latter-day scholars are writing histories of the silent era without including the primary material found in Brownlow or Pratt. D.J. Wenden's short book, *The Birth of the Movies,* takes the medium to the coming of sound; and Harry Geduld's *The Birth of the Talkies* is actually a study of the efforts of the industry to develop a sound system. He starts with Edison and takes the reader through the early stages of sound technology that eventually led to "You ain't heard nothing yet."

An important anthology on the early silent era is *Film Before Griffith,* edited by John Fell. The essays in this volume cover the development of the industry from the early 1890s until about 1908 and present readers with history too often neglected in the brief histories mentioned above. The most complete history of early film is *American Silent Film* by William K. Everson. This is a thoroughly scholarly study of film from the beginnings to the coming of sound. Much has been uncovered about the earliest years since this book was written, but it still remains the most useful general survey of the period.

And last there is a charming and intriguing book sponsored by the American Film Institute called *The American Film Heritage,* edited by Tom Shales and others. It includes essays by scholars on films, filmmakers, studios, and themes of the silent era. Often the essay subject is little known to the general public, and the book becomes part of the AFI's effort at rediscovering the lost heritage of the medium.

Naturally other eras in film history have received similar attention. Books such as Andrew Bergman's *We're in the Money,* about the Depression, and Penelope Houston's *The Contemporary Cinema, 1945–1963* devote themselves to particular periods.

Some of the histories concentrate on the role Hollywood has played in the development of American culture. Hortense Powdermaker was one of the first to take an anthropological look at Hollywood in her book *Hollywood: The Dream Factory.* The book is a bit dated now, but it has set standards for a particular method of considering the medium. The American Film Institute sponsored a book by Garth Jowett that is a general history with an emphasis on Hollywood and its impact. Jowett includes much history of the controversies originated by Hollywood and is especially detailed on the problems of censorship. A delightful book for the fan of the popular film, edited by Todd McCarthy and Charles Flynn, is entitled Kings of the B's. The focus of the book is on the many minor directors who worked within the Hollywood system to produce countless movies that may be aesthetically insignificant but culturally powerful. In addition to history and criticism, the book includes a valuable filmography for 325 directors who are given scant attention in other histories.

Tino Balio's *The American Film Industry* is an anthology of essays on the industry that made the movies. Some were written by people who were part of the industry during its development and others by scholar historians. It is the best so far of an emerging field of study into the practices of the industry. The book is historically organized around the chronological period of the subject of each essay.

And there is a large group of books concentrating on single studios and their roles within the Hollywood industry. Studies such as Charles Higham's *Warner Brothers* and Rochelle Larkin's *Hail Columbia* explore the inner workings of a studio and the escapades of the moguls who made it successful.

The area of film criticism is large, diverse, and eclectic, but perhaps the best critical research tools can be divided into smaller categories. Many of the best can be considered introductions to film. The fact that a book is intended as an introduction to the subject and was published for the many students who may be taking their first film course should not suggest that the book is necessarily superficial. In fact, a number of them delve deeply into the aesthetics of the medium. One of the earliest scholars to publish an introduction was Lewis Jacobs in his anthology, *Introduction to the Art of the Movies.* This book is a collection of essays on image, movement, time and space, color, and sound-standard topics to be covered in an introduction.

During the 1960s a number of introductions came out, and several have remained highly regarded. Ernest Lindgren's *The Art of the Film* has sections on mechanics, techniques, and criticism; and *The Film Experience,* by Roy Huss and Norman Silverstein, deals with continuity, rhythm, structure, image, and point of view.

Of the introductions written during the 1970s by single authors, Louis Giannetti's *Understanding Movies* has proved to be most durable. His chapters deal with the picture, movement, editing, sound, drama, literature, and theory. A similar book by Richard Blumenberg, *Critical Focus: An Introduction to Film,* was written by a teacher and scholar with some experience as a filmmaker. After an introduction that defines the medium and relates it to the other arts, Blumenberg devotes sections to the narrative film, the documentary, and the experimental film.

Elements of Film by Lee R. Bobker is perhaps the best of the introductions in the area of technique. None of the others explains the technical side of the art in prose as easy to understand. Of the anthologies that serve as introductions, the best is a large book by Gerald Mast and Marshall Cohen, *Film Theory and Criticism.* They have shown discretion in the authors whose essays they have chosen to reprint, and their categories (reality, language, theory, literature and film, genre, artists, and audience) cover a wide range of film criticism. Not many of the introductions deal with the aesthetics of the short film, but one by David Sohn does. *Film: The Critical Eye* discusses films distributed by Pyramid Films, but its general discussion helps to create understanding of a type of film often overlooked.

More recently, James Monaco has written *How to Read a Film.* He covers a full range of film studies from technique to history. George Wead and George Lellis have focused their book, *Film: Form and Function,* on Hollywood and the alternatives to the Hollywood traditions. This introduction to film also discusses movie techniques. For an example of an introduction to film studies which mixes close analysis of films and filmmakers with history and technical understanding, the reader might consult Lewis Jacobs's *The Emergence of Film Art: The Evolution and Development of the Motion Picture as an Art, from 1900 to the Present.*

These introductions for the most part are based on the writings of film theorists whose work is earlier and more complex. Once the students have passed the need for the introductions, they will find the work of the theorists challenging and fascinating. As early as 1915 the poet Vachel Lindsay published a curious book that was part theory and part encomium on what was then a new art form. In fact his title, *The Art of the Moving Picture,* would have surprised many people who would not have called this entertainment form an art.

Much of the early theory was developed by the Russians, some of whom learned their lessons by watching films made by Americans who wrote little about the theory. Sergei Eisenstein (*The Film Sense, Film Form, and Film Essays and a Lecture*) and V. I. Pudovkin (*Film Technique and Film Acting*) were directors who, through their writings, helped to establish the language of film criticism while at the same time coming to an understanding of how film works.

They were followed by the French and the German. Of the French, Béla Balázs was also a director; his *Theory of Film* was a summary of his thoughts on the use of the camera and editing. André Bazin was not a director but a mentor of the directors who make up the French New Wave and editor of *Cahiers du Cinéma,* the most important French cinema journal. *What Is Cinema?* contains a sample of his extensive criticism. Siegfried Kracauer was a German who came to America to escape the Nazis. His book, *Theory of Film,* is basically a general theory with an emphasis on acting, sound, and music. The book, however, does range into many areas, including a notable chapter on the film and the novel. Most recently, important film theory has again been coming from France, where the theory of semiotics has been developed. The semiotics of film is a linguistic approach to the study of film in which visuals are seen as signs between the sender and viewer. The leading proponent of this theory is Christian Metz, whose book *Film Language* is the easiest of his works to understand, but the beginner should be warned that semiotics is not a simple approach to film.

There are several anthologies of essays that attempt to give an overview of film criticism. Richard Dyer MacCann's *Film: A Montage of Theories* is well known. His essays are by the best-known writers of film theory from Eisenstein to Bergman and cover the nature of film, film and the other arts, the reality of film, and the future of the medium. More recent is *The Major Film Theories,* by J. Dudley Andrew. This book analyzes the work of the major theorists, who are separated into three broad groups: the formative tradition, realist film theory, and contemporary French film theory. MacCann covers more theorists, but Andrew is more up-to-date.

One of the types of film criticism that both scholars and film viewers have found most useful is the study of film genre, although there is some debate over the meaning of the word *genre* when applied to film. As far as this essay is concerned, *genre* will refer to simply to film types, without much regard for the important scholarly debate over definition. It is admitted that "fantasy" may well overlap with "Western" and that "comedy" may not be a genre at all, but there is not space enough here to resolve that controversy.

There are several books that deal with the general concept of genre. *Beyond Formula* by Stanley J. Solomon devotes a chapter to each of the important genres: Western, musical, horror, crime, detective, and war. Each chapter begins with a general discussion of the genre and its characteristics. It then discusses in depth seven or eight feature-length films of the genre.

American Film Genres by Stuart M. Kaminsky begins with an intelligent essay on film genre, then moves to a discussion of comparative genre (samurai and Western), literary adaptation of genre, horror and science fiction, musicals, comedy, and genre directors (such as Donald Siegel and John Ford).

Film Genre: Theory and Criticism opens with six essays on the theory of genre. The editor, Barry K. Grant, has selected essays on several major genres: screwball comedy, disaster, epic, gangster, horror, musical, sports, Western, and science fiction.

The guides to the fantasy films, including horror films and science fiction, are numerous. Walt Lee in the *Reference Guide to Fantastic Films* packs a lot of information about horror, science fiction, and fantasy films into a short space. He includes data about the cast, director, running time, source and type of fantasy, and a brief bibliography for each film. Less complete but valuable is a checklist compiled by Donald C. Willis, *Horror and Science Fiction Films.* He has included some 4,400 titles and has given a one-sentence plot description, lacking in Lee. *The Science Fiction Film Source Book* by David Wingrove contains a brief history of the genre, a chronology of important science fiction films, and a survey of films and serials. Roy Huss and T. J. Ross have concentrated on the horror film alone in their book *Focus on the Horror Film,* an anthology of essays on gothic horror, monster terror, and the psychological thriller. And Carlos Clarens does not overburden the excellent text of *An Illustrated History of the Horror Film* with too many photos. *The Horror Film Handbook* by Alan Frank gives credits and brief synopses for important horror films. *The Aurum Film Encyclopedia: Horror,* edited by Phil Hardy and others, arranges its discussion by decades. It too gives credits and a brief history of horror film production. A special type of horror film is covered in James Ursini and Alain Silver's *The Vampire Film,* but *In Search of Dracula,* by Raymond T. McNally and Radu Florescu, is more reliable even though its chief focus is not on films.

The standard book on the Western, by George N. Fenin and William K. Everson, is simply titled *The Western.* It traces the history of the genre, discusses the major films and even many of the minor ones, and includes enough photographs to stir memories of Saturday afternoons of long ago— sitting in small theaters, munching popcorn, and watching heroes on beautiful horses. An excellent reference guide to study about the Western is *Western Films: An Annotated Critical Bibliography,* by John G. Nachbar. This book, with both author and subject indexes, includes an intelligent and scholarly introduction and useful annotations. Phil Hardy has also edited *The Aurum Film Encyclopedia: The Western.* It includes an overview essay on the genre and a decade-by-decade survey of the important Western films.

The most useful guide to the gangster pictures is *The Great Gangster Pictures,* by James Robert Parish and Michael R. Pitts. This book is basically an index to the credits, distributors, and running times of the movies in this genre, but an introductory essay on the history of the genre and brief critical comments about the individual films raise it beyond the level of an index.

John Kobal's *Gotta Sing, Gotta Dance* is a popular history of the musicals; it is a good place to begin the study of that genre. Unfortunately, the needed analysis of movie is yet to be written.

Comedy is a diverse and complex genre, if in fact it is a genre at all. The books on the movie comedies are numerous, and it is most difficult to select one or two as the point at which one might begin a study. Gerald Mast's *The Comic Mind* is a major study with an emphasis on the silent comedians. As with most of Mast's work, this book is both theoretical and historical. Walter Kerr in *The Silent Clowns* presents a historically oriented study of the greats.

The serials that so many of us remember from those Saturday afternoons of our youth are well remembered and studied in *Continued Next Week: A History of the Moving Picture Serial,* by Kalton C. Lahue. This excellent history is complemented by an extensive appendix that includes the credits and other data about the serials. Ken Weiss and Ed Goodgold have indexed the serials in *To Be Continued.*

Several books deal with the narrative in film. John Fell's excellent *Film and the Narrative Tradition* traces the development of cinematic narrative in the early years of the medium. He looks back to nineteenth-century art forms for the source of film narrative. In *Narration in Light: Studies in Cinematic Point of View,* George M. Wilson discusses the narrative and narrators in major filmmakers such as Alfred Hitchcock and Josef von Sternberg. And David Bordwell's *Narration in the Fiction Film* also discusses theories of cinematic story telling. He analyzes the Hollywood narrative tradition, experimental films, and the European modernist films.

The history of work in documentary film is ably recorded in both *Nonfiction Film,* by Richard Meran Barsam, and *Documentary: A History of Nonfiction Film,* by Erik Barnouw. Both are solid, but the latter especially emphasizes the images and themes of the documentaries rather than the personalities.

Two anthologies have selected essays on the theory of the documentary as well as the history. *The Documentary Tradition,* edited by Lewis Jacobs, contains essays on the leading films and filmmakers from *Nanook* to *Woodstock.* Arranged according to the decades of the films studied, the essays also include general theory. Another of Barsam's books is *Nonfiction Film: Theory and Criticism.* This anthology includes essays on the idea of the documentary, its history, its artists, and its films.

Finally, Roy Levin's *Documentary Explorations* is a series of interviews with the major makers of documentary films. Included are Frederick Wiseman and Richard Leacock and six other Americans as well as a number of Europeans.

One of the most important, but often overlooked, areas of film production is the experimental film. This area is difficult to define, even difficult to name. Whether it goes by the term *experimental film, underground film, independent film,* or whatever, it is concerned with the efforts of the film-maker to expand the knowledge and technology of the medium. The basic study of the experimental film is by Sheldon Renan, *An Introduction to the American Underground Film.* This important book contains definition, history, and theory as well as studies of the important filmmakers and films. The appendix includes an excellent list of significant experimental films and an all too brief bibliography.

The history of the underground movement is told in two good books: *Underground Film: A Critical History,* by Parker Tyler, and *Experimental Cinema,* by David Curtis. The latter book emphasizes the economic aspect of the experimental films, an important subject since these films are rarely shown in big money markets.

Two interesting anthologies of essays on the experimental film have been published. Gregory Battcock edited *The New American Cinema,* which includes essays by critics, such as Andrew Sarris, and filmmakers, such as Stan VanDerBeck and Stan Brakhage. P. Adams Sitney's *Film Culture Reader* is a collection of the most important essays from the journal that bills itself as "America's Independent Motion Picture Magazine." The essays give history and criticism, but the emphasis is on theory.

The best study of the technology of the experimental film is *Expanded Cinema.* This outstanding book by Gene Youngblood begins with a difficult but sound discussion of the nature of the experimental film and its effect on audiences. The first chapter is as much sociology as film criticism. His second and third chapters deal with the theory and cosmic consciousness of this type of film, and the latter part of the book considers in depth the technology of the major attempts at expanding the limits of the medium.

Much paper and ink are taken up discussing the relationship that exists between film and the other arts—literature, theater, music, dance, even architecture—perhaps because, to a large extent, film is a synthesis of the arts. A good general introduction can be found in an anthology edited by T. J. Ross, *Film and the Liberal Arts.* The essays here compare and contrast film with literature, the visual arts, and music. An index to the relationship is *Filmed Books and Plays, 1928–1983* by A. G. S. Enser. The book contains indexes to the authors, films, and changes in original titles. It is by no means complete, but it is a good place to begin the study of the relationship between film and novels and the theater. That relationship between film and the theater is further explored by Nicholas Vardac in *Stage to Screen,* a study of theatrical method from David Garrick to D. W. Griffith; and critics, filmmakers, and playwrights have commented on that relationship in *Focus on Film and Theatre,* edited by James Hurt.

Perhaps the best known of the books dealing with the relationship between literature and film is George Bluestone's *Novels into Film*. He begins with a theoretical essay and then analyzes several major adaptations, such as *The Grapes of Wrath* and *The Ox Bow Incident*. Overall the book provides a good introduction to the relationship, but it is more limited in scope than its title and first chapter suggest. More valuable as introduction because it is more general and more theoretical is Robert Richardson's *Literature and Film*. Richardson has a good background in both media, and the result is a basic resource. His is one of the few books to pay much attention to the relationship between poetry and film, as most books concentrate on fiction or theater. Other studies abound, such as Geoffrey Wagner's thought-provoking (at times it is just provoking) *The Novel and the Cinema* and John Harrington's anthology *Literature and/as Film*. There is a series of books dealing with the adaptation of short stories into film under the general editorship of Gerald Barrett and Thomas Erskin. Titles include "An Occurrence at Owl Creek Bridge" and "The Rocking-Horse Winner." Each of the volumes is introduced by a solid essay on the problems and nature of adaptation. Fred Marcus has published a book called *Short Story/Short Film* that will be very useful to the researcher working with the shorter material. He gives the story, a story board, and film continuity, as well as analysis.

Recently much attention has been paid to the role played by women and minorities in film and their image as portrayed by the films. For instance, books analyzing the depiction of women on the screen have been written by Marjorie Rosen (*Popcorn Venus*), Molly Haskell (*From Reverence to Rape*), and Joan Mellon (*Women and Their Sexuality in the New Film*). These books all combine history with criticism. Reference guides to women in film include a valuable book by Sharon Smith, *Women Who Make Movies*. Her brief essay on each filmmaker, analyzes the woman's career and mentions her most important films. Smith, of course, deals with the better-known women filmmakers, such as Elaine May and Eleanor Perry, but she also devotes some space to the women who are just beginning but will be known soon (with a little luck). Bonnie Dawson's book *Women's Films in Print* is an annotated guide to some 800 films by women. A brief bibliography for each film is included when possible. Kaye Sullivan, in *Films for, by, and About Women*, provides brief descriptions of features and shorts that have women as either their subjects or creators. Louise Heck-Rabi writes on some of the best-known women filmmakers in *Women Filmmakers: A Critical Reception*. She deals with the critical reputations of eleven filmmakers, including Maya Deren, Mai Zetterling, and Shirley Clarke. And finally, in *Women and Film: Both Sides of the Camera*, Ann E. Kaplan compares the view of women in the classical Hollywood tradition, which was dominated by men, with that of the independent feminist filmmakers, which clearly has a new perspective.

There have also been released solid books on the role of the black in film.

Several have been critical histories. Donald Bogle calls his *Toms, Coons, Mullatoes, Mammies, and Blacks* an "interpretative history of blacks in American films." Lindsay Patterson has edited an anthology of essays that considers both the image of the black in film and the black's role in the film industry. His *Black Films and Film-makers* is notable for its contributors as well as its subject. Daniel Leab in *From Sambo to Superspade* demonstrates the progress—or more accurately the lack of progress—of the black screen image from *Birth of a Nation* to *Shaft*. The most scholarly of the critical histories of the black on the screen is by Thomas Cripps. *Slow Fade to Black* is an excellent study of the black in American film from 1900 to 1942. The reference guides to blacks and film, however, are somewhat less satisfactory. Anne Powers has published *Blacks in American Movies: A Selected Bibliography*. This book is fair, but uneven and at times pedestrian. It includes both an author and subject index, as well as an occasional brief annotation. Richard Maynard has written a guide for teachers who wish to use films about blacks in the classroom. *The Black Man On Film: Racial Stereotyping* includes essays and a practical filmography; its chief flaw lies in its brevity. Two recent filmographies provide reference materials for those who wish to identify films presenting a black perspective: *The Afro-American Cinematic Experience: An Annotated Bibliography and Filmography* by Marshall Hyatt, and *Frame by Frame: A Black Filmography* by Phyllis Rauch Klotman. Each includes films not listed in the other, so both should be consulted.

A popular form of film criticism is the interview; the current expression for this device is *oral history*, history recorded through the actual words of the men and women who made history. Film and comics are probably the only art forms so far whose entire history can be recorded in this manner. This is the method and virtue of Kevin Brownlow's *The Parade's Gone By*, mentioned in the section of this essay on history. Other interviews with movie people abound, but most often they are published in journals and must be discovered through the various guides to periodicals. Some few have been published in book form.

For some years now the American Film Institute has been publishing the written record of interviews held by the staff and students at the AFI West Coast facility. Many movie makers—directors, actors, others—have talked informally with the students and staff, and the results have been transcribed. The transcriptions were first published separately as *Dialogue on Film;* more recently they have been included as the centerfold of *American Film*. The AFI says that they have an additional 300 interviews that will not be published, but are on file at their offices on both coasts.

The first important published book of interviews was probably that of Andrew Sarris, *Interviews with Film Directors*. He reprints interviews with forty directors, most of which were conducted by people other than himself. He believes that the results support his theory about the importance of the role of the director in the movie-making process. He has been followed by others interested chiefly in directors. Eric Sherman and Martin Rubin, in *The Director's Event,* interviewed Peter Bogdanovich, Samuel Fuller, Abraham Polonsky, Budd Boetticher, and Arthur Penn. Charles Thomas Samuels interviewed no Americans, but in *Encountering Directors* he has recorded interviews with filmmakers, such as Alfred Hitchcock and Ingmar Bergman, who have been especially influential in this country. And in *The Men Who Made the Movies,* Richard Schickel gives the transcripts of his televised interviews with Frank Capra, George Cukor, Howard Hawks, Alfred Hitchcock, Vincente Minnelli, King Vidor, Raoul Walsh, and William Wellman.

Probably the form of criticism most people see most often is the movie review published in the daily newspaper or monthly magazine. Naturally reviews serve a different purpose than does the in-depth scholarly article, but the review can provide the researcher with valuable material. It can suggest the public reaction to the film at the time it was released; it can cite needed data about the production of the film. For many films in many libraries the review may be the only printed material available. *Readers' Guide* and the *Humanities Index* both list reviews under "Moving Picture Plays" for the year in which the review appeared.

Stephen Bowles's *Index to Critical Film Reviews in British and American Film Periodicals* is a three-volume guide to the reviews published in thirty-one journals. It is useful but the list of journals is not complete. The critic, rather than the journal, becomes the emphasis for Richard Heinzkill in *Film Criticism: An Index to Critics' Anthologies.* A number of the better critics, such as Andrew Sarris, Pauline Kael, and John Simon, have had their reviews, originally published in periodicals, collected and published in book form. Heinzkill has indexed the work of twenty-seven such reviewers, and through his list it is possible to begin the study of either films or critics.

There are a few books that reprint reviews from a number of critics. *The New York Times Film Reviews, 1913–1980* is a massive eight-volume collection of all the film reviews published in the *Times.* Included are the reviews of Bosley Crowther, Vincent Canby, Frank S. Nugent, and others. Reviews from *Variety* have also been collected in a multivolume set: *Variety Film Reviews, 1907–1980.* Both the *New York Times* and *Variety* sets are well indexed. Stanley Kauffman has edited a book of reviews: *American Film Criticism* is a collection of one or two reviews of many of the important films from the beginning to *Citizen Kane. American Film Directors,* edited by Stanley Hochman, is a collection of excerpted reviews of the important films of major American directors.

This essay is not intended as a how-to guide to making movies, but some knowledge of technique is essential to the critic. The critic must know what each of the persons involved in the process does even if he or she does not want to make a film personally.

First, a critic must develop a vocabulary of technical terms. Raymond

Spottiswoode's *A Grammar of the Film* discusses the art of film production and helps with definition of the terms. It is now somewhat old and hard to read, but useful. More up-to-date is *An Illustrated Glossary of Film Terms* by Harry Geduld and Ronald Gottesman. The definitions are brief, and even complicated matters are not discussed in depth, but as a guide it does what it is supposed to.

The entire process of film production is given an overview in several books. John Quick and Tom La Bare have written a *Handbook of Film Production,* which is an easy method of studying all the work that goes into the production of a film. More ambitious are two volumes sponsored by the American Film Institute. Eric Sherman in *Directing the Film* covers in depth the contribution of the directors, while Donald Chase considers the rest of the collaborators in *Filmmaking: The Collaborative Art.* There are many other books that deal with the individual contributions of members of the production team, but these general guides are a good place to begin.

Some of the best film criticism is that written about a single film, but space here does not permit a list of the books on single films any more than it permits lists of books on individual actors or directors. The researchers should consult the card catalog at the local library or search through the bibliographies mentioned earlier in this essay. The researcher should be aware that there is a large range of types of books about individual films—some are historic, others technical, some analytic.

The range of books on film is large, and this bibliographic essay is by necessity highly selective. As the moviegoing audience has become better educated, the demand for intelligent books to provide background and interpretation has increased. This list can only point in the direction of the appropriate books and offer the encouragement that many of them can enhance watching the movies themselves.

BIBLIOGRAPHY

Books

Aceto, Vincent J., Jane Graves, and Fred Silva. *Film Literature Index*. Albany, N.Y.: Filmdex. Annual.

Allen, Nancy. *Film Study Collections*. New York: Frederick Ungar, 1979.

Andrew, J. Dudley. *The Major Film Theories*. New York: Oxford University Press, 1976.

Anobile, Richard J. *Casablanca*. New York: Universe Books, 1974.

————. *The General*. New York: Universe Books, 1975.

Armour, Robert A. *Film: A Reference Guide*. Westport, Conn.: Greenwood Press, 1980.

Aros, Andrew, *A Title Guide to the Talkies, 1964 Through 1974*. Metuchen, N.J.: Scarecrow Press, 1977.

Arvidson, Linda. *When the Movies Were Young*. New York: Benjamin Blom, 1968.

Balázs, Béla. *Theory of the Film*. New York: Arno Press, 1972.

Balio, Tino, ed. *The American Film Industry*. Madison: University of Wisconsin Press, 1985.

Barnouw, Erik. *Documentary: A History of the Non-fiction Film*. New York: Oxford University Press, 1983.

Barrett, Gerald R., and Thomas L. Erskine. *From Fiction into Film: Ambrose Bierce's "An Occurrence at Owl Creek Bridge."* Encino, Calif.: Dickenson, 1973.

————. *From Fiction to Film: D. H. Lawrence's "The Rocking-Horse Winner."* Encino, Calif.: Dickenson, 1974.

Barsam, Richard Meran. *Nonfiction Film*. New York: E. P. Dutton, 1973.

————, ed. *Nonfiction Film: Theory and Criticism*. New York: E. P. Dutton, 1976.

Battock, Gregory, ed. *The New American Cinema*. New York: E. P. Dutton, 1967.

Bawden, Liz-Anne. *The Oxford Companion to Film*. New York: Oxford University Press, 1976.

Bazin, André. *What Is Cinema?* Berkeley: University of California Press, 1967.

Bergman, Andrew. *We're in the Money*. New York: New York University Press, 1971.

Bluestone, George. *Novels into Film*. Berkeley: University of California Press, 1957.

Blumenberg, Richard. *Critical Focus: An Introduction to Film*. Belmont, Calif.: Wadsworth, 1975.

Bobker, Lee R. *Elements of Film*. New York: Harcourt, Brace and World, 1979.

Bogle, Donald. *Toms, Coons, Mulattoes, Mammies, and Blacks*. New York: Viking, 1973.

Bohn, Thomas W., and Richard L. Stromgren. *Light and Shadows*. Port Washington, N.Y.: Alfred Publishing, 1975.

Bordwell, David. *Narration in the Fiction Film*. Madison: Wisconsin University Press, 1985.

Bowles, Stephen E. *Index to Critical Film Reviews in British and American Film Periodicals*. 3 vols. New York: Burt Franklin, 1979.

Braudy, Leo, and Morris Dickstein. *Great Film Directors: A Critical Anthology*. New York: Oxford University Press, 1981.

Brownlow, Kevin. *The Parade's Gone By*. Berkeley: University of California Press, 1976.

Bukalski, Peter J. *Film Research: A Critical Bibliography*. Boston: G. K. Hall, 1972.

Catalogue of Copyright Entries: Motion Pictures. 4 vols. Washington, D.C.: Library of Congress, 1951, 1953, 1960, 1971.

Chase, Donald. *Filmmaking: The Collaborative Art*. Boston: Little, Brown, 1975.

Clarens, Carlos. *An Illustrated History of the Horror Film*. New York: Capricorn Books, 1967.

Cook, David A. *A History of Narrative Film*. New York: W. W. Norton, 1987.

Coursodon, Jean-Pierre, and Pierre Sauvage. *American Directors*. New York: McGraw-Hill, 1983.

Cowie, Peter, ed. *International Film Guide*. London: Tantivy. Annual.

Cripps, Thomas. *Slow Fade to Black*. New York: Oxford University Press, 1977.

Curtis, David. *Experimental Cinema*. New York: Dell, 1971.

Dawson, Bonnie. *Women's Films in Print*. San Francisco: Booklegger Press, 1975.

DeNitto, Dennis, and William Herman. *Film and The Critical Eye*. New York: Macmillan, 1975.

Dickinson, Thorold. *A Discovery of Cinema*. New York: Oxford University Press, 1971.

Dimmitt, Richard Betrand. *An Actor Guide to the Talkies, 1949–1964*. Metuchen, N.J.: Scarecrow Press, 1967–68.

———. *A Title Guide to the Talkies, 1927–1963*, Metuchen, N.J.: Scarecrow Press, 1965.

Eisenstein, Sergei. *Film Essays and a Lecture*. New York: Praeger, 1970.

———. *Film Forum*. New York: Harcourt, Brace and World, 1949.

———. *The Film Sense*. New York: Harcourt, Brace and World, 1947.

Ellis, Jack C., Charles Derry, and Sharon Kern. *The Film Book Bibliography, 1940–1975*. Metuchen, N.J.: Scarecrow Press, 1979.

Elsas, Diana, ed. *Factfile: Film and Television Periodicals in English*. Washington, D.C.: American Film Institute, 1977.

Enser, A.G.S. *Filmed Books and Plays, 1928–1983*. Aldershot: Gower, 1985.

Everson, William K. *American Silent Film*. New York: Oxford University Press, 1978.

Fell, John L. *Film and the Narrative Tradition*. Norman: Oklahoma University Press, 1986.

———. *Film: An Introduction*. New York: Praeger, 1975.

———. *A History of Films*. New York: Holt, Rinehart and Winston, 1979.

———, ed. *Film Before Griffith*. Berkeley: University of California Press, 1983.

Fenin, George N., and William K. Everson. *The Western*. New York: Orion, 1962.

Frank, Alan. *The Horror Film Handbook*. Totowa, N.J.: Barnes and Noble, 1982.

Friar, Ralph E., and Natasha A. Friar. *The Only Good Indian . . . The Hollywood Gospel*. New York: Drama Book Specialists, 1972.

Geduld, Harry M. *The Birth of the Talkies*. Bloomington: University of Indiana Press, 1975.

Geduld, Harry M. and Ronald Gottesman. *An Illustrated Glossary of Film Terms*. New York: Holt, Rinehart and Winston, 1973.

Giannetti, Louis D. *Understanding Movies*. Englewood Cliffs, N.J.: Prentice-Hall, 1987.

Gish, Lillian. *The Movies, Mr. Griffith, and Me*. Englewood Cliffs, N.J.: Prentice-Hall, 1969.

Grant, Barry K., ed. *Film Genre: Theory and Criticism*. Metuchen, N.J.: Scarecrow Press, 1977.

Halliwell, Leslie. *The Filmgoer's Companion*. New York: Granada, 1977.

Hardy, Phil. *The Aurum Film Encyclopedia: The Western*. London: Aurum, 1983.

Hardy, Phil, et al. *The Aurum Film Encyclopedia: Horror*. London: Aurum, 1985.

Harrington, John. *Literature and/as Film*. Englewood Cliffs, N.J.: Prentice-Hall, 1977.

Haskell, Molly. *From Reverence to Rape*. New York: Holt, Rinehart and Winston, 1974.

Heck-Rabi, Louise. *Women Filmmakers: A Critical Reception*. Metuchen, N.J.: Scarecrow Press, 1984.

Heinzkill, Richard. *Film Criticism: An Index to Critics' Anthologies*. Metuchen, N.J.: Scarecrow Press, 1975.

Higham, Charles. *Warner Brothers*. New York: Scribner's, 1975.

Hochman, Stanley, ed. *American Film Directors*. New York: Frederick Ungar, 1974.

Houston, Penelope. *The Contemporary Cinema, 1945–1963*. Baltimore: Penguin Books, 1963.

Humanities Index. New York: H. W. Wilson. Annual.

Hurt, James, ed. *Focus on Film and Theatre*. Englewood Cliffs, N.J.: Prentice-Hall, 1974.

Huss, Roy, and Norman Silverstein. *The Film Experience*. New York: Dell, 1969.

Huss, Roy, and T. J. Ross, eds. *Focus on the Horror Film*. Englewood Cliffs, N.J.: Prentice-Hall, 1972.

Hyatt, Marshall. *The Afro-American Cinematic Experience: An Annotated Bibliography and Filmography*. Wilmington, Del.: Scholarly Resources, 1983.

Jacobs, Lewis, ed. *The Documentary Tradition*. New York: W. W. Norton, 1979.

————. *The Emergence of Film Art: The Evolution and Development of the Motion Picture as an Art, from 1900 to the Present*. New York: W. W. Norton, 1979.

————. *Introduction to the Art of the Movies*. New York: Noonday Press, 1960.

————. *The Movies as Medium*. New York: Hippocrene, 1973.

————. *The Rise of the American Film*. New York: Teachers College Press, 1968.

Jones, Karen. *International Index to Film Periodicals*. New York: St. Martin's Press. Annual.

Jowett, Garth. *Film: The Democratic Art*. Boston: Little, Brown, 1976.

Kaminsky, Stuart M. *American Film Genres: Approaches to a Critical Theory of Popular Film*. New York: Dell, 1974.

Kaplan, Ann E. *Women and Film: Both Sides of the Camera*. New York: Methuen, 1983.

Katz, Ephraim. *The Film Encyclopedia*. New York: Crowell, 1979.

Katz, John Stuart, ed. *Perspectives on the Study of Film*. Boston: Little, Brown, 1971.

Kauffman, Stanley, and Bruce Henstell, eds. *American Film Criticism*. Westport, Conn.: Greenwood Press, 1979.

Kawin, Bruce. *How Movies Work*. New York: Macmillan, 1987.

Kerr, Walter. *The Silent Clowns*. New York: Alfred A. Knopf, 1979.

Klotman, Phyllis Rauch. *Frame by Frame: A Black Filmography*. Bloomington: Indiana University Press, 1979.

Knight, Arthur. *The Liveliest Art: A Panoramic History of the Movies*. New York: New American Library, 1979.

Kobal, John. *Gotta Sing, Gotta Dance*. New York: Kamlyn, 1971.

Kracauer, Siegfried. *Theory of Film*. New York: Oxford University Press, 1960.

Krafsur, Richard, ed. *The American Film Institute Catalogue of Motion Pictures: Feature Films, 1961–70*. New York: R. R. Bowker, 1976.

Lahue, Kalton C. *Continued Next Week: A History of the Moving Picture Serial*. Norman: University of Oklahoma Press, 1964.

Langman, Larry. *A Guide to American Screenwriters: The Sound Era 1929–1982*. 2 vols. New York: Garland, 1984.

Larkin, Rochelle. *Hail Columbia*. New Rochelle, N.Y.: Arlington House, 1975.

Leab, Daniel J. *From Sambo to Superspade*. Boston: Houghton Mifflin, 1975.

Lee, Walt. *Reference Guide to Fantastic Films: Science Fiction, Fantasy and Horror*. Los Angeles: Chelsea-Lee Books, 1974.

Leonard, Harold. *The Film Index: A Bibliography*. New York: Arno Press, 1970.

Levin, G. Roy. *Documentary Explorations*. Garden City, N.Y.: Doubleday-Anchor, 1971.

Limbacher, James. *Feature Films on 8mm and 16mm*. New York: R. R. Bowker, 1985.

Lindgren, Ernest. *The Art of the Film*. New York: Macmillan, 1963.

Lindsay, Vachel. *The Art of the Moving Picture*. New York: Liveright, 1970.

MacCann, Richard Dyer, ed. *Film: A Montage of Theories*. New York: E. P. Dutton, 1966.

MacCann, Richard Dyer, and Edward S. Perry. *The New Film Index*. New York: E. P. Dutton, 1975.

McCarthy, Todd, and Charles Flynn. *Kings of the B's*. New York: E. P. Dutton, 1975.

McCarty, Clifford. *Published Screenplays: A Checklist*. Kent, Ohio: Kent State University Press, 1971.

McNally, Raymond T., and Radu Florescu. *In Search of Dracula*. New York: Galahad Books, 1972.

Magill, Frank N. *Magill's Cinema Annual, 1986: A Survey of the Films of 1985*. Englewood Cliffs, N.J.: Salem Press, 1986.

———. *Magill's Survey of Cinema: English Language Films*. Englewood Cliffs, N.J.: Salem Press, 1980, 1981.

———. *Magill's Survey of Cinema: Foreign Language Films*. Englewood Cliffs. N.J.: Salem Press, 1985.

Manchel, Frank. *Film Study: A Resource Guide*. Rutherford, N.J.: Fairleigh Dickinson University Press, 1973.

Manvell, Roger, ed. *The International Encyclopedia of Film*. New York: Crown, 1972.

Marcus, Fred H. *Short Story/Short Film*. Englewood Cliffs, N.J.: Prentice-Hall, 1977.

Martin, Leonard. *The Great Movie Shorts*. New York: Crown, 1972.

Mast, Gerald. *The Comic Mind*. Chicago: University of Chicago Press, 1979.

———. *A Short History of the Movies*. 4th ed. New York: Pegasus, 1981.

Mast, Gerald, and Marshall Cohen, eds. *Film Theory and Criticism*. New York: Oxford University Press, 1985.

Maynard, Richard. *The Black Man on Film: Racial Stereotyping*. Rochelle Park, N.J.: Hayden, 1974.

———. *The Celluloid Curriculum*. Rochelle Park, N.J.: Hayden, 1971.

Mellon, Joan. *Women and Their Sexuality in the New Film*. New York: Dell, 1973.

Metz, Christian. *Film Language*. New York: Oxford University Press, 1974.

Monaco, James. *How to Read a Film*. New York: Oxford University Press, 1981.

Munden, Kenneth W., ed. *The American Film Institute Catalogue of Motion Pictures Produced in the United States, Feature Films, 1921–1930*. New York: R. R. Bowker, 1971.

Nachbar, John G. *Western Films: An Annotated Critical Bibliography*. New York: Garland, 1975.

The New York Times Film Reviews, 1913–1980. 8 vols. New York: New York Times/Arno Press, 1970.

Niver, Kemp R. *Motion Pictures from the Library of Congress Paper Print Collection, 1894–1912*. Berkeley: University of California Press, 1967.

Parish, James Robert, and Michael R. Pitts. *Film Directors: A Guide to Their American Films*. Metuchen, N.J.: Scarecrow Press, 1974.

———. *The Great Gangster Pictures*. Metuchen, N.J.: Scarecrow Press, 1976.

Patterson, Lindsay, ed. *Black Films and Film-makers*. New York: Dodd, Mead, 1975.

Poteet, G. Howard, ed. *The Complete Guide to Film Study*. Urbana, Ill.: National Council of Teachers of English, 1972.

———. *Published Radio, Television, and Film Scripts: A Bibliography*. Troy, N.Y.: Whitson Publishing, 1975.

Powdermaker, Hortense. *Hollywood: The Dream Factory*. Salem, N.H.: Ayer, 1979.

Powers, Anne. *Blacks in American Movies: A Selected Bibliography*. Metuchen, N.J.: Scarecrow Press, 1974.

Pratt, George C. *Spellbound in Darkness*. Greenwich, Conn.: New York Graphic Society, 1973.

Pudovkin, V. I. *Film Technique and Film Acting*. New York: Grove Press, 1970.

Quick, John, and Tom La Bare. *Handbook of Film Production*. New York: Macmillan, 1972.

Quinland, David. *The Illustrated Directory of Film Character Actors*. London: B. T. Batsford, 1985.

———. *Quinland's Illustrated Directory of Film Stars*. London: B. T. Batsford, 1986.

Readers' Guide to Periodical Literature. New York: H. W. Wilson. Annual.

Rehrauer, George. *The Macmillan Film Bibliography*. 2 vols. New York: Macmillan, 1982.

Renan, Sheldon. *An Introduction to the American Underground Film*. New York: E. P. Dutton, 1967.

Rhode, Eric. *A History of the Cinema from Its Origins to 1970*. New York: Da Capo Press, 1985.

Richardson, Robert. *Literature and Film*. New York: Garland, 1985.

Rosen, Marjorie. *Popcorn Venus*. New York: Avon, 1974.

Ross, T. J. *Film and the Liberal Arts*. New York: Holt, Rinehart and Winston, 1970.

Rotha, Paul, with Richard Griffith. *The Film Till Now*. London: Spring Books, 1967.

Sadoul, Georges. *Dictionary of Filmmakers*. Berkeley: University of California Press, 1972.

———. *Dictionary of Films*. Berkeley: University of California Press, 1965, 1972.

Samuels, Charles Thomas. *Encountering Directors*. New York: Capricorn, 1972.

Sarris, Andrew. *Interviews with Film Directors*. New York: Avon, 1967.

Schickel, Richard. *The Men Who Made the Movies*. New York: Atheneum, 1975.

Schuster, Mel. *Motion Picture Directors: A Bibliography of Magazine and Periodical Articles, 1900–1972*. Metuchen, N.J.: Scarecrow Press, 1973.

———. *Motion Picture Performers: A Bibliography of Magazine and Periodical Articles, 1900–1969*. Metuchen, N.J.: Scarecrow Press, 1971.

Shales, Tom, et al. *The American Film Heritage*. Washington, D.C.: Acropolis Books, 1972.

Sherman, Eric. *Directing the Film*. Boston: Little, Brown, 1976.

Sherman, Eric, and Martin Rubin. *The Director's Event*. New York: New American Library, 1969.

Sitney, P. Adams, ed. *Film Culture Reader*. New York: Praeger, 1970.

Smith, Sharon. *Women Who Make Movies*. New York: Hopkins and Blake, 1975.

Sohn, David A. *Film: The Critical Eye*. Dayton, Ohio: Pflaum, 1970.

Solomon, Stanley J. *Beyond Formula*. New York: Harcourt Brace Jovanovich, 1976.

Spottiswoode, Raymond. *A Grammar of the Film*. Berkeley: University of California Press, 1969.

Steinberg, Cobbett S. *Film Facts*. New York: Facts on File, 1980.

Sullivan, Kaye. *Films for, by, and About Women*. Metuchen, N.J.: Scarecrow Press, 1980.

Thomson, David. *A Biographical Dictionary of Film*. New York: William Morrow, 1976.

Truitt, Evelyn Mack. *Who Was Who on Screen*. New York: R. R. Bowker, 1984.

Tyler, Parker. *Underground Film: A Critical History*. New York: Grove Press, 1969.

Ursini, James, and Alain Silver. *The Vampire Film*. Cranbury, N.J.: A. S. Barnes, 1975.

Vardac, A. Nicholas. *Stage to Screen*. New York: Ayer, 1968.

Variety Film Reviews, 1907–1980. New York: Garland, 1983.

Wagner, Geoffrey. *The Novel and the Cinema*. Rutherford, N.J.: Fairleigh Dickinson University Press, 1975.

Walls, Howard Lamarr. *Motion Pictures, 1894–1912, Identified from the Records of the U.S. Copyright Office*. Washington, D.C.: Library of Congress, 1953.

Wead, George, and George Lellis. *Film: Form and Function*. Boston: Houghton Mifflin, 1981.

Weber, Olga S. *North American Film and Video Directory*. New York: R. R. Bowker, 1976.

Weinberg, Herman G. *The Complete Greed*. New York: Arno Press, 1972.

Weiss, Ken, and Ed Goodgold. *To Be Continued*. New York: Crown, 1972.

Wenden, D. J. *The Birth of the Movies*. New York: E. P. Dutton, 1974.

Who Wrote the Movie and What Else Did He Write? Los Angeles: Academy of Motion Picture Arts and Sciences and Writers' Guild of America, 1970.

Willis, Donald C. *Horror and Science Fiction Films: A Checklist*. Metuchen, N.J.: Scarecrow Press, 1972.

Wilson, George M. *Narration in Light: Studies in Cinematic Point of View*. Baltimore: Johns Hopkins University Press, 1986.

Wingrove, David. *The Science Fiction Film Source Book*. London: Longman, 1985.

Youngblood, Gene. *Expanded Cinema*. New York: E. P. Dutton, 1970.

Periodicals

American Cinematographer, Los Angeles, 1919–.

American Film. Washington, D.C., 1975–.

Cinema Journal. Philadelphia, 1961–.

Dialogue on Film. Beverly Hills, Calif., 1972–75.

Film Culture. New York, 1962–.

Film Quarterly. Berkeley, Calif., 1945–.

Literature/Film Quarterly. Salisbury, Md., 1973–.

Media and Methods. Philadelphia, 1965–.

Foodways

CHARLES CAMP

Few subjects occupy a larger place in the American consciousness than food. In both a literal and figurative sense, food serves to define individual and group identities; culturally acquired and nurtured matters of taste demark ethnic, regional, racial, and spiritual differences among Americans that otherwise might lack concrete expression. Indeed, within the maze of identities that characterizes contemporary American society, food offers one of the oldest and most evocative systems of cultural identification. While many characteristics of American ethnic groups, for example, have been obscured in our postindustrial society, we sense and know the difference between Italian and Greek pastries and between a Polish sausage and the common hotdog. We may lack very scientific procedures for describing the differences between these foods, but we regularly employ such distinctions as a way of defining (and celebrating) ethnic cultural diversity.

The past decades have seen an explosion of interest in food that apparently draws its energy from a variety of sources. The back-to-nature and whole-earth movements of the 1960s have contributed an increased public sensitivity to matters of diet and to the economic system that supplies most Americans with their daily bread. Interest in old-time ways of life, which led to something of a boom for American folk-life studies, also sparked a more general curiosity about home cooking and other aspects of American domestic life. In the early 1970s, American industry began to catch up with European competitors in the manufacture of home cooking equipment that would permit the average American cook to produce virtually any dish desired. With the elevation of the Cuisinart food processor to the status of a mid–1970s icon, food became a general grid for plotting status and social position. *Time* and *Newsweek* covers heralded the "Cooking Boom," and, overnight, dozens of magazines, cookbooks, courses, and television programs sprang up to meet an ever-growing appetite for information.

The groundwork for the present food boom lies, of course, in the long-standing love affair that well-to-do Americans have had with French and other continental cuisine. As part of the social heritage that defined the elite, gourmet cooking (as it has been traditionally termed) places food within a European symbolic system that most Americans have found difficult to understand, much less imitate. The food boom brought together grass-roots interest in American foodstuffs and domestic traditions and a system of defining social achievement and status that was previously restricted to the wealthier classes. The result is a curious mixture of American and gourmet styles, but also a refreshingly open consideration of the variety of American cookery.

As might be expected for an area of expression that has only recently found public acceptance, scholars have been reluctant to devote much energy to the study of food in American culture. Folklorists, anthropologists, and nutritionists have not often explored the behavioral aspects of food preparation and use, but some investigations of American foodways have yielded interesting information. To some extent, the multidisciplinary study of American foodways has been hindered by a lack of agreement on the basic unit of study. Nutritionists have been chiefly interested in foods and their nutritional properties. Anthropologists have focused on the role of food in the everyday life of primitive peoples and have occasionally studied the employment of food as a symbol in industrial cultures. Folklorists have studied the beliefs and customary practices related to food, but have recently begun to consider in a more consciously ethnographic fashion the relationship of food to other aspects of life in traditional communities.

In popular as well as anthropological works, the terminology of food research has never been adequate to the task of describing or analyzing food-related behavior. In common American speech, we use the same word-food-to describe the raw materials from which meals are prepared and the meals themselves. Nutritionists refer to patterns of food consumption and behavior as "food habits." Anthropologists commonly refer to the food culture of a self-defined group as the group's "ethnocuisine." And folklorists use the term "foodways" to describe the relationship between food and culture in the same way that "folkways" was formerly used to examine the traditions in traditional ways of life. The common denominator among these terms, and the unifying theme of this essay, is *culture*. Food *in* culture, food as a *symbol* of cultural identity, the preparation and consumption of food as a culture *unto itself*-these are some of the ways in which the relationship of food and culture can be explored.

There is much written about food that does not contribute to this field of study. Most cookbooks, which are simply collections of the author-editor's favorite recipes, have little to say about what people eat and why they do so. Books and articles about specific foods, their history, and their biological properties are most often stripped of the cultural "clothing" of the cooking and eating processes that reveal the cultural character of food-related behavior. Scientific monographs on the diet of primitive people offer lists of foods consumed by such peoples, but without the information about daily life that would permit reweaving the fabric of social life created by the interaction of food and culture.

What is useful to the study of food and American culture is the type of information that relates foods and/or techniques for their preparation and consumption to a specific locale, or group, or time of year. Occasionally, such information is found in unlikely places, including restaurant guides, newspaper advertisements, and food industry trade association publications. But if the study of food in American culture is to focus on the connections between food and culture, we must be willing to search for new sources rather than simply rely on existing information.

HISTORIC OUTLINE

The history of American food mirrors the history of American society, with its periodic fluctuations between a longing admiration of European ways of life and an intense pride in things distinctively American. With the exception of Native American contributions to American foodways, the development of a distinctively American food pattern has consisted of adapting a much larger range of native foodstuffs to immigrant cookery styles (and vice versa). Unlike European cookery, during the eighteenth and nineteenth century American food was noted for the quality of foodstuff (meat, fruits, and vegetables chiefly) and not for the quality of preparation. The domination of the food industry in nineteenth-century America by descendants of prominent English families did not advance the concept of a truly American way of eating, although, by mid-century, American oysters, shrimp, beef, and whiskey had begun to distinguish themselves.

Although European travelers in America often describe the crudity of American inns and other eateries, the simplicity of American foods and the bountiful supply of beef, seafood, and wild fowl impressed many visitors. What average Americans ate during that time is more difficult to determine; but it is clear that in the style of the log cabin, in which native materials are combined as simply as possible, the everyday diet of early Americans was based chiefly on local crops and meat and game supplies. This dependence on local foodstuffs defined the regional character of American cookery-a feature that is perhaps the most obvious distinction of American foodways.

The development of industrialized food technology and the use of railroads for shipping livestock and foodstuffs allowed for a wider choice of materials for the late nineteenth-century American cook. However, at the end of the century, most Americans had established a balance between the ethnic traditions in which their culture (and approach to food) was based and the regional food supplies. The result-a Texas German food style distinctively different from a mid-Atlantic German style, for example-has not changed markedly in this century, despite the growing diversity of foodstuffs available to the average cook.

The goal of American agriculture and food technologists to supply the average cook with food supplies that defy season and locale was reached with the development of mechanized food preservation and transportation industries. With summer produce available year round, both frozen and fresh, the last physical limitation on American cookery was removed and the last regional boundaries were struck down. Restaurant systems that made use of standardized food technology quickly developed, and it was soon possible to follow a chain of franchised fast-food restaurants across the country in a string of virtually identical meals.

While critics at the time lamented the passing of cookery traditions that were grounded in time and space, it has become plain that Americans have developed a pluralistic approach to food much like the double vision with which they perceive popular entertainment, music, and other aspects of daily life. Frozen vegetables and syndicated fast food have found their place in American life, but Americans still eat ten-times as many tomatoes in the summer as in the winter, and the consumption of sausage, soups, and barbecue still varies widely from region to region.

REFERENCE WORKS

The principal academic disciplines that have examined American foodways are anthropology, nutrition and health, sociology, geography, and folklore. By combining similar approaches and including some general publications, these fields can be reduced to three: nutrition and health, history and geography, and social sciences. Since most of the folkloristic study of foodways is of a social-scientific nature, I have included works in this area under social sciences. The books and articles discussed here and listed in the bibliography cross many academic battle lines, including the division between scholarly and popular works. The purpose of this outline is not only to discuss significant writings in each of the disciplines that has studied American foodways, but also to provide, through this discussion, a clearer notion of the different ways in which each academic field approaches the subject.

Nutrition and Health

Although the fields of nutrition and health have contributed more information on American foodways than all other disciplines combined, relatively little of this information is accessible or useful to the student of American culture. As a whole, nutritionists deal with the description of culture only when it is necessary to deal with specific nutritional questions. Consequently, much of the literature cited here, while precise in the description of food habits, is thin on the correlation of food and culture. Among basic reference works in the field, the *Cumulated Index Medicus,* compiled by the U.S. Department of Health, Education and Welfare, is the standard research index. Diet and nutrition studies from all major American and international journals are indexed quarterly. *Nutrition Abstracts and Reviews* is a monthly index and review of international nutrition research and includes topics related to food and culture. Joseph Dommers Vehling's *America's Table* is a dictionary of food terminology, useful primarily because it is the only work of its kind. The U.S. Department of Agriculture *Experimental Station Record* can be very difficult to use, but it offers the only widely available tool for sorting the annual flood of state circulars, bulletins, and special publications, many of which describe in fine detail the foodways of particular areas of the United States.

Of the score of food-related bibliographies published two stand out. The best general review of scholarship in foodways within the fields of health and nutrition is Christine S. Wilson's "Food Habits: A Selected Annotated Bibliography"—a surprisingly thorough treatment of contemporary research. Marguerite Patten's *Books for Cooks* is primarily a listing of cookbooks and other general works on food, with no particular concern for culture. If nothing else, the Patten bibliography reveals the sharp increase in publications on American food in recent years.

Waldo Lincoln's list of American cookery books published between 1742 and 1860 is a basic reference work much closer in approach and purpose to books noted in the history and geography section of this outline, but it is listed here with other bibliographies and guides to the literature for the sake of convenience. Lincoln's work was made current to 1960 by Bob Brown and Eleanor Parker, *Culinary Americana* 1860–1960, but unfortunately the coverage these authors bring to the post-Civil War era is much less complete than Lincoln's prewar coverage.

Much of the nutritionists' contribution to American foodways research lies in the development of quantitative data gathering methods. The publications of the National Research Council's Committee on Food Habits in this area represent the highest refinement of survey techniques, along with their inherent shortcomings. The quality of these surveys unfortunately derives in part from the narrowing of the research on food habits to the development of per capita consumption and diet profile statistics, neither of which is especially useful in the analysis of cultural aspects of food.

Among the approaches used by nutritionists, one of the most compatible with studies of American culture is the definition of culture patterns and the correlation of food habits with systems of social organization. Nutritionists view food patterns as the quantification of individual food behaviors and the expression of shared attitudes toward or consumption of particular foods. Patterns differ from food habits in the respect that the former are often based on extensive or repeated surveys, while the latter may be the expression of individualized or occasional eating habits. Clark F. Le Gros's hypothesis that food habits form the basis for more complex economic and social structures is not generally shared by fellow nutritionists. Edith M. Barber, E. N. Todhunter, and M. R. Trulson view contemporary food patterns as the result of historical processes—chiefly economic—which initially shape and gradually narrow the range of possible food habits. Faith Clark and Arthur H. Niehoff reject the inevitability of this historical model in favor of a more open-ended view of food patterns as the generalization of smaller-scale food-related behaviors which are themselves in constant flux.

In the nutritional literature, social and economic considerations are often combined, especially where the focus of analysis is the relationship between food and culture. Magnus Pyke and M. E. Lowenberg survey food-related behaviors that are affected or shaped by social patterns, while M. B. Loeb offers an often-assumed, but seldom-stated, alternative to more conventional social analyses. By pointing out that food habits tend to reinforce and extend the social systems of which they are a part, Loeb reverses the emphases of other studies, which ascribe a greater degree of social continuity to status systems and other cultural organizations than the food habit complex.

Among those few writers who span the fields of nutrition and culture, Magnus Pyke's works come closest to drawing a substantial correlation between diet and behavior on a theoretical level. Pyke contends that American foods have found acceptance in Europe not because of their economic or nutritional advantages but because of cultural associations attached to them. In a 1975 essay, Pyke demonstrates how deeply issues of cultural meaning penetrate the study of food habits and the widespread association of foodways and other culturally based systems of meaning.

Nutritionists have written in considerable detail about the dietary habits and resultant problems of regional, ethnic, age, and sex groups. In retrospect, many of the older studies of this kind are most revealing as social documents rather than as foodways studies. Such is the case for a 1917 publication on Massachusetts's working women, which reveals growing public and government concern for this work force expressed through dietary reforms. Studies of minority religious groups, including Seventh-Day

Adventists (Doris E. Phillips and Mary A. Bass), Muslims (A. H Sakr), and Jews (B. Cassell), necessarily take cultural characteristics of group members into account when constructing dietary profiles since belief systems enter actively into matters of dietary choice and regulation.

Perhaps the most notable contribution of nutritionists to the study of American foodways and culture is, ironically, least known to contemporary scholars. In the 1930s and 1940s, the U.S. Department of Agriculture coordinated a special nutritional research effort in the southeastern states in response to reports of deteriorating public health. The health conditions were attributed to the combination of a depressed economy and a series of blights and droughts that reduced existing food supplies. The studies of diet-related diseases and general dietary practices in the Southeast comprise a unique social record, as well as the flowering of a method of regional nutritional analysis. Dorothy Dickins's work in Mississippi and Ada Moser's South Carolina research place nutritional concerns within cultural contexts that give them a social as well as a nutritional accuracy and importance. Although Dickins's work is limited to Mississippi, her techniques, which include yearly household inventories, in-depth personal interviews, photographs of houses and cooking areas, and detailed descriptions of everyday meals, established a high standard for regional studies in other areas.

Unfortunately, the bulletins and circulars in which Dickins's work and that of many other nutritionists who were part of the larger research project were published are often difficult to obtain. Like the general contribution of nutritionists to American foodways research, there is much concerning Dickins's work that may continue to remain beyond the reach of foodways scholars.

History and Geography

The works discussed in this category are a mixed group of popular and scholarly writings about cookery, food in history, foodways and cultural geography, and other historical topics related to American food. Among these works, several are concerned with the description of cookery traditions defined by historical period, region, or ethnic group. Of these, only two— *James Beard's American Cookery* and *The American Heritage Cookbook*—are actual cookbooks. Special note is made of these books because they offer more to the reader than recipes and they share a concern for historical relationships between certain foods and aspects of American culture.

Prominent among other general works on American cookery are the books in the Time-Life American Cooking series. The two survey books in this series, written by James Patrick Shenton and Dale Brown, are especially useful, although the excellent photographs often take precedence over more detailed written descriptions of food patterns. The regional studies that comprise the remainder of the series (Dale Brown, Peter S. Feibleman, Jonathan Norton Leonard, Eugene Walter, and Jose Wilson) offer a good introduction to the cookery of an American region, including information on customs related to the preparation or eating of foods distinctive to a particular area. The books are lavishly illustrated, and, while the series does vary in quality by author (Brown and Wilson topping the list), it is a good source for general information. The format of the Time-Life publications (an oversize book of texts and photographs accompanied by a smaller, spiral-bound collection of recipes) is well suited to the material and recommends the series to library as well as to home use. Of similar but somewhat more limited value is Raymond Sokolov's *Fading Feast,* which links regional (especially endangered) foodstuffs with descriptions of local food events and recipes, for such dishes as morel soufflé and persimmon pudding.

With the exception of the modified cookbooks discussed above, there are relatively few general works on American cookery that explore cultural matters. Waverly Root and Richard de Rochemont's *Eating in America* is the most recent and, with certain qualifications, the most thorough general history of American eating habits. The work that has long held this title, Richard Osborn Cummings's *The American and His Food,* is more comprehensive in terms of social classes represented, but lacks the historical detail found in *Eating in America.* The shortcomings of Root and de Rochemont's work stem from the authors' fairly narrow definition of foodways and the restriction of their study to materials that describe the foodways of the elite class almost exclusively. Ironically, Waverly Root has written a book that avoids this very problem in *The Food of France,* a work whose subject has little to do with American cookery, but whose approach provides an interesting model for regional studies of American food.

More scholarly general treatments of food and culture include Rupert B. Vance's writings on the relationship of geography and health—diet providing the key to this relationship—and Max Sorre's excellent essay on food and cultural geography. G. L. Jordan, *Changing Food Habits in Relation to Land Utilization in the United States,* and Charlotte Elizabeth Biester, *Some Factors in the Development of American Cookbooks,* offer more focused studies, and they are the ones that are perhaps more difficult to acquire, but they point out important general considerations in the study of American foodways. Biester examines some of the historical issues that pertain to American cookbooks. In so doing, she raises significant questions regarding the value of such books as historical sources. William Woys Weaver's study (and reprint) of Elizabeth Ellicott Lea's 1845 *Domestic Cookery* answers many of these questions and provides a model for the measurement of the impact of printed materials upon cooks as well as cookery. Laura Shapiro extends these lines of influence in her recent book *Perfection Salad,* which explores the effects the turn-of-the-century "scientific cookery" movement had upon public tastes.

Calvin Trillin's books on American food, *American Fried Alice, Let's Eat,* and *Third Helpings,* are worthy of special note in this context simply because among those writers whose work reaches a general readership, Trillin has the most to say about the relationship between American food and culture. Of his three books on food, *American Fried* is the best, since more of its pages are devoted to the description of regional food specialties and to his search for what is genuinely American in American food. *Alice, Let's Eat* and *Third Helpings* deal with much of the same material as the earlier *American Fried,* but in less detail and with less emphasis on the foods themselves. Despite these qualifications, Trillin's books offer the freshest and most accessible approach to American food to emerge from the past decade, and *American Fried* may find a continuing usefulness as a text for American studies or foodways courses.

More specialized books that deal with American "popular" foods have reached the commercial market. Michael Lasky's *The Complete Junk Food Book* is similar to other works of its idiom (*The Complete Book of Running, The Robot Book, The Cat Book,* and so on) in the sense that much information has been gathered together on a particular subject, but the author has not taken great pains to make sense of it. Some interesting comments are made on the organization of the American fast-food industry, and there is something stimulating about seeing foods like Fritos, Sugar Babies, and Hi-C described in specific terms. But Lasky fails to explore in detail the matter that might have yielded a more interesting analysis—the cultural attachment Americans share for foods of this type. Paul Dickson's *Chow* is similarly a compendium of information on a type of food—in this case military—but the narrowness of the chosen subject provides for a better overall treatment. Dickson has also compiled an interesting collection of photographs and illustrations that depict scenes of food preparation and eating in military settings. Since the latter half of *Chow* consists of military versions of standard American recipes, the photographs do much to relieve the dreariness of the subject matter.

Among recent books on specific foods and foodstuffs, Sally Levitt Steinberg's *The Donut Book* expands upon the popularity of one of America's best-loved foods by sketching connections between the donut and the social, literary, and advertising worlds in which it has attained a high degree of association with such verities as good conversation, good humor, and circularity. Two recent studies of red peppers are somewhat more serious, but no less circumspect. *Peppers: The Domesticated Capsicum* by Jean Andrews is a beautiful, almost reverential album of the pepper family, replete with full agricultural data, color line drawings of all subspecies, and detailed notes about their surprisingly varied uses. Richard Schweid's *Hot Peppers* examines the *capsicum* in its American nexus—New Iberia, Louisiana—where tabasco and Cajun culture commingle.

It is interesting, if somewhat ironic, to note that some of the best general foodways research focuses on the architecture of the food world, as vernacular landscape as well as cookery and eating locations. Philip Langdon's *Orange Roofs, Golden Arches* and the less recent Hirshorn and Izenour study of White Tower restaurants are important documents—evocative as well as descriptive of fast food's sense of space and place. Equally evocative are two books on Seattle's Pike Place Market. Alice Shorett and Murray Morgan understand the market*place* as a political as well as a commercial and culinary crossroads. John Stamets's book of market photographs is an excellent complement; one might hope for further photographic study of markets and other food-centered locales that meets this high standard.

Social Sciences

As was the case with the previous group of works, the books and articles discussed in this category comprise a mixed body of writings that examines American foodways from a social-scientific perspective and offers analysis or theory pertaining to the social description of American food-related behavior. The works included here are a more select group than the nutritional studies, being limited to works chiefly concerned with the social scientific study of food and culture rather than ethnographies that include information about foodways.

Prominent among the research conducted by social scientists in the area of American foodways is the work of the National Research Council's Committee on Food Habits. Although the committee actively functioned for only five years (1941–45), the research and publications it sponsored are principally responsible for labeling the early 1940s as the "golden age" of American foodways research. Under the leadership of anthropologist Margaret Mead, the committee conducted wide-ranging research into the food habits of American ethnic minorities, refined field methods for the documentation of foodways, and served as a forum for the exchange of theories regarding the role of food-related behaviors within the American social system. The major publications of the Committee on Food Habits, *The Problem of Changing Food Habits* (1943) and the *Manual for the Study of Food Habits* (1945), brought to the attention of scholars and policymakers in various federal agencies the wealth of research that social scientists had to offer in the area of foodways and attempted to redefine the goals of food habit research in order to include behavioral as well as dietary considerations.

Much of the committee's work remained unfinished when the unit was dissolved in 1945, but Mead prepared a summary report and an updated bibliography on food habits, published by the National Research Council in 1964, entitled *Food Habits Research: Problems of the 1960s*. Outside her work with the committee, Mead wrote prolifically about the relationship between food and culture throughout the 1940s and 1950s. Although many of the articles listed in the bibliography are simply restatements of the

Committee on Food Habits' goals, Mead also wrote on regional patterns in American diet and the concept of culture change as it pertains to food-related behaviors.

Other committee alumni who wrote on noncommittee topics include John Bennett, Margaret Cussler, and Mary Louise de Give. Bennett's 1946 article "An Interpretation of the Scope and Implications of Social Scientific Research in Human Subsistence" is perhaps the single most important article in the field, offering not only a careful analysis of then-current research, but also an insightful critique of social-scientific research strategies most often employed in foodways studies. Bennett's other writings, most of which detail his work in southern Illinois, provide a model for the analysis of field data, which goes beyond the statistical profiles of previous research. Cussler and De Give's *Twixt the Cup and the Lip* is an unusual mixture of anthropology and dietetics and is a landmark in the field of American foodways research. Although the authors' fieldwork was limited to the southeastern United States, the information they provide on the foodways of that region is extensive and thoughtfully analyzed.

Several anthropologists have been concerned with questions of cultural interpretation and symbolism inherent in food systems and behavior. Among general studies, Claude Lévi-Strauss's "The Culinary Triangle" is perhaps most accessible and most widely applicable, but as Edmund Leach points out in *Culture and Communication,* it is not without its theoretical problems. Leach's concern with symbolic languages and the conscious manipulation of food behaviors for social ends is echoed in the writings of Octavio Paz and Roland Barthes. The latter's semiotic analysis of contemporary popular culture provides an approach to the study of food that is both object-and behavior-oriented.

Anthropologists Marvin Harris and Mary Douglas have explored the cultural basis of dietary avoidances and preferences from two different critical perspectives. Harris approaches ritual "treatments" of pork and potlatch ceremonies as cultural paradoxes, while Douglas uses Jewish dietary practices as a key to understanding not only nonfood-related group behaviors but also the cultural and historical premises upon which such behaviors are based. Douglas has most recently examined the link between food and festivity in American culture. The case studies reported in her more recently edited *Food in the Social Order* are less than satisfying, but Douglas's lengthy introduction provides a concise and up-to-date summary of work in this field.

I have chosen to discuss folklife studies of American foodways within the context of social-scientific inquiries as a body of research distinct from that of anthropology or sociology, not because folklorists have not been influenced in their work by social scientists, but because as a whole folklife foodways research has traditionally reflected the range of professional interests and methods that has typified food habits research in general. Among general works on traditional cookery, Jay Anderson's survey of American research, "Scholarship on Contemporary American Folk Foodways," and Don Yoder's chapter on folk cookery in Richard Dorson's *Folklore and Folklife* are most useful. Yoder has also outlined a method for the use of historical documents in his 1971 study of American foodways and has demonstrated the usefulness of this approach in the description of the history and social meanings of foods important to the folk culture of the Pennsylvania Germans. A useful collection of current folkloristic work in foodways, and a logical extension of Yoder's well-laid groundwork, is Michael Owen Jones, Bruce Giuliano, and Roberta Krell's *Foodways and Eating Habits.* Another collection of essays which complements Jones's attention to identity in foodways is *Ethnic and Regional Foodways in the United States,* edited by Linda Keller Brown and Kay Mussell. Both books provide a good sampling of what folklorists interested in food and culture are doing at the moment, with Jones's concern with market research an important, if not definitive, difference.

Other studies of specific foods that emphasize the description of the cooking process and its cultural context include Thomas G. Burton and Ambrose N. Manning's study of folk preservation and canning techniques in rural Tennessee and R. Dodson's early account of tortilla making. John Gregory Bourke's more extensive description of folk foods of the Rio Grande Valley appeared in the *Journal of American Folklore* in 1895 and represents an original, if not entirely successful, attempt to define the importance of cultural continuities in the perpetuation of a cookery tradition. N. D. Humphrey and B. Chang offer accounts of food habits that reflect the values of the ethnic cultures in which they are followed. The difference between the nutritionist and the student of culture is made clear in a comparison of these accounts. Chang defines Chinese dietary beliefs in terms of their nutritional rather than ideational referrent, while, for Humphrey, the dietary practices of a group of northern Mexican Americans are of folkloric interest by nature of their deviation from accepted public food habits and medical beliefs.

Among more theoretical writings on folklore and food, Marjorie Sackett outlines a method for using "folk recipes" as cultural characteristics by which the migration of new ideas and culture groups into a community can be measured. Unfortunately, the difference between folk and other recipes is not adequately spelled out, and the usefulness of this method is weakened. British folklorist Venetia Newall draws a less literal means of describing culture change and tradition that makes use of foods and cookery techniques as well as specific recipes. Although Newall's examples are drawn from Jamaican cultures in the Caribbean and in England, the broader basis of comparison and the attention to the social context of the cookery tradition make the conclusions regarding food and culture more widely applicable.

RESEARCH SOURCES

The previous section provided an overview of the scholarly and popular literature on American foodways within the framework of the major academic fields that have explored the relationship of food and culture. In this section, I shall offer some additional sources of information on foodways, ranging from popular publications, organizations, museums, films, and courses, to field trips and self-education projects suitable for scholastic or personal use. The materials I have included here represent my own view of what I find helpful in dealing with food and culture and the places where interests in specific aspects of this subject might be best explored.

General Circulation Publications and Journals

Magazines and newspapers have long carried regular features and columns on food, although these articles have not generally dealt with cultural concerns until recently. Among the bright spots in magazine coverage of American foodways are Raymond Sokolov's monthly articles on specific foods in *Natural History,* the best of which are collected in the aforementioned *Fading Feast,* and Calvin Trillin's U.S. Journal series in the *New Yorker.* Trillin's pieces tend to be longer than Sokolov's and explore a specific food event or locale in greater detail, but they are published on an occasional basis. Sokolov also publishes occasional articles in the *International Review of Food and Wine* and other food-oriented magazines.

A new international journal that holds some promise is *Food and Foodways,* which is concerned less with American materials and issues than readers might wish, but does begin to address the need for periodic publication of foodways scholarship. (The journal is distributed in the United States by Harwood Academic Publishers, P.O. Box 786, Cooper Station, New York 10276.)

The number of magazines that deal exclusively with food and wine is ever increasing, although few articles deal with *American* food, let alone cultural aspects of American food. The four major national food magazines, *Bon Appétit, Cuisine, International Review of Food and Wine,* and *Gourmet,* appeal to an audience that is apparently concerned with international, and especially continental, cookery. As a result, they have little to offer the student of American foodways. Often, local food magazines or restaurant guides supply the best information on local foods, although such magazines often cater to similarly gourmet tastes and sensibilities.

In the area of restaurants, there has been a mushrooming of book-length city restaurant guides in recent years. Although they do not always tell the whole story of an area's food culture (many people still eat at home these days), they do provide an interesting characterization of the ethnic groups, regional styles, and cultural self-image of specific cities. Many of the current guides are part of a new wave of restaurant criticism that has followed upon the success of the *Underground Gourmet* series begun by Simon and Schuster in 1966. The *Underground Gourmet* books attempted to enlarge the pool of restaurants commonly reviewed and the criteria normally used to review them by applying a more democratic view of cookery and a more open view of what constitutes a good meal. Considering the series as a whole, some books are better than others; Richard Collin's *New Orleans Underground Gourmet* and Milton Glaser and Jerome Snyder's original New York guide head the list. While the chatty style of these guides is shared by the San Francisco and Washington D.C. authors, R. B. Read and Judith and Milton Viorst, these last two books lack the insight into food and culture that makes Collin's book something more than a list of restaurants. If the *Underground Gourmet* series remains in print or in library collections long after the restaurant information is out of date, years from now we will have a unique record of the ethnic and regional character of some of the major American cities during the 1970s.

Richard Collin has written widely on food in addition to his work on the *New Orleans Underground Gourmet*. His *New Orleans Restaurant Guide* is not as interesting as the *Gourmet* and is poorly organized, but it charts the author's growing preoccupation with the cultural aspects of the eating experiences he records. Collin's two cookbooks are very much grounded in the New Orleans tradition, and they are as educational as they are useful, but both are unfortunately often difficult to locate outside the New Orleans vicinity.

In New York City, the selection of places to eat and the guarding of "inside" information on excellent but unknown eateries are matters of urban folklore. But for outsiders, the wealth of literature on this single cookery scene can be stimulating. Gael Greene's book on New York restaurants, *Bite,* is not a guide per se, but rather an exploration of the economic and cultural intricacies of living in New York expressed in terms of food. Craig Claiborne's *New York Times Guide to Dining Out in New York* is a more conventional review of restaurants, but it is an interesting counterpart to Glaser and Snyder and Greene both in terms of what is reviewed and what is not. As was mentioned above, restaurant guides do not offer the kind of ethnographic information we might wish to have on American foodways, but as ephemeral publications that are part *of* as well as a commentary *on* popular cultural behavior, they have much to offer the student of American foodways.

Organizations and Trade Publications

Few fields of American industry are as well organized and publicized as food growers, processors, and merchandisers. Organizations range from the 20-member Bee Industries Association and 5 member Associated Pimiento Canners to the 3,400-member Independent Grocers Alliance and the 13,000-member National Restaurant Association. Most trade organizations, even those with fairly small memberships, are in business to promote the distribution and use of their product or service. Consequently, they frequently distribute information on the history and uses of food crops and products or the function of a particular food-related service within the American diet and economy. A brief list of organizations and trade publications follows the bibliography, but readers are encouraged to follow individual interests by contacting organizations whose work or products are relevant to more general concerns.

Libraries, Museums, and Special Collections

Many major national associations in the fields of nutrition and home economics maintain libraries for the use of their membership and, with special permission, the use of interested scholars and students. The American Home Economics Association, the National Association of Food Chains, and the National Canners Association all maintain libraries in the Washington, D.C., area. These libraries, along with the National Agriculture Library in Beltsville, Maryland, and the Library of Congress, are good sources for general works on American foodways and for special collections deposited by organization members or private scholars. In addition, many public and academic libraries have special collections in local culture that often include church-published local cookbooks and other ephemera unobtainable through other sources.

Most local museums acquire cooking equipment of historic importance or local significance, but some folk museums or museums of everyday life have explored the relationship of food and culture in greater detail. The Smithsonian Institution's Museum of History and Technology maintains a special collection of early American cooking equipment. Plymouth Plantation, Old Sturbridge Village, and Colonial Williamsburg, to name only a few, have conducted extensive research on the history of local foodways in addition to the preservation of artifacts. Williamsburg has also published monographs on the subject, including Jane Carson's excellent *Colonial Virginia Cookery*. In studying the development of a cooking technique or style, an examination of the equipment used in the preparation of food during an earlier period can be of considerable benefit.

Films

Many trade associations have produced promotional films on American foods and their history that may be of use to contemporary scholars and interested students. Such films often lack the sort of cultural information we might wish to have, and some take liberties with the facts in order to make promotional points, but they can be integrated within courses and other educational programs for effective use. Only a few films have been made by folklorists or anthropologists that explore the relationship between food and culture. Prominent among these are Les Blank's films about Louisiana Cajun life, Texas-Mexican border culture, and New Orleans's Mardi Gras festivities. Although Blank's primary subject in each of these films is not food, but music, dance, or custom, the filmmaker has an ability to show the relationship between foodways and other expressive forms within a folk group. The films that deal with these three groups are *Spend It All, Chulas Fronteras,* and *Always for Pleasure,* respectively. Readers may also wish to consider Blank's opus *Garlic Is as Good as Ten Mothers.* Further information on all of these can be obtained from Flower Films, Box 9195, E1 Cerrito, California 94709. Another film recommended for classroom use in connection with foodways, folklore, and history is *Maple Sugar Farmer,* a portrait of a sugar-maker and the sugar-making process, distributed by the University of Michigan Audio-Visual Education Center, 416 4th Street, Ann Arbor, Michigan 48109.

Courses, Field Research and Self-Education

Teachers have long used field trips to factories of various kinds as educational experiences for their students, and many food-related industries are accustomed to dealing with requests by individuals or groups to view the inside of their operations. Even when the subject of study is an older non-industrial food complex, there is often much to be learned by visiting dairies, mills, distilleries, and other food processing facilities. Tours and special information on specific topics must usually be arranged with the plant superintendent of the facility you wish to visit. Field research in American foodways is an activity that can be entered into by individuals or student groups with a minimum of experience in field techniques since every member of our society has a basic grasp of the subject matter. Unlike some culture areas that appear exotic or esoteric to the uninitiated, the study of foodways offers a shared and comparative experience upon which discussions of cultural variation and change may be based. Information about food is easily obtainable both from peers and from members of other social groups without encountering the resistance that frequently discourages the novice fieldworker. Students may, of course, use themselves as the first informants in a research project.

BIBLIOGRAPHY

Books and Articles

The American Heritage Cookbook and Illustrated History of American Eating and Drinking. New York: American Heritage Publishing, 1964.

Anderson, Jay Allan. "Scholarship on Contemporary American Folk Foodways." *Ethnologia Europaea*, 5 (1971), 56–63.

Andrews, Jean. *Peppers: The Domesticated Capsicums*. Austin: University of Texas Press, 1984.

Barber, Edith M. "The Development of the American Food Pattern." *Journal of the American Dietetic Association*, 24 (July 1948), 586–91.

Barthes, Roland. "Ornamental Cookery." In *Mythologies*. Paris: Editions du Seuil, 1957, pp. 78–80.

———. "Toward a Psychosociology of Contemporary Food Consumption." In Elborg Forster and Robert Forster, eds., *European Diet from Pre-industrial to Modern Times*. New York: Harper and Row, 1975, pp. 47–59.

Beard, James A. *James Beard's American Cookery*. Boston: Little, Brown, 1972.

Bennett, John. "Food and Culture in Southern Illinois." *American Sociological Review*, 7 (October 1942), 645–60.

———. "An Interpretation of the Scope and Implications of Social Scientific Research in Human Subsistence." *American Anthropologist*, 48 (October 1946), 553–73.

Biester, Charlotte Elizabeth. *Some Factors in the Development of American Cookbooks*. Field Study Number 2. Ann Arbor, Mich.: University Microfilms, 1950.

Bourke, John Gregory. "The Folk Foods of the Rio Grande Valley and of Northern Mexico." *Journal of American Folklore*, 8 (January–March 1895), 41–71.

Brown, Bob, and Eleanor Parker. *Culinary Americana: 1860–1960*. New York: Roving Eye Press, 1961.

Brown, Dale. *American Cooking*. New York: Time, Inc., 1968.

———. *American Cooking: The Northwest*. New York: Time, Inc., 1970.

Brown, Linda Keller, and Kay Mussell, eds. *Ethnic and Regional Foodways in the United States: The Performance of Group Identity*. Knoxville: University of Tennessee Press, 1984.

Burton, Thomas G., and Ambrose N. Manning. *Folk Methods of Preserving and Processing Food*. East Tennessee University Monograph Series, No. 3. Johnson City, Tenn.: Institute of Regional Studies, 1966, 27–31.

Carson, Jane. *Colonial Virginia Cookery*. Williamsburg, Va.: Colonial Williamsburg, 1968.

Cassell, B. "Jewish Dietary Laws and Food Customs." *Public Health Nursing*, 32 (November 1940), 685–87.

Chang, B. "Some Dietary Beliefs in Chinese Folk Culture." *Journal of the American Dietetic Association*, 65 (October 1974), 436–38.

Claiborne, Craig. *The New York Times Guide to Dining Out in New York*. Rev. ed. New York: Atheneum, 1968.

Clark, Faith, ed. *Symposium III: The Changing Patterns of Consumption of Food*. International Congress of Food Science and Technology. Proceedings of the Congress Symposia, 1962. Vol. 5. New York: Gordon and Breach Science Publications, 1967, 159–254.

Collin, Richard. *New Orleans Restaurant Guide*. New Orleans: Strether and Swann, 1977.

———. *New Orleans Underground Gourmet*. New York: Simon and Schuster, 1973.

———. *The Pleasures of Seafood*. New York: Holt, Rinehart and Winston, 1977.

Committee on Food Habits, National Research Council. *Manual for the Study of Food*

Habits. Bulletin of the National Research Council No. 111, January 1945. Washington, D.C.: National Research Council, 1945.

———. *The Problem of Changing Food Habits*. Bulletin of the National Research Council No. 108, October 1943. Washington, D.C.: National Research Council, 1943.

Cummings, Richard Osborn. *The American and His Food: A History of Food Habits in the United States*. Chicago: University of Chicago Press, 1940.

Cussler, Margaret, and Mary Louise de Give. *Twixt the Cup and the Lip: Psychological and Socio-cultural Factors Affecting Food Habits*. New York: Twayne, 1952.

Dickins, Dorothy. "Changing Pattern of Food Preparation of Small Town Families in Mississippi." *Mississippi Agricultural Experimental Station Bulletin*, 415 (1945), 1–56.

———. "Food Preparation of Owner and Cropper Farm Families in the Shortleaf Pine Area of Mississippi." *Social Forces*, 22 (October 1943), 56–63.

Dickins, Dorothy, and R. N. Ford. "Geophagy Among Mississippi Negro School Children." *American Sociological Review*, 7 (February 1942), 59–65.

Dickson, Paul. *Chow: A Cook's Tour of Military Food*. New York: New American Library, 1978.

Dodson, R. "Tortilla Making." In *In the Shadow of History*. Texas Folklore Society Publications No. 15 (1939), 1–18.

Douglas, Mary. "The Abominations of Leviticus." In *Purity and Danger*. New York: Praeger, 1966, pp. 41–57.

———. "Deciphering a Meal." In Clifford Geertz, ed., *Myth, Symbol, and Culture*. New York: W. W. Norton, 1971, 61–81.

———, ed. *Food in the Social Order: Studies of Food and Festivities in Three American Communities*. New York: Russell Sage Foundation, 1984.

Feibleman, Peter S., and the Editors of Time-Life Books. *American Cooking: Creole and Acadian*. New York: Time, Inc., 1971.

Glaser, Milton, and Jerome Snyder. *The Underground Gourmet*. Rev. ed. New York: Simon and Schuster, 1970.

Greene, Gael. *Bite*. New York: W. W. Norton, 1971.

Harris, Marvin. *Cows, Pigs, Wars, and Witches: The Riddles of Culture*. New York: Random House, 1974.

Hirshorn, Paul, and Steven Izenour. *White Towers*. Cambridge, Mass.: MIT Press, 1979.

Humphrey, N. D. "Some Dietary and Health Practices of Detroit Mexicans." *Journal of American Folklore*, 58 (July 1945), 255–58.

Jones, Michael Owens, Bruce Giuliano, and Roberta Krell, eds. *Foodways and Eating Habits: Directions for Research*. Los Angeles: California Folklore Society, 1981.

Jordan, G. L. *Changing Food Habits in Relation to Land Utilization in the United States*. Carbondale: University of Illinois Press, 1933.

Kroc, Ray. *Grinding It Out: The Making of McDonald's*. Chicago: Henry Regnery, 1977.

Langdon, Philip. *Orange Roofs, Golden Arches: The Architecture of American Chain Restaurants*. New York: Alfred A. Knopf, 1986.

Lasky, Michael S. *The Complete Junk Food Book*. New York: McGraw-Hill, 1977.

Leach, Edmund. "Cooking." In *Culture and Communication*. New York: Cambridge University Press, 1976, pp. 60–61.

Le Gros, Clark F. "Human Food Habits as Determining the Basic Patterns of Economic and Social Life." *Nutrition,* 22 (January 1966), 134–45.

Leonard, Jonathan Norton, and the Editors of Time-Life Books. *American Cooking: New England.* New York: Time, Inc., 1970.

———. *American Cooking: The Great West.* New York: Time, Inc., 1971.

Lévi-Strauss, Claude. "The Culinary Triangle." *Partisan Review,* 33 (Fall 1966), 586–95.

Lincoln, Waldo. *American Cookery Books, 1742–1860.* Worcester, Mass.: American Antiquarian Society, 1954.

Loeb, M. B. "The Social Functions of Food Habits." *Journal of Applied Nutrition,* 4 (1951), 227–29.

Lowenberg, M. E. "Socio-cultural Basis of Food Habits." *Food Technology,* 24 (1970), 27–32.

Massachusetts State Department of Health. *The Food of Working Women in Boston.* Studies in Economic Relations of Women, Vol. 10. Boston: Women's Educational and Industrial Union, Department of Research, 1917.

Mead, Margaret. "The Challenge of Cross-Cultural Research." *Journal of the American Dietetic Association,* 45 (December 1964), 413–14.

———. "Dietary Patterns and Food Habits." *Journal of the American Dietetic Association,* 19 (January 1943), 1–5.

———. *Food Habits Research: Problems of the 1960s.* Publication 1225. Washington, D.C.: National Research Council 1964.

Moser, Ada M. *Farm Family Diets in the Lower Coastal Plains of South Carolina.* Bulletin 319. South Carolina Agricultural Experimental Station, 1939.

———. *Food Habits of South Carolina Farm Families.* Bulletin 343. South Carolina Agricultural Experimental Station, 1942.

Newall, Venetia. "Selected Jamaican Foodways in Homeland and in England." In Linda Degh, Henry Glassie, and Felix J. Oinas, eds., *Folklore Today.* Bloomington: Indiana University Press, 1976, pp. 369–77.

Niehoff, Arthur H. "Food Habits and Cultural Patterns." In Nutrition Foundation, *Food Science and Society.* New York: Nutrition Foundation, 1969, pp. 45–52.

Patten, Marguerite. *Books for Cooks: Bibliography of Cookery.* N.p., 1975.

Paz, Octavio. "Eroticism and Gastrostrophy." *Daedalus,* 101 (Fall 1972), 67–85.

Phillips, Doris E., and Mary A. Bass. "Food Preservation Practices of Selected Homemakers in East Tennessee." *Ecology of Food and Nutrition,* 5 (Winter 1976), 26–39.

Pyke, Magnus. *Food and Society.* London: John Murray, 1968.

———. "The Influence of American Foods and Food Technology in Europe." In C. W. E. Bigsby, ed., *Superculture: American Popular Culture and Europe.* Bowling Green, Ohio: Bowling Green University Popular Press, 1975, pp. 83–95.

Read, R. B. *The San Francisco Underground Gourmet.* New York: Simon and Schuster, 1969.

Root, Waverly. *The Food of France.* New York: Alfred A. Knopf, 1958.

Root, Waverly, and Richard de Rochement. *Eating in America: A History.* New York: William Morrow, 1976.

Sackett, Marjorie. "Folk Recipes as a Measure of Intercultural Penetration." *Journal of American Folklore,* 85 (January–March 1972), 77–91.

Sakr, A. H. "Dietary Regulations and Food Habits of Muslims." *Journal of the American Dietetic Association,* 58 (February 1971), 123–26.

Schweid, Richard. *Hot Peppers: Cajuns and Capsicum in New Iberia, Louisiana.* Seattle: Madrona, 1980.

Shapiro, Laura. *Perfection Salad: Women and Cooking at the Turn of the Century.* New York: Farrar, Straus and Giroux, 1986.

Shenton, James Patrick, et al. *American Cooking: The Melting Pot.* New York: Time, Inc., 1971.

Shorett, Alice, and Murray Morgan. *The Pike Place Market: People, Politics, and Produce.* Seattle: Pacific Search Press, 1982.

Sokolov, Raymond. *Fading Feast: A Compendium of Disappearing American Regional Foods.* New York: Farrar, Straus and Giroux, 1981.

Sorre, Max. "The Geography of Diet." In Phillip L. Wagner and Marvin W. Mikesell, eds., *Readings in Cultural Geography.* Chicago: University of Chicago Press, 1962, pp. 445–56.

Stamets, John. *Portrait of a Market: Photographs of Seattle's Pike Place Market.* Seattle: Real Comet Press, 1987.

Steinberg, Sally Levitt. *The Donut Book.* New York: Alfred A. Knopf, 1987.

Stern, Jane, and Michael Stern. *Roadfood.* New York: Random House, 1977.

Todhunter, E. N. "The History of Food Patterns in the U.S.A." In *Proceedings of the Third International Congress on Dietetics.* New York: Nutrition Foundation, 1961.

Trillin, Calvin. *Alice, Let's Eat.* New York: Random House, 1978.

———. *American Fried.* New York: Penguin Books, 1975.

———. *Third Helpings.* New Haven and New York: Ticknor and Fields, 1983.

Trulson, M. R. "The American Diet: Past and Present." *American Journal of Clinical Nutrition,* 7 (January–February 1959), 91–97.

U.S. Department of Agriculture. *Experimental Station Record.* Washington, D.C.: U.S. Department of Agriculture, 1889–.

U.S. Department of Health, Education and Welfare. *Cumulated Index Medicus.* Washington, D.C.: National Institutes of Health, Public Health Service, 1959–.

Vance, Rupert B. "Climate, Diet, and Human Adequacy." In *Human Geography of the South.* Chapel Hill: University of North Carolina Press, 1932, pp. 411–41.

Vehling, Joseph Dommers. *America's Table.* Chicago: Hostends, 1950.

Viorst, Judith, and Milton Viorst. *The Washington, DC Underground Gourmet.* New York: Simon and Schuster, 1970.

Walter, Eugene. *American Cooking: Southern Style.* New York: Time, Inc., 1971.

Weaver, William Woys, ed. *A Quaker Woman's Cookbook: The Domestic Cookery of Elizabeth Ellicott Lea.* Philadelphia: University of Pennsylvania Press, 1982.

Welsch, Roger. "We Are What We Eat: Omaha Food as Symbol." *Keystone Folklore Quarterly,* 16 (Winter 1971), 165–70.

Wilson, Christine S. "Food Habits: A Selected Annotated Bibliography." *Journal of Nutrition Education,* 5 (January–March 1973), supplement 1, 36–72.

Wilson, Jose. *American Cooking: The Eastern Heartland.* New York: Time, Inc., 1971.

Yoder, Don. "Folk Cookery." In Richard M. Dorson, ed., *Folklore and Folklife: An Introduction.* Chicago: University of Chicago Press, 1972, pp. 325–50.

———. "Historical Sources for American Foodways Research and Plans for an

American Foodways Archive." *Pennsylvania Folklife,* 20 (Spring 1971), 16–29.

———. "Sauerkraut in the Pennsylvania Folk Culture." *Pennsylvania Folklife,* 12 (Summer 1961), 56–59.

———. "Schnitz in the Pennsylvania Folk Culture." *Pennsylvania Folklife,* 12 (Fall 1961), 56–59.

Periodicals

Bon Appétit. Los Angeles, 1955–.
Cuisine. Santa Barbara, Calif., 1970–.
The Digest. Philadelphia, 1977–.
Ecology of Food and Nutrition. London, 1971–.
Food and Foodways. London, 1986–.
Gourmet. New York, 1941–.
International Review of Food and Wine. New York, 1958–.
Journal of Nutrition Education. Berkeley, Calif., 1969–.
Journal of the American Dietetic Association. Chicago, 1925–.
Natural History. New York, 1900–.
The New Yorker. New York, 1924–.
Nutrition Abstracts and Reviews. Boston, 1942–.

Organizations and Trade Publications

Catfish Farmers of America	*The Commercial Fish Farmer*
P.O. Box 2451	
Little Rock, Ark. 72203	
Shellfish Institute of North America	*Shellfish Soundings*
212 Washington Ave., Suite 9	
Baltimore, Md. 21204	
American Frozen Food Institute	*Frozen Food Report*
919 18th St. N.W.	
Washington, D.C. 20006	
American Spice Trade Association	*Spiceletter*
Box 1267	
Englewood Cliffs, N.J. 07632	
American Sugar Cane League	*The Sugar Bulletin*
416 Whitney Bldg.	
New Orleans, La. 70130	

Chocolate Manufacturers Assoc. of the   *The Story of Chocolate*
U.S.A
7900 Westpark Dr. Suite 514
McLean, Va. 22101

Independent Grocers Alliance   *Grocergram*
Distributing Co.
5725 E. River Rd.
Chicago, Ill. 60631

International Federation of Beekeepers'   *Apiatica*
Associations
Corso Vittorio Emanuele 101
00186 Rome, Italy

National Association of Chewing Gum   *The Story of Chewing Gum*
Manufacturers
366 Madison Ave.
New York, N.Y. 10017

National Canners Association   *Canned Food Pack Statistics*
1133 20th St. N.W.
Washington, D.C. 20036

National Hot Dog & Sausage Council   *Hot Dog Fact Sheet*
400 W. Madison
Chicago, Ill. 60606

National Macaroni Manufacturers   *Macaroni Journal*
Association
P.O. Box 336
Palatine, Ill. 60067

Games and Toys

BERNARD MERGEN

Games and toys, as part of the larger topic of play, have been studied by anthropologists, folklorists, psychologists, and historians for a century, and there is general agreement that both are significant in shaping individual personality and cultures. While the use of games and toys is not limited to childhood, it is obvious that in our society these terms are usually reserved for children's activities, with the prefix "adult" attached to games and toys that are not primarily meant for minors. On the other hand, as Jac Remise has pointed out, most toys are made by adults to appeal and sell to other adults.[1] When is a painted replica of a soldier a toy, and when is it a miniature? When is throwing a ball a game, and when is it a sport? Purpose and context can help make some useful distinctions, but the study of games and toys quickly leads to related subjects such as leisure, child development, education, sport, and recreation. Indeed, it is difficult to abstract games and toys from the whole study of work and play.

Games must be subdivided into at least three categories: physical skill, strategy, and chance. Most games involve some combination of the three, and, more often than not, some kind of competition is involved between teams, players, or an individual with himself. Competition may be the key element in distinguishing between games and play since most recent definitions of play emphasize process rather than any specific activity. As Stephen Miller has written: "There are goals in play, but these are of less importance in themselves than as embodiments of the process involved in obtaining them. Process in play is not streamlined toward dealing with goals in the shortest possible way, but is voluntarily elaborated, complicated, in various patterned ways."[2] All games are played, but not all play is a game. Similarly, all toys are played with, but not all play involves toys. Toys may be thought of as props in activities that may involve competition, chance, learning fantasy, entertainment, or even "doing nothing." Games and toys, especially those of children, provide us with material for understanding the development of the mind—of imagination and communication, of ritual and innovation.

HISTORIC OUTLINE

The games and toys of colonial children were those of their British, French, Dutch, and German ancestors. Paintings and engravings by Pieter Breughel, Jacob Cats, and other Dutch artists show children playing tag, blindman's buff, jump rope, and leapfrog. They also depict a variety of stilts, hoops, tops, dolls, kites, and musical instruments. The sixteenth-and seventeenth-century child had a rich assortment of playthings, and there is no reason to suppose that the colonial child did not share in this abundance. Neither the rigors of frontier life nor the strictness of New England Puritanism could eliminate games and toys. Peter Wagner has recently noted that as early as 1649, Thomas Shepard castigated his congregation for spending the Sabbath "in rioting and wantonness, in sports and foolishness."[3].

Prosperity and changing values brought even greater variety to the toy market in the eighteenth century. Benjamin Franklin recalled buying imported toys in Boston in 1713, and English, German, and American potters made miniature dishes and tea sets in increasing quantities. The earliest surviving dolls' house, now in the collection of the Van Cortlandt Museum in New York City, is believed to date from 1774. If we extend the definition of toys, as Katharine McClinton does, to include "antiques of American childhood,"[4] we find interesting examples of silver whistles with coral and bells that were given as christening presents. These small noisemakers are often shown in eighteenth-century portraits of children, either held in a hand or worn on a silver chain around the child's neck. Silver-smiths also made nursing bottles, porringers, and vessels with long spouts called "pap-boats" for the children of wealthy Americans. Pottery cradles made in England also found their way to the colonies, where they were sold for christening and birthday presents.

Older children and adults played with ivory or hardwood "cup and ball" toys, in which the object was to catch the ball in the cup or on the point of the handle that fitted into a small hole in the ball. Battledore and shuttlecock were popular outdoor games, as were marbles and ball games. Each game had its season; marbles came first, in the early spring, followed by kites, tops, and hoops. In New York, the sequence was slightly different, according to the adage: "Top-time's gone, kite-time's come, and April Fool's day will soon be here." Ball games—rudimentary forms of soccer and baseball—were played on holidays. According to William Wells Newell, "In Boston, *Fast-day* (the first Thursday of April) was particularly devoted to this sport. In England, the playing of ball at Easter-tide seems to have been a custom of the festival, inherited probably from pre–Christian ages. Foot-ball was a regular amusement on the afternoon of a New England Thanksgiving."[5] Bowling, hand ball, and hockey were other forms of ball games in seventeenth-and eighteenth-century America.

Indoor games of the same period included backgammon, chess, billiards, and various card games. As early as 1775, the *Pennsylvania Packet* advertised a card game to teach geography; but the heyday of educational card and board games was in the nineteenth century. The appearance of animals in many eighteenth-century family portraits suggests that pets were important elements in children's play. Dogs, cats, birds, squirrels, lambs, and even deer were part of the domestic scene. The legacy of Puritanism clouded the enjoyment of some of this kind of play, however, since the 1773 edition of *The New England Primer* illustrated the letter C with the rhyme: "The Cat doth play, And after slay." Samuel Goodrich described another indoor pastime of late eighteenth-century boys: "During my youthful days I found the penknife a source of great amusement, even instruction. Many a long winter evening, many a dull, drizzly day . . . have I spent in great ecstasy making candlerods or some other simple article of household goods, for my mother, or in perfecting toys for myself and my young friends."[6]

A generation later, Edward Everett Hale grew up with "an infinite variety of amusements—almost everything we wanted for purposes of manufacture or invention. Whalebone, spiral springs, pulleys and catgut, for perpetual motion or locomotive carriages, rollers and planks for floats . . . good blocks for building, carpenter's tools, a work-bench, and printing materials. . . . When we became chemists we might have sulphuric acid, nitric acid, litmus paper, or whatever we desired, so our allowance would stand it. I was not more than seven years old when I burned off my eyebrows by igniting gun-powder with my burning glass."[7] The 1830s and 1840s witnessed the birth of the American toy and game industry. William S. Tower, a carpenter in South Hingham, Massachusetts, organized a guild of toymakers in the late 1830s, and Franklin Peale exhibited a small steam locomotive made by Matthias Baldwin at the Peale family's Philadelphia museum. For the next forty years, wooden and metal toys were usually produced as a sideline by craftsmen engaged in cabinetmaking or tool manufacturing.

Paper toys and games were developed by stationers and lithographers. The titles of some board and card games echo the concerns of the period. In 1843, W. & B. Ives of Salem, Massachusetts, issued a highly moralistic board game, "The Mansion of Happiness," intended to teach young Americans to practice the virtues of industry, honesty, and sobriety. The following year introduced "The Game of Pope or Pagan or the Missionary Campaign or the Siege of the Stronghold of Satan by the Christian Army."

By the 1860s, moralism began to be replaced by current events and an emphasis on material success. Milton Bradley's tremendously popular "The Checkered Game of Life," which appeared in 1860, alternated squares printed with "wealth," "happiness," "industry," and "ambition," with others labeled "gambling," "poverty," "jail," and "suicide."

"In 1868," according to McClinton, "four games of war and patriotism were packaged together under the title "The Union Games'"[8] Anagrams, puzzles, Zoetropes (a slotted revolving drum that gives the viewer the sense of moving pictures), and conversation cards gained in popularity through the 1860s. Conversation cards, which printed questions such as "Have you ever been in love?" and "What is your favorite food?," were intended to enliven the "cold and ceremonious" social gatherings that European travelers often found in the United States. The McLoughlin Brothers' catalog of 1867 lists seven kinds of conversation cards, including "Loves and Likes," " Comical Conversation Cards," "Conversations on Marriage," and "Quizzical Questions and Quaint Replies." Another type of game involving dialogue is illustrated by "Japhet Jenkins and Sally Jones visit to Boston," copyrighted in 1867. In this game, cards with brief sentences are shuffled and dealt to the players, who take turns reading them and filling in blanks in a book that tells the adventures of a pair of country bumpkins visiting the city.

In 1883, sixteen-year-old George S. Parker invented his first game, the "Game of Banking." Subsequent games also reflected the concerns of the Gilded Age. "The Game of Moneta: or Money Makes Money" appeared in the Montgomery Ward catalog of 1889, and a "Game of Business" came out in 1895. One of the most popular games of the period was marketed by the Crandalls in 1889 under the name "Pigs in Clover." This puzzle required the player to maneuver four marbles through a maze into a cardboard enclosure. Hundreds of thousands were sold, and the game seems to have been especially popular in Washington, D.C., where the symbolism of the spoils system was obvious. Political election games appeared regularly in the late nineteenth century, and an interesting study could be done by comparing the "Centennial Presidential Game" of 1876 with the "Presidential Election" game of 1892, "Politics" of the 1950s, and "Bigwig" in 1973.

Games and toys were inspired by every conceivable event. The Chicago Columbian Exposition of 1893 was commemorated in games, puzzles, and building blocks. "Sherlock Holmes" and "The Amusing Game of Innocence Abroad" profited from the popularity of the books that preceded them. "White Squadron Picture Puzzles" helped to make the names of the war ships *Baltimore, Chicago,* and *Monterey* familiar to American children. The 1886 catalog of sporting goods and games sold by the Peck & Snyder Company lists chess, checkers, lotto, dominoes, Parcheesi, cards, bagatelle, cribbage, tetotums or spinning dice, and dice, as well as a board game called

"The Monopolist." "On the board," the catalog reads, "the great struggle between Capital and Labor can be fought out to the satisfaction of all parties, and, if the players are successful, they can break the Monopolist, and become Monopolists themselves." Again, it would be instructive to compare this game with the well-known Parker Brothers game, "Monopoly," introduced in 1935. Robert H. Canary's essay on "Monopoly," and the 1950s "Game of Life" and James M. Hughes's comparison of "Monopoly" and "The Cities Game" are suggestive beginnings. The "Class Struggle" game, marketed in 1978 by political science professor Bertell Ollman, offers still another point of comparison.

The plethora of games in the twentieth century reveals much about American culture. Since most of these games involve elements of chance as well as strategy, they may reflect a growing uncertainty about the future and the desire to prepare individuals "to endure bad times in the hope of brighter futures." This is the hypothesis advanced by J. M. Roberts and Brian Sutton-Smith in their work on "Child Training and Game Involvement" in non-Western societies. Luck has always played a significant, if neglected, role in American thought, and a study of gambling games, especially among children, would be rewarding. The problem, of course, is that like other illegal activities, few records exist that describe gambling games. One of the few comes from Stewart Culin, an anthropologist and museum curator, who described "Street Games of Boys in Brooklyn, New York" in 1891. Culin found a game that the boys called "Pictures," which was played by shooting the cards found in cigarette packages toward a wall, the winner being the boy whose card landed nearest the wall. The winner then threw all the cards into the air and kept the ones that fell face up. Culin's ten-year-old informant claimed to be ignorant of the related game—penny pitching. "It was regarded among his associates as a vulgar game, and only practiced by bootblacks and boys of the lowest class, such as compose the 'gangs' that are a well-known feature of street life among the boys of our cities."[9]

There are many other kinds of toys that parallel adult activities. Toy models of steam engines, trains, telegraphs, telephones, washing machines, automobiles, and airplanes appeared soon after their introduction in the adult world. In some cases, an inventor seems to have no clear purpose and tries out his invention in toy form. Edison put one of his early phonograph cylinders in a "Talking Doll" in 1890. Dolls' houses and doll house furniture are obvious examples of toys that follow the fashion and changes in technology. Building materials are another example. In 1901, a British inventor, Frank Hornby, patented a set of construction materials made of thin strips of metal with perforations for nuts and bolts. His "Mechanics Made Easy," or "Meccano," was soon copied in the United States as "Erector" sets, allowing American children to build skyscraper skeletons to mirror those outside their bedroom windows. Charles Pajeau's 1914 patent for "Tinkertoys" followed the same general idea of building in outline, but his colorful rods, knobs, and pulleys seem closer to the abstract forms of the Armory Show than to the cantilever of the Queensboro Bridge. Pajeau may also have borrowed his idea from Friedrich Froebel, whose rods, strings, and balls inspired the young Frank Lloyd Wright in 1876.

Occasionally, however, the power of toys to mold the habits and talents of children fails. During World War I, Edward Hurley, chairman of the United States Shipping Board, decided that Americans should learn the value of the merchant marine and persuaded the Ives Toy Manufacturing Company to make a copy of the standard merchant ship being constructed by the Emergency Fleet Corporation. In his letter to the company, Hurley wrote: "It is none too early to begin waking Americans to the importance of ships, putting ships and the sea into their daily thought and work, and making ships appeal to the imagination of everybody in the country. We want to reach the children as well as the grown-ups, and, in this connection knowing how closely toys follow popular interest and what an educative value they have, it has been in my mind to have this great new national interest before the men who invent and design your goods."[10] When the Ives catalog for 1919 appeared, the advertising copy echoed Hurley's patriotic note: A boy "can get thoroughly interested in the great game of commerce and the big Merchant marine of his country. He can talk it, play it and interest his chums in it. . . . Who knows but what it may lead them into the big business of transportation by sea that is going to play such a wonderful part in the future world trade of the United States?" The ironic end to this effort to build support for an American merchant marine was the bankruptcy of the Ives Company in 1929, a collapse that Ives's accountants attributed in part to poor sales of the toy merchant fleet.

Turning from toys to games played without equipment, the historical record is strongest for the years since 1883, when folklorists, psychologists, and anthropologists first began to study children's play systematically. In that year, William Wells Newell, linguist, poet, and folklorist, published *Games and Songs of American Children*. This collection of almost 200 folksongs and counting-out rhymes, clapping and ring games, tag and guessing games gives us a sense of the complexity and formality of games in the 1870s. Few adults or children today would be willing to memorize the long poem, "Knights of Spain," that accompanied a popular kissing game. Some songs, such as the familiar "Barbara Allen," were used to circumvent the religious ban on dancing. As the ballad was sung, couples kept time with slow movements without changing place. Newell's research showed that most American games and songs had British and European origins. He was impressed by the conservatism of children in preserving these games, but he was also afraid that increased immigration, urbanization, and industrialization were destroying traditional games.

There is some evidence that cities made play difficult. In 1892, Washington, D.C., passed an ordinance that declared it unlawful "for any person or persons to play the game of football, or any other game with a ball, in any of the streets, avenues, or alleys in the cities of Washington and Georgetown; nor shall it be lawful for any person or persons to play the game of bandy, shindy, or any other game by which a ball, stone, or other substance is struck or propelled by any stick, cane, or other substance in any street, avenue, or alley."[11] In the same year, Helen and Robert Lynd tell us, Muncie, Indiana, made it illegal to pitch quoits or coins, to play cricket, bandy, cat, townball, or any other game of public amusement, or to discharge a gun, pistol, or firearm on Sunday. Both laws tell us a great deal about the play life of small cities and towns and about the kinds of games and where they were played. Whether the motive was a reformist hope that play could be regulated in school yards and playgrounds, or a conservative desire to maintain fundamental religious values, the 1890s and the early twentieth century saw numerous efforts to redefine games and play.

Observers unanimously agreed that most children were "doing nothing" and wasting their time when they were not working. A survey in Milwaukee, Wisconsin, in 1911, put the percentages at 19 percent working, 31 percent playing, and 50 percent doing nothing on a typical November day.[12] A similar survey in Cleveland, Ohio, on June 23, 1913, found 10 percent working, 50 percent playing, and 40 percent of the city's children doing nothing.[13] Of those who were playing, 43 percent were described as "just fooling." Doing nothing and just fooling were categories that included breaking windows, chalking suggestive words on buildings, standing around on corners, fighting, looking at pictures of women in tights on billboards, stealing, and gambling with dice, cards, buttons, marbles, and beer bottle tags. Joseph Lee, Luther Gulick, Henry Curtis, and others sought to improve opportunities for urban recreation under the supervision of professional playground directors. The founding of the Playground Association in 1906 and the publication the following year of the first issue of *The Playground* (now *Parks and Recreation*) mark the beginnings of highly organized children's games and play in the United States.

Typical of the way in which traditional games were appropriated by the recreation movement is a list published in the *Seventh Annual Report of the Department of Playgrounds* of Washington, D.C., in 1918. Games were divided into "Low Organized Games," "High Organized Games," "Quiet Games," "Races," "Relay," and "Memory and Sense Games." An example of each included "Prisoners Base," "Basketball," "Boiler Burst," "Wheelbarrow," "All up Indian Club," and "Ghosts." Early surveys of games and play suggest that there have been important changes in game preferences among American children. For example, T. R. Croswell, who studied about 2,000 schoolchildren in Worcester, Massachusetts, in 1896, found only 4 of 1,000 boys playing cowboys and Indians and only 2 who mentioned playing with toy soldiers. Girls' game preferences seem to have changed more than boys' in the past century, with many more girls playing games that were played exclusively by boys in the past, such as leapfrog and red rover. Boys and girls now play few singing and dialogue games such as those recorded by Newell, and many of the rhymes that were recited with those games are now used in jump rope.

Brian Sutton-Smith argues that children's play has become more sophisticated and that fantasy play and games involving the manipulation of symbols have been encouraged by middle-class parents.[14] Playground planners in the United States are trying to introduce "Adventure Playgrounds," in which children are encouraged to organize and develop their own games and to build their own play structures. A new vocabulary has entered the playground movement: "loose parts," "ambiguity," "flexibility," "diversity," "change," and "open-endedness." The contemporary student of games is faced with a bewildering variety of theories and an equally confusing body of raw data. Games, toys, and play serve many functions, not the least of which is to help cope with a chaotic, violent, and even dangerous world. We should not be surprised to find much that is shocking in play, but we must try to understand what is actually going on, rather than impose preconceived definitions of what play is and what it is not. We must try to discover what games and toys mean to the players. For that, we may well begin with ourselves.

The 1980s have seen the commercial development of home computer games, the cultural impact of which is not yet measurable. Two things seem clear, however: first, that these games will continue to compete for the free time of the players, thereby reducing time for other activities, and second, that children as young as six can learn to play games on the computer, so that a new generation is growing up that is completely at ease with electronic games that were formerly played with dice on boards and with more sophisticated interactive games that further encourage solitary play. Children under seven are being introduced to electronic learning aids such as Speak & Spell, Sesame Street, and Whiz Kid, but the favorite toys continue to be action figures such as G.I. Joe, robots like the Transformers, baby dolls like the Cabbage Patch Kids, and fashion dolls such as Barbie. The popularity of weapons such as Laser Tag and Phasor Force Guns has sparked renewed debate among psychiatrists and child development experts.

REFERENCE WORKS

Since definitions of games, toys, and play vary widely, and because so little basic research has been done, this section will list several kinds of reference material. First, and most basic, are the handful of bibliographies that list primary and secondary works on games and play. For games in general, including those used in education and by the military, the most complete bibliography is in *The Study of Games,* edited by Elliott M. Avedon and Brian Sutton-Smith. Their book is also an anthology of articles on the historical, anthropological, and folkloristic aspects of games.

Child's Play, edited by R. E. Herron and Brian Sutton-Smith, is also an anthology with a bibliography of over 700 items on the theory of play and on psychological studies of children's play. It should be supplemented with Helen B. Schwartzman's "Research on Children's Play: An Overview and Some Predictions" and "Works on Play: A Bibliography," both of which may be found in *Studies in the Anthropology of Play: Papers in Memory of B. Allan Tindall,* edited by Phillips Stevens, Jr. Schwartzman's bibliography of over 250 items combines both psychological and anthropological studies and includes publications through 1976. Barbara Kirshenblatt-Gimblett's *Speech Play* contains an excellent bibliographical essay on the linguistic and cultural aspects of play. Jean-Leo's *Jouets, jeux, livres d'enfant: repertoire bibliographique d'ouvrages utiles aux collectionneurs et aux chercheurs, augmente de nombreux articles inedits* is a useful starting place for foreign-language books and articles.

There is no bibliography on American toys, but Roland Renson and B. Van Reusel have published a brief list of works on European toys. Moreover, the distinction between reference works and general histories of toys and dolls is not clear. Among those books that are basically catalogs of different types of toys and games, *The Collector's Encyclopedia of Dolls* by Dorothy, Elizabeth, and Evelyn Coleman ranks high. Leslie Daiken's *Children's Toys Throughout the Ages* is typical of an older, collector's approach to the subject, but it is useful for its discussion of various definitions of toys. Daiken's *World of Toys: A Guide to the Principal Public and Private Collections in Great Britain* is also a useful starting place for the study of eighteenth-and nineteenth-century toys, especially since the United States imported a great many British and European toys.

For this country, the basic reference work is still Louis Hertz's 1947 guide, *The Handbook of Old American Toys,* which has a brief introduction to such topics as classification, identification, materials, and terminology. Hertz arranges his study by tin toys, cast iron, clockwork, wooden, steam, banks, cannon, cap pistols, musical toys, electric toys, trains, toy household equipment, games, wheel toys, and dolls. His more recent book, *The Toy Collector,* has useful chapters on research as well as a guide to manufacturers and to identification marks. Another excellent work is Katharine McClinton's *Antiques of American Childhood,* a guide that expands the definition of toy to include children's costumes, buttons, furniture, dishes, and needlework.

Specialized reference works include Ann E. Grinham's *Japanese Games and Toys;* Ceil Chandler's *Toys and Dolls Made in Occupied Japan* Kenny Harman's *Comic Strip Toys;* Gwen White's *Toys and Dolls: Marks and Labels;* Cecil Gibson's *A History of British Dinky Toys: Model Car and Vehicle Issues, 1934–1964;* and Linda Hannas's *The English Jigsaw Puzzle, 1760–1890; with* a *Descriptive Check-list of Puzzles in the Museums of Great Britain and the Author's Collection.* Fred Ferretti's *The Great American Marble Book* contains color illustrations of dozens of different kinds of marbles and the games played with them. Ferretti's *The Great American Book of Sidewalk, Stoop, Dirt, Curb, and Alley Games* is less successful because it only touches on each kind of game. A more satisfying collection is Alan Milberg's *Street Games.* Although they are not reference books in the usual sense, the Ferretti and Milberg books provide 1970s comparisons to the great collections of Douglas, Gomme, Newell, and the Opies.

Newell's classic *Games and Songs of American Children* has been cited above, but it is the British who provide the most comprehensive game surveys. *The Traditional Games of England, Scotland, and Ireland* by Alice Gomme, *London Street Games* by Norman Douglas, and *Children's Games in Street and Playground* by Iona and Peter Opie supply a detailed history of games of the past century. The Opies more recent *The Lore and Language of School Children* adds still more to our knowledge of outdoor play. Roger D. Abrahams's *Jump-Rope Rhymes: A Dictionary,* Bess Lomax Hawes and Bessie Jones's *Step It Down: Games, Plays, Songs and Stories from the Afro-American Heritage,* and Paul G. Brewster's *American Nonsinging Games* are the only American surveys since Newell that attempt a wide sample of selected types of play, although Mary and Herbert Knapp provide a useful beginning in *One Potato, Two Potato . . . The Secret Education of American Children.* For native Americans, Stewart Culin's *Games of North American Indians* remains unsurpassed. Brian Sutton-Smith's *The Games of New Zealand Children* and *A History of Children's Play: New Zealand, 1840–1950* offer an inventory of play from another transplanted English society.

Perhaps the most useful reference works for the student of games and toys are still the catalogs of the toy manufacturers and retailers and their trade publications. Some of the catalogs have been reprinted. Peck & Snyder's *Sporting Goods and Games 1886* has been published by the Pyne Press and contains an overwhelming assortment of uniforms, equipment, magic tricks, joke books and play scripts, microscopes and telescopes, steam toys, and magic lanterns. *The Wonderful World of Toys, Games and Dolls,* edited by Joseph J. Schroeder, Jr., contains reprints from the catalogs of F.A.O. Schwartz, Montgomery Ward, Marshall Field, and other stores from 1862 to 1930. By far the most important trade journal is *Playthings,* which has been published monthly since 1903. Each issue has articles on toy manufacturing and advertising from most of the large firms. Other trade journals include *Toy World,* which was published in San Francisco in the 1920s and which merged with *Toys and Novelties* (now *Toys*) in 1936; and *Toy Manufacturer,* published in Atlanta. For the German toy industry, *Das Spielzeug,* published in Bamberg, provides trade information.

There are also several magazines and newspapers published by and for collectors: *Antique Toy World, Collectibles Monthly, Miniature Collector,* and

Toy Trains are good examples. These publications are useful for discovering private collections, and they often contain articles on toy and doll manufacturers. There are three published censuses of toy manufacturers—one in 1927, one in 1931, and another in 1940. The Department of Commerce also sponsored two studies of the international toy business—Jeannette M. Calvin's *International Trade in Toys* in 1926 and E. D. Schutrumpf's *World Trade in Toys* in 1939. Both volumes contain detailed statistics on exports and imports of toys in all industrialized countries. *Willson's Canadian Toy, Notion and Station Directory* provides a basic list of toy firms in that country, while *The Toy Trader and Exporter and Toy Trader Year Book* serve the British industry.

RESEARCH COLLECTIONS

Almost every museum and historical society has a collection of games, toys, and dolls that is used for an annual Christmas display. The student of games and toys should always begin research with a visit to the local museum. The next step would be to identify private collectors and collections. There are, however, a number of museums throughout the country with large and growing collections of toys. The following cannot claim to be a complete list of all the significant doll and toy collections, but it does represent a good sample of the museums that responded to the letter of inquiry I sent to about forty institutions in the summer of 1978. The museums are listed with the address and name of the appropriate curator when available. Researchers should always write in advance to the institution they wish to visit, so that the curator has time to assemble relevant materials.

The Atlanta Historical Society (P.O. Box 12423, Atlanta 30355) has a few items relating to nineteenth-and twentieth-century children's play. It has recently acquired a collection of twenty-six dolls. Lisa Reynolds, curator, has a special interest in the toy collection. There is also a new Toy Museum of Atlanta (2800 Peachtree Road, NW, Atlanta 30305). The Atwater Kent Museum (15 South Seventh Street, Philadelphia 19106) has a small collection of eighteenth-, nineteenth-, and twentieth-century dolls, as well as some iron toys and some blocks and board games. The Bucks County Historical Society and the Mercer Museum (Pine Street, Doylestown, Pennsylvania 18901) have a small collection accessible by appointment with Laurie J. Rufe, curator. Among the animals, banks, blocks, dolls, dolls' houses, games, puppets, rocking horses, tops, and wagons is a coffin made for a doll owned by Ella Good of Solebury, Pennsylvania, in about 1850.

A small, uncataloged collection of dolls, doll house furnishings, board games, trucks, and cars is available by appointment at the Chicago Historical Society (Clark Street at North Avenue, Chicago 60614). The Children's Museum (30th Street and Meridian, Indianapolis 46208) is one of the largest and most comprehensive children's museums. It has educational programs and exhibits of many kinds, and a permanent exhibit of toys opened in December 1978. The museum owns a well-documented collection of over 1,000 toy cars from the 1950s and has one of the largest toy train collections in the country. Mary Jane Teeters is curator of dolls and Judi Ryan is head of the Department of Collections. Colonial Williamsburg (P.O. Box C, Williamsburg, Virginia 23185) has a number of games and toys. There is no catalog, but there are files available to scholars for research by appointment.

The Colorado Historical Society (The Colorado Heritage Center, 1300 Broadway, Denver 80203) has a good collection of toys, including household items, board games, guns, ships, toy soldiers, cowboys, Indians, and badges. A collection of about 200 dolls and a few toys may be examined in the Daughters of the American Revolution Museum (1776 D Street, NW, Washington, D.C. 20006). The Essex Institute (Salem, Massachusetts 01970) has dolls, dolls' houses, trains, and cast-iron wagons. An illustrated book, *Dolls and Toys at the Essex Institute,* by Madeline and Richard Merrill, describes the collection. Kenneth Wilson, director of collections, Greenfield Village and the Henry Ford Museum (Dearborn, Michigan 48121), describes the toys and games in his institution as "too numerous to mention." The Maryland Historical Society (201 West Monument Street, Baltimore 21201) has a large and varied toy collection, including some outstanding dolls' houses reflecting the architectural styles of the state.

A small collection of dolls, both homemade and commercial, a football game played with marbles, and a number of games taken from comic strips may be found at the Nevada Historical Society (1650 North Virginia Street, Reno 89503). The Museum of International Folk Art, a division of the Museum of New Mexico (Box 2087, Santa Fe 87503) has a few contemporary toys, and its curators are negotiating for the purchase of the Girard Foundation Collection of 75,000 folk toys. This collection is partially described in Alexander H. Girard's *El Encanto de un Pueblo. The Magic of a People: Folk Art and Toys from the Collection of the Girard Foundation.* The Newport Historical Society (82 Touro Street, Newport, Rhode Island 02840) has a limited number of toys, but a large collection of dolls and furnished dolls' houses. One of the best exhibits of dolls' houses may be found in the Museum of the City of New York (1220 Fifth Avenue, New York 10029). John Noble, curator, has published widely on dolls. In the same city, the New-York Historical Society (170 Central Park West at 77th Street, New York 10024) has an extensive collection of nineteenth-century carved animals by Wilhelm Schimmel; a peddler's cart dated 1884 with miniature pots and pans; a walking doll patented in 1862 and sold under the name "Autoperipatetikos"; circus toys, including ball-jointed wooden animals, from Albert Schoenhut's 1902 "Humpty Dumpty Circus"; and tin toys from George W. Brown of Forestville, Connecticut, made in 1856.

Old Salem (Drawer F, Salem Station, Winston-Salem, North Carolina 27108) has late eighteenth-and nineteenth-century toys, games, dolls, and books that are displayed in a Boys' School Museum. Old Sturbridge Village Sturbridge, Massachusetts 01566) has four or five hundred toys, games, dolls, and dolls' tea sets exhibited in its buildings. *Child Life in New England* by Elizabeth George Speare draws on this collection. The Perelman Antique Toy Museum (270 South Second Street, Philadelphia 19106) has 225 of the 243 known types of mechanical banks made between 1867 and 1902. This private museum also contains many cap pistols and automata. The Seattle Historical Society (2161 East Hamlin Street, McCurdy Park, Seattle, Washington 98112) has a collection of over 2,000 dolls, several hundred toys and games, and several hundred books on marionettes and puppetry. A large collection of marionettes, as well as doll furniture, building blocks, mechanical toys, models, banks, stuffed toys, and games, is exhibited in the Toy Shop at the Shelburne Museum (Shelburne, Vermont 05482). Shelburne also has several hundred dolls in its variety unit and a small, but good, research library.

Both the National Museum of History and Technology and the National Museum of Natural History of the Smithsonian Institution (Washington, D.C. 20560) have collections relating to games and toys. In the former, the Division of Domestic Life of the Department of Cultural History has the Sears, Roebuck Collection of cast-iron toys. Some interesting material on nineteenth-century games and toys may be gleaned from the 1,700 lithographs in the Harry T. Peters "America on Stone" Collection. The Division of Extractive Industries of the Department of Industries administers the millions of items in the Warshaw Collection of Business Americana, some of which relate to games and toys. The ethnographic collections of the Natural History Museum contain games and toys from around the world. The museum's library has the Human Relations Area File, which facilitates cross-cultural comparisons of games and toys. Genre paintings often contain data on games and toys, and the collections of the National Gallery of Art, the Hirshhorn Museum and Sculpture Garden, the National Portrait Gallery, the Freer Gallery of Art, and the National Collection of Fine Arts should all be consulted. The library of the National Collection of Fine Arts houses the Inventory of American Painting executed before 1914, a computerized index of 175,000 paintings in public and private collections throughout the country. There are several entries under the subject classification "Sports and Games." The staff of the children's area of the Festival of American Folklife, especially Kate Rinzler, have gathered considerable material on games and children's lore. Tapes, videotapes, and publications are available from the Office of American and Folklife Studies. The two newest Smithsonian museums—the National Air and Space Museum and the Museum of African Art—can provide information on toys and games in their respective areas of specialization.

Finally, also in Washington, four other institutions have valuable information on games and toys. The Library of Congress (Washington, D.C. 20540), through its rare book collections, folk music division, and in its vast holdings of prints and photographs, contains an unequalled store of material on games and toys. Within the Prints and Photographs Division, for example, the Farm Security Administration and Office of War Information photographs of America in the 1930s and 1940s, the Frances Benjamin Johnston and Theodor Horydczak collections, and the George Grantham Bain Collection are especially rich on play, games, and toys in the period 1890 to 1945. The Copyright Division of the Library of Congress should also be consulted, as should the Patent Office (2021 Jefferson Davis Highway, Arlington, Virginia 20231). Another rich source for visual material is the Audio-Visual Division of the National Archives and Records Service. Here, for example, you can find the Helen Levitt photographs of children's chalk drawings in the streets of New York in the late 1930s and thousands of feet of motion picture film of children playing in the years 1914 to 1934, taken by cameramen for the Ford Motor Company. For color photographs of play and games in the 1970s, the files of Documerica at the Environmental Protection Agency (401 M Street, SW, Washington, D.C. 20460) contain some good examples.

The large collection of games and toys owned by the Society for the Preservation of New England Antiquities (Harrison Gray Otis House, 141 Cambridge Street, Boston 02114) is in storage and is inaccessible to scholars. Fortunately, this is not the case with the superb collections of the Margaret Woodbury Strong Museum (700 Allen Creek Road, Rochester, New York 14618). Here one can see many of the 25,000 dolls, 600 dolls' houses, and thousands of models, miniatures, toys, and playing cards that the museum owns. A new building is planned for 1979, which will provide more exhibit space. A knowledgeable staff, including H. J. Swinney, director; Lawrence L. Belles, chief curator; Mr. and Mrs. Blair Whitton, specialist curators; and Barbara Jendrick, curator of paper dolls, is also available. The Washington Dolls' House and Toy Museum (5236 44th Street, NW, Washington, D.C. 20015) is a small private museum founded by Flora Gill Jacobs, author of several books on dolls' houses and furniture. Mrs. Jacobs has a small, but excellent, collection of Schoenhut animals, including a circus, a Theodore Roosevelt safari, a Bliss village, and some games. A recent acquisition—an elaborate dolls' house made in Puebla, Mexico, in the early twentieth century—provides an interesting contrast to the houses made north of the Rio Grande.

Perhaps the finest collection of paper dolls and toys in the United States can be found in the library of the Winterthur Museum (Winterthur, Delaware 19735). The Maxine Waldron Collection of Children's Books and Paper Toys contains hundreds of items, mostly American, but with some English and European paper dolls, games, peep shows, panoramas, paper soldiers, valentines, and Christmas cards and decorations. Among the rare items are the "Protean Figure of Metamorphic Costumes" published by S. and J. Fuller in 1811; "Flora, the Game of Flowers"; "Newton's New Game of Virtue Rewarded and Vice Punished"; and the paper dolls, "Lady of New York," "The Virtuous Girl," "Jenny Lind," "Little Henry," and "Ellen, or the Naughty Girl Reclaimed." Some of the other games, dolls, and toys in the Winterthur's collections may be seen in the rooms of the museum. Last, but not least, the State Historical Society of Wisconsin (816 State Street, Madison 53706) has a large collection of children's toys and games dating from the 1850s to the present. An annual Christmas exhibit, emphasizing playthings of Wisconsin children, displays some of the society's material. Carol T. Larsen, registrar of the museum, has a special interest in the subject of games and toys.

The Please Touch Museum in Philadelphia has created a Childlife Center to collect toys, children's clothing and furniture, and the archival records of organizations dealing with children and children's play, particularly in the Delaware Valley. A major acquisition is the Child Development Association (CDA) Consortium archives. The CDA was founded in 1972 to assess the competence of child-care personnel and to grant credentials to persons assessed as competent. The records cover the years 1971 to 1985 and are being supplemented by an oral history project. Another important research collection may be found at the Western Kentucky University Folklore, Folklife, and Oral History Archive in Bowling Green, Kentucky. The archive contains material on play, games, toys, and toymaking in the region.

HISTORY AND CRITICISM

Games and toys have drawn attention from four kinds of writers—hobbyists and collectors, who are usually interested in a fairly narrow aspect of the subject; moralists, who select examples from children's play to make points about the corruption of society; psychologists, who use games and toys to study human development; and a handful of historians, who have attempted to make the subject a respectable part of social history. Among the first of the serious collectors was Louis Hertz, whose numerous books have been cited throughout this chapter. One of his best contributions to the history of toys is *Messrs. Ives of Bridgeport,* a study of the Ives Manufacturing Company's sixty years of toymaking. Another pioneer collector who has written well-researched books on dolls' houses is Flora Gill Jacobs. Her *A History of Dolls' Houses,* which first appeared in 1953, is a fascinating account of these objects from the sixteenth century to the present. Her introduction contains one of the few discussions of what seems to be a universal human attraction for smallness and miniaturization. Her illustrations and text reveal a number of interesting details about the relation of dolls' houses to the "larger" world, including the fact that a California bungalow doll's house appeared in 1920, a doll's swimming pool in 1928, and a Frank Lloyd Wright-style house in 1936. Wooden furniture was rapidly replaced by metal after 1922, when Tootsietoy began to produce doll furniture for the mass market, and metal was challenged by plastic after 1946. Mrs. Jacobs's *Dolls' Houses in America: Historic Preservation in Miniature* continues her studies and develops the thesis that many regional architectural styles survive in unaltered form in these "toys."

Toys in America by Inez and Marshall McClintock falls between a collector's reference work and a historian's interpretative survey. Although they suspected "that toys might give some insight into our entire society: that the amount of play, the number and nature of toys might reveal a great deal about any stage of our history," they stick to descriptive narrative history and fail to prove "that toys and games were indeed accurate mirrors of the adult world." The same may be said of Jac Remise and Jean Fondin's *The Golden Age of Toys,* which was first published in Switzerland in 1967. The beautiful photographs, many in color, more than compensate for the lack of interpretation in the text, however. Patrick Murray's *Toys,* Charles Best's *Cast Iron Toy Pistols, 1870–1940: A Collector's Guide,* Betty Cadbury's *Playthings Past,* and David Pressland's *The Art of the Tin Toy* are all good examples of the excellent work done by curators and collectors in recent years.

Ever since 1882 when Herbert Spencer proclaimed the "gospel of relaxation," moralists and social critics have used games and play to argue that society is in desperate need of reform. Thus, in 1928, Stuart Chase attacked a hedonistic and mass-minded America in his essay on "Play" in Charles Beard's *Whither Mankind.* Twenty years later, David Riesman reversed Chase and found evidence for the development of "autonomous" man in the sphere of games and play. In *The Lonely Crowd,* Riesman went so far as to warn that "a conspiracy of silence about leisure and play is its best protection." The 1950s was a decade of great debate among sociologists and social critics about the proper uses of leisure. In France, both Roland Barthes and Roger Caillois published on the meaning of toys and games. Barthes, in *Mythologies,* saw toys as microcosms of the materialism of the adult world, while Caillois took a more detached stance in *Les Jeux et les hommes,* which was published in English as *Man, Play, and Games.* Nevertheless, Caillois moralizes about the loss of courtesy in competitive games and the corruption of masks into uniforms in contemporary society. This kind of criticism continued in the 1970s in an interesting variety of forms.

Stanley Aronowitz has written of "The Egalitarian Promise of Children's Games," and Frank and Theresa Caplan, owners of Creative Playthings from 1944 to 1966, have expounded on *The Power of Play.* The Caplans drew on an impressive range of authorities from Cicero to Jean Piaget, but often overstated their case and frequently expressed a regrettable ethnocentrism: "We believe the Mexican, Asiatic, and Indian child for whom there is no lively play during early childhood loses the ability to create imaginary situations. An examination of the play materials of these cultures shows them to be made of clay, papier-mâché, and flimsy wood, none of which lend themselves to active use . . . Introduce the rubber or vinyl doll, building blocks, and other unbreakable toys, and we maintain that the innate playfulness of these children would quickly be given active support." Two years earlier, in 1971, Edward M. Swartz had attacked the toy industry for unsafe toys and deceptive advertising. *Toys That Don't Care* follows Ralph Nader and other consumer advocates in finding considerable hazards in the marketplace. The industry lashed back with a moralist of its own. Marvin Kaye, former editor of *Toys*, wrote *A Toy Is Born* as a partial refutation of Swartz. Most of Kaye's book consists of brief chapters on well-known manufacturers—Lionel, Parker Brothers, Lesney, and others. Most readers will be touched by nostalgia for their childhoods when they read about the invention of Silly Putty at General Electric in 1945, Wham-O's first Frisbee in 1956, and Hasbro's G.I. Joe of 1963, but few will be convinced by Kaye's defense of the toy industry since the Child Protection and Toy Safety Act of 1969.

The third group of game and toy scholars is the psychologist. Beginning with G. Stanley Hall's studies in the 1880s, an impressive body of literature has developed. These are usefully summarized in Susanna Miller's *The Psychology of Play*. Among the major theorists in child development, Erik Erikson is the most readable. His *Childhood and Society* has influenced research in half a dozen fields in the past thirty years. Erikson's insistence on the opportunity for children to develop their imaginations through play has done much to make the study of play respectable. Recently, he has summarized these beliefs in a new book, *Toys and Reasons,* which takes its title from a line by William Blake: "The child's toys and the old man's reasons are the fruits of the two seasons." Jean Piaget has gone further than Erikson in arguing that play is essential for the development of adult intelligence. Throughout his work, but especially in *Play, Dreams and Imitation in Childhood,* Piaget reduces play to a function of thought and limits the role of play in creativity and innovation. This role is restored in Jerome Singer's *The Child's World of Make-Believe: Experimental Studies of Imaginative Play*. The importance of fantasy is recognized by Jerome S. Bruner in several important studies and by Catherine Garvey in her book, *Play*.

A few studies are difficult to categorize, but remain important landmarks in the study of play. Roger G. Barker and Herbert F. Wright's *One Boy's Day: A Specific Record of Behavior* is the minute-by-minute record of a seven-year-old midwestern boy on April 26, 1949. The description, gathered by observers, parents, and teachers, illustrates the difficulty of labeling any particular activity as "play." *Six Cultures: Studies of Child Rearing,* edited by Beatrice B. Whiting, contains data on the Nyansongo of Kenya, the Rajputs of India, the Taira of Okinawa, the Mixtecans of Mexico, the

Tarong of the Philippines, and "the New Englanders of Orchard Town"; but all the ethnographies are disappointingly sketchy on play. A much better description of American children at play appears in Sue Parrott's "Games Children Play: Ethnography of a Second-Grade Recess." Mexican children's games are well covered by Cecilia Gil de Partearroyo's *Links into Past: A Folkloric Study of Mexican Children Relative to Their Singing Games* and by Michael Maccoby's "Games and Social Character in a Mexican Village." Herbert Berry III and John Roberts provide a link between psychological and anthropological theories in their "Infant Socialization and Games of Chance," while Clifford Geertz offers an interpretation of a whole culture through its games in "Deep Play: Notes on the Balinese Cockfight." Another recent attempt to synthesize several theories of play is Mihaly Csikszentmihalyi's *Beyond Boredom and Anxiety: The Experience of Play in Work and Games*. Although his work is confined to adult behavior, Csikszentmihalyi's idea that play is a state between boredom and anxiety has applications to children's activities as well.

A note should be added on the application of psychological theories by playground planners and landscape architects. Beginning with Marjorie Allen's *Planning for Play* in 1969, a large number of books and articles have argued the necessity of including children in the planning process and making basic materials such as water, dirt, and wood available in playgrounds. Although playgrounds are still seen as a place where children should learn, the arrangement of equipment and the supervision tends to be much less didactic than in the past. This trend may be followed in M. Paul Friedberg's *Play and Interplay: A Manifesto for New Design in Urban Recreational Environment*, Paul Hogan's *Playground for Free*, Richard Dattner's *Design for Play*, and Robin Moore's "Anarchy Zone: Encounters in a Schoolyard."

Historians, too, may trace their interest in games and toys back to the nineteenth century. E. B. Tylor, the British anthropologist, published "The History of Games" in *The Fortnightly Review* in 1879, and Alice Morse Earle anticipated the revival of interest in the seventeenth and eighteenth centuries in 1899, with her *Child Life in Colonial Days*. The rediscovery of play in the 1880s left little time for stocktaking, however, and it is not until the 1920s and 1930s that historical studies began to appear. Clarence Rainwater published his history of playground reform, *The Play Movement in the United States: A Study of Community Recreation*, in 1922. The unwanted free time of the unemployed in the Depression led Jesse Steiner to a reassessment of leisure in *Americans at Play: Recent Trends in Recreation and Leisure Time Activities*, published in 1933. At the end of that decade, Foster Rhea Dulles completed *America Learns to Play*, which is chiefly concerned with adult play, but which still provides the only comprehensive history of games and sports in this country.

Although it was not published in English until after his death, *Homo Ludens: A Study of the Play Element in Culture*, by Johan Huizinga, first appeared in 1938. *Homo Ludens* remains today the one great study of play. Part history, part anthropology, part philosophy, *Homo Ludens* is, as Robert Anchor has pointed out, "neither a history of play, nor a history of the idea of play, nor a study of play as one among many other human activities. Rather it is a morphology of play, a study of play as a structure that manifests itself in all spheres of human culture."[15] Huizinga's chapter titles—"The Play-Concept as Expressed in Language," "Play and Contest as Civilizing Functions," "Play and Law," "Play and War," "Playing and Knowing"— suggest that he, too, thought that play was didactic. But his definition of play as "a voluntary activity or occupation executed within certain fixed limits of time and place, according to rules freely accepted but absolutely binding, having its aim in itself and accompanied by a feeling of tension, joy and the consciousness that it is 'different' from 'ordinary life,' " obviates any specific goal in play. Writing at a time when Hitler's uniformed Nazis were staging their pageants of conquest, Huizinga was critical of the corruption of play he observed in their rituals, yet he was convinced that civilization arose in play. *Homo Ludens* remains a rich and subtle cultural history from which all students of games, toys, and play can profit.

Since 1960, historians of childhood and children's play have been influenced by Philippe Aries's *Centuries of Childhood*. Aries's chapter on the games and toys of the French court in the seventeenth and eighteenth centuries is interesting, but his thesis that a period of childhood did not exist at that time has limited value for American historians. There is good evidence that our colonial ancestors did recognize several stages of childhood and youth, as Ross Beales shows in his essay, "In Search of the Historical Child: Miniature Adulthood and Youth in Colonial New England." J. H. Plumb has done work on the history of childhood in England, while the sociologists Elizabeth and John Child have explored "Children and Leisure" in contemporary Britain. In the United States, the major work on games and play has been done by Brian Sutton-Smith, now at the University of Pennsylvania. Many of his pioneering articles have been reprinted in his *The Folkgames of Children*. From the historical standpoint, special attention should be given the essay he coauthored with B. G. Rosenberg, "Sixty Years of Historical Change in the Game Preferences of American Children." Sutton-Smith's *Toys as Culture* (1986) is a thorough discussion of the multiple meanings of toys and playthings. Sutton-Smith explores the paradox of the toy in the family context, in which an adult gives a toy to a child with the message, "Here is a trivial object that shows that I love you, now go and play with it by yourself and try to learn something from it."

Beginning in the early 1970s, a number of scholars began to place games and play in the context of cultural history. Bernard Mergen's book-length study, *Play and Playthings*, attempted to organize a variety of materials by psychologists, anthropologists, educators, and historians on children's play. Richard Knapp's doctoral dissertation, "Play for America: The National Recreation Association, 1906–1950," and Dominick Cavallo's *Muscles and Morals: Organized Playgrounds and Urban Reform, 1880–1920* provide a good overview of the organization and motivation of the early playground advocates. Dorothy Howard's beautiful and insightful autobiography, *Dorothy's World: Childhood in Sabine Bottom 1902–1910,* adds information on rural child life. Cary Goodman's *Choosing Sides: Playground and Street Life on the Lower East Side* and David Nasaw's *Children of the City: At Work and at Play* fill in many details of immigrant child life in New York City in the early twentieth century. Gary Alan Fine and Thomas J. Schlereth have each written on the possibilities of approaching children's games and toys through folklore and the study of material culture.

Dolls and games have been studied by Marilyn Ferris Motz and Paula Petrik. A forthcoming book by Petrik will fill many of the gaps in our knowledge of the business of toy manufacturing and retailing. Miriam Formanek-Brunell's doctoral dissertation, "Dolls and Dollars: The Rise of the Doll Industry and the Construction of Modern Girlhood, 1890–1930," adds significantly to our understanding of play as a form of socialization. Robin C. Moore's *Childhood's Domain: Play and Place in Child Development* focuses on spaces where children play as well as on the objects they play with. Three new periodicals provide current reports on games and toys from various perspectives: the *Children's Folklore Newsletter, Children's Environment Quarterly,* and *Play and Culture.*

For further comparisons with the history of games and toys in other countries, a half-dozen studies are available. Karl Ewald Fritzsch's *An Illustrated History of Toys* is especially good on German toy production. A *History of Toys* by Lady Antonia Fraser presents a popular survey. Closer to home, Musée de Quebec's *Le Jouet dans l'univers de l'enfant, 1800–1925,* Robert Lionel Séguin's *Les Jouets anciens du Quebec,* and Harry Symons's *Playthings of Yesterday: Harry Symons Introduces the Percy Band Collection* offer some basic information on the history of Canadian toys. Séguin's book suggests that toys in Quebec and the northeastern United States are basically similar, but that the Quebecois had some unusual folk toys such as the *pite* or *tapecul*—a narrow sled with a vertical post in the middle and a handle for sledding or skiing standing up. South of the border, *Los Juegos Infantiles en las Escuelas Rurales* by Ramón Garcia Ruiz is an older study that still has much merit, while Francisco Javier Hernández's *El Juguete Popular en México: estudio de interpretacion* is a scholarly monograph on toys from the pre-Hispanic period to the present. Aida Reboredo's *Jugar es un Acto Politico* is a critique of the ideological domination of Third World countries by the toy industry of the United States. The author, a Mexican sociologist, also presents some interesting evidence on the ways in which toys are perceived by children in her country.

ANTHOLOGIES AND REPRINTS

The anthologies by Elliott Avedon and Brian Sutton-Smith and by R. E. Herron and Sutton-Smith have already been mentioned, as has Phillips Stevens's *Studies in the Anthropology of Play,* which is made up of papers presented at the second annual meeting of the Association for the Anthropological Study of Play. The proceedings of the first meeting of TAASP were published as *The Anthropological Study of Play: Problems and Prospects,* edited by David F. Lancy and B. Allan Tindall. The proceedings of the third meeting, edited by Michael Salter, are titled *Play: Anthropological Perspectives.* A fourth volume was edited by Helen B. Schwartzman. A useful reprinting of early articles is *A Children's Games Anthology: Studies in Folklore and Anthropology.* For recent scholarship in psychology, see Jerome Bruner and associates, *Play—Its Role in Development and Evolution.* Curiously, Robert H. Bremmer's three-volume anthology, *Children and Youth in America: A Documentary History,* has nothing on games and toys. Barbara Finkelstein's collection, *Regulated Children/Liberated Children: Education in Psychohistorical Perspective,* contains several useful essays that set the context for further studies of children's games and toys, as does Joseph M. Hawes and N. Ray Hiner's *American Childhood: A Research Guide and Historical Handbook.*

NOTES

1. Jac Remise, *The Golden Age of Toys* (Greenwich, Conn.: New York Graphic Society, 1967), p. 11.
2. Stephen Miller, "Ends, Means, and Galumphing: Some Leitmotifs of Play," *American Anthropologist,* 75 (February 1973), 97.
3. Peter Wagner, "Literary Evidence of Sport in Colonial New England: The American Puritan Jeremiad," Stadion, 2 (1976), 235.
4. Katharine McClinton, *Antiques of American Childhood* (New York: Bramhall House, 1970).
5. William Wells Newell, *Games and Songs of American Children* (New York: Harper and Brothers, 1883), p. 176.
6. Elizabeth George Speare, Child Life in New England 1790–1840 (Sturbridge, Mass.: Old Sturbridge Booklet Series, 1961), p. 18.
7. Ibid., p. 19
8. McClinton, p. 227.
9. Stewart Culin, "Street Games of Boys in Brooklyn, New York," Journal of American Folklore, 4 (July–September 1891), 234–35.
10. *Emergency Fleet News,* January 1, 1919, p. 9.
11. U.S. Department of Labor, Children's Bureau, *Facilities for Children's Play in the District of Columbia* (Washington, D.C.: Government Printing Office, 1917), p. 68.
12. *The Playground,* 6 (May 1912), 51.
13. George Johnson, Education Through Recreation (Cleveland: Survey Committee of the Cleveland Foundation, 1916), p. 49.

14. Brian Sutton-Smith, "The Two Cultures of Games," in *The Folkgames of Children* (Austin.: Published for the American Folklore Society by the University of Texas, 1972), pp. 295–311.

15. Robert Anchor, "History and Play: Johan Huizinga and His Critics," *History and Theory*, 17 (February 1978), 77–78.

BIBLIOGRAPHY

Books and Articles

Abrahams, Roger D. *Jump-Rope Rhymes: A Dictionary*. Austin: University of Texas Press, 1969.

Allen, Marjorie. *Planning for Play*. Cambridge, Mass.: MIT Press, 1969.

Aries, Philippe. *Centuries of Childhood*. New York: Alfred A. Knopf, 1962.

Aronowitz, Stanley. "Together and Equal: The Egalitarian Promise of Children's Games." *Social Policies*, 4 (November/December 1973), 78–84.

Avedon, Elliott M., and Brian Sutton-Smith, eds. *The Study of Games*. New York: Wiley, 1971.

Babcock, William Henry. "Games of Washington Children." *American Anthropologist*, 1 (July 1888), 243–84.

Barenholtz, Bernard, and Inez McClintock. *American Antique Toys, 1830–1900*. New York: Harry N. Abrams, 1986.

Barker, Roger G., and Herbert F. Wright. *One Boy's Day: A Specific Record of Behavior*. New York: Harper, 1951.

Barthes, Roland. *Mythologies*. New York: Hill and Wang, 1972.

Beales, Ross W. "In Search of the Historical Child: Miniature Adulthood and Youth in Colonial New England." *American Quarterly*, 27 (October 1975), 379–98.

Berry, Herbert, III, and John Roberts. "Infant Socialization and Games of Chance." Ethnology, II (July 1972), 296–308.

Best, Charles W. *Cast Iron Toy Pistols, 1870–1940: A Collector's Guide*. Englewood, Colo.: Rocky Mountain Arms and Antiques, 1973.

Bremner, Robert H., et al., eds. *Children and Youth in America: A Documentary History*. 3 vols. Cambridge, Mass.: Harvard University Press, 1970.

Brewster, Paul G., *American Nonsinging Games*. Norman: University of Oklahoma Press, 1953.

———, *Children's Games and Rhymes*. Chapel Hill: University of North Carolina Press, 1952.

Bruner, Jerome S., Alosin Jolly, and Kathy Sylva, eds. *Play—Its Role in Development and Evolution*. New York: Basic Books, 1976.

Burns, Thomas A. "The *Game of Life:* Idealism, Reality, and Fantasy in the Nineteenth-and Twentieth-Century Versions of a Milton Bradley Game." The *Canadian Review of American Studies*, 9 (Spring 1978), 50–83.

Cadbury, Betty. *Playthings Past*. Newton Abbot, England: David and Charles, 1976.

Caillois, Roger. *Man, Play, and Games*. London: Thames and Hudson, 1962.

Calvin, Jeannette M., comp. *International Trade in Toys.* Washington, D.C.:Government Printing Office, 1926.

Canary, Robert H. "Playing the Game of *Life.*" *Journal of Popular Culture,* 1 (Spring 1968), 427–32.

Caplan, Frank, and Theresa Caplan. *The Power of Play.* Garden City, N.Y.: Anchor Press/Doubleday, 1973.

Cavallo, Dominick. *Muscles and Morals: Organized Playgrounds and Urban Reform, 1880–1920.* Philadelphia: University of Pennsylvania Press, 1981.

Champlin, John D., and Arthur E. Bostwick. The Young Folks' Cyclopaedia of Games and Sports. New York: H. Holt, 1890.

Chandler, Ceil. Toys and Dolls Made in Occupied Japan. Houston: Chandler's Discriminating Junk, 1973.

Chase, Stuart. "Play." In *Whither Mankind.* Edited by Charles Beard. New York: Longmans, Green, 1928.

Child, Elizabeth, and John Child. "Children and Leisure." In *Leisure and Society in Britain.* Edited by M. Smith, S. Parker, and C. Smith. London: Allen Lane, 1973, pp. 135–47.

A Children's Game Anthology: Studies in Folklore and Anthropology. New York: Arno Press, 1976.

Coleman, Dorothy S., Elizabeth A. Coleman, and Evelyn J. Coleman. *The Collector's Encyclopedia of Dolls.* New York: Crown, 1968.

Croswell, T. R. "Amusements of Worcester School Children." *Pedagogical Seminary,* 6 (September 1899), 314–71.

Csikszentmihalyi, Mihaly. Beyond Boredom and Anxiety: The Experience of Play in Work and Games. San Francisco: Jossey-Bass, 1975.

Csikszentmihalyi, Mihaly, and Stith Bennett. "An Exploratory Model of Play." *American Anthropologist,* 73 (1971), 45–58.

Culin, Stewart. *Games of North American Indians.* Twenty-fourth Annual Report to the Bureau of Ethnology. Washington, D.C.: Government Printing Office, 1907.

———. "Street Games of Boys in Brooklyn, New York." *Journal of American Folklore,* 4 (July–September 1891), 221–37.

Daiken, Leslie. *Children's Toys Throughout the Ages.* New York: Praeger, 1953.

———. *World of Toys: A Guide to the Principal Public and Private Collections in Great Britain.* Kent: Lambarde Press, 1963.

Dattner, Richard. *Design for Play.* Cambridge, Mass.: MIT Press, 1974.

Douglas, Norman. *London Street Games.* London: St. Catherine Press, 1916.

Dulles, Foster Rhea. *America Learns to Play.* New York: Appleton-Century, 1940.

Earle, Alice Morse. *Child Life in Colonial Days.* New York: Macmillan, 1899.

Erikson, Erik. *Childhood and Society.* New York: W. W. Norton, 1950.

———. *Toys and Reasons.* New York: W. W. Norton, 1977.

Ferretti, Fred. *The Great American Marble Book.* New York: Workman, 1973.

———. *The Great American Book of Sidewalk, Stoop, Dirt, Curb, and Alley Games.* New York: Workman, 1975.

Fine, Gary Alan, "Children and Their Culture: Exploring Newell's Paradox." *Western Folklore,* 39 (July 1980), 170–83.

Finkelstein, Barbara, ed. *Regulated Children/Liberated Children: Education in Psychohistorical Perspective.* New York: Psychohistory Press, 1979.

Formanek-Brunell, Miriam. "Dolls and Dollars: The Rise of the Doll Industry and the Construction of Modern Girlhood, 1890–1930." Ph.D. dissertation, Rutgers University, in progress.

Fraser, Lady Antonia. *A History of Toys*. New York: Spring Books, 1972.

Friedberg, M. Paul. *Play and Interplay: A Manifesto for New Design in Urban Recreational Environment*. New York: Macmillan, 1970.

Fritzsch, Karl Ewald. *An Illustrated History of Toys*. Leipzig: Edition Leipzig, 1968.

Garvey, Catherine. *Play*. Cambridge, Mass.: Harvard University Press, 1977.

Geertz, Clifford. "Deep Play: Notes on the Balinese Cockfight." *Daedalus*, 101 (Winter 1972), 1–37.

Gibson, Cecil. *A History of British Dinky Toys: Model Car and Vehicle Issues, 1934–1964*. Hemel Hempstead: Model Aeronautical Press, 1966.

Gil de Partearroyo, Cecilia. *Links into Past: A Folkloric Study of Mexican Children Relative to Their Singing Games*. Mexico: Editorial Jus, 1953.

Girard, Alexander H. *El Encanto de un Pueblo. The Magic of a People: Folk Art and Toys from the Collection of the Girard Foundation*. New York: Viking, 1968.

Gomme, Alice. *The Traditional Games of England, Scotland and Ireland*. 2 vols. London: D. Nutt, 1894–98.

Goodman, Cary. *Choosing Sides: Playground and Street Life on the Lower East Side*. New York: Schocken Books, 1979.

Grinham, Ann E. *Japanese Games and Toys*. Tokyo: Hitachi, 1973.

Hall, G. Stanley. "The Contents of Children's Minds." *Princeton Review*, II (May 1883), 249–72.

Hannas, Linda. *The English Jigsaw Puzzle, 1760–1890, with a Descriptive Check-list of Puzzles in the Museums of Great Britain and the Author's Collection*. London: Wayland, 1972.

Harman, Kenny. *Comic Strip Toys*. Des Moines, Iowa: Wallace-Homestead Books, 1975.

Hawes, Bess Lomax, and Bessie Jones. *Step It Down: Games, Plays, Songs and Stories from the Afro-American Heritage*. New York: Harper and Row, 1972.

Hawes, Joseph M., and N. Ray Hiner, eds. *American Childhood: A Research Guide and Historical Handbook*. Westport, Conn.: Greenwood Press, 1985.

Hernández, Francisco Javier. *El Juguete Popular en México: estudio de interpretacion*. Mexico: Ediciones Mexicanas, 1950.

Herron, R. E., and Brian Sutton-Smith, eds. *Child's Play*. New York: Wiley, 1971.

Hertz, Louis. The Handbook of Old American Toys. Wethersfield, Conn.: Mark Haber, 1947.

———. *Messrs. Ives of Bridgeport*. Wethersfield, Conn.: Mark Haber, 1950.

———. *The Toy Collector*. New York: Funk and Wagnalls, 1969.

Hogan, Paul. *Playgrounds for Free*. Cambridge, Mass.: MIT Press, 1974.

Howard, Dorothy. *Dorothy's World: Childhood in Sabine Bottom 1902–1910*. New York: Prentice-Hall, 1977.

Hughes, James M. "A Tale of Two Games: An Image of the City." *Journal of Popular Culture*, 6 (Fall 1972), 357–62.

Huizinga, Johan. *Homo Ludens: A Study of the Play Element in Culture*. London: Routledge and Kegan Paul, 1949.

Jacobs, Flora Gill. *Dolls' Houses in America: Historic Preservation in Miniature*. New York: Scribner's, 1974.

———. *A History of Dolls' Houses*. New York: Scribner's, 1953, 1964.

Jean-Leo. *Jouets, jeux, livres d'enfant: repertoire bibliographique d'ouvrages utiles aux collectionneurs et aux chercheurs, augmente de nombreux articles inedits*. Bruxelles: Le Grenier du collecionneur, 1974.

Kadzielski, Mark A. "'As a Flower Needs Sunshine': The Origins of Organized Children's Recreation in Philadelphia, 1886–1911." *Journal of Sport History*, 4 (Summer 1977), 169–88.

Kaye, Marvin. *A Toy Is Born*. New York: Stein and Day, 1973.

Kirshenblatt-Gimblett, Barbara, ed. *Speech Play*. Philadelphia: University of Pennsylvania Press, 1976.

Knapp, Mary, and Herbert Knapp. *One Potato, Two Potato . . . The Secret Education of American Children*. New York: W. W. Norton, 1976.

Knapp, Richard. "Play for America: The National Recreation Association, 1906–1950." Ph.D. dissertation, Duke University, 1971.

Lancy, David F., and B. Allan Tindall, eds. *The Anthropological Study of Play: Problems and Prospects*. Cornwall, N.Y.: Leisure Press, 1976.

McClintock, Inez, and Marshall McClintock. *Toys in America*. Washington, D.C.: Public Affairs Press, 1961.

McClinton, Katharine. *Antiques of American Childhood*. New York: Bramhall House, 1970.

Maccoby, Michael, et al. "Games and Social Character in a Mexican Village." *Psychiatry*, 2 (May 1964), 150–62.

McGhee, Zach. "A Study of the Play Life of Some South Carolina Children." *Pedagogical Seminary*, 7 (December 1900), 459–78.

Mechling, Jay. "Sacred and Profane Play in the Boy Scouts of America." In *Play and Culture*. Edited by Helen B. Schwartzman. West Point, N.Y.: Leisure Press, 1980, pp. 206–13.

Mergen, Bernard. *Play and Playthings: A Reference Guide*. Westport, Conn.: Greenwood Press, 1982.

Milberg, Alan. *Street Games*. New York: McGraw-Hill, 1976.

Miller, Stephen. "Ends, Means, and Galumphing: Some Leitmotifs of Play." *American Anthropologist*, 75 (February 1973), 87–98.

Miller, Susanna. *The Psychology of Play*. New York: Pelican Books, 1968.

Moore, Robin. "Anarchy Zone: Encounters in a Schoolyard." *Landscape Architecture*, 69 (October 1974), 364–71.

———. *Childhood's Domain: Play and Place in Child Development*. London: Croom Helm, 1986.

Motz, Marilyn Ferris. "Maternal Virgin: The Girl and Her Doll in Nineteenth-Century America." In *Objects of Special Devotion: Fetishism in Popular Culture*. Edited by Ray Browne. Bowling Green, Ohio: Bowling Green State University Popular Press, 1982, pp. 54–69.

Murray, Patrick. *Toys*. London: Studio Vista, 1968.

Nasaw, David. *Children of the City: At Work and at Play*. Garden City, N.Y.: Doubleday, 1985.

Newell, William Wells. *Games and Songs of American Children*. New York: Harper and Brothers, 1883.

Opie, Iona, and Peter Opie. *Children's Games in Street and Playground*. Oxford: Clarendon Press, 1969.

————. *The Lore and Language of School Children*. Ox- ford: Clarendon Press, 1960.

Page, Hilary Fisher. *Toys in Wartime*. London: G. Allen and Unwin, 1942.

Parrott, Sue. "Games Children Play: Ethnography of a Second-Grade Recess." In *The Cultural Experience: Ethnography in Complex Society*. Edited by James Spradley and David McCurdy. Chicago: Science Research Associates, 1976, pp. 207–19.

Petrik, Paula. "The House that Parcheesi Built: Selchow & Righter Company." *Business History Review*, 60 (Autumn 1986), 410–37.

Piaget, Jean. *Play, Dreams and Imitation in Childhood*. New York: W. W. Norton, 1962.

Plumb, J. H. "The New World of Children in Eighteenth-Century England." *Past and Present*, 67 (May 1975), 64–93.

Pressland, David. *The Art of the Tin Toy*. New York: Crown, 1976.

Rainwater, Clarence. *The Play Movement in the United States: A Study of Community Recreation*. Chicago: University of Chicago Press, 1922.

Reboredo, Aida. *Jugar es un Acto Politico. El jugete industrial: recurso de dominacion*. Mexico: Nueva Imagen, 1983.

Remise, Jac, and Jean Fondin. *The Golden Age of Toys*. Greenwich, Conn.: New York Graphic Society, 1967.

Renson, Roland, and B. Van Reusel. "Toy Bibliography." In Association for the Anthropological Study of Play *Newsletter*, 4 (Spring 1978), 17–18.

Riesman, David. *The Lonely Crowd*. New Haven: Yale University Press, 1950.

Roberts, J. M., M. J. Arth, and R. R. Bush. "Games in Culture." *American Anthropologist*, 61 (1959), 597–605.

Roberts, J. M., and Brian Sutton-Smith. "Child Training and Game Involvement." *Ethnology*, 1 (1962), 166–85.

Rosenberg, B. G., and Brian Sutton-Smith. "Sixty Years of Historical Change in the Game Preferences of American Children." *Journal of American Folklore*, 74 (January-March 1961), 17–46.

Ruiz, Ramón Garcia. *Los Juegos Infantiles en las Escuelas Rurales*. Mexico City: El Nacional, 1938.

Salter, Michael. *Play: Anthropological Perspectives*. West Point, N.Y. Association for the Anthropological Study of Play, 1978.

Scheffler, Lilian. "The Study of Traditional Games in Mexico: Bibliographical Analysis and Current Research." In *The Anthropological Study of Play: Problems and Prospects*. Edited by David Lancy and B. Allan Tindall. Cornwall, N.Y.: Leisure Press, 1976, pp. 58–66.

Schlereth, Thomas J. "The Material Culture of Childhood: Problems and Potential in Historical Explanation." *Material History Bulletin*, 21 (Spring 1985), 1–14.

Schroeder, Joseph J., Jr., ed. *The Wonderful World of Toys, Games and Dolls*. Northfield, Ill.: Digest Books, 1971.

Schutrumpf, E. D. *World Trade in Toys*. Washington, D.C.: Government Printing Office, 1939.

Schwartzman, Helen B. *Transformations: The Anthropology of Children's Play*. New York: Plenum Press, 1978.

Séguin, Robert-Lionel. *Les Jouets anciens du Quebec*. Montreal: Lemeac, 1969.

Singer, Jerome L. *The Child's World of Make-Believe: Experimental Studies of Imaginative Play*. New York: Academic Press, 1973.

Snow, Robert E., and David E. Wright. "Coney Island: A Case Study in Popular Culture and Technical Change." *Journal of Popular Culture*, 9 (Spring 1976), 960–75.

Speare, Elizabeth George. *Child Life in New England 1790–1840*. Sturbridge, Mass.: Old Sturbridge Village Booklet Series, 1961.

Sporting Goods and Games 1886: Peck & Snyder. Princeton, N.J.: The Pyne Press, 1971.

Steiner, Jesse Frederick. *Americans at Play: Recent Trends in Recreation and Leisure Time Activities*. New York: McGraw-Hill, 1933.

Stevens, Phillips, Jr., ed. *Studies in the Anthropology of Play: Papers in Memory of B. Allan Tindall*. West Point, N.Y.: Leisure Press, 1977.

Sutton-Smith, Brian. *The Folkgames of Children*. Austin: Published for the American Folklore Society by the University of Texas, 1972.

———. *The Games of New Zealand Children*. Berkeley: University of California Press, 1959.

———. *A History of Children's Play: New Zealand, 1840–1950*. Philadelphia: University of Pennsylvania Press, 1981.

———. *Toys as Culture*. New York: Gardner Press, 1986.

Swartz, Edward M. *Toys That Don't Care*. Boston: Gambit, 1971.

Symons, Harry. *Playthings of Yesterday: Harry Symons Introduces the Percy Band Collection*. Toronto: Ryerson Press, 1963.

Tylor, E. B. "The History of Games." *The Fortnightly Review*, 31 (n.s. 25) (1879), 735–47.

U.S. Bureau of Census. *Census of Manufacturers: 1927. Carriages and sleds, children's toys, games, and playground equipment, sporting and athletic goods, not including firearms or ammunition*. Washington, D.C.: Government Printing Office, 1929.

———. *Census of Manufacturers: 1931*. Washington, D.C.: Government Printing Office, 1931.

———. *Sixteenth Census of the United States 1940. Manufacturers: 1939. Toys and Sporting and Athletic Goods*. Washington, D.C.: Government Printing Office, 1941.

White, Gwen. *Toys and Dolls: Marks and Labels*. Newton, Mass.: C. T. Branford, 1975.

Whiting, Beatrice B., ed. *Six Cultures: Studies of Child Rearing*. New York: Wiley, 1963.

Willson's Canadian Toy, Notion and Stationery Directory. Toronto: Willson's Directories, 1956.

Yoffie, Lea Rachel Clara. "Three Generations of Children's Singing Games in St. Louis." *Journal of American Folklore*, 60 (January-March 1947), 1–151.

Periodicals

Antique Toy World. Chicago, 1970–.

Children's Environment Quarterly. New York, 1984–.

Children's Folklore Newsletter. Greenville, N.C., 1978–.

Collectibles Monthly. York, Pa., 1977–.

The Doll Reader. Riverdale, Md., 1973–.

Good Toys. New York, 1986–.

Miniature Collector. New York, 1976–.

Play and Culture. Champaign, Ill., 1988–.

The Playground. New York, 1907–15; Cooperstown, N.Y., 1916–23; Greenwich, Conn., 1923–24; New York, 1924–29; *Playground and Recreation,* New York, 1929–30; *Recreation*, New York, 1931–65; *Parks and Recreation*, Arlington, Va., 1966–.

Playthings. New York, 1903–.

Das Spielzeug. Bamberg, Germany, 1909–.

Toy and Hobby World. New York, 1963–.

Toy Manufacturer. Atlanta, 1957–.

Toy Retailer (title varies). Atlanta, Ga., 1953–62.

Toys. New York, 1972–.

Toys and Games. Montreal, 1973–.

Toys and Novelties. Chicago, 1909–72.

Toys and Playthings. Montreal, 1957–.

Toys International. London, 1962–.

The Toy Trader and Exporter. London, 1908–.

Toy Trader Year Book. Watford, England, 1969–.

Toy Trains. Silver Spring, Md., 1951–.

Toy Wholesaler. Atlanta, 1959–.

Toy World. San Francisco, 1927–36.

Gardening

PATSY G. HAMMONTREE

The term *gardening* is an inclusive one, meaning both ornamental gardening and vegetable gardening. In American popular culture, however, a reference to a garden more often than not means a vegetable garden. And though horticulture and gardening mean the same thing, horticulture is generally used to refer to ornamental gardening. Ornamental gardening is an important part of American culture, but it is the vegetable garden that is the major preoccupation of many Americans. This chapter will restrict itself to the study of vegetable gardening.

Gardening is a topic of conversation almost as popular as the weather. In the fall, individuals ask, "Is your garden ploughed?" In the winter, gardeners discuss seed catalogs. And in the early spring they begin to till the soil and plant seeds. And though the fundamental purpose of a garden is utilitarian—to grow food—in American culture gardening is more nearly a recreation. It is one of the major sporting propositions in this country.

The National Gardening Association, through its publication *Gardens for All,* commissioned a Gallup poll on gardening in the United States. The results of the poll revealed that vegetable gardening is the fifth most popular recreational activity in the country. A number of gardening books refer to the poll in making points about gardening. Gardening is especially suited to Americans. It permits American individualism and self-reliance to thrive, and it also allows for creativity. Producing a successful, well-arranged garden is artistry. But because gardening is the ultimate challenge, it remains popular because it satisfies the American desire to compete. The competition works on levels from the spiritual to the frivolous. A gardener competes with the mystery of birth. A seed is planted in the dark soil, appearing at its own secretly appointed time, beginning anew the cycle of the seasons and philosophically the cycle of birth, growth, death, and growth again. The gardener competes with the elements and unpredictable weather conditions. Both drought and excessive rain can damage a crop; hail storms can beat plants into the ground; strong winds can bend and break plants. The gardener is at the mercy of insects and plant diseases, competing by means of the miracle of chemicals or age-old methods of outwitting his adversaries. And the gardener competes with himself—with his accomplishments in last season's garden.

When the crop reaches fruition, gardeners compete with their family, friends, and professional growers. Titles of articles in gardening magazines attest to the competitive spirit. For example, a recent *Southern Living* article by T. Steadman was entitled "Get a Jump on Spring."[1] The person who grows the first ripe tomato is a community celebrity. Competition is given official endorsement by organizations which in August and September hand out prizes at regional and state fairs for the largest tomato, the largest pumpkin, the largest watermelon, and so forth. According to Peter Chan in *Better Gardens the Chinese Way,* in 1976, 1,400 people entered the *Sunset Magazine* contest for the best garden.[2] 4-H Clubs and similar young people's organizations encourage such competition by giving prizes and awards for those who excel. Even those with the highest intentions, such as Alice Skelsey and Gloria Huckaby, who encourage children to become interested gardeners in their child's book, *Growing Up Green,* endorse competition with the imagery of sections entitled "Pumpkin Derby," and "Bean Olympics," to name two. Within the cultural context, gardening becomes a recreational sport.

Gardening even has its own folklore and its own heroes, such as Johnny Appleseed, Luther Burbank, George Washington Carver, and Euell Gibbons, to name a few.

During the sexual revolution of the seventies, some gardening articles reflected the imagery of the time, for example, a 1972 *American Home* essay by L. V. Powers entitled "Today's Vegetable Turn-On."[3] Perhaps only in popular culture could there be titles filled with puns such as "Great Hoe-Down,"[4] "Beat the Southern Broccoli Blues,"[5] "Meet the Hotheads: Growing Lettuce in the South,"[6] and "Laugh at Food Prices—Hoe! Hoe! Hoe!"[7] If further proof is needed, one should consider a Duane Newcomb manual, *Mobile Home Gardening Guide,* commissioned by the Trail-R-Club of America.

No longer need gardeners rely on the drab *Farmer's Almanac*. Starwood Publishers puts out a line of glossy, full-color calendars with gardening advice suited to regional weather zones. Nor need gardeners read encyclopedias and manuals. The Publishers Central Bureau now advertises *The Victory Garden Vegetable Video* from PBS's highly acclaimed "Victory Garden" program, produced, the description says, "just for home video, covering, in 60 minutes, 31 projects in color." And Garden Way Publishing has prepared a set of step-by-step audio cassettes, packaged with printed material in case the gardener wants to be old-fashioned. Titles include such hits as "Grow the Best Tomatoes" and "Grow Fifteen Herbs for the Kitchen." Garden master Dave Schaefer narrates the half-hour tapes.

Most newspapers, even weeklies, have a regular gardening column, and many general interest magazines also feature gardening articles. But when a subject is on both video and audio, its time in popular culture has come.

HISTORIC OUTLINE

Gardening in the Americas began with the Indians in North, Central, and South America. Three of the most popular garden items in the United States are indigenous to Central and South America: corn, called maize by the American Indians; tomatoes, called *tomatl* or *xtomatl* by the Mayans[8] and potatoes, called *papas* by the pre-Inca Indians of the Andes mountains.[9] North American settlers, beginning with the Pilgrims, brought European seeds and cultivation methods with them, but gardening began here long before their arrival, and it began elsewhere in the world long before that.

Gardening as people currently define it has a long ancestry, reaching back to the Middle East, where the first plots of what can be called cultivations appeared. According to Anthony Huxley in *An Illustrated History of Gardening,* the earliest cultivators apparently lived around Jericho in Palestine about 8000 B.C. The cultivation of such plots seems to have evolved both from the wild grains, which grew in the area, and from seeds and pits casually spat out or dropped by persons having eaten wild fruits. These seeds eventually reappeared as trees, growing within the areas of habitation and leading finally to selected planting of grains and fruit trees as well as seeds collected from wild plants. Gardens then moved throughout the Middle East and eventually to Europe through Greece. Huxley approximates the dates for organized cultivation in Greece at sometime before 6000 B.C.; in Egypt and Crete, 5000 B.C.; China, 5000 B.C., and in South America, 2500 B.C.[10]

In "The History of Vegetables," in his *The Perfect Vegetable and Herb Garden,* Roy Genders remarks that though using very primitive cultivation methods, the Egyptians had highly productive vegetable gardens. Genders provides the following list of Egyptian food-producing plants: almond, barley, broad bean, cabbage, chicory, dates, endive, figs, garlic, grapes, leek, lettuce, melon, olive, onion, pea, radish, shallot, watercress, and wheat. Genders also points out that only two significant food crops were not grown by the Egyptians. One was rice, which has to have its roots submerged in water and originates in Asia. The other was the potato.[11]

Both Greeks and Romans had vegetable gardens. The Romans left evidence of having rapidly advanced gardening, due in part to their technical skills. Huxley states, "By the second century B.C. [the Romans] had developed farming, market gardening, and decorative gardening to new levels." He contends that the Romans "laid the foundations of gardening ideals."[12]

During the Middle Ages, gardening was essentially nonexistent among the populace, being maintained primarily by monks within the monasteries. Edward Hyams reports in *A History of Gardens and Gardening* that the monks who founded monasteries adopted the Roman idea of having gardening academies as well as the Roman practice of agriculture estates, which were self-supporting, and thus planted and cultivated varied gardens which both taught other monks cultivation and provided food for the monastery. He also suggests that the vegetable gardens of monasteries owe a debt to St. Benedict, who placed great stock in both the potential for self-sufficiency and the work discipline associated with a garden. Hyams credits the monasteries with having improved gardening techniques during the Middle Ages as well as preserving plants and herbs which might otherwise have been lost.[13]

Yet, according to Hyams, the feudal system allowed the populace to have some exposure to gardening. He remarks: "The advancement of gardening in the eleventh and twelfth centuries in Europe was not solely in ecclesiastical hands. Secular lords were soon learning the worth of a garden from the church."[14] And by having gardens planted within the castle walls, the upper classes had certain foods for themselves, meaning that lower classes benefited to a minimal degree. Chaucer in "The Summoner's Tale," gives evidence of at least bulbous plants being popular when he says of the pilgrim Summoner: "Well loved he garlic, onions, and the leek."

As might be expected, during the Renaissance emphasis in gardening was more on ornamentals than on vegetables. Though the populace no doubt planted gardens to feed themselves, high culture dictated having an elaborately designed garden. During the Commonwealth in England, however, Oliver Cromwell, a man of utilitarian bent, eliminated luxury gardens to stress the growing of foods. With the restoration of Charles II, elaborate luxury gardens again prevailed. Nevertheless, the rural British—and city dwellers who could participate in community gardens—have continued to grow vegetables.

In North America gardening by English settlers began, of course, with subsistence planting. The Pilgrims, who landed in the Northeast, followed by the Dutch and the Swedes, came prepared to grow food crops. They brought seeds with them, and as soon as weather permitted they began cultivation. Households had both a kitchen garden and an herb garden. When living conditions permitted, settlers also had flower gardens, but non–utilitarian gardens were planted only after the residents could provide food for themselves. As an indication of the colonists' interest in gardening, three prominent early Americans, Washington, Jefferson, and Franklin, wrote a great deal about gardening. Jefferson's gardening books are still popular; Robert Baron has recently edited and published *The Garden and Farm Books of Thomas Jefferson.*

The Spanish armies and their camp followers were more interested in taking territory—and in finding precious metals—than in forming settlements. Nevertheless, the earliest Spanish settlement in St. Augustine, Florida, had gardens attached to the houses. According to Huxley, garden cultivation in Spanish territories was done by the priests, who came after the soldiers and who built missions in the Southeast and the Southwest. From those early gardens we have most of our citrus fruits as well as peaches.

It is commonplace to think of the native American Indians as primarily hunters and gatherers, and of course they were. But surprisingly, many of them also had gardens by the time the Pilgrims arrived. In his *Story of Gardening* Richardson Wright remarks that the Indians were not given to gardening, yet he goes on to list the rather varied composition of their gardens: two kinds of maize, beans, pumpkins, squash, groundnut, Jerusalem artichoke, wild onions, as well as sunflowers for oil, tobacco for smoking, and gourds for containers.[15] A look at the contents of the Indian garden reveals a great similarity to contemporary choices in planting.

Throughout the seventeenth, eighteenth, and nineteenth centuries, North American gardening moved with the frontier as settlers relocated and created new gardens in new home clearings. Gardening methods tended to follow the pattern of the country from which immigrants came. For settlers, gardens were an absolute necessity, the means of survival. In the Rocky Mountain states, gardening was not then—and is not now—a simple task, as a recent article in *Sunset Magazine,* "How Three Bountiful Colorado Gardens Solved Mountain Problems," indicates.[16] Pioneers who preferred a richer soil and a longer growing season, however, moved on until they reached California, Oregon, and Washington.

People who have remained within the boundaries of large cities have also found ways to practice gardening. Many city home lots are large enough to accommodate a small garden, but space is always a consideration in a city, a topic addressed by Duane Newcome in *The Postage Stamp Garden Book.* Certainly tenement dwellers in preceding centuries did not have ready access to garden plots—nor do most apartment dwellers of today. But in many large cities there now is space either for rent as a garden plot or for public community gardening. Most persons who wish to garden can accommodate themselves. Community gardening is consistently popular, with Mary Lee Coe's *Growing with Community Gardening* serving as a testimony to its wide-ranging interest.

During the American Civil War, gardening was a major source of food for both sides. Farmers living on small southern farms practiced gardening as diligently as did those on large plantations. Farms of varying sizes in the

Northeast and Midwest had suitably sized provision gardens. Gardening was even more important after the war. Rural dwellers who were not landowners either rented space for a vegetable garden or participated in sharecropping, a practice still followed in parts of the United States. Though few farms were as isolated in the late 1800s as in pioneer times, a significant number still had to be almost totally self-sufficient. Having a garden was a necessity. It was the family's sole source of vegetables, which were preserved for the winter through canning and drying. Because of the United States' vast rural areas and its longtime dependence on agriculture, the country remained largely pastoral—in mood and tone, if not in reality—until early in the twentieth century.

In 1934 Richardson Wright remarked in *Story of Gardening:* "It would be interesting to trace the effect of political and religious upheavals in the world's gardening. What Russia under the Soviets is doing today in agriculture, England did under the Commonwealth."[17] Wright assesses gardening popularity in worldwide terms, but there is also value in doing a similar assessment of individual countries. To a large extent the economic and military history of the United States is reflected in the history of gardening, particularly in the twentieth century. Though the backyard garden has never disappeared from favor in this country, neither has interest in it always remained at a high level of intensity. Once individuals could purchase foodstuffs instead of being compelled to raise what they ate, gardening took on its recreational characteristics. But despite being recreational, vegetable gardening in the twentieth century has tended to increase or decrease in relation to environmental circumstances.

During the first fourteen years of the century gardening continued to be more a necessity than a choice. It retained a pastoral quality—in part because it was the nation's lingering connection to its agricultural past. As America moved increasingly toward being an industrial nation, it became more compartmentalized and consumer-oriented. Nevertheless, the very joy of gardening was not an easy habit to break. For example, "Garden Plots of the Bridge Builders," a 1911 magazine article, shows the recreational preference of a group of steel workers.[18]

But beginning in 1915, a national emergency changed the tempo of gardening, making it once again a significant part of the nation's existence. World War I created a need for increased food production, and the chosen source was home gardening, called during the war "defense gardens." The need aroused a strong sense of nationalism. Adolph Kruhm, the James Underwood Crockett of early twentieth-century gardening publications, wrote in *Home Vegetable Gardening from A to Z:* "April 15, 1917 will go down as one of the most momentous days in American history quite apart from the fact that it marked our entrance into the world War. It will be remembered by gardeners throughout the land as the day when the President asked every citizen to recognize the importance of home gardening as a means to help feed the world."[19] The president called for 10,000 gardens each year. Until the end of the war in 1918, publications on gardening greatly increased. But at the end of the conflict, gardening returned in mood to a more serene pastoral exercise.

The Great Depression of the 1930s marked another trauma in the country, and again gardening became a means to relieve hunger. The listings for the period in *Readers' Guide to Periodical Literature* show that gardening advice increased by more than 60 percent. There is no record, however, of the extent to which people took the advice. Many simply did not have the money to buy seed and fertilizer for cultivation. There were spots of elective gardening, however. In his popular-history narrative *The Glory and the Dream,* William Manchester mentions that the Bonus Army, which marched on Washington in 1932, cultivated small garden plots during the period they camped out in the city. Like the construction workers in the earlier part of the century, these men, in the midst of concrete and chaos, chose to spend some of their waiting time cultivating a garden—not entirely for food. The garden provided recreational diversion for them, but it also made a political statement, indicating that they were willing to wait for a response from the government for quite a period of time—as long as it takes a garden to mature. Before the gardens came to fruition, however, the protestors were evicted from their squatters' lots and removed from the city.

The succeeding national crisis, World War II, once more channeled the nation's energies into food production. The call went out from the Roosevelt administration to utilize all possible space into what were this time called "victory gardens." Charles Nissley's 1942 *Home Vegetable Gardening* offered cautionary remarks, providing insight into the emotional reaction to gardening during World War I: "We should avoid the mistakes of the First World War when the home owner was urged to plow up his lawn, his flower beds, and even his tennis court to grow vegetables. In too many cases, such ventures were dismal failures from the standpoint of the production of foodstuffs"[20] What Nissley does not acknowledge, however, is the psychological benefits of such a venture. Even if the food production quota was not met, the participating citizens considered themselves to be making a contribution to the war effort. From 1942 to 1945, victory gardens achieved the same result. Indeed, the enthusiasm and support with which the call for victory gardens was answered reveals the intense patriotism of the populace.

Periodical articles of the time carried rousing challenges to American nationalism. The titles also indicate the optimism with which potential gardeners approached the venture. For instance, a 1942 issue of the *Rotarian* carried an article by G. T. Donoghue, "Put That Dirt to Work!"[21] In a February 1943 issue of the *Christian Science Monitor* an article by E. M. Eaton encouraged, "They Haven't Rationed Your Own Back Yard," adopting just the right tone of defiance to inspire patriotic Americans.[22] Generating further interest in participation was D. W. Bailey's "Make Your First Line of Defense in the Back Yard" in a February 1942 issue of *House Beautiful*.[23] Through gardening, Americans could believe they had some control over their lives even though unpredictability enveloped most of the world. In the last year of the war, members of the military, like the bridge builders and members of the Bonus Army before them, found sustenance for body and spirit in gardening. In a February 1945 issue of *Better Homes and Gardens*, C. Ford's article has a title that speaks for itself: "G.I.s Garden Around the World."[24]

As the country readjusted during the post-World War II period, growing vegetables was left largely to commercial food producers. The building boom of the late forties did not need to rely on gardening space as a marketing device. Buyers waited on long lists to purchase a home. Seemingly, the interest in home ownership would have inspired a regeneration of the pastoral feeling. Instead, the homeowners' consuming interest was in the new home appliances available for the first time. The civilian population could now benefit from the technology which had for four years been concentrated on the war effort. The remaining years of the forties and the entire decade of the fifties saw little interest in the pastoral aspects of living. Popular interest continued to turn to technological advancements; consequently, gardening receded as a recreational activity. Not even the Korean War inspired gardeners to cultivate for increased food production. Very few "defense" gardening articles appeared in periodicals throughout the duration of the Korean War.

The decade of the sixties, however, became the counterpoint to technology as a new romanticism swept the country. Once again gardening reflected the country's social and political changes. Rebelling against American involvement in the Vietnam War and against the technological emphasis of American culture, large numbers of Americans created a new value system. Much popular sentiment turned toward preservation—both of human lives and of the environment. There were no victory or defense gardens to mark the conflict in Southeast Asia.

Two distinct gardening philosophies emerged early in the sixties: the chemical and the organic. Organic gardening became the watchword for a new generation of cultivators. Ecological concerns dominated, giving rise to many publications offering information and advice on how to grow vegetables without using insecticides and herbicides. Though technology was on the whole loudly denounced, technical skills did introduce two new methods of growing plants: solar power and hydroponic gardening. Both methods were embraced by ecology-minded Americans: in this instance, technology worked to the good, providing a natural means to grow food. *Organiculture* and *sustainable agriculture,* new terms for the anti-technology—primarily anti-chemical—philosophy, began to appear in gardening publications. Moreover, many new publications devoted to organic gardening became available.

The frontier spirit re-emerged as popular interest focused on self-sufficiency. Unquestionably, the country was in the midst of another romantic movement, and one of its major manifestations was in a kind of spiritualism related to vegetable gardening. Indicating the mood of those who had rediscovered the soil is M. A. Roche's 1964 essay in *Flower Grower,* "Happiness Is a Thing Called Vegetable Gardening."[25] But *true* happiness could come to the novitiates only if they practiced organic gardening.

Emerging as a shaman of the new gardening religion was Robert Rodale, a prolific writer who also founded Rodale Press of Emmaus, Pennsylvania, which began publishing *Organic Gardening and Farming,* a monthly periodical that later became *Rodale's Organic Gardening.* The publication addressed the efficacy of organic gardening in articles with such titles as "Organic Gardeners Grow 'Em Big!" by M. C. Goldman.[26] The Rodale Press also publishes books and has been a major source of information on vegetable gardening for those adhering to the organiculture philosophy. The press's success in both books and periodicals attests to the power of this new movement in the history of vegetable gardening.

In fact, the ecological movement essentially took control of gardening in the sixties and seventies. The obsession with protecting the environment became a religious fervor to purify everything, even the digestive system. Rodale's article in *Organic Gardening and Farming* titled "Holistic Gardening" reflects both the movement away from mainstream gardening techniques and an increased sense of mission about the practice.[27]

One significant offshoot of the new gardening evangelism has been a movement to preserve food flavor. An increasing number of tasteless fresh fruits and vegetables have been presented for public consumption. Drawing public attention to this insidious trend is a beneficial side-effect of popular interest in ecology. Technological advancements in shipping have meant that fruits and vegetables once available only within a limited growing period are now available year round. Availability, however, has not meant enhanced flavor; instead, in many cases flavor has disappeared. Tomatoes, for example, are for sale every month of the year—if the purchaser does not mind a taste similar to styrofoam. In *The Great American Tomato Book,* Robert Hendrickson shows that concern over the loss of tomato flavor has reached the nation's legislative body. He cites as an example Representative James A. Burke of Massachussetts demonstrating the intractability of what he describes as one of the "rocklike store-bought spheres." In an Agricultural Subcommittee hearing, Burke drops a "shipped tomato" on a table and watches it bounce off as support of his assertion that such tomatoes do not qualify to be called by that name. The fall did not even break the tomato's skin.[28] Shipped tomatoes, like many other fruits and vegetables, are now grown for stability in transportation, not for flavor. Strawberries, too, now travel well, and they are of a magnificent size, but they taste more like apples than strawberries. And though green onions can now be had the year round, the eater often bites into a hollow stalk, virtually devoid of the onion's familiar pungent taste.

By taking note of a serious loss of flavor in foods, the ecology-minded have drawn useful attention to the gradual extinction of many seeds which produce succulent fruits and vegetables. The seeds for many such plants are in some cases lost forever. To prevent further loss, interested people have formed organizations to collect and preserve what are now known as "heirloom vegetables." Even the business community has recognized the movement, a sure sign of national establishment. For example, S. D. Atchison wrote an article in 1987 for *Business Week* entitled "Growing Food with That Ol' Time Flavor."[29] Addressing an audience who has personal knowledge of that "old time flavor," Eliot Tozer, in "Heirloom Seeds: The New Collectibles,"[30] writes to the Americans who may be able to provide badly needed help in saving seeds of heirloom plants. Many older Americans who have gardened all their lives, particularly residents in rural areas, continue to save seeds from the slowly disappearing plants.

More abstract and literally much closer to a form of spiritualism is the use of gardening for therapy. In *Modern Home Gardening* Clyde Calvin and Donald Knutson remark, "Gardeners universally find pleasure in working with the soil and plants and this involvement with nature reduces pressures and tensions."[31] Calvin and Knutson speak rather casually, however, treating the curative results of gardening as being incidental. Others speak of them in a more direct fashion. For instance, a 1976 issue of *Science Digest* features an article entitled "Hortitherapy."[32] A 1973 issue of *Parks and Conservation,* a pamphlet of the parks system, includes an article by E. Stainbrooke, "Man's Psychic Need for Nature."[33] A more folksy approach appears in a 1978 issue of *Organic Gardening and Farming*: John Wellencamp's "Just Plough Your Problems into the Garden."[34] Though most of these publications appeared in the late seventies, paralleling the entire organic-ecological movement, there remains a serious interest in carefully monitored programs that use gardening for psychological therapy.

For all the philosophizing about ecology in the sixties and early seventies, actual cultivation of home gardens increased very little. It took the inflation of the late seventies to affect home gardeners. The high prices of food and other consumer goods highly motivated diverse people either to turn the back yard into a garden, to rent a garden plot, or to participate in a community garden. It was during this period that community gardening achieved a marked increase, generating the founding of the National Gardening Association in Burlington, Vermont. A nonprofit, member-supported organization, it has helped many other communities establish and operate community gardening projects.

Adding to the popular interest in gardening in the late seventies was a raised consciousness about good health. Ecology and its offspring, organiculture, remained influential throughout the rest of the decade. During this period, herb gardens re-emerged as important cultivations. Herbs are one of the constants in growing foodstuffs, having appeared in the earliest forms of humankind's gardens. They were used in the Middle East, the Orient, and Europe for medicines, for religious purposes, and for seasoning foods. For centuries, much of the success of food preparation depended on herbs. Because much of the meat consumed was wild game, herbs were needed in its preparation to overcome its strong, off-putting flavor. Monasteries maintained herb gardens. So did early families, placing the kitchen garden and the herb garden in close proximity. In the late 1970s and the early 1980s, a United States obsession with cooking foods untainted by fats and sodium made herbs again an important ingredient. Herbs effectively season both meats and vegetables, providing a pleasant flavor and eliminating the need for other less healthy seasonings. Herb gardening once more is popular.

The history of gardening in the eighties has been largely uneventful. The organic-ecological movement is still influential. Community gardening, though not as widespread as during the inflationary period of the preceding decade, is still actively pursued. Dedicated gardeners continue to talk of soil preparation in the fall, begin to search seed catalogs in the winter, turn the soil early in the spring, and plant as soon as weather conditions permit. The decade has not seen large numbers of new converts to gardening. The economic and social conditions are too stable. Gardening in the United States reaches a frenzied state only under threatening circumstances.

There does appear to be a movement back to technology, however. A number of publications now promote the use of computers in gardening. Examples are a February 1984 *Mechanics Illustrated* article by B. Benn, "Use a Computer Service to Increase Your Garden Harvest,"[35] and a 1986 *Saturday Evening Post* article by C. Faris, "Gardening by Computer."[36]

The methodical procedure of gardening is also being revolutionized by being brought into the fast-is-better contemporary culture. Joining the fast-food industry in general, and Jiffy Lube, Lens Crafters, instant pudding, and instant coffee in particular, is instant gardening. Derek Fell has authored a paperback (fast reading, only ninety-six pages) entitled *The One-Minute Gardener*.[37] Two periodical articles also advocate quicker gardening: a March 1987 article in *Sunset* entitled "The Believe-It-or-Not One-Day Vegetable Garden"[38] and more recently, Derek Fell's "The Twenty-Minute Vegetable Garden"[39] Speed is an important ingredient of gardening history in contemporary culture.

REFERENCE WORKS

There has been little comprehensive bibliographic work done on vegetable gardening. No indexes or abstracts exist which give the researcher help in locating gardening literature. Most gardening books, particularly gardening manuals and other how-to books, include bibliographies, but the quality is uneven. Some authors provide carefully detailed information, while others give nothing more than titles and prices of available books and periodicals. Since authors of gardening books consider principally the needs of their gardening readers, naturally they do not provide exhaustive bibliographic information. The one annotated bibliography, *Gardening: A Guide to the Literature,* compiled by Richard T. Isaacson, is invaluable. It is not as complete as a researcher might wish, but it is far superior to any other source to which the researcher can turn. Isaacson states in his introduction that the bibliography is not comprehensive, and he gives his rationale for what he includes and excludes. Isaacson knows gardening and he knows the literature. The book is arranged well; the annotations are concise and to the point.

The Isaacson work's major drawback for the person interested specifically in vegetable gardening is that the book also includes information on landscape design and ornamental gardening plants. Nevertheless, the book's arrangement gives access to particular information. Isaacson provides a useful list of general gardening periodicals as well as periodicals of regional interest. He includes names and addresses of organizations for persons interested in plants as well as providing information on libraries that have gardening interests and collections. This book is a major source for work on gardening.

A traditional index, the *Readers' Guide to Periodical Literature,* is unwieldy but useful as a source for gardening articles. *The Farm and Garden Index,* equally cumbersome, is another important source for periodicals. Like the *Readers' Guide,* this index does not annotate the articles; consequently, the researcher often has higher expectations than the located article fulfills. Moreover, because this index covers large commercial planting as well as home gardening, the researcher needs to look extra carefully at the titles to avoid fruitless searches. Nevertheless, it covers some gardening periodicals not indexed elsewhere and is therefore a useful source.

A seemingly unlikely source is *Home Gardening in International Development: What the Literature Shows* by Leslie Brownrigg, published in 1985 by the League for International Food Education under a grant from the U.S. Agency for International Development. It is designed primarily to give information on gardening projects internationally, many of which receive economic assistance from the United States. Although there is much material about Asia and Europe that is not useful, the annotated bibliography and the inventories of international organizations involved in home gardening and their projects include information on U.S. publications and agencies. The book is somewhat confusing in its format, but the extensive appendixes reward a patient researcher.

The Brooklyn Botanic Garden Record, published quarterly, provides a helpful list of recent books, magazines, and articles as well as state experimental station bulletins. The list is selected, but it is annotated.

Richard Nichols's *Plant Doctor in His Vegetable Garden,* published in 1976, has a useful annotated bibliography. His commentary in the annotations is to the point and gives the researcher a good sense of the quality of the publications. *Bibliography of Garden Books,* prepared by Richardson L. Wright in 1943, is helpful if one is interested in an overview of publications on garden books. It is, of course, dated. Since some things in gardening never change, many of the books listed are useful within a restricted need. Also dated is Paul F. Frese's *100 Best Books for the Gardener's Library,* first published in 1948 and revised in 1952. The provided list is beneficial in research on gardening techniques at the middle of the century.

Gardening encyclopedias, manuals, and handbooks tend to present information in similar ways. Most of them give details about times to plant particular vegetables, identify and illustrate plants, suggest ways to deal with weeds and insects, and recommend gardening tools. They distinguish themselves in part by the quality of illustrations as well as by the thoroughness of content. Gardening dictionaries also are similar in naming and defining techniques and in describing plants.

One of the best sources available is the work by Liberty H. Bailey, a name familiar to most gardeners. The most current and complete reference to cultivated plants is Bailey's *Hortus Third: A Concise Dictionary of Plants Cultivated in the United States and Canada,* considered the authority on gardening plants by people in diverse fields of study. The plants are arranged alphabetically by genus, including the complete family of the plant, the authorities in the field of study, and botanical descriptions. There is also a detailed glossary of botanical terms. This book is thorough, scholarly, and reliable.

The *Vegetable Gardening Encyclopedia* by the editors of *Consumer Guide* is also a first-rate source. The work is exactly what one has come to expect from the Consumer Guide organization, a balanced and fair report. The book is written in simple, easy-to-read language which at the same time does not demean the reader's intelligence. The graphs and charts are easy to comprehend; the illustrations, all in black and white, are clear and useful. Specific calendar information on when the first and last frost can be expected in regions of the United States helps both planters and researchers. Garden pests are identified with illustrations, in addition to explanations of their favorite plant food and of the best ways to destroy these insects. Beneficial insects are identified so that the gardener will not eradicate the garden helpers. At the same time, there are suggestions on how to destroy plant-eating insects. Along with recipes at the end of the book, there are canning guides. Additionally, the editors provide a list of state cooperative extension service offices. There is practical information on a variety of topics, making the book useful for research. This book gives the researcher a view of the complete cycle of gardening from preparation of ground through preparation and preservation of foods for the table.

The Time-Life Encyclopedia of Gardening is a multivolume series, each volume on a different gardening topic, prepared by different editors. The volume entitled *Vegetables and Fruits* is edited by James Underwood Crockett. As is common with Time-Life publications, the books are well illustrated with photographs, graphs, and drawings. Because the books are aimed at a general audience, they are more useful for beginning gardeners than for researchers. Another multivolume work, Thomas H. Everett's *The New York Botanical Garden Illustrated Encyclopedia of Horticulture,* is not as simplified and is invaluable for a researcher. It gives extensive cross-references and details on the ancestry of each plant. The advice on cultivation is intellectually stimulating as well as informative. The book is an excellent source of information for gardeners—either novice or experienced.

In *Gardening: A Guide to the Literature,* Richard Isaacson calls Donald Wyman's *Wyman's Gardening Encyclopedia* "the best one-volume gardening encyclopedia." Because Professor Wyman is himself a gardener, his explanations are presented in an exceptionally clear and informative way. Wyman includes helpful details on the likelihood a plant has of thriving in different climate zones. It is an excellent reference for gardeners and is useful to researchers as a means of verifying information.

The Encyclopedia of Gardening Techniques was edited by Christopher Brickell under the guidance of the Royal Horticultural Society, England. It would seem to be of little use to American gardeners. The edition distributed in the United States, however, provides information on climate and growing seasons applicable to American regions. The book is divided into sections with large Arabic numbers denoting distinct points of information on separate vegetables, making details easy to locate. There is an abundance of illustrations done in subdued shades of gray and green. This book is an excellent source of step-by-step guidance on growing plants, and its format makes it quite useful for research.

The National Gardening Association's *Gardening: The Complete Guide to Growing America's Favorite Fresh Fruits and Vegetables* is edited by Genoa Shepley and Anne Eldridge. The slick pages are filled with glossy color pictures of all aspects of gardening. There are details on every stage of planting and growing vegetables. This book will be of great help to anyone seeking a dependable source of gardening information. Its handsome presentation makes it a pleasure to browse through. Another useful source book is Joan Lee Faust's *The New York Times Book of Vegetable Gardening.* Faust's sense of humor and her thoroughness make this book a pleasant and useful source.

Since most gardening books base their information on northern or eastern planting, it is important to examine handbooks from other regions. An excellent source of information is the *Home Garden Handbook: A Month-by-Month Checklist,* edited by H. C. Thompson. The book is published by

Oxmoor House, publishers of the excellent magazine *Southern Living*. The southern climate creates a need for details not found in other gardening manuals.

Whether a believer in chemical gardening or in organic gardening, the gardener must come to terms with weeds. It is impossible to escape weeds, even with sophisticated method. They are as persistent and pervasive as insects. Nor can research in gardening be complete without an understanding of weeds. An excellent dictonary-handbook is Mea Allen's *Weeds: The Unbidden Guests in Our Gardens,* which illustrates and describes weeds. A glossary and a good bibliography are included in this interesting and informative work. Also beneficial for general information is F. F. Rockwell's *10,000 Garden Questions Answered by Twenty Experts.* Published in 1959, the book is dated; nevertheless, it contains helpful information.

There are two additional imperative needs for gardeners: an almanac and seed catalogs. At one time, the gardener had only the almanac for advice on weather conditions and the correct times for planting. Popular gardening today has more sophisticated methods. Indeed, the almanac is still an invaluable source, but Starwood Publishers has provided something easier on the eyes: a glossy gardener's calendar. Versions are published for different regions of the country. A U.S. Department of Agriculture map is printed on each version with information suited to the particular weather zone specified. The company publishes calendars both for ornamentals and for vegetables and herbs. Each monthly leaf covers "Outdoors" and "Indoors," informing when to prune, when to fertilize, and how to carry out successful garden maintenance. The luxuriant photographs are in full color, quite a contrast to the drab almanac.

Many garden catalogs are free, but gardeners not on a mailing list need a source. Barbara J. Barton has provided *Gardening by Mail: A Source Book.* This reference book for mail-order gardening amply covers the varied sources for seeds, plants, and even worms—for those who want a particular kind of cultivation.

Additional sources for help are local county agent's offices, the state departments of agriculture, and the U.S. Department of Agriculture. Also useful as a source is the Superintendent of Documents, U.S. Government Printing Office, Washington, D. C. 20402, and for pamphlets and other material, Garden Resources of Washington (G.R.O.W.), 1419 V Street NW, Room 300, Washington, D.C.

The above list does not cover the surfeit of gardening books, but it provides the most useful sources for gardening research. An exhaustive annotated list of gardening publications would comprise a volume in itself.

RESEARCH COLLECTIONS

Research in vegetable gardening is not restricted to libraries. While a number of libraries mantain book collections on gardening, equally as many botanical gardens and arboretums have book repositories. Additionally, it is necessary to do some research at experimental farms or at living historical farms and museums.

Traditional library collections are largely in the East, although one important repository is in Cleveland, at the Garden Center of Greater Cleveland, Eleanor Square Library, 11030 East Blvd., Cleveland, Ohio 44106. Since Richard T. Isaacson, compiler of *Gardening: A Guide to the Literature* is librarian at Eleanor Square, research work there has an additional advantage. The Horticultural Society of New York Library on 128 West 57th Street, New York, New York 10019 contains a useful collection of gardening material. A traditional place of research, Smithsonian Institution Libraries, offers helpful information at the Botany Library at 10th and Constitution, Washington, D. C. 20560. Researchers can find wide-ranging material on plants, including, of course, ornamentals.

A little less orthodox is the Rodale Experiment Station, 33 East Minor Street, Emmaus, Pennsylvania 18049. With the increasing interest in subsistence agriculture, the Rodale organization has become a major center in advancing organic gardening. The station maintains a library of almost 15,000 books and bound periodicals. It subscribes to 800 journals and files subjects related to its own publications. Researchers can benefit from work in the library if the topic is related in any way to organic gardening.

The United States Department of Agriculture maintains its National Agriculture Library in Beltsville, Maryland. The library holds the largest collection of documents related to agriculture in the United States. Gardening is only a division of the collection, but the computerized data base, AGRICOLA, offers maximum efficiency in locating particular items. Moreover, access to AGRICOLA is available through several commercial vendors as well as at land grant universities throughout the United States. A further benefit is the comprehensive bibliographies that the library data base publishes on an irregular basis. Reference services are available at the library itself from 8:00 A.M. to 4:30 P.M. on federal work days. The library also maintains a Small Grains Collection at the Plant Genetics and Germplasm Institute at the Beltsville site.

RAIN Information and Referral Center, 2278 Northwest Irving Street, Portland, Oregon 97210, maintains a small library of 4,000 volumes. The library is open only three days a week. The center also publishes a bimonthly journal, answers phone and written inquiries, and conducts workshops. Though the library collection is small, people in the Northwest can take advantage of the library's general services.

There are several Botanical gardens that maintain libraries. For the Chicago Botanic Garden Library, P.O. Box 400, Glencoe, Illinois 60022, it is advisable to make a reservation. The Denver Botanic Gardens, 909 York Street, Denver, Colorado 80206, maintains a research collection and operates an outreach community gardening project. Hunt Institute for Botanical

Documentation, Hunt Botanical Library, Carnegie-Mellon University, Pittsburgh, Pennsylvania 15213, has an extensive botanical history collection. The New York Botanical Gardens Library, Bronx, New York 10458, has the largest North American botanical library. In the Midwest, the Missouri Botanical Garden Library, 4344 Shaw Blvd., St. Louis, Missouri 63166–0299, is a superior resource for botanical information. The library answers inquires and the laboratories analyze data. There is a herbarium which has an excellent collection of tropical plants. The Royal Botanical Garden's Hamilton Library in Hamilton, Ontario, Canada, maintains a collection specializing in Canadian garden history.

Libraries affiliated with arboretums are located in the East, Midwest, and West. The Harvard University Arnold Arboretum and Gray Herbarium Libraries, 22 Divinity Avenue, Cambridge, Massachusetts 02138, are excellent sources, as is the Farlow Reference Library at Harvard. Both the Minnesota Landscape Arboretum Andersen Horticultural Library, 3675 Arboretum Drive, Chahassen, Minnesota 55317, and the Los Angeles State and County Arboretum Plant Science Library, 301 N. Baldwin Avenue, Arcadia, California 91006, are good sources for research.

An experimental group working under the name PLENTY maintains a working farm called, appropriately enough, The Farm, 156 Drakes Lane, Summertown, Tennessee 38483. For a number of years, the communal farm residents, composed of former Californians who settled in the small Tennessee town in the sixties, were not particularly receptive to researchers; but now that the organization is established, they permit observation and limited research regarding their experimental garden methods. Persons interested in heirloom gardening can gather primary information at the National Seed Storage Laboratory, Fort Collins, Colorado 80521. The facility is the major seed bank in the United States.

There are a number of living historical farms and museums in all areas of the United States. A particularly interesting one is the Acadian House Museum, St. Martinville, Louisiana 70582. There are too many of these living museums to list here, but anyone interested can get information from the Association of Living Historical Farms and Museums, c/o The Smithsonian, Washington, D.C. 20560.

HISTORY AND CRITICISM

There is no gardening criticism in the traditional scholarly sense. Most evaluations of material on gardening come from gardeners who favor one method over another; organic gardeners are particularly strong in their opinions. All articles and books recommending the use of chemicals are evaluated as being errors in judgment by organic gardeners. And though they do criticize the concept of chemical gardening, it is not traditional criticism in that the writers address only the attitude on chemicals. Writers about gardening are such an affable and optimistic group on the whole that, with the preceding exception, they are more nearly a brotherhood than competitors. An article in *U.S. News and World Report* during the frenzy of gardening to fight inflation, however, sounds a note of caution, deromanticizing the gardener's view of vegetable growing: "You Can Save by Gardening—But Watch for the Pitfalls."

There are a number of gardening histories, but rarely do they adhere to scholarly requirements. Many of the writers include bibliographies but neglect other forms of documentation. One distinct exception is *Growing with Community Gardening*, Mary Lee Coe's history of community gardening, in which she provides complete documentation and a helpful bibliography. A large number of the general gardening books are also useful as sources for historical information. Several authors consider it imperative to include a section either in the introduction or at the end of the book on the history of gardening. For example, Calvin and Knutson's *Modern Home Gardening* includes an informative section titled "Origins of Agriculture and Gardening" in the introduction. Roy Genders's *The Perfect Vegetable and Herb Garden* devotes an entire division to "The History of Vegetables," and *America's Garden Book* by James and Louise Bush-Brown offers a useful section, "Historical Background." *The Great American Tomato Book* by Robert Hendrickson gives a great deal of space to the history of the tomato, and in *Famine on the Wind* Carefoot and Sprott write page after page on the history of the potato.

A History of Horticulture in America to 1860 by Ulysses P. Headrick is a serious, scholarly study, but, as the title denotes, its contents cover only a limited segment of history. An article by John A. Wott, "A Short History of Consumer Horticulture," in *Hortscience,* is suitable only for a cursory look because it is derivative, failing to go beyond the books and articles already available.

Of the books devoted entirely to the history of gardening, none deals solely with vegetable gardening. Anthony Huxley's *An Illustrated History of Gardening* is a well-written, intellectually engaging, and visually rewarding book, having an abundance of illustrations and photographs. But it devotes more space to ornamental gardening than to vegetable gardening. Huxley provides a thorough history of cultural cultivation. This book is the most useful for general information on gardening history. One can only wish that the book had more documentation, even though there is a helpful bibliography. Richardson Wright's *Story of Gardening* is good reading, but, like Huxley, he gives over a major portion of the book to ornamental gardening. Wright includes a bibliography, but it is essentially useless because it is seriously incomplete in its information. Other books that seem promising in their titles, such as Carlton B. Lees's *Gardens, Plants, and Man* and Julia S. Berrall's *The Garden: An Illustrated History,* are lovely to look at but useless as histories of vegetable gardening since both books deal with flowers, lawns, trees, and shrubs—but not vegetables.

Although there is a plethora of gardening books, missing is a strong scholarly book on the history of gardening in general or on vegetable gardening in particular. There are, of course, scholarly books on agriculture—the raising of commercial crops and experimental studies for commercial gardening. But there is nothing on small home gardening. The absence of serious studies reflects the cultural view that gardening is important as a popular topic but not as a scholarly one.

Gardening Periodicals

Gardening periodicals have a more scholarly cast than gardening books because a number of the agricultural journals also include home gardening articles. For instance, *American Horticulturist,* a glossy monthly magazine published by the American Horticulture Society, has many home gardening subscribers. The *Avant Gardener,* a monthly in newsletter format designed for serious gardeners, is published by the Horticultural Data Processors. A periodical favored by gardeners is the quarterly *The Brooklyn Botanic Garden Record.*

Diversity is a specialized bimonthly publication for the plant genetic resources community. It is useful for information on heirloom seeds. Also aimed at a special audience is *The Herb Quarterly.*

Of general interest as well as featuring articles on community gardening is *National Gardening,* a monthly publication of the National Gardening Association. In the same category is *Family Handyman* (incorporating *Home Gardening*), which has a national circulation and covers all home gardening activities. It is published nine times a year from July through December.

Twenty-five years ago, *Weeds Today,* published quarterly by the Weed Science Society of America, could have been categorized as general interest—even though it deals with a specialized subject. Now, however, the magazine must be qualified as being of interest only to those who accept chemical gardening. For the backyard gardener who uses herbicides, this answers many questions about identification, life cycle, habitat, and control of the ubiquitous weed. *Popular Gardening,* exactly suited for popular culture, ceased publication in 1968.

Organic gardeners have a surfeit of publications, but if all except the two following periodicals ceased publication, the needs of these gardeners could be satisfied: the monthly Rodale's *Organic Gardening* (described as "the bible of the organic movement") and the equally ecologically dedicated *Mother Earth News,* a bi-monthly.

Two monthly publications, *Flower and Garden* and *Sunset Magazine,* are published in regional editions. Both have a varied table of contents. Urban gardeners have the *City Harvester,* which promotes urban gardening and features articles to achieve that end. The *Journal of Community Gardening* anticipates problems and provides information for the country's growing segment of community gardeners.

ANTHOLOGIES AND REPRINTS

Vegetable gardening has very little in the way of anthologies or reprints. Because of the renewed interest in community gardening in the mid-seventies, *Horticulture* offered a reprint issue of the victory gardening articles published by the magazine during World War II. The date of publication is July 1976; J. Nelson wrote an introduction to accompany the reprinted issue, which is useful primarily for historical and cultural research.

In 1959 Joseph Wood Krutch edited an anthology, *The Gardener's World,* published by Putnam. The collection is a useful source, but the material is dated.

NOTES

1. T. Steadman, "Get a Jump on Spring," *Southern Living,* 22 (January 1987), 70–71.

2. Peter Chan, with Spencer Gill, *Better Gardens the Chinese Way* (Portland Maine: Graphic Arts Center, 1977).

3. L. V. Powers, "Today's Vegetable Turn-On." *American Home,* 75 (March 1972), 86–87.

4. "Great Hoe-Down," *Time,* 105 (May 5, 1975), 63–64.

5. B. Pleasant, "Beat the Southern Broccoli Blues," *Rodale's Organic Gardening,* 34 (November 1987), 80.

6. B. Pleasant, "Meet the Hotheads: Growing Head Lettuce in the South," *Rodale's Organic Gardening,* 35 (January 1988), 36.

7 T. Tilling, "Laugh at Food Prices—Hoe, Hoe, Hoe!" *Saturday Evening Post,* 254 (May-June 1982), 70–72.

8. Robert Hendrickson, *The Great American Tomato Book* (New York: Double-day, 1977), p. ix.

9. G. L. Carefoot and E. R. Sprott, *Famine on the Wind: Man's Battle Against Plant Disease* (Chicago: Rand McNally, 1981), p. 70.

10. Anthony Huxley, *An Illustrated History of Gardening* (New York: Paddington Press, 1978), p. 9.

11. Roy Genders, *The Perfect Vegetable and Herb Garden* (New York: Drake, 1972), p. 123.

12. Huxley, p. 10.

13. Edward Hyams, *A History of Gardens and Gardening* (New York: Praeger, 1971), pp. 89–90.

14. Ibid., p. 91.

15 Richardson Wright, *Story of Gardening* (New York: Dover, 1934), pp. 259–60.

16. "How Three Bountiful Colorado Gardens Solved Mountain Problems," *Sunset Magazine* (May 1987), 264–65.

17. Wright, p. 248.

18. "Garden Plots of the Bridge Builders," *Survey*, 26 (May 27, 1911), 323–24.

19. Adolph Kruhm, *Home Vegetable Gardening from A to Z* (New York: Doubleday, 1918), p. v.

20. William Martin, Introduction to *Home Vegetable Gardening*, by Charles H. Nissley (New Brunswick, N.J.: Rutgers University Press, 1942), p. 14.

21. G. T. Donoghue, "Put That Dirt to Work!" *Rotarian*, 60 (April 1942), 39.

22. E. M. Eaton, "They Haven't Rationed Your Own Back Yard," *Christian Science Monitor Weekly Magazine* (February 13, 1943), 8–9.

23. D. W. Bailey, "Make Your First Line of Defense in the Back Yard," *House Beautiful*, 84 (February 1942), 56–57, 97.

24. C. Ford, "G.I.s Garden Around the World" *Better Homes and Gardens*, 23 (February 1945), 23.

25. M. A. Roche, "Happiness Is a Thing Called Vegetable Gardening," *Flower Grower*, 51 (January 1964), 40–42.

26. M. C. Goldman, "Organic Gardeners Grow 'Em Big," *Organic Gardening and Farming*, 16 (June 1969), 43–45.

27. Robert Rodale, "Holistic Gardening," *Organic Gardening and Farming*, 25 (May 1978), 36–38.

28. Hendrickson, p. xi.

29. S. D. Atchison, "Growing Food with That Ol' Time Flavor," *Business Week* (March 2, 1987), 106.

30. Eliot Tozer, "Heirloom Seeds: The New Collectibles," *Modern Maturity*, 31 (April-May 1988), 24–28.

31. Clyde Calvin and Donald M. Knutson, *Modern Home Gardening Techniques* (New York: Wiley, 1983), p. 9.

32. "Hortitherapy," *Science Digest*, 80 (October 1976), 10.

33. E. Stainbrook "Man's Psychic Need for Nature," *Parks and Conservation* (September 1973), 22–23.

34. John Wellencamp, "Just Plough Your Problems into the Garden," *Organic Gardening and Farming*, 25 (January 1978), 158.

35. B. Benn, "Use a Computer Service to Increase Your Garden Harvest," *Mechanics Illustrated*, 80 (February 1984), p. 48.

36 C. Faris. "Gardening by Computer," *Saturday Evening Post*, 258 (April 1986), 32.

37. Derek Fell, *The One-Minute Gardener* (Philadelphia: Running Press, 1988).

38. "The Believe-It-or-Not One-Day Vegetable Garden," *Sunset Magazine* (March 1987), 88–91.

39. Derek Fell, "The Twenty-Minute Vegetable Garden," *Flower and Garden* (February-March 1988), 50–51.

BIBLIOGRAPHY

Books and Articles

Allen, Mea. *Weeds: The Unbidden Guests in Our Gardens*. New York: Viking, 1978.

Atchinson, S. D. "Growing Food with That Ol' Time Flavor." *Business Week* (March 2, 1987), 106.

Bailey, D. W. "Make Your First Line of Defense in the Back Yard." *House Beautiful,* (February 1942), 56–57, 97.

Bailey, Liberty H. *Hortus Third: A Concise Dictionary of Plants Cultivated in the United States and Canada.* New York: Macmillan, 1976.

Baron, Robert C. *The Garden and Farm Books of Thomas Jefferson.* Golden, Colo.: Fulcrum, 1988.

Barton, Barbara J. *Gardening by Mail: A Source Book.* Sebastopol, Calif.: Tusker Press, 1988.

"The Believe-It-or-Not One-Day Vegetable Garden." *Sunset Magazine* (March 1987), 88–91.

Benn, B. "Use a Computer Service to Increase Your Garden Harvest." *Mechanics Illustrated,* 80 (February 1984), 48.

Berrall, Julia S. *The Garden: An Illustrated History.* New York: Viking, 1966.

Brickell, Christopher, ed. *The Encyclopedia of Gardening Techniques.* New York: Exeter Books, 1984.

Brownrigg, Leslie. *Home Gardening in International Development: What the Literature Shows.* Washington, D.C.: League for International Food Education, 1985.

Bush-Brown, James, and Louise Bush-Brown. *America's Garden Book.* New York: Scribner's, 1980.

Calvin, Clyde L., and Donald M. Knutson. *Modern Home Gardening.* New York: Wiley, 1983.

Carefoot, G. L., and E. R. Sprott. *Famine on the Wind: Man's Battle Against Plant Disease.* Chicago: Rand McNally, 1981.

Coe, Mary Lee. *Growing with Community Gardening.* Taftsville, Vt.: Countryman Press, 1978.

Chan, Peter, with Spencer Gill. *Better Vegetable Gardens the Chinese Way.* Portland Maine: Graphic Arts Center, 1977.

Crockett, James Underwood. *Vegetables and Fruits: The Time-Life Encyclopedia of Gardening.* New York: Time-Life Books, 1972.

Donoghue, G. T. "Put That Dirt to Work!" *Rotarian,* 60 (April 1942), 39.

Eaton, E. M. "They Haven't Rationed Your Own Back Yard." *Christian Science Monitor Weekly Magazine* (February 13, 1943), 8–9.

Everett, Thomas. *The New York Botanical Garden Illustrated Encyclopedia of Horticulture.* 10 vols. New York: Garland, 1980–82.

Faris, C. "Gardening by Computer." *Saturday Evening Post,* 258 (April 1986), 32.

Farm and Garden Index. Wooster, Ohio: Bell and Howell Microphoto, 1978–.

Faust, Joan Lee. *The New York Times Book of Vegetable Gardening.* New York: Quadrangle, 1975.

Fell, Derek. *The One-Minute Gardener.* Philadelphia: Running Press, 1988.

———. "The Twenty-Minute Vegetable Garden." *Flower and Garden* (February–March 1988), 50–51.

Ford, C. "G.I.s Garden Around the World." *Better Homes and Gardens,* 23 (February 1945), 23, 88.

Frese, Paul. *100 Best Books for the Gardener's Library.* Norwood, Mass.: Holliston Mills, 1952.

"Garden Plots of the Bridge Builders." *Survey* 26 (May 27, 1911), 323–24.

Genders, Roy. *The Perfect Vegetable and Herb Garden.* New York: Drake, 1972.

Goldman, M. C. "Organic Gardeners Grow 'Em Big!" *Organic Gardening and Farming,* (June 1969), 43–45.

"Great Hoe-Down." *Time,* 105 (May 5, 1975), 63–64.

Headrick, Ulysses P. *A History of Horticulture in America to 1860.* New York: Oxford University Press, 1950.

Hendrickson, Robert. *The Great American Tomato Book.* New York: Doubleday, 1977.

"Hortitherapy." *Science Digest,* 80 (October 1976), 10.

"How Three Bountiful Colorado Gardens Solved Mountain Problems." *Sunset Magazine* (May 1987), 264–65.

Hunter, Beatrice T. *Gardening Without Poisons.* Boston: Houghton Mifflin, 1964.

Huxley, Anthony. *An Illustrated History of Gardening.* New York: Paddington Press, 1978.

Hyams, Edward. *A History of Gardens and Gardening.* New York: Praeger, 1971.

Isaacson, Richard T. *Gardening: A Guide to the Literature.* New York: Garland, 1985.

Jabs, Carolyn. *The Heirloom Gardener.* San Francisco: Sierra Club Books, 1984.

Kruhm, Adolph. *Home Vegetable Gardening from A to Z.* New York: Doubleday, 1981.

Krutch, Joseph Wood, ed. *The Gardener's World.* New York: Putnam, 1959.

Lees, Carlton B. *Gardens, Plants, and Man.* Englewood Cliffs, N.J.: Prentice-Hall, 1970.

Manchester, William. *The Glory and the Dream: A Narrative History of America, 1932–1972.* Boston: Little, Brown, 1974.

Martin, William H. Introduction to *Home Vegetable Gardening,* by Charles H. Nissley. New Brunswick N.J.: Rutgers University Press, 1942.

Nelson, J., ed. "Reprints of the Victory Garden Articles." *Horticulture,* 54 (July 1976), 25–40.

Newcomb, Duane. *Mobile Home Gardening Guide.* Beverly Hills, Calif.: Trail-R-Club of America, 1963.

———. *The Postage Stamp Garden Book: How to Grow All the Food You Can Eat in Very Little Space.* Los Angeles: J. P. Tarcher, 1975.

Nichols, Richard. *Plant Doctor in His Vegetable Garden.* Philadelphia: Running Press, 1976.

Percival, Bob. *Organic Vegetable Gardening.* Blue Ridge Summit, Pa.: TAB Books, 1984.

Pleasant, B. "Beat the Southern Broccoli Blues." *Rodale's Organic Gardening,* 34 (November 1987), 80, 103–4.

———. "Meet the Hotheads: Growing Head Lettuce in the South." *Rodale's Organic Gardening,* 35 (January 1988), 36, 86, 91.

Powers, L. V. "Today's Vegetable Turn-On." *American Home,* 75 (March 1972), 86–87, 103.

Readers Guide to Periodical Literature. New York: H. W. Wilson, 1900.

Roche, M. A. "Happiness Is a Thing Called Vegetable Gardening." *Flower Grower,* 51 (January 1964), 40–42, 66.

Rockwell, F. F. *10,000 Garden Questions Answered by Twenty Experts.* New York: Doubleday, 1959.

Rodale, Robert. "Holistic Gardening." *Organic Gardening and Farming,* 25 (May 1978), 36–38.

Shepley, Genoa, and Anne Eldridge. *Gardening: The Complete Guide to Growing America's Favorite Fresh Fruits and Vegetables.* Reading, Mass.: Addison-Wesley, 1986.

Skelsey, Alice, and Gloria Huckaby. *Growing Up Green: Children and Parents Gardening Together.* New York: Workman, 1973.

Stainbrooke, E. "Man's Psychic Need for Nature." *Parks and Conservation* (September 1973), 22–23.

Steadman, T. "Get a Jump on Spring," *Southern Living,* 22 (January 1987), 70–71.

Thompson, Bob. *The New Victory Garden.* Boston: Little, Brown, 1988.

Thompson, H. C. ed. *Home Garden Handbook: A Month-by-Month Checklist.* Birmingham Ala.: Oxmoor House, 1975.

Tilling, T. "Laugh at Food Prices—Hoe! Hoe! Hoe!" *Saturday Evening Post,* 254 (May-June 1982), 70–72.

Tozer, Eliot. "Heirloom Seeds: The New Collectibles." *Modern Maturity,* 31 (April-May 1988), 24–28.

Vegetable Gardening Encyclopedia. Editors of *Consumer Guide.* New York: Galahad Books, 1982.

Wellencamp, John. "Just Plough Your Problems into the Garden." *Organic Gardening and Farming,* 25 (January 1978), 158.

Wott, John A. "A Short History of Consumer Horticulture." *Horticulture-Science,* 17 (June 1982), 313–16.

Wright, Richardson. *Bibliography of Garden Books.* New York: Saturday Review of Literature, 1943.

———. *Story of Gardening.* New York: Dover, 1934.

Wyman, Donald. *Wyman's Gardening Encyclopedia.* Rev. ed. New York: Macmillan, 1988.

"You Can Save by Gardening—But Watch for the Pitfalls." *US. News and World Report* 78 (March 31, 1975), 42–43.

Periodicals

American Horticulturist. Mt. Vernon, Va., 1922–.
Avant Gardener. New York, 1968–.
Brooklyn Botanic Garden Record. New York, 1945–.
City Harvester. Newark, 1978–.
Diversity. Arlington, Va., 1982–.
Family Handyman (incorporating *Home Gardening*). New York, 1951–.
Flower and Garden. Kansas City, 1957–.
The Herb Quarterly. Newfane, Vt., 1979–.
Journal of Community Gardening. Milwaukee, 1973–.
Mother Earth News. Hendersonville, N.C., 1970–.
National Gardening. Burlington, Vt., 1978–.
Rodale's Organic Gardening (formerly ROM Organic Gardening and Farming). Emmaus, Pa., 1942–.
Popular Gardening. London, 1950–70.
Southern Living. Birmingham, Ala., 1966–.
Sunset Magazine. Menlo Park, Calif., 1949–.
Weeds Today. Champaign, Ill., 1937–.

Graffiti

LISA N. HOWORTH

Of all the many overlooked aspects of American urban popular culture, graffiti has become the most difficult manifestation to ignore. A ubiquitous feature of the landscape of most large American cities, graffiti has been embraced by urban and youth cultures around the world in the same way that other phenomena of American popular culture have been: rock and roll, bluejeans, and hamburgers, to list a few notable examples.

For centuries a means of marking one's presence ("I was here") or making a particular scatological, political, sexual, or intellectual statement, graffiti has transcended limitations imposed by the written word and has evolved into a full-blown art. The questions and problems presented by graffiti are many, and of both an aesthetic and sociological nature. What are the psychological and sociological implications? What are the messages of graffiti, and what does it tell us about the writers? What does it say about society? Are the fantastic and original subway car paintings illuminating the underground transit system of New York City to be considered vandalism or art? And, if art, is it folk, or is it fine? Is it still graffiti when it is transferred to canvas, sold in a gallery, and hung on a living room wall? The message, medium, and significance of graffiti metamorphose rapidly—practically from year to year and certainly from decade to decade—and it seems barometric in response to other cultural phenomena, such as official campaigns to eradicate it, rock and roll trends, or the climate of the art world.

Traditionally, graffiti has been researched and discussed as an age-old method of simple communication. Psychologists have studied graffiti as a manifestation of certain identifiable patterns in individual human behavior.

Sociologists have scrutinized it in search of clues about society—how people view themselves as a part of or separated from society, and how those views are expressed. Folklorists have examined graffiti for the linguistic evidence it can provide. Many of these studies, done before the 1940s, have looked at graffiti as the action of individuals in a psychosocial context.

The great significance of graffiti as an important artifact of several subcultures was not investigated until recent years after graffiti had flowered into a popular art with connections to other facets of urban popular culture: dance, music, television, comic books, drugs, and computers. Even more recently graffiti has been given serious consideration as a "high" art and therefore as a marketable commodity.

For the purposes of this chapter, it is useful to discuss graffiti as two forms: graffiti and graffiti art. Graffiti will be discussed as the traditional, monochromatic initials, names, and messages found inscribed on tree trunks, in cement, on bridge overpasses, and on the walls of "private" areas such as public restrooms. Traditional graffiti continues to be common throughout the United States and is not usually associated exclusively with any particular environment.

Graffiti art, however, is strictly an urban phenomenon and will be considered here as the colorful spray-painted names, messages, and three-dimensional images that began appearing on walls, subway trains, and handball courts in the mid–1970s. In addition to being a popular urban art form, graffiti art is also identified with smaller subcultures, such as the youth and ethnic cultures of a city. Graffiti art is a melting pot of pop influences, drawing images and inspiration from 1960s nostalgia, music, dance, television, comic books, and computer graphics and jargon. Because a good deal of research has already been compiled on traditional graffiti, and because graffiti art is a relatively new phenomenon and the research is scant, ephemeral, and involves a variety of media, the greater part of this chapter will be devoted to graffiti art.

HISTORIC OUTLINE

The folklorist Alan Dundes has pointed out that while it is academically acceptable to study graffiti of past cultures, there is something less permissible about scholarly investigations of graffiti in our own time. Since Dundes made this observation, nearly a quarter of a century has elapsed, during which time graffiti in America has evolved into a phenomenon with powerful cultural and sociological implications. Its dimensions as a cultural phenomenon have expanded and metamorphosed from the traditional marking of public surfaces with names and initials to the spectacular street murals featured in *Colors,* the 1988 Dennis Hopper film about gang violence in Los Angeles, to contemporary works of art offered for sale for thousands of dollars by the prestigious and highly proper auction houses of Sotheby and Christie. Those who are interested in the study of popular culture in America should be very thankful that a handful of "graffiti watchers" has been observing and documenting this ephemeral and rapidly changing phenomenon because it is such a rich source of cultural information, revealing a great deal not only about widely disparate societal groups but also about urban American popular arts.

The history of graffiti is as old as that of mankind. Wherever there have been people and inviting, unmarked surfaces, there have been the scrawled gesticulations signifying ritual, warning, decoration, or simply existence. The word itself, *graffiti*, originates with the Italian verb *graffiare*, meaning "to scratch," an infinitive that might evoke images from lovers' optimistic inscriptions on trees to the magical beasts adorning the caves of Lascaux. In fact, some who study graffiti view it as having come full circle from the subterranean corridors of prehistoric Europe to the subterranean corridors of modern New York City. What began as a primitive art form evolved and grew in complexity until it was elevated (or reduced) to a neo-primitive high art form.

Written rather than pictorial graffiti has its origins in Western culture with the Greeks, whose common people were the first to learn to write and therefore to express themselves graphically. Many examples exist from the ancient Athenian marketplace. Most are obscene.

The Romans were great graffitists, too, and, interestingly, much of their graffiti dealt with either sexual and scatological subjects or politics, and, not infrequently, both, in the same inscription. The eruption of Vesuvius in A.D. 79 preserved a great deal of Pompeiian graffiti on a vast array of subjects. Other ancient people who apparently practiced graffiti-writing were the Mayans at Tikal, Guatemala, whose graffiti can be dated between 100 B.C. and A.D. 700, and the Phrygians of what is now central Turkey, whose writings have been dated about 1200 B.C.

Medieval England had its share of graffitists who chose to incise walls, pillars, and floors of churches, monasteries, and dungeons. The Tower of London features quite a few grim inscriptions, some in blood, by those incarcerated within, many awaiting execution. During the earthy eighteenth century there was an incredible flowering of graffiti, inspired by literature and encompassing a variety of themes from love to admonishments about health and disease. So prevalent and elaborately witty were these English inscriptions that Hurlo Thrumbo was inspired to collect examples found in taverns and inns. He published his anthology, *The Merry-Thought, or The Glass Window Bog-House Miscellany,* in 1731, describing it in his own words as "by persons of the first Rank and Figure in Great Britain; relating to Love, Matrimony, Drunkenness, Sobriety, Ranting, Scandal, Politics, Gaming and many other Subjects, Serious and Comical." This eighteenth-century propensity for graffiti-writing was evidently transplanted in the New World, as Daniel Boone's legendary inscription on a Tennessee tree,

"D. Boon Cilled a BAR in THE YEAR 1760," attests. Even earlier examples of colonial graffiti exist at Williamsburg, where the elegant rubbed brick of the Public Records Office bears initials of many F.F.Vs., including Blairs and Carters, leading one to suspect that if we could examine the hold of the *Mayflower* we would find it to have been liberally inscribed with initials, complaints about seasickness, hopeful religious messages, and griping about less than ideal accommodations.

For two centuries American graffiti adhered closely to traditional subject matter as described by Thrumbo—that is, it mostly had to do with some of the baser aspects of life: drinking, defecating, and politicking. Although ubiquitous in the United States, no serious scholarly attention was granted to graffiti until the twentieth century, when folklorist Allen Walker Read published *Lexical Evidence from Folk Epigraphy in Western North America: A Glossarial Study of the Low Element in the English Vocabulary*. Based on examples he had gathered in public latrines throughout the western United States and Canada, Read's study examined the linguistic significance of words that occurred frequently in graffiti, such as *bitch*, comparing the colloquial usage with the standard definitions found in dictionaries. Read's pioneering work not only identified graffiti as worthy of serious study but also revealed the interesting discrepancy between the way words are supposed to be used in American language and the way people actually use them.

Most traditional American graffiti is very specific in regard to place, time, or situation, but a few examples have become internationally recognized. Such an example is the omnipresent and elusive Kilroy of the mischievous graffiti brag, "Kilroy was here." Kilroy was always depicted as hanging onto and peering over a wall, and he could be drawn very rapidly with a minimal number of marks. The mascot of World War II (military humor and iconography is another understudied area of popular culture), Kilroy's platypus-like visage could be found from the Marshall Islands to the Arc de Triomphe. There is some speculation that Kilroy was born of the old Army–Air Force rivalry, in which he represented the lowly infantry sergeant who could always beat everyone, especially the Air Force, to any scene. A Freudian interpretation goes so far as to suggest that the Kilroy legend is Oedipal in origin: the enemy being the father and the territory occupied by the enemy the mother that Kilroy desires to possess. It seems a little more likely that Kilroy was simply a product of G.I. humor and bluster, the indomitable American spirit in the face of adversity.

In the post–World War II years, graffiti, like many things in America, began to change slightly in character. In the 1950s, America experienced the rapid growth of its first real culture of youth—a vigorous, vital phenomenon that has had as much to do with the world's image of the United States as anything has. Also occurring in the fifties was a growing ethnic pride and identity among different racial groups and nationalities. For both these cultures—youth and ethnic—graffiti became a useful medium of communication, especially when the two cultures overlapped. Mexican-American gangs, for instance, were first formed in Los Angeles after the war and began to rely on graffiti to mark territories and to propagandize. A rival gang would know better, for instance, than to try to frequent a neighborhood in which "BLOODS" appeared many times. For the first time, graffiti became an expression of groups and not only the individual.

In the late 1960s, graffiti changed again, this time becoming again the medium of the individual, but with a difference. "Tagging," or writing one's initials and street number, became popular in New York City and touched off a graffiti explosion that has lasted twenty years. What made tagging different from simple vandalism or initialing was its territorial significance as well as its representation of an even more powerful subculture of youth with little regard for the values and laws of established society. As graffiti proliferated, the subculture developed aesthetic values and standards all its own.

The spark that ignited this graffiti explosion was "TAKI 183." In 1969 New Yorkers began to see the mysterious name and number everywhere. It appeared in subways, on walls along Broadway, at Kennedy International Airport, and in the "bedroom" suburbs of New Jersey and Connecticut. An enterprising New York Times reporter finally identified Taki as a teenage Greek immigrant from a blue-collar neighborhood on the edge of Manhattan. His real name was Demetrius, Taki being the Greek diminutive of that name, and his family home was on 183rd Street. Although Taki put his first "tag" or initial on an ice-cream truck in the summer of 1970, he recalled having been inspired as early as 1967 by "JULIO 204," whose tag appeared around their neighborhood. Taki's ambitions were greater than Julio's, and because his job as a messenger took him by subway to all five boroughs of the city, his tag became a sort of neo-Kilroy in the New York City area. Taki is also credited with popularizing the wide magic marker as a tagging medium, eventually enabling graffitists to enhance their names with interesting calligraphic effects.

Before long, New York and Philadelphia were covered with a blizzard of graffiti spawned by Taki imitators. Immediately, there were innovations and refinements in technique. In 1972, Super-Kool 223 was one of the first writers to discover that by using spray paint instead of or in combination with markers, large areas could be painted very rapidly and draw more attention. Super-Kool purportedly also discovered that by replacing the narrow caps of spray paint cans with "fat caps" from oven cleaner or spray starch, broader or smoother areas could be painted. Distinctly different styles developed. Bronx style was characterized by bubble letters, Brooklyn used a curious, almost ancient Celtic style featuring flourishes and arrows, and Broadway or Manhattan style had long, slim letters and was thought to have been imported from Philadelphia by a writer named Topcat, who claimed to have learned it from Cornbread. Styles merged, resulting in Wild Style—Brooklyn structured lettering crossed with Manhattan spray techniques.

No surface was spared, but the subway system became the preferred medium for several reasons. Subway trains provided a means of communicating with other writers in distant neighborhoods. The Number 5 train, for instance, one of the subway lines preferred by writers, takes four hours to traverse the city from the Bronx to Brooklyn, guaranteeing a very wide audience. Tagging trains could also be very dangerous, and writers found the increased element of risk attractive. Despite the spontaneity of their work, graffiti writers have a studied knowledge of the transit system and know exactly where trains are parked and which trains have the best surfaces for painting.

City authorities became alarmed at the unchecked proliferation of graffiti. On October 10, 1972, the New York City Council unanimously passed a tough anti-graffiti bill which made it unlawful to carry spray paint in a public building. Convictions could carry fines of up to $500 and up to three months in prison. Special compounds were invented to remove graffiti from trains and buildings. By 1973, New York City was spending $10 million a year to combat graffiti without making an appreciable dent. The city even went so far as to implement an attack-dog program, which, not surprisingly, seemed only to stimulate the phenomenon.

As efforts to eradicate graffiti intensified, so did the challenge to create ever more daring and spectacular graffiti tags. Individual writers or "style masters," and gangs or "crews" like the Ex-Vandals, the Independent Writers, and Wanted—the largest group, with seventy members—vied to create the most original and outrageous pieces, further stimulating the frenzy of graffiti activity. One important artistic development was "3D," which added the illusion of mass and depth to a tag. Shading, highlighting, and overlapping letters also enhanced the name, which became less recognizable as a word and more like an abstract or pop art painting. Graffiti grew enormously in size, culminating with the first "top-to-bottom whole car": the ultimate achievement in which the tag covers an entire subway car— windows, doors, and all. In addition to scale and color, composition was carefully planned, as were decorative motifs like stars, clouds, flames, checkerboards, cracks, and polka dots. Writers had also begun incorporating illustrative material like television, cartoon, and comic book characters into their work. Subway graffiti has featured Mickey Mouse, Pluto, Donald Duck, Felix the Cat, Dondi, the Pink Panther, Deputy Dog, Howard the Duck, the Silver Surfer, the Incredible Hulk, Cheech Wizard, and characters from *ZAP* comics of the 1960s, most notably R. Crumb's Mr. Natural and Rick Griffin's winged eyeball.

These "style wars," or aesthetic experiments, underscored the difference between graffiti and graffiti art. Graffiti became something more than a way of "watching your name go by," and writers became something more than vandals. An underground subculture had developed with an art form, value system, and language all its own. No longer "toys," or beginners who were proficient only at "tagging," graffiti artists became "bombers" who executed "throw ups," the large-scale works on train exteriors; "downs," a painting or large signature below a train's windows; or "masterpieces," which generally featured an ambitious theme and elaborate technique, like the John Lennon memorial train created by Lady Pink and Iz the Wiz in 1981.

By the 1980s graffiti art had come off the walls and trains and into a number of small, unfashionable galleries like Fashion Moda in the South Bronx. The Times Square Show in 1980 was followed by the New York/New Wave Show in 1981, and before long exclusive SoHo and 57th Street galleries were hanging work by graffiti writers. Graffiti artists were commissioned to paint backdrops for the Twyla Tharp dance troupe and to design nightclubs, Mardi Gras floats, magazine covers, record jackets, billboards, postcards, and upholstery. Graffiti art has inspired textile design, clothing, and jewelry. Major exhibitions of paintings inspired by American graffiti art have been mounted in cities around the world, attracting serious critical attention and making graffiti, like pork bellies, a marketable commodity. In 1985 a painting by a former American graffitist, Jean-Michel Basquiat, commanded $20,900 in a Christie's auction—the same price paid for a DeKooning in the same sale. Another former graffitist, Keith Haring, became an instant celebrity when his neo-neoprimitive graffiti-inspired work was featured in *People* magazine.

At present, there are signs that interest in graffiti art has diminished for a number of reasons. Young graffiti artists who were bombing the trains in the late seventies and early eighties are now adults, and a new generation has grown up totally accustomed to seeing graffiti around them; consequently, the thrill is gone. Also, some of the major graffiti writers have now become "post-graffiti" artists. In addition, New York City officials have managed to make the trains much less accessible and have developed very efficient cleaning programs. The only subway lines that can easily be "hit" are the B, 5, R, and N lines, and these have old cars and provide limited public exposure. More active graffiti scenes imitating that of New York are developing in San Francisco and Chicago. In Los Angeles, the graffiti scene has split. On one hand there is Hip-Hop graffiti art on buildings, walls, and ball courts instead of subways, and on the other hand there is a return to gang graffiti with threatening and territorial messages.

Graffiti's evolution illustrates a wild ride on the roller coaster of American culture. Beginning as a monochromatic, personalized scrawling, it metamorphosed into awesome, lush creations bursting with sensuous color, finally becoming a formal art form we see in galleries today. Do graffitists deserve praise or blame? Are their impulses creative or destructive? Is graffiti art merely a fad, or is it portentous of a direction art is to take? What are the implications of the change of context—from street and subway to gallery and canvas? Is graffiti art fine or folk?

There is certainly evidence to support the fact that it has much in common with what is generally considered to be "high" art. There is a strong and identifiable aesthetic theory in graffiti art. Because it is illegal it is a radical art, making a social statement and having evolved out of a social condition not unlike American Social Realism and Mexican mural art of the 1930s. It is not officially acceptable, which is what gives it its vitality. It breaks frontiers, and therefore can be seen to have historic precedent in other pioneering American art movements like the Ashcan school and abstract expressionism. There are obvious similarities to pop art, conceptual art, and New Realism. Some see graffiti art as being as cataclysmic a development as the frescoes of Giotto. The painter Frank Stella suggests that graffiti artists have something in common with Caravaggio and painters of sixteenth-century Rome, particularly in regard to their rebellion against the spatial confinement of the traditional easel painting. Some see graffiti as having precedent in all of modern abstract painting. In his poetic 1974 essay, *The Faith of Graffiti,* Norman Mailer said: "Art had been rolling down the fall-line from Cezanne to Frank Stella, from Gauguin to Mathieu. On such a map, subway graffiti was an alluvial delta, the mud-caked mouth of a hundred painterly streams."[1]

Some graffiti artists have academic backgrounds and seem to have used graffiti as a fertile medium for their art, not without a certain self-consciousness. Keith Haring, with his black-and-white "new wave Aztec" style, is an example. Raised far from the urban ghetto, in Kutztown, Pennsylvania, Haring studied commercial art in Pittsburgh and then spent two years at Manhattan's School of Visual Arts. He has also studied semiotics and lists some of his influences as Aztec art, Pierre Alechinsky, and Jean Dubuffet. He began his graffiti career by scribbling on spaces intended for advertisements on the walls of subway stations.

Some art critics see graffiti art as marking the end of modernist arrogance and elitism and as a reaction against the institutionalized and commercialized art of today, although plenty of graffiti artists are happy to be selling works on canvas. Other critics have refused to envision graffiti art as a positive force in the future of art, however. Robert Hughes predicts that the current art market will soon crash, beginning with a slide brought about by the entrance of graffiti into the art world. Critic Barbara Rose excluded any graffiti art from her important 1979 "crystal ball" exhibition, "American Painting: The Eighties."

Some characteristics of graffiti art as it appears on the street constitute elements frequently used to define "folk art." Quite clearly, graffiti art demonstrates much that is "folk" in urban culture, although folklorists seem reluctant to recognize it as such or to bestow the respectable label of "folk art" upon it. There is certainly a communal aesthetic shared by a group of artists and their audience in graffiti art. Critic Harold Rosenberg has said that "the graffiti in New York subways are probably the largest spontaneous outpouring and group showing of folk art that have ever taken place."[2] There is a tradition in which forms are perfected and passed on, and this transmission is carried out in an apparently informal, but highly systematic way. Graffiti art relies on words, signs, and images that have universality and that are meant to be taken at face value, like Haring's radiant child, or Bil Blast's 1982 masterpiece, *Sky's the Limit*. Reviews of graffiti shows are fraught with words like "shamanistic," "primal," "primordial," and "orgiastic." Graffiti art is often reflective of roots in other cultures, such as the work of Basquiat, whose parents are Haitians, or the Hispanic graffiti of the Los Angeles ghetto. Graffiti incorporates the everyday elements of popular culture, drawing imagery and tags from cars (Futura 2000), baseball players (Cey I for Ron Cey), comic strips, drugs, and even from computer jargon and graphics. It is vividly decorative, sometimes visionary or surreal, and certainly is a reaction against the stark colorlessness of modern architecture and the bleakness of the ghetto environment. Most graffiti artists are unschooled; sometimes they are self-taught, but more frequently learn through an informal apprenticeship, during which the tools, techniques, jargon, ritual, and protocol of graffiti are passed along. As artist Futura 2000 has pointed out, "I wouldn't mind going to art school if I could get a scholarship, but it would probably interfere with my work."[3] Regarding the problem of defining folk art, collector Herbert Hemphill has stated, "It seems a waste of time to backtrack into semantics while the art can disappear, undocumented and unappreciated."[4] Certainly, this admonishment applies to graffiti art.

It must be said that once graffiti is painted on canvas, hung in galleries, museums, and other "legitimate" spaces, and bought and sold commercially, it becomes something else. It may or may not be "art," but by breaking with the traditional medium for graffiti—forbidden public surfaces—and by removing the taboo, it no longer is graffiti. It is the vandalism aesthetic that gives graffiti its validity. Once the element of risk is removed and the spontaneity with it, graffiti loses its vitality and its very essence. Painted on buildings and subways, graffiti is an authentic urban folk art, but when it becomes discovered by the galleries and dealers who cater to high culture, its aesthetic is debased.

Will graffiti art endure, and will it have a lasting impact or influence on art or other aspects of American culture? There are already signs that graffiti art has come full circle and is again becoming a method of communicating gang territorial parameters and warnings. But graffiti art has already lasted longer than many art movements, Fauvism and Impressionism, for instance, and who is to say that the impact of graffiti on art may not be as great? Norman Mailer believed that "the beginning of another millennium of vision" may be vested in graffiti art.[5] As long as cities are stark, impersonal, and oppressive, the creative urge will be stimulated. In 200 or 2,000 years, the questions of labeling or categorizing graffiti as one thing or another will not be as important as what it will be able to tell us about urban dwellers in America in the late twentieth century.

REFERENCE WORKS

Because of the underground or avant-garde nature of graffiti, it is a difficult if not fruitless topic to approach through general reference works. Entries on traditional graffiti can be found in some general encyclopedias like the *Academic American* and *Encyclopedia Americana,* but even the latest editions make no mention of subway art.

General reference works on social science, psychology, folklore, and art consistently fail to include graffiti at all. To get at information on graffiti, the best approach is through periodical indexes. *Art Index* is notoriously slow to catch on to new trends—before 1980, looking up the word *graffiti* yielded only articles on Attic vases and Etruscan art. Other indexes dealing specifically with art are *Arts and Humanities Citation Index, Artbibliographies Modern,* and *RILA: Répertoire international de la littérature de l'art.* Among specialized indexes, the Modern Language Association's *MLA International Bibliography of Books and Articles on the Modern Languages and Literatures* includes articles on graffiti in the fourth section, "General Literature and Related Topics," subsection "Folk Literature." *Psychological Abstracts* might yield articles dealing with that aspect of graffiti. The *Readers' Guide* is a good general index, as are some of the machine indexes, like the *Magazine Index* and *Infotrac;* the latter is currently on video disc but will soon be available on CD-ROM. These indexes are also very useful because they often index publications not indexed elsewhere, like *New York* magazine or *Los Angeles.* Newspapers like the *New York Times* and the *Los Angeles Times* have their own indexes and are extremely rich sources, in the case of graffiti providing a real chronicle of its rise and metamorphosis and efforts to combat it.

Collections of examples of traditional graffiti abound. Most sources represent specific kinds of graffiti relating to feminism, politics, sports, sex, ethnic humor, and so on. Already mentioned is Read's pioneering graffiti glossary. The *Encyclopedia of Graffiti* by Robert Reisner and Lorraine Wechsler includes hundreds of examples of graffiti, organized by subject; most were gathered by the authors. Books by Henry Chalfant and Steven Hager include glossaries of graffiti jargon. Other sources are amusing collections like the books compiled by Richard Hammerstein and Maria Haan dealing with sports-related graffiti in four college athletic conferences.

RESEARCH COLLECTIONS

There is, of course, little archival material available on graffiti, and its very nature precludes its being collectible or preservable. Some of the "alternative artspace" galleries that first showed graffiti-inspired paintings are still going strong, like Fashion Moda in the South Bronx. Another gallery that shows post-graffiti painting is Sidney Janis, at 110 West 57th Street, New York. In a school yard at 106th Street and Park Avenue there is the "Graffiti Hall of Fame," where graffiti artists may paint on ball court walls. In Paris, there is reportedly a graffiti museum under the directorship of Serge Raymond.

HISTORY AND CRITICISM

Studies of graffiti in America are best divided, like the subject itself, into two separate entities: traditional graffiti and graffiti art. Research on traditional graffiti can also be grouped further into studies of its psychological and sociological aspects.

A good place to begin researching graffiti would be Robert Reisner's *Graffiti: Two Thousand Years of Wall Writing*. A general history, Reisner's work includes information on the significance of caste and class, graffiti as art and literature, as well as illustrations and a compendium of selected graffiti organized by subject.

It would be impossible to discuss graffiti as a popular art without first consulting some of the standard works on popular culture, such as Russel B. Nye's *The Unembarrassed Muse: The Popular Arts in America*. Herbert J. Gans's *Popular Culture and High Culture* identifies graffiti as a popular art of the last of his five "taste cultures"—the quasi-folk low culture. Graffitists are characterized as poor, mostly non–white, unskilled, blue-collar workers with little education whose tastes include tabloids, comic books, adventure films, and television soap operas. Graffiti, like other aspects of Gans's quasi-folk low culture, is overwhelmingly a male activity.

The psychological and sociological aspects of graffiti have been well explored and provide a number of intriguing perspectives. A thorough and entertaining examination has been provided by Ernest L. Abel and Barbara E. Buckley in *The Handwriting on the Wall: Toward a Sociology and Psychology of Graffiti*. The authors discuss the history of graffiti and review the many theories about its psychological motivations. Among the various motivational forces they identify are sex (heterosexual, autosexual, and homosexual), humor, defecation, and surprisingly, smell. Abel and Buckley define two types of graffiti, public and private, differentiate between male and female graffiti, and also make the shortsighted statement that after its heyday in 1972–73 graffiti artistry began to disappear.

More specific studies theorize in graphic detail about the psychological inspiration for American graffiti. A landmark study by the folklorist Alan Dundes suggests that with scatological graffiti the motivation "is related to an infantile desire to play with feces and to artistically smear it around."[6] In his paper, "Here I Sit—A Study of American Latrinalia," Dundes equates defecation and this "smearing impulse" with writing, and coins the term *latrinalia* to describe the inscriptions relating to excretory functions commonly written on the walls of public restrooms. Another important article is W. J. Gadpaille's "Graffiti: Its Psychodynamic Significance," which concentrates on sexual graffiti. Gadpaille differentiates between male and female graffiti, pointing out a male preoccupation with penis size, and cites statistics from Kinsey that show that most (75 per cent) sexual graffiti is homosexual. In "Graffiti: Some Observations and Speculations," Harvey D. Lomas looks at the psychological significance of the wall itself and the need of the graffiti writer to possess or destroy the wall.

Some attempts have been made to study graffiti scientifically. Notably, David Ley and Roman Cybriwsky have written "Urban Graffiti as Territorial Markers," in which they pinpoint occurrences of graffiti on distribution maps in order to delineate the territories of various Philadelphia street gangs. They point out the importance of learning to read the "diagnostic indicators" of the behavioral environment, stating that if "the scholar is unable to interpret the visible, then the invisible meaning of place will be beyond his grasp."[7] Stocker, Dutcher, Hargrove, and Cook's "Social Analysis of Graffiti" is a midway report of a study that has analyzed graffiti gathered at three American universities in order to determine specific social attitudes that are evident.

Jill Posener's *Spray It Loud* is a black-and-white photodocumentation of political graffiti. Although British, the book is a good representation of graffiti-writing that has been inspired by contemporary social concerns: nuclear warfare, smoking, and feminism. Posener believes in graffiti as an effective political weapon when it is a complement to other actions such as demonstrations or campaigns.

Other sources document ethnic graffiti, such as Gusmano Cesaretti's *Street Writers: A Guided Tour of Chicano Graffiti*. Cesaretti's photographic essay is accompanied by text in the form of the words of a young Los Angeles *plaquito,* or street writer, who describes the major inspiration for the graffiti of the *cholos* (gang members): their Mexican heritage (Aztec and Spanish), and territorial demarcation.

Much of what is known and remembered about graffiti art in years to come will be due to the spectacular and thorough photodocumentation of Henry Chalfant. In two extraordinary books Chalfant's photographs have captured the sensational artwork that is often literally "here today gone tomorrow." (Five hundred "pieces" that no longer exist were photographed over a five-year period.) To truly understand the visual impact and appeal of graffiti art and its significance as a popular art, one would have to refer to Chalfant's books: *Subway Art* (co-authored with Martha Cooper) and *Spraycan Art* (co-authored with James Prigoff). No other sources represent the dazzling colors and fantastic designs with such fidelity. In *Subway Art* the authors have managed a rapport with graffiti writers that facilitated a revealing glimpse into style, technique, and materials. *Spraycan Art* looks at the phenomenon in the eighties, recognizing the spread of graffiti art to Europe, Australia, and New Zealand as well as new trends: painting on racquetball courts, computer influences, and the appearance of Japanese comic book characters. Craig Castleman's *Getting Up* provides the other side of the story: interviews with police. Another fascinating and essential source is Steven Hager's *Hip Hop: The Illustrated History of Break Dancing, Rap Music, and Graffiti*, which documents the important connections of graffiti with other urban popular arts. Hager identifies "Hip Hop" as an urban subculture that has created art forms all its own. Included is a great deal of how-to information: how to dress, how to use spray paint appropriately, how to "backspin" records. Richard Goldstein's December 1980 article in the *Village Voice* was the first to link rap music and graffiti.

The first and best source to refer to regarding the aesthetics of graffiti art would be Norman Mailer's landmark essay, *The Faith of Graffiti*. Dubbing himself the "Aesthetic Investigator," Mailer endowed graffiti with a number of apocalyptic properties as well as noble historic associations with art from the caves of Lascaux to Giotto, Michelangelo, Picasso, and Pollock. In this essay, Mailer also relates a dream which could have been the inspiration for Keith Haring's subway station work. Most of the thoughtful considerations of graffiti exist as periodical articles. Two very informative ones are Suzi Gablik's "Report from New York: The Graffiti Question," which examines questions posed by graffiti's entrance into the gallery, and Francesca Alinova's "Twenty-First Century Slang," which accepts graffiti as art and scrutinizes the iconography of works on canvas by Keith Haring and others. Cynthia Nadelman's "Graffiti Is a Thing That's Kind of Hard to Explain" is also important. A feisty radical defense is Rene Ricord's "The Radiant Child." Few current books on contemporary art even mention graffiti, but Edward Lucie-Smith's *American Art Now* and Harold Rosenberg's *Art on the Edge* are two exceptions. Lucie-Smith differentiates between graffiti artists and post-graffiti artists who have made the transition from subway to canvas. In *Working Space*, Frank Stella's collection of Charles Eliot Norton lectures given at Harvard, the painter acknowledges his own interest and debt to graffiti art by taking the book's title from a "piece" on a New York street. Any researcher wishing to understand the place of post-graffiti art in the contemporary art scene would do very well to consult two invaluable sources: auction catalogs from Sotheby's (980 Madison Avenue, New York, New York 10021), and Christie's (502 Park Avenue, New York, New York 10022–1199). Although few libraries collect them, subscriptions are available and include not only the catalogs, with prices the art is expected to fetch, but a list of "prices realized," which is sent after the auction occurs.

AUDIO VISUAL RESOURCES

Fortunately, several films exist which either document the graffiti phenomenon or prominently feature graffiti or graffiti writers. Anyone wishing to understand the graffiti art phenomenon must see *Style Wars,* an excellent documentary co-produced by Henry Chalfant in 1984. It is the best single source on the subject and includes interviews with the artists (available through New Day Films in New Jersey or Tony Silver Films in New York). Based on *Style Wars* and produced in 1985 by Harry Belafonte, *Beat Street* is a 35mm feature film that was responsible for spreading the culture of "Hip Hop" around the United States and the world. Directed in 1983 by Charlie Ahearn, *Wild Style* is a 35mm docudrama on the street culture of Hip Hop. Famous graffitists and break dancers like the Rock Steady Crew, Lee Quinones, and Lady Pink are featured. In 1985, Twentieth Century Fox (Interscope Productions) released a mediocre feature film entitled *Turk 182* in which a young graffiti artist is portrayed unrealistically but sympathetically. In Dennis Hopper's 1988 film *Colors,* several scenes are staged with Los Angeles graffiti art in the background, providing a good look at some excellent examples, but unfortunately creating the impression that Hip-Hop street murals are associated with violent, drug-trafficking youth gangs. Musician Malcolm McLaren's rock video *Buffalo Gals* was shot in front of Bil Blast's 1982 masterpiece, *Sky's the Limit.* A television documentary on graffiti, "The Writing on the Wall," was produced by New Jersey Network and aired on New Jersey Educational Television on February 6, 1987. Finally, an audiotape, "Young Graffiti Artists," in which several graffiti artists were interviewed in 1982, is available from National Public Radio.

NOTES

1. Norman Mailer, *The Faith of Graffiti* (New York: Praeger, 1974), p. [8].

2. Harold Rosenberg, *Art on the Edge* (Chicago: University of Chicago Press, 1971), p. 295.

3. Suzi Gablik, "Report from New York: The Graffiti Question," *Art in America,* 70 (October 1982), 36.

4. "Folk Art Meeting: Calm and Placid on the Surface . . . ," *Folklife Center News,* 7 (January-March 1984), 5.

5. Mailer, p. [16].

6. Alan Dundes, "Here I Sit—A Study of American Latrinalia," *Kroeber Anthropological Society Papers,* 34 (Spring 1966), 104.

7. David Ley and Roman Cybriwsky, "Urban Graffiti as Territorial Markers," *Annals of the Association of American Geographers,* 64 (December 1974), 505.

BIBLIOGRAPHY

Books and Articles

Abel, Ernest L., and Barbara E. Buckley. *The Handwriting on the Wall: Toward a Sociology and Psychology of Graffiti*. Westport, Conn.: Greenwood Press, 1977.

Academic American Encyclopedia. Danbury, Conn.: Grolier, 1980-.

Alinova, Francesca. "Twenty-First Century Slang." *Flash Art*, 114 (November 1983), 23–31, 59.

Artbibliographies Modern. Santa Barbara, Calif.: ABC Clio, 1969-.

Art Index. Bronx, N. Y.: H. W. Wilson, 1929-.

Arts and Humanities Citation Index. Philadelphia: Institute for Scientific Information, 1976-.

Ashbery, John. "Graffiti on Canvas." *Newsweek*, 101 (April 18, 1983); 94.

Brassai. *Graffiti*. Stuttgart: C. Beiser Verlag,1960.

Castleman, Craig. *Getting Up: Subway Graffiti in New York*. Cambridge, Mass. MIT Press, 1982.

Cesaretti, Gusmano. *Street Writers: A Guided Tour of Chicano Graffiti*. Los Angeles: Acrobat Books, 1975.

Chalfant, Henry, and James Prigoff. *Spraycan Art*. London: Thames and Hudson, 1987.

Cooper, Martha, and Henry Chalfant. *Subway Art*. New York: Holt, Rinehart and Winston, 1984.

Dundes, Alan. "Here I Sit—A Study of American Latrinalia." *Kroeber Anthropological Society Papers*, 34 (Spring 1966), 91–105.

Encyclopedia Americana. Danbury, Conn.: Grolier, 1918-.

"Folk Art Meeting: Calm and Placid on the Surface . . . "

Folklife Center News (Library of Congress), 7 (January-March 1984, 4–5, 13.

Fried, Frederick. *America's Forgotten Folk Arts*. New York: Pantheon, 1978.

Gablik, Suzi. "Report from New York: The Graffiti Question." *Art in America*, 70 (October 1982), 33–37, 39.

Gadpaille, W. J. "Graffiti: Its Psychodynamic Significance." *Sexual Behavior*, (November 1971), 45–51.

Gans, Herbert J. *Popular Culture and High Culture*. New York: Basic Books, 1975.

Goldstein, Richard. "The Fire Down Below." *Village Voice*, 25 (December 24, 1980), 55.

——. "This Thing Has Gotten Completely Out of Hand." *New York Magazine* (March 26, 1973), 33–39.

Hager, Steven. *Hip Hop: The Illustrated History of Break Dancing, Rap Music, and Graffiti*. New York: St. Martin's Press, 1984.

Hammerstein, Richard, and Maria N. Haan. *Graffiti in the Big Ten*. New York: Warner Books, 1981.

——. *Graffiti in the Ivy League, Seven Sisters, and Thereabouts*. New York: Warner Books, 1981.

——. *Graffiti in the PAC Conference*. New York: Warner Books, 1981.

——. *Graffiti in the Southwest Conference*. New York: Warner Books, 1981.

Haring, Keith. *Art in Transit: Subway Drawings by Keith Haring*. New York: Harmony Books, 1984.

Horowitz, Carl F. "Portrait of the Artist as a Young Vandal: The Aesthetics of Paint Graffiti." *Journal of American Culture,* 2 (Fall 1979), 376–91.

Huber, Joerg. *Paris Graffiti.* London: Thames and Hudson, 1986.

Ingham, Curtis. "Graffiti: The Soapbox of the Seventies." *Ms.,* 4 (September 1975), 65–67.

Jundis, Orvy. "Graffiti Cartoons and Comics: Is There a Connection?" *Witty World,* 3 (Spring 1988), 18–19.

Leary, Bill. *Graffiti.* Greenwich, Conn.: Fawcett, 1969.

Ley, David, and Roman Cybriwsky. "Urban Graffiti as Territorial Markers." *Annals of the Association of American Geographers,* 64 (December 1974), 491–505.

Lomas, Harvey D. "Graffiti: Some Observations and Speculations." *Psychoanalytical Review,* 60 (Spring 1973), 71–89.

Lucie-Smith, Edward. *American Art Now.* New York: William Morrow, 1985.

Mailer, Norman. *The Faith of Graffiti.* New York: Praeger, 1974. (Also published in *Esquire,* 81 [May 1974], 77–88, 154, 157–58.)

MLA International Bibliography of Books and Articles on the Modern Languages and Literatures. New York: Modern Language Association of America, 1921–.

Mockridge, Norton. *The Scrawl of the Wild: What People Write on Walls—and Why.* New York: Paperback Library, 1969.

Nadelman, Cynthia. "Graffiti Is a Thing That's Kind of Hard to Explain." *ARTnews,* 81 (October 1982), 76–78.

Nye, Russel B. *The Unembarrassed Muse: The Popular Arts in America.* New York: Dial Press, 1970.

Posener, Jill. *Spray It Loud.* London: Routledge and Kegan Paul, 1982.

Psychological Abstracts. Arlington, Va.: American Psychological Association, 1927–.

Read, Allen Walker. *Lexical Evidence from Folk Epigraphy in Western North America: A Glossarial Study of the Low Element in the English Vocabulary.* Paris: Privately printed, 1935.

Readers' Guide to Periodical Literature. Bronx, N.Y.: H. W. Wilson, 1890–.

Reisner, Robert. *Graffiti: Two Thousand Years of Wall Writing.* Chicago: Cowles Book Co., 1971.

Reisner, Robert, and Lorraine Wechsler. *Encyclopedia of Graffiti.* New York: Macmillan, 1974.

Ricard, Rene. "The Radiant Child." *Artforum,* 20 (December 1981), 35–43.

RILA: Répertoire international de la littérature de l'art. Williamstown, Mass.: J. Paul Getty Trust, 1975–.

Rosenberg, Harold. *Art on the Edge.* Chicago: University of Chicago Press, 1971.

Small, Michael. "Drawing on Walls, Clothes and Subways, Keith Haring Earns Favor with Art Lovers High and Low." *People Weekly* (December 5, 1983), 147.

Stella, Frank. *Working Space.* Cambridge, Mass.: Harvard University Press, 1986.

Stocker, Terrance L., Linda W. Dutcher, Stephen M. Hargrove, and Edwin A. Cook. "Social Analysis of Graffiti." *Journal of American Folklore,* 85 (October–December 1972), 356–66.

"Taki 183 Spawns Pen Pals." *New York Times* July 21, 1971, p. 37.

Thrumbo, Hurlo. *The Merry-Thought, or The Glass-Window Bog House Miscellany.* London: 1731. Reprint. Los Angeles: Augustan Reprint Society, 1982.

Periodicals

Art and Design. London, 1985–.
Art Direction. New York, 1949–.
Artforum. New York, 1962–.
Art in America. Marion, Ohio, 1913–.
ARTnews. Farmingdale, N.Y., 1902–.
Arts. New York, 1983–.
Artweek. Oakland, Calif., 1970–.
Bolletino d'Arte. Rome, 1907–.
Domus. Milan, 1950–.
Flash Art. Milan, 1977–.
Journal of American Culture. Bowling Green, Ohio, 1978–.
Journal of American Folklore. Washington, D.C., 1888–
Journal of Popular Culture. Bowling Green, Ohio, 1967–.
Los Angeles: The Magazine of Southern California. Los Angeles, 1960–.
Los Angeles Times. 1881–.
Maledicta. Waukesha, Wis., 1977–.
New York Magazine. New York, 1968–.
New York Times. New York, 1851–.
Print. Bethesda, Md., 1940–.
Studio International. New York, 1893–.
Village Voice. New York, 1955–.